DEFENDERS OF JAPAN

GARREN MULLOY

Defenders of Japan

The Post-Imperial Armed Forces, 1946–2016

A History

OXFORD
UNIVERSITY PRESS

Oxford University Press is a department of the
University of Oxford. It furthers the University's objective
of excellence in research, scholarship, and education
by publishing worldwide.

Oxford   New York
Auckland   Cape Town   Dar es Salaam   Hong Kong   Karachi
Kuala Lumpur   Madrid   Melbourne   Mexico City   Nairobi
New Delhi   Shanghai   Taipei   Toronto

With offices in
Argentina   Austria   Brazil   Chile   Czech Republic   France   Greece
Guatemala   Hungary   Italy   Japan   Poland   Portugal   Singapore
South Korea   Switzerland   Thailand   Turkey   Ukraine   Vietnam

Oxford is a registered trade mark of Oxford University Press
in the UK and certain other countries.

Published in the United States of America by
Oxford University Press
198 Madison Avenue, New York, NY 10016

Copyright © Garren Mulloy 2021

All rights reserved. No part of this publication may be reproduced,
stored in a retrieval system, or transmitted, in any form or by any means,
without the prior permission in writing of Oxford University Press,
or as expressly permitted by law, by license, or under terms agreed with
the appropriate reproduction rights organization. Inquiries concerning
reproduction outside the scope of the above should be sent to the
Rights Department, Oxford University Press, at the address above.

You must not circulate this work in any other form
and you must impose this same condition on any acquirer.

Library of Congress Cataloging-in-Publication Data is available
Garren Mulloy.
Defenders of Japan: The Post-Imperial Armed Forces, 1946–2016: A History.
ISBN: 9780197606155

Printed in the United Kingdom on acid-free paper
by Bell and Bain Ltd, Glasgow

CONTENTS

Abbreviations and Acronyms	ix
Note on Transcription	xvii
Acknowledgements	xix
Preface	xxv

Introduction	1
1. Post-war Military Roots: Japan's Conflicted Military Legacy	11
Post-War Japanese Fighters	13
Holdouts	13
Converts	14
Captives	14
Pathway to the JSDF	17
Imperial Legacy	17
Korean War	20
Korean War: Shipping	21
Korean War: Casualties	22
Korean War: Japan in Reserve	24
Vietnam Coda	25
Re-arming	26
NPR	26
Transition	33
Safety Forces	34
Conclusion	36
2. Cold War Defenders of Japan	39
Establishment of the Forces	39
Foundations	40

CONTENTS

US Forces Japan	44
Recruitment	45
Ground Self-Defense Force	48
Establishment	48
Defence Build-up and Defence Tasks	49
Formations	54
Defence Plans	56
Natural Defence	59
Society and Culture	62
Conclusion	65
Maritime Self-Defense Force	66
Establishment	67
Defence Build-Up and Tasks	69
The Fleet of 1975	75
The Second Cold War	83
Naval Aviation	85
MSDF Force Culture	87
Conclusion	89
Air Self-Defense Force	91
Establishment	91
Defence Build-up and Tasks	93
The 1976 Shock	99
Close Air Support (CAS), Maritime-Strike/Support	102
Air-Defence Resilience	104
ASDF-USAF	107
ASDF Culture and Safety	108
Conclusion	112
Chapter Conclusion	112
3. Transition to Post-Cold War Challenges	117
1 The Socio-Economics of Japanese Defence	118
2 Overseas Despatch: A Journey with Few Maps	121
Gulf Crisis	122
Japan's Peacekeeping Pre-history	123
Legal Revisions	126
Overseas Operations	130
Legacies of ODO	156
3 Threats Close to Home: East Asia in the Corridor of Uncertainty	159

CONTENTS

	Regional Challenges: Russia	160
	Regional Challenges: China	165
	Regional Challenges: The Democratic People's Republic of Korea (DPRK)	182
	Chapter Conclusion	187
4.	**Defenders of Japan Present and Future**	191
	Changing Defence	192
	Striking Power	198
	Strategic Approaches	200
	Partnerships	205
	Mobility	207
	Civilians Serving	209
	Reserves	209
	Officials	210
	Intelligence	211
	Technology Procurement	214
	Defence Procurement	214
	Defence Exports	216
	Overseas and Back	217
	Indian Ocean	218
	Iraq	218
	Anti-Piracy	221
	Banda-Aceh	224
	Haiti	224
	South Sudan	226
	Exercises	227
	JSDF and the 'Triple Crises'	230
	JSDF Disaster Response Experience	230
	March 2011 Response	231
	JSDF-USFJ *Tomodachi*	232
	Non-US Cooperation	234
	Nuclear Operations	235
	Aftermath	236
	Force Culture	238
	Training and Education	238
	Officer Training	240
	GSDF Training	242

CONTENTS

MSDF Training	242
ASDF Training	243
Training Air Space	243
Women	244
Mental Health	246
Japan is Back!	247
Amphibious Jointness	250
Amphibious Air-Support	254
Expeditionary Challenges: East China Sea	256
South China Sea	258
Western Pacific	260
Yellow Sea	260
Arctic	261
Conclusion	262
Conclusion	265
Notes	281
Index	387

ABBREVIATIONS AND ACRONYMS

1TAG	1st Tactical Airlift Group
A2/AD	Anti-Access Area Denial
AAM	Air to air missile
AAW	Anti-aircraft warfare
ACSA	Acquisition and Cross-Servicing Agreement
ADC	Air Defense Command (*Kōkūsōtai*)
ADF	Australian Defence Forces
ADIZ	Air Defense Identification Zone
ADMM	ASEAN Defence Ministers' Meeting
ADTC	Air Development and Test Command
AEW	Airborne Early Warning
AFV	Armoured fighting vehicle
ANA	All Nippon Airways
AOE	Fast combat support ship/replenishment vessel
AOR	Combat stores ship/replenishment vessel (also AFS)
APC	Armoured personnel carrier
ARDB	Amphibious Rapid Deployment Brigade (*Suirikukidōdan*)
ARDR	Amphibious Rapid Deployment Regiments (*Suirikuki-dōrentai*)
ARF	ASEAN Regional Forum
ARV	Armoured reconnaissance vehicle
ASC	Air Support Command (*Kōkūshienjūdan*)
ASDF	Air Self-Defense Force (*Kōkūjieitai*)
ASEAN	Association of Southeast Asian Nations
ASIS	Australian Secret Intelligence Service
ASO	Allied-Support Operations

ABBREVIATIONS AND ACRONYMS

ASW	Antisubmarine warfare
ATC	Air traffic control
ATgC	Air Training Command (*Kōkūkyōikushūdan*)
ATLA	Acquisition, Technology and Logistics Agency
AWACS	Airborne Warning and Control Systems
BADGE	Base Air Defense Ground Environment
BMD	Ballistic missile defence
BPND	Basic Policy for National Defense (*Kokubōno kihonhōshin*)
BRI	Belt and Road Initiative
C3	Command, Control, Communications
C4-ISR	Command, Control, Communications, Computers-Intelligence, Surveillance, Reconnaissance
CADF	Central Air Defense Force
CAS	Cabinet Secretariat (*Naikakukanbō*)
CAS	Close Air Support
CCA	Close Combat Attack
CCG	Chinese Coast Guard
CCP	Chinese Communist Party
CDU	Cyber Defense Unit
CGPS	UN Contact Group on Piracy off the Coast of Somalia
CIA	Central Intelligence Agency
CIC	Combat information centre
CIMIC	Civil-military cooperation
CIRO	Cabinet Intelligence Research Office (*Naikakujōhō chōsashitsu*)
CIVPOL	Civilian police (in UN operations)
CLB	Cabinet Legislation Bureau (*Naikakuhōseikyoku*)
CRF	Central Readiness Force
CSD	Collective self-defence
CSF	Coastal Safety Force
CSIC	Cabinet Satellite Intelligence Center (*Naikakueiseijōhō sentaa*)
CTBT	Comprehensive Test-Ban Treaty
CTF	Combined task force
CTO	Counter-Terrorism Operations
CWC	Chemical Weapons Convention
DAPE	Deployment Air Force for Counter-Piracy Enforcement
DBP	Defense Build-up Plan

ABBREVIATIONS AND ACRONYMS

DCI	Director of Cabinet Intelligence
DDR	Demobilization, disarming, and reintegration
DFAA	Defense Facilities Administration Agency (*Bōeishisetsuchō*)
DIH	Defense Intelligence Headquarters (*Jōhōhonbu*)
DOD	Department of Defense
DPJ	Democratic Party of Japan (*Minshutō*)
DPRK	Democratic People's Republic of Korea
ECS	East China Sea
EEZ	Exclusive Economic Zone
ELINT	Electronic Intelligence
EOD	Explosive Ordnance Disposal (*fuhatsudanshori*)
EU	European Union
FAC	Forward air control
FEC/FECOM	Far East Command
FIR	Flight Information Regions
FMS	Foreign Military Sales
FOIP	Free and Open Indo-Pacific
FONOPS	Freedom of navigation exercises
FRAM	Fleet Rehabilitation and Modernization
GAO	Government Accountability Office
GCC	Ground Component Command (*Rikujōsōtai*)
GSDF	Ground Self-Defense Force (*Rikujōjieitai*)
GSO	Ground Staff Office (*Rikujō bakuryōkanbu*)
GSOMIA	General Security of Military Information Agreement
HAC	Honourable Artillery Company
HA/DR	Humanitarian assistance/disaster relief
HAS	Hardened Aircraft Shelters
HUMINT	Human intelligence
IAEA	International Atomic Energy Agency
ICBM	Inter-continental ballistic missile
IDF	Israeli Defense Force
IED	Improvised Explosive Device
IISS	International Institute for Strategic Studies
IJA	Imperial Japanese Army (*Teikokurikgun*)
IJN	Imperial Japanese Navy (*Teikokukaigun*)
IMF	International Monetary Fund
INTERFET	International Force East Timor
IPCC	International Peace Cooperation Corps

ABBREVIATIONS AND ACRONYMS

IPCH	International Peace Cooperation Headquarters (*Kokusaiheiwakyōryoku honbujimukyoku*) IPCL
	International Peace Cooperation Law (*Kokusaiheiwakyōryokuhō*)
IPSL	International Peace Support Law (*Kokusaiheiwashienhō*)
IRSG	Iraq Reconstruction and Support Group
ISPC	Information Security Policy Council
JADGE	Japan Air Defense Ground Environment
JASSM	Joint Air-to-Surface Stand-off Missile
JATEC	Japan Technical Committee for Assistance to US Anti-War Deserters
JCG	Japan Coast Guard (*Kaijōhoanchō*)
J-CON	Japanese contingent, UNDOF
JCP	Japan Communist Party
JCS	Joint Chiefs of Staff
JDA	Japan Defense Agency (*Bōeichō*)
JDAM	Joint Direct-Attack Munitions
JFT-TH	Joint Task Force-Tohoku
JICA	Japan International Cooperation Agency
JS	Japan Ship
JSC	Joint Staff College (*Tōgōbakuryōgakkō*)
JSDF	Japan Self-Defense Forces (*Jieitai*)
JSM	Joint Strike Missile
JSP	Japan Socialist Party (*Shamintō*)
JSP	Japanese Surrendered Personnel
KEDO	Korean Peninsula Energy Development Organization
KHI	Kawasaki Heavy Industries
KMT	Kuomintang
LAV	Light Armoured Vehicle
LCAC	Landing Craft Air-Cushion
LDP	Liberal-Democratic Party (*Jimintō*)
LRASM	Long Range Anti-Ship Missile
LST	Landing Ship, Tank
MAAG-J	Military Assistance and Advisory Group Japan
MAP	Military Assistance Program
MBT	Main Battle Tank
MCV	Manoeuvre Combat Vehicle (*Kidōsentōsha*)
MDAO	Mutual Defense Assistance Office

ABBREVIATIONS AND ACRONYMS

MDAP	Mutual Defense Assistance Plan
MEU	Marine Expeditionary Unit
MHI	Mitsubishi Heavy Industry
MICV	Mechanized infantry combat vehicle
MINUSTAH	UN Stabilization Mission in Haiti
MITI	Ministry of International Trade and Industry (*Tsūshō-sangyōshō*)
MLIT	Ministry of Land, Infrastructure, Transport and Tourism (*Kokudokōtsūshō*)
MNF	Multinational Force, Iraq
MOD	Ministry of Defense (*Bōeishō*)
MOF	Ministry of Finance (*Zaimushō*)
MOFA	Ministry of Foreign Affairs (*Gaimushō*)
MOJ	Ministry of Justice (*Hōmushō*)
MSA	Maritime Safety Agency (*Kaijōhoanchō*)
MSB	Maritime Safety Board
MSDF	Maritime Self-Defense Force (*Kaijōjieitai*)
MSF	Maritime Safety Force
MSO	Maritime Staff Office (*Kaijō bakuryōkanbu*)
MSTS	Military Sea Transportation Service
MTB	Motor-torpedo boat
MTDP	Mid-Term/Medium-Term Defense Program
NADF	Northern Air Defense Force
NAO	National Audit Office
NATO	North Atlantic Treaty Organisation
NBC	Nuclear, biological, chemical
NDA	National Defense Academy (*Bōeidaigakkō*)
NDC	National Defense Council (*Kokubōkaigi*)
NDMC	National Defense Medical College (*Bōeiikadaigakkō*)
NDPO	National Defense Program Outline (*Taikō*)
NEI	Netherlands East Indies
NGO	Non-governmental Organisation
NHK	*Nippon Hōsō Kyōkai*
NIDC	National Institute for Defense Studies (*Bōeikenkyūsho*)
NISC	National Information Security Center (from 2015 National center of Incident readiness and Strategy for Cybersecurity, NISC)
NPA	National Police Agency (*Keisatsuchō*)

ABBREVIATIONS AND ACRONYMS

NPR	National Police Reserve (*Keisatsuyobitai*)
NPT	Non-Proliferation Treaty
NRP	National Rural Police (*Kokkachihōkeisatsu*)
NSA	National Safety Agency (*Hoanchō*)
NSC	National Security Council (*Kokkaanzenhoshōkaigi*)
NSF	National Safety Forces (*Hoantai*)
NSL	New security laws
NSS	National Security Strategy
NTWD	Navy Theater-Wide Defense
OCA	Offensive counter-air
ODA	Official Development Assistance
ODO	Overseas Despatch Operations
OECD	Organisation for Economic Cooperation and Development
ONUMOZ	UN Operation in Mozambique
OSP	Offshore procurement
PARC	LDP Policy Affairs Research Council (*Seimuchōsakai*)
PCRS	Primary Casualty Receiving Ship
PFI	Private Finance Initiative
PGM	Precision-guided munitions
PJHQ	Permanent Joint Headquarters (PJHQ
PLA	People's Liberation Army
PLAAF	People's Liberation Army Air Force
PLAN	People's Liberation Army Navy
PMO	Prime Minister's Office
POW	Prisoners of War
PRC	People's Republic of China
PSI	Proliferation Security Initiative
PKO	Peacekeeping Operation (*heiwaijikatsudō*)
PSO	Peace Support Operations (*heiwashienkatsudō*)
PTSD	Post-Traumatic Stress Disorder
RA	Regional Army (*hōmentai*)
RAA	Reciprocal Access Agreement
RAF	Royal Air Force
RAAF	Royal Australian Air Force
RAN	Royal Australian Navy
R&D	Research and development
RAS	Replenish(ment) at sea (or underway replenishment, UNREP)

ABBREVIATIONS AND ACRONYMS

RCDS	Royal College of Defence Studies
RCN	Royal Canadian Navy
ReCAAP	Regional Cooperation Agreement on Combating Piracy and Armed
RFA	Royal Fleet Auxiliary
RIMPAC	Rim of the Pacific exercises
RLO	Regional Liaison Office
RN	Royal Navy
ROC	Republic of China (Taiwan)
ROCN	Republic of China Navy
ROE	Rules of Engagement
ROK	Republic of Korea
RRU	Refugee Relief Unit
SACO	Special Action Committee on Okinawa (*Okinawanikansuru tokubetsukōdōiinkai*)
SAG	Special Airlift Group (*Tokubetsukokuyusotai*)
SAM	Surface to air missile
SAR	Search and Rescue
SAR	Synthetic-aperture radar
SAS	Special Air Service
SCAP	Supreme Commander of the Allied Powers
SCAJAP	Control Authority for the Japanese Merchant Marine
SCO	Shanghai Cooperation Organisation
SCS	Static Covert Surveillance
SCC	Security Consultative Committee
SCJ	Science Council of Japan
SCS	South China Sea
SDC	Subcommittee for Defense Cooperation
SDR	Strategic Defence Review
SDSR	Strategic Defence and Security Review
SEAC	South-East Asia Command
SEALDs	Students Emergency Action for Liberal Democracy
SIGINT	Signals Intelligence
SIPRI	Stockholm International Peace Research Institute
SLBM	Submarine-launched ballistic missiles
SLOC	Sea Lines of Communications
SOFA	Status of Forces Agreement
SOSUS	Sound Surveillance System

ABBREVIATIONS AND ACRONYMS

SSBN	Ballistic missile submarine
SSF	Safety Security Force (*Keibitai*)
SSM	Surface-to-surface (anti-ship) missile
SRSG	Special Representative of the Secretary-General
STA	Surveillance and Target Acquisition
STOL	Short-take-off and landing
STOVL	Short-take-off-vertical-landing
TAS	Training Air Spaces (*kunrenkūiku*)
TEPCO	Tokyo Electric Power Company
TMD	Theatre missile defence
TRDI	Technical Research and Development Institute
UAV	Unmanned Aerial Vehicle
UK	United Kingdom of Great Britain and Northern Ireland
UN	United Nations
UNCLOS	UN Convention on the Law of the Sea
UNDOF	UN Disengagement Force
UNDPKO	UN Department of Peacekeeping Operations (from 2019 UN Department of Peace Operations, UNDPO)
UNESCO	UN Educational, Scientific and Cultural Organization
UNHCR	UN High Commissioner for Refugees
UNMISET	UN Mission of Support for East Timor
UNMISS	UN Mission in South Sudan
UNMO	UN military observer
UNOGIL	UN Observation Group in Lebanon
UNSC	UN Security Council
UNTAC	UN Transitional Authority for Cambodia
UNV	UN Volunteer
USA	United States of America
USAF	US Air Force
USFJ	US Forces Japan
USMC	US Marine Corps
USN	US Navy
USSR	Union of Soviet Socialist Republics
UXO	Unexploded ordnance
WADF	Western Air Defense Force
WAIR	Western Army Infantry Regiment
WFP	World Food Program
WMD	Weapons of Mass Destruction
WTO	World Trade Organisation

NOTE ON TRANSCRIPTION

When writing a work on Japan, explanation should be made of how Japanese names and terms are rendered into English. Full roman (*romaji*) transcription is provided of important institutions, laws, terms, and phrases, such as the Japanese Ministry of Defense (MOD *Bōeishō*). Individual names are written in the family-personal name order most common in Japan, and also in China, Korea, and Taiwan, such as Nakasone Yasuhiro, Abe Shinzo, and Mao Zedong, with Western names provided in the usual personal-family order, such as Barack Obama. Japanese is a relatively simple language to write in English, the one complication being extended vowels, thus resulting in use of macrons to indicate long vowel pronunciation, such as Kōno Yōhei, to provide students of Japan and Japanese with the most accurate rendering to aid further research. However, a slight complication is that several Japanese choose not to apply macrons to their names, or apply alternative forms, so that a surname could be rendered alternatively as Sato, Satō, or Satoh. This volume attempts to follow Japanese standards, with macrons, except where it appears that individuals have an alternative preference. Therefore, Abe Shinzo appears to be preferred (personally and officially) to Abe Shinzō, the form that most accurately expresses Japanese pronunciation. Any mistakes of such preferences are the author's alone, as are mistakes with transcription of non-Japanese names where modern international standards are utilised.

The same basic rule of transcription is applied to place names, with Tokyo and Hokkaido being preferred to Tōkyō and Hokkaidō as they constitute standard usage by the Japanese government and the respective local authorities. Where there is significant controversy regarding a place name, such as Takeshima in Japan, Dokdo in Korea, both are provided, but where common international usage is established, such as the Sea of Japan, then this form is

NOTE ON TRANSCRIPTION

utilised without judgement being made on the respective values of contesting claims. Similarly, China is used to refer to the People's Republic, and Taiwan to the Republic of China, as Korea refers to the Republic of Korea, and North Korea to the Democratic People's Republic of Korea as means of shorthand for readers' convenience.

ACKNOWLEDGEMENTS

This book would not have appeared if not for the imagination of Michael Dwyer of Hurst & Co. He sought me out and 'persuaded me' to write the manuscript, and despite my many delays he retained faith in the value of the work. He has always been a joy to work and talk with, despite pressures upon a small company such as Hurst during normal times, and the extraordinary circumstances of the abnormal global corona virus pandemic. Thank you Michael, and to all of the lovely people I worked with at Hurst, such as Daisy, Maren and many others over the years.

It is a tricky matter to acknowledge everyone who has helped in the production of this book. Mainly due to the range and depth of people, but also many of them would rather remain anonymous, being public servants limited in their ability to be associated with a publication. Therefore, in keeping with the structure of the book, I shall try to conform to chronology.

Many thanks to my parents, who took me to local libraries and helped develop a love and respect for books and information, and who filled the house with talk/argument of politics and current affairs, and my sister and brothers who were part of this slightly mad and always entertaining world and provided me with support and love throughout. Also, to the many teachers who filled my life, providing good examples of being a teacher, who by sixth form had helped me find direction in the study of history and politics. I must also thank my lecturers at the University of Dundee who showed great patience, in particular C.J. Bartlett, who inspired me and encouraged my research on Yugoslavia in the early Cold War, and although I have strayed far from that focus he was the first person who suggested I could possibly make an academic career.

In Japan, I owe much to the many people in Nikko City and Tochigi Prefecture who first welcomed me, and gave me so many opportunities to

ACKNOWLEDGEMENTS

pursue interests that kept me in Japan long beyond my initial one-year plan. I must acknowledge the support provided by the Ministry of Education scholarship that introduced me to research at the University of Tsukuba, and to the fine colleagues, friends, and students I worked with at Shonan Fujisawa Campus, Keio University, where I had my first experience of life as a career academic. Naturally, I must thank my friends and colleagues, past and present, at Daito Bunka University who have put up with my questions and failings for many years, and the university itself which generously supported my sabbatical in Cambridge and multiple research projects. Having a University President, Faculty Dean, and Head of Department who you can ask advice on anything, and can count on as friends is a great benefit of any faculty position, and sharing most of this time with a friend like Edward Mergel brought light and laughter to every day.

In research, there are so many debts to be honoured there simply isn't adequate space. Reinhard Drifte was the first person to show enthusiasm for my PhD proposal, and supported me throughout the very long process. He has also been a constant friend and support since then, offering sage advice, which I have sometimes taken but always valued, and I always look forward to the next meeting. One of the most significant influences on my early development as a researcher in Japan was Tadokoro Masayuki, who encountered me by chance at the National Defense Academy, and immediately made me a research collaborator, and friend of himself and his family. Through him I was able to engage with a broad range of Japanese and overseas scholars, participate in conferences, a historical book project, and develop as a researcher, and I thank him for his generosity. He introduced me to Watanabe Akio and the Research Institute for Peace and Security (RIPS), where I further broadened my network of contacts. Watanabe sensei was always engaging, as too was his successor, Nishihara Masashi, and all of the distinguished members, staff, and associates of RIPS, far too numerous to mention.

Among academics in Japan, there are many to whom I owe thanks. Aoi Chiyuki of the University of Tokyo has been a great friend over the years, and is one of the exceptional academics in Japan able to fully grasp defence and military issues, and feel comfortable in addressing them within the context of peace operations, foreign policy, and strategy. Her opinion and comment is always valued. Wilhelm Vosse has been a great friend and collaborator over the years, and provides me with a grounding in the 'less military' sphere, balanced with our 'third musketeer' Thomas Wilkins of the University of Sydney, and Senior Fellow of The Japan Institute for International Affairs (JIIA).

ACKNOWLEDGEMENTS

When Wilhelm, Tom, and I gather time vanishes and volume levels reach critical levels, all in the pursuit of academic truth and purity. Hosoya Yuichi has been another I have enjoyed engaging with, despite limited opportunities in recent years, and he is another member of the 'Tadokoro Group' who so much enjoyed researching on the Royal Navy in the 19th century, blissfully detached from consideration of present-day politics.

Outside of Japan, but a frequent and welcome visitor, Alessio Patalano, King's College, London, is the ever cheerful, positive, and focused friend who always raises my spirits, as well as being a superb scholar of maritime security, and has thankfully, occasionally corrected some of my conclusions. In a similar vein, Christopher W. Hughes of the University of Warwick has quietly offered advice over the years, and among all the talented Japan security scholars his work stands out for its quality and balance. Chris and I have found ourselves examining very similar subjects, and on more than one occasion he has announced himself in complete agreement with me, 'right up until the conclusion.' This remains a most re-assuring thought. Like Chris, Paul Midford of the Norwegian University of Science and Technology in Trondheim has also conducted similar research to my own, but possesses such an astonishing breadth of interests and detailed knowledge that any meeting is both enjoyable and illuminating, and I always value his comments. In Cambridge, John Nilsson-Wright and Barak Kushner proved most welcoming and engaging during my sabbatical and beyond, and Barak particularly encouraged my research of post-war Japanese conflict issues, resulting in my contributing a chapter to the book he edited with Andrew Levidis in 2020. Together with Sherzod Muminov, Barak and Andrew proved the most supportive and gracious of project leaders.

At the University of St Andrews, Catherine Jones has become a good friend and finely complimentary research colleague. Complimentary, as we rarely research the same subjects, but contribute supporting elements. Cath has several rare qualities. Not only is she gifted and diligent, but she is also generous with her time, very popular, and an excellent networker, forming links, groups, and creating communities with seeming ease, but actually founded upon scholarly curiosity, perseverance, and plain hard work. Thanks to her, I participated in several conferences and workshops, and we co-edited a special issue of the *Australian Journal of International Affairs* in February 2020, the authors becoming a real 'community.' Due to Cath and the other members, Rikard Jalkebro (St Andrews), Alistair Cook (NTU, Singapore), Vanessa Newby (Leiden), and Hirono Miwa (Ritsumeikan), I greatly expanded my under-

ACKNOWLEDGEMENTS

standing of peace, humanitarian assistance, and disaster relief operations in Asia, and the roles played by Japan. I hope that our community can expand and continue this work, possibly addressing some of the human security issues resulting from the corona virus pandemic and climate change.

In Japan, this book would not have been possible without the great cooperation of many members of the Japan Self-Defense Forces. So many of them showed extreme patience in explaining issues, correcting perceptions, or simply providing connections to colleagues, and I could never hope to list them all. Their contributions were largely off the record, although several were bold enough to provide direct quotations, but all were generous with their time, as were many researchers at the National Institute for Defense Studies, their unmatched knowledge of security matters provided priceless resources despite the limitations of disclosure and security that they work within. I was also lucky to encounter many engaging officials of the Defense Agency and Ministry of Defense, Ministry of Foreign Affairs, Cabinet Office, National Police Agency, and the Japan International Cooperation Agency (JICA) amongst others. In many ways, they are the largely unacknowledged actors in Japanese security, and I was often greatly impressed by their openness, critical thinking, and imagination, and yet also sympathised with their frustrations. They too remain largely anonymous. The one retired public official I would mention, only because I am sure he wouldn't mind in the least, would be former GSDF Lt-Gen. Yamaguchi Noboru, whom I met through Prof. Tadokoro, and who while serving in the JSDF proved uniquely open, engaging, critical, and internationally oriented. His subsequent academic career has predictably flourished due to those qualities, and I always look forward to meeting him at one of the security research events in Tokyo where our paths cross. There are many other present and former officials, uniformed and civilian who could also be singled out, but who would prefer to remain anonymous, as would many members of the diplomatic community in Tokyo who have proved wonderfully engaging company over the years.

I must also apologise to several people for my research. Among them were politicians and officials whom I have ambushed with questions at odd moments. These included an impressive trio of Ogata Sadako, Akashi Yasushi, and John Sanderson, all leading UNTAC veterans, whom I managed to badger into answering my questions in various corridors, doorways, and catering venues during one UN event. My excuse is that I was new to such field work, only 32, and knew no better. I have also very much annoyed some officials by my questions, and certainly without meaning to, but perhaps my

ACKNOWLEDGEMENTS

inelegant Japanese, direct questions, and critical comments clearly exhausted several people's patience. Also apologies to the many journalists whom I have talked with over the years. Their role is so vital, and yet I feel that I often revert to interviewer and receive more than I provide, certainly in terms of value.

And final thanks to family and friends. They provide support through good times and bad, and even endure my many 'boring but true' anecdotes with more grace than they should really be forced to muster. I know it must be a strain to be around me at times, and my family in Britain grew used to me arriving from Japan with a suitcase full of research material and locking myself away in my mother and step-dad's back bedroom, using a family term, 'The Teesside Prisoner of Zenda.' I would like to say that my term has ended and I shall be free to have fun with you soon. But I suspect the next project will always be on the horizon.

PREFACE

The origins of this book can be traced to July 1993, arriving in an endlessly fascinating and confusing Japan on the JET Program, as a young assistant language teacher at Nikko High School, with five words of Japanese. Having previously been unable to gain funding for a doctoral proposal examining Yugoslavia's early Cold War position, my attention became drawn to the last few months of Japan's first peacekeeping mission in Cambodia, and in particular to the role played by the Japan Self-Defense Forces (JSDF). Pre-internet access to information was limited, but as overseas operations proliferated it seemed not only a richly fresh area for research, but also one which most politicians and journalists had little understanding of. With few published references available, for someone who had studied security with a (very modest) background of service as a British Army reservist, the opportunities and dire need appeared evident. This eventually resulted in my PhD from Newcastle University, and expansion of interests in various aspects of Japanese politics, diplomacy, and security. During a wonderful sabbatical at the University of Cambridge, I began to envisage a large-scale study of Japanese defence, combining historical and international relations approaches, with IR theory lightly applied as a subtle analytical tool aiding understanding rather than as a hammer or crowbar to shape or shift events. While preparing to depart Cambridge in 2014, a Faculty colleague recommended me to Michael Dwyer of Hurst & Co., who explained with startling clarity his idea for a book on Japanese security, in a few minutes describing most of my comprehensive study concept. The only regret is that it took far longer to realise than initially planned.

The need for the book seemed as obvious as for my initial peacekeeping research. Japanese defence was little understood inside and outside Japan, many policy makers and shapers appeared to have little greater insight and knowledge than the general public, and in meeting with overseas visitors I often unwittingly acted as interpreter of Japanese security 'uniqueness,' a most uncomfortable position. Regularly having to explain to gifted politicians, officials, and scholars why Japan was unable or unwilling to act in certain ways, and attempting to communicate their concerns to influential Japanese stretched my limited capabilities, but was also obviously a burden to more able colleagues and research associates. A comprehensive study of Japanese defence and security was required beyond the numerous extant works on the constitution, US alliance, and politics, and few works on defence. Evaluating the JSDF and other security institutions in similar ways to equivalent bodies in other countries appeared an obvious but largely ignored approach. Pre-JSDF armed forces, including war-legacy troops in the post-war, post-imperial confusion of Japan's supposedly 'long peace,' were even more neglected, the 'long history' of post-war defence needing to be fully inclusive to dispel lingering myths and provide contemporary context for the at times seemingly odd development pathways of Japan's defenders.

The increasing sense of crisis between Japan and China, and the second coming of Abe Shinzo, provided a sense of urgency and added context. Abe's multiple security reforms, culminating in large scale protests against New Security Laws in 2015, prompted an old friend, Hosoya Yuichi, who had served on the Advisory Panel that shaped elements of the Laws, to write a book on Japanese security politics, out of frustration at ill-informed discussion.[1] His skill was in being able to craft the original draft in little over three weeks, while my effort has taken significantly longer. I hope it may be of some use to general and specialist readers, the 'Japan curious' as well as Japanophiles (or –phobes), those without interest in military affairs as well as *gunji otaku* (military nerds), and that it also provides sufficient coverage, context, and complexity for students and researchers. The detail may seem dull in parts, and no single work can cover all relevant issues, but at least it may provide a suitable gateway for understanding the complexities facing the defenders of Japan throughout seven decades and beyond, and a motivation for scholars to produce far better works on related issues.

INTRODUCTION

The purpose of this book is to provide insight into the various defenders of Japan after 1945, and attempt to answer some of the most common fundamental questions related to Japanese defence. Most prominent among these defenders are the existentially controversial Japan Self-Defense Forces (*Jieitai* JSDF), which have sought domestic legitimacy and international respect as military-equivalent armed forces within an overtly pacifist constitutional order. No other national institution more dramatically embodies the conflicted nature of Japanese identity: the Forces encompass historical legacy burdens, liberal-internationalist engagement, and realist security duties, they are broadly appreciated for disaster relief and national defence capabilities, and yet seek legitimacy for their very existence. Counterparts in overseas armed forces and United Nations' missions constantly wonder why the Forces are unable to perform certain tasks, avoid particular terms, are equipped and trained as one of the world's leading militaries and, while being proud of their professional qualities, still shrink from such recognition. For students and specialists of Japan alike, the defence of the country often appears a mysterious balancing act conducted in a dimly lit venue with a critical audience judging performances by rules that are ill-defined, rapidly revised, and with seemingly little relevance to external standards or events.

This work attempts to illuminate the arena of Japanese defence by focusing upon the actors, the defenders of Japan. While these are primarily the JSDF, the Forces are not the only parties engaged in defence activities. During the post-war occupation, United States armed forces constituted Japan's primary security actors, and they continued this role during the Cold War as JSDF capabilities gradually developed. Coastguard forces also grew in importance, gaining prominence in disputes and conflicts with neighbouring states, and thus became the first Japanese armed forces, purely civilian, to engage in armed combat and inflict fatal casualties. Support for armed forces has come from civilian officials of agencies and ministries in technical, intelligence, and policy roles, who were engaged in an undeclared, ill-defined battle for control and influence over Japan's defence with both those they support, the armed forces, and those they serve, the politicians. Notions of civilian control in a democracy would appear to indicate democratic control through parliament and cabinet, but in Japan this is nuanced by the experiences of war and empire, when such institutions became corrupted by military, political, and corporate influences, and officials could be regarded as the last bastion of just, legal, civilian control.

That such notions retain relevance well into the twenty-first century indicates the enduring legacies of war and empire upon Japan, and these strike the visitor beyond the iconic impact of Hiroshima's *genbaku* dome. The country is awash with peace symbolism and references, and at the same time bereft of war memorials, a stark contrast for visitors from North America or most of Europe. This post-war embrace of peace and pacifist norms, not least in the occupation-imposed but long-cherished 'peace constitution', remains a prominent aspect of Japanese society that leaves its citizens with a healthy disdain for conflict. It also has denuded knowledge of the defence and security of the nation, and Japan's role in numerous conflicts around Asia following defeat in 1945 and into the early Cold War. This volume aims to bridge the gap of knowledge between imperial regime, demilitarisation, and the founding of post-imperial forces, eventually leading to the establishment of the JSDF. The starting point of 1946 indicates the transition from demobilisation to demilitarisation: the first civilian armed forces were founded with former Imperial Naval minesweepers, who played an unlikely pivotal role in Japanese strategic security and rearmament. The story of neglected post-war defenders of Japan must begin with those continuing in combat beyond the Japanese surrender, sometimes allied with former enemies, and the way they were treated by their own and other governments. This helps towards a tentative understanding of Japanese treatment of its military servants and the shaping of perceptions that would greatly influence the emergence of Japan's new armed forces.

While it is impossible to provide, in this single volume, the definitive history of post-war Japanese defence, or even of the JSDF, this book aims to draw upon diverse scholarly approaches to provide a more rounded view of the defence actors during Japan's long peace. Even among the armed forces, the

INTRODUCTION

distinct institutions have rarely been examined together. Post-war remnants are often treated as footnotes or postscripts to war studies. Occupation-era, post-imperial legacy and new para-military forces often brushed over as little more than minor participants in broader colonial independence struggles, the inevitable precursors to the Self-Defense Forces. Even the JSDF have been the subject of surprisingly few extensive studies, are often treated with limited cross-referencing between the Forces, and, apart from richly-researched naval cooperation, the studies of US-Japan defence cooperation by armed forces have been surprisingly limited. This contrasts with the broad range of policy, diplomacy, and trade studies related to Japanese defence and security. There have similarly been few works relating JSDF defence and security duties with the roles of domestic civilian agencies/ministries, particularly the Defense Agency (JDA)/Ministry of Defense (MOD), Ministry of Foreign Affairs (MOFA), police, and coastguards.[1] The JSDF are often criticised for insufficient 'jointness', but this could be an equal criticism of security research neglect of joint Force and civil-military cooperation issues in Japanese defence.

The mysteries of Japanese defence are numerous for many Japanese, even among members of the Self-Defense Forces. With such a complex subject, it seems inadequate for research to focus on just one question, but the one most frequently asked by non-Japanese diplomatic and military practitioners when considering the legal architecture, institutions, politics, and social pressures, is: how did Japanese defence end up like this? Often that leads to a subsequent question: how will it then develop? To understand both those questions requires seeing them as part of a larger research puzzle. The shedding of militarism and imperialism during the occupation period was a spontaneous, organic act reinforced by the new US-drafted constitution, particularly the pacifist Article 9, by active purging and prosecution, as well as by the policies of demobilisation and demilitarisation. This was the period in which pacifist norms flourished in society, helped along by official policy, wartime memories, and by political and social movements. How and why were military remnants retained or allowed to survive, how were veterans of war treated, and how did society and politicians react to war in Korea and consequent threats to Japan? To what degree were internal and external security threats appreciated, and what means were developed to counter them? Since there was no inevitable route to the JSDF, why were the Forces founded, from what roots, and why were there three of them? Did they receive equal support from their citizens, government, and US allies? Given that they emerged during the early stages of the Cold War in an alliance with the US, did the Forces develop as inte-

3

grated elements of US strategy or to some domestic strategic plan? As they evolved in such different ways, what were their overarching designs, how were they developed, for what purposes, and how long did such plans remain relevant—and indeed, do they remain relevant?

This is quite a puzzle, but given the changes in Self-Defense Forces' roles and structure since the end of the Cold War, the questions proliferate. How did the Forces adapt to post-Cold War challenges and threats, and with what degree of success? Indeed, how effective does the defence of Japan seem now compared to previous periods, and how well prepared does it appear to meet future threats and challenges? Given Japan's relative economic and demographic decline, is the future of Japanese defence sustainable, and are the Japanese willing to attempt sustaining their defences? Why, in spite of a public perception of increased regional threats, have Japanese defence resources remained so little changed from the late Cold War period? This may indicate dislocation between policy, public opinion, and threat assessment, or it may indicate that Japan's defence accords to values different from those widely assumed in realist theories. While this puzzle may seem daunting and disparate, there are clear links between present day efforts for defending islands and intercepting missiles to post-war demilitarisation and cautious founding of para-military police reserves. The links are the perception of what is considered acceptable in civil society, navigating between extant pacifist norms, Japanese self-identification, internal and external pressures, and the constant elements of international-liberalism with realpolitik realism. This is the process that resulted in what became known as the Yoshida Doctrine, and whose institutionalisation went well beyond what its creator thought possible or advisable. The final part of the puzzle addressed in this study is the attempt to determine whether Yoshida's Doctrine remains in its original or altered form, or whether it has been displaced by other approaches amid Japan's decades of decline amid threats.

The structure of this volume may seem rather unambitious. Themes such as militarism, civilian control, or International Relations (IR) theory in Japanese defence could occupy whole chapters, as could studies of each Force, each civilian actor, and obviously the constitution, but such an approach would involve a dislocation from chronology, confusing for many non-specialist readers, while also reducing the degree of integrated study of actors, events, and themes required to address the research puzzle. Therefore, the structure is based upon simple division into four periods, and, within each period, by subjects. The post-war and early Cold War period is covered in

INTRODUCTION

Chapter One, which examines Japan's conflicted military legacy in the post-imperial era. This includes Japan's war-legacy personnel and conflicts, the development of para-military forces and first post-war casualties, an assessment of the impact these had upon society, politics, and the emerging Forces' structures, tasks, culture, and capabilities. Chapter Two examines the unique foundations of the three Forces, how they developed during the Cold War, as institutions and within Cold War defence and security plans and strategy, and how effectively they conducted their core tasks and duties. Each Force is examined in turn, not only for defence capabilities, but also for social-cultural characteristics, with extensive cross-referencing and contextualisation, including how seriously security threats were assessed and measures taken to secure Japan in conjunction with US forces and Japanese civilian agencies. Chapter Three examines the post-Cold War period and the way Japan and the JSDF dealt with emerging security challenges, as well as domestic issues in a new era of uncertainty. These include the economic and demographic challenges of the post-bubble period from the early 1990s and attendant resource-allocation pressures for Japanese defence. The major challenges posed by the Gulf War are examined, and Japan's response to the socially and politically radical step of JSDF overseas missions, which by cautious management became normative Force roles. The chapter concludes with JSDF efforts to meet extant and emergent East Asian threats and challenges, by examining the three main security challenges from the Cold War to the twenty-first century: Russia, China, and North Korea. Chapter Four examines the Forces as the primary defenders of Japan in the post-post-Cold War period of the new century, how they coordinate with civilian defence and security actors, as well as present and future concerns for Japanese security. This includes whether expansion of Japanese security legislation and potentially expeditionary and offensive capabilities constitute significant challenges to the legacy of the Yoshida Doctrine and to the post-war social and political recognition of Japan as a pacifist or pacific state. It culminates with an exploration of what past and present developments will mean for the future of Japanese defence beyond 2016. The end date signifies the point at which new security legislation was enacted and 'operationalised;' when JSDF troops and civilians found themselves amid a violent African civil conflict, providing a case study test for the new legislation; and the year Donald Trump was elected US President, challenging Tokyo to assume more of the financial burden for the defence of Japan. The conclusion assesses how the research puzzle and its myriad questions have been addressed and, it is hoped, answered, and considers what the world beyond 2016 will mean for the defenders of Japan.

This volume is based upon the uneven but increasingly rich extant scholarship covering the period and issues. Japanese primary sources include Diet records, white papers, and official publications. The Freedom of Information mechanism while welcome can often impose a heavy filter on research efforts, such as when attempts to gain access to JSDF *hakenshi* (despatch histories) result in less than 1 per cent of the documents requested being released, with most content redacted. Semi-official resources, as well as unofficial conversations and interviews with retired and serving personnel are vital resources, with only a few listed as official, including names and titles. This study relies upon two decades of collecting documents and building contacts in the Japan defence community, gaining some degree of trust, and therefore few names are provided. Where possible sources are given in English media to facilitate the non-Japanese specialists, but many are only available in Japanese. Scholars may be more sensitive than general readers to the nature of many sources, and the forms of theoretical analysis applied in this volume. While it is the stated aim of this work to be a history, employing historical sources and archive material, it draws upon several disciplines. Primarily the goal is to combine historical and political science materials and approaches in as seamless a manner as possible, but there is also recourse to sociological, anthropological, and psychological scholarship to provide insight into aspects of institutions. This is an eclectic approach that, it is hoped, provides more benefits than frustrations for the reader. The narrative concentrates upon empirical evidence, and attempts to weave a 'middle path' through historical approaches and IR theories by embracing a balanced 'analytical eclecticism.' This balanced approach utilises IR-theories as part of a 'tool kit,' to be employed as required to aid understanding without imposing an odious burden of theoretical dogmatism, a strategy that has been pioneered by Katzenstein and Okawara, and Glenn Hook et al.[2]

In attempting to write on Japanese military institutions the obvious starting point is the impeccable study of the Imperial Navy, *Kaigun*, by Evans and Peattie, the most complete work on any Japanese military institution, which focuses upon Japan's naval strategy, tactics, and technology, and 'the evolving interrelationship of the three.'[3] Evans and Peattie were unable to consider education and training, civil-military relations, administration, economic and budget factors, let alone the more nuanced issues of social relations and institutional culture. This study therefore aspires to draw together the elements

INTRODUCTION

that *Kaigun* examined with those that it did not, but for multiple Japanese institutions, and utilising both historical and IR methodologies. This ambitious attempt has been made with full acknowledgement that it will probably fail to be a fully comprehensive study of its subject, but nonetheless it is hoped the attempt will provide value for a broad range of readers. *Kaigun* does not provide a model, merely a standard to aim for. The motivation for writing this book was the great frustration that a single-volume comprehensive study of the Self-Defense Forces did not exist. The diverse, fractured, uneven scholarship for the period and subjects covered in this work demonstrates the need for a unifying study.

Extant scholarship of post-war imperial legacy forces of the Japanese empire has generally been treated in country-area specific terms (Indochina, China etc.), or through examining family-individual histories. In both cases, aspects of colonial liberation have been to the fore, rather than the forces or personnel in terms of Japanese security or in consideration of their suffering.[4] They have been largely ignored, in stark contrast to returning Japanese prisoners of war held in Siberia, whose records were declared UNESCO heritage collection items in 2015.[5] Japanese para-military forces, between empire and JSDF, have been researched more thoroughly in recent years, but unevenly. These included the (initially only in Japanese) sole work considered by many to be a semi-official history of the birth of the JSDF, by Frank Kowalski.[6] Subsequently, the number and quality of works on this period and later defence subjects greatly increased, with Thomas French's illuminating work a particular case in point.[7] The range of books critically dealing with the post-1954 Forces expanded, while works analysing the Forces in defence and security terms tended to be written by retired officers or conservative bodies, often with a fascination with hardware that bordered on the comic-book.[8] Indeed, the JSDF have been the subject of many *manga*, which primarily focus upon heroics and hardware that liberal narratives might assert had been rejected by Japanese society.[9]

Among the academic works attempting to rationally analyse the JSDF there has been a preponderance of studies on naval affairs, from James Auer's ground-breaking work on early Japanese naval forces, through Agawa and Graham, to the pre-dominant Alessio Patalano.[10] Ground Self-Defense Force (GSDF) studies tended to be the domain of former-soldiers and anti-militarists, with few academic contributions, the exception being a detailed and insightful work edited by Eldridge and Midford focusing on the 'search for legitimacy,' which has few comparable peers.[11] Apart from personal recollec-

7

tions and technical aviation works, scholarship on the Air Self-Defense Force (ASDF) has been extremely limited.[12] The exception is the companion piece to Auer, Michael Hughes' 1972 doctoral study of Japanese airpower, illustrating the unique contribution of English-language research to Japanese security studies, as well as the relative poverty in the field as this remains the most comprehensive work on the ASDF.[13] Covering the three Forces together and bringing aspects of their development into contemporary relevance, Sado Akihiro stands out among independent, civilian academics focusing upon the JSDF, outside of the National Defense Academy (NDA) and National Institute for Defense Studies (NIDS), which provide a wealth of material, but are limited in their ability to be critical of Japanese defence issues.[14] Insightful academic works that have sought balanced study of Japanese defence within the context of political and social changes have been few but often of high quality; Martin Weinstein producing a notable early work, with the end of the 1990s seeing a number of works raising the possibility of 'Japan as a Normal Power.'[15] Christopher W. Hughes has been one of the refreshingly critical scholars, in good company with Richard Samuels, Kenneth Pyle, Sheila Smith, Reinhard Drifte, Michael Green, and Andrew Oros among others producing excellent scholarship that has been extensively cited. This volume attempts to marry elements of their comprehensive approaches with a more detailed study of the JSDF within a context of policy and strategy transformation.[16]

This survey of literature illustrates that this book has been written to address the fact that there is no single volume that unifies the study of the three Forces, with civilian and US actors, within an assessment of Japanese defence throughout the period of Japan's long peace. The closest in intent would be the excellent work cited by Sheila Smith. However, her focus is more upon the later periods, the diplomacy and the politics, than the operational issues of defence and security, in particular with her detailed examination of the US-Japan alliance. Smith's work is outstanding, but it does not aim to examine the Self-Defense Forces as institutions nor their relative effectiveness, efficiency, and quality, or other defence actors of various periods in equivalent terms.[17]

As previously stated, the vast scale of the subject matter means that it won't be possible to aim for a truly comprehensive study within the limits of one single volume. Nevertheless, it is hoped that this attempt will encourage others to pursue similar projects drawing upon even more diverse material. Over the coming decades, the defenders of Japan are likely to face a series of challenges unprecedented in the post-imperial era. It seems only fair to attempt to

INTRODUCTION

understand their complex histories and critically explain their particular traits, ties, and sensitivities. This book argues that the JSDF have developed in an unbalanced, unorthodox, and yet highly capable manner influenced by imperial legacies and post-war social values, well-suited to disaster relief duties, adaptable to overseas operations with parameters, and with niche capabilities in defence and human security roles representative of modern Japan. Japanese strategy and defence policy appear to place increased emphasis upon firstly shaping the international security environment through engagement and partnership, secondly deterring regional challengers from attempting to pressure Japan, and finally countering threats to Japanese territory or interests, the JSDF integrated within all three aspects. However, in the midst of increased regional tension and the apparent drift towards leaders exhibiting heightened nationalist sympathies, there is the danger that the lack of civil-military trust and intimacy may result in a temptation to utilise military strength at the political level despite Force misgivings and contrary advice. The lack of 'joint consideration' and overly restrictive 'civilian control' rather than coordination also increases the risk that military planning and advice could lack comprehensive and consistent preparation and 'whole of government' integration. Ill-informed utilisation of armed forces, including increasingly 'militarised foreign and security policy' far more than fanciful notions of a return to a 'militarised society,' appears to be one of the greatest potential hazards facing the defenders of Japan and those being defended. Developments appear to indicate that national defence responsibilities are being taken more seriously than they have been for much of the preceding seventy years, but that Japanese politics, society, and the armed forces face difficult challenges and choices ahead of them. They can be informed of such challenges and choices by consideration of where Japan's defenders have come from, the challenges they have faced, and how they have adapted and developed.

1

POST-WAR MILITARY ROOTS

JAPAN'S CONFLICTED MILITARY LEGACY

Japan's post-war demilitarisation, 'peace constitution,' and post-war armed forces demonstrate transformative ways in which imperial-military legacies and responsibilities were managed, processed, and sanitised. This entailed erasing most imperial-military traces, adopting 'state pacifism,' and from 1946 establishing 'sanitary' armed forces that were overtly identified as non-military. Occupation-supervised demilitarisation and pacification measures actually facilitated rearmament by 'cleansing' perceptions of lingering imperial legacies. Newly sanitised liberal-democratic Japan was thereby able to cast a new security identity, the Self-Defense Forces (JSDF), which eventually became valued and utilised within US Cold War security strategies. Imperial legacies nonetheless lingered within the JSDF while seemingly evaporating from public consciousness.

Japanese who served in conflict during this 'blank' period are largely absent from post-war narratives. Ex-combatants were met with indifference or rejection, notable exceptions illustrating arbitrary shunning of imperial legacies and embracing of post-war pacifism. Official 'para-civilians' in the Korean and Vietnam Wars provided Japan's first post-war combat fatalities, largely concealed to avoid association with casualties of empire. This chapter examines the demilitarisation and rearming of post-imperial Japan, and the way some Japanese continued as combatants beyond the surrender. It depicts civilians despatched to war zones, how para-military constabulary forces transformed into quasi-military defence forces, and how defence institutions, cultures, and doctrines developed in the pursuit of post-imperial legitimacy and filial US alliance security amid a broader struggle for national identity.[1]

The early-stage development of the JSDF should be considered in the context of presumed nascent militarism within an environment of overwhelming liberal-democratic pacifism. The Forces have remained existentially controversial within the 1947 constitutional system of Article 9, whereby 'land, sea, and air forces, as well as other war potential, will never be maintained. The right of belligerency of the state will not be recognized.' Born out of para-military police and remnants of imperial-naval legacy, delivered unto a war-renouncing, anti-militarist social culture, the JSDF's institutional and operational development was shaped by controversies concerning status and legitimacy.[2] Constitutional interpreted limits have been thoroughly examined in extant scholarship, and this book assesses those limitations' influence on the Forces to comprehend how they could be evaluated and behave so differently from other armed forces, including the Imperial Japanese Navy and Army (IJN/IJA).[3] The Forces' most obvious Cold War public roles were in snow festivals, sports events, and Godzilla films, despite becoming armed forces equivalent to other US allies. Derided as 'tax thieves,' accorded scant regard, and grudging respect for relief activities, the JSDF were a 'shadow military' with an equivocal social and constitutional existence. Their unconventional, unbalanced development is less surprising than their emerging professional capabilities. This chapter assesses the influence their unconventional establishment had upon eventual capabilities, cultures, and perceptions of the Forces.

Japanese security 1946–54 is often described as a blank period (*kūhakuki*), a vacuous nothingness.[4] For such an empty period there was much activity. Among Japan's post-war para-military forces, the police reserve was initially tasked with internal security duties and the quelling of communist insurrection. Consequently JSDF duties were primarily directed towards external security and national defence within a US-led strategic containment of Soviet power. West Germany rearmed within a pluralistic security community, embracing the norms of collective defence of a liberal-democratic bloc, thereby diffusing wartime legacy concerns, whereas Japan rearmed under US tutelage without reassuring multilateral institutions.[5] A common assumption of the 1946–54 period is that the imperial military was disarmed, demobilised, and returned to a devastated, peaceful Japan. There is limited awareness of many thousands of veterans who died in captivity or combat, disregarded in the dominant narrative of post-war, post-imperial peaceful Japan.⁶ Their stories might have cultivated more deeply nuanced notions of peace and pacifism.

Post-War Japanese Fighters

According to a persistent post-war myth, Japanese have not fought in wars since August 1945, and imperialism suddenly transmuted into pacifism. The confused coda to war began three days after the Emperor's ceasefire broadcast on 15 August 1945, Japanese troops being ordered to defend the Kuril Islands against Soviet invasion, but only to a minimal extent, conducting confused combat within a ceasefire until the surrender agreement was signed on 2 September 1945.⁷ The reality for Japanese troops overseas was often a confused pattern of belligerency legacies, divided loyalties, and conflicting ideologies. Some were belligerents by volition, some followed orders, while the most pitiable followed false imperial orders. Their stories are all the more wretched for being largely unknown and unlamented, in contrast to well-documented privations of prisoners of war in Siberia.⁸ The three main categories are 'holdouts,' 'converts,' and 'captives.'

Holdouts

The most famous Japanese post-war fighters were 'holdout' troops who resisted capture. Small bands and individuals eventually emerged from jungles, driven by hunger, sickness, loneliness, and propaganda. The most famous was Lt. Onoda Hiroo, an IJA intelligence officer who survived Philippine jungles until coaxed out in 1974, when rather surprisingly he was lauded and welcomed home by approximately 70,000 well-wishers.⁹ He was referred to as 'the living spirit of the war dead,' and his stoic reaction to repatriation, and unease in post-war Japan, added to his appeal.¹⁰ This was in stark contrast to prevailing socio-political norms of anti-militarism and anti-imperialism, and marked a turning point in attitudes to veterans and their narratives. Onoda became a celebrity-activist, until his death in January 2014, aged ninety-one. The same treatment was not extended to Private Nakamura Teruo, who surrendered in Indonesia nine months after Onoda. He was looked on with suspicion by Japanese authorities and media, for as a Taiwan-born aboriginal volunteer he fit neither Japanese-veteran, nor conscript-victim model. Considered more curiosity than hero, the Japanese government limited its contacts after he chose repatriation to Taiwan, where he died in 1979.¹¹

Converts

Japanese personnel were deeply involved in the post-1945 conflicts throughout Asia. In Indo-China, fading Japanese imperial power was displaced by Anglo-French imperial and native communist influences, with hundreds of IJA 'converts' joining Viet-min independence fighters, while 'captives' served Allied forces. The Tokyo Foundation's research reveals the remarkable extent of Japanese involvement in the Viet-min struggle.[12] The main 'convert' motivations were personal ties, fear of capture (war-crime trials), and ideological commitment to Japan's imperial yet counter-colonialist Greater East Asia Co-prosperity Sphere (*Daitōa-kyoeiken*).[13] Their numbers have been estimated at 700–800, and those returning to Japan after 1954 were met by official uncertainty whether they should be treated as communist infiltrators, IJA veterans, or refugees.[14]

On 2 September, the Viet-min declared independence and within three months up to 3,000 Japanese troops had deserted. British Maj.-Gen Gracey insisted that Japanese forces maintain law and order until British forces relieved them under 'General Order Number One,' facilitating Ho Chi Minh's legitimisation of the 'national resistance struggle against both Japanese and French colonialism.'[15] Lord Louis Mountbatten, Supreme Allied Commander South-East Asia Command (SAC-SEAC), used Japanese troops throughout Indo-China to make up for insufficient British numbers until December 1946, thus confirming the Allied-Japanese anti-independence alliance.[16] The British referred to 'Japanese Surrendered Personnel' (JSP), rather than Prisoners of War (POW), in order to utilise them for tasks well beyond Geneva and Hague Convention limits, conflicting with independence forces and US anti-imperial policies in assuming responsibility for their own and vast, undeveloped French and Dutch colonies. SEAC retained JSP for as long as possible, including in military roles, although the majority undertook construction labouring, as they did under US control, albeit on smaller scales and for much shorter periods.[17]

Captives

As Euan McKay stated, the JSP 'turned out to be a huge asset,' as British authorities could neither replace them nor rapidly repatriate them or the 53,171 Japanese civilians within SEAC.[18] The Japanese cultural historian Aida Yūji laboured under such harsh JSP conditions in Burma that it influenced much of his later work critiquing western rationalism, although Oba Sadao claims that conditions in Indonesia were more amenable under the British than under Indonesian or even Japanese control.[19] The British relied upon JSP, particularly given cases of British 'minor mutinies' due to conditions and slow demobilisation, using Japanese troops which had retained their weapons and command structures to maintain order, for food production, infrastructure work, and ordnance disposal tasks.[20] The last JSP were not repatriated until late 1947, and McKay has shown that the British attempted to prevent any written record of their experiences surviving.[21]

The situation in Netherlands East Indies (NEI) was complicated by the Japanese having made vague promise of independence, with an Indonesian PETA (*Pembela Tanah Air*—Defenders of the Homeland) militia of over 50,000 having been formed. Under surrender terms Japanese forces were required to both disarm and to maintain security, an obvious contradiction not easily reconciled. Sukarno announced independence, the 16 August declaration was drafted in IJN Rear-Admiral Matsui's residence and printed by the Naval Office Press, but opposed by IJA Marshal Terauchi and General Yamamoto, indicating the fragmented state of Japanese imperial policy and cooperation with the Allies.[22] British forces arrived in NEI on 8 September, but before landing in Surabaya, Java on 3 October 1945, Japanese troops were attacked and passed weapons to PETA.[23] In Bandung, General Mabuchi used tanks to re-assert IJA authority, yet refused to shoot locals who threatened allied personnel.[24] In Central Java, General Nakamura, in a weaker position, ordered arms to be transferred to PETA, which was later reversed by British orders, thereby stoking resentment.[25] Hundreds of Japanese were killed in Semarang, and perhaps 2000 locals in Japanese reprisals.[26] As Richard McMillan states, the British '[...] came to rely on Japanese assistance to an embarrassing extent.'[27] A Gurkha detachment surrounded in Magelang had to be relieved by an IJA company with British support, an Anglo-Japanese combined operation repeated in Bandung in December, IJA tanks and artillery were supporting British operations, with an IJA major being recommended for the Distinguished Service Order (not awarded).[28] Combined operations reached their peak in Surabaya, when Anglo-Japanese forces assaulted the city despite bitter resistance.[29] Tanks were used in urban conflict, 600 British troops were killed, IJA artillery and infantry were integrated within British battle groups and studied for counter-insurgency and stabilisation duties.[30]

Over 300,000 JSP across South-East Asia were not repatriated until late 1946 under the appallingly titled 'Operation Nipoff', reported as 'guarding military stores.' The last of them left NEI on 4 May 1947, 1,057 Japanese having died on Java alone since the surrender, 544 of them in combat.[31] British imperial poverty meant that American ships repatriated JSP, paid for by the Japanese government.[32] Japanese ill-treatment of allied POWs eventually overwhelmed new-found fraternal feelings, with 584 war crime suspects detained in Sumatra, while another 551 disappeared, and 324 veterans remained in Indonesia, forming their 'left-behind' association.[33] Many Japanese were regarded as Indonesian liberation heroes, such as Ueda Kaneo, who from the 1960s worked for Toyota in Jakarta, settling and marrying there, only returning to Japan in 1984 with five fellow veterans to meet relatives and clarify their imperial-service pensions.[34] Veterans were invited to Indonesian independence anniversary commemorations. Ono Sakari was the last survivor, and, on his death aged ninety-four in 2014, was accorded a state military funeral in the cemetery of national heroes.[35] Ota Atsushi has illustrated literary portrayals of IJA soldiers in NEI as kind and egalitarian, their hosts gracious and accepting, Japanese superiors brutishly incompetent.[36] Common 'memories' of resisting aggression thereby became part of a shared, edited memorialisation, leaving Japanese as colonial aggressors largely ignored, until interest was revived in the 1990s with the 'comfort women' research.[37]

The most extreme examples of Japanese 'captive' veterans were in China. Rotem Kowner has illustrated the breadth and depth of their presence under both Kuomintang (KMT) and communist command.[38] Both sides used propaganda to convince Japanese troops to defect. IJA veterans were particularly prized thanks to their artillery and aviation skills, with some serving into the Korean War.[39] One notable case involved 2,600 IJA troops in Shanxi Province, told by their commander to follow (false) imperial orders to fight for the KMT until 1949, by which time 550 had died, 1,600 were repatriated, and 450 remained in Taiwan. Some, such as Okumura Waichi, were not repatriated until 1954, their cases for compensation finally rejected by the Supreme Court in 2005, unlike former Siberian POWs who were granted full pay and pensions during captivity.[40] The normalising of relations with China aided repatriation, the steady procession raising questions concerning 'returned veterans' which sometimes resulted in grudging receptions.[41] Repatriations have occasionally appeared as a state device depicting Japanese as equal victims of war, with few efforts to lessen the stresses of transition for the repatriated.[42] The government made no connection between these combat veterans and the newly established forces eventually transformed into the JSDF, but facilitated former-IJA/IJN figures to serve, and to rise to the highest ranks.

Pathway to the JSDF

The JSDF were founded on 1 July 1954. Many consider this a relatively simple matter, for the immediate post-war period Japan 'did without' armed forces until the Korean and Cold Wars. It was American insistence that resulted in the Forces: the '*kūhakuki*' phenomenon. The reality, however, is that Japanese forces served from late 1945, existing in a twilight zone between eras, which included combat service during Japan's Long Peace. This story does not readily fit with post-war narratives of eschewing militarism, embracing defeat and peace, and founding an international-liberal, pacific Japan. This explains why the pacifist narrative is so pervading and the history of Japan's post-war forces so obscure but so important in the history of Japanese defence.

The continuation of armed forces does not mean that Japan avoided demilitarisation, or maintained forces for stealthy remilitarisation: the mundane reality fitted neither dominant left/right, 'liberation-course'/'reverse-course' narratives.[43] Some have equated former-IJN minesweepers with 'naval forces,' in spite of their being (initially) civilian, technical coastguard units. In establishing Japanese forces, allied sensitivities were considered. Britain had few qualms, and assisted minesweeping capabilities, as it did in Germany, while Australia and New Zealand held decidedly negative views.[44] The British were more concerned with Japan having an unfair economic advantage if it were to be allowed to forgo the 'burdens' of defence contributions: 'the main concern of Western policy will be to ensure that Japan fully undertakes her responsibilities for defence, rather than that she oversteps them.'[45] The Korean Constabulary provided a model of police forces (with Japanese officers, under US command), for maintaining order, national defence, and facilitating US withdrawal by 1949, but was compromised by use against social protests, poor officer candidates, premature military transformation (1948), and poor combat performance in 1950.[46] Such experiences shaped US attitudes to the National Police Reserve (NPR) and Maritime Safety Force (MSF) in Japan.[47]

Imperial Legacy

Two leading experts on Japanese naval affairs, James Auer and Alessio Patalano, identified how pre- and post-war Japanese maritime forces experienced continuity of culture, with the MSDF displaying pride in that heritage.[48] The ASDF also expressed nostalgia for imperial aviation pioneers, not least wartime pilots and aircraft engineers, but there was little evident sense of IJA/GSDF continuity beyond Regional Army structures resembling IJA Regional Military Districts.[49] US Initial Post-Surrender Policy stated: 'Japan will be completely disarmed and demilitarized. The authority of the militarists and the influence of militarism will be totally eliminated from her political, economic, and social life;' the demilitarisation of Japan became 'the primary tasks of the military occupation.'[50] Militarisation had been endemic, with training incorporated into school lessons, and civilians in the Volunteer Fighting Corps (*Kokumingiyōsentōtai*), akin to the British Home Guard, being expected to allow themselves to be slaughtered resisting invasion, but after the August ceasefire only a few pilots attempted futile, last-stand attacks.[51]

Under the First Demobilization Ministry the IJA abolished itself under SCAP supervision, demobilising most personnel within Japan by December 1945 and scrapping military equipment.[52] The Second Demobilization Ministry scrapped the IJN fleet and demobilised personnel by September 1946, while simultaneously operating over 300 ex-IJN minesweepers, reduced to 160 by October 1946.[53] So extensive was demilitarisation that although some IJN escort and minesweeping vessels survived, IJA-legacy hardware was limited to trucks and uniforms, for some veterans their only clothes.[54] The process was also industrial: by December 1947, aircraft and munitions tooling had been dismantled or destroyed, and the 1946 Pauley Report on reparations even recommended banning ball-bearing and aluminium production to prevent Japanese military or trading resurrection.[55]

Demobilisation and demilitarisation occurred within constitutional reform asserting civilian power primacy. It was accompanied by broad 'purging,' an arbitrarily administrative rather than judicial process that pushed thousands of Japanese from their careers, and even saw the removal of martial statues, now considered unsavoury.[56] Even popular authors were at risk, such as Hino Ashihei, purged for his autobiographical novel *Barley and Soldiers* (*mugi to heitai*) 'an Eastern counterpart to Erich Remarque's *All Quiet on the Western Front.*'[57] More deeply in society, Prime Minister Yoshida Shigeru 'embraced defeat' in John Dower's terms, demonstrating an indivisible loyalty to Washington in order to secure Japan, and also recognised new Japan's anti-militarist, pacifist character.[58] Yoshida stated in 1946, 'Many recent conflicts have occurred under the guise of self-defense. Thus the recognition of self-defense will only invite war.'[59] Some assumed that Washington might enforce a 'Swiss settlement' of unarmed neutrality upon Japan, a principle that had received support in Japanese society during the Meiji period, and one that

Yoshida briefly (conveniently) supported in June 1946.[60] Although, owing to economic concerns, neither Yoshida nor the Foreign Minister Ashida Hitoshi were eager to rapidly rearm, both were realists wary of the illusory benefits of neutrality, and wished to revive Japan's prestige and power, primarily through economic means.[61]

The respective Demobilization Ministries were replaced by the Demobilization Bureaux in June 1946, under the Ministry of Health and Welfare (ex-IJA), and the Prime Minister's Office (PMO, ex-IJN). Tessa Morris-Suzuki suggests that 'transwar' institutions preserved traditions and provided cultural and operational continuity. The PMO-managed 'naval' forces constituted Japan's only armed forces beyond police and continued with the same command structure and technical routines, their 'transwar' establishment coinciding with the International Military Tribunal for the Far East and the formulation of the post-war constitution: conclusion and commencement.[62] IJN Admiral Yonai Mitsumasa cannily understood that future naval forces would emerge from this force and carefully selected staff officers.[63] Repatriation of six million overseas Japanese, the restoration of inter-island communications, and food imports were given to the Control Authority for the Japanese Merchant Marine (SCAJAP), together with the battered remnants of Japan's merchant fleet and over two hundred Japanese-crewed US vessels.[64] The transwar environment was encapsulated by the crew of the IJN destroyer *Yukikaze* who saw extensive wartime service before aiding US occupation commanders in anti-smuggling and repatriation roles for over 50,000 Japanese, and transferred their 'unsinkable' ship to the Republic of China navy in Taiwan as reparations in 1947.[65] In January 1947, the minesweeping force was reassigned to the Civilian Merchant Marine Committee, then the General Maritime Bureau of the Transport Ministry, thence transitioned through Maritime Safety Board (MSB), and Maritime Safety Agency (MSA) identities.[66] Remarkably, the changes barely impacted upon Captain Tamura Kyuzō's minesweeping command disposing of approximately 100,000 mines, which Agawa Naoyuki suggests had killed 1,294 in the post-war period.[67] There were over 9,000 minesweeping peak personnel, but by late 1948 this had been reduced to approximately 1,500, with fifty-two vessels.[68] From April 1948, the MSB/MSA became a de facto coast-guard force, although as Patalano states, 'it exceeded the normal functions of an organisation of this kind,' combining naval and civil functions.[69] After two years of relative calm the return of war would make MSA excess capacities appear most fortuitous, for the UN, US, and Japanese 'navalists.'

Korean War

Although the MSA continued 'naval operations' under a civilian banner, this was not a continuation of the IJN by other means, but rather a well-planned continuation of naval expertise to meet urgent requirements of civil security and maritime safety for economic recovery. The 'remilitarisation' of Japan, if it occurred, began with the outbreak of the Korean War on 25 June 1950. This was declared a heaven-sent piece of good fortune by Prime Minister Yoshida ('a gift of the Gods') and by US Ambassador Murphy ('a godsend'), even though both were primarily concerned with reviving the moribund economy.[70] The invasion was a long-held concern, expressed by former foreign minister Komura Jutarō and shared by Yoshida: 'The peninsula of Korea thrusts itself, like a menacing dagger, from the Continent toward the vital parts of Japan.'[71] The Ministry of Foreign Affairs (MOFA) on 19 August declared that fighting for democracy in Korea was no different from preserving democracy in Japan, thus legitimising the first post-war war.[72]

Japan clearly wished to avoid damaging Korean War entanglements, but war ensured comprehensive US security and immense economic investment. SCAP Directive Number 3 (September 1945) had banned aircraft development and production, and yet by 1952 this had been repealed with rapid industrial military redevelopment.[73] An urgent operational requirement for landmines in late June was met by the arrival of 3,000 in Pusan on 18 July.[74] Richard Samuels has illustrated how the remilitarisation of Japanese industry was not simply US-imposed but a united effort. Purged *zaibatsu* conglomerates were reformed and 'remilitarised' through contracts, with more than three-quarters of US special procurement in Japan being munitions and military equipment.[75] Japanese firms were naturally eager for this situation to continue, while in the US Japanese demilitarisation was increasingly regarded as having been a mistake. Despite the sudden industrial military boom, there was no remilitarisation of society, although war-related employment was welcomed. Japanese security policy remained founded upon the Ashida memorandum, enshrined within the 1951 Security Treaty, whereby Japan would assume responsibility for its domestic security while the United States guaranteed Japan's external security. Japan providing its own internal security was quite a step considering how the police had struggled to maintain order in industrial disputes, and is indicative of how rapidly the Korean War had impacted upon policy and social attitudes.[76]

Korean War: Shipping

The initial Japanese involvement in the Korean War was passive, as an allied base. Within days however this turned into active participation, but with little official acknowledgement, most war studies lacking Japanese references.[77] The civilian contribution was considerable, such as at the Sasebo naval base, Nagasaki, where by 'mid-November 1950 [...] Japanese stevedoring had been used in ammunition handling [...] equivalent to that of a thousand-man labor battalion.'[78] Japanese were first mobilised for operations as a result of US naval deficiencies: of 3,000 USN large amphibious warfare ships in 1945, only 158 remained in 1948, and only just avoided being scrapped in 1949.[79] Japanese-manned SCAJAP Pacific War-surplus Landing Ship Tank (LST) were mobilised from their daily roles as civilian inter-island ferries in Japan, transporting the US Army 24th Division from its Japan base to Korea. Forty such LST were mobilised by 15 July (Group 96–3), their coordination complicated by language and signalling issues.[80] These '*Maru*' vessels enabled the Incheon landings of September 1950, where 'Japanese crews manned thirty-seven of the forty-seven LST's in the Marine convoy,' making the operation possible.[81] This expanded with further landings at Wonsan, Hungnam, and Pohang, USN personnel aiding navigation and communications, and Japanese crews providing 'yeoman service throughout the war.'[82] SCAJAP service was so highly valued that after the occupation thirty-three SCAJAP LSTs were transferred to the US Military Sea Transportation Service (MSTS) with their Japanese crews, and their service repeated in Vietnam.[83]

In addition to merchant sailors, the numbers of Japanese civilians engaged in logistical duties in Korea was also impressive, stevedores being employed at Incheon, and in the evacuation of Heungnam, the 'Korean Dunkirk.'[84] Beyond the initial emergency, Korean authorities demanded Japanese be withdrawn from Korea or arrested, a clear legacy of empire that stymied US efforts to increase Japanese roles.[85] In Japan, workers repaired massive quantities of US equipment from trucks and tanks through to ships and aircraft.[86] Reinhard Drifte estimates that over 150,000 civilians were employed on over 2,000 US bases in Japan to support Korean War operations, even though 'the government retreated behind the Potsdam Declaration' that Japan provide facilities for occupation authorities even when 'absolutely clear that these bases were not used solely for occupation purposes but rather for US strategic purposes in the Far East.'[87] While military-industrial revival had been enabled by war, SCAP's 1947 Operation Roll-up had assembled Japanese engineers to repair equipment, offsetting budget cuts on the US military.[88]

Korean War: Casualties

In order to utilise their advantage of amphibious manoeuvre the USN required a minesweeping force it did not possess. The ROK Navy had a small and largely ineffective force, the Wonson minesweeping group including ten USN, eight Japanese, and one ROKN vessel.[89] The experienced MSA perfectly matched US requirements, problems being primarily political—despatching a civilian force to a combat zone, anticipated communist and trade union disruption, and Korean hostility to recent colonial oppressors. The order (not request) of 15 October 1950 was direct from Commander Naval Force, Far East, Admiral Joy, to Ministry of Transportation (not via PMO or SCAP), stating 'The Japanese Government is hereby directed to assemble twenty (20) Japanese Minesweepers, one guinea pig and four other Japanese Maritime Safety vessel [...] for such minesweeping operations as will be designated in future directives.'[90] Post-facto approval by the Japanese government was a face-saving formality, most crew accounts portraying distinctly limited enthusiasm and confidence—they were after all civilians on (lightly) armed vessels, entering a war zone for hazardous service, in secrecy and with urgency.[91]

The Japanese force gathered near Moji, Shimonoseki, Kyushu, and sailed for Korean waters. Task Group 95–66 under Captain Tamura, had been urged by MSA-DG Ōkubo Takeo: 'To regain Japan's independence, we must overcome this challenge and win international trust'.[92] Task Group 95–66 was divided into First Squadron (five ships), which swept Incheon for twenty-one days from 11 October 1950, while Second Squadron, Wonson, operated for nine days from 10 October. Second Squadron was particularly unfortunate, receiving artillery fire and losing minesweeper *MS14* to a mine, leading to Japan's first post-war 'naval' casualties, one fatality and eighteen injured.[93] The inherent operational risks were obvious when two ROK Navy vessels struck mines, with one of them sinking.[94] Minesweeping continued, the Japanese returning to Wonson (twenty-six days) and Incheon (six days) in November and December, latterly under local Royal Navy command.[95] Of an estimated 3,000 mines the Japanese accounted for only thirty-three compared to over 300 swept by allies, but it seems the Japanese operated efficiently, despite reports of crews being discharged for lack of diligence, and Fourth Squadron losing *MS30* due to grounding.[96]

The legacies of the operation have been noted by Auer, Agawa, and Patalano, but it is not clear how prominent they were to contemporary observers. Stealthy despatch was an operational priority, but keeping operations shrouded from public scrutiny was clearly a political priority. The *Sankei Shimbun* ran a series of articles on the operation, but only in January 1954, even though it had been raised in the Diet in 1952 by Nakasone Yasuhiro.[97] This revealed the disquiet of MSA and political leaders as to mission constitutionality, and sensitivity towards the bereaved family, who were discreetly granted standard mission allowances and undisclosed consolation payments from the Japanese and US governments (¥1,853,672 and ¥4,000,000, respectively).[98] The mission never assumed prominence in Japanese post-war narratives, unlike the 1955 *Lucky Dragon No. 5* radioactive contamination incident, but continued as a niche controversy, provoking Diet questions in 1987 that were relevant to discussion of Japanese participation in the Straits of Hormuz minesweeping under Nakasone.[99] It raised more interest than the twenty-two Japanese sailors who were lost when US Army tug *LT-636* was mined one month after *MS14*; their fate would provide a model for later service in Vietnam, where all such losses and any expectation of Japanese responsibility for them was dismissed by a senior MOFA official who stated that under US occupation Japan was little more than a vassal state.[100] The Korean War was not to be the final controversy of Japanese overseas minesweeping missions, nor the end of Korea's importance to Japanese security.

There has been no comprehensive compilation of Japanese Korean War casualties incurred in supporting US Forces, but Kimura Yasuyuki quotes US estimates that up to December 1951 there were 381, fifty-nine of them fatal.[101] Tessa Morris-Suzuki has illustrated how at least 120 Japanese served with US forces in Korea, many uniformed and armed, and two becoming DPRK prisoners. Yet when a 2019 NHK documentary investigated, it discovered bereaved families who had been informed by US authorities that Japanese casualties were effectively criminals, outside of US responsibilities. This was refuted by multiple US Army veterans as well as by records of Japanese volunteering for military support service, but when the MOD was approached the flat response was that any investigation would be 'difficult' (*konnan*), beyond Japanese responsibilities.[102] A single Japanese-DPRK soldier was taken prisoner by UN forces, but hundreds of Japanese are thought to have died while serving with the communists.[103] The US military cooperated with Mindan, the pro-South Korean organisation in Japan, to recruit 644 volunteer ethnic Korean residents of Japan, of whom 135 were killed or missing in action before the scheme was curtailed in October 1950.[104] Ishimaru Yasuzo estimates that approximately 8,000 Japanese crew served in Korean War roles, 1,200 of them in minesweeping, with one killed and seventy-nine injured in operations, another three dead and eighteen injured in non-operational circumstances, with 254 Japanese casualties aboard transport vessels of whom twenty-two died on duty, four committed suicide, and 208 suffered from self-inflicted wounds.[105] Clearly the Japanese Korean War experience was far from glorious, but Alessio Patalano has identified it as highly significant in the formation of a US-supported Japanese naval capacity, ultimately the MSDF.[106] He also asserts that Japanese civilian status was largely irrelevant due to MSA minesweepers being within integrated-allied naval command, flying the UN flag, and clearly operating as naval forces, which explains the post-war decisions to separate civilian coastguard from naval (and minesweeping) duties.[107] Status issues certainly appeared meaningless considering fatalities and Japan-US avoidance of responsibilities, but such issues were to dog the civilian and later 'military' forces of Japan for decades.

Korean War: Japan in Reserve

Throughout the first year of war UN resilience and the security of Japan were in doubt. This can be seen in the US-FEC contingency Operation Plan (OPLAN) No. 1–51 for relocating the Korean Government, forces, and civilians to Cheju-do, and OPLAN No. 4–51, evacuating to Japan or Saipan.[108] In January 1951, US Army units were withdrawn to Japan, where they formed a composite brigade—probably a relief and recuperation measure, but suggesting that contingency planning was underway to secure Japan. These became the GHQ Reserve, and from 12 March 1951, a GHQ Reserve Corps (National Guard) was established in Sendai, supervising 'ground defense and general security for Hokkaido, and for Honshu north and east of the western boundaries of Niigata, Nagano, and Shizuoka prefectures,' until XVI Corps assumed responsibility from May 1951.[109]

Despite invasion being unlikely a 1951 CIA assessment stated that the Soviet Union and People's Republic of China (PRC) 'have decided to invade Japan in the event Japanese rearmament takes place.' While admitting intelligence discrepancies, it claimed 'fairly consistent' indications that Japan was being targeted, even though those that showed that the CIA Director-General and Director of Naval Intelligence disagreed with the threat assessment were scored through by hand, but neither the nature nor scale of dissension is clear.[110] Domestic security was the main Japanese government concern, and ethnic Korean and Chinese residents, communist and socialist groupings, and possible DPRK infiltrators provoked fears of destabilisation and thus compounded concerns of police weaknesses. During the Korean War internal and external threat perceptions presaged the foundation of new para-military security forces that would evolve into the JSDF.

Vietnam Coda

Japan hosted the US during the Vietnam War in a manner similar to 1950, with Japanese citizens even drafted into US military service under visa conditions. One was despatched to Vietnam, deserted in Hiroshima but was subsequently pilloried for his military, deserter, and atomic bomb survivor status, with little discernible pattern to the anger or discrimination.[111] A critical 1965 TV Vietnam War documentary series had episodes prohibited from being broadcast, so sensitive was the issue considered in non-belligerent Japan.[112] Foreign Minister Shiina Etsusaburo stated in May 1966 that 'Japan is not neutral' in the Vietnam War, although his successor Miki Takeo denied the right of Japanese intervention, despite 'the government [...] quietly helping to recruit civilian seamen through the transportation ministry to staff LST's [sic] and other cargo vessels in the war theater.'[113] The *Asahi Shimbun* exposed how twenty-eight Japanese and twenty South Korean-crewed vessels under US naval control, the men wearing US uniforms, transported supplies to Vietnam.[114] The first Japanese crewman casualty was shot in Da Nang in November 1964, and over the next two years a further eight Japanese died and over 100 were injured during US LST duty. The Japanese government denied not only responsibility but also any right to comment, despite state recruitment, seemingly torn between domestic norms and alliance demands, not least with Korea deploying combat troops in Vietnam.[115] Unconfirmed reports of JSDF pilots from Hokkaido flying Vietnam 'black operations' aside, for most citizens the War was 'over there,' only becoming a Japanese issue with widespread anti-war demonstrations, and the underground Japan Technical Committee for Assistance to US Anti-War Deserters (JATEC) establishing an escape-line for deserting US personnel.[116] US security dependency directly paralleled Korea, but far more radical steps were taken at home during the Korean War to secure Japan and ensure that the occupation would end on favourable terms.

Re-arming

NPR

The genesis of the GSDF is the most politically complex of the three Self-Defense Forces. From police reserve origins, it became a 'safety force,' in turn civilian, para-military, and quasi-military, with rearmament not equating to remilitarisation. While the line of imperial naval forces may appear to have been (thinly) maintained with legitimising minesweeping and fisheries-protection roles, and the air force created with limited imperial legacy, the ground forces were unfortunate enough to combine controversial legacy, questionable legitimacy, and dubious political propriety in one package. Unsurprisingly, the GSDF struggled to win public acclaim; in Eldridge and Midford's terms it has long been 'searching for legitimacy.'

The mundane reality of GSDF establishment is not easily accommodated in left/right-wing narratives.[117] US pressure for such forces, particularly after June 1950, was strong but not monolithic, with hardliners such as head of intelligence (G2) General Willoughby, MacArthur's 'loveable fascist,' pushing for ground forces, while substantial liberal groupings within SCAP resisted 'remilitarisation.'[118] The US State Department officer for Japan (Green) in July 1950 wondered 'whether standing FEC policy decisions would obstruct any plans which the U.S. might have for turning over to the Japanese increased responsibility for maintaining internal security and defense. These plans might range anywhere from an improved police force to the defensive rearmament of Japan.'[119] John Foster Dulles, later Secretary of State, from 1951 was a proponent of full rearmament for Japan and Germany within US Cold War strategy.[120] There were differing opinions on whether Japan should have police or military forces, the urgent despatch of US units to Korea resulting in a potential security vacuum. The prevailing narrative that Prime Minister Yoshida accepted Japanese 'forces' as a necessary evil to satisfy American demands and deflect more extensive rearmament demands contains elements of truth while being misleading. From 1947, the Japanese government was cognisant of domestic security threats, particularly the Japan Communist Party (JCP), requiring para-military auxiliary police forces, which would thereby be characterised as repressive. This has cultivated an alternative narrative of 'rearmament' under guise of Korean War securitisation for primarily domestic political ends, avoided while the US Army reinforced Japanese police, such as during 1947–8, when US armoured vehicles were deployed to control strikers and demonstrators, indicating the limitations of police capabilities.

'Weak and impotent Japan was putty waiting to be molded by the force of war in Korea' in Maeda Tetsuo's critical view; the 'Memo on Increasing the Japanese Police Force' of 9 July 1950 'was an order [...] since the Yoshida cabinet had made no request for any sort of increase,' a view supported by Kaihara Osamu, a police official in the NPR and JSDF.[121] The memo called for a 75,000-man police reserve, and an increase of 8,000 in the Maritime Safety Force (MSF). The NPR came into (nominal) existence on 10 August 1950, despite never being debated in the Diet, Yoshida issuing Government Ordinance 260 realising that urgency and conforming to US requests were greater priorities. Maeda's 'alternative-rearmament' narrative regards the Reserve as essentially military, albeit different from the IJA, controlled by Ministry of Home Affairs' Hayashi Keizo, 'a court official with no military history,' but under de facto American command.[122] SCAP military history section's ex-IJN/IJA officers under G2 Gen. Willoughby as a staff-in-waiting for Japan's resurrected military supported such conspiracy theses.[123] There is, however, little evidence and Ordinance 260 reveals a hurriedly formed police auxiliary, reinforcing the prefectural National Rural Police (NRP), US military assistance for uniforms, equipment, and training based upon necessity. Like the legal basis, expediencies bred conspiracies but did not prove them, and conspirators, such as Willoughby and Colonel Hattori, were repeatedly marginalised.

The 1947 Truman Doctrine indicated US Cold War approaches, and US Secretary of the Army Kenneth Royall praised Japan's military-industrial capacity, suggesting it might be utilised by the US. This was reinforced by George Kennan, US architect of 'containment,' who visited Tokyo proposing his 'Kennan Restoration.'[124] US Joint Staff Planners (JSP) studied employment of Japanese armed forces from March 1946 despite demobilisation policies, but without policy recommendations.[125] US Far East Command defensive plans (FEC Plans Baker 62/65), however, presumed atomic weapons would secure Japan rather than troops, NSC 13/2 (October 1948) emphasising 'economy first' approaches with strengthened police and coastguards.[126] Kuzuhara Kazumi asserts that MacArthur saw the NPR as a projection of the new Japanese constitution and identity, a non-military according with his New Year's Day 1950 address that Japan held the right to self-defence, and his resistance to Dulles rearmament demands just before the Korean War.[127] SCAP's 8 July letter to Yoshida explicitly authorises the Reserve as an extension of the NRP, founded in September 1947 to redress overenthusiastic cuts to imperial-era police forces.[128] This contrasts with the Far East Command

(FEC) official history of the NPR that 'the new police unit was actually a military organization,' shared by Frank Kowalski, SCAP Military Advisory Group (MAG) chief of staff and key figure in establishing the NPR.[129] Kowalski's direct commander, General Shepherd, told him that the NPR constituted 'the beginning of the Japanese army.'[130]

It seems that over-reliance upon later US source materials skewed scholarship of the NPR as a 'covert military,' while the views of Reserve members were more nuanced. Kowalski's account brims with anecdotes of how Japanese derided the NPR as being 'unmilitary-like,' and the Reservists unworthy of respect, with the views of recruits in Japanese accounts similarly lacking martial pride or a sense of inherited military legacy.[131] Thomas French's most impressive study of the NPR takes issue with the assumption that authorisation was effectively a SCAP order, to which the government meekly acceded, neglecting substantial evidence that repeated requests for expanded police forces had been dismissed by GHQ.[132] The Reserve had its roots in police shortcomings that followed post-war demobilisation and fragmentation, and which resulted in 'nearly 1,400 local autonomous police forces' by early 1948, the National Rural Police (NRP) comprising 30,000 officers, compared to 95,000 in municipal police forces.[133] The police 'gap' was identified by Kennan during his 1948 Japan visit, when he noted that 'Japan's central police establishment had been destroyed. She had no effective means of combatting the Communist penetration.'[134] NRP were frequently overwhelmed by industrial unrest following the third wave of 'Red Purges' from 1948. The initial SCAP purge of January 1946 naturally focused upon war criminals and associates, while the second wave (1947) resulted in mass purges.[135] Masuda Hiroshi (referencing John Montgomery) lists IJA/IJN veterans as 79.4 per cent or more than 167,000 of the purged.[136] The third wave appeared more repressive and 'left-focused,' with John Dower and Hirata Tetsuo estimating that from December 1948 to November 1950 over 27,000 were summarily dismissed, including professors and journalists.[137] US purge and NPR influence can be seen in Richard Samuels' contention that General Marquat, SCAP Economic and Science Section chief, utilised the secret 'M-Fund' (source of fantastic speculation) to stimulate the economy, quell left-wing forces, and fund the formation of the NPR.[138]

Such turmoil was common in Europe, and Australia deployed troops during a 1949 coal strike.[139] In Japan, the JCP, unsullied by imperial-military loyalties, secured a record thirty-five Diet seats and 9.7 per cent of votes in January 1949, despite Yoshida's Democratic Liberal Party winning a healthy majority. The 'Red Purge' was interpreted as an order descending from SCAP, with the government seen to be implementing rather than shaping policy. Samuels quotes Yoshida saying that the NPR was 'a means of national defense with forces not equipped to conduct wars.'[140] The defence envisioned countered subversion, and JCP membership reached 150,000 by 1950, later reducing due to the Korean War and Communist sabotage.[141] Fear of communism was strong, yet Martin Weinstein also references Yoshida and Ashida's concerns of 'Swiss-style' idyllic, neutrality illusions. 'Mr. Yoshida and Mr. Ashida did not want simply to hand Japan's security problems over [...] making Japan into an American military dependency.'[142] Ashida was vehement that what emerged as the Yoshida line, that military forces were unconstitutional but the NPR and JSDF were not, was an unprincipled trick. He advocated constitutional revision and considered democratisation Japan's fundamental transformation, ensuring the end of imperial wars, which, as Ueda Makiko illustrates, drove his robust critique of Yoshida's security policies.[143]

This bitter rivalry was not between left and right, but intra-conservative—between the overt, direct, de jure Ashida, and the covert, indirect, de facto Yoshida. It extended to SCAP, with G2 attempting to sabotage Government Section by attacking their 'protégés,' the Socialist-Liberal/Democrat Katayama-Ashida axis, and by the Government Section retaliating and attempting to break up the Democratic Liberal Party, and to displace Yoshida for Yamazaki Takeshi.[144] Ashida supported the NPR for domestic security, and military-volunteer forces for Japan's external security, advocating including Socialists within peace treaty formulation, fearing that the Yoshida line 'forced the putative bearers of postwar democracy-workers, housewives, youth and progressive thinkers [...] into advocating "unarmed neutrality", "non-aggression" and "anti-Americanism."'[145] Unfortunately for him, and perhaps for Japanese defence, 'Ashida's rearmament movement became distorted', finding unfortunate bedfellows among former-IJA/IJN nationalists, with the appeals to 'traditional nationalism' and modern democracy eventually becoming incompatible.[146] And yet he did not monopolise contradictions, responding to Yoshida's elegantly obtuse remarks on the JSDF being 'an army without war potential' and 'not engaged in rearmament,' that Yoshida was 'trying to convince us that a heron is actually a crow.'[147] The Yoshida doctrine, as it emerged, was clear and appealing: 'Light rearmament, reliance on the United States for security, and an emphasis on the economy and trade'.[148] But how light? How reliant? What security? It later emerged that Yoshida was secretly encouraging socialist leaders to demonstrate against rearmament during Dulles' visit to Tokyo to restrain US demands for increased defence spending.[149]

One striking aspect of the NPR was its rapid formation, with only eleven days from announcements to swearing in 74,580 police officers from among 382,003 applicants.[150] Recruitment was managed by the NRP, also under the Prime Minister's Office (PMO), but directed through prefectural police committees.[151] There was no military Reserve element, which added to the attraction of appealing terms and conditions. Of one thousand NPR initial officer candidate positions, two hundred were reserved for transferred agency-ministry personnel, with 10,899 applicants for eight hundred positions. In 1951, there were 2,758 former-IJA/IJN officer applicants for eight hundred positions.[152] Rapid recruitment nullified plans for training cadres and phased recruitment, sudden induction resulting in US trainers and Japanese assistants, of uneven quality, swamped by recruits of varied capacities.[153] Gen. Willoughby and Col. Hattori Takushiro hatched a plan listing approximately four hundred former military officers as a de facto NPR cadre, the preparations only scuppered by timely SCAP intervention.[154]

Hattori was profiled by Robert Guillain in 1952 as prospective leader of a 'new Japanese army,' 'one of the main points of contact between General Willoughby and SCAP on the one hand and former Japanese army personnel on the other.'[155] However, soon afterwards, Hattori was identified by the CIA in a plot of uncertain provenance to assassinate Yoshida, and his career thereafter was limited to military history.[156] Shibayama Futoshi's impressive study of the period identifies numerous unrepentant and expectant veterans. He notes CIA concerns regarding former Foreign Minister and Korea Governor-General Ugaki Kazushige's 'underground government' group of several thousand aiming to revive Japan's military and participate in Chinese, Indo-China, Indonesian, and Korean conflicts, sharing virulent anti-communist sentiment with noted nationalist Kodama Yoshio, and even Dulles.[157] The CIA tracked Hattori until 1957 due to his espoused desire to abolish the JSDF for their 'betrayals,' even though many ex-IJA officers similarly loathed his SCAP service 'betrayal.'[158] The NPR was problematic for veterans' groups, who reviled it as 'unmilitary' and ill-disciplined, vastly overpaid, and potentially frustrating a military revival.[159] It was only from 1951 that former imperial officers were inducted, four hundred entering the NPR Academy. There is a contention that 'the government decided that the NPR would not be adequately staffed or imbued with a sufficiently strong military spirit unless it availed itself of the service of the most experienced soldiers,' but perhaps such sentiment belonged to Willoughby and Hattori.[160] Cold War pragmatism in providing effective security forces was superseding post-war sensitivities.

In stark contrast to G2 scheming, Hayashi Keizo was installed as the Chief of the General Group, the policy-civilian leader of the NPR, with Masuhara Keikichi as the Director-General, the civilian-uniformed head. Neither had police experience and both had only limited military service, Kowalski believing Hayashi's appointment was at the suggestion of the emperor, while Masuhara had been Governor of Kagawa Prefecture.[161] Both were regarded as 'safe hands,' and resisted imposing military methods or large numbers of former-military officers, and the NPR accordingly developed as a hybrid, neither conventional police, nor military. Little more than former-IJA caps and training areas vacated by US troops deployed to Korea suggested military heritage, although training was conducted by US instructors in drill and weapon handling. Japanese NRP led police procedure, administration, and management, with all the usual confusion ensuing that one can imagine from such mixed training and languages. It became clear that those with previous command experience, mainly NCOs, were best suited for similar Reserve roles, and an organic equalisation process occurred. The largest group of recruits were agricultural workers (40 per cent), mostly IJA/IJN veterans, 44.5 per cent having served as enlisted men, and 7.3 per cent as officers, with senior officers, convicts, and revolutionary party members (mainly JCP) barred.[162] Many command positions were initially filled by National Rural Police.

The thirteen week training programme, which French asserts was not 'militarised' due to the time devoted to riot-control (20.7 per cent), did, however, include 'Field Formations,' a bland label for section/platoon/company manoeuvres distinctly military in nature. Together with drill and guard duty (over 25 per cent), carbine handling (7.7 per cent), scouting and camouflage (5.4 per cent), and 'field fortifications' (trench-digging, 3.8 per cent), the pattern appears far more military than police.[163] While Reserve culture and society were 'civilian-constabulary' in nature, and distinct from harsh IJA brutality, it was a hybrid with complementary police and military qualities, but it seems the emphasis upon military aspects was partly due to US Army trainers' limited skill range. Training implementation varied, Kuzuhara insisting it was US Army controlled, but the majority of instructors were Japanese NRP, who naturally emphasised civil police roles.[164]

One odd aspect was that 10,000 NPR recruits were rapidly transported to Hokkaido before completing training, despite the stated aim being domestic security. Kowalski claims this was to deter Soviet invasion, his memory possibly influenced by the later Cold War context of his memoirs, although CIA reports suggested such a (surely remote) threat.[165] The NPR were eventually well balanced across Japan given training area limitations, even though Hokkaido did receive large allocations of the successor National Safety Force (NSF) as it expanded with heavier weapons, as the hybrid-force became distinctly 'more-military.'[166] Thomas French supports his thesis of the NPR as an internal rather than external security force by highlighting their deployment away from the north from late 1950, with over 15,000 moved 'to new homes in Kanto and Kansai, near the major urban and industrial conurbations which held the vast majority of JCP supporters.'[167] However, far from Osaka and Tokyo, large numbers were dispatched to Matsumoto (Nagano), Takada (Niigata), and Fukuchiyama (Kyoto). These relatively rural areas have common points: Takada (now Joetsu) port, Fukuchiyama, near the Sea of Japan and Maizuru naval base, and Matsumoto, 100km from the Sea of Japan while more than 200km from either Tokyo or Nagoya. These locations would be ideal for countering an external security threat from Korea or Vladivostok, or supporting US forces countering such threats. Even those moved 'to Camp Utsunomiya, near Tokyo' were 120km from the capital.[168] Former IJA and vacated US bases in northern Tokyo/southern Saitama, such as Camp Nerima, would have been obvious choices for urban stabilisation missions. French correctly counters that there were few movements of personnel to Kyushu or south-west Honshu, closer to Korea, and that US naval and air command rendered invasion impossible.[169] But this should not rule out concerns for both internal and external security of DPRK infiltration, as occurred during the Cold War. French and Weinstein rightly assert that the NPR, NSF, and GSDF were relatively slow to move their 'centre of gravity' to Hokkaido, despite transformation into an overtly external security force, with the implication that political priorities remained internal.[170]

Former IJA weapons and uniforms were discarded, as the US-supplied M1 carbine was ideal for domestic duties. Despite limited combat utility, Yoshida and MacArthur's resistance meant that the NPR was not being provided with artillery.[171] It later received M-24 'Special Vehicles' (*tokusha*), and tanks (*sensha*: 'war vehicles'), but the NPR was civilian, like the French National Gendarmerie with which it shared civil arrest powers, even though none were recorded. More remarkably, given its counter-subversion foundation, the NPR was never deployed for counter-demonstration roles, despite units mobilised (usually without ammunition) for the Suita Incident (Osaka anti-military demonstration) and peace treaty enactment ceremony following a fatal riot before the Imperial Palace.[172] NPR 'tanks' were low-value US surplus, of limited combat effectiveness, used by the US for internal security, including during the 1948 Toho Studio strike.[173] Artillery would have been prioritised for military forces, Kuzuhara and French disagreeing upon when heavy-weapon training began, policy and logistical realities diverging, and the official history suitably vague.[174] Limited training was introduced for machine guns and mortars, later light anti-tank weapons, artillery and tanks introduced during transition to the NSF.

Japanese and US governments seemingly agreed on slender invasion threats, yet disagreed about appropriate levels of Japanese contributions to national defence, although not on the essential roles that Japanese forces should initially assume. A 1948 CIA Report stated: 'The key factor in the postwar development of Japan and the relationship of that development to US security is Japanese economic rehabilitation.' However, as in many contemporary CIA reports doubt was cast upon Japan's new pacifist identity: 'Japan's manpower [...] if mobilized and assured of logistical support could contain hostile forces of large size on the Asiatic continent.' 'Militarily Japan is now defenseless and must rely for protection from aggression upon the armed might of some other nation or nations having sufficient strength and willingness to guarantee Japanese sovereignty.'[175] This provides an alternative view of Japanese rearmament, and of the four US Army divisions stationed in Japan, 'constabulary units' by default, and, as became clear in Korea, largely unfit for combat.[176] The NPR by contrast was trained up for civilian-constabulary roles rather than downgraded to them, and later stretched to fill defence gaps left by departed US forces.

Transition

From spring 1951, former imperial officers gained commissions, with Maeda estimating the eventual number in the JSDF at over 5,000.[177] Many rose to prominence: Kurisu Hiroomi was commissioned in the IJN but became (via the NPR) GSDF Chief of Staff. The highest positions remained dominated by civilians, with Hayashi Keizo heading the NPR, the NSF, and the GSDF, retiring as Chairman, Joint Staff Council in 1964. As the first generation of civilian leaders retired, former imperial officers came to occupy important positions, the majority of MSDF admirals being Naval Academy graduates by 1970. Itaya Takaichi was typical, as an IJN academy graduate in 1932, Coastal Safety Force Commander in 1952, rising to Chairman of the Joint Staff

Council in 1969, when Vice-Admiral Ibuki Shoichi was appointed C-in-C of the Self-Defense Fleet, two years below him in the IJN academy.[178] By 1970, an exceptional 96 per cent of MSDF Captains and 80 per cent of Commanders were ex-IJN, but in 1987 the last imperial officers retired.[179] As imperial-legacy personnel increased in number and influence the institutions became increasingly similar to military forces, with infantry and armour eroding police culture. The maritime forces, although undertaking typical coastguard patrol roles, also had extensive naval minesweeping duties, and with the CSF (Coastal Safety Force) transformed from a hybrid coastguard-naval institution into a more conventional naval force. Sebata Takao argues that 'there is no grand strategy in Japan's defense policy' and that the most important policy formulation factor is a 'tug of war among the politician and bureaucrats rather than by a single rational choice.'[180] A combination of political acquiescence and US pressure resulted in the transformation to the NSF, and ultimately the JSDF, after a period of flux and political machinations regarding respective 'armed' and 'police' forces.[181] There was little evident strategy beyond confirming independence.

Safety Forces

From 1952, the NPR transitioned to National Safety Forces (NSF), under a National Safety Board (NSB, later Agency), expanded from 75,000 to 110,000 personnel, and by 1954 had acquired artillery, aircraft, tanks, respective training schools and academies.[182] Recruitment was extensive and despite many members leaving after two years' service new recruits were rapidly enrolled, new specialist schools facilitating technical training.[183] Apart from name changes, training shifted focus onto battalions and regiments. Heavy weapons were available after March 1954 through the US Mutual Defense Assistance Plan (MDAP), so that brigade strength training became a realisable goal.[184] Kusunoki provides ample evidence that NSF members had mixed feelings regarding their quasi-defensive roles, from 'run away from war,' to doubts about national defence capabilities, even impatience at political vacillation towards rearmament.[185] The NSF provided an interregnum of flux between the NPR and JSDF, which the official history attempts to veneer with cogent development. However it fails to illustrate how politicians or Force leaders regarded the institution, let alone how members understood their roles. The 1951 San Francisco Peace Treaty signalled the turning point, not least as it was accompanied by the Treaty of Mutual Cooperation and

POST-WAR MILITARY ROOTS

Security Between the United States and Japan, the Security Treaty or *Anpō*, which divided defence responsibilities along Ashida-memo lines, making the US responsible for guaranteeing Japan from external threats, but also giving her a potential role in Japanese domestic security, until revised in 1960.[186] In February 1952, a treaty agreement under Article III was reached on USFJ bases, which stated the US desire that Japan 'increasingly assume responsibility for its own defense [...] always avoiding armament which would be an offensive threat.'[187] Japan would henceforth be responsible for internal and an increasing degree of external defence and security. The NPR had achieved its limited goals and was being regarded as less of an aberration and more as a normal internal security entity. After 1951, Japan's leaders increasingly felt the pressure to extensively rearm, and momentum gained pace and purpose due to US pressures and desire to access US military aid. The National Safety Agency (*Hoanchō* NSA) was established under PMO direction on 1 August 1952, the NPR re-born as the National Safety Force (*Hoantai* NSF) in October, together with the Coastal Security Force (CSF) later Safety Security Force (*Keibitai* SSF), uniting ground and maritime elements.[188]

The Coastal Safety Force had been founded on 26 April 1952, in Yokosuka, based on the MSA's imperial ancestry and joint US-Japan naval-planning 'Y-committee,' which determined that Japanese maritime forces become distinctly naval rather than coast-guard, and eventually won Yoshida's agreement.[189] The 'Y-Committee' facilitated CSF functional engagement with the USN and US aid, and the post-war blue-water fleet was founded with ex-USN warships. The committee had a small former-IJN membership, but several retired senior officers unofficially influenced proceedings, so that 'imperial experience was exactly where it was supposed to be, in the background of the process.'[190] In parallel, journalist Itō Masanori 'remobilised' himself as a security commentator, particularly on naval issues, and conducted a vigorous campaign through *Sankei Shimbun* columns to re-awaken Japanese appreciation of naval forces, widely respected in a perceived pacifist nation. Alessio Patalano has shown how, rather than becoming entwined in political, constitutional, and legal details, 'Itō by contrast, sought to shift the focus of public attention to the fundamental relationship between a nation and its armed forces' and attempted to shape the tangible sense of 'military sensitivity generated by the trauma of defeat.'[191] Most commentators focused upon threats to the constitution, rather than the security threats they were created to counter, a persistent Cold War phenomenon. NSA/NSF/CSF formation allowed Japan to reap the benefits of US aid and training with few changes in duties.

The NSF introduced the *hōmentai*, 'regional groups/armies' with artillery, from October 1952, and became a military training force, with 67,000 cadets accepted in 1952 and an influx of equipment. The NSF aviation school illustrates the transformation towards the JSDF embedded within NSF education and training.[192]

Conclusion

This chapter has illustrated that Japan's 'long peace' included thousands of Japanese engaged in conflict. The 1946–54 period can be regarded as the continuation of war beyond state control, but not without state knowledge. Startling inconsistencies between how state and society regarded Japanese in conflicts were conditioned by local conditions and contemporary events. Pro-communist freedom fighters may have been welcomed home in 1946, but not in 1954. Troops that followed orders and fought with the Allies were treated with much the same disdain as other war veterans, their unique ordeals ignored, while those in China were the most wretched and abused. The last holdouts perfectly illustrated society's double standards: the Japanese officer lauded, the Taiwanese-native shunned. Former Imperial Navy personnel who continued to serve in hazardous minesweeping were accorded scant regard, possibly even less while serving in a war zone in near-secrecy, with the Japanese government accorded little more respect by US authorities. Japanese Korean War casualties were unknown, left without memorials, the government preferring not to acknowledge them despite being partly responsible, as with sailors killed during Vietnam War service. Politicians praying at Yasukuni Shrine have not obviously atoned for the state's responsibility for Japan's civilian, nor its military, post-war 'long peace' casualties.

The foundations of post-war Japan coincided with those of the MSA and NPR. They in turn provided a pathway for the JSDF, and yet were civilian, performing para-military police, and distinctly 'para-naval' minesweeping duties, not inevitably constituting cadres for military-naval expansion. The NPR performed no military tasks despite martial training, its characterisation as a 'shadow army' being as misleading as the 'created by and for the US' thesis, the Japanese government from 1947 onwards having repeatedly requested increased police capabilities. As it acquired heavier weaponry the Reserve transitioned towards a new, more martial identity, and yet even the NSF was not military as much as pre-military, enabling the eventual development of clearly non-police armed forces. The CSF emerged as more obviously 'navy' than the NSF did as 'army', and with USN vessels and instructors the mentoring relationship was born, Korean War experience having clearly indicated the naval value of Japan to the USN in the Cold War.

These institutional developments reflected contemporary internal and external events: the Korean War highlighted internal security requirements as US units withdrew, and, as JCP support declined, internal-external threat perceptions became more nuanced. The realisation that the Cold War would be prolonged and global increased US pressure upon Japan to rearm and assume increased burdens for external security, with consequent transformation towards the NSF and the JSDF as Yoshida's 'minimal possible demonstration' to retain US support and limit economic effects of rearmament. As this 'demonstration' became increasingly 'military', Yoshida's pragmatism appeared ever more stretched, highlighting Ashida's accusation of dishonesty, yet both influential characters would be marginalised by the '1955 system' in which the JSDF would develop. Post-war extemporisation would be transformed and sustained by Cold War contingency as the Yoshida Doctrine, which he came to regret, morphed from recovery mechanism to default grand strategy. What became increasingly clear with the passage of time was that Yoshida had uniquely, and often by cunning and deception, imposed his personal concept of conservative national strategy upon Japanese defence, planning and encouraging rearmament, and yet also encouraging opposition to remilitarisation and excessive US demands for Japanese contribution to western Cold War strategy. No politician since Yoshida has had such an obvious shaping effect upon the defence of Japan, and, as will emerge in the following chapter, such shaping during the Cold War was a far more nuanced process of negotiation, balancing, internal-external pressure, and the emergence of officials as more influential shapers than either political or uniformed leaders.

Japanese defence and security institutions, even in the twenty-first century, continue to owe certain qualities to those Yoshida-era police and coast-guard origins, including police officials in security leadership roles. In 2015, the Ground Self-Defense Force issued a new emblem displaying 'From 1950,' the first acknowledgement of police reserve antecedents. As usual the MSDF preceded them, celebrating a CSF sixtieth 'anniversary' in April 2012.[193] As will become clear in Chapter Two, this naval confidence in heritage, identity, and roles would continue as a dominant theme throughout the Cold War, as would the Ground Force's less clearly defined roles, troubled sense of lineage, and search for legitimacy.

2

COLD WAR DEFENDERS OF JAPAN

Establishment of the Forces

The establishment of the Japan Self-Defense Forces from post-war civilian para-military institutions was momentous: Japan had seemingly begun assuming ownership of its national defence and constitution through post-occupation mediated interpretations. How the Forces were founded and developed, and how they matured during the Cold War is the subject of this chapter, through examining the processes, policies, personalities and events that shaped the institutions, their capabilities and cultures. Starting out with meagre resources and limited confidence, the JSDF would conclude the Cold War as among the world's most capable and best resourced armed forces, but with a lingering lack of confidence in their identity and legitimacy. This chapter outlines how each Force developed in a unique manner, largely dissimilar to each other and distinct from other equivalent armed forces, yet significantly shaped by their respective US relationships, and their diverse perceptions of security threats. The lack of threat perception consensus, dearth of government strategic direction, and relative freedom for the Forces to forge separate conflict contingency plans for separate security threats is striking. Civilian control rhetoric dominated the evolution of the Forces, but this was one-dimensional control that sought to prevent rather than enable actions, simultaneously isolating the Forces and political masters and debilitating integration of strategic considerations into security policy. While all of the fundamental blocks for constructing a defence establishment were present, the architecture and binding elements were distinctly lacking coherence. This can be traced to the legal, constitutional and sociopolitical contexts of their establishment.

Foundations

The Forces were founded on 1 July 1954, amid a flurry of restructuring that established the Japan Defense Agency (JDA; *Bōeichō*), with residual NPR/NSF associations ended by a new, independent National Police Agency (NPA).[1] The Procurement Agency (*Chōtatsuchō*) supported the Forces before being succeeded in 1962 by the Defense Facilities Administration Agency (DFAA; *Bōeishisetsuchō*), which was tasked with building up and modernising facilities that they (and US Forces Japan) would require. The DFAA was, like the JDA, under Prime Minister's Office (PMO) direction without ministry status or full cabinet representation (the Director-General, DG-JDA, was granted cabinet membership). Even though the National Defense Council (*Kokubōkaigi*) was established in 1954, it didn't meet until 1956, and thereafter failed to become a key policy or strategy body. Being chaired by the Prime Minister and composed of politicians and officials with almost no Forces input, it largely acted as a budget-planner and censor for more ambitious defence plans.[2] The JDA, as a recent, lowly civil service institution, inherited many of its officials from the Ministry of Finance (MOF), the Ministry of Foreign Affairs (MOFA), and the Ministry of International Trade and Industry (MITI), and had many other officials 'parachuted in'. The lingering influence of police officials was an unanticipated consequence given the 1954 separation, and it continued into the 1980s, the JDA not gaining a 'home grown' top-rank administrative vice-minister until Nishihiro Seiki's appointment in 1988.[3] JDA and JSDF development clearly required careful mediation between internal and external pressures.

The constitutionally controversial nature of the JSDF embodied three fundamental problems of status that only slightly varied:

1. De facto military status and the imperial legacy.
2. Constitutional status in relation to Article 9.
3. Assigned roles: national defence, civil support, and 'miscellaneous duties.'

The principle that Japan could repeat imperial-era mistakes, compounded by the failure of leaders to adequately atone for colonial and wartime aggression, together with perceived 'remilitarisation,' disturbed many observers.[4] In this pessimistic view Article 9 constituted a 'cork in a bottle' that if 'popped' could lead to 'reversion' to militarism. This 'cork' analogy was also applied to the US both as defender of Japan, and of Asia against Japan, mitigating the need for Japanese military power with implied presumptions of to-be-repeated imperial-era atrocities.[5] This book is not concerned with Japan's constitutional history, but such matters have importance in shaping the Forces and their perception. Indeed, the constitutional issue has long been widely regarded as the defining matter of Japanese armed forces, posing an existential challenge to them and often clouding rational evaluation of defence capabilities. Article 9 provides the foundations as well as a paradox for pacifist norms, clearly prohibiting a military, which Japan seemingly maintains:

> Aspiring sincerely to an international peace based on justice and order, the Japanese people forever renounce war as a sovereign right of the nation and the threat or use of force as means of settling international disputes.
>
> In order to accomplish the aim of the preceding paragraph, land, sea, and air forces, as well as other war potential, will never be maintained. The right of belligerency of the state will not be recognized.

As Glenn D. Hook and Gavan McCormack have stated, it is Article 9 'which provides the basis for state pacifism,' and for restrictions not explicitly stated in the constitution, such as the self-denial of the right of collective defence, and defence export restrictions. The justification provided for the foundation of the JSDF was that they were not military forces (*guntai*) but self-defence forces (*jieitai*), their roles non-belligerent (national defence, civil support, and 'miscellaneous duties'). The Forces were rejected by the leading opposition, the Japan Socialist Party (JSP), as 'unconstitutional yet legal,' and by the JCP as lacking legitimacy as Japan's defenders. The JSP position transformed in 1984–95 as the party approached electoral success to displace the LDP, while the JCP gradually changed its nuanced position to resemble the former JSP stance.[6] The government repeatedly committed to the United Nations Charter, Article 51: 'Nothing in the present Charter shall impair the inherent right of collective or individual self-defense if an armed attack occurs against a member of the United Nations, until the Security Council has taken the measures necessary to maintain international peace and security.'[7] Successive governments incrementally broadened JSDF 'legitimate' roles, usually in accordance with reinterpretations by the Cabinet Legislation Bureau (CLB), responsible for providing (supposedly) independent official advice, but no attempt was made (until 2006) to resolve the constitutional paradox of a 'non-military' JSDF, equipped as a military, for military duties.[8] Internal-

41

security roles expanded to national defence, later including sea-lane defence, regional security, and ODO, the notion of purely national defence being diluted within the stated contexts of UN and US alliance duties.

The post-1954 duties of the GSDF changed little from those of the NSF, but for the MSDF and ASDF the early years involved expansion and technological advancement under US instructors only gradually displaced by Japanese personnel assuming expanded responsibilities. The Forces were initially largely without operational approaches, other than borrowed US doctrines and tactics. The SDF Law (*Jieitaihō*) stated what the Forces were compelled and prohibited to do, but with little notion of purpose or procedure.[9] The 1957 Basic Policy for National Defense (BPND) was the first attempt to provide strategic security direction. Its political rather than operational utility resulted in it being left unchanged for nineteen years, the essence remaining to this day, with four (overtly idealistic) approaches: (1) To support the activities of the United Nations and promote international cooperation, thereby contributing to world peace; (2) To promote public welfare and patriotism, thereby establishing a sound basis for Japan's security; (3) To incrementally develop capabilities for self-defence, with regard to the nation's resources and prevailing domestic situation; (4) To deal with external aggression based on the Japan-US security arrangements, pending United Nations capacity to deter and repel such aggression.[10] These themes remained constant: 'UN-centricity,' peace norms within security policy, gradual Force expansion, and US alliance dependence. The inclusion of UN references continued attempts to 'sell' the 1951 Security Treaty to the Japanese public, particularly USFJ bases. Yoshida remarked that he used UN-centric references like 'a "silk hat" to dress up this unattractive reality,' and Reinhard Drifte has illustrated how Yoshida used them to garner domestic support and to emphasise domestic restraints on policy to parry US pressure for further defence expansion.[11] Ann Sherif shows how UN-centric rhetoric became imperative after the *Lucky Dragon No. 5* (*Daigofukuryū-maru*) atomic-test radiation incident energised 'peace activism.'[12]

From 1957, the JDA, with few policymaking powers, seconded officials, and rigorous 'civilian control,' administered rather than governed defence.[13] The BPND united JSDF, US alliance, and international peace elements, paralleling the 1956 Basic Atomic Energy Law's nuclear-peace unity. This could be viewed as a pragmatic or cynical Yoshida-legacy demonstration that despite rearmament Japan remained dedicated to pacifist norms. The illogical duality of 'armed-pacifism' was the 'least-worst' solution for a divided country. This became embedded from 1955 with Liberal-Democratic Party (LDP) administrations opposed by the JSP, which rejected the legitimacy of the Forces, establishing the bipolar LDP-JSP government-opposition '1955 order'. Despite the 1957 BPND, Japan still had, in James Auer's phrase, 'a non-policy' on defence planning and strategy in order to avoid domestic conflict, being unable to conduct operations, 'other than perhaps to sweep mines, [for] which there was a capability [...] before the SDF.'[14] The three-year First Defense Build-up Plan (DBP; *ichijibō*) succeeded by three five-year DBP, seemingly strident programmes to boost defence capabilities, demonstrating Japanese compliance with the 1953 Ikeda/Robertson talks on defence capabilities, and thereby facilitating reduced US Forces Japan. Despite such advances, however, as Kent Calder stated, Japanese defence was politically 'an orphan' with few friends in broader society.[15]

Civilian control (*bunmintōsei*) became the mantra for subjugating the Forces as institutions not to be trusted due to imperial-era legacies, and by inference due to their constitutional status. JSDF members were designated 'special civil servants,' partly to reinforce civilian jurisdiction and partly to conform with Article 9.[16] Hikotani Takako suggested that 'civilian control' to prevent military dominance of government actually resulted in limiting defence transparency, due to fear that it would appear to challenge civilian authority.[17] It also marginalised JSDF defence advice, and retarded planning, training, and doctrinal development, and led to officers being forcibly retired for protocol breaches, such as GSDF General Kurisu who dared to state the inadequacies of contingency planning.[18] Civilian control could also be characterised as official-bureaucratic control (*bunkantōsei*), bureaucracy dominating both nominal political masters as well as subordinate uniformed officers. Maruyama Takashi illustrates expansive JDA spending plans blocked by the CLB and MOF, while Nishihiro Seiki details JDA Internal Bureau assertions of authority during struggles with JSDF officers.[19] Ian Gow portrays a window of equality between uniformed and civilian officials in access to NSF leadership in the PMO 1952–4, which reverted to civilian-only access after 1954, JDA Internal Bureau domination frustrating uniformed efforts to influence planning.[20]

There were authors who in the wake of the 1963 'Three Arrows' planning scandal, the 1970 'coup de théâtre' of Mishima Yukio, and the 1973 Chilean coup d'état conjectured about the possibilities of a JSDF coup, with suggestions that an attempt of former-IJA officers to attract GSDF officers was planned and foiled by police in 1961.[21] Coming just after the unprecedented

1960 *Anpō* Security Treaty revision demonstrations where it was feared the GSDF might be called upon to reinforce stretched police, such suggestions were truly alarming. One JSDF Major more fancifully suggested in 1992 that Japan needed a coup to eradicate corruption, thus rapidly accelerating his retirement.[22] Civil society should have been perversely reassured by the response to Mishima's exhortations for the GSDF to rise up and save Japan. Troops jeered and ridiculed him, and the disappointed would-be hero committed suicide; however it was later revealed that GSDF Colonel Yamamoto Kiyokatsu had aided Mishima and given training to his group, including on psychological warfare, but despite being investigated by police Yamamoto was promoted to Brigadier-General less than two years later.[23] Society perhaps had even less confidence in civilian leaders. The first DG-JDA, Kimura Tokutarō, purged for war crimes, when Justice Minister in 1951 seemingly sought to recruit 200,000 nationalists and gangsters to 'secure' Japan amid Communist-led disturbances. By contrast, the 'Three Arrows' scandal was merely a JSDF attempt to inject some realistic defence scenarios to 'professionalise' planning exercises neglected by civilian leaders. As a former-JDA official stated, 'the truth is that plans about required defense capability were really not taken seriously inside the JDA.'[24] The trust deficit also resulted in limited defence intelligence capability and continuing reliance upon the United States.

US Forces

From 1945 onwards, US Forces Japan (USFJ) were the primary defenders of Japan. They were gradually reduced as the JSDF expanded, from 260,000 personnel (with 2,824 facilities) in 1952, to 117,000 (565) by 1956, until 1960, when personnel stabilised at 46,000, and reducing again to 34,700 in 1966 due to Vietnam demands.[25] Peace in Vietnam resulted in USFJ increases despite Okinawa's reversion in 1972, the most notable change being the first forward-basing of a USN aircraft carrier group (*USS Midway*) in Yokosuka from October 1973, providing a major USN Asian presence, and bolstering Japan's defences. It also provoked the ire of left-wing protesters, apparently angry with the Japan-US alliance, the Japanese government, and the US government, in that order. Few referenced the vessel name irritating MSDF IJN-veterans.[26] But while USFJ could prove an irritant to some Japanese, only those in Okinawa, under full US occupation 1945–72 with the massive post-reversion foreign military presence, could most fully appreciate the burdens of hosting US forces, and question their 'security.'

However, USFJ would remain as a major part of Japan's defences within the unequal treaty system, many members dying while serving in Japan, including aircrew shot down while flying close to Soviet, North Korean, and Chinese airspace from Japanese bases.[27] USFJ provided initial Force training and tactical development, emphasizing future JSDF training specialists, but the mentors were aiming to depart rapidly. Within five years the ASDF and particularly the MSDF enjoyed intimate US 'mentor-mentored' relations that matured into mutual respect and support, the naval-alliance relationship incorporating 'joint exercises and intelligence sharing since the 1950s.'[28] The GSDF, meanwhile, lacked an intimate mentor relationship, becoming a 'political and defence orphan.' Japanese defence was shared between the JSDF and USFJ in the 1960 Security Treaty, yet apart from burgeoning naval relations there was no significant attempt to operationalise alliance security until the 1978 Guidelines, and the predominant USFJ stance until 1973 was reduction and withdrawal.[29] The Forces meanwhile focused upon recruiting and equipping.

Recruitment

Force Recruitment was not initially problematic as the post-Korean War economic slump resulted in major redundancies and the JSDF provided steady employment, with a diversity of specialisations and specialist schools. In 1952, NSF recruitment had seen 214,429 applicants for 63,940 positions. The JSDF 1954 figure was 170,434 for 55,000 positions, but just over 50,000 were enrolled, leading to recruitment intakes expanding from one to four by 1956, when recruitment for 42,000 positions resulted in only 39,693 being accepted from over 200,000 applicants. By 1959, positions had reduced to 25,300, but from 151,467 applicants more than 2,000 posts remained unfilled, the economic upturn clearly having an effect, as was the demographic dip of men born in wartime.[30] There were fewer problems in recruiting officer candidates, with 316 applicants applying for twenty-five foreign language officer positions, but the ratio of applicants to positions began to decline in the late 1950s.[31] The ability to recruit became more serious during the 1960s 'income-doubling' economy, and although the MSDF and ASDF usually achieved their targets, the GSDF consistently fell short. The first Japanese defence white paper in 1970 explicitly stated the challenges of recruiting 30,000 every year to two- to three-year contracts, and retaining highly skilled personnel, such as nurses, with approximately 60 per cent of positions vacant.[32] It failed, however, to indicate that mediocre pay, conditions, housing, and low public esteem had significantly impacted upon recruitment and retention.

Unsurprisingly, air-crew service and the National Defense Academy (NDA) proved popular. Flying training candidate applicants contended with an applicant-success ratio of between eight and eighteen to one. The first (1952) Academy intake contended with a twenty-nine to one acceptance ratio, while NDA recruitment by 1959 stabilised at a nine to one ratio.[33] These figures were consistent with higher-level universities in Japan, and the appeal of free education, with a stipend, and no compulsory Force service requirement upon graduation was probably greater than patriotism. The JSDF has relied upon certain regions for the majority of its recruits (the same pattern applies to the US and the UK), lessening numbers of applicants from metropolitan centres, and increasingly depending upon distressed areas for recruits.[34] In Japan, the north and west followed traditions, with IJN officers from Kyushu samurai clans and IJA officers of modest Tohoku noblemen prominent, while the JSDF proportionally recruited few from Tokyo and Osaka and yet many from Hokkaido and Tohoku (north-east, particularly Aomori, Miyagi, Fukushima) and Kyushu (south-west, especially Fukuoka, Nagasaki, Kumamoto, Kagoshima) prefectures.

JSDF Overall Recruitment by Prefecture 1980

Hokkaido	24,114	Tokyo	7,173	Fukuoka	11,144
Aomori	8,425	Kanagawa	4,497	Nagasaki	9,863
Miyagi	7,977	Osaka	2,898	Kumamoto	13,646
Fukushima	7,248	–	–	Kagoshima	14,278

The imbalance is stark, Nagasaki providing ten times the recruits (per capita) of Tokyo.[35]

Population by Prefecture 1980

Hokkaido	5,575,989	Tokyo	11,618,281	Fukuoka	4,553,461
Aomori	1,523,907	Kanagawa	6,924,348	Nagasaki	1,590,563
Miyagi	2,082,230	Osaka	8,473,446	Kumamoto	1,790,327
Fukushima	2,035,272	–	–	Kagoshima	1,784,623

While Tokyo contributed 30 per cent fewer recruits than Hokkaido, despite more than double the population, it provided almost 30 per cent of all officer candidates, compared to Hokkaido's 10 per cent. Among 'provincial' areas, only Fukuoka contributed officer candidates in numbers significantly above the average. It seems that northern Japan was providing much JSDF manpower, and land area, without achieving concomitant influence within the officer corps.[36]

Officer Candidate Recruitment by Prefecture 1980

Hokkaido 10%	Miyagi 12.6%	Tokyo 29.7%	Fukuoka 19.9%

The NPR was established with extreme haste, succeeded, within two years, by the rapidly expanded NSF, and then, without experience building or consolidation, the JSDF were founded and expanded. The GSDF grew significantly, but the MSDF and ASDF experienced more dramatic growth, from lower base figures and with highly technical professions. The MSDF (92 per cent) and ASDF (at 94.2) recruited quite successfully, held more career appeal, and their establishments were far smaller than the GSDF. In 1973, GSDF personnel comprised less than 86 per cent of the 180,000 establishment, and never achieved more than 90 per cent during the Cold War.

JSDF Establishment Personnel

	1954	1955	1956	1958	1960	1967	1969	1973	1980
GSDF	130,000	150,000	160,000	170,000	171,500	173,000	179,000	180,000	180,000
MSDF	15,800	19,400	22,700	25,400	32,100	36,600	37,800	41,400	43,900
ASDF	6,300	10,300	14,400	26,600	38,300	40,700	41,200	44,600	46,200

JSDF Actual Personnel[37]

	1970	1973	1980
GSDF	157,600	154,000	154,500
MSDF	36,900	38,100	40,500
ASDF	41,400	40,900	43,500

Despite the 'bubble' economy drawing workers into corporations, the JSDF reached record recruitment levels during the 1980s, as joining became increasingly regarded as a rightful career, and the legitimacy of the Forces considered less controversial. The bubble period also accelerated movement of young workers from the provinces to metropolitan areas, JSDF service providing a 'boomerang' compensatory effect of returning personnel to provincial areas. The GSDF as the largest force required the greatest budget, and developed a profile that became synonymous for all Forces, as a provider of rescue and relief amid crisis. It shall be the first Force examined in detail.

Ground Self-Defense Force

The MSDF may lay claim to an unbroken imperial naval lineage. The GSDF by contrast was content to break Imperial Army legacies. One of its defining qualities has been the desire to be regarded as a professional army, in the same way that the MSDF and ASDF effortlessly manage as navy and air force respectively.[38] The NPR legacy was also something the GSDF failed to dwell upon, seemingly equally ill at ease with police origins (until 2015), and it had the most obvious of Cold War national defence roles. The secondary domestic security role was an NPR continuation, even if 'military' reinforcing of the police was an uncomfortable notion. Disaster rescue and relief roles were also continued, and therefore the GSDF should have been secure in its duties and confident of its abilities. However, these were lacking for much of the Cold War. The Force received US equipment and training, but the 1957 BPND, rather than providing development focus, facilitated withdrawal of most US Army units and their mentoring potential. The Force also failed to establish strong joint/inter-service planning or doctrine development with the MSDF and ASDF. In many ways the GSDF were 'left alone,' highly regarded among neither military professionals nor civilians, and struggling for defence relevance. The 'post-war Japanese army' developed unconventionally, its professional combat and non-combat capabilities tied to a deep civilian support and cooperation ethos unmatched by deep public support.

Establishment

The GSDF had a larger capability base upon which to build than the other Forces, but also faced the challenge of re-equipping tens of thousands of troops rather than making gradual qualitative improvements. Manpower rose rapidly, from 110,000 at the establishing of the NSF to 130,000 in one year, and to 170,000 in 1956.[39] Economic growth impacted upon recruitment and retention. Most personnel were retained on two-year terms of service and could leave upon completion, the most skilled being sought by civilian employers. Not only quantitative problems impacted upon recruitment, as candidate quality was a significant issue, and one which shocked a GSDF colonel who entered officer candidate school in 1982 and considered one third of graduates to be of extremely limited ability.[40] The primary problem was meeting the expansion demands of the Japanese and US governments, 170,000 in the first DBP and 180,000 by the fourth, while also improving quality. Nakamura Ryuhei, former GSDF Chief of Staff, suggests the targets were the maximum figures that could be justified to the MOF and Japanese public.[41] Numerical recruitment rather than capability targets were provided, but once a formation had been established there was little impetus to evaluate or improve quality. Initially, US MAP aid provided (surplus) armoured fighting vehicles (AFV), artillery, small arms, and support weapons, at times ill suited to needs. The GSDF could scarcely reject rifles producing such recoil that average marksmanship suffered, due to the all-consuming need to establish units rather than capabilities. With such scant regard to quality it is hardly surprising that professional esteem was suboptimal.

Defence Build-up and Defence Tasks

From the modest NSF scale, GSDF armoured forces underwent dramatic increases from 244 tanks in 1952 to 1,000 by 1966, with equivalent quantitative improvements in other AFV, artillery, and aircraft. US military aid terminated in 1967.[42] It was announced in 1963 that Japan would receive 225 M-41 light tanks under US MAP funding, and yet the JDA would also spend approximately ¥13 trillion on AFV for the 7th Mechanized Division, exceeding the cost of three MSDF submarines.[43] Japan received fewer than 150 M-41s due to MAP reductions, and the fact that they were inferior to the new domestic Type-61 (type-number indicating acceptance year)—though the model remained in service until the 1980s. The premier 7th Division received a plethora of AFV in the early 1960s, including fifty-nine Type-61 MBT, forty-one Type-60 self-propelled recoilless rifles, twenty-five self-propelled mortars, forty-five self-propelled artillery guns (SPG), twenty-three anti-aircraft SPG, and fifteen repair, recovery, and bridging vehicles. No new armoured personnel carriers (APC) were provided, despite existing vehicles being obsolete war surplus, even though funds were allocated for an ASDF Nike-Hercules surface-to-air missile (SAM) regiment costing more than re-equipping 7th Division.[44] This pattern was repeated beyond the Cold War—tanks and artillery were increased rather than infantry APC, obsolete vehicles retained for quantitative capability images, and large numbers of armoured formations facilitated. Only in aviation could real progress be seen, with helicopter totals doubling to 270 in 1966–73, and exceeding 400 by 1989, almost equalling ASDF aircraft numbers and with quality enhancement that few armies could match.[45]

While listing materiel may seem a puerile accounting exercise, it illustrates where investment was focused, what nature of Force was being developed, and to a degree its character and purpose. With capable air and naval forces, light, mobile ground forces able to rapidly re-deploy could have been developed, and GSDF aviation capabilities suggest such a route, but the focus was clearly upon hard, heavy forces with maximum firepower. This was based upon the premise of a Soviet invasion threat, concentrated in the north. The GSDF was unable to provide unilateral defence, but would have to rely upon US reinforcements if the invading force were above a nominal threshold, which in the late 1970s was vaguely 'four-five divisions.'[46] A US assessment in 1964 stated that 'GSDF strength has remained over the past three years at about 85% of authorized strength' and that, although comprising '13 divisions, some divisions are at only 50–60% of strength; available manpower is sufficient for only 9 full-strength divisions.'[47] US thinking was that air power could compensate for this shortfall, but it was unclear who was expected to provide this.

GSDF officers of different eras have expressed distinctly underwhelming impressions of ASDF close air support (CAS) capabilities, hence the perceived need for extensive artillery and aviation forces to compensate for the 'CAS-gap.' Some personnel also doubted the capabilities of the MSDF (without the USN) to deter or defeat an amphibious assault on Hokkaido, and this appears to have driven GSDF investment in land-based surface-to-surface anti-ship missiles (SSM). The Type-88 SSM entered service more than two decades later than the equivalent Swedish Rb08A system (1967), despite enhancing GSDF capabilities against the invasion threat that drove development of expensive hard-heavy forces.[48] The similar Soviet SS-N-2 missile was deployed to Cuba in 1962 to deter invasion, and demonstrated its effectiveness in sinking Israeli and Pakistani naval vessels (1967, 1971).[49] One retired officer involved with Type-88 development noted ASDF and MSDF resistance to the GSDF acquiring such a maritime defence role. The GSDF naturally wished to expand its capabilities. In its search for legitimacy it also sought salient relevance within a 'Force relevance promotion' effort, and deployed defence-based arguments to gain a sea-strike force capability despite domestic naval and air opposition.[50]

The GSDF operated through Regional Armies, without centralised GSDF command (until 2018). The first was Northern Army (1952, NSF), for Hokkaido, the others followed in 1955 (Western Army) and 1960 (North-Eastern, Eastern, Middle).⁵¹ Initially, these Armies controlled relatively weak 'regional forces' (*kankutai*), multiple battalion-regiment formations but not field formations of brigade/divisional level capable of multi-arms coordination (infantry with artillery, armour etc.). They were not capable of field manoeuvres and their development into brigades (later divisions) was a priority. In the first wave, this resulted in the nominal formation of six divisions (*shidan*) and four combined brigades (*konseidan*).⁵² The latter differed from conventional brigades by being combined-arms forces with balanced armour-artillery-infantry elements, and consequently less manpower with greater firepower.⁵³ They were larger equivalent versions of NATO/Commonwealth battle groups in Iraq and Afghanistan, or USMC Marine Expeditionary Units (MEU).⁵⁴ Command of combined brigades would have been challenging, given that they included only one infantry regiment, compared to three battalions in most Commonwealth brigades allowing fluid movement, interchange, and support between battalions.

Clearly the most valued units were armoured. Hunter-Chester has suggested that US-Japan contingency planning discussions from the late 1970s resulted in the GSDF 'changing its posture [...] creating a heavier, tank-centric force,' but this fails to account for the great early investment in armoured forces.⁵⁵ Armoured formations did become 'heavier' throughout the Cold War, with more and heavier artillery. The first *kokusanka* Type-61 tank was more powerful than US-aid models, and, being lighter than NATO equivalents was more easily transportable in Japan (with restrictive tunnels and bridge loadings), cheaper than imported models due to the weak yen, and lacked the performance-degrading ergonomic pedal-reach problems of US vehicles.⁵⁶ The second DBP targeted thirteen divisions, each reduced in manpower (*c.* 7,000–9,000) from the regional force units (12,000), possibly driven by recruitment problems or pro-active anticipation rather than reactive planning.⁵⁷ Sado reflects on GSDF officers' comments that smaller formations were intended to make Japanese divisions more manoeuvrable than US divisions, given Japan's mountainous terrain and consequent command and control difficulties.⁵⁸ However, GSDF officers have insisted that concentration upon armoured-artillery units allowed each (smaller) division to have equivalent scales of tank-artillery resources to larger divisions, a vital requirement given endemic under-manning, particularly of infantry. MSDF and US officers have suggested that ensuring GSDF command positions was a prime motivation, each division being commanded by a lieutenant-general (three star) rather than a major-general (two star) in most armies (with larger divisions). The Chief of Ground Staff stated in 1972 that the thirteen divisions and 180,000 personnel establishment were required to secure Japanese territory, and that, although more divisions would be militarily desirable, such demands could weaken national security by reducing public support.[59]

The thirteen division re-organisation appears to have been completed by 1962, with four divisions in Hokkaido (Northern Army), two each in Tohoku (North-Eastern) and Kanto-Koshinetsu (Eastern), three in Kinki, Chugoku, Shikoku (Middle), and two in Kyushu (Western Army).[60] Of these new divisions, the 7th Mechanized (Hokkaido) was the most prominent, after being founded as a composite brigade in 1955, becoming 7th Armored Division in 1981.[61] This division received high investment priority and enjoyed a famous IJA lineage, being headquartered immediately besides the Hokkaido Gokoku Shrine, a place of IJA and JSDF pilgrimage.[62] Examining units within 7th Division also reveals emerging priorities. The NSF 1st Independent Special Vehicle [tank] Battalion formed in November 1952, becoming the 101st Special Vehicle Battalion in 1954, undergoing further name changes before finally becoming the 73rd Tank Regiment in 7th Division in 1982. Initially equipped with ex-US war surplus, the regiment didn't receive Type-61s until 1969, despite being a key frontline unit. The first Type-74s arrived in 1979, five years after acceptance, while the Type-90 entered regimental service only in 1999.[63] This regiment, within one of the most important divisions in the GSDF, prioritised for modernisation, waited on average more than seven years to be equipped with the latest tank models due to fractional defence budgeting and *kokusanka* priorities.[64] The lack of urgency contrasted with contemporary defence white papers highlighting Soviet invasion threats from 1979 and government efforts to address them.[65]

The emphasis upon heavy formations may seem a natural response to invasion fears, yet there was little sense of alarm in early JDA public pronouncements. With tight budgets and recruitment problems, it is remarkable that the government emphasized the 180,000 target, particularly as personnel costs were (and remain) the largest item in defence expenditure. The Chief of Ground Staff acknowledged that a Swiss-style in-depth national citizenry defence was unacceptable, conscription politically taboo and probably unconstitutional.[66] Former DG-JDA Funada Naka in 1969 proposed a one million man Swiss militia-style 'local defense corps,' but was widely ridiculed despite his concern for the inadequacy of JSDF reserves, and limited Cold War contingency planning.[67] The small-division approach suited the defence of Japan, but this did not necessarily mean thirteen small, heavy divisions, and it could be conjectured that without US pressure the GSDF would have produced a much smaller force target and thereby attracted less funding. Ironically, the United States eventually preferred air and naval investment prioritisation.

In addition to the development of armoured-artillery units, field engineering and medical units for Force support as well as disaster-relief operations were prioritised. Engineering units had been vital in IJA China and Pacific War operations, and GSDF bridging, earth moving, and other capabilities were impressive. Taking account of its Hokkaido presence, the GSDF also made substantial investments in snow-vehicles, and tested equipment for cold weather operations, even though older AFV were often open-topped.[68] Snow capabilities were proven during civil support activities, including medical evacuations that utilised sleighs and even tanks.[69] From inception, based on IJA experiences of cholera in China, water purification became an area of Force expertise, with extensive purification equipment and bathing facilities.[70] For similar reasons, the failings of wartime medical care resulted in a comprehensive GSDF medical service, not least as one of the welfare measures with which to appeal to recruits and their families.

Specialist units, such as the parachute regiment at Narashino, Chiba, received priority in training and equipment, even though it is not clear why, given that such forces had no obvious national defence role. Parachute forces started with twenty men in Fukuoka in 1954, but with US training and equipment developed into the 101st Airborne Battalion (1956), and 1st Airborne Brigade (*Dai-ichikūteidan*; 1958) under former-IJA Major Kinugasa Hayao, later JCS Chairman.[71] Membership became the pathway to prestigious ranger qualification as 1st Airborne was the sole contingency force under DG-JDA direct command, including responding to disasters, accidents, and incursions as an 'emergency counterforce'—effectively 'special forces' but without the micro-elite status of US Delta Force or UK/Australia/New Zealand Special Air Service (SAS) units.[72] The GSDF would not prepare such forces until 2000 (see Chapter Four).

Airborne forces developed in parallel to GSDF aviation, resulting by 1959 in a light-infantry manoeuvre reserve centred about the 1st Helicopter Brigade (*Dai-ichi herikoputaadan*), which from 1968 was based in Kisarazu, near Narashino. The Third DBP (1967–71) provided an additional eighty-three large and medium helicopters, thereby establishing a 1,800-man helicopter regiment, with a considerable portion of aviation assets deployed in the Northern and North Eastern Armies. Up to ten helicopter squadrons were allocated to command, liaison, and transport roles, with the central reserve of four squadrons held in Tokyo and Utsunomiya, a main training base.[73] Mitsubishi Heavy Industry (MHI) license-built H-19/S-55 transport craft, able to lift a ten-man section, entered service in 1959. From 1966, the V-107/CH-46, able to lift 4.5-tonnes or 25 troops, was introduced, and, from 1962, the ubiquitous UH-1 Huey, which would serve for over sixty years.[74] By the 1970s, the GSDF was a major 'air power,' complemented from 1985 with anti-tank regiments of licence-produced AH-1S Huey Cobra gunships to address the 'CAS-gap.'[75] US forces define Close Air Support as 'air action by fixed-wing (FW) and rotary-wing (RW) aircraft against hostile targets that are in close proximity to friendly forces, and requires detailed integration of each air mission with fire and movement of those forces.'[76] The GSDF received limited ASDF CAS training or defence planning support, hence GSDF aviation and artillery investment. This was laudable, but not in line with US practice that designated army assets for Close Combat Attack (CCA). Nor does US CCA include the use of non-aviation indirect fire weapons, such as mortars and artillery, which raises issues of interoperability with US Marine Corps (USMC) and Army units.[77] The GSDF expanded its aviation partly to compensate for limited confidence in the ASDF and JSDF joint planning.

Formations

As outlined, the Regional Armies controlled 'regional forces' (*kankutai*) and brigades, re-organised by 1960 into a total GSDF force structure of six divisions and four combined brigades, and into thirteen divisions (nominally) by 1962, even though unit histories suggest that many were below strength. A (1970s) divisional establishment would be either 9,000 troops (seven), or 7,000 (five divisions), 7th Division having a 6,500 establishment. In a mechanized infantry division, there would be four infantry regiments (without brigade-level command) each of 1,200 troops in three infantry battalions, unlike Commonwealth practice of two brigades, each of three battalions of *c*.700 troops each. Combat support units comprised an artillery regiment (1,900 troops, four batteries, ten guns each), a tank battalion/regiment (450, two squadrons, fifteen tanks each), an anti-tank company (130 troops, twelve 106mm recoilless rifles), and a military police company (100). Field support included an engineering battalion (540 troops), a signals battalion (350), and medical, ordnance, supply, and transport companies (100–180 each), with another 1,450 troops in logistical support roles, 170 in the divisional command headquarters, and even a divisional band.[78] Thus, this division would have an establishment of 9,000, though they were often under-strength.

Such a division would be powerful due to its artillery, and locally manoeuvrable with four independent infantry regiments, but without an integral reconnaissance force unless infantry or armoured units were detached, intelligence and situational awareness limitations could hamper commanders. These formations would clearly be challenging to command in high intensity operations, without a subordinate brigade-level and with limited APC. They would also be smaller than equivalent NATO and Soviet divisions, the latter usually comprising 13,000–15,000 troops with integral reconnaissance, armour, artillery, aviation and CAS, although the Northern Army also had the unique 1st Artillery Brigade to supplement the firepower of its divisions.[79] Soviet airborne divisions were much smaller, approximately 6,500 troops with airdropped AFV and artillery, while the Soviet Naval Infantry's sole division, with the Pacific Fleet, had over 8,000 personnel with tank, artillery, and SAM units.[80] Japanese divisions by comparison had additional anti-aircraft and aviation assets provided, particularly in Hokkaido, but major deficiencies, such as limited and elderly APC provision, indicated quantitative and qualitative problems.

Into the 1980s, the GSDF retained outdated tanks with few upgrades, the accompanying infantry also provided with inadequate numbers of APC, and those they possessed had comparatively inferior mobility, protection, and firepower. From wartime half-tracks, through the first domestic Type-60, without nuclear, biological, chemical (NBC) or night vision equipment, to the improved Type-73, of which only 340 were produced compared to 873 Type-74 tanks, Japan invested little in relatively cheap infantry vehicles.[81] The Soviets introduced BMP and BMD Mechanized Infantry Combat Vehicles (MICV), APC with enhanced firepower and protection, prompting NATO responses with Marder (Germany), AMX-10P (France), Bradley (US), and Warrior (UK), while Japan's limited-production Type-89 entered service after the Cold War. Only one anti-tank AFV was introduced, the small, cheap Type-60, the first domestic post-war AFV with meagre armour and weather protection. Effective for 1960 but rapidly rendered obsolete, it remained in production until 1979 and in service until 2001, supplemented by the first domestic anti-tank guided weapon (ATGW), the Type-64 Medium Anti-Tank (MAT); this was an impressive feat that demonstrated 'spin-on' from

Japan's electronics industry.[82] From the 1980s, 'spin-on' produced various highly effective domestic missiles, but the GSDF soldiered on with obsolete weaponry, such as the M-20, an NPR-era bazooka, which was in frontline service into the 1980s and in reserve service in 2019—in Edwardian First Sea Lord Jackie Fisher's term, 'a miser's hoard of useless junk.'[83] Former US Defense Secretary James Schlesinger commented to DG-JDA Sakata in 1976, 'If you keep spending money the way you are now, in five years you'll end up with a military that has people but old weapons.'[84] With 80 per cent of GSDF and half of ASDF/MSDF budgets devoted to personnel expenses, it appeared that 'building-up' both quantity and quality were beyond budgetary means. Until the late 1970s, most GSDF artillery was of Pacific War vintage, but with new *kokusan* equipment increasingly expensive (with an appreciating yen), reluctance to replace was rational.[85] US offshore procurement (OSP) had been immense, with 9,000 Japanese-manufactured trucks ordered for the Forces in 1957, so the end of such aid was keenly felt.[86]

While a national citizenry defence may have been impossible, the GSDF concentrated upon fulfilling numerical targets rather than capability, with the exception of firepower. This was a reasonable counter to limited invasion threats, but did not match the notion of Japanese armed forces tightly integrated into US Cold War planning. An extensive 1965 State Department memo from Assistant Secretary of State for Far Eastern Affairs, William P. Bundy, suggested that Japan should develop 'high quality forces on the Swedish model with a sizeable ready reserve,' presenting 'a hard nut to crack.' He also supported cuts in GSDF manpower if 'the resources saved are devoted to modernization of the ground forces, modernization and possible expansion of the air and maritime forces, and formation of organized reserves,' which appear to have been widespread US goals, but ones which Japan chose not to follow.[87] Given this alliance perspective on GSDF configuration, the nature of GSDF operational planning requires examination.

Defence Plans

The basic GSDF Cold War planning scenarios were to reinforce police seizure of agents and insurgents, repel small-scale incursions by air or amphibious assault, and delay and frustrate large-scale invasion forces in manoeuvre warfare, depleting enemy forces and isolating them from resupply and reinforcement.[88] The legal basis was Article 78 of the SDF Law, for mobilisation 'when regular police capabilities are insufficient to assure public safety,' based upon cabinet orders, ratified by the Diet within twenty days, and Article 81 providing local government requests for JSDF mobilisation.[89] Units trained in their respective designated areas, and, it seems, became somewhat adept, not least due to the degree of repetition and lack of operational and geographic variation in GSDF exercises. Hokkaido was the main defence focus, had the largest military training areas and greatest unit concentration. Other Armies suffered from limited training resources, with few opportunities for large-formation training, while some divisions appeared to plan to operate in traditional territorial defence patterns. The exceptions were the airborne and aviation forces, and a secret body detailed by Richard J. Samuels as having been based in Nayoro Camp, Hokkaido, from the GSDF Intelligence Training Academy (*chōsagakkō*) for 'stay behind' sabotage tasks against invading forces. Despite being small and clandestine, such limited intelligence forces were the only GSDF personnel to continue US military and CIA mentoring, but little is known of the scale of GSDF intelligence capacity through the Ground Staff G-2.[90]

GSDF serving and retired personnel have lamented the lack of joint training with the MSDF and ASDF, and combined training with USFJ. Defensive plans were intended to be coordinated, but little was achieved, and the GSDF was left to develop means to defend Hokkaido. Indeed, Kusunoki states that the US prepared to defend Honshu south of Sendai (towards Tokyo), and was 'willing to listen but would not comment' upon matters further north, without comment upon USFJ use of tactical nuclear weapons.[91] This is partly contradicted by *Map Exercise Fuji*, a USFJ-JSDF 1957 command post exercise, 'in which atomic weapons were played,' at US Army Camp Drake, north of Tokyo.[92] The US Joint Chiefs asserted in 1958 that '(the SDF) must eventually be equipped with the most modern conventional and atomic weapons.' GSDF Staff College taught how to fight in an atomic environment using US Command and General Staff College content, but officers relate how JSP Diet criticism in 1968 resulted in NBC training being curtailed.[93] Shibayama suggests that JSDF defence capabilities reduced the likelihood of US atomic weapon use.[94]

Regardless of the nuclear issue, Hokkaido was a difficult defensive proposition, due to its size and topography with four distinct coastlines suitable for amphibious assault, and rolling farmland ideal for armoured forces. The western Ishikari River area, including Sapporo and Asahikawa, was identified as vital, not only for infrastructure and communications, but also as a west coast landing that could bypass Sapporo south-eastwards, severing land communications with Hakodate and Honshu in a force-decapitation manoeuvre, through what one USMC officer considered 'Japan's Fulda Gap.'[95] There was also the possibility of a limited flanking invasion of Niigata, much closer to Tokyo and further from Soviet bases, and a high-risk venture given proximity of Japanese air bases. With such planning difficulties there were few opportunities for extensive forward coastal-defence planning beyond mobile light-infantry battalions countering small landing craft and amphibious vehicles, nor would such a disposition have been advisable if airborne forces were considered a significant threat. Denmark and Sweden adopted coastal defence fortifications reinforced by SSM during the Cold War, but they had large conscript armies with extensive reserves. The Combined Annual Plan (CAP) produced by the JDA provided the main civilian prescript for unit operations, designating what defence role each formation (usually division) would aim to plan and train for, but these appeared to be pro-forma with little evolution.[96]

The Northern Army was headquartered in Sapporo, the four divisional areas being Asahikawa (north-centre, 2nd Div.), Obihiro (east, 5th Div.), Higashi Chitose (south-east, 7th Div.), and Makomanai (south, 11th Div.), with satellite camps hosting units. These dispositions provided the flexibility to counter potential invasion attempts towards the coast or inland, and protected the major routes of communication, municipalities, as well as the Ishikari Plain, although cities, such as Nemuro and Wakkanai, were essentially written off. An example of location-function difficulties was Camp Bekkai, approximately 50km from the Sea of Okhotsk, which from 1965 hosted the 27th Infantry Regiment responsible for coastal defence.[97] Former GSDF Chief of Staff and Chief of Staff, Joint Staff Kurisu Hiroomi insisted that Soviet forces could have attacked the eastern portion of Hokkaido and resisted efforts to repel them, given the light GSDF covering forces. Kurisu also estimated GSDF ammunition supply at two to three weeks, with little prospect of significant replenishment.[98] Others estimated far more pessimistically.

From a European-NATO perspective, greater Force concentration and reinforcement provision might have seemed natural. The British Army during the 1970s based approximately one third of its personnel and most modern equipment in Germany, with regular and reserve reinforcements doubling personnel in annual exercises, and held multi-national brigade-level reinforcement exercises in Norway. The GSDF rarely conducted such reinforcement exercises, being primarily small units limited by civilian, ASDF, and MSDF transport capacities. James Auer states that 'the U.S. never considered the Soviet Union would invade Japan,' but late Cold War defence white papers provide a differing Japanese perspective.[99] Indeed, Auer asserts that the late Cold War US-Japan defence exercise planning was framed around 'the unlikely scenario of a direct invasion of Japan [...] the easiest one politically for the Japanese [...] since that was the scenario the Japanese could do fairly easily, that was the first one selected.'[100] This is supported by Vice-Admiral Sakonjo Naotoshi, who stated that in US-Japan defence discussions following the 1978 Guidelines, the US side (civilian-military) considered GSDF estimates of Soviet invasion to be unrealistic and exaggerated, particularly given Soviet amphibious limitations. According to him, this partly helped to justify the 180,000 troops and armoured investments, but also to ensure a US reinforcement response.[101] Therefore 'research on the Japanese contingency went forward concerning an imagined, unlikely situation.' Two bilateral plans were prepared yet 'treated with such secrecy that they were locked away' and not disclosed to political leaders (with considerable implications for civilian control in both countries). William Perry (later US Defense Secretary) suggested Soviet invasion (Plan 5051) could be managed by Hokkaido police.[102] Indeed, Nishihiro Seiki, closely involved in JDA Cold War planning, suggests that 1960s GSDF expansion driven by US Army reductions in Japan was not to counter 'an external threat, it was intended for the maintenance of the public peace;' to protect USFJ facilities, the JSDF 'emphasized their role as police over that of defenders against an invasion' until 'the first half of the 1970s.'[103] There were attempts at contingency planning, such as the 1963 Three Arrows Study, a joint venture with eighty-four JSDF officers examining a realistic scenario of Korean conflict, which revealed major planning, legal, and capability deficiencies and poor alliance coordination.[104] The scandal that broke upon its revelation stunted joint Force contingency planning for decades and sustained the civilian control mania that excluded the Forces from providing Diet testimony. The priority in subsequent combined operational planning was based upon GSDF limited capabilities rather than inherent importance for national defence.

Natural Defence

The failure to hold reinforcement exercises was due to JSDF reluctance to invest in expensive training, as well as the desire to avoid commercial disruption. Basing divisions away from the north was driven by the need to provide both national defences and natural disaster contingency resources. All forty-seven prefectures hosted GSDF bases, other than Nara, due to NPR police reinforcement and domestic humanitarian assistance/disaster relief (HA/DR) legacies.[105] The first NPR disaster relief duties occurred in July 1951, when a commander responded to local appeals in Fukuchiyama City, Kyoto, receiving local praise, but incurring punishment for failing to obtain PMO approval, in an early demonstration of civilian control.[106] The first national mobilisation, and the first large-scale deployment with ASDF and USFJ personnel, followed the 1959 Ise Bay Typhoon that devastated Nagoya and killed more than 5,000 people.[107] This firmly established GSDF 'highly constabulary, less masculine, and civilianized identities' as the primary national rescue and relief force, reinforcing its socio-political legitimacy.[108] This proved decisive for Force involvement in domestic relief operations. Examples can be found for every GSDF division. The 10th Division, in Moriyama City (Nagoya), was at the centre of 1959 typhoon rescue and relief activities only three months after (brigade) formation, and 1962–81 participated in seven rescue, relief, and infrastructure support missions. The most intense was the Hidagawa Bus Accident on 18 August 1968, when a landslide swept away two buses, killing 106, with twelve missing presumed dead, and overwhelming Gifu Prefectural authorities. The division provided 3,462 of 7,891 GSDF personnel despatched, with 1,237 ASDF, and twenty-three MSDF divers.[109] In extremis joint operations occurred naturally, but they were neither jointly planned nor trained for.

Under the SDF Law, local requests could be made to the DG-JDA, but there were emergency provisions for direct local requests to Forces for civil-military cooperation (CIMIC), and even for GSDF commanders to undertake rescue and relief duties without official request. These were based upon a 1978 SDF Law revision resulting from the Large-Scale Earthquake Countermeasures Law. The law also assigned the Forces as reconnaissance elements for the National Headquarters for Earthquake Disaster Prevention. After the 1995 Hanshin earthquake, commanders again hesitated, but criticism was directed at the Murayama cabinet's caution rather than GSDF units.[110] The CIMIC pattern was repeated throughout the Cold War, the only GSDF operational deployments being HA/DR, such as the gruesome recovery of corpses in the aftermath of the 1985 Japan Airlines JL123 crash, and Explosive Ordnance Disposal (EOD *fuhatsudanshori*).[111] As in other war-ravaged countries, this work was frequent and dangerous, equivalent to MSDF minesweeping, but with one deviation: EOD cases continued long after the post-war period: the GSDF was called to an average 30 incidents per week during 2001 in Kanto alone, which experienced 5,854 such cases 1994–2014.[112] However, most duties were 'less-military,' such as the 25th Infantry Regiment, 6th Division (Hokkaido), which from May 1964 to January 1965 fought mountain fires, removed snow, and captured a rogue bear. No role was too obscurely related to defence, including planting crops, picking apples, and aiding sporting events, seemingly at odds with frontline duties.[113] This though became the essence of the Cold War GSDF—combat training and community tasks.

The abstraction from defence duties is more easily understood in conjunction with the quest to shape public opinion in the ongoing 'search for legitimacy,' in which local environments influenced CIMIC interaction. Rural communities tended to be more positive than urban ones, partly as the drain of young people to urban areas depleted the local workforce and services, such as volunteer fire-fighters. GSDF bases provided economic stimulus and infrastructure services, but rural-urban divisions were not universal. Significant cities, such as Yokosuka, Kanagawa, and Kisarazu, Chiba, on opposite sides of Tokyo Bay within an hour's commute of Tokyo, hosted various JSDF facilities and endeavoured to foster relations, often involving city centre parades. One GSDF officer in Kanazawa, Ishikawa, a sophisticated yet *inaka* (provincial) city, attempted to coordinate Force events with local groups but was consequently inundated with anti-JSDF protests concerning a summer festival invitation to local people.[114] The contrast between cities was as stark as between rural and urban, but as usual the starkest exception was Hokkaido.

The prominence of the GSDF in Hokkaido was not always part of a smooth interaction, and there were significant protests, but the sheer scale and depth of involvement of particularly Ground Forces in Hokkaido life is remarkable.[115] This could be interpreted as an extension of the imperial-era 'colonial Hokkaido'—not through design but by an extension of central control of the island as a 'special case.'[116] Ann Irish illustrates the intrusiveness of the Hokkaido Development Bureau, as 'Tokyo officials felt the need to continue control of Hokkaido development […] on the Cold War's front line.'[117] However, many local communities relied upon the GSDF for essential services, as only from 1974 did all Hokkaido municipal bodies have civil fire and ambulance provision.[118] Many municipalities lobbied to host GSDF facilities, in the expectation of 'people's livelihood support' payments, as well as land requirement compensation. In Takikawa, following the bankruptcy of a local chemical company, the municipality attracted a GSDF base in 1955, with personnel and families boosting the population above the 30,000 threshold to become a city. Sasaki Tomoyuki details cases of agricultural, infrastructure, and cultural support by the GSDF in Hokkaido communities, some forming

JSDF Cooperation Associations (*Jieitaikyōryokukai*), and one successfully appealing in 1965 for a GSDF base to replace a failed coal mine.[119]

Force involvement in public life in Hokkaido has been well documented, but in other areas there is far less recognition of engagement in public works projects as 'training exercises.' These were localised, such as the construction of a school in Ogose Town, Saitama Prefecture, 1969–70, scarcely acknowledged during anniversary events, even while remembered by former students and staff.[120] The Japan Teachers' Union's (*Nikkyōso*) antagonism toward the Forces was and remains prominent.[121] In Ogose, a large secular war memorial, the Tomb for Unknown Soldiers of the World (*Sekaimumeisenshi no haka*) was constructed 1953–5 by the NSF-GSDF with local residents. The dubious secular nature of the memorial and Force involvement could seem questionable, but little controversy surrounded the project.[122] The lack of fanfare was matched in extensive road and bridge projects undertaken by 9th Engineer Battalion in Tohoku, such as the 'battle' to build Route 339 between Kodamari Village and Cape Tappi on the inhospitable north-west coast of Aomori.[123] Along the route, GSDF plaques and memorial stones record these achievements, but there is little broader acknowledgement of such Force contributions to society.

Society and Culture

An examination of JSDF culture requires not only a study of how the Forces train and operate, but also an account of the values instilled and represented, including interactions with Force families and broader society. GSDF culture developed from a police base and a rejection of IJA legacies, and sought alternative models as local servants, rescuers, and homeland defenders, often in that order. Local communities rarely felt excessive burdens from GSDF bases, due to restrictive regulations and their relatively small number. The residents of Gotenba, Shizuoka, 'enjoyed' almost constant live-fire training, but theirs was a rare case in Honshu. The examples of Hokkaido, particularly the Eniwa case, in which the Northern Army attempted to prosecute a family for obstructing live firing at the Shimamatsu training area, immediately adjacent to their farm and despite repeated requests to provide advanced notice of firing, projected a contrasting model.[124] Despite positive GSDF images in Hokkaido, such local incidents repeatedly occurred, demonstrating an arrogance of Forces determined to prove their worth as defenders, and ignoring other aspects of Force culture.

The numbers of GSDF who retired in base areas is significant, and this, combined with the positive economic impact upon often depressed areas, as well as PR exercises like the annual Kita-Utsunomiya helicopter 'joy-rides,' helped develop positive impressions.[125] Responses to disasters have done more than anything to promote Force legitimacy. This has been enhanced by television coverage, culminating in high profile post-Cold War operations in Hanshin, Niigata, Tohoku, and Kumamoto, and in countering the Coronavirus pandemic. GSDF engineering capabilities and massive helicopter lift provides an independence to respond with limited ASDF or MSDF support. Criticism of tardy Hanshin deployments directed towards the Murayama administration led to the GSDF response system being reinforced.[126] The ultimate expression of the GSDF's role in times of emergency came with the Triple Disaster in Tohoku following the Great East Japan Earthquake of 11 March 2011, and it was this experience that confirmed the GSDF as the one reliable national institution during crises. Such duties obviously directly served the society that had long lived with the Forces' ambiguous status, but such was the scale of GSDF social service that personnel became accustomed and comfortable with such roles, to the extent that it was this CIMIC capacity that facilitated GSDF overseas despatches.

The role of women within the NSF and GSDF was initially highly circumscribed and restricted to nursing, which, according to the academic Tanaka Jirō, in his testimony to the Diet, provided an engaging contrast with the imperial military.[127] The JDA pioneered expanding GSDF duties from nursing to administration, signals and support areas in 1968, despite opposition from the GSDF high command.[128] By 1975, the GSDF was annually recruiting over 300 women, with 2,820 serving JSDF women, which rose to 966 GSDF female recruits and over 9,000 female personnel in 1992. Sato Fumika illustrates how this recruitment boom coincided with defence expansion and male recruitment problems, doubling women's numbers and percentage of the Forces 1986–91, and coinciding with Japan's first equal opportunities law.[129] Female GSDF personnel reached 6,484 (of 9,908 JSDF total) by 1998, despite obviously highly gendered career barriers and discrimination, women continued to gain promotion and expand their specialist areas.[130] The darker side of this development was presented in a 1999 report that 18 per cent of JSDF-JDA female personnel had experienced sexual harassment.[131] Sato provides examples of politicians' comments from 1985, such as Suzuki Muneo (LDP): 'young men will decide to enroll in the NDA and contribute to national defense so that they can find good wives. I recommend thinking that way.' A female opposition Diet member remarked of comments such as 'women are not physically appropriate for such military actions' that they 'illustrate the sexist logic that underlies popular images of women' in the Forces.[132]

In considering GSDF culture and lingering imperial influences, religion requires examination that it rarely receives, as Shinto rites and symbols became integrated into imperial-military culture. This came to the fore with the issue of the Yasukuni Shrine, when it became known that fourteen executed Class-A war criminals, including Tōjō Hideki, had been enshrined in 1978. Feelings were inflamed by Prime Minister Nakasone's 1985 visit, even though it emerged that Emperor Hirohito refrained from adding to his eight post-war visits up to 1975 due to the war criminals' enshrinement.[133] Yasukuni remains a dilemma for *izoku*, the families of fallen IJA/IJN veterans, who seek to worship their ancestors, and who lack alternatives, such as Endo Ayako, who annually visited the shrine on 7 April, the day her father, the ship's doctor of battleship *Yamato*, died in 1945.[134] Visits by JDA-JSDF personnel to *Gokoku* (Nation Defence) Shrines have been less controversial, despite raising constitutional and cultural questions.[135]

Article 20 of the constitution states that no religious body may 'receive any privileges from the State,' with the latter obliged to 'refrain from religious education or any other religious activity.' A Tsu City court ruling in 1965 found a *jichinsai* Shinto blessing ceremony for municipal buildings and related payments acceptable based on 'ideas current in society.'[136] This became relevant in the case of Nakaya Takafumi, a GSDF member who died in a work traffic accident in Yamaguchi in 1968, and received a Buddhist funeral based on his father's wishes, to which his Christian wife, Yasuko, consented. From 1964, the JSDF Veterans Association had urged enshrinement in Yamaguchi *Gokoku* Shrine, from 1970 receiving cooperation from the JDA Regional Liaison Office (RLO). Despite Nakaya Yasuko's protests, her husband was enshrined in April 1972. The Supreme Court ruled RLO action had only an 'indirect relation with the religion,' and had intended to 'make SDF members in active service proud of their life and death.'[137] An RLO official told Mrs. Nakaya that 'it was natural [...] because he had died for the State,' another insisting that 'Gokoku Shrine is an official religion,' illustrating constitutional ignorance and insensitivity.[138] The JDA conducted secular services from 1957, and constructed a secular JSDF memorial in 1962, which in 1998 moved to JDA Ichigaya, with 1,737 JDA/JSDF personnel lost during service memorialised (*kenshō*) up to 2004.[139]

Skabelund and Ishikawa report Christian JSDF personnel experiencing little or no workplace discrimination, but significant congregation prejudice against their profession, mainly due to imperial state Shinto militarism and the perceived Christian affinity with Article 9.[140] Major Yatabe Minoru, being publicly eviscerated by a church minister for his JSDF 'life of sin,' compounded contemporary victimisation of JSDF members and families by verbal abuse as 'tax thieves,' or discrimination in local government services.[141] This view was not so unusual at the time, with one commentator noting that 'for decades the Self-Defense Forces were considered people who "live under a rock."'[142, 143]

Shinto worship has not been encouraged, rather selective cultural legacies of imperial and post-imperial military service have been venerated, even while the GSDF generally rejects imperial heritage. The GSDF Kasumigaura Base Public Relations Center includes an 'Ōka Corner' for IJN suicide rocket-planes, displays on Fujita Nobuo, the only Japanese pilot to bomb the US mainland, and extensive memorialisation of Fujita Tamiko, the wartime bus-driver venerated as 'Sky-goddess' (*Ōzora no Megami*). André Hertrich illustrates that among over 130 JSDF museums, many combine imperial and Force elements with broader history, such as the Northern Territories issue.[144] Japanese society appears little conflicted by religion, although magazine *AERA* noted in 2015 that of twenty Abe cabinet members fifteen belonged to the nationalist *Nipponkaigi* group, but nineteen to the Shinto Association of Spiritual Leadership (*Shintoseijirenmei*).[145]

Conclusion

There were 156,216 GSDF personnel in 1988 despite an establishment of 180,000, nominally reinforced by over 40,000 reservists, but with dubious training and equipment. When compared to the British Army, the GSDF of the late Cold War was approximately the same (regular) size, and with similar tank and airborne forces, but far greater provision of artillery, organic aviation, and HA/DR-related equipment. Relative GSDF weaknesses were armoured reconnaissance vehicles (ARV) and APC, few reserves or special forces, and poor forward air control (FAC) skills, with limited reinforcement, joint, or combined training, and without combat experience. British forces possessed at least five times the ARV and four times the GSDF APC provision, and despite the often tribal instincts of Cold War British forces, they regularly trained together with joint CAS and amphibious support roles prominently to the fore. Knowing a potential enemy's location, direction, action, and strength constitute fundamental military requirements, which were not well met by the GSDF. Even within a (seemingly unlikely) single scenario of Soviet invasion, due to the variety of potential amphibious and airborne assault locations this situational awareness limitation would have greatly hampered operations. The failure to maximise limited GSDF infantry assets through modern APC/AIFV is difficult to understand. Light infantry valued for flexibility and air-mobility only constituted one brigade until 2002, but heavy (armoured) infantry were also generally neglected compared to tanks and artillery, compounding poor reconnaissance capabilities. The development of reserves would also have been logical for reinforcement and as the repository of niche skills, as in the US, the UK, and Australia. However, as with most aspects of JSDF investments, those for training, personnel incentives, and military 'software' were overshadowed by 'hard and heavy' 'industrial military' expenditure.[146] The GSDF would have been well advised to have attempted to do what it gradually attempted in the next century, to develop smaller, lighter, more mobile forces for more diverse, flexible operations more closely matched to national defence requirements. It later came to more fully appreciate the value of both female and reserve personnel, but both were largely neglected during the Cold War.

The GSDF became effective but unbalanced, with HA/DR niche skills, impressive aviation, and some excellent but uneven equipment, but lacked reserves of personnel, equipment, and ordnance to sustain its planned operations. It failed to effectively engage with other Forces for integrated defence planning, and thereby often appeared peripheral to Japanese defence. Blame for this can be assigned to the PMO, JDA, and JSDF culture of raising alarm of existential threats and failing to develop capacities to meet them. By becoming 'harder and heavier' in Hokkaido, the GSDF established an institutional culture that was difficult to change with shifting security challenges. Accompanying this 'hard and heavy' culture was a softer, 'less masculine' CIMIC identity that readily engaged with communities and civilians. This came to define and distinguish the Force as unique among armies, for its professionalism and devotion to civil, support tasks, and its place within international peace operations. In international engagement, however, the GSDF lagged far behind the MSDF, the first Force to train overseas and with the most intimate international partnership.

Maritime Self-Defense Force

The MSDF was born with both imperial lineage and local and broader strategic imperatives shared between Tokyo and Washington. Japanese maritime forces had proven themselves vital to US Korean War operations, and there were security concerns that the new navy and the US Navy could jointly address. The Ground Force had proved useful for the US only in the sense that they allowed withdrawal of American ground forces. The MSDF was the only Force providing complimentary capacities, enhancing USN capabilities, and holding doctrines and plans closely integrated with its US partner. The mentor-mentee relationship developed into a partnership of near-peers, albeit of vastly different resources. The USN developed many such close relationships, not least with the Royal Navy and Royal Australian Navy, but the degree of Navy involvement within the MSDF is unique, and regarded as almost universally positive by both parties. The concomitant relationships with the ASDF and GSDF, and often the JDA, were far less intimate and trusting, with the consequence that Japanese naval planning often appeared to ignore some basic JSDF and policy requirements. With little strategic direction from the Prime Minister's Office or Defense Agency, the MSDF defined 'national defence' by its own parameters, in USN partnership, and through imperial-era experiences. There is no mystery as to why the MSDF is by far the most studied of the Forces.

Establishment

Numerous scholars, veterans, and even the official history conceive of the initial phase of MSDF development as a drive for scale with limited funds and consequences for quality and capability. A 1956 JDA study illustrated the potential vulnerability of Japan and its coastal and oceanic trade to Soviet naval and aviation threats, as well as potential effects upon US Cold War planning, thereby providing the justification (if any were needed) for the development of a capable fleet.[147] This premise was founded upon bitter Pacific War lessons when Japanese oceanic and coastal trade had been paralysed by Allied submarine, mine, and air action. The USN held an overwhelming advantage of resources over the Soviet Navy in the Cold War, but it also lacked the contiguous seaways and close proximity of major Soviet naval and air bases. The estimate of Japan's land area is approximately 380,000sqkm, while its total claimed EEZ waters equalled approximately 4,050,000sqkm.[148] The main MSDF-perceived naval threat to Japan was therefore blockade and economic ruin rather than amphibious landings.

The 1954 SDF Law assigned no specific tasks to the MSDF other than to defend the nation from aggression, to preserve peace, and maintain national security in conjunction with the other Forces.[149] As Auer states, in the MSDF 'Minesweeping crews were the only groups within the organization that really knew definitely what they were supposed to do,' while others just trained as best they could with (relatively) new equipment, often under US instructors.[150] Initial training was, like the ships and instructors, focused upon anti-submarine warfare (ASW), but deeper long-term planning was being applied.

The minesweeping flotillas as the most obvious imperial legacy forces formed the initial professional core, but by 1961 the naval structure had settled into a recognisable, sustainable pattern. The Maritime Staff Office provided direction, but many command tasks were devolved to the Self-Defense Fleet (*Jieikantai*), the main combat strength with the Fleet Escort Force of up to four escort flotillas, each of six or eight destroyers/escorts. The Fleet also eventually controlled the Fleet Air Force, Fleet Submarine Force, and Mine Warfare Force, as well as replenishment and transport forces, making it an operational command far larger than any GSDF or ASDF equivalent, and more powerful than most comparable navies. The other operational commands were the five Regional District Forces (*Chihōtai*), very much the MSDF second rank, each usually assigned two destroyer divisions, each of two (older) ships, mine countermeasure (MCM) vessels, and limited coastal combat craft.[151]

The heart of the MSDF could be regarded as Yokosuka, home to the Self-Defense Fleet, intelligence functions, and within metres of the USN base; whereas the soul was Kure-Etajima, Hiroshima, the home of the Officer Candidate School (*Kanbukohoseigakkō*) naval academy. Personnel could expect to spend a proportion of their service in these Meiji-period workshops of western industrial modernity. By contrast, northern Japan had relatively few MSDF facilities, Mutsu and Hachinohe, Aomori, three small facilities in Hokkaido, at Hakodate (minesweepers), Yoichi (from 1971, coastal forces), and Wakkanai (from 1974, signals-intelligence, with GSDF, ASDF, and USFJ). The next MSDF bases were the Second Fleet Air Wing (*Dai2kōkūgun*) at Hachinohe, Aomori, shared with ASDF and civil traffic from 1957 to the mid-1970s, and Yokosuka and Atsugi, south-west of Tokyo.[152] The MSDF directly contributed the smallest proportion of its resources to territorial defence, with the least northern profile of the Forces. The submarine force when established was concentrated at Yokosuka and Kure, but base location was not a crucial factor, and similar arguments could be made for the escort flotillas and air forces tasked with non-coastal defence roles. Limited investment in island-territorial defence illustrated differing

Force threat perceptions and priorities, a situation enabled by limited JDA and PMO defence direction.

Defence Build-Up and Tasks

Japanese naval and mercantile shipbuilding had been highly capable between the wars. Kevork considered 'the IJN [...] represented the forefront of ship building and after the war would bequeath to private industry a significant capability [...] of personnel, infrastructure, technology and know-how'.[153] Under SCAP, Japanese shipyards had been repairing and scrapping, with (small) merchant construction eventually encouraged, but due to the 'holiday' and overseas technical advances, Japanese naval construction could not be rapidly restarted.[154] In 1952, preliminary research on future defence planning was conducted by an Organisational Investigation Committee (*Seidochōsaiinkai*), and with input from naval and civilian experts a thirteen-year naval build-up was proposed, with an ambitious total fleet goal of 475,000-tonnes, anticipated to consume approximately 8 per cent of government expenditure. Fleet roles were outlined as being sea-lane defence, primarily carrying out convoy and ASW techniques with homeland defence a subsidiary role.[155] Part of the commentary on the lack of investment in the MSDF is derived from the failure to meet this incredibly ambitious goal. For comparison, 2016 MSDF tonnage was 466,100 tonnes.[156]

Threats to Japanese maritime trade and communications, airspace, and territory, appear to have been obvious, but the MSDF had limited scope within the First Defense Build-up Plan (1958–60) to address them. As the 1956 study illustrated, the potential vulnerability of Japan's maritime trade to eventual Soviet hostile military action underlined the need to reconstitute and maintain a modern fleet, and it was on this that the MSDF and industry were focused.[157] They achieved an increase to 99,000-tonnes commissioned escort vessels by the first plan's conclusion, of the designated 124,000-tonnes target for 1962, the shortfall due to shipbuilding and new technology bottlenecks.[158] By the end of the Second DBP, the MSDF achieved only 116,000 tonnes of the 143,700-tonne target, but over 97 per cent of its aviation target, with 228 aircraft in service by 1966.[159] Technical matters were being resolved, but financial issues were often to the fore, subject to both Ministry of Finance (MOF) and Diet criticism. JDA Finance Bureau Chief Ueda Katsurō detailed to the House of Councillors Budget Committee in 1963 how two MSDF escort vessels were estimated to cost ¥7.166 trillion, one submarine ¥3.972 trillion, whereas two ASDF helicopters cost ¥425 million, receiving harsh comments related to their relative costs and values.[160] With stated ASW aims, members could see the value of the escorts far above that of submarines, and by comparison to either helicopters appeared alluringly inexpensive. Such criticisms would impact upon procurement, but not as much as might be expected in a liberal democracy. Technical defence matters were largely considered the realm of specialists; however, several opposition and governing side Diet members made pointed contributions to defence dialogue.[161] The example from 1963 is prominent for the rarity of Cold War Diet committees examining defence details. In the 1955 system opposition parties were largely ignored, most detailed defence consideration being undertaken within the JDA, MOF, and the LDP Policy Affairs Research Council (*seimuchōsakai*) and its subsidiary divisions (*bukai*). Additionally, the informal, fluid *bōeizoku* 'defence tribe' of interested Diet members lobbied for industrial and economic goals in addition to defence priorities.[162]

Japan's wartime mercantile resources had been devastated by USN action, and in addition to ASW escorts the MSDF attempted to rebuild its submarine capabilities.[163] It seems remarkable that Japan was able to commission its first indigenous submarine in 1960, based upon the efforts of ex-IJN officers in a 'Submarine Study Group' from March 1954.[164] The Maritime Staff Office (MSO) submitted a request to the Technical Research and Development Institute (TRDI) and established an 'Undersea Weapons Study Group' chaired by Yoshimatsu Tamori (ex-IJN, later MSDF Vice-Admiral) with representatives of the JDA Internal Bureau, and the Kawasaki-Mitsubishi Submarine Study Group.[165] One might have anticipated the IJN experience of losing 127 of 160 boats in the Pacific War to have blunted submarine interest, but enthusiasm was undiminished. Boyd and Yoshida suggest that reversion to IJN doctrines occurred during the Cold War, as submarines were regarded as vital to the two stages of naval war: attrition against superior enemy fleet to degrade their advantages, and the decisive battle.[166] It seems, however, unlikely that the MSDF sought such roles against Soviet forces, as submarine capabilities were initially slight and finely focused upon limiting naval movement by deterring navigation of the 'major straits,' containing until the USN was able to manage the threat, most likely through decisive strike options.

This focus on submarines demonstrated a nexus of five elements: IJN legacy, USN mentoring, domestic design and production, demonstrating distinct MSDF capabilities, and the deterrent value of submarines able to constitute a submerged 'fleet in being.' Soviet naval commanders would have been wary, as was the British fleet commander with Argentina's sole operational submarine for much of the Falklands War.[167] Submarine development is largely masked by the nature of the craft often displaying only subtle generational changes and little hint of capabilities. A conservative, war-derivative design was a 'safety-first' choice for 'underwater target ship' (*Suichūmokuhyōkan*), rather than submarine (*Sensuikan*). Vice-Minister Masuhara Keikichi, and DGs-JDA Sugihara Arata and Funada Naka all stated that two ordered boats would be 'target ships for training,' and not offensive weapons, paralleling GSDF 'special vehicles.'[168]

The first indigenous submarine, *Oyashio*, depended upon US support, but was a Japanese design, and Japan, with remarkable rapidity, developed a production pattern averaging one boat per year, progressing, from the late 1960s, to a tear-drop hull design (*Uzushio*-class).[169] From this point, the MSDF would develop some of the world's most advanced diesel craft as an independent innovator, while incorporating such overseas developments as Air-Independent Propulsion (AIP) and sensors.[170] The submarine force provided ASW and anti-surface capabilities, as well as intelligence gathering, ideally suited to Japan's relatively shallow near-waters but also able to operate in deep Pacific roles. Lacking such a small-boat force, the USN could rely upon the MSDF for inshore roles, replicating concentration on MCM warfare, thus not only defending Japanese ports and sea-lanes, but also providing niche capabilities to the US Seventh Fleet.

MSDF expansion based upon increased hull-numbers was subject to intense MOF scrutiny, and alarmed socio-political sensitivities towards Japan once more possessing a 'great fleet.' One long running saga involved a helicopter carrier, highly valued for more effective ASW and MCM operations and greater flexibility. As Alessio Patalano has detailed, the 'lost decade' without commissioned Japanese submarines and technical advances, as well as the prescient Soviet submarine threat, provided an imperative for anti-submarine capabilities, ideally provided by shipborne ASW helicopters.[171] The US Joint Strategic Plans Committee drafting the Military Assistance Program received USN and USMC recommendations, and USAF and Army objections, for the provision of a surplus aircraft carrier to Japan for East Asian security, which was ultimately rejected by the Joint Chiefs of Staff in February 1957.[172] The MSO initially studied a 6,000–7,000-tonne small helicopter carrier (CVH)—it was not included in the 1959 DBP revisions, nor was the subsequent 11,000-tonne CVH-b, developed in consultation with the US Military

Assistance and Advisory Group Japan (MAAG-J). Kōda states that this CVH-b with eighteen helicopters failed to gain approval primarily due to the 1960 Security Treaty revision demonstrations and socio-political sensitivities, and was dropped in 1961: 'the first demise of the JMSDF helicopter carrier.'[173] Even without the treaty controversy such a programme would have presented significant political and technical challenges. Given the (ill-informed) controversies aroused by the flat-top appearance of later MSDF vessels, it would have been a brave government that defended much larger aviation ships. As Patalano states, the CVH project had 'failed to gain any civilian support,' as would an initial attempt in 1989 for a combined 5,500-tonne LST/MCM aviation vessel, which eventually emerged as *Ōsumi*.[174] Kōda admits that the CVH 'might have become a hard-to-remove (and self-imposed) obstacle for future force planning,' and, given the state of helicopter art in 1960, 'it is doubtful if this [...] group could have achieved its mission.'[175] That USN Adm. Zumwalt was also unable to introduce the similar Sea Control Ship illustrates the obstacles even for great navies.

Four uncontroversial hybrid-design ships that emerged from this process did give long service. The *Haruna* and *Shirane*-classes were commissioned 1973–81 and formed the core of the Escort Division flotillas in the 8–6 and later 8–8 flotilla group concept, for over thirty years, when Kōda composed a fond farewell to the *Shirane*-class.[176] These were destroyer-helicopter vessels (DDH) carrying a destroyer armament and three medium ASW helicopters, two DDH supported by five escort destroyers (DD), with one guided-missile destroyer (DDG) providing anti-aircraft warfare (AAW) capability. This eight-ship six-helicopter force became the basis of two large escort flotillas, the main combat force of the MSDF and the distillation of Japanese ASW operational concepts.[177] Providing the vessels was a challenge, but actualising the operational concept took even longer, with the first two flotillas only becoming operational in 1981, despite the concept having being developed in 1965 and included within the Third DBP from 1967. The shift to an 8–8 force was due to enhanced submarine and air threats, each flotilla being reformed with only one DDH, two DDG, and all five DD being upgraded with a helicopter and short-range surface-air missiles (SAM), a process not completed until the mid- to late 1980s, but resulting in an expansion to four DDH-centred flotilla groups.[178] These flotillas were well suited to an operational scenario of escorting a convoy, but were not able to 'dominate' areas like a USN taskforce. They took time to work up into effective units, which was particularly difficult for the DDH as they formed the 'core' of the conceptual structure, without relief vessels and therefore under significant operational stress. DDG were initially scarce, the first suffering extensive problems, and it is interesting that the MSDF regarded air threats so lightly, given IJN experience and the proximity of Soviet bases. It required the late 1970s emergence of the Tu-22 Backfire bomber before anti-aircraft warfare (AAW) was accorded a prominent role. The Soviet maritime air threat was acknowledged by the USN, but considered less relevant to Atlantic operations, as it could not be reinforced by short-ranged aircraft, whereas Soviet bases within sight of the Soya Straits presented rather different air-defence dynamics.[179]

The greatest weakness of the 8–8 concept involved operational expectations and logistics. The flotillas would remain at sea for extended periods, consuming large quantities of fuel (and munitions in operations), therefore requiring replenishing, yet the MSDF in 1975 had only one tanker, the small, slow *Hamana* (1962). The next replenishment ship (AOE) was the larger and faster *Sagami* (1979), which also carried limited munitions/dry-stores cargo. These ships had barely sufficient fuel to replenish an eight-ship flotilla, let alone provide aviation fuel for eight helicopters, and were vulnerable to attack, being merchant-form vessels incapable of self-defence.[180] Their elimination would have compromised flotilla performance far more than the loss of an escort, and yet they were far cheaper to produce and crew, particularly given Japanese ship-building expertise. As force capability multipliers they rivalled DDH flagships, and yet the MSDF built so few, concentrating resources upon expensive warships and aircraft to improve combat capabilities, despite such capabilities being unsustainable without AOE.

The neglect of inexpensive and yet vital force-multiplier capabilities can also be seen in mine-warfare. The Force was adept and well practised at MCM, with continuous 'live' missions to sweep war-legacy mines with vessels and MCM helicopters. Despite this, the MSDF failed to invest in efforts to rapidly and effectively close the vital 'three straits' with mine-laying vessels, notwithstanding Soviet mines having limited Japanese domestic shipping 1950–5, and killing civilians onshore.[181] Sekino and Patalano demonstrate that the relatively shallow (*c.*100m) straits were ideal for denial by mining.[182] The MSDF had the capacity to lay mines by submarines and aircraft, but such methods were time consuming and those craft had limited load capabilities as well as alternate roles to perform. In 1975, there were only one large and one small Japanese minelayer, mainly for training, while the Danish navy's strait-access-denial duties involved four large and three small minelayers, and the North Koreans had proven adept at using wooden barges to simply and effectively sow mines in 1950.[183] The contrast between minelayer and minesweeper priorities reflects the impact of war and the post-war period. The MSDF by 1955 operated fifty war-legacy ex-USN LSSL patrol boats and sixty-seven MCM vessels, inherited roles regenerated by regular MCM construction, twenty-four *Kasado*-class commissioned in the 1950s–60s and eighteen *Takami*-class in the 1960s–70s.[184] Frontline regional District command forces were also reinforced by MCM 'mother-ships' (*sōkaibokan*). Unsurprisingly, the first detailed operational planning for JSDF overseas missions envisioned an MSDF MCM flotilla being despatched to the Persian Gulf in 1987, and such a force did precede peacekeeping missions overseas in 1991.[185]

Unlike replenishment and minelaying, the limited nature of Japanese amphibious lift capacity is far easier to understand as a requirement rather than as a doctrinal choice that served the GSDF; it was regarded as a subsidiary role worth little investment. Three ex-USN wartime LST were commissioned in 1961 (*Ōsumi*-class) to assume such duties, replaced in the 1970s by six smaller, domestic LST, but total lift-capacity was only 955 troops plus light vehicles. They served well into the 1990s, but this was not an army reinforcement transport capability.[186] Unlike in 1950, Japanese amphibious capabilities were not a USN force-enhancement factor, nor did the role significantly influence Cold War operational or investment planning.

The only Cold War coastal defence forces were ten motor-torpedo boats, the smallest possible combat vessels, mainly less than 100-tonnes, carrying one 40mm gun and a pair of torpedoes practically identical to wartime MTB craft, most in commission 1956–1972. They were typical of coastal forces developed worldwide, cheap to build and operate, with only eighteen crewmen, but unlike many in Europe they were not later refitted with SSM.[187] All served under Yokosuka and Kure District commands, rather than in northern areas, for little apparent benefit.[188] The only subsequent development consisted of five boats commissioned 1971–5, with two guns and four torpedo tubes, replacing half the previous boats until the early 1990s, and, though fine boats, they were outdated in the missile age. These were deployed to Maizuru District covering the Sea of Japan, and the newly-formed Coastal Defense Group (*Bōbitai*) Yoichi, Onimata District, covering Aomori and Hokkaido. Here, five small, outmoded boats between two bases constituted a token coastal defence, until three (ultimately unsuccessful) Italian-designed *Ichigo*-class hydrofoil missile-craft were commissioned 1993–5.[189] This lack of MSDF interest was mirrored by USN Adm. Zumwalt's frustrated reform plans to introduce a High-Low Mix of cheaper, smaller vessels that revealed sharp divisions and an obsessive approach to 'bigger-better' naval technology.[190] Suggestions of such approaches can also be divined by studying the MSDF in the second half of the Cold War.

The Fleet of 1975

An examination of the MSDF in 1975 provides a snapshot of a seemingly effective but limited-spectrum force at the conclusion of the Fourth DBP. With over 41,000 naval personnel, and 5,000 civilian staff, the Force had increased from 58,000 to 168,000 tonnes, and from fifty to 290 aircraft. During thirty years of peace, Japanese maritime forces had been transformed from civilian, coastal vessels into an ocean-going navy, which operated more than fifty major combat vessels and fifteen submarines, obviously specializing in anti-submarine and anti-mine warfare.[191] From an initially subordinate role to the USN, two decades had transformed this relationship into strategic partnership. The MSDF hoped to secure Japan's 'three straits,' as gatekeepers against Soviet Pacific Fleet vessels attempting to enter the Pacific Ocean and East and South China Seas. From the 1970s, this role appeared crucial, as the Soviet Navy deployed ballistic missile submarines (SSBN) and thereby existentially threatened the United States. Soviet Naval expert Michael MccGwire countered that Soviet Cold War naval policy was aimed at deterring attacks upon and threats to the Soviet homeland, and that Soviet Admiral Gorshkov fully appreciating the threats posed by the MSDF in addition to the USN, for both blockade and sea-air assault.[192]

The importance of the MSDF to US strategy thus grew throughout the Cold War to a greater extent than it did for the other Forces. Changing Soviet naval investment patterns had been noted, but most shocking were the huge, interconnected global naval exercises of 1970 that were eventually identified as *Exercise Okean* (Ocean), and which involved practically the entire Soviet navy.[193] The USN consequently shifted from regional to global approaches to counter Soviet naval globalism, with the MSDF forming a vital support for the Seventh Fleet in Asia. However, James Auer describes the Force of the early 1970s as 'an aimless force of limited capability,' the result of political leaders failing to produce cogent defence policy and strategy. He also wondered whether the 'shield of the Seventh Fleet over Japan' might be fading, with post-Vietnam plans for major withdrawals.[194] However, the MSDF had begun ASW exercises using USN nuclear submarines (SSN) 'targets,' as Washington was focused upon Japan developing these and AAW capabilities rather than counter-invasion forces.[195] Indeed, Auer claimed, even after 'three defense buildup programs, no responsible person claims that the MSDF has the ability to close or even effectively monitor the Tsushima, Tsugaru, and Soya Straits'.[196] The three straits would not be accorded twenty-four hour surface patrols until May 1983, but one account suggests that, in close cooperation with the USN, MSDF submarines began operations countering Soviet vessels in waters close to the Soviet coast in 'the riskiest operation we ever experienced.'[197] The dissonance between stated tasks and capacities to undertake them was clearly apparent to contemporaries, and the process by which the defence programmes were drafted illustrates the depth of the problems. Nishihiro drafted several of the programmes, once by default, as the responsible official 'gave up on it since it would have been miserable to complete it under the circumstances,' continuing extant trends with relatively little input from the Forces.[198]

Minister for Foreign Affairs Aichi Kiichi stated in a 1969 *Foreign Affairs* article that the JSDF were 'guaranteeing the primary defense of Japan' with 'conventional firepower greater than that of the Imperial forces at their wartime peak,' signalling a rejection of a 'little Japan' mentality.[199] This desire to demonstrate Japanese defensive efforts smacked of delusional hubris, and JDA Vice-Minister Obata Hisao stated soon after that he thought the GSDF and ASDF had approximately half the resources and capabilities required for them to undertake their duties, while the MSDF had only one-third.[200] Most ministries complain about resources, but the Obata remark resonates with comments made by Auer and MSDF veterans to paint a picture of a capable force that was not able to undertake part of its core duties. The Force was adept at ASW but had limited range, technology, and operational sustainability. Coastal defence was seemingly beyond Force capabilities, amphibious transport and minelaying were also clearly limited, as was AAW capacity, an anomaly given Soviet proximity. Auer's frustration with the statements of Aichi and others intended for US audiences concerning the power of Japanese defences is understandable.

Mid-Cold War, mid-détente, 1975 provides a transitional moment in MSDF development, between the first defence white paper (*bōeihakusho*) in 1970, the 1976 MiG-25 scandal (see below) and the National Defense Program Outline (NDPO *Taikō*) replacing 'build-up' plans, 1978 US-Japan Guidelines, and the Soviet invasion of Afghanistan. While the situation seemed relatively calm, David Walsh states that US threat perceptions were transforming dramatically, so that while 'in 1976 only a handful of analysts were expressing alarm over what they saw as a shift in the military balance in the USSR's favor, by 1980 their views were central in the debate over US national security policy.'[201] He identifies declining US defence budgets from 1973 and equivalent Soviet increases, Soviet regimes proliferating in Africa and Asia, and the invasion of Afghanistan as indicators of a shifting strategic balance that created a 'second Cold War,' which was soon felt in Tokyo.[202]

In Japan, the mid-1970s appeared a time for stabilisation following the Nixon shock, the oil shock, and the end of the Arab-Israeli wars. Japan's economic growth faltered and defence expansion appeared to plateau. One year before the 1976 NDPO, the Miki cabinet indicated the 1 per cent of GDP limit on defence spending, previously observed from 1967, would be formally adopted counter-intuitively to enable increased defence spending despite opposition. The naval post-war period ended as the MSDF became a Japanese trained and equipped Force.[203] The 1976 NDPO was innovative, providing a JSDF 'standard defence posture' (*kibanteki bōeiryoku*) concept. This had been framed by Kubo Takuya and Sakata Michita following Kubo's 'KB-thesis' paper, but was also developed by Nishihiro Seki and Hoshuyama Noboru, and adopted after considerable struggles between JDA and JSDF cliques, thereby altering the nature of risk assessment in defence planning.[204] While more realistic and sustainable than 'build-up plans,' it enabled consideration of a defence plateau having been reached, but, like the 1 per cent limit, actually enabled sustained defence expansion. In 1976, however, the JDA appeared ready to abandon the concept of securing Japan against invasion, the essence of previous 'necessary defence force' concepts, the NDPO 'limited defence' seen as a limited holding action awaiting US 'rescue.' This minimal approach displaced previous 'threat perceptions' based upon Soviet capability for broader assessments of risk including diplomatic relations. This left the Forces perplexed. The GSDF faced their basic defence role being dismissed, while within the MSDF ex-IJN senior officers were appalled at the regression, with fundamental implications for USN relations.[205] In naval terms, the NDPO proposed stability, with the MSDF considered to have reached maturity. By contrast, Aizawa Teruaki quotes 1976 Chief of Maritime Staff Nakamura Teiji who had been 'consistently asserting that the MSDF, which is well behind in capabilities development, will face serious issues if the status quo decision stands.' Nakamura argued that NDPO drafts had stated that the defence build-up had been 'largely completed,' based upon the diktat of Finance Minister Ōhira Masayoshi rather than actual Force enhancement, and that the MSDF was far short of completing its capability build-up.[206]

The gap between political and naval sides is unsurprising. Auer described how through US-Japan combined exercises and doctrinal harmony 'in the 1960s and 1970s, the two navies were far beyond where the (1978) Guidelines started' and that 'the Guidelines, were in some ways a reflection of a jealousy, particularly on the part of the GSDF, that they didn't have the kind of interaction and connection' as existed between the navies.[207] Politicians and policy were effectively attempting to catch up with MSDF practice. In May 1972, Commander in Chief of the Self-Defense Fleet Kitamura Kenichi reportedly made references to the MSDF preference for nuclear-powered submarines and aircraft carriers. The ensuing media frenzy focused upon the 'sensationally raised problems' relating to nuclear power and Article 9.[208] However, the subsequent Diet session on 31 May 1972 not only included opposition attacks upon Kitamura, the MSDF, and the government, but also some unusually insightful discussions of naval issues. DG-JDA Ezaki Masumi and particularly JDA Defense Policy Bureau Director Kubo Takuya, a prominent defence 'insider-commentator', defended the Agency, MSDF, and policy, disagreeing with the basis of the Kitamura position. Taunted by opposition Diet members eager to expose his contradictions, he admitted that guaranteeing the MSDF had both adequate resources and clearly defined, limited operational missions was fundamentally impossible.[209] MSDF Chief of Staff Ishida Suteo defended Kitamura's off-the-record personal comments, and both were forced to resign, illustrating the sensitivity of feeling, and the need for discretion in raising capability issues.[210] Ishida described 'the realisation of the US-Japan Alliance as the presence of the US Seventh Fleet,' and, given JSDF limitations, this appears a decent summation, though hypocritical if Japan were to rely upon US nuclear-powered warships but be prohibited from discussing their utility.[211] Even the official history emphasises that USN cooperation was vital, not least due to Japan lacking credible strike capabilities, but such bold statements were also unacceptable in the 1970s.[212]

Little reference was made in Japan to US plans for the withdrawal of the USN from Yokosuka to Sasebo, Nagasaki, and major cuts to USFJ as part of an Asia-wide drawdown. Senior USN officers in the US and Japan had publicly refused to contemplate the reductions, particularly that of the US Naval Ship Repair Facility (SRF), due to the importance of the base.[213] However, within four years drawdown plans were being drafted, driven by 1969 Nixon (Guam) doctrine statements on 'Vietnamization' and budgetary restrictions.[214] Not only did the reversal of the decision in 1972 and the subsequent forward basing of the *USS Midway* from 1973 bring relief to Japanese planners fearing the fate of national defence plans, but it also focused minds on the imperative for combined coordination that aided progress to the Guideline revisions.[215]

There have been suggestions that the MSDF was either internally conflicted or externally in contention with the JDA or other Forces to fulfil either a homeland defence role, as a largely coastal force, or else defend Japan's Sea Lines Of Communications (SLOC). Euan Graham details the efforts of Kaihara Osamu to restrict MSDF oceanic ambitions, as a broad 'sea lane defence' was beyond the resources of even the USN given the scale of Soviet submarine forces by the 1970s. By contrast, homeland defence appeared a viable proposition.[216] Kōda Yōji has insisted that it is 'inappropriate to consider separately the operations required for each mission,' with the MSDF addressing 'the homeland-defense mission by giving full priority to the warfare capabilities, especially ASW, required for the SLOC-protection mission, in the belief that it can best contribute to Japan's homeland security by defeating invasion forces at sea.'[217] This logically asserts that developing naval capabilities for one scenario provides capabilities for others, but also has limitations. Kōda's assertion is based upon Japanese security relying on US reinforcements, particularly USN carrier strike groups (CSG), with the MSDF effectively securing areas within which the CSG can conduct 'strike operations against enemy naval forces and land targets.' This was characterised as the MSDF-USN Alliance 'shield and spear' approach, with Japan providing the shield for the mobile, offensive US spear. Japan would defend, sanitise, and escort trade, the US would strike and defeat, and therefore 'ASW was made the main pillar of JMSDF missions.'[218] Naturally, the MSDF would counter invasion, but that would not be its main role.

This logic is neat and plays to respective strengths, but poses fundamental problems. As the MSDF failed to develop credible capacity to defeat invasion until the late 1980s, it was placing complete confidence in the USN never having equal, competing demands upon resources. The MSDF also appeared to be relying on the ASDF to conduct anti-invasion operations, in addition to anti-aircraft warfare (AAW) for fleet protection, an ability it largely lacked until the late 1980s. The development of GSDF SSM capabilities was partly a reaction to MSDF abrogation of territorial defence responsibilities considered existentially vital by ground forces, in contrast to a homeland defence-alliance approach considered existentially vital by naval forces. The GSDF also had a 'Force relevance promotion' and ground-budget defence agenda, but it wisely deployed defence arguments to win its sea-strike force capability against naval and air resistance.[219] In this, as in many aspects, it is the MSDF-USN relationship that appears close, trusting, and 'joined-up,' rather than JSDF approaches.

Sado Akihiro asserts that the consequences of Admiral Ishida's 'realisation of the US-Japan Alliance' statement proved increasingly problematic during the late Cold War, for the Force interpreted the 1976 NDPG and 1978 US-Japan Guidelines as conforming to their combined MSDF-USN notion of SLOC-defence. Thereby, the MSDF planned and prepared for a significantly more expansive and potentially risky role that would also prove more resource-consuming. This was beyond the understanding of the JDA Internal Bureau, which interpreted Japanese policy as a more traditional and limited 'sea-lane defence.'[220] Sado illustrates the differences with two maritime maps. The first indicates two SLOC routes, one 270x1,512km south-west of Kyushu, south of Okinawa and Taiwan, the second 432x1,800km, south-south east of Honshu towards the Mariana Islands, expressing MSDF-USN planning concepts. Seemingly, JDA and MOFA understanding of sea-lane defence was conveyed in a second general map of Japanese EEZ and Air-Defense Identification Zone (ADIZ) without specific SLOC. There was no great secrecy, but an astonishing lack of coordination and direction, even if Sado may be regarded as over-reacting to two maps. Auer however relates seeing an MSDF map with 'Nakamura Lines' in 1971, which accords with Sado's MSDF-USN version, drawn by MSDF Chief of Staff Vice-Admiral Nakamura Teiiji and seemingly forming MSDF policy.[221] This sense of fundamental strategic confusion was expressed in the 1983 defence white paper, which outlined disparate views on 'sea-lane defence,' and provided only the vaguest parameters ('about 1,000-nautical miles') and conditions within which the MSDF could use force ('depending on the situation').[222]

This confusion had partly arisen as a result of the unexpected controversy that had resulted from Prime Minister Suzuki's May 1981 Joint Communiqué with President Reagan, concerning references to the Security Treaty and maritime security. Suzuki's reference to '1000-miles' was made the day after the White House communiqué, at the National Press Club press conference, seemingly without strategic consciousness. The US side sought clarification from the Japanese embassy, upon which it was a simple DOD map-exercise to determine that Tokyo-Guam, and Osaka-Bashi Channel (Philippines-Taiwan), seemingly fulfilled US 'Northwest Pacific sea-lane' demands.[223] Euan Graham describes how the declarations created distinctly different impressions in Tokyo and Washington, thereby both spreading confusion and allowing different actors to believe in differing consequences of events: USFJ identifyed differing positions, JDA insisted that sea-lane defence formed part of 'contingencies' under Article VI of SOFA, while MOFA considered this under Article V, unilateral Japanese emergency.[224] Foreign Minister Itō was forced to resign for having seemingly conceded the notion of collective defence, and for having dared use the accurate term *dōmei* (alliance) to describe the relationship.[225] Upon returning to Japan, Suzuki backtracked on hard commitments to defend contiguous seaways out to 1,000nm, which was understandable given that he merely agreed 'an appropriate division of roles between Japan and the United States. He stated that Japan [...] will seek to make even greater efforts for improving its defense capabilities in Japanese territories and in its surrounding sea and air space, and for further alleviating the financial burden of U.S. forces in Japan.'[226]

The Suzuki statement was clearly a response to the pressure exerted by the Reagan administration, and the particular urging for greater allied defence efforts by Alexander Haig and Casper Weinberger. The Japanese had been sounded out on assuming greater responsibility for Northwest Pacific sea-lane defence, which, as Foreign Minister Itō, with MOFA prompting, suggested would imply (inappropriate) regional security roles. Although the suggestion has often been made that the Suzuki statement set the strategic position of Japan-US 'shield-and-spear' defence, contemporary officials state that this basic principle had been agreed several years before.[227] Peter Woolley references JDA-DG Mihara Asao stating that 'important sea-lanes within 1,000 miles' could be subject to JSDF defence, particularly in Saipan-Taiwan waters.[228] Prime Minister Nakasone, when welcoming President Reagan to Japan in 1983 made one pointed comment: 'With respect to the improvement of our defense capability, I wish to continue to make further efforts along the lines of the joint communiqué of May 1981.'[229] This attracted little controversy, despite being part of a much more expansive approach to defence spending and naval cooperation, including assuming greater defence responsibilities within a 'burden-sharing offensive' to gain greater leverage over US trade and security policies. Suzuki had the misfortune of failing to bow sufficiently deeply before the honorific standards of post-war pacifism, towards which two years later his successor would give no more than a passing nod. In 1983, opposition Diet members questioned SLOC defence, asking how Japan would protect maritime trade and economic security if the US was involved in a conflict or contingency in Europe and/or the Middle East.[230] The Nakasone cabinet response was as expected: Japan was developing its defensive power and was confident that the US would abide by the conditions of the Security Treaty.²³¹ The non-answer of government that was attempting to demonstrate its commitment to the US alliance and to expanding MSDF capabilities was as disappointing as it was predictable.

Few recognised that a significant shift was also taking place within Japanese merchant shipping, and the lack of discourse between JDA, Ministry of Transport, and MITI appears marked. Protecting maritime trade was designated as a vital task, but it was becoming increasingly difficult to identify what exactly was Japanese shipping. From the 1970s, Japanese shippers were allowed to increasingly use foreign chartered-vessels, both as independent charters and *Shikumisen*, a complex device using public loans for foreign owners to buy Japanese-produced vessels, leased-back to Japanese shipping companies.²³² By 1980, foreign-chartered shipping exceeded Japanese-flagged within the nominally Japanese merchant fleet, Japanese-flagged vessels reduced from 449 in 1990 to ninety-nine by 2004, while foreign-chartered tonnage reached almost ten times that of Japanese-flagged.²³³ Many Japanese officials struggling to separate constitutional collective-defence controversies from SLOC-defence issues simply chose to ignore the fundamental issue of whose ships the MSDF could or might defend.

In a US-Japan Security Subcommittee meeting in June 1981, the US produced an MSDF force outline for expanded SLOC-defence commitments, which appeared remarkably similar to MSDF proposals, with the addition of expanded fuel and munitions reserves.²³⁴ This was not adopted, but through mysterious, mutual *gaiatsu* external pressure leverage, much of it eventuated particularly for aviation, boosting P-3C patrol and ASDF F-15J fighter squadrons.²³⁵ Despite JDA and MOF resistance, by the 1986–90 Mid-Term Defense Program (MTDP), air and SLOC defence improvements, as well as counter-invasion measures, received enhanced prioritisation, but the 1986 defence white paper is more striking for its continuity than radical transformation. The prescribed duties of the MSDF remained coastal defence (with little investment), ASW operations, and (vague) escorting of shipping, but priorities were evidently changing.²³⁶ The MSDF-USN hope for seventy escorts and twenty-five submarines, with major qualitative improvements, was unrealistic and untenable for personnel limitations. By the 1990s, the MSDF was coming up against an inflexible barrier to expansion: the lack of recruits willing and capable of serving. The navy thereafter struggled with being over-shipped and under-manned.

MSDF vessels do require further study, for investments illuminate that motivations and aspirations were clearly focused upon underwater threats, to the detriment of other capabilities. The destroyer *Amatsukaze* was (from 1965) the only SAM-equipped ship, while in 1975 twenty-two vessels were equipped with modern ASROC ASW systems. *Amatsukaze*'s Tartar SAM-system had proved a technical, training, and budgetary strain, and was provided with minimal ammunition reserves (fifty rounds in 1971).[237] *Amatsukaze* 'was too expensive to build in large numbers, so the JMSDF traded quantity for its superb AAW capability,' worried that this 'leap in the dark' might have devoured resources, despite Germany, Australia, and Italy managing to avoid such pitfalls.[238] Many Japanese vessels retained obsolete weaponry, such as the *Yamagumo*-class commissioned 1966–78, typical MSDF Cold War escorts, with excellent ASW weaponry but air and surface combat capabilities often worse than in IJN destroyers.[239] The *Akuzuki*-class (1960) carried three 5-inch and four 3-inch guns, one of the heaviest but least effective MSDF gun armaments when facing jet aircraft, and yet limited ASW capabilities and surface-warfare capabilities were not addressed until the small frigate *Ishikari* (1981) was fitted with Harpoon SSM.[240] The subsequent twelve ship *Hatsuyuki*-class (1982–7) combined SSM, SAM, and ASW systems, with gun armament, helicopter, gas-turbine propulsion, and integrated combat system (ICS) in the classic late-Cold War Japanese warship template, equal to multipurpose vessels in any navy.[241] MSDF officers relate that SSM capabilities were enhanced primarily to counter Soviet Pacific Fleet cruisers, rather than amphibious forces. As previously noted, the GSDF acquired such capabilities approximately twenty years after Sweden and Denmark, while the ASDF acquired the ASM-1 Type-80 missile from 1981. The imperative for such weapons can be traced to the emergence of the second phase of the Cold War, in which air and naval competition was particularly intense.

The Second Cold War

The period from 1976 was marked by a greater emphasis upon qualitative improvements, but the pace of naval construction barely faltered as relations with the Soviet bloc cooled. On average two-three escorts, one submarine, and two MCM vessels ordered per year.[242] In the mid-1970s, the MSDF was approximately the size of the Italian Navy in manpower and amphibious lift, but had fewer SAM and helicopter capabilities.[243] However, the Suzuki and Nakasone cabinets accelerated the expansion and range of capabilities to such an extent that Japan once again came to be regarded as a great naval power. Whilst retaining and improving MCM and ASW expertise, the Force also greatly augmented AAW and surface warfare capacities: three *Tachikaze*-class DDG, with long-range SM-1MR SAM, were commissioned 1976–83, accompanied by heavy investments in naval aviation.[244] In the 1980s, the first major FRAM (Fleet Rehabilitation and Modernization) refits commenced, two *Takatsuki*-class and both *Haruna*-class destroyers were refitted with Sea Sparrow SAM, upgraded fire-control systems (FCS), radar, combat information centre (CIC), Close-in Weapon System (CIWS) defence against SSM, with improved aviation capabilities.[245] This was followed post-1976 by a re-emphasis on qualitative improvements, with additional impetus provided by 1982 Falklands Conflict lessons for navies (without carriers) operating in hostile air environments.[246]

Proximity to Soviet (and Chinese) territory and sea lanes provided not only security challenges but also opportunities. The MSDF was estimated to have at least fourteen electronic surveillance sites within Japan, and shared responsibility for straits surveillance with the GSDF.[247] The USN installed SOSUS submarine Sound Surveillance System in Japan's restricted waterways, as in the Greenland-Iceland-UK Gap, but with the advantage and hazard of contiguous waters with Soviet territory. This had been strongly urged by former IJN officer and naval commentator Sekino Hideo not only for intelligence, but also to facilitate limited MSDF resources, particularly aircraft, being rapidly focused for maximum effect.[248] Tanter and Ball provide a wealth of detail on Electronic Intelligence (ELINT) and submarine surveillance sites as well as intimate MSDF-USN workings, almost equivalent to 'Five Eyes' intelligence relationships with 'intimate' US allies, and this has seemingly provided a valuable return on investment.[249]

The investment in combat vessels during the Cold War was obvious, but this would be overshadowed by the decisions made in the mid-1980s to pursue procurement of the cutting-edge USN AEGIS system. The AEGIS process was long and complex, but it required intricate US-Japan technology transfer negotiations, massive investment in a new DDG class (*Kongō*) that improved upon USN designs (*Arleigh Burke*), and an equally great investment for training and maintenance. AEGIS remained the premier naval combat system for four decades, the defining symbol of symbiosis with the USN. However, it has its critics, unexpectedly several of them within the MSDF, including the effusive Kōda Yōji who has praised the system's abilities but decried the 'resource consumption system' that has pared other projects.[250] Before resources became constricted, the end of the Cold War was a period of astonishing investment in training ships, most converted escorts/submarines, but three purpose-built, the AAW training ships *Tenryu* and *Kurobe*, with remote drone launchers, and *Kashima*, a large and sophisticated midshipman training vessel constructed to plush 'bubble-era' standards. Great attention was paid to support ships for minesweepers and submarines (including rescue ships), cable repair and survey vessels, and a large, destroyer-type weapon trials ship, *Asuka*, purpose-built to test AEGIS systems, unique outside the USN.[251] There was logistical investment in three *Towada*-class AOE (1987–90), providing one replenishment vessel for each escort flotilla, most of them equipped with self-defence CIWS facilities. The Antarctic research ship *Shirase* was commissioned in 1982 as the largest MSDF vessel, able to operate two helicopters and navigate through ice. Obvious limitations remained in transport, and constraints in AOE provision would be experienced, but the MSDF would develop into one of the world's great naval aviation forces.

Naval Aviation

The MSDF Aviation Component can be traced back to the Safety Security Force in August 1952, with the helicopter and fixed-wing components being established in 1953.[252] Former-IJN personnel cooperated in creating the ASDF, but were equally adamant that the new naval force would regain maritime aviation capacity.[253] Naval aviation might have been an ASDF responsibility had it not been for USN aviation advocates engaged in a 'war of independence' with the USAF. The US provided 217 aircraft to the MSDF as well as extensive technology, training, and other support.[254] From 1956, the MSDF began to receive modern P2V-7 Neptune twin-engine maritime reconnaissance aircraft produced under licence with USN prompting, and the smaller S2F-1 Tracker.[255] The rate of expansion was such that the MSDF was operating eighteen helicopters and sixty-four modern maritime patrol aircraft in its fleet by 1958.[256]

The squadrons were initially under District command, until the Fleet Air Force was established under the Self-Defense Fleet in September 1961, with Fleet Air Wings (*Kōkūgun*), an Air Development Squadron, and Air Training Command.[257] Domestic production boosted the P2V-7 fleet to forty-eight aircraft by 1964, with an improved (Japanese) P2J version and unique *kokusanka* PS-1 flying boat, resulting in approximately 130 patrol aircraft by 1972, over half of which were P-2J. In support aircraft, the YS-11 was chosen as an MSDF transport, particularly to distant island bases such as Iwo Jima, as a result of *kokusanka* credentials rather than operational capabilities. The

MSDF finally assumed control of all naval aviation training in 1969, US MAP funding having ended in 1967, and the MAAG-J being reduced in size and scope and, as Mutual Defense Assistance Office (MDAO, 1969), signalling the shift from mentor to partner.[258] The subsequent modernisation of MSDF fixed-wing aviation became rather complex, owing to the nexus of *kokusanka* aspirations, US reluctance to divulge secret technology, and the expanding Lockheed scandal that threatened to spill over into military contracts. A 2016 NHK investigation discovered that the potential purchase of P-3C or S-3 Viking by Japan had been subject to both dubious practices and criminal investigation that sullied JDA procurement.[259] Aizawa Teruaki illustrates how the Maritime Staff Office had conflicted views on whether to pursue a *kokusanka* project or Lockheed's P-3C, with MOF pressure facilitating P-3C orders from 1978.[260]

Aizawa suggests that the decision to operate 100 P-3C was not based upon SLOC prioritisation above homeland defence, but rather aircraft quality, the qualitative leap being less area 'coverage' than 'hunting capability.'[261] In quantity, the new force replaced approximately 130 P2J, in line with post-1976 consolidation, within a '220 aircraft' force concept, one which the MSDF had hoped would include a shift from 'Eight-Six' to 'Eight-Eight' groups, with an increase to five escort groups—but which did not eventuate.[262] The qualitative P-3C improvement compensated for this, and the 100 aircraft might well have been eighty if the fifth flotilla had boosted helicopter numbers. Helicopter numbers had already greatly increased through the escort flotilla concept and through the initial S-55 (H19) craft, the first five of which crashed, indicating early difficulties. They formed both ASW and search and rescue (SAR) units, being replaced by larger HSS-1 (S-58), HSS-2 (S-62) Sea King, and KV-107.[263] Ishikawa Junichi has detailed how enhanced DDH and HSS-2 capabilities were matched to expand ASW capacity, one aircraft able to prosecute contacts for extended periods at significant ranges, in the worst weather conditions, even though more than a dozen were lost.[264] Numbers of aircraft increased thanks to Nakasone largesse with shore-based MCH-53 minesweeping helicopters, investments matching USN desires, which provided naval operational synergy and political advantage in demonstrating Japan's value to US companies. The contrast between MSDF and ASDF aviation programmes' effects upon bilateral relations is remarkable, constituting minor quibbling over P-3C system exports compared to rancour over fighter jet technology transfers. The increase of Air Wings to six in 1981, and seven in 1987, outstripped the quantitative increase in surface ship hulls but matched the qualitative fleet improvements, reflecting greater MSDF mission range and capabilities.

MSDF Force Culture

MSDF culture naturally possesses similarities with as well as legacies of the IJN. These may appear as tired clichés, but they are regenerated and reinforced, and have been extensively researched by Patalano, Agawa, and Koizumi.[265] Beyond 'navy curry Fridays,' the 'rising sun' flag (also used by other Forces) appeared prominently from the earliest days, and ship-naming conventions of the IJN were partly continued, considered 'neutral,' as they are inspired by natural phenomena, such as rain and wind, with certain names avoided. The MSDF had no *Yamato* (the Japan Coast Guard did, a Yokohama tug). In the twenty-first century the naming convention reached post-imperial zenith with the large, hybrid DDH flat-tops *Hyūga* and *Ise*, following the conventions of IJN hybrid battleship-carriers.

Part of the appeal of the MSDF is that it most obviously is naval, rather than military. The history that has arisen from the legacy of war has often depicted the IJN as the 'good service,' made up of 'the good Japanese' compared to the IJA 'barbarians. No such history can survive significant scrutiny, but the image persists, for the IJN helped to quell the 1936 '2–26' mutiny, and resisted IJA efforts to expand the war on the Asian continent. During research on prisoner of war camps, local residents of the site of the Ōfuna Transitory Prison Camp, Kamakura, insisted that while not knowing any details they were sure that Allied prisoners were treated well as 'it was run by the navy, not the army.' Former resident Louis Zamperini, airman and Olympian, who was beaten and starved at Ōfuna for a year, might disagree, but the internal and external vilification of the Army and contrasting praise of the Navy endures.[266]

Skabelund and Ishikawa have illustrated the range of unofficial and yet officially coordinated shrine-related events, from naval personnel visiting the Tōgō Shrine in Harajuku, Tokyo, to blessing ceremonies for new projects.[267] In barracks and aboard most MSDF vessels, there are small altars or *kamidama* shelves, which are also treated as minor 'crew welfare' services, akin to a domestic *butsudan* (Buddhist altar). Most personnel appear not to ascribe great significance to such rituals, several sailors describing the small shrine on *JS Akitsugi* during the 2012 Fleet Review as being 'homely,' and any imperial-era legacy being dismissed as less important than 'navy curry.'[268] Sailors appear less concerned with religious iconography than academics. Similarly, naval images remain popular, and the post-war destruction of military statues was not extended to that of Admiral Tōgō, which stands before the British-built battleship *Mikasa* in Yokosuka, a museum 'demilitarised' during the occupation and quickly 'remilitarised' with USN assistance. Today it is a symbol of Japanese heritage, victory in battle, technological development, and UK and US alliances. It is scarcely conceivable that members of the Imperial family would visit IJA remnants, but this famous IJN artefact has been so blessed.

Gradually former IJN officers were admitted and rose to prominence, the majority of MSDF admirals comprising Naval Academy graduates, 96 per cent of Captains, and 80 per cent of Commanders by 1970.[269] Compared with the other Forces, the MSDF had a relatively large (retired) presence in the Diet and industry, even though officers have complained that sea service precludes the contacts that GSDF officers build with local and national politicians.[270] The MSDF has also conducted PR outreach to civil society, with aircraft flying snow to children in Okinawa, or even familiarisation flights for university students, all of which were generally regarded as healthy experiences for the young, rather than as wasted resources.[271] The same can be said for the Fleet Review (*Kankanshiki*), held twenty-eight times from 1957 to 2015, which attracted just over 1,000 guests aboard vessels at sea in 1961, and over 50,000 in 2012 despite grey skies and choppy seas.[272]

The greatest naval PR efforts have been conducted through specified duties, particularly disaster relief efforts, often for small island communities, and inland, such as the 1968 Hidagawa Landslide and after the 2011 tsunami, when MSDF divers were tasked with recovering bodies.[273] The Force led Japan's response to the Gulf War in 1991, and has supported overseas HA/DR and UN peace operations from the first voyage to Cambodia in 1992 (see Chapter Three). The MSDF could be regarded as the most outwardly focused Force, pioneering 'overseas training,' with the JDA Establishment Law, amended by Cabinet Order and despite Diet and CLB resistance, eventually permitting MSDF training cruises to Midway Island and Hawaii in 1958.[274] From this the principle 'that JSDF units should not go abroad was adjusted many times as need and opportunity arose,' and the navy was at the forefront of internationalising Force culture.[275] Establishment laws also provided for defence attaché staff (*bōeichūzaikan*) despatched from the 1960s, Japan and Britain having a reciprocal naval attaché relationship.[276]

In addition to attachés and training cruises, MSDF ships began port calls for defence diplomacy ('training') to Europe in 1967, and Africa in 1970. As

Wooley states, 'The deployment of warships to distant oceans where they would not be in harm's way was simply not a media event', as training visits expanded to diplomacy, and then USN combined exercises, and ultimately multinational exercises through RIMPAC.[277] The Rim of the Pacific naval exercises, held annually from 1971 between the US, Canada, Australia, and New Zealand, welcomed Japan in 1980. Japanese participation was bilateral through the Security Treaty, while other navies attended 'by coincidence'.[278] RIMPAC participation combined with the building programme and USN cooperation as 'soft' defence diplomacy with 'hard' edged functional engagement. Participation in these 'best of the best' exercises, and extensive international naval interaction, ensured that the MSDF had significant numbers of English speakers, which further facilitated overseas engagements and boosted Force profile and status.

The MSDF has been strongly criticised for its actions and responses to accidents involving warships. Considering the scale of ship movements, there have been relatively few incidents, but those that have occurred have been serious. The 1988 sinking of a fishing boat, the *Fuji Maru No. 1*, by the Japanese submarine *Nadashio* and the inadequate rescue effort by the MSDF was considered to illustrate broader JSDF rescue management problems.[279] The 2,250-tonne submarine collided with the 154-tonne ship in good conditions in Tokyo Bay, killing thirty and injuring sixteen, with only three rescued by the submarine.[280] The official civil investigation found the submarine primarily responsible, but accepted mitigating circumstances for its limited rescue effort. Christopher Hood's extensive study indicated suggestions by 'conspiracy authors' that an MSDF *Fire Bee* target drone possibly shared culpability for the JAL JL123 crash in 1985. Naval vessels were exercising in Sagami Bay at the time and location that the aircraft shed part of its tail, possibly due to avoiding action.[281] Despite such examples, however, among the Forces the MSDF appears to hold a position of prestige, partly as a result of its heritage, partly becaue of its resources and technical acumen, and partly due to its obvious distance from civil society, an important factor in reducing potential friction.

Conclusion

The MSDF is one of the world's most powerful and respected navies. In almost every aspect of combat capabilities it ranks among the most technically capable, with a fleet that during 2016–2020 had slightly more warships than the Royal Navy and the French Marine Nationale combined, almost the same number of submarines (although without nuclear capabilities), and far larger and very sophisticated naval aviation, on top of operating in tandem with one of the largest coastguard services. The direction that former-IJN personnel contributed to this progress has been noted, and both Auer and Patalano have acknowledged IJN individuals' and legacy influences on forming this Force and ensuring that it developed in lockstep with its USN ally. The nature of this relationship may be unique in its intimacy, but MSDF culture, personnel, and vessels remained distinctively Japanese, and more than in any other Force, or possibly any other Japanese civil institution, pre-war imperial and post-war secular-democratic traits have been blended to a largely positive and constructive end. The concern raised in this section has been that the intimacy and pace of MSDF-USN cooperation precluded the forms of civilian control exerted upon the other Forces. The MSDF seemingly planned its doctrines and operational scenarios more in tune with US than with Japanese Cold War security needs, civilian security policy struggling to keep pace and thereby becoming partly navy-led. Owing to the alliance, these elements may be regarded as indivisible but in law they were distinct, and this legal aberration of duty and civilian control persisted.

MSDF capability gaps have also been noted. Sealift provision was limited, as were logistics for much of the Cold War, and the addressing of AAW and surface warfare failings came towards the end of the period in which it was assumed that Japan faced significant existential threats. The lack of investment or attention in national defence towards coastal defence further illustrates the lack of joint defence planning by the JDA and the Forces. The MSDF and ASDF appeared to cooperate to some degree, but the GSDF was, as usual, largely left to its own devices, and therefore developed a maritime territorial-defence role-capability parallel to and separate from the MSDF. This neglect was part of the Force culture, focused upon blue-water ocean security, cooperation with the USN and increasingly other partners, and at the highest level of naval technologies and investments, that contrasts so sharply with the low-level roots of coastal minesweeping in which the Force remained adept. And it is such skills that presented the prized value and most limiting factor for the MSDF as it entered the post-Cold War period. Its massive investments, particularly in the AEGIS programme, depended upon not only sustaining high levels of funding for a heavily resource-concentrated venture, but also on attracting sufficient numbers of young people willing to spend years training to operate such systems and then remain in the service. The MSDF had spent considerable time demanding ever greater resources, and through skill and USN leverage had largely achieved its goals, but was then faced with the task of sustaining the achievement. The ASDF confronted similar technical issues, but was far less enmeshed within US partner strategic plans, and among the three Forces faced the most limited critique, until scandals and deaths exposed glaring capability gaps.

Air Self-Defense Force

The ASDF developed like the other Forces in ways that may not immediately appear altogether logical or natural, but may be traced to imperial legacies, domestic interests, USAF patronage, and intra-JSDF relations origins. By the 1980s, the ASDF had emerged as a technically adept air force, experiencing a similar qualitative growth to the MSDF, with greatly extended range of operations and capabilities. The Air Self-Defense Force faced less criticism of imperial legacies than the other Forces, and presented a rather 'cleaner' and less complicated face to the nation. Defending skies has a universally glamourous aspect, and the ASDF has played adeptly to that image, to the extent that during the Cold War and beyond it rarely sullied itself with serious attention to other aspects of its defence roles, such as directly supporting ground forces. This is a curiosity, for the independent air force was born as a result of the great exertions of IJA and IJN veteran aviators, as well as the conviction within the (relatively newly independent) US Air Force (USAF) that Japan also required an equivalent force. Even more curiously, the intimate USAF-ASDF mentor-mentee relationship faded significantly during the Cold War, and while it later revived, it would take North Korean ballistic missiles to recast it into an approximation of the intimacy of the USN-MSDF model. Despite these aspects, the ASDF grew to become an advanced, respected air force, and Japan a producer of licensed and original military aircraft. Considering that aviation started at base zero in 1951, this was a significant achievement.

Establishment

Establishment of the ASDF constituted a major innovation: the IJA-IJN, which had previously possessed separate air arms,'disbanded and disarmed by December 1945, with the Force coming into being as a result of coincidental American and Japanese pressure groups.[282] Former-IJA-IJN aviation officers combined to create the 1950 'Military Aviation Reconstruction Group' (*Kōkūsenryoku saikengurūpu*) and lobbied the USAF Far Eastern Command (FEC) for a Japanese aviation force, while similar concepts were emerging among US defence planners.[283] The Group was influenced by the context of the Korean War and impending NPR formation, but the strength of will among former imperial aviators to disregard prior service boundaries is extraordinary given previous animosities.[284] Masuda details US priorities for Japanese aviation as maritime rather than territorial defences, Shibayama supporting the contention that from US, British, and most Japanese perspectives maritime issues dominated defence considerations.[285] Actual Force planning was a tightly negotiated mediation process through SCAP, USAF, USN, Department of Defense (DoD), State Department, and others, but a July 1952 'declaration of independence' was the position paper for General Otto P. Weyland, Commander of the Far East Air Forces (FEAF). It was developed in consultation with former-IJN aviators and indirectly submitted to Yoshida.[286] The cadre of former IJA officers quickly realised they needed 'IJN-allies' if an independent air force was to be realised, who would partly be drawn from 'Y-committee' members.[287] Ura Shigeru (ex-IJA, ASDF Chief of Staff 1964–6), stated that the group began communicating directly with US military authorities prior to 1952, but that year was the point at which the US began to request equivalent and complimentary air force development plans.[288]

Both SCAP and the US Joint Chiefs supported an independent Japanese air force, apparently motivated by over forty Soviet overflights of Hokkaido while the USAF was stretched by Korean War duties. Ambassador Murphy reported in 1952 that General Clark had discouraged the development of Japanese military aviation, partly as it appeared to ignore ground force planning requirements and to be USAF-focused.[289] However, by August 1953, a JCS recommendation to form an independent Japanese air force was formally received by the Yoshida cabinet, and approved as a 'three Force' plan in December.[290] Initially, Prime Minister Yoshida had 'opposed an air force because he felt it utilized "offensive weapons," and foresaw serious economic and technical difficulties', but bowed to pressure and defence logic, particularly the (defensive) Battle of Britain example, rather than Japanese defence against US bombing.[291] The result was the formation of an Aviation Preparation Office (*Kōkūjunbishitsu*) on 1 February 1954, with forty-seven NSA officials led by Yamada Makoto as a fledgling civilian air staff to prepare recruitment, basing, as well as equipment and training plans for the new

ASDF.[292] Initial DoD plans envisaged 257 combat and sixty-two support aircraft, costing the US $184 million 'for joint defense with US forces', and stating air defence as the initial aim.[293] Gen. Weyland had contacted NSA Director Masuhara the previous October, and had selected Col. Le Bailly and Maj. Brown to provide technical advice and training leadership. They surveyed facilities, serving personnel, and potential recruits, so that by 1 July 1954 the new ASDF had an actionable plan for rapid expansion despite the obvious technical difficulties involved.[294] DG-JDA Kimura Tokutarō announced to the press that the Air Self-Defense Force would be the principal weapon for the defence of Japan.[295]

The vital role of the USAF is evident in the formation of the ASDF. It should also be noted that the first ASDF Chief of Staff was Uemura Kentarō, a former Interior Ministry official, who was succeeded after two years by his deputy, Sanagi Sadamu, a former-IJN aviator, who was in turn succeeded after three years by the irrepressible Genda Minoru, one of Japan's most famous naval aviators.[296] They represented the three great influences upon the ASDF: police officials, USAF officers, and former imperial-era aviators. The aviation ban until 1951 and subsequent technical advances created a significant knowledge gap, Japan trailing in not only jets, but helicopters, radar, and systems, and requiring US technical and financial support.[297] The NSF Air Section establishment proceeded slowly, researching, gaining technical familiarity, and establishing a training base at Hamamatsu South, although most training was conducted on USAF bases.[298] The NSF Aviation School was established on 15 October 1952, with thirty-five US-gifted aircraft, increasing to 146 by 1954, with 6,738 personnel.[299] These included 559 officers and 2,574 men from the NSF, and eighty-five officers and 253 CSF transfer volunteers, while 570 former-IJA/IJN officers, 478 administrative staff, and 2,000 airmen-cadets were recruited.[300] Expansion was dramatic, the ASDF operating 269 T-33A and 302 F-86F jet-aircraft by 1958, most domestically produced, and the Fuji T-1A jet-trainer, Japan's first domestically designed jet aircraft.

Defence Build-up and Tasks

It was clear that ASDF planning was lacking structure, resulting aircraft type and squadron balance decisions being frequently altered.[301] By 31 March 1957, the ASDF had 542 aircraft but only one operational fighter squadron, with most of the 131 fighters in operational conversion units, indicating the steep learning curve.³⁰² The first defence build-up plan ambitiously envisaged 777 combat aircraft in thirty-three squadrons, but the ASDF possessed only ninety-one qualified pilots, due to selection and training delays. Particularly the scarcity of English-language skills was a problem, since USAF responsibility for air defence and air traffic control (ATC) entailed all pilots and controllers communicating in English at all times.³⁰³ US reports indicate a huge gap between Japan's defence budget, US military aid (averaging over $100-million per annum), and the $200-million per-annum cost of the first six-year defence plan.³⁰⁴ Japan's USFJ contribution amounted to $82–$148 million, consuming almost all MAP funds, while Japan's air budget was ¥6.6 billion in 1954 rising to ¥42.7 billion ($118.6 million) in 1960, the US funding the majority of the F-86F programme.³⁰⁵ Aviation was consistently the most expensive element in defence procurement due to the weak yen and the reliance upon imports, which accounted for over 90 per cent of equipment costs in 1960. Otake Hideo detailed how such costs provoked more determined Diet opposition than any other defence procurement issue into the early 1970s.³⁰⁶ However, Nishihiro Seiki relates how in the 1950s and 1960s the JDA struggled to find things to spend its money on, so disconnected were budgets, perceived needs, and procurement opportunities.³⁰⁷

Kaihara Osamu, Chief of the First Section Defense Bureau, JDA, complained to the Pentagon that outlandishly impractical 'expansion plans' were being produced by USAF, which the ASDF then enthusiastically lobbied for in a '*gaiatsu* conspiracy' that would become all too familiar. The USAF produced a 2,000 aircraft plan in 1957 when the ASDF couldn't effectively operate one hundred fighters, which was vigorously pressed by former-IJN admiral Hoshina Zenshiro, Prime Minister Kishi's defence advisor-confidant, and 'the arms industry's key advocate' in the LDP and Diet.³⁰⁸ Only in 1958 was the ASDF able to intercept aircraft, assuming national responsibility by July 1960.³⁰⁹ The gradual building of ASDF defence capabilities was natural considering the Japanese aviation experience gap, even though the fact that more than a year passed between the reversion of Okinawa in May 1972 and the ASDF assuming local air defence duties appears less reasonable.³¹⁰ Michael Hughes's critical 1972 commentary is prescient:

> The failure to examine the force structure rigorously has led to misinterpretations of the basis of Japan's attitude toward military means of effecting national security policy.
>
> [...] Japan's leaders have not perceived any threat, and therefore, the bureaucracy has not been required to reach a consensus on military policies.

[...] The force structure illustrates the isolation in which the uniformed planners work; it also indicates the industrial influence and economic motivation in defense development.

The irreconciled, and in some cases contradictory policy proposals, have resulted in a force structure capable of exercising a variety of future options, but having limited operational capacity.[311]

He identifies the lack of obvious threat assessment, poor evaluation of roles and capabilities, and civilian control restrictions effecting little reference to professional military advice, airmen being left to muddle through with little direction from above other than the imposition of *kokusanka* priorities.

Under the ASDF Chief of Staff and the Air Staff Office the main ASDF strength was initially concentrated in the Air Command (*Kōkūshūdan*), and from August 1958 the Air Defense Command (ADC *Kōkūsōtai*), at Fuchū, Tokyo. The ADC eventually commanded the Northern Air Defense Force (NADF), as well as the Central (CADF), and from 1961 the Western (WADF), with the Southwestern Composite Air Division, Okinawa, being established in 1973.[312] Air Support Command (ASC *Kōkūshienjūdan*) was initially formed in 1958 as Transport Command (*Yusōdan*) with an air-rescue wing and air traffic control and meteorological groups, and gradually assumed flight-checking functions with a dedicated squadron. From 1987, ASC established the Special Airlift Group (SAG *Tokubetsukōkūyusōtai*) operating Boeing-747 aircraft for Imperial Household and cabinet members. Air Training Command (ATgC *Kōkūkyōikushūdan*) was founded at Hamamatsu in 1964 to provide a single structure for the burst of training activity and proliferation of schools, as well as flight training previously under US supervision. While USAF cooperation continued, 1964 marked the point by which the ASDF became essentially self-training, and with the command and control architecture that remains in place.[313]

The three main commands during the Cold War, later supplemented by Air Development and Test Command (ADTC) and Air Materiel Command Headquarters (AMCH), were listed in the SDF Law, with their respective duties, structure, and cooperative responsibilities, yet without stated responsibilities towards the other Forces, even for transport, rescue, and ATC.[314] This was reflected in the 1970 Defense White Paper that listed particular ASDF duties as maintaining radar stations and scrambling to intercept intruders, but little else other than assisting in emergencies.[315] For such an important defence institution it seems remarkable that so little guidance could have been provided, not least towards joint or general cooperation with the GSDF, MSDF, and even USAF, all of which indicated the oddly isolated manner in which the air force developed.

ASDF development was less dramatic than hoped for, but consistently concentrated resources upon training aircraft, light-fighters, and air-defence weaponry, with logistical support capabilities only gradually being targeted for investment. Thirty-six US-gifted wartime C-46 transporters, plus twelve bought from Taiwan, were only removed from service with the introduction of the Kawasaki C-1 (1974–9), despite being obsolete.[316] The C-1, though modern and possessing short-take-off and landing (STOL) capabilities as well as fine speed, lacked range-payload to reach Okinawa.[317] ASDF transport was seemingly developed with little reference to GSDF requirements, as the C-46 and YS-11 were only capable of light transport and paratrooper training roles. The YS-11 and C-1 were *kokusanka* projects to aid Japan's aviation industry. Chalmers Johnson's majestic study of Ministry of International Trade and Industry (MITI) illustrates care for 'national projects,' with defence and aviation notable priorities.[318] The YS-11 was produced, like the C-1, by a coalition of domestic producers under MITI guidance, the first ordered as war reparations for the Philippines.[319] Yamamura Takashi considers the YS-11 a commercial failure, managed on imperial-military lines that discounted customer requirements to demonstrate national 'spirit.'[320] The C-1 was a larger, more expensive, purely military project, which denuded ASDF transport resources until two C-130H were ordered in 1981. Further incremental orders by 1990 provided the ASDF with twelve aircraft, equivalent to Belgium's fleet, even though the C-1 logged over fifty years of service.[321] MITI-directed *kokusanka* projects enhanced neither ASDF nor GSDF capabilities compared to the C-130H.[322] *Kokusanka* prioritisation was later lessened by budget constraints, diluted through 'defence tribe' (*bōeizoku*) influence (partly, ironically, due to Nakasone's defence budget largesse, and partly due to efforts made by Sakata and others to broaden defence discussions), and by the prominence of perceived national project cost overruns.[323]

The ASDF primarily targeted air defence capabilities, its core duty, and wished to procure the best US jet-fighters available both for their technical qualities as well as to facilitate production, training, and development. The first non-US imported service aircraft, from 1992, was the BAe U-125.[324] The ASDF acquired the transonic F-86F, the supersonic F-104J, and then the multi-purpose, combat-proven twin-seat, twin-engine F-4EJ that in many ways became the defining ASDF Cold War combat aircraft.[325] Richard Samuels notes that even machine tools and logbooks were provided for

Japanese F86F and F104J production, whereas the dauntingly complex F-4EJ was the first fighter built in Japan without US subsidies.[326] Unit costs reached approximately ¥4 billion by 1977 ($14 million, over $20 million by 1979), more than double that of US-produced aircraft.[327]

Qualitative improvements contributed to the quantitative decreases from over 1,100 in the early 1960s to 430 combat aircraft under the 1976 NDPO, as F-4EJ and Mitsubishi F-1 fleets expanded and F-86Fs retired to training.[328] The JDA lobbied for air-to-air missiles (AAM) as early as 1957, with AIM-7 Sparrow, AIM-9 Sidewinder, and AIM-4 Falcon entering service, the latter rapidly withdrawn as a disappointment.[329] From 1970 the first Japanese AAM entered service (AAM-1/Type-69), a 'non-copy' Sidewinder 'cousin'—a move motivated by import costs.[330] The Japanese government decried a unilateral US decision to withdraw eight air-defence artillery battalions, prompting a face-saving announcement that withdrawal was by Japanese request, but this gradual transfer of responsibilities was a troubled process of budget, training, and political sensitivities.[331] USAF frustration at the tardiness of ASDF development was evident, the US seemingly expected to fill every capability gap, while the Japanese focused on manned-aircraft, while signally failing to gain public approval for USAF airbase runway extensions.[332] US officials were baffled by JDA reticence to utilise civilian weather rockets for defence due to Japanese scientists' pacifist leanings.[333] USAF operation of twenty-four early warning radar sites around Japan, costing ¥10–15 billion annually, equivalent to one-tenth of the Japanese defence budget, became a contentious issue: the US urged Japan to take it on, while the JDA suggested an equal split.[334] Japan assumed responsibility in stages up to the mid-1970s, but few systems improvements were made before the mid-1980s. Several USFJ veterans were surprised to find few changes, one commenting on a 2003 visit that the operations and maintenance areas were 'like a time warp.'[335]

The radar stations and air traffic control (ATC) systems provided surveillance and management of Japan's Air Defense Identification Zone (ADIZ), established in 1969 and extended in 1972 to Okinawa Prefecture. Still, following USAF practice, this only covered half of the Yonaguni Islands chain until a 2010 revision, conducted insensitively towards Taiwanese sensitivities.[336] The Japan ADIZ never included Korean-controlled Takeshima/Dokdo, and since both countries' ADIZ were established under USAF protocols, there has been little contention, in contrast with maritime demarcation issues.[337] The Zone ensures that legitimate air traffic is recognised, and that all other traffic is identified and potentially challenged, coexisting with Flight

Information Regions (FIRs) for seamless international ATC across national boundaries.[338] Japan is covered by Fukuoka FIR, which covers a vastly greater area than the ADIZ, which does not include the south-eastern portion of the EEZ, while FIR far exceeds the EEZ as a means for civilian aviation management and cooperation.[339] The Japanese ADIZ places no burden on air traffic not seeking to land in Japan or enter (twelve nautical-mile) territorial air space, equivalent to the maritime right of innocent passage, with few contentious points, until the Chinese East China Sea ADIZ declaration of 2013. From 1969, when all civil ATC reverted to Japan, the ADIZ was coordinated by the Japan-US Base Air Defense Ground Environment (BADGE) System.

USAF influence lingered long after the end of the occupation. The US Country Team in Japan indicated that the economy even in 1957–8 could support a defence budget of 5 per cent 'without adverse economic effect' rather than the 2 per cent of 1954–7.[340] The ASDF even had difficulty in spending its budget, with a quarter of funds held over from 1955 and 1956, due to base delays (USAF withdrawal, land acquisition), preparation of specifications (lack of specialists), and import of equipment.[341] However, following the inaugural Japanese-American Committee on Security in August 1957, US Ambassador MacArthur, Gen. Smith, and Minister-Counsellor Horsey with Prime Minister Kishi, Foreign Minister Fujiyama, and DG-JDA Tsushima covered the transition of air defence duties from USAF to ASDF.[342] ASDF Chief of Staff Genda was noticeably absent, more for Japanese civilian control sensitivities than American concerns.

Four great shocks had transformative effects upon ASDF development. A fatal air crash that killed 162 on 30 July 1971 and had been caused by ASDF controllers resulted in operational and cultural changes for the Force. The shooting down of Korean Airlines Flight 007 in September 1983 by Soviet fighters reinforced Soviet threat perceptions, wreckage and body parts being discovered on Hokkaido beaches, with JSDF SIGINT intercepts of Soviet air defence communications being used (with little consultation) by the US to expose fallacious Soviet denials.[343] The 1998 launch of a North Korean Taepodong-1 ballistic missile over Japan brought home the reality of DPRK missile programmes, and prompted ASDF (and MSDF) ballistic missile defence (BMD) investments (see Chapter Three). However, for core ASDF capabilities, the landing at Hakodate Airport of Soviet Air Defence Force pilot Lt. Victor Belenko's MiG-25 fighter on 6 September 1976 was unrivalled, and coincided with the deepening frost of the second Cold War.

The 1976 Shock

From 1958, the ASDF began air defence interceptions, 'scrambles', the alert take-off of two fighter aircraft, initially F-86F, under fighter-director control to deter, escort away, or force a landing of unauthorised aircraft approaching Japanese airspace. That year there were twenty-five scrambles, full air-defence missions assumed from July 1960, not just 'a primary mission, it has been *the* primary mission. The other air power roles [...] relegated to less than secondary roles.'[344] The F-104J first scrambled on 1 December 1964, the ASDF's first air-superiority F-4EJ fighter on 1 November 1975, interception missions peaking at 426 in 1967, and 798 in 1978, before reaching 944 scrambles in 1984, which stood unrivalled until 2014.[345] There were twenty-nine recorded intrusions into Japanese airspace 1967–2000, yet it was not until 9 December 1987 that an F-4EJ from Naha made the first ASDF live-munitions interception (Soviet Tu-16J Badger electronic intelligence (ELINT) aircraft), firing 20mm cannon warning-shots, indicating that although scrambles were common and threat perceptions heightened, air defence had been cautiously conducted.[346] The 1976 incident saw an inexperienced squadron with new aircraft, acting cautiously under inadequate ground control. Critical voices included Kaihara Osamu, NDC Secretary-General, and Ogawa Raita, former Zero-pilot and editor of *Kōkū Shimbun*, who 'deplored the vulnerability of the radar network and the bases.' Ogawa, particularly critical of the command structure, stated in 1971, 'there is no complete air defense weapon system.'[347]

Lt. Belenko flew low to avoid Soviet interception as he attempted to defect, climbing to attract ASDF attention over Hokkaido, to enable interceptors to escort him to an appropriate base, which the two F-4EJ scrambled from Chitose Air Base (AB) failed to achieve. The 1977 Defense White Paper devoted an entire chapter to this incident and systematic air defence failures, but it is alleged that the ASDF were ordered to destroy most related documentation, and that police, JDA, and MOFA squabbled over jurisdiction issues.[348] Despite hosting the best equipped defence sector, the Force had failed to intercept an 'enemy' aircraft that was attempting to be intercepted, illustrating ASDF neglect of not only transport and CAS capabilities, but also core air defences. JDA Director-General Sakata Michita described the MiG-25 incident and the Lockheed Scandal as the two most trying events in his career.[349] While the 1976 crisis was short-lived (the Lockheed Scandal saga, which implicated Genda and led to the arrest of former Prime Minister Tanaka Kakuei in 1976, and conviction in 1983, also created two 'Lockheed

Scandal elections'), coming mid-Scandal it provided a weapon with which to beat the besieged Miki cabinet. With a 15 September cabinet reshuffle, a new foreign minister, a split LDP, and a Diet Lockheed investigation committee, the MiG-25 issue was, unusually, left to the DG-JDA.

Consequences of the 1976 interception failure rapidly followed. DG-JDA Sakata established jurisdiction over the MiG-25, enabling examination by US and Japanese technical staff, and despatched an ASDF team investigating the next fighter aircraft (already preferring the F-15) to the US. Foreign Minister Miyazawa Kiichi managed the US transfer of Belenko, while Sakata (with Miyazawa's brother, Yasushi, a senior JDA official) dealt with the aircraft's disassembly, movement, examination, and return to the USSR.[350] The examination and Belenko's debrief provoked consternation, as MiG-25 interception-control systems and 'dated' technology solved complex problems quickly, cheaply, and reliably, with over 400 aircraft in squadron service highlighting capability gaps with contemporary Japanese and US forces.[351] Diet scrutiny was surprisingly limited, pre-occupied as it was with the Lockheed Scandal. JSP House of Representatives member Ōide Shun, with deft flexibility of logic, attacked the inability to defend Japanese airspace, and the innate ridiculousness of attempting to do so given Soviet superiority, utilising a JDA comic-book, *Leave the Defense of Japan's Skies to Us*, for both purposes. Sakata politely avoided such bait, dismissed suggestions of anti-Soviet conspiracies, and focused upon the need to provide credible air defence, for which Airborne Early Warning (AEW) aircraft had become obviously necessary, due to the base vulnerability to surprise attack.[352] The delay in the AEW order, despite a 1974 ASDF capability study, had been due to MOF parsimony and MITI *kokusanka* insistence, a FY-1976 request refused as post-oil shock equipment budgets shrank. It was also influenced by the lingering influence of Tanaka Kakuei's 1973 espousal of 'peacetime defence capability' (*heiwajino bōeiryoku*), contrasting with the brief but bruising attempts of then JDA-DG Nakasone to massively increase defence spending and ambitions in his novel 1970 defence white paper as part of his 'autonomous defence' (*jishubōei*) concept.[353] Post-Belenko, five AEW aircraft were ordered, filling the curious gap in air and maritime security, a further oddity being that the MSDF had operated an AEW-capable system it had failed to exploit either for national or fleet defence.[354]

From July 1957, nineteen MDAP-gifted ex-USN TBM-Avenger aircraft began training MSDF aircrews for the more sophisticated P2V-7 Neptune, ten being TBM3W 'hunters,' with AN/APS-20 radar.[355] The AN/APS-20 was the first AEW radar in carrier-borne service from 1951, used by the USAF in

Vietnam, and in British Royal Navy, then Royal Air Force service, until 1991.[356] The Forces may not have realised AN/APS-20 AEW potential, but the ASDF experimented with F-86D fire-control radar (AN/APG-36) in a C-46D transporter, whereas MSDF AN/APS-20 were discarded.[357] Despite the UK example, MSDF assets remained underutilised, which emphasised the poverty of JSDF joint approaches and technology sharing, not unlike 'stove-piped' imperial-era radar developments. Funada's ridiculed 1969 defence reform proposals included radar systems for maritime security, presumed to include AEW.[358] The proximity of Soviet airbases, limitations of land-based radar, and ASDF fleet air-defence responsibilities would indicate that AEW should have been a joint-Force priority rather than a reaction to airspace intrusion, but the MSDF met Backfire/missile-driven air-threat assessments by investing in AEGIS.[359]

The F-104J replacement effort resulted in the ASDF favouring the F-15 (USAF), MSDF favouring the F-14 (USN), and JDA Internal Bureau favouring the F-16 (USAF, 120 aircraft for the cost of 50 F-14 or 80 F-15).[360] An evaluation mission visited the US and an Internal Bureau announcement had been expected in September 1976.[361] Owing to Belenko's flight, the ASDF with USAF support argued for both the F-15 and more (123) aircraft, but the recommendation was delayed due to financial considerations and a MITI *kokusanka* rearguard effort. The eventual US Foreign Military Sales (FMS) agreement was for 100 licence-produced F-15J, to equip only four of five F-104J squadrons; F-4EJ production extended until 1981 to form a sixth F-4EJ squadron, less capable than the F-15J, but significantly cheaper (despite F-4EJ itself being far more expensive than USAF F-4E).[362] Owing to political pressure in 1973 the JDA retracted an ASDF in-flight refuelling plan and removed (and stored) refuelling equipment from aircraft, but from 1984 the refuelling issue returned, with sea-lane defence and Iwo Jima flights raised as justifications, but increased Soviet aircraft threat perceptions as vital drivers, even though it would be 2010 before ASDF tanker-aircraft entered service.[363] The F-15J gave the ASDF greatly increased capabilities, such as target detection range, but despite great scramble capability Combat Air Patrols (CAP) were limited by an aerial refuelling gap compounded by limited USAF cooperation, non-'frontline' and only during 'contingencies' (*yūji*).[364] AEW capability was obviously welcome, but limited by processing commands through ground-based rather than air-based controllers.[365]

The 1976–7 period, therefore saw the ASDF embarrassed but thereby gained AEW capability and the world's most advanced fighter aircraft amid difficult US-Japan trade relations, just when détente was flagging and the second Cold War approaching.[366] It also tightened the ASDF-USAF relationship, which had weakened during the Vietnam War. Like Taepodong, the MiG-25 incident illustrated to the public that greater air defence investment was required and that Japan, while peaceful, remained vulnerable. Despite Diet criticism of the government, DG-JDA Sakata had also found himself in agreement with several opposition members and at odds with cabinet colleagues and officials, illustrating that a broader spectrum of politicians were rationally approaching defence and security issues than may have been immediately apparent.[367]

From 1980, ASDF configuration changed little other than the enlargement and renaming of Air Support Command, establishment of the AEW Group and additions to technical schools.[368] The three regional Air Defence Forces and the South-Western Composite Air Division continued with qualitative improvements in ground-radar systems and aircraft, with further F-15J orders sanctioned in 1982 and 1985.[369] The 1976 NDPO (*Taiko*) established ten air-defence squadrons (250 aircraft), and three maritime-strike/ground-attack squadrons (100), clearly indicating prioritisation of tasks and the 'second rank' nature of support-strike capabilities in the ASDF.[370]

Close Air Support (CAS), Maritime-Strike/Support

With such an indistinct outline of ASDF required duties, and consequent capabilities, it was hardly surprising that GSDF/MSDF support duties were neglected, and maritime and ground-strike capabilities became increasingly unbalanced. In 1971, Genda Minoru derided sea-lane defence capabilities and insisted that the ASDF focus upon this task in cooperation with the MSDF, as otherwise the country faced repeating the disasters of 1944–5.[371] Hughes claims that four of seven F-86F squadrons trained for ground/maritime support roles in 1970, and studied with forward air-controllers (FAC) several times a year, but with such limited range and payload that they would be unable to reach northern Hokkaido from their Misawa base, and, if forward-based (Chitose AB), envisaged only five minutes loiter-time.[372] The same squadrons were equally limited for maritime strike, with no radar or navigation systems and outmoded weapons, but at least they trained more realistically, with forty-eight total sorties per year against ships. The problems experienced 1969–71 included an MSDF 'enemy fleet' being missed while the ASDF attacked the 'friendly fleet,' and a Soviet warship mistakenly 'attacked,' luckily without further consequences.³⁷³ The ASDF replaced the F-86F with F-1 'support fighters' (*shiensentōki*), designated for maritime strike and ground attack with much greater capabilities in the former than latter role, due to inertial maritime strike radar with secondary air-combat capability, but lacking equivalent inertial navigation attack systems of the remarkably similar Anglo-French SEPECAT Jaguar.³⁷⁴ Leading military analyst Ebata Kensuke therefore derided the F-1 'support fighter': 'as far as GSDF operations are concerned, it provides almost no support.'³⁷⁵

The lack of precision-guided munitions (PGM) was noted by the JDA, but only addressed with the anti-ship ASM-1, CAS roles depending upon 'dumb' bombs, rockets, and cannons, as in the Korean War. The ASDF lacked CAS cluster munitions until after the Cold War, or CAS PGM, which were first ordered in 2005.³⁷⁶ Ebata asserts that CAS was marginalised by the F-4EJ having its inertial bombing computer removed, by the fear of pacifist ire at adopting an aircraft associated with bombing Vietnam, which was quietly reinstalled in the 1981–7 *kai* (modification) programme.³⁷⁷ This embodied the *senshubōei* approach of 'exclusively defensive defence,' which precluded any system or practice not judged entirely defensive, a significant hazard to Cold War defence planning. CAS capability gaps were not uniquely Japanese. Commonly 'supporters' (pilots) wish to fly faster, higher, and with maximum stealth and range, while the 'supported' (ground troops) generally desire slower, lower, and longer air presence.³⁷⁸ ASDF priorities were set at air defence and area denial, meaning sole ASDF missions with (some) joint ASDF-MSDF missions. The GSDF-support CAS role was and remains a lesser priority. Test pilot Jeffrey Quill also encountered NATO air staffs 'dominated by the "fighter jockey" mentality, [who] could not bring themselves to see [how] an aircraft without Mach 2 performance [...] could be of any use to anyone.'³⁷⁹ The aircraft in question was the Jaguar, the F-1's distant relation, and yet NATO air forces became converts to and adept in CAS/interdiction roles, without equivalence in Japan. Hughes has suggested that the GSDF and MSDF rebuffed ASDF cooperation efforts as they hoped to develop their own organic capabilities, including those for the MSDF Harrier, but Force criticisms of air combat priorities have proved prolonged and persistent.³⁸⁰

Italy and Germany developed cheap, light CAS fighters, and many countries operated jet training aircraft in 'swing' weapons-training/CAS roles. The ASDF took neither path. Partly, the DBP aircraft/squadron numerical limit provoked a dash for high-end quality rather than overall capabilities, but it appears that the ASDF were simply, in the words of a USAF officer, 'happiest when flying at 30,000-feet, not interested in much else, and with ideas on CAS that the Air Force gave up in Vietnam.'[381] One wonders what ASDF CAS plans were. Unfortunately, most sources have been noticeably reticent, their discomfort notable yet absent when discussing air defence. The poverty of Japanese CAS is due primarily to ASDF neglect, but also to a lack of GSDF engagement, with the JDA demonstrating control but deficient leadership. Expertise rested almost solely with Force personnel, as the Joint Staff Council was unable or unwilling to enforce joint planning or integration. The weakness of the JSC was that it rarely enacted defence enhancements favouring one Force over another. It was a balancing and mediation office, interceding and negotiating for the Forces with politicians and officials. Doctrine and planning for anti-shipping strikes were developed with the accompanying technology, illustrating ASDF joint planning capacity, but its heart was in national air defence.

Air-Defence Resilience

Providing resilience to armed forces involves improving their ability to avoid destruction before they can deploy, and being able to sustain operations. This commonly involves making bases and equipment difficult to destroy in surprise, pre-emptive attacks, such as Pearl Harbor in 1941, or Egyptian airfields in 1967. Air defence resilience can be improved through overall base defences and 'hardening,' with hard shelters and bunkers, such as Hardened Aircraft Shelters (HAS), but their size and resilience vary from shrapnel to nuclear protection. While 'hardening' began throughout NATO from the 1960s, the 'hardest' HAS are in Saudi Arabia, Taiwan, and Switzerland's fantastic mountain complexes, while Sweden relied upon disbursement using public roads as runways to dilute potential targets.[382] Most airbases without HAS have underground storage, earthwork 'berms' and revetments (reinforced walls), or dispersal over larger areas, reducing potential damage but increasing operational complexities. Sidoti's definitive study highlights active and passive defences, deep dispersal, alternate bases, and efforts made to ensure that surviving bases, personnel, and aircraft are not 'logistically isolated.'[383]

Japan constructed underground aircraft factories and hardened shelters in 1945, but during the Cold War there were few HAS, limited revetments, and little dispersal despite Cold War ASDF assumption of a massive, initial surprise attack to destroy Japanese airpower.[384] Chitose AB, important and spacious, was provided with paired HAS adjacent to the apron, protective berms, ordnance and fuel stores within close proximity, but this remained an exception.[385] Komatsu AB, Ishikawa, the only fighter base on the Sea of Japan, was provided with only lightweight shelters, dispersal often proving difficult given land availability, and the sharing of many bases with civilian airports, such as Naha, Komatsu, and Hyakuri, although Chitose AB is also shared. The JSDF tends not to lavish money on its bases, and visitors to USFJ facilities find them a plush contrast, many JSDF bases appearing, in the words of one former USMC officer, 'tattered [...] *boroi* (worn-out)'.[386] Limited base hardening appears peculiar given the supposed Soviet threat immediacy, and starkly contrasts with NATO bases. Kaihara Osamu noted in 1975 how easily Soviet aircraft could launch surprise attacks, rapidly knocking out radar, command and control, as well as aircraft and runways.[387] From the mid-1980s, defences (gun-missile) were strengthened, but reliance upon ASDF air defences to prevent a debilitating *coup de main* while neglecting resilience was a high-risk approach.[388]

Although runway vulnerability was obvious, the ASDF undertook limited alternative contingency preparations, unlike West Germany, Switzerland, Sweden, Taiwan, and Korea, which conducted regular exercises of fighters operating from highways, German events featuring on television and attracting significant crowds.[389] In Britain, there were few such exercises, but Harrier squadrons performed regular 'field' exercises, and Jaguars test-flew from meadows and motorways.[390] Throughout most of the Cold War the ASDF relied upon nineteen air bases (including Okinawa), five shared with civilian airports. Thirteen GSDF runways were mainly short, for helicopters, the MSDF maintaining twelve heliports and long runways for maritime reconnaissance aircraft.[391] ASDF base provision was consistent but puzzling. It operated the longest JSDF runways (Chitose AB, 3000/2700m), necessitating basing Boeing-747s in Hokkaido, only four ASDF bases having twin-runways, allowing safer operations in challenging weather conditions and optimising operational effectiveness.[392] This provided few options for fighter or large transport aircraft operations requiring 1800m-plus runways.[393] Fighter aircraft can operate within more restricted parameters than airliners but heat, humidity, and wind must be included within ordnance and fuel-load factoring, as well as potential runway damage after attacks, and the ASDF never prioritised STOL or rough-field capabilities for its combat aircraft, despite enhanced operational sustainability.[394] There are numerous small ex-IJA/IJN airfields utilised for civil aviation, such as Honda Airport in Okegawa, Saitama, with a 700m runway, but the Aviation Law (*Kōkūhō*) stipulates that JSDF use requires Ministry of Land, Infrastructure, Transport and Tourism (until 2001, Ministry of Transport) permissions that the JDA did not apply for.[395] ASDF sources relate how landing-take-off 'touch and go' drills were practiced at Yakumo Sub-Base, 80km north of Hakodate, and ex-ASDF base Nakashibetsu Airport but without documentation.[396]

Despite a significant military footprint, Hokkaido was not deeply prepared for air conflict. There were few investments in mobile radar or ground-crew capabilities to enable 'field squadrons' to flexibly service alternative sites, the main resilience investment being in *Kōkūshisetsutai* (Air Civil-Engineering Groups) for combat damage repair and snow clearing.[397] The ASDF might have prepared numerous regular and reserve bases, but for much of the Cold War there were only three fighter bases in northern Japan. The most northerly and main NADF base was Chitose, Hokkaido; the most 'southerly' northern base Matsushima, Miyagi, over 500km from Chitose and over 250km from Misawa, Aomori, the 'middle' base, shared from the 1980s with the USAF, with one 3,000m runway. Matsushima has primarily been a training base under 4 Wing, ATC, part of Central Air Defense Force (CADF) area rather than NADF, which means that few Matsushima aircraft would directly support Chitose.[398] In Korea by contrast, the USAF 51st Fighter Wing was based less than 100km from the DPRK border (Osan AB), providing CAS with hardened shelters and fuel supplies, and the largest base security in the Pacific Air Forces, indicating the differing perceptions of conventional invasion.[399] Kaihara Osamu estimated in 1971 that the ASDF 'would last one hour in a Soviet attack,' whereas one USAF officer 'suggested five minutes.'[400]

By 1964, the ASDF was operating an extensive network of radar stations, including nine in the NADF, but the only fighter squadrons were 203rd (F-104J) and 103rd (F-86D) at Chitose AB, and 3rd (F-86D) at Hachinohe AB, Aomori, later transferred to the MSDF.[401] By contrast, Western Air Command (Kyushu/Western Honshu) controlled five fighter squadrons, despite few scrambles and Okinawan airspace under USAF control.[402] During the fourth DBP, NADF forces changed little other than by the addition of further Nike-Hercules SAM, particularly during the 1980s, when Patriot PAC-2 replaced Nike-Hercules, and *kokusanka* medium Type-81 and light Type-91 SAM introduced, so that by the end of the Cold War ground-based air defence partly offset resilience weaknesses.[403] However, the fundamental imbalance of the GSDF looking 'north,' while the MSDF looked 'south,' was matched by the ASDF not knowing where it was looking. By 1981, NADF deployed 2 Wing (Chitose F-104J/F-4EJ fighters) and 3 Wing (Misawa, F-1 'support'), each of two squadrons, thirty-six aircraft. The next combat squadrons were 7 Wing (Central ADF) F-4EJ at Hyakuri, Ibaraki, over 900km from Chitose AB.[404] If the ASDF was deploying so few units to the most vulnerable area five years after the Belenko shock, amid a chilly second Cold War, its priorities were not readily apparent.

ASDF-USAF

The end of occupation and establishment of the JSDF provides a potential mid-1950s hinge of transition from defended to self-defending, and yet US defence of Japan continued long after the occupation with an extensive transition period, particularly for the ASDF. Iruma AB, Saitama, 35km northwest of Tokyo, illustrates this gradual transition, from IJA aerodrome, US Johnson Field, and from 1958, Iruma AB as a shared ASDF-USAF facility, passing to ASDF command by 1963, with USAF support functions continuing until 1978. The common signposts of end of occupation (1952), ASDF foundation (1954), and treaty revision (1960) clearly had little immediate impact on defensive responsibilities.[405] This was replicated in expensively constructed radar and signals monitoring stations, such as at Wakkanai, Hokkaido, vital for monitoring Soviet movements and signals, including USAF-USN cooperation monitoring Soviet Soya Strait submarine movements (coded 'Cointreau') and TU-95B maritime reconnaissance aircraft flights ('Drambui').[406] The JSDF assumed responsibility from 1972 as USAF personnel trained their ASDF successors, but until at least 1983 a US presence was maintained, as it was through the shared BADGE system.[407]

USAF connections were also maintained through technical training missions in the US, such as initial pilot and engineering training for F-104 and F-4 fighters, and Nike-Hercules SAM training; in 1957, US officials even encouraged arming these missiles with nuclear warheads.[408] Of the less amenable alliance-related duties, ASDF personnel had to deal with uncomfortable demonstrations at USAF shared bases, particularly during the Vietnam War, which negatively raised Force profile.[409] The Vietnam War also saw many USAF units leave Japan, weakening the air alliance; only in July 1984 did F-16 fighters of USAF 432 Wing return, to Misawa AB, where the first ASDF AEW unit had formed the previous year.[410] The US Air Force remained in Japan during the mid-Cold War without fighters to aid transition of aviation control to the ASDF, also indicating limited US threat perception. This gradually changed with escalating Korean tensions, with the 1968 *USS Pueblo* seizure and the shooting down of a USN Atsugi-based surveillance aircraft in 1969 with thirty-one crew killed. This resulted in temporary reinforcements, but the Misawa return came late in the Cold War, and the USAF-ASDF relationship lacked the intimacy of the naval partnership.[411]

ASDF Culture and Safety

As a 'new' service, the ASDF often appeared less encumbered with imperial legacy baggage. Focusing upon the latest technology, compatibility with USAF, and the glamorous profession of defending blue skies, the predominant image of the ASDF was of a technically adept, professional force represented by the Blue Impulse aerobatic display team. Blue Impulse forged itself in popular consciousness by 'painting' the five-ring Olympic symbol above Tokyo at the 1964 Olympic Games opening ceremony.[412] As Paul Midford has noted, the first post-Olympic opinion polls on the JSDF illustrated positive impressions of the Forces.[413] Blue Impulse repeated their Olympic feat, writing 'EXPO 70' above the Osaka World Exposition, but in November 1982, during a public display at Hamamatsu, a pilot was killed and twelve civilians injured.[414]

While crashes were inevitable in training, those involving the ASDF generally appeared to raise less ire than those of USFJ. On Yokohama Bluff a 1980 statue, 'The love of mother and children,' represented a mother and children killed when a USMC RF-4B fighter crashed in 1977.[415] It resembles a 1981 statue in Ninomiya, Kanagawa, of a girl in air-raid protection hood, holding a glass rabbit she held when killed by a US P-51 fighter in 1945. The two statues clearly indicate that Japanese are victims of US military aircraft in peace and war. ASDF crashes tend to elicit sympathy for bereaved service families, with one former-IJA pilot (Major Kobayashi Teruhiko) lauded for emulating the 'old spirit' by ordering his pupil to eject prior to fatally crashing in June 1957.[416] The ASDF follows IJA/IJN practice in posthumously promoting 'lost' pilots.[417] While the Force has lost a significant number of aircraft, the first major incident occurring when a C-46 crashed off Tottori in March 1957 and killing seventeen, many were in the early days of pilot training, particularly as they were becoming accustomed to jet technology.[418] Certain types suffered high rates, such as eight F-4EJ lost 1973–9, most likely due to unfamiliarity with such a large and complex aircraft, but it was surprising for a twin-engine type with an inherently greater safety margin. By contrast, the ASDF operated 230 single-engine F-104J/DJ,

1962–86, losing thirty-six aircraft (16 per cent), while Canadian F-104 losses were 44 per cent, and West Germany's 32 per cent, many at low level, reflecting ASDF 'flying high' culture.[419]

A notable contrast to tolerance of ASDF crashes involved a T-33 training jet approaching Iruma AB on 22 November 1999, killing both crew members. The issue raised possible ASDF negligence, but media outrage focused upon damage to electricity supplies, with homes and trains blacked out, rather than the fatalities.[420] There was little attention given to air crews flying obsolete aircraft, other than in Diet debates where opposition members who had opposed greater defence spending attacked poor ASDF investment without either obvious irony or shame.[421] The government provided answers on the crash but not on the nature of risking operating unfit aircraft.[422] The incident featured in no defence white papers, unlike the 30 July 1971 collision of an ANA Boeing 727 with an F-86F over Iwate, which killed 162, but where the ASDF pilot and trainee ejected safely.[423] Two ASDF ground controllers, using inherited occupation-era systems separate from civilian ATC, were found guilty and imprisoned for negligence, the government being forced to fundamentally change ATC procedures with ASDF controller duties integrated into the BADGE system.[424] The most shocking accident, nationally memorialised, was of Japan Airlines (JAL) 123 which crashed into a Gunma mountain on 12 August 1985, with 520 fatalities and only four survivors. The ASDF and GSDF mobilised personnel, but institutional faults resulted in damning indictments.[425] A USAF C-130 identified and reported the crash site, enabling a US helicopter to arrive quickly, only to be ordered to withdraw so as to allow the ASDF SAR operations.[426] However, the ASDF repeatedly misidentified the site, the delay probably causing the death of several survivors to exposure, despite the flight's distress signal being tracked and reported by Hyakuri AB, which scrambled two F-4EJ fighters.[427] Nagano Police and several media helicopters reached the correct location, but the ASDF and GSDF remained confused, partly, Christopher Hood correctly contends, due to the lack of local relief maps, and confusion between nautical miles and kilometres.[428]

There were few people of public notoriety associated with the ASDF, other than former-IJA/IJN officers, such as Genda Minoru, but one was the novelist, commentator, and aspiring revolutionary Mishima Yukio, photographed in an ASDF F-104DJ at Hyakuri in 1967.[429] This association was less pronounced than Mishima's GSDF involvement, and therefore there was little adverse publicity, the ASDF budgeting to 'entertain' prominent citizens for public relations.⁴³⁰ The first Japanese astronauts were notably civilian, with Yui Kimiya being the first ASDF member to be selected for space training in 2009, twenty-four years after selection began.⁴³¹ The exception of notoriety was ASDF Chief of Staff, Tamogami Toshio, who was not only the first ASDF chief to be forced from his position for outspoken comments on his 'unique' historical views of imperial-legacy war issues, but also the first to be found guilty of crimes.⁴³² He unfortunately received a degree of attention unbefitting his professional capacity or historical knowledge.⁴³³

There is far less opposition to ASDF than USFJ bases, but certain facilities have inspired niche local opposition. Hyakuri AB, shared with Ibaraki Airport, 'Tokyo's Third Airport,' had been an IJN air station and there was considerable opposition from local farmers when aviation resumed in the late 1950s, and activist groups sustained opposition thereafter.⁴³⁴ The opposition mirrors that to Narita Airport, which prompted a specific law countering protests and sabotage which resembled anti-terrorism rather than transportation policies.⁴³⁵ The ASDF similarly failed to ameliorate opposition, clumsily displaying cluster bombs at a 2008 open day, despite a previous government statement banning such munitions. Chief of Staff Tamogami's influence was suspected, as he had previously expressed ASDF shame for submitting before farmers, with the Force relaying upon PR open days and air shows rather than through negotiations.⁴³⁶ In order to generate positive publicity, the ASDF regularly held 'rolling out' ceremonies equivalent to MSDF ship launching, often with a religious presence, Shinto priests inaugurating into service the first domestically designed jet aircraft, Fuji T1A.⁴³⁷ In one less conventional ceremony, at Iruma AB in November 1965, the USAF presented the ASDF with an IJN Ōka rocket-powered suicide aircraft.⁴³⁸ It was not altogether clear what the USAF intention was nor how the ASDF accommodated this generosity.

Negative ASDF images have been rare other than Tamogami, accidents, and a minor scandal involving furniture contracts.⁴³⁹ ASDF personnel have guarded against base protests at Hyakuri and at shared USAF facilities. However, in 1969 a law suit began that lasted almost fifteen years, and involved retired Chief of Staff Genda, and serving Chief, Ogata Kagetoshi, giving courtroom evidence concerning a Nike-Hercules SAM site in Naganuma, Hokkaido. The real accused were the JDA and cabinet. The military specialists Takahashi Hajime and Yamada Akira contended that, rather than defending Japanese interests, the missiles defended US Misawa AB, and could provoke rather than deter attacks. In a normalised pattern, the plaintiffs won their case, overturned on appeal, and after many years of rancour the government's position was confirmed.[440]

As part of recruitment drives the ASDF emphasised how well their personnel were paid and treated.[441] Despite such PR efforts an ASDF fighter squadron technician complained of the lack of civilian employment opportunities to utilise skills developed in military service, and fear for a post-ASDF future.[442] One of the most promising promotion opportunities was provided by the 'frontline operational' role of the ASDF, the Air Rescue Wing (*kōkūkyūnandan*), which from 1961 established an enviable reputation for dedication in mountain rescue, accident assistance, and disaster relief operations, even featuring in TV drama and cinema.[443] Women were first recruited to the ASDF from April 1974, three officers commissioned from civilian applicants and three GSDF transfer officers in charge of fifteen enlisted administrative personnel, but from 1986 non-flying specialisations were opened, and from 1994 flying training.[444] The ASDF lacks the 'rough' image of the GSDF or the distant MSDF image, and Sabine Frühstück has noted how the blue sky images have found appeal among Japanese women.[445] The numbers of women increased, as did the areas of specialisation, and by 1998, only fifteen of 1,552 female personnel were medical specialists, in contrast with early recruitment.[446] Women increased by 166 per cent, to 2,578, officers by 268 per cent, and NCOs rising 283 per cent 1998–2015, the Force offering stable, fairly well-paid, pensioned careers in contrast to many female career options in Japan.[447]

The ASDF was concerned at the prospect of losing pilots to civilian aviation, with each taking three years, four months and ¥40,870,000 to train (in 1961) for even a relatively simple jet fighter. The JDA in coordination with the MOF and Ministry of Transport allegedly established an effective public-private cartel restricting the free movement of JSDF pilots from public to private sectors. They utilised the 'stick' of threatening to withdraw licenses while offering a 'carrot' of overlooking established 'private cartel' practices.[448] This protected JSDF interests, allowed a planned retirement and post-JSDF career path for senior pilots, thereby providing a planned stream of senior pilots for civil aviation, with remaining JSDF reservists available during contingencies. Present air crew generally deny knowledge that such a public corporatist system remains, but assert that there are unspecified pressures brought to bear to retain valuable personnel. While the ASDF had minor recruiting problems, often 8 per cent below strength mid-Cold War, retaining highly trained individuals on two-three year terms of service proved challenging, despite positive depictions of Force culture.

Conclusion

As a new service established in a period almost devoid of aviation activity, the ASDF developed surprisingly well into a large and capable air force. It was reliant upon both US and imperial-veteran influences for development, as well as massive public investment, particularly in *kokusanka* projects, and despite several major accidents raising concerns regarding safety culture, it has retained a comparatively positive image. During the Cold War the abiding public images were of rescue missions, Blue Impulse displays, and conventional air defence scrambles. In several ways the ASDF developed along a similar pathway to the MSDF despite the great differences in imperial legacies and force continuation, and the ASDF appeared to prepare plans with more regard for the MSDF than either gave to the GSDF. The obvious AEW gap is puzzling for both Forces, as was the concentration upon only one element of combat forces and relative neglect of logistical support, but the relative lack of combat capabilities is most striking. This is excusable in the MSDF for its concentration upon ASW and MCM. Air defence, however, was the reason Yoshida agreed to establish the ASDF, it was the image that it had created and nurtured, and in the one instance when this was tested, it was found to be pitifully ill-prepared, despite massive investment. The 1976 shock was keenly felt, and this can be seen to have changed investment patterns and elements of culture more than any other event or policy. Owing to Japan's unprecedented long peace, there was no equivalent shock to illustrate the limitations of ASDF CAS capabilities to counter (presumed) Soviet invasion threats, its lack of resilient preparation for wartime contingencies, or the effects of its limited investment in air transport capabilities until the 1990s. The ASDF also failed to develop active reserve forces, which, given personnel issues, appears self-defeating. Air like Ground and Maritime Forces developed extensive capabilities to meet Cold War commitments only at its conclusion, but in time to find application in emerging post-Cold War confrontations with China and North Korea.

Chapter Conclusion

In this chapter the JSDF have been examined during their establishment and Cold War development. Their inception involved unique, rushed, and complex processes for each Force that failed to address attendant constitutional, political, and social controversies. The Forces attempted to address legality and legitimacy issues within their limited realms, which successive governments avoided partly for fear of being defeated by a supposedly pacifist Japanese public, encapsulating Ashida's critique of Yoshida, as shown in Chapter One. This avoidance approach that feared public sentiment was accompanied by JSDF/JDA publicity efforts, which utilised the JSDF for supporting sports and entertainment to curry public opinion.This ranged from the Olympics and *ekiden* road race events through to regular appearances in cinema and television dramas, most notably as the (often defeated) defenders of Japan against Godzilla and associated monsters. One of the more remarkable publicity events was a Defence Expo (*daibōeihaku*) featuring JSDF equipment, from 15 March to 31 May 1966, in a popular theme park, Yokohama Dreamworld. Missiles, tanks, and aircraft were exhibited, with skydiving, tank driving, and special forces displays, helicopter 'joy rides' thrilling and impressing, all presented as a modernist combination of defence and science.[449] How could ten weeks of JSDF events within a major tourist attraction near Tokyo not have provoked scandal or riots, only six years after the Security Treaty demonstrations, if attitudes to the JSDF were as one-dimensionally pacifist as some accounts suggest? Opinions on the Forces gradually shifted over time, and public appreciation grew during the Cold War, partly due to increasing appreciation of security threats, particularly after the 1976 shock, with Backfire bombers, Afghanistan invasion, and Korean Airline shoot-down, but mainly due to Force human security efforts. The JSDF became legitimate disaster rescue and relief responders, and this beyond all else led to increasing public support and publicity, with the GSDF naturally to the fore—even though, in spite of its best efforts, it remained sullied by imperial association.

The exceptional features of the Forces' establishment environment and constitutional status, and the unequal nature of defence responsibilities under the 1960 Security Treaty, have often detracted from rational analysis of JSDF development, capabilities, and characteristics. The more notable features have been the frequently vexing challenges of quantitative and qualitative improvements and the mediation and balancing challenges they provided for budget priorities, the significant technical challenges of new equipment, and the dearth of joint approaches to planning and fundamental defensive preparations. Limited interest within the MSDF and ASDF to support the GSDF homeland defence role was notable, as was GSDF responsibility for creating a hard-heavy force with a seemingly one-dimensional and unlikely combat mission, but the ASDF-MSDF AEW cooperation failure was 'stovepipe' sectionalism at its worst with major defence implications. The meta-failure was of civilian control of Japanese defence.

Neither Prime Minister's Office nor Defense Agency attempted to force a jointly focused approach, let alone cogent strategy upon the Forces, with the result that the services essentially planned three different Cold War scenarios with only the slightest reference between them, in an example of what Aoi Chiyuki refers to as the separateness of civilian control.[450] Each scenario was conducted with fine intentions and with naturally divided responsibilities, but in modern combat operations the lack of coordination would have held the potential for national disaster. The JDA felt able to force through the recruitment of women and the 1976 NDPO, both unpopular with the Forces, but not many of the fundamental elements of existential defence. This reflected not only the subordinate position of the Agency, but also a basic responsibility gap in defence, security, and strategic planning. Officials were clearly dominant within JDA power structures, but no single office, ministry or agency was responsible for strategy other than the limited PMO, nor seemingly willing to assume responsibility unless as budget competition or turf war. The Diet was largely peripheral to consideration of national defence, other than the sea lane security, budgetary issues, and scandals noted, and lacked standing committees on defence and security issues until after the Cold War. Discussions by default were often being conducted within closed LDP policy committees, largely divorced from JSDF advice.[451] While the *bōeizoku* pressed defence interests within the Diet and particularly within the LDP, these were far from cogent. Some were pet projects of one service or industry, and the interplay of *kokusanka* interests and defence ultimately proved to splinter the *bōeizoku*. Those pressing for defence resources clashed with those advocating expensive *kokusanka* projects, for pork-barrel politicking, or long-term industrial goals.

The failure of JSDF civilian control was not of reversion to an imperial-military identity, but of civilian failure to provide sufficient direction of purpose and strategy to the Forces, leaving them with little option but to invent their own. These were lightly managed by officials and politicians and diverged during the Cold War, only re-converging by its conclusion, raising the unanswerable questions of who was actually controlling Japan's defence during the Cold War, and for what purpose. There was no Yoshida scheming to impose a plan or vision, Kishi, Tanaka, Suzuki, and Nakasone paling by comparison with the old master's ability to set a course that bitter opponents would actually tolerate and sustain. Even the nature of Cold War threat perception lacked consensus, for each Force relied upon subtly different perceptions to justify its own chosen approaches and investment patterns, differing threat portrayals utilised by the JDA, PMO, MOF, and the Forces to increase or limit defence budgets. As always, the MSDF was the outlier, formulating plans that were not only largely removed from Air and Ground Forces but also from stated Japanese government policy. The Navy provided, somewhat clandestinely, an alternative approach to strategy and defence, a collective security approach, tightly bound with Washington, far in advance of Guidelines revisions and Japanese law up until 2016, when the rest of Japan appeared to eventually catch up to the naval-strategic reality.

The development of the Forces, how they adapted to diverse security challenges and the changing Japanese society of the post-Cold War is the subject of the next chapter, but it is clear that during the Cold War capabilities grew dramatically, albeit in unbalanced ways and diverse directions that cannot be readily explained by IR theory or examination of defence white papers. The 1990s were marked by both institutional continuity and changing threat perceptions for Japan's defenders. The GSDF continued to value the hard-heavy approach concentrated in the north long after northern threats had evaporated, the ASDF similarly aspired to air defence above all else but tentatively invested in air-lift, and the MSDF continued its qualitative and quantitative USN lock-step expansion, the only Force highly valued in US Cold War strategy. However, by the mid-1990s the ASDF and MSDF had reluctantly realised that they were required to support the GSDF in varied overseas operations and that by extension all three Forces would by necessity become more diversely international actors. This newly acquired identity provided the Self-Defense Forces with enhanced status and legitimacy, as had domestic disaster relief duties, and eventually meeting emerging regional security challenges would enhance their legitimacy as national defenders. In the new millennium, national defence capabilities so expensively prepared during the Cold War would become valued for securing Japan against emerging threats. The nature of post-Cold War security challenges is the subject of Chapter Three.

3

TRANSITION TO POST-COLD WAR CHALLENGES

The end of the Cold War only gradually emerged in East Asia, lacking the iconic symbolism of Europe. Soviet-Russian power and presence faded but 1989 marked deepening tensions, as Tiananmen Square suggested that rapprochement and convergence with China had stalled, although the 'rising China' issue only gained prominence a decade later, together with the unconventional challenges of North Korea. For Japan, the end of the Cold War brought few immediate changes in defence and security policies, despite improving regional relations.[1] The US alliance remained central, qualitative defence improvements and budget increases sustained Cold War patterns, and the economy appeared ready to achieve 'Japan as Number One' status. As Kenneth Pyle paraphrased multiple contemporary observers, 'The Cold War is over [...] and Japan has won.'[2] The bursting of Japan's economic bubble and decade of unprecedented recession damaged Japanese power and prestige, but also critically damaged national confidence, Brad Glosserman characterising an unhappy and anxious country equivocating over whether to accept 'little Japan' decline, 'great Japan' rebirth, or ruin.[3] Post-Cold War Japan transitioned to a new millennium, and hubris was displaced by a realisation that Japan faced combined future-shocks of a rapidly ageing and decreasing population in concert with unexpected local and global security challenges.

This chapter examines the transition to these post-Cold War challenges, socio-economic influences upon Japanese defence, the post-Cold War regional security issues that provided opportunities and ever increasing challenges, primarily of Russia, China, and North Korea, and broader questioning of security identity that facilitated the tangible transformation from Cold War 'national' to post-Cold War 'international' Japanese defence and security approaches. Force developments provide insight into Japan's transition from the Cold War to the twenty-first century, and from potential to actual operations overseas. The Self-Defense Forces and coastguards emerge as perhaps unexpectedly central to security policy, and with enhanced legitimacy and respect. The first challenge considered is that of socio-economic factors and their impact upon Japanese defence.

1 The Socio-Economics of Japanese Defence

The post-Cold War brought few changes in defence budget trajectory. The 'bubble-period' increases continued as the economy flagged and deflated. By 1995, National Defense Policy Outline realities indicated less expansive budgeting, first pausing (1998), peaking (2002), and gently declining (until 2014). This was not a peace dividend, as reducing threats saw budgets rising, but an acknowledgement of bleak economic prospects. In 1955, the defence budget (¥134.9 billion) constituted 13.6 per cent of government expenditure (general account), slightly above education and significantly higher than social security, but had barely risen since 1950 (¥131 billion).[4] By 1965, defence had declined to 8.2 per cent (¥301.4 billion), 6.2 per cent by 1975 (¥1.3273 trillion), while social security rose to 18.5 per cent by 1975.[5] From 2008, the defence budget comprised less than 6 per cent of government expenditure, with 4.99 per cent in 2014, but regularly was one of the global top five.[6] A 'defence budget bubble' saw a rise of 9.6 per cent in 1965, and of 21.4 per cent in 1975, amid the 'dash for growth.' Under the 1980s Nakasone administrations the 1 per cent GNP defence budget limit (nominal, the true figure being approximately 1.2 per cent or more, see below) was slightly exceeded (1.004–1.013 per cent, 1986–8), but budgets grew annually by approximately 7 per cent, declining after 1996 (¥4.9414 trillion).

Japanese Stated Defence Expenditure

Year	Defence Budget (¥-billion)	Percentage of Public Spending	Percentage of GDP/GNP
1952	104.12	11.9	2.78
1955	134.9	13.6	1.78
1965	301.4	8.2	1.07

1975	1,327.3	6.2	0.84
1985	3,137.1	5.98	0.997
1995	4,723.6	6.65	0.949-GDP/
			0.959 GNP thereafter
2002	4,939.5	6.08	0.995
2008	4,742.6	5.71	0.900
2014	4,783.8	4.99	0.956
2016	4,860.7	5.03	0.937
2017	4,8996	5.03	0.885

Economic under-performance resulted in insecure finances, with the OECD's greatest gross public debt, 215.9 per cent of GDP (2016), and economic growth of 1per cent (2010–2015), alarming in the context of an ageing and declining population, with pensions equalling 412 per cent of education budgets. The 'Three Arrows' of 'Abe-nomics' attempted to stimulate consumption, but to little effect, with limited start-up enterprises and low levels of unemployment indicating a lack of spare capacity to stimulate.[7] As Patrick Imam of the IMF stated, 'monetary policy also has a weakened effect on the economy due to changing demographics,' with a pattern developing of mild demand upturns followed by declines.[8] Japan's economy is beyond the scope of this book, but economics and demographics greatly impact Japan's armed forces.

Japan Population[9]

	Recorded Population		Future Estimate
1946	75,750,000	2030	116,618,000
1955	90,077,000 (inc. Okinawa)	2040	107,276,000
1967	100,196,000	2050	97,076,000
2002	127,486,000	2060	86,737,000
2008	128,084,000	2100	49,591,000
2014	127,083,000		
2019	126,131,000		

Declining Japanese birth rates have been understood since the number of under-fifteens first declined in 1978, reducing over 30 per cent by 1997, when over-sixty-fives outnumbered under-fifteens.[10] Government predictions of population development are alarming, and effects upon the Forces were clear by 1993 when the GSDF retained only 146,114 of its 180,000 establishment personnel (81.2 per cent).[11] By March 2017, the GSDF figure exceeded 90 per cent (138,126 of 150,856) with the MSDF and ASDF sustaining similar levels, but all Forces faced demographic 'hollowing' problems as recruits and other ranks (ORs) drastically reduced.[12] *Tōyō Keizai* magazine revealed a profound JSDF age shift, personnel in their forties and fifties increasing as younger ORs hollowed out. In 1991, the largest single age group was of twenty-year-olds, while by 2014 this was thirty-nine-year olds, the average age increasing from an already high thirty-two point two to thirty-six. Although 93.5 per cent of warrant officer and officer positions were occupied, 25 per cent of OR positions remained unfilled.[13] By March 2017, 'missing privates' had reached 30.5 per cent, the JCP reporting desperate Force recruiters soliciting high school students.[14] Recruitment and retention efforts of corporations and public bodies will also likely impact upon Forces facing increased defence and support duties.[15]

The second challenge to Japan's post-Cold War expectation of peace posed the most immediate problems, and while being essentially short-term, it redefined how Japanese imagined their security identity. The invasion of Kuwait by Iraq in 1990 should not have had such definitive effects, but an unlikely chain of events and decisions resulted fifteen years later in armed Japanese troops being mortared in southern Iraq. The journey began with Japanese politicians, citizens, and Force members being asked to 'think the unthinkable.' In the face of significant opposition, Japanese sailors were despatched for overseas operations for the first time since the Korean War, ironically once more for minesweeping. Bizarrely, the Gulf crisis led the Japanese government to engage in United Nations peacekeeping operations (UN-PKO), the invasion of Kuwait resulting in GSDF troops building bridges in Cambodia. This journey overseas may appear the least relevant of the three post-Cold War security challenges to the defence of Japan, but it readjusted JSDF roles within Japanese foreign and security policy, redefined Japan as an international actor, and transformed public and Force concepts of operational duties. Despite initial and vitriolic opposition prior to the Forces' first overseas operations, personnel were generally welcomed home as exemplar representatives of Japanese international peace cooperation, cast as liberal internationalists, with Japanese security no longer considered in purely national nor alliance terms.

This second section examines the journey and background to Japan's struggles with overseas missions. Operational details are explained in detail, for the first JSDF overseas despatch operations (ODO) established new norms and practices for subsequent operations.

2 Overseas Despatch: A Journey with Few Maps

Kent Calder drew attention to the apparently abnormal nature of Japanese defence-related decision making processes. There was seemingly little public imperative to maintain benchmark levels of capabilities given constant political and social forces prioritising of non-defence issues, with little pro-defence lobby in politics or society. Calder identified JSDF development as having usually been driven by external rather than internal factors. Even by the early 1990s, when Japan's defence budget had become the world's third largest, the enduring image was of a civilian, pacific state.[16] If Japan had crossed the Rubicon and become a significant military power, it had done so heavily disguised. It was apparent that the Rubicon of JSDF ODO had been driven by external pressure (*gaiatsu*), and that this was intended to be noticed. It was not altogether clear, though, what exactly the JSDF were being despatched for, or indeed why. ODO rationales were influenced by attitudes towards Article 9, essentially drawing a line between JSDF acceptors and rejecters. The latter, rejecting Force legitimacy, opposed overseas despatch, the former accepted Force legitimacy, but with subtle differences regarding what the JSDF constituted and what overseas roles they might play. Sugawa Kiyoshi presented three rationales concerning Japanese attitudes towards the JSDF. He assessed each concerning JSDF UN peace operations:

> Alliance Supremacists: 'Japan will be willing to participate in UN peacekeeping and peace enforcement operations when the U.S. is ready to get involved. When the UN is paralyzed [...] Japan under this rationale would act almost unconditionally with the U.S.'

> UN Believers: 'Based on a faith in the UN system as a legitimate conflict resolution mechanism and a strong aspiration to make a contribution to the UN [...] push Japan to dramatically expand its support for UN operations, both peacekeeping and peace enforcement.'

> New Realists: support UN-PKO 'that demand the overt use of force to the extent that such operations would address critical Japanese national interests'. Some would claim that, 'Japan should have the option to participate in multilateral military operations even without UN authorization, as long as a Japanese vital interest is at stake.'[17]

While the overt Japanese government position in 1991 was both 'UN Believer' and 'Alliance Supremacist,' by the early years of the twenty-first century 'New Realism' had also been integrated, whilst projecting the façade of 'liberal international actor.' In considering JSDF overseas despatch, little can be accepted at face value, for almost everything has a symbolic cultural and/ or political aspect, and central to this is the iconic 'peace constitution.' Article 9 provided the basis for normative restrictions upon policy and approaches not explicitly stated in the constitution, such as self-denial of the right of collective security and overseas despatch.[18] The Japanese people by 1991 had largely accepted, if not warmly embraced, the JSDF, with limited appetite for abolition, but there was no great swell of public support for overseas missions.[19] As Katahara Eiichi stated, from the 1980s, Japan experienced 'the emergence of a greater public consensus on the fundamentals of Japan's security policy—namely its maintenance of the SDF and the Japan-US security arrangements' despite widespread respect for Article 9.[20] Attitudes to the constitution and revision were very different from those in the twenty-first century. In 1993, Foreign Minister Watanabe Michio was forced to withdraw comments on constitutional revision, and DG-JDA Nakanishi Keisuke was forced to resign and retract comments that 'it is wrong to cling with religious zeal to a document written half a century ago.'[21] By 2006, Abe Shinzo had become Prime Minister with an avowedly revisionist manifesto. JSDF ODO were a taboo that once scarcely dared be mentioned but which rapidly became normalised, operationalised, and eventually lauded as evidence of Japan's liberal-international credentials.

While there are many who regard constitutional revision as vital to JSDF ODO, including a leading newspaper, many scholars consider the issue peripheral.[22] Aoi Chiyuki has stated that the Five Conditions of UN-PKO participation and Rules of Engagement (ROE) for JSDF ODO were too restrictive for fully effective peacekeeping, but that these could be reformed, 'within the framework of the present constitution.'[23] National Institute for Defense Studies (NIDS) researchers voiced concerns that constitutional revision controversies were unhelpful, as they threatened politicising security policy and stunting legislative and doctrinal innovations. The 2004 Araki Report similarly emphasised concentration upon policy reform within extant constitutional interpretations.[24] There appeared to be more concern that legal, rather than constitutional, issues required urgent attention, and the sudden and unexpected challenges of the Gulf crisis resulted in legal reform coming to the fore.[25]

Gulf Crisis

The normative legacy of Article 9 profoundly shaped the mediation processes that enabled JSDF ODO. This mediation was often tortuous, and primarily driven by external factors, to clearly demonstrate Japanese burden sharing and the end of Cold War 'bandwaggoning' or 'free-riding,' limiting Japanese exposure to risk. The painful emergence of Japanese ODO was prompted by the Gulf War, when, as US Ambassador Armacost commented, 'Japan's conduct distressed its friends and angered its critics;, leading to it being labelled 'The Scrooge of Asia.'[26] Former diplomat Togo Kazuhiko characterised the events as 'Japan's defeat in 1991,' since its closest allies and oil providers derided slow and seemingly grudging offers of financial aid and insistence that it could not despatch troops.[27] The critique by US Secretary of State James Baker that Japan's '"checkbook diplomacy," like our "dollar diplomacy" of an earlier era, is clearly too narrow,' concerning Japan's $13 billion coalition contribution, was keenly felt.[28] The impetus to assuage US critics and preserve the alliance led to efforts to pass a peacekeeping-enabling bill that allowed for Gulf despatch but avoided JSDF participation. This eventually collapsed with the Kaifu administration, Japan 'falling short' of other nations' contributions of non-combat personnel, such as Korea's military medical team.[29] The result was a financial contribution and post-conflict MSDF Persian Gulf minesweeping despatch, and eventually UN-PKO dispatches to ameliorate criticism. Japan's second major utilisation of JSDF ODO for alliance reinforcement came in the wake of the 9/11 terror attacks in 2001, when MSDF vessels were despatched on patrol and refuelling missions, with the GSDF ultimately deployed to Iraq.[30] Despite domestic opposition, Prime Minister Koizumi's priority was to demonstrate allegiance to the US, with China and North Korea looming larger than Iraq.[31] The mediation required in 1991 between the conflicting influences of domestic opinion, international criticism, and long-standing norms and interpretations of Japanese law and the constitution, however, was such that there was initially little confidence in success.

Japan's Peacekeeping Pre-history

Japan was not simply dragged from detached pacifism and presented with a demand for military deployments. UN Membership from 1956, the year of the first 'classic' UN-PKO (UNEF, Egypt), brought Japanese mission participation into focus, with UN Secretary-General Dag Hammarskjold requesting despatch of ten JSDF observers to the UN Observation Group in Lebanon (UNOGIL), 1958, which Japan had helped establish. DG-JDA Satō Gisen, an unorthodox Buddhist priest defence chief, suggested personnel despatched for 'training purposes' under the SDF Law (as with MSDF training cruises), but Foreign Minister Fujiyama stated that new legislation was required.[32] A despatch-supporting Diet member countered that, 'to refuse the SDF despatch to UNOGIL [...] was to tarnish Japan's authority as a member of the UN and the Security Council. [...] To join UNOGIL is not for warfare but for peace and for preventive measures.'[33] The Kishi government advocated UNOGIL as a new international security norm, asserting its liberal, neutral credentials, while also enabling US Lebanon withdrawal as a loyal ally.[34]

The government feared domestic opposition, ODO controversies potentially imperilling ratification of the 1960 US-Japan Security Treaty.[35] The controversy deflated Japan's UN status and ambitions, complicated by Ambassador to the UN Matsudaira's 1961 statement that refusal to send observers had compromised his position and Japan's 'UN-centric foreign policy.' CLB Director-General Hayashi Shūzō stated that JSDF ODO 'would not pose problems relating to the First Clause of Article 9' if unarmed, unmilitary-like, or if all UN members contributed to enforcement operations, which 'would not be an act of a sovereign nation' but of international society.[36] From this point, Japan distinguished between 'military elements' involving potential use of force (Peacekeeping Force, PKF) to be avoided, and 'other elements' unlikely to involve force (PKO). The obvious problem of differentiating between 'force' and 'operation' remained unaddressed, but *haken*, (neutral) despatch was preferred to *hahei*, despatch of troops (for war).[37]

MOFA drafted a 1966 'United Nations Cooperation Bill' for JSDF UN-PKO despatch, but the prevailing socio-political atmosphere made implementation impractical.[38] Prime Minister Satō Eisaku referred to potential South-East Asian UN-PKO in 1969, as MOFA aspired to UNSC reform and a permanent Security Council seat.[39] MOFA eventually provided thirty-one civilian electoral observers, and even proposed sending JSDF officers, 'temporarily' on the reserve list, as unarmed observers.[40] Reinhard Drifte has indicated how the 1960s marked the point from which Japan's 'UN-centric' foreign policy sharply declined, displaced by prioritising the US alliance and the increasing diplomatic value of ODA.[41] As UN-PKO settled into a 'classical' pattern, with only three new missions 1970–1988, it was considered possible that UN legitimacy and Japan's 'pacifist norms' would converge and permit a limited reinterpretation of the constitution sufficient for JSDF missions. From 1981, Japan proposed improved UN fact-finding capabilities to enhance preventive diplomacy.[42] Dore and Watanabe note Prime Minister Takeshita promoting Japan's preventive diplomacy initiatives in 1988 within this progression towards peace operations.[43] Seemingly, the MOFA UN

Bureau Director decided in 1989 that Japanese staff should be sent to every civilian UN electoral mission, but there were few suitable opportunities.[44] Constitutional reinterpretation for ODO awaited a political imperative, which arrived in 1990.

Murakami Tomoaki has posed the pertinent question, 'how and why did Japanese governments change policy so rapidly, and why when faced with difficult choices did they choose UNPKO?'[45] How did the invasion of Kuwait lead the JSDF to Cambodia? UNSC membership and ameliorating US criticism were critically important for MOFA, and while the JDA/JSDF considered international engagement for status enhancement, was aware of the risks. There was no logical progression from Kuwait to Cambodia, but many suspected that previous mercantilist approaches had run their course. JSDF ODO provided a utilitarian mediation device between domestic and foreign pressures, 'in part intended to help Japan's bid to get a permanent seat on the United Nations Security Council,' a view believed shared by UN Secretaries-General.[46] UK Foreign Secretary Douglas Hurd told Prime Minister Miyazawa Kiichi in 1993 that 'Any permanent member of the Security Council needs to take a full part in UN Peacekeeping Activities.'[47] UN-PKO was one tangible means of demonstrating Japanese international assertiveness and burden sharing, while mediating between conflicting external pressures and domestic norms and legal restrictions, with Richard Samuels identifying the crucial Cabinet Legislation Bureau (CLB) role in mediating constitutional re-interpretation.[48] Japanese UNSC aspirations were naive given China's veto, but also vague as to membership benefits. Naivety and vagueness were defining qualities in planning ODO legislation, which consisted of short-term reactions with few longer-term plans, and little evident strategy.

Japanese government personnel were despatched overseas through four instruments: Official Development Assistance (ODA) legislation, ministerial establishment laws, disaster relief legislation, and International Peace Cooperation (IPC) legislation. Only the latter allows despatch of JSDF units. Establishment laws (such as the SDF Law) provided for defence attachés (*bōeichūzaikanseido*), overseas training, and MOFA UN election monitors from 1989.[49] Government reluctance to consider revision for overseas operations is indicative of the legal-constitutional and political problems envisaged: were the Forces appropriate national actors, should they utilise force, and how might lethal force be legally accommodated?[50] A 1954 House of Councillors resolution stated that JSDF overseas despatch 'should not be put into practice', but premier Miyazawa considered that this 'does not entail any constitutional problem' as only non-belligerent missions were proposed.[51]

Legal Revisions

The Iraqi invasion of Kuwait led to pressure upon Japan to despatch JSDF units, as a political imperative demonstrating 'New World Order' cooperation. A Bill on Cooperation with United Nations Peacekeeping Operations was submitted to the Diet on 16 October 1990, allowing a 2,000 strong Peacekeeping Contingent of ('resting') JSDF) 'civilian volunteers.'[52] Administrative Vice-Minister Kuriyama Shōichi insisted only civilian personnel be selected, while Treaty Bureau head Yanai Shunji insisted that only JSDF could participate, a conflict of opinion that illustrated MOFA divisions.[53] Yamaguchi Jirō contends that LDP 'fixer' Ozawa Ichirō's attempts to force the bill through the Diet, to wake up the 'peace-fogged Japanese people,' made matters worse, with the bill being withdrawn due to broad opposition, rather than intrinsic impracticalities, and Prime Minister Kaifu Toshiki being replaced by Miyazawa.[54] Eventual passage of the Act on Cooperation for United Nations Peacekeeping Operations and Other Operations (*Kokusairengō heiwaijikatsudōtō nitaisurukyoryoku ni kansuruhōritsu*), the International Peace Cooperation Law (IPCL *Kokusaiheiwakyōryokuhō*), was (slightly) less controversial, JSDF despatch being balanced with international-liberalist affirmations.[55] The IPCL eventually passed on 15 June 1992 despite 'ox-walk' delaying tactics in 190 hours of Diet deliberation.[56] Public opinion polls indicated a small majority in favour, but most preferred aid for refugees rather than military forces, with youth particularly opposed to military despatch. Murakami Yasusuke conjectured that 'the Japanese became a nation of hypocrites' in supporting neutrality while benefiting from US free trade and security, with the Yoshida Doctrine 'sapping the intellectual integrity of Japanese pacifism.'[57] LDP election gains in July 1992 were not necessarily indicative of IPCL support, but 'piggybacking' with the June 1992 Disaster Relief Reform Bill and ODA Charter provided a comfortingly liberal context.[58] Retroactive Diet approval requirements placated opponents, as did Disaster Relief Law revision allowing JSDF participation. According to Yanai Shunji, the JDA and JSDF were passive observers, awaiting orders and lacking any role in the most significant Japanese security reform for decades, executors rather than shapers of policy.[59]

The IPCL re-instated the JSDF as national representatives, assigned to the International Peace Cooperation Corps (IPCC) administered by the

International Peace Cooperation Headquarters (IPCH), within the Prime Minister's Office (from January 2001, Cabinet Office (*naikakufu*)) with IPCC insignia, together with despatched police and officials.⁶⁰ The Forces operated within tight limitations, some specifically stated in the IPCL, others ephemerally associated with socio-political norms and the SDF Law, under which miscellaneous duties included sporting and cultural event support, in addition to ODO, until 2007.⁶¹ As the Araki Report stated, 'international peace cooperation has been regarded as an incidental duty of the SDF, but given the growing importance of such cooperative efforts, they should be redefined as one of its primary missions.'⁶² With MOD establishment in 2007, ODO was mainstreamed as a JSDF 'primary role,' although national defence remained a 'primary mission' with ODO, contingency missions, and civil-support roles collectively termed 'secondary missions,' within the 'primary role.'⁶³ Prime Minister Abe stated: 'While adhering to the principles of the Constitution, Japanese will no longer shy away from carrying out overseas activities involving the SDF, if it is for the sake of international peace and stability.'⁶⁴ However, the 2008 defence white paper stated that MOD status 'does not assign new missions to the SDF nor does it alter the nature [...] of SDF activities.'⁶⁵ Not for the first time, major defence reform resulted in new patterns resembling the old.

The IPCL was an example of umbrella legislation, an enabling instrument and not a 'general law,' Diet approval being required for each despatch and mission-renewal.⁶⁶ The government strongly differentiated between the *hontaigyōmu*, 'main body' PKF, and the *kohochiikishien*, 'rear-area support' for Peace Support Operations (PSO). The IPCL, therefore, provided specific tasks that could be conducted, drafted with little reference to JSDF professionals. The 'Five Conditions for PKO Participation' (*PKO sankagogensoku*) were:⁶⁷

1. Ceasefire (peace process with ceasefire).
2. Consent (host nation and parties' agreement).
3. Impartiality (neutral mission-stance).
4. Self-Defence (minimal force).
5. Suspension and termination (if conditions breached).

Six 'frozen activities' precluded JSDF participation in 'core peacekeeping tasks':

(a) Disarmament;
(b) Collection, storage, or disposal of weapons;
(c) Stationing/patrolling in buffer zones;

(d) Inspection/monitoring weapon imports/exports;
(e) Designation of ceasefire/conflict boundaries;
(f) Assisting prisoner-of-war exchange.[68]

These were considered risk-laden assignments 'for core units of PKF [...] separately prescribed in law,' until 'unfrozen' in 2001.[69] It was clear that the JSDF were to be prevented from conducting any duties not explicitly listed in law, as an overseas extension of 'civilian control.' The frozen duties were not unique. German and Italian troops are prohibited from public order duties, while British troops can use firearms to defend lives, not property.[70] However, the JSDF were restricted by the extremely detailed IPCL stating which tasks they could undertake, certain tasks being solely civilian, others 'frozen'. Hirano Ryuichi refers to the '*Pojiristo*' and '*Negaristo*': the 'positive' and 'negative list' activities limiting ODO.[71] Not only were certain duties frozen or forbidden, but JSDF were supposedly confined to activities listed in the IPCL, thereby greatly limiting operational flexibility, contingency planning, and field command. The IPCL stated that '"International Peace Cooperation Assignments" shall mean the following tasks', and listed (a)–(f) the six 'frozen' duties (above), (g)–(i) civilian election and police monitoring/mentoring, and (j)–(p) JSDF ODO duties, (q) being 'any other' duties. JSDF designated duties were:

(j) Medical/sanitation measures;
(k) Search/rescue for affected people, assistance for repatriation;
(l) Distribution of food, clothing, medical supplies etc. for affected people;
(m) Installation of facilities for affected people;
(n) Repair/maintenance of conflict damaged facilities for affected people;
(o) Pollution reduction measures;
(p) Additional transport, storage, communication, construction/repair duties in addition to (a) to (o) items.[72]

The contentious issuing and use of weapons by the JSDF was strictly limited, by IPCH order ('borrowed' from the JSDF, which managed them).[73] Article 24 allowed weapons to be issued by command decision, but use to be controlled by each JSDF member, rather than superiors, and not be used for UN mission defence. IPCC members '[...] may use such small arms and light weapons within the limits judged reasonably necessary according to the circumstances, when reasonable grounds are found for the unavoidable necessity to protect the lives or bodies of themselves, [or] other Corps Personnel who are with them on the scene,' conforming to minimal self-defence force under

(1907) Penal Code Articles 36–37.[74] The rules were not only strict, but contradicted the basic premise of armed forces: officers and NCOs providing leadership and orders. JSDF officers insisted that they had no Rules of Engagement (ROE), merely (confidential) guidelines, but interviews reveal that beyond legal restriction was the fear of violating implicit rules, and the stigma of being the first Japanese to use force, either sustaining or inflicting casualties.

Following IPCL passage and SDF Law revision there was a legislative hiatus. IPCL revision was due in 1995, but delayed until 1998, allowing commanders to authorise use of force, thereby relieving contingents 'of their psychological burden which was felt under the previous provisions.'[75] Common sense also permitted cooperation for election monitoring activities, allowing the Law to catch up with operational practice in Cambodia. More radically JSDF humanitarian missions were permitted without requiring ceasefire confirmation.[76] Discussions concerning 'unfreezing' duties revealed much official and political opposition, despite Prime Minister Obuchi Keizō acknowledging constitutional compliance, the main opposition party preferring broader security policy reviews.[77] The 'unfreezing' eventually arrived in November 2001, with opposition support, indicating shifting security related norms and JSDF image through the decade.[78] The 'Law on Working Conditions of Defense Agency Officials Despatched to International Organizations' was also revised, and a GSDF officer was despatched to the UN Department of Peacekeeping Operations (UNDPKO) Military Planning Section.[79]

Shinoda Tomohito has stated that 'a legal framework has been slowly but surely established and strengthened since the 1990s, with the 1992 International Peace Cooperation Law, the 1999 Regional Crisis Law, the 2001 anti-terrorism law, the 2003 emergency law, and the 2003 Iraq law.'[80] There is no Cambodia-Iraq ODO connection, but controversies and perceptions of success surrounding the former mission facilitated passage of later controversial despatch laws. Iraq despatch would have been barely imaginable without successful operations throughout the 1990s. Although Bhubhindar Singh's suggestion that early UN-PKO led directly to expanding the JSDF operational area in support of US forces overstates the case, despatch tolerance was raised by perceptions of success presented within a liberal-international context.[81] In an October 2004 Cabinet Office poll, 51.9 per cent considered 'contribution to international peace' as the most important consideration for Japan's foreign policy.[82] Legal reforms affecting JSDF ODO appeared to match evolving Japanese public opinion and 'pacifist' norms, until the events of 2015.

Overseas Operations

The JSDF has undertaken five ODO variants, HA/DR Operations often combined:

1. UN Peace Operations, commonly referred to as Peacekeeping Operations (UN-PKO *heiwaijikatsudō*) although actually Peace Support Operations (PSO *heiwashienkatsudō*).
2/3. Humanitarian Assistance/Disaster Relief Operations (HA/DR *jindōshien/ kinkyūenjo katsudō*).
4. Allied-Support Operations (ASO).
5. Counter-Terrorism Operations (CTO), generally within ASO.

The JSDF prepared for the evacuation of Japanese nationals from conflict areas, but the Gulf War illustrated the difficulties, with former Ambassador Katakura Kunio commenting on the obstacles to evacuating from Kuwait.[83] A Special Cabinet Order of 29 January 1991 allowed ASDF aircraft use for evacuations, which was later annulled, and a precedent for ODO without legislation.[84] The ASDF trained with MOFA in March 1995 to prepare for an emergency evacuation from South-East Asia during civil disturbances, and Prime Minister Hashimoto dispatched three ASDF C-130H aircraft to Thailand on 12 July 1997 (Clause 8, Article 100, SDF Law) anticipating evacuation from Cambodia.[85] The attempt was farcically unsuccessful since the aircraft departed after the unrest had subsided, and Cambodia refused the ASDF entry.[86]

Minesweeping Again

Japan's first overseas operational despatch of the JSDF involved the same capabilities as the first post-war despatch of para-military forces during the Korean War, similar to planning under the Nakasone administration.[87] MSDF minesweeping and support vessels were sent to the Persian Gulf in April 1991 as the minimum tangible contribution that Japan could make under US pressure. Its effectiveness was largely overlooked despite media coverage, some scholars insisting that the 1992 Cambodia despatch was the first JSDF ODO.[88] The MSDF Maritime Staff Office had prepared contingency plans 1987–8, and as the US had largely delegated Cold War minesweeping duties to the MSDF and NATO allies, the post-Gulf War effort would be a coalition effort, including Germany's first extra-NATO-area operation.[89] The MSDF were able to contribute niche capability and extensive overseas experience. Despatch was authorised (24 April, JSDF Law, Article 99) for the safety of Japanese shipping in international waters, enabled by a subtle yet important shift in legal interpretation.[90] Based upon solid MSO planning, the force sailed within two days on their thirty-two day, 13,000km voyage, consisting of four *Hatsushima-class* minesweepers, minesweeping support-ship *Hayase*, and replenishment vessel (AOE) *Tokiwa*, transiting via the Philippines, Singapore, Malaysia, Sri Lanka, and Pakistan, and arriving in Dubai on 27 May, suggesting an absence of urgency.[91] The MSDF role also included provision of services and goods to allied ships, an understated yet important precedent, repeated in the Indian Ocean. The MSDF group began its first box-pattern search routine on 5 June 1991, discovering its first mine 19 June.[92] Thereafter the pace quickened, with sixteen mines disposed of on 1 July, and thirty-four cleared in total, which Glenn Hook has suggested 'was of greater symbolic importance than the task performed', given that approximately 1,200 mines had been laid.[93] The mission completed without loss, injury, or damage, the vessels returned via the same route, arriving in Kure on 30 October 1991 to a welcoming fanfare. Mission success was measured primarily in the impression made upon the US and other partners, and in absence of casualties and controversies, rather than naval capabilities. Defence diplomacy activities undertaken during port calls, and professional and social events amongst the minesweeping groups were also useful, including visiting an Iranian naval base, where the MSDF crews were warmly received.[94]

As effective for the immediate political crisis as the MSDF mission had proven, it was apparent that Japan faced pressure to play more substantial roles, so as to demonstrate international 'burden sharing.' An unlikely path had been mapped from the Persian Gulf to Cambodia, as well as a range of operations of which the JSDF were technically capable but which they were largely ill-prepared to undertake.

Japanese Peacekeeping: Cambodia

Japanese participation in the United Nations Transitional Authority for Cambodia (UNTAC) was noteworthy both as the first JSDF UN-PKO deployment and as it was incorporated into a long-term comprehensive involvement in settling the Cambodian problem, the Japanese government's first comprehensive peace-making effort.[95] This appeared a nascent strategic approach, with diplomatic, financial, civil, and military elements coordinated towards a common goal.⁹⁶ UNTAC was widely regarded as a great JSDF success, but initial expectations included alarmist language concerning rampaging Japanese soldiery, echoed overseas, with Singaporean Prime Minister Lee Kuan Yew comparing JSDF overseas deployments to handing chocolate liquors to a former alcoholic.⁹⁷ The abiding and enduring images, however, were of diligent personnel attempting to improve local conditions, the murders of a Japanese UN Volunteer (UNV) and a police inspector emphasizing the precarious nature of the mission, all of which made the absence of JSDF casualties all the more noteworthy. UNTAC is crucial for understanding the perception of Japanese ODO as peaceful, liberal, and constructive, providing a JSDF operational template. The JDA and MOFA assumed this template represented 'UN-PKO success,' without defining or measuring effectiveness, efficiency, quality, or 'success.'

The Paris Peace Accords (Comprehensive Political Settlement of the Cambodia Conflict) of 23 October 1991 led to the Supreme National Council of Cambodia (SNC) delegating to the UN 'all powers necessary' to implement the Accords.⁹⁸ The Japanese head of mission Special Representative of the Secretary-General (SRSG) Akashi Yasushi and UNTAC military commander Lt-General John Sanderson were both conscious that this was not an enforcement operation and that use of force and local resistance could become significant issues.⁹⁹ Their fears were compounded by delays in receiving infantry, engineering, and police contingents, as 'the critical problem confronted by UNTAC [...] was how to discharge its responsibility for filling a political vacuum in the face of obstructive violence by contending Cambodian parties.'¹⁰⁰ Sanderson believed that military contingents 'were sent to Cambodia at a rate too slow to seize advantage of the dynamics and goodwill prevailing at the signing in Paris, [which] in itself reflects a profound lack of understanding of the nature of these undertakings.'¹⁰¹ Japanese contingents were among those despatched without significant haste.

UNTAC was unique in its authority. The SRSG directly supervised agencies/ministries, established a legal system, and was able to strike down laws.¹⁰² While UNTAC's civilian effort focused upon elections, de-militarisation involved combatants withdrawing to cantonment areas, with weapons under UNTAC military supervision.¹⁰³ UNTAC proceeded with escalating tension as the Khmer Rouge promoted its spoiling campaign, but the election was held in May 1993 with almost 90 per cent participation, the United National Front (FUNCINPEC) of Prince Sihanouk winning over 45 per cent of votes. Despite problems, the broad-ranging, innovative, and challenging mission, with inexperienced personnel, was regarded as a UN landmark.[104]

The 16,000 strong military force was mainly tasked with verification of Vietnamese withdrawal, cantonment and disarmament, weapon disposal, mine clearing, and education.[105] The force was designed around twelve composite infantry battalions, and with enhanced logistical components each should have comprised highly capable units reinforcing 485 unarmed UN military observers (UNMOs). Unfortunately, the infantry, apart from French and Dutch units, were generally inadequate, some even lacking cooking equipment.[106] Additionally, the engineering units of Thailand, China, and Japan deployed months late. With such limited competences available, and poor local infrastructure, JSDF engineering capability was greatly valued, but highly dependent upon mediation of political and legal despatch mechanisms in the absence of consensus. The involvement of Akashi Yasushi, and Ogata Sadako as UNHCR, aided mediation, as two such prominent Japanese serving in UN-PKO without JSDF personnel could have been as damaging as the Gulf War debacle. Fujiwara Kiichi is adamant that, although security deteriorated, the 'civil war was brought under control [...] by multilateral consent [...] not military intervention,' and because of its role in this process 'other countries positively welcomed Japan's participation.'[107] Trevor Findlay noted that if the UNTAC mandate had been transformed 'to one of enforcement, the Japanese would have been obliged, constitutionally, to withdraw, and would perhaps have been followed by the Australians.'[108] Akashi compared UN-PKO to a shop window: 'an easy task to physically break [...] but quite difficult politically and psychologically.'[109]

JSDF preparations were complicated by the absence of despatch laws. A civilian 'Cambodia survey team' deployed on 1 July 1992, while on 27 July a handful of JSDF officers were despatched to the Swedish Armed Forces UN School for UN Military Observer training.[110] In August 1992, the DG-JDA, Miyashita Sohei, ordered a second survey team including JSDF and police representatives to assess needs and infrastructure.[111] The JSDF despatch was confirmed as legal, and established by Cabinet Order 165 under the IPCL, from 11 September 1992 until 31 October 1993.[112] The JSDF deployed a 600-strong GSDF engineering battalion (*Shisetsukabutai*), under Lt.-Colonel Watanabe Takashi, and eight independent UNMO. Addtionally, seventy-five Japanese civilian police (CIVPOL) under NPA Superintendent Yamazaki Hiroto were deployed separately from the JSDF, although like the troops Japanese police in UNTAC were also IPCC members.[113] Additionally, 400

133

MSDF and 120 ASDF personnel, nationally rather than UN funded, provided logistical support within the IPCC and 2,000 personnel IPCL limit.[114] The commanding officer was assigned by Lieutenant-General Uno Shōji GOC (General-Officer-Commanding) Middle Army (*Chūbuhōmentai*), under the army-rotation system, a composite force being raised from volunteers, of varying degrees of enthusiasm.[115] The first contingent had less than three months between passage of the IPCL and despatch, mostly spent assembling personnel, equipment, and information, with only rudimentary language training. One officer supporting the GSDF dispatch relates how a MOFA briefing provided information on Cambodian factions, UNTAC, and Cambodian society and culture, but in terms of risk only mentioned heat, disease, and land mines, with conflict issues dismissed as irrelevant.[116]

JSDF strategic logistical limitations were evident, as six ASDF C-130H, without aerial-refuelling, staged through Okinawa, the Philippines, and Thailand, the GSDF contingent commander and staff arriving 25 September 1992. Most heavy equipment was transported by two MSDF LST (*Miura*, *Ojika*), small, shallow draft (therefore rolling severely), and extremely uncomfortable for the equipment specialists and journalists aboard, accompanied by a replenishment vessel (AOE *Towada*).[117] They departed Kure on 17 September 1992, arriving in Cambodia 2 October, the majority of personnel following by charter flight on 13 October.[118] The slowness of despatch was criticized by Akashi and others, the Japanese being among the last UNTAC arrivals.[119]

The JSDF Camp Takeo, south-west of Phnom Penh, initially tented before being replaced by prefabricated buildings, and including an impressive bathhouse, was established within the French infantry battalion area, one of the safest in Cambodia, the result of extensive lobbying including of SRSG Akashi by Prime Minister Miyazawa.[120] As Akashi later asked, 'what good would it have done to have the JSDF operating in a less safe area? They would have been able to achieve less.'[121] DG-JDA Miyashita 'said he would prefer to avoid areas where land-mine disposal is the primary job, adding that ideally the troops will be where they can go about their duties in calm and quiet.'[122] Japan's request was not unique—French infantry successfully lobbied for transfer to Takeo and Kompong Som with 'palm-fringed white sand beaches nearby' rather than northern jungles.[123] The strong impression that 'Japanese military personnel were assigned to relatively safe areas with more luxurious quarters than other UN troops' belied the first contingent experience of austere, tented accommodation, basic plumbing, and few amenities.[124] When the engineering battalion arrived, Camp Takeo was still incomplete, with temperatures above 40 C, and the *Nikkei Shimbun* reporting that newly arriving troops would be welcomed by land mines, heatstroke, and homelessness.[125] JSDF UNMOs experienced rough and hazardous conditions, while transport units were temporarily despatched to basic Branch Billeting Areas (*hakenchi*) in Kampot (with a French infantry company) and later Sihanoukville; there was a ban on travelling at night, as all efforts were being made to avoid combat or (frequent) traffic accidents.[126] The Japanese government took such an exception to negative reporting in *The New York Times* that Suzuki Katsunari, Executive Secretary of the IPCH, responded in an open letter to ask, 'What is the rationale for criticizing a country's efforts to provide comfort to its personnel as they carry out their mission?'[127]

The MSDF and ASDF transported and supported the GSDF in UNTAC. The MSDF provided fresh water, food, and other stores, their vessels playing an unexpectedly important medical support role, as well as serving as a miniature Japanese recreation centre.[128] The ASDF provided weekly airlifts into Pochentong airbase, via Thailand and the Philippines.[129] The GSDF engineering battalion was tasked with repairing and maintaining roads and bridges, particularly those connecting the capital and main port, Sihanoukville, and won praise for their professionalism, despite the limitation of having to return to base before dusk. The first contingent 'despatch establishment battalion' (*hakenshisetsudaitai*) prepared Camp Takeo, and established working practices and security arrangements.[130] Despite being risk averse, JSDF attention to security appears limited. Even though there was widespread belief to the contrary, each member of the engineering battalion was allocated a rifle or pistol, but no support weapons, which were held in a storage container behind barbed wire.[131] Weapons were only distributed in the event of contingencies or as part of the regular camp guard—one infantry squad (twelve) supplemented by other troops, with extreme limitations on use of force.[132] Fear of being considered in violation of the IPCL was stronger than the desire to maximise security, and there were no slit trenches to protect personnel in case of attack, or fire trenches to defend the camp, and no sandbagging or 'hardening.'[133] In a publication distributed to JSDF families in 1992, the JDA stated that 'there is no possibility of the SDF being drawn into an armed confrontation.'[134] Security planning appeared to be equally faith-based.

The engineering battalion possessed heavy moving and lifting equipment, and an impressive array of prefabricated bridging equipment, which saved time and enabled independent operations. General Sanderson remarked upon GSDF technical capabilities and wrote that the 'success of UNTAC is attributed as much to the retention of the peacekeeping ethos as to any other factor.'[135] There was a minor controversy over three GSDF liaison officers at UNTAC headquarters, providing a link between UNTAC-HQ and GSDF engineers, innocuously coordinating work programmes. Ill-informed controversy in Tokyo speculated that staff duties might involve PKF planning, the government denying any participation in military planning or 'other sensitive activities.'[136] This indicated the lack of understanding of multilateral operations and as well as the prevalent restrictive atmosphere.

Initially, GSDF engineering work was focused on repairing Takeo's terrible roads, which had contributed to UNTAC's burgeoning accident record.[137] The GSDF repaired 175km of main roads, disposed of fifty unexploded ordnance (UXO) items, and built forty bridges.[138] As Japanese capabilities were realized, the GSDF additionally purified water, delivered food and water, and conducted sanitation work, sanctioned by Cabinet in December 1992, and even constructed a freight container yard at Sihanoukville.[139] This extension of duties was large-scale and complex. Water purification was a niche capability based upon disaster relief experience, and, as a natural extension, basic medical care became a significant and unexpected mission duty. Initially tasked with contingent health care, the small medical unit performed admirably in difficult conditions after the February 1993 cabinet decision allowing treatment of locals and UN personnel.[140] The seventeen clinical personnel dealt with up to 600 patients daily rather than the planned twenty-four, treating approximately 7,000 in total, with almost 10 per cent suffering from malaria, whereas no contingent personnel were affected due to preventative medicine.[141]

Fujii Tatsuya of the JSDF Central Hospital noted how JSDF clinics were unprepared and lacked training to deal with large numbers of local people suffering from multiple minor ailments with no obvious physical cause, eventually diagnosed as Post-Traumatic Stress Disorder (PTSD).[142] The GSDF clinic was able to perform only basic services and minor operations, concentrating mainly on prevention. Serious cases were transferred to hospital or air-lifted to Thailand, in cooperation with a Swiss Red Cross group and the Indo-German Field Hospital. The JSDF pooled know-how on tropical maladies with other contingents, formalizing short training courses, recognizing their initially poor understanding of PTSD and tropical diseases, and limited nursing staff due to being a sanitation unit. After UNTAC, the JDA utilised the University of Tokyo Tropical Diseases course to broaden the skills base of JSDF medical staff.[143] The GSDF also established a dental clinic in a tent under a palm tree, replaced by an air-conditioned prefabricated building from December 1992, with only four personnel, cooperating with MSDF colleagues aboard *JS-Tokiwa*, although, surprisingly, most patients were Japanese.[144] The greatest single performance degrading factor involved living in tents in a tropical climate. This resulted in significant investment in prefabricated air-conditioned buildings from December 1992—a virtue was made of the cost when the facilities were donated to Takeo City, to much local acclaim.

A more significant change accompanied the Cambodian election campaign. UNTAC's mandate included demobilization, disarming, and reintegration (DDR) in cantonment areas, but KR rejection resulted in violence, including attacks on contingents, and thirty Uruguayan troops kidnapped in December 1992.[145] This led UNTAC command to utilise 'spare' DDR-tasked infantry for security patrols after the KR declared an election boycott, and to request all engineering units to commence electoral security patrols in their areas.[146] The Japanese were the only unit to decline, as the phrase 'patrol' (*keibi*) denoted PKF duties, excluded by the IPCL. This provoked an UNTAC-HQ officer to comment that it was based on a meaningless differentiation of an 'O' and an 'F' when GSDF-paved roads were used by UNTAC infantry.[147] The situation further deteriorated when a twenty-five-year-old Japanese District Electoral Supervisor, Nakata Atsuhito, was murdered with his local interpreter by a disgruntled job applicant on 8 April 1993, the day after the second GSDF UNTAC contingent had been despatched.[148] This led to speculation that the IPCL five conditions had been breached and that the contingent might be withdrawn, despite denials from UNHCR Ogata.[149] Australia expressed concern, and when Indonesian soldiers were attacked, 'even members of the rubber-stamp Indonesian parliament called for the recall of the Indonesian battalion.'[150] Such sensitivities were not uniquely Japanese, despite UN criticisms.[151]

The Japanese government resolved to continue the mission, with Cabinet Secretary Kōno Yōhei and Foreign Minister Mutō Kabun declaring that the five conditions remained intact.[152] The cabinet after considering UNTAC requests eventually broadened GSDF contingent duties, ordering GSDF troops to engage in 'information gathering,' while delivering ballot boxes to polling stations. Ambassador Imagawa states that UNTAC personnel pushed hard for this expansion, SRSG Akashi decisively concurring (fearing Japanese withdrawal), but the extent of cabinet consensus is unclear.[153] Expanded duties were coordinated between IPCH Director Yanai Shunji and JDA Administrative Vice-minister Hatakeyama Shigeru. Initially, armed GSDF infantry in Type-82 armoured vehicles visited voting stations, ostensibly to deliver supplies, but actually to reassure staff, with support for other contingents allowed if required.[154]

Such further expanded duties were not for GSDF force protection, but to protect and reassure electoral staff by 'information gathering,' de facto security patrols placing Japanese troops at greater risk. Second contingent members were regularly provided with weapons, helmets, and protective vests, in a significant concession to PKO practice and common sense, utilising the Type-82's imposing 'APC-like' presence to good 'security effect.'[155] *Tokyo Shimbun* journalist Kiroku Hanai, serving as an election monitor, stated that although 'French troops were to protect our polling station, they did not protect us. We felt relieved when the SDF visited the station on the pretext of collecting information. It may be inappropriate for Japanese to be protected by troops of other countries while the SDF troops are at hand.'[156] Maeda Tetsuo contends that GSDF members 'abandoned road repair work and put on helmets and bulletproof vests and began carrying small arms.'[157] He was also critical of expanded duties including 'information gathering,' which he refers to as 'camouflage' for patrolling, in which he is quite correct.[158] Colonel Ishioroshi, the second contingent commander, directly refuted Maeda's claims by placing JSDF PSO duties within the overall mission of supporting the election process, initially by engineering work, and later by other official duties.[159] Both Maeda and Ishioroshi are right: patrols were conducted, beyond IPCL duties, and they contributed to the peace process. The former considers this to have been irresponsible and the latter considers this to have been efficacious and legitimate.

One GSDF Captain in UNTAC explained that Japanese troops were wary of provoking an armed response, both as they were unsure of Japan's responses to such an incident, and to their personal abilities in combat.[160] The latter point is often overlooked. The Japanese had no operational experience, were mainly engineers and technical specialists, with limited local knowledge, and were faced by experienced, committed, and heavily armed forces. A GSDF officer engaged in planning UNTAC stated after the operation how he 'had difficulty explaining why the Japanese troops could not engage in guard duty although our troops were regarded the same as others. As for the use of arms, SDF soldiers felt psychologically burdened when told to use their weapons at their own discretion, since [...] [this] is usually controlled by superior officers.'[161] The use of weapons was to be 'the absolute last resort.'[162] The contingent commander keenly felt the gap between UN-PKO practice and JSDF UNTAC practice:

> what is basic common sense for the militaries of nations taking part in PKOs is not recognized by Japan. The Japanese military units deployed in Cambodia initially confronted the disparity between the Rules of Engagement (ROE) for UNTAC, and the Japanese rules [...] Japanese PKO personnel were only able to defend themselves and other unit members in the same area of operation as themselves. Moreover, the use of weapons in legitimate defense [...] was left to the judgment of the individual, and appeared to be outside the standards of conduct for troops.[163]

The *Yomiuri Shimbun* reported that the GSDF had been requested by a Tunisian infantry unit to help construct their camp, but the Japanese had refused due to PKF-contribution concerns.[164] General Sanderson was adamant that defence of UNTAC's mandated objective was vital: 'Self-defense meant not only an individual's defense of himself alone; it also meant collective action.'[165] Japanese troops were clearly conflicted as a result of the contradictory demands of local and home commands. The murders of Nakata in April and Okayama Prefectural Police Inspector Takada Haruyuki in May 1993 provoked diverse reactions. Home Affairs Minister Murata Keijiro and others called for the withdrawal of all UNTAC members from dangerous areas, including the junior minister and future Prime Minister Koizumi Junichiro.[166] However, the government realised that complete JSDF mission withdrawal would be disastrous for Japan and UNTAC, and thus modified operational duties and security practices to continue the mission.[167] This flexibility and determination (as well as good fortune) entailed that UNTAC was the first of several JSDF ODO rather than a single failed attempt, as with Japanese police unit ODO.

The eight UNMO selected among JSDF officers with international experience and language skills were deployed along the borders of Cambodia and integrated with international colleagues.[168] One of the problems was that they were essentially left to fend for themselves in a country they hardly knew. Major-General Fukui related how he was placed in a team with four others of different nationalities in Phnom Penh, given a Toyota Land Cruiser, a radio, $130 daily allowance, and told to arrange his own accommodation. For a professional soldier accustomed to home and mess life it was a surprising challenge.[169] The newly established IPCH was responsible for the coordination of data collection, surveys, and all pre-despatch business, in addition to the UNMO, who were often requested to disburse grants.[170] This placed strain upon isolated officers, with one JSDF UNMO being regularly fired upon while investigating ceasefire violations.[171] Japanese UNTAC UNMO had at least attended the Swedish Peacekeeping Training Centre for sixteen days' training, unlike other JSDF colleagues.[172] While the situation in Cambodia cannot be compared to that in Rwanda, the roles of UNMOs in both countries often placed them in direct contact with armed groups.[173]

General Sanderson, despite praising the JSDF contribution, also commented on contingents preferring to provide 'passive' logistics units, to emphasize the humanitarian nature of their work, avoiding risk and thereby burdening other contingents.[174] 'In UNTAC's case this was true of at least the Japanese contingent, which gained a reputation for refusing to take any risks, withdrawing to their base well before sunset, for example, in order to avoid possible contact with the Khmer Rouge.'[175] Kenneth Pyle reports that UN officials were dismayed by the special circumstances of the JSDF, and even Akashi referred to them as 'maidens.'[176] Marrack Goulding describes visiting the GSDF engineering contingent and finding them 'overwhelmed by their responsibility for ensuring that it was a success.'[177] Political and media expectations were perhaps unreasonable, and one of the prime causes of cumulative and traumatic stress disorders is a gap between expectations and experiences, compounded by third party expectations. The JSDF were poorly prepared for stress illnesses, and had not been well served by pre-despatch briefings. The GSDF appeared to have few personnel with foreign language skills, complicating the ability to contribute to the mission, with limited experience of overseas standards, languages, customs, and mission expectations. Watanabe has described how they 'had absolutely no experience with this type of multinational framework, and I remember how we were able to learn a lot from the PKO that the military organizations in other countries knew as a matter of course.'[178]

It appears that JSDF actions elicited hope and confidence in local people, as these were the first large-scale infrastructure projects in the country for decades. The later expansion of roles by the JSDF, with delivery of goods and services to other UNTAC units and medical services, was effective, and the ability to purify vast amounts of water was a unique capability that would become a hallmark of JSDF ODO. Despite limited medical resources the JSDF provided a great deal of health care coverage, and won a great deal of praise and trust in the process. Robert McNamara stated in 1968, 'security is development, and without development there can be no security.'[179] Nathaniel Fick argued that a failure to interact humanely with local populations can have serious implications: 'When we retreat behind body armor and concrete barriers, it becomes impossible to understand the society we claim to defend.'[180] While 'information gathering' was not seemingly a grander scheme combining human and traditional security, the effect was nonetheless positive. How effective the overall Japanese mission was in improving the security within Takeo Province is impossible to assess, but despite such tasks not being overtly mandated the Force did effectively contribute to the security of its operational area.

Working efficiency was greatly hampered by the imposition of late-working bans, as well as poor English skills, a constant frustration for UNTAC veterans often forced to communicate with other contingents via Japanese NGO staff, a remarkable planning gaffe for a country with Japan's resources.[181] Until the request to deliver goods and services to other UNTAC contingents there was little cooperation with other national contingents, apart from the French, who provided additional camp security.[182] Infrastructure task forces could have been despatched to other areas and contingents, but this was not considered, and only in the provision of medical services did the JSDF truly cooperate internationally, seemingly for fear of exceeding legal restrictions.

In assessing the quality of JSDF UNTAC contributions, the engineering work was of undoubtedly high quality, as was provision of health care. While Japan transported 300 vehicles to Cambodia, it did not provide helicopters, despite UNTAC having at most twenty-four available in a hazardous country of limited infrastructure. Japan could have provided a quality airlift capability from its impressive fleet, but the JSDF has never operated helicopters within a UN-PKO, and has demonstrated an aversion to discussing the issue (see Chapter Four).[183] The cargo facility at Sihanoukville, of little direct benefit to the Japanese, demonstrated project management and engineering contribution to the mission, together with the UNMO contribution, despite operating in the most difficult circumstances of any JSDF personnel. The MSDF were able to provide a quality support service, while the ASDF was limited by aircraft range-payload despite the best efforts of crews.

Another aspect of the quality of the Japanese contribution can be assessed by looking at the least military aspects of its work and life in Cambodia. JSDF personnel like those of some other contingents made friends with locals, played sports with children, and generally attempted to make the lives of the local population better. This included a Takeo *Bon Odori* festival, which provides an insight into Japanese culture with the sort of activities that cannot be trained or ordered but develops organically. The Pakistani and Bangladeshi contingents likewise provided English classes and sporting events, the Pakistanis even establishing an English radio service.[184] The French forces, by contrast, were characterised as being cold and lacking engagement with locals, other than professionally or sexually.[185] French troops shot in the air to disperse Cambodians 'stealing' discarded French plastic water bottles around the shared camp perimeter, so the GSDF collected and washed the bottles for local people.[186] This was not the result of training or doctrine, but of socialisation and education, all people being accorded 'civilian respect' within a comprehensive 'human security' approach that was instinctive of personnel and units rather than instructed.

Some UNTAC contingents, the Bulgarians and Uruguayans in particular, were noted for poor treatment of locals, including extortion and sexual harassment.[187] The JSDF contingents were notable for avoiding SRSG Akashi's unfortunate explanation of 'hot-blooded soldiers' giving chase to 'young beautiful beings of the opposite sex.'[188] Judy Ledgerwood states that although '21 peacekeepers died in Cambodia as a result of hostile action, more than twice that number (47) were diagnosed as being HIV-positive [...] the true figure is probably as high as 150. The German field hospital treated more than 5,000 incidents of sexually transmitted diseases.'[189] While no published statistics exist, the JSDF seem to have avoided sexual diseases and sexual harassment, partly by force-culture and discipline, and partly by recreation breaks in Thailand. Among other contingents, performance and morale varied, with experienced peacekeepers, such as the Irish and Australians, withdrawing labour over bonus disparities.[190] Equivalent engineering battalions were provided by China and Thailand. The Chinese appear to have been targeted by KR forces, with two troops killed in May 1993, while it was alleged that the Thai battalion opened a (highly profitable) restaurant in Battambang.[191] Neither force offered the extensive capabilities of the GSDF.

The despatch of JSDF personnel to Cambodia was the most significant change in Japan's security policies and international role in four decades. The principle that the state was internationally represented by its armed forces was initially unsettling for many Japanese. UNTAC was conducted under a cloud of uncertainty, but also in an environment of increased expectation of Japanese contributions to international society. Every mission detail was judged by criteria that were determined more by imperial and political legacies than performance standards. The JSDF UNTAC deployment thus became an inverted mission, where what did not occur was often considered more important than operational achievements. Watanabe considers that 'it can be argued that the Cambodia PKO opened the door for Japan and the SDF to move from bilateral to multilateral relations.'[192] However, it is clear that significant capability gaps remained in hardware and software, which the US relationship had done little to address, and perhaps the over-arching bilateral relationship had stunted greater efforts at multilateral military cooperation.

Domestic media coverage was, for the JSDF, almost wholly positive by summer 1993. This was aided by unusual openness, rapidly altering JDA 'press club' rules, admitting critical media, and adroit management of over 300 Japanese media personnel.[193] However, official follow-up activities and research were poor. Less than one and a half pages space was devoted to JSDF UNTAC activities in the 1994 defence white paper, compared with five and a half pages for Persian Gulf minesweeping.[194] In the 1996 and 1998 White Papers 'UNTAC' was not mentioned, with little more published 1995–2000.[195] Even more telling was the JSDF attitude to despatch histories, compiled but little used with restricted circulation, never published, and with very few personnel debriefed or engaged to record, analyse, or utilise their experiences for Forces' 'lessons learned,' and without repository of ODO experience.[196] The effort expended to mediate the JSDF despatch, to commence operations, and expand duties under intense pressure, which was a significant feat, and the JSDF performed effectively, to high standards of quality, and with significant efficiency. Yet, the failure to follow through with operational analysis, to 'learn lessons,' meant that much that would have been of value was squandered and expertise dissipated, rather than being utilised in successive missions. This would be evident in the second UN-PKO despatch to Mozambique.

Peacekeeping-Light: Mozambique

The despatch of JSDF to the UN Operation in Mozambique (ONUMOZ) occurred just a month after the second contingent had joined UNTAC, concurrent ODO not being ideal, but the opportunity arose from a UNSG request and MOFA pressing to build upon UNTAC momentum.[197] ONUMOZ participation was initially rejected by Chief Cabinet Secretary and acting-Foreign Minister Kōno Yōhei. This led to surprisingly vociferous denunciations from LDP politicians and MOFA officials, who pilloried Kōno as 'a coward,' and his decision 'comical.'[198] The decision was reversed with the

26 March despatch of a survey team, and the cabinet confirmation of 27 April 1993.[199] The government favoured contributing a full contingent but was frustrated by IPCL personnel limitations that entailed either controversial reductions in UNTAC, or a smaller ONUMOZ unit, resulting in the first non-self-supporting JSDF ODO, mirrored in limited media coverage and research scholarship. The IPCL 2,000 personnel limit resulted in only fifty personnel per JSDF rotation, Mozambique fitting MOFA's aspirations and being seen as preferable to the hazards of Somalia or Bosnia. Japanese profile was low, contrasting with the largesse in UNTAC. Extra-contributions made upon UN request boosted the power of one radio transmitter, while Germany donated an entire radio station.[200] Compared with UNTAC, ONUMOZ was clearly the less-favoured sibling.

ONUMOZ, one-third the size and one-quarter the budget of UNTAC, was a longer mission, established by Security Council Resolution 797 (1992) on 16 December 1992.[201] The mandate centred upon ceasefire monitoring, DDR, human rights monitoring, refugee assistance, electoral support, and 'security arrangements for vital infrastructures,' related to JSDF activities.[202] In early 1993, 6,500 troops were deployed under SRSG Aldo Ajello, the main duties being humanitarian assistance to 3.7 million displaced people, and a DDR programme overseen by 354 UNMO. UNHCR aided the repatriation of 1.3 million refugees, and by mid-1994 some 75 per cent of internally displaced people had been resettled. The UN did not consider it dangerous, but of an estimated 1.5 million rifles the DDR programme recorded only 46,193 small arms surrendered.[203] Unlike in Cambodia, there were no specific 'spoiler' groups, and demobilization continued more successfully than disarmament despite National Mine Clearance Plan delays.[204] The elections in October 1994 gave FRELIMO victory in elections, with the government and president inaugurated in December 1994, when ONUMOZ's mandate ended.[205]

JSDF ONUMOZ problems derived from small, non-independent contingent status, local conditions, and rushed deployment that hampered learning lessons from UNTAC. Indeed, many deployed personnel were given ten vaccination injections in one month, and had little time to prepare for deployment. This was compounded by limited information. Briefings and pre-departure training comprised basic skills such as Movement Control Units (MCU), team-work development in working and social events to unite disparate volunteers, as well as language training. The contingent commander attended the JSDF Kodaira Foreign Language School on his own volition, studying English and Portuguese expressions in his free time. Most personnel had only two-three weeks of basic training, but local knowledge was complemented by briefings provided by trading companies with experience of Mozambique. One hundred volunteers were trained for ONUMOZ, with only the best forty-eight selected for the first 'semi-joint' contingent of GSDF and ASDF personnel. In addition to the MCU, the JSDF also deployed five staff officers to act in headquarters liaison roles in Maputo, the Central Region HQ in Beira, and the Southern Region HQ in Matola.[206]

Contingent transport was by commercial charter container vessel for heavy equipment, and chartered Antonov aircraft, while commander Major Nakano Shigenori and five HQ staff arrived by scheduled airlines on 13 May.[207] Additional personnel arrived on chartered airlines, with all unit members assembled by 17 May, who unloaded jumbled equipment they had not packed.[208] The ASDF flew ONUMOZ support missions, again hampered by C-130H limitations, the 7,200-km one-way flights requiring four to five days via five countries, with Nairobi used as a hub, as during the Rwanda/Zaire despatch, for two aircraft and fifty personnel (exceeding the ONMUOZ contingent total).[209] Thereafter, civilian scheduled flights were used to transport most supplies, with the ASDF reserved for sensitive equipment, VIPs, and New Year presents.[210] Contingent equipment included twenty vehicles, specialist loading equipment, and personal weapons, which as in UNTAC were only issued when the security situation deteriorated.[211] The UN vetoed the Japanese suggestion of staying in a Maputo hotel, and proposed billeting the JSDF with a Bangladesh logistics battalion. This was coolly received by the GSDF who preferred a 'western' host, resulting in their being billeted with, and dependent upon, the Portuguese Army for basic services and infrastructure.[212] The problems of tented accommodation obvious from UNTAC were not implemented, and water and electricity were rationed, but it seems from interviews that the first contingent had basic expectations, while the second contingent apparently expected to walk into a fully-functioning 'African Camp Takeo,' and were rudely shocked.

The main duty was Movement Control (MOVECON), the processing of passengers and freight, by two MCU, entailing small group duties, precluding credible self-defence capability while in transit.[213] The Beira/Dondo duty was rotated so that troops could regularly return to the main Japanese contingent area, which required a long journey through unsafe areas, the JSDF depending upon Italian or Portuguese escorts as bandit attacks increased during 1994.[214] This 'collective security' was considered highly sensitive, in light of accusations that JSDF UN-PKO were breaching legal-constitutional prohibitions, but became an established operational norm that benefited the mission.[215] Twenty-six ONUMOZ members died, and JSDF reliance upon other contingents for integrated security ensured that there were no Japanese casualties.[216]

The language and general communications situation in ONUMOZ was as poor as in Cambodia, but the contingent commander discovered that younger personnel more easily and more enthusiastically learned languages and communicated by non-verbal means, readily adapting to challenging environments. He therefore rotated younger members in the roles which required the greatest degree of external communications, and attempted to utilise the skills of more experienced older men in less exposed ways, frustrated by GSDF high average age entailing many middle-aged personnel of limited mission utility. JSDF staff officers provided liaison and communications between ONUMOZ-HQ, JSDF units, and the IPCH, resulting in them being sequentially under-utilised and overworked, as well as hampered by poor transport, with some feeling unable to be more pro-active due to limited Japanese presence.[217] The staff officers did relieve some of the strain of English communication from the MOVECON-HQ, particularly by providing précis of ONUMOZ documents, but they were always 'on-call' and required to draft reports for Tokyo.[218] One staff officer stating that the significance of these reports was that, were a breach of IPCL 'five conditions' included, then the contingent could be required to abandon their duties and mission partners, staff officers drafting contingency withdrawal plans.[219] Formation of a 'support team' within the PMO communicated effectively with the JDA complimented by MOFA in Tokyo and Maputo, and JSDF officers felt confidence in being able to request information and/or guidance.[220] This demonstrated civilian assets reinforcing military forces in a cooperative rather than controlling function, and both the Cambodia and Mozambique missions are replete with examples of JSDF personnel valuing the contributions of civilian officials.

The effectiveness of the MOVECON can be judged by the length of their despatch and the scale of their work, being the only developed-country contingent to remain in service until end of mission.[221] The JSDF contingent worked efficiently, but the commander acknowledged that many of their duties could have been competently undertaken by civilian personnel, and they did indeed cooperate closely with civilians.[222] The Forces illustrated their versatility in dealing with Soviet helicopters and steam trains, proving a surprisingly cheap, predictably high-quality capability with a light footprint.²²³ With limited ASDF and no MSDF support, the contingent provided a high quality service of light logistical strains, but was unable to expand its contributions.²²⁴

The limited learning from UNTAC marks ONUMOZ as an example of neglected operational analysis, with inadequate language skills, pre-despatch training, and resources. Yet the Mozambique case, with a niche capability and a light footprint, provided an alternative model for JSDF ODO for technical operations in close cooperation with other contingents and civilians, in a far more integrated manner than UNTAC, and for a longer duration. ONUMOZ provided an example that could be seen in later deployments to Golan and Honduras, acting as a compact 'capability multiplier,' highly dependent upon individual command competence rather than systemic Force planning. Although the mission was regarded by the government as resembling UNTAC, for the JSDF it was a completely new model, making quite different demands on personnel, and not altogether a comfortable experience. The JSDF did not appear to suffer from lack of operational quality in their work, but whether the 'light-footprint' approach was as effective as it was (relatively) cheap and efficient is unclear. As in UNTAC, while the JSDF could claim that their operation was a success, good fortune and the cooperation of allies played a significant part in avoiding casualties, being inevitably dependent upon controversial collective defence.

The conclusion of initial JSDF UN-PKO revealed the two predominant mission types, large-scale, heavy logistical support, and small-scale, light support, as well as the benefits of each. From 1995, both the JDA and MOFA would search for missions which each considered ideal. The UNTAC-model was considered optimum, but most potential UN missions were considered too dangerous or lacked sufficient international profile. The compromise was a small-scale mission, without any awareness that Japanese troops would spend almost seventeen years in the Golan Heights.

JSDF UN-PKO Missions 1992–2017:

UN Transitional Authority in Cambodia (UNTAC)	09/1992~09/93	c.610 troops (x2)
UN Operation in Mozambique (ONUMOZ)	05/1993~01/95	c.50 troops (x3)
UN Disengagement Force (UNDOF) Golan Heights	02/1996~01/2013	c.40 troops (x25)

UN Mission of Support for East Timor (UNMISET)	02/2002~05/04	c.650 troops (x3.5)
UN Mission in Nepal (UNMIN)	03/2007~01/11	6 observers (x4)
UN Mission in Sudan (UNMIS)	10/2008~09/11	2 staff officers (x3)
UN Mission in Timor L'Este (UNMIT)	09/2010~09/12	2 observers (x2)
UN Stabilisation Mission in Haiti (MINUSTAH)	02/2010~03/13	c.350 troops (x6)
UN Mission in South Sudan (UNMISS)	11/2011~05/17	c. 350 troops (x11)

HA/DR-Humanitarian Assistance: Zaire/Rwanda

The despatch of JSDF personnel to Zaire originated with the genocide in neighbouring Rwanda from April 1994, Hutu troops and militia murdering Tutsis and moderate Hutus, escalating into genocide that killed approximately 800,000.[225] This and defeat of Hutu forces by Tutsi rebels prompted approximately two million, including Hutu militia, to flee, creating the Great Lakes Refugee Crisis.[226] Japan provided financial support but also considered capitalising upon the achievements of UNTAC and ONUMOZ (still on-going), and set a precedent for IPCL Humanitarian Assistance duties. The mission was characterised by despatch difficulty, unilateral command (non-UN), and safety concerns. Compared with ONUMOZ, media coverage was extensive, the government emphasising the 'non-military' humanitarian nature of the mission.

The Japanese government had dramatically changed since UNTAC. The LDP had been replaced by a diverse coalition under Prime Minister Hosokawa Morihiro, then Hata Tsutomu, before being displaced by a 'grand coalition' of LDP, JSP, and New Party Sakigake under Socialist Prime Minister Murayama Tomiichi. While the government had rejected a mission in Macedonia, it approved the Goma, Zaire despatch, after being requested by UNHCR Ogata Sadako.[227] Goma was chosen due to the UNHCR request, as the choice of US, French, Dutch, and Israeli militaries, and due to uncertain conditions within Rwanda. Interviewees have commented on desired proximity to US units as USAF logistical assistance had been requested (but not provided), and French units in order to repeat UNTAC security 'cooperation.' The mission was despatched under Cabinet Order 295, following survey team reports in August 1994, outside UN command despite erroneous reports.[228] The GSDF Billeting Area was next to Goma airport, convenient for ASDF supply flights, close to a French Army unit, Goma General Hospital, and UNHCR headquarters.[229]

The 290 GSDF troops were supported by 180 ASDF personnel, with four C-130H aircraft, but heavy equipment, such as water purification systems, refrigeration, and a field hospital, with eighty vehicles, entailed commercial 'wet lease' Antonov airlift. This provoked ASDF concerns, as Cold War fears persisted and former Soviet Air Force crews landing at ASDF bases was disconcerting, while the GSDF commander was more concerned that USAF aircraft had been requested and refused.[230] Despite the survey team report that security in Goma was deteriorating, the Murayama government rejected fifty additional security personnel.[231] Also, despite GSDF requests to transport two-three machine guns, political debates were conducted over several days on television until one such weapon was allowed, plus personal side arms for non-medical personnel, and a Status of Forces Agreement (SOFA) reached with the Zairean government.[232]

The first ASDF aircraft departed on 16 September 1994, travelling to Goma via Thailand, the Maldives, Seychelles, and Nairobi, Kenya, where the ASDF and ten MOFA, JDA, and JICA staff established a coordinating office in close cooperation with British command, control, and communications (C3), coordinating all aid efforts amid limited aviation infrastructure.[233] The GSDF Refugee Relief Unit (RRU) advance party of twenty-three departed on 21 September, followed by the ASDF support team's three aircraft, the main RRU leaving from 30 September, with the final 'wave' not arriving until late October.[234] Forty-one RRU medical staff (clinical-surgical) with over 200 support staff, provided medical care, disease prevention, and approximately 70,000 tonnes of filtered water in a display of Japanese niche capabilities, with a notable security element.[235]

Refugee Relief Unit (RRU) Staff-Patients[236]

RRU Staff:	Clinical 23	Surgical 18	Hygiene 9	Prevention 16
Security 50	Water 43	Admin. 68	Medical-HQ 4	Mission-HQ 29
In-patients Treated 70	Out-patients Treated 2100	Combined Daily Average 30		

As during UNTAC, the conditions in tented accommodation were harsh, and staff sought specialist advice in Japan and conducted field research into cholera and malaria, as well as ways to mitigate HIV risks.[237] The ASDF flew almost 100 Nairobi-Goma shuttles, the first direct cooperation between the JSDF, UNHCR, and NGOs.[238] JDA personnel coordinated with British staff in Nairobi, from which relations blossomed, leading to a JDA Nairobi veteran being the first Japanese civilian attending the Royal College of Defence Studies (RCDS).[239] The RRU departed Zaire from 15 to 25 December 1994, and the commander Lt.-Colonel Kamimoto Mitsunobu stated that 'when faced with a million refugees [...] we inexperienced people did what we had to do for international cooperation,' indicating how overwhelming many aspects of the mission had been for troops.[240]

The contribution to refugee relief was undoubtedly successful. The medical and disease prevention work was of a high quality, and the provision of fresh water highly effective, but the number of cases treated was limited as the RRU undertook full surgery. Takahara Takao has stated that there was 'great scepticism about the relevance and effectiveness of sending the SDF to a refugee camp for just three months. There were also anxieties over whether SDF personnel might be put in a situation where the single machine gun which they brought with them had to be used.'[241] One GSDF participant and UNTAC veteran admitted that in Cambodia 'success' had been measured primarily by an absence of Japanese casualties, while in Goma the RRU determined success by saved lives. A GSDF translator found great differences in cooperating with UNHCR and NGOs and their different notions of security, something brought home to him by seeing Zairean soldiers with their legs blown off at Goma hospital.[242] The RRU had only one French speaker, so relied upon NGO staff to compensate for their deficiencies as in UNTAC.[243]

When the JDA refused a UNHCR request to search for a missing aid worker due to risk issues, the aid community was obviously unhappy, particularly the NGOs that assisted the GSDF—something the RRU commander acknowledged and attempted to ameliorate by discreetly lending assistance.[244] The commander was initially worried by physical dangers in the mission, but later became more concerned with longer-term PTSD, and that 100 NGO workers and journalists in close proximity could damage the contingent's reputation.[245] Media coverage was extensive, with journalists vying to present images of GSDF personnel, and particularly the single machine gun, the media mood changing with deaths of journalists in a plane crash.[246] The first JSDF Humanitarian Assistance mission was professionally conducted in a harsh natural and security environment. Goma in 1994 became one of the least secure places on earth, but the RRU was so lightly armed that it is questionable if they could have defended themselves, let alone protected others, in a situation that would surely have been compounded by legal limitations. Absence of combat could be considered proof of commensurate deployment, but it appears that once more Japanese ODO depended upon good fortune and collective self-defence.

HA/DR-Disaster Relief: Honduras

The JSDF disaster relief mission to Honduras was unusual as a 'mission of opportunity' to set a precedent demonstrating their third IPC mission capability. It was a distant, brief, small-footprint, unarmed mission, providing medical services usually associated with Japanese civilian units, without engineering capabilities. It stretched ASDF airlift capacity to the limits and demonstrated the need for much deeper logistical investment, and, until the 2010 mission to Haiti, Honduras was also the most rapid JSDF overseas deployment.

Hurricane Mitch devastated Central America from 27 October to 1 November 1998, killing at least 7,000 Hondurans.[247] Following an appeal from the Honduran government, MOFA consulted with the Cabinet Office and JDA, made a formal request to the DG-JDA on 9 November, and immediately despatched a JDA/MOFA survey team.[248] The JDA began assembling a unit under the provisions of the 1987 Law Concerning Dispatch of International Disaster Relief Teams (IDR Law), as amended in 1992, providing for JSDF/civilian despatch, personnel not being IPCC members nor IPCH-coordinated.[249] The survey team reported on 12 November and the next day DG-JDA Nukaga Fukushiro issued JSDF orders.[250] JDA enthusiasm provided 'a chance to dispense with its shame' for not having conducted an IDR mission, despite thirty-nine civilian JDRT having been despatched over the preceding decade.[251] Six ASDF C-130H departed Komaki AB, Nagoya, 13 November 1998, flying via US bases in Guam, Marshall Islands, Hawaii, California, and Texas, into Toncontin Airport near Tegucigalpa on 17 November, where the GSDF offloaded 20 tonnes of equipment.[252] The USAF provided ASDF refuelling and services for the slow, hard, uncomfortable ASDF unit only able to deliver a 20-tonne load, while GSDF personnel arrived in Tegucigalpa by a comfortable commercial flight on 15 November.[253]

The contrast was also stark within the mission. The ASDF element had 105 personnel, the GSDF only eighty, aided by twenty MOFA and JICA staff, indicating the air-lift burden.[254] The medical contingent conducted emergency medical assistance and disease prevention duties from 17 to 30 November, having rehearsed the role within GSDF Middle Army for over a year.[255] Their equipment was limited due to ASDF airlift, hence only one pick-up truck, but this 'logistics-light' force nonetheless treated huge numbers of patients.[256] The GSDF contingent comprised a medical treatment unit (*chiryōtai*), disease prevention unit (*bōeikitai*), and supporting elements.[257] The medical treatment team had one paediatric (*shōnika*), three internal medicine (*naika*), and two surgery (*gaika*) specialists, but as 70 per cent of patients were women and children the paediatrician was overwhelmed.[258] The GSDF augmented their capabilities by using 'tele-medicine' equipment (pioneering in 1998) to cooperate with the JSDF Central Hospital and the GSDF School of Field Medicine, so that approximately three hours were required between referral and diagnosis, video examinations aiding treatment.[259] The GSDF personnel were also able to rely upon MOFA and JICA staff for translation assistance, as well as local medical students.[260]

Honduras IDR Mission[261]

GSDF Personnel	Medical 23	Prevention 15	Support 42
In-patients 0	Out-patients 4031	Daily Average 288	–

For such a small force so lightly deployed for such a short time, the numbers of patients treated was impressive, and there was genuine local appreciation, despite the fleeting Japanese involvement.[262] The single vehicle was limiting, being pressed into service as an ambulance, and despite lacking equipment, JICA and MOFA staff travelled in requisitioned school buses.[263] The security situation was not as calm as MOFA briefings had portrayed, and the JSDF relied upon Honduran troops to assist them, despite being busy with their relief duties.[264]

Without heavy airlift, it is difficult to see what more significant contribution the JSDF could have made to the post-disaster recovery efforts, the ASDF making maximum efforts to support the mission. As a demonstration of a capability for rapid deployment in a disaster relief role the Honduras despatch appeared to have been successful. Lt.-General Yamaguchi Noboru GSDF Research Division commander believed the mission was wisely kept short, as the effectiveness of such small forces, operating at a high tempo, rapidly deteriorates, while the natural inclination of commanders is to stay longer and attempt more.[265] For the JSDF, the most significant lesson was to demonstrate a disaster relief mission capability, and comprehensive HA/DR expertise.

TRANSITION TO POST-COLD WAR CHALLENGES

JSDF HA/DR Overseas Operations

Zaire/Rwanda	09~12/1994	First HA operation
Honduras	11~12/1998	First DR operation
Turkey	09~11/1999	MSDF transport supplies
Timor-Leste/West Timor	11/1999~02/2000	Refugee relief
Afghanistan	10/2001	ASDF transport supplies
Iraq	03~08/2003	ASDF/MSDF transport supplies
Iran	12/2003~01/2004	ASDF transport supplies
Thailand	12/2004~01/2005	MSDF destroyer tsunami relief
Indonesia	01~03/2005	Tsunami relief. First GSDF helicopter ODO, and first JSDF joint liaison/coordination centre
Russia	08/2005	Submarine rescue mission
Pakistan	10~12/2005	ASDF/GSDF transport supplies
Indonesia	06/2006	Medical-sanitation support,
Indonesia	10/2009	Medical support
Haiti	01~02/2010	Earthquake medical relief
New Zealand	02~03/2011	Earthquake medical relief
Philippines	11~12/2013	Post-typhoon relief and recovery
Ghana	12/2014	ASDF transport supplies (Ebola)
Nepal	04~05/2015	Earthquake medical relief
New Zealand	11/2016	Earthquake relief

First Generation ODO in Perspective

Up to 1992, forty Japanese civilians participated in five UN missions, and up to 2020 approximately 11,000 JSDF personnel participated in nine UN-PKO, plus several thousand more in non-UN HA/DR operations, and far more in Allied Support and Counter-Terrorism Operations. In the twenty-first century Japan had seemingly moved beyond the limited scope of UN-PKO and HA/DR missions, with deployments in support of 'Operation Enduring Freedom-Maritime Interdiction Operation,' in Iraq, and within anti-piracy efforts in the Gulf of Aden. Despite the varied legal frameworks of these new missions, the operating norms and standards remain remarkably similar to those of the first generation of JSDF ODO. Legally, restrictions only gradually eased, and the Forces and government retained their disdain for robust missions, much as they retained their less martial emphasis upon civil-military cooperation and engagement.

The second wave of JSDF missions, in the Golan Heights, Turkey, and East and West Timor, were balanced between short-term, immediate response HA/DR deployments, and longer-term UN-PKO. The UN Mission of Support for East Timor (UNMISET) deployment from 2002 was the largest JSDF overseas mission, with over 650 personnel. It was also the first to deploy with female troops, prefabricated buildings (rather than tents), and Korean-language interpreters to facilitate communication with neighbouring ROK units, both an operational and defence diplomacy measure.[266] The JSDF trained locals to use engineering vehicles donated upon withdrawal, and in many ways, UNMISET, based upon UNTAC lessons, provided a model for the Iraq despatch.[267] It also faced unusual challenges. There were anti-Japanese demonstrations in Dili based upon war-legacy issues, and there were the first allegations of sexual harassment by JSDF personnel, resulting in strict curfews.[268] UNMISET, despite these negative aspects, developed into the culmination of JSDF ODO experience. It was the first UN-PKO mission launched since the 1998 IPCL reform and the unfreezing of 'six tasks' in 2001, there was significant recycling of personnel from previous ODO, and security was reinforced with a company-strength infantry presence. Based upon the development of the Japan Platform experience, Japanese NGO and JICA projects were actively supported, and there was a greater degree of cooperation with other contingents.[269] In East Timor, the JDA and JSDF appeared to have eventually learned lessons from a decade of overseas missions.

The MSDF HA mission to Turkey by contrast was simple, delivering supplies after the August 1999 earthquake killed at least 18,000 people.[270] The MSDF despatched three ships on 23 September, the LST *Ōsumi*, minesweeper support-ship *Bungo*, and AOE *Tokiwa*, arriving off Istanbul 19 October.[271] While the intentions were unquestionable, a chartered container vessel would have travelled as fast, more cheaply, and would have been more suited to the load carried.[272] As a defence diplomacy and training exercise it was doubtless effective, being the longest-range MSDF operation, replacing scheduled training exercises, but questions remain regarding efficient use of resources, no matter how ultimately effective.[273] For West Timor, the UNHCR made a formal request to Japan for refugee relief assistance in November 1999 following the independence referendum and INTERFET multi-national mission in East Timor. An ASDF preparatory group was despatched on 22 November, with the main force two days later, remaining until 21 February 2000.²⁷⁴ The 113 ASDF personnel with five aircraft transported relief supplies from Surabaya, Java, to Kupang, delivering 400 tonnes in a simple, low-risk, effective logistical support operation, well within ASDF capabilities.²⁷⁵

The third JSDF UN-PKO was the UN Disengagement Force (UNDOF) in the Golan Heights of Syria and Israel, one of the least known and most remarkable Japanese operations. It was unusual in not being a nation-building 'UNTAC-type' mission, but a classical 'blue helmet' security mission, providing a buffer between two countries that fought ferociously over the Heights in 1973, Japan's first ceasefire observation mission, and first JSDF Middle East presence.²⁷⁶ Additionally, UNDOF provided MOFA with a constant demonstration of UN burden sharing while the JSDF and JDA/MOD valued the small but high-value 'PKO School,' as 'UNDOF showed [...] how effective peacekeeping can be if certain conditions are met.'²⁷⁷ The Japanese contingent (J-CON) despatched from January 1996 was the first UN-PKO for the Murayama cabinet, apparently under LDP pressure.²⁷⁸ J-CON commenced duties from 1 February 1996, with forty-three personnel, and a plethora of equipment, including individual weapons and two machine guns, supported by ASDF flights to Damascus.²⁷⁹

UNDOF was unique as the only permanent mission that Japan joined, the longest at seventeen years, the most integrated with other contingents and the mission profile, and it became not only the training ground for peace operations, but also led to the first systematic pre-departure training programme. UNDOF was the mission that transformed JSDF ODO efforts from ad hoc improvisation into dedicated professional concern. J-CON constituted only approximately 4 per cent of UNDOF, or 2.89 per cent of UN-assessed personnel (twelve to fifteen troops being nationally funded), but through its snow clearing, engineering, and repairs it became a vital mission component.²⁸⁰ Major Sato Masahisa was the first J-CON commander with UNTAC planning and survey experience, later '*hige no Sato*' ('moustache-Sato') GSDF contingent commander in Iraq.²⁸¹ The main focus of preparation was on core transport and engineering tasks, including operating unfamiliar UN equipment, volunteers were plentiful, and motivation high.²⁸² J-CON was not required to transport arms, ammunition, or armed troops, but its 'swing capabilities' included snow removal, an unglamorous but vital task to maintain communications and operations, well rehearsed due to experience in Hokkaido.²⁸³

From the late 1990s pre-deployment training was systemized: specialist training (engineering/transport), team work-group ethos, and language and culture (English, Arabic, and regional studies).[284] For the first time, combat and contingency ROE were carefully explained and rehearsed, the assumption being that J-CON troops would withdraw to bunkers, defending their immediate area within the mission defence plan. Ministries were reluctant to discuss security concerns, but J-CON contributed to and yet relied upon other contingents for mission defence.[285]

While the UNDOF area has never been 'invaded,' in May 1997, two UNDOF Austrian soldiers were shot and killed while on patrol, and four others died 2005–2008, from various causes.[286] One Japanese staff member raised the issue of Israeli bombing of Syria in October 2003 over-flying the UNDOF Area, and former contingent commanders expressed concerns over the possibility of becoming terrorist targets.[287] The eventual withdrawal of J-CON in 2013 was apparently due to the escalating civil war in Syria and perceived threats to Japanese personnel. The loss to the mission was significant, as J-Con capabilities were so highly valued, but it seems the greater loss was to the JSDF, UNDOF being the Forces' only constant, low-cost, high-return operational experience. From 2003 it integrated MSDF and ASDF personnel, from 2004 female troops, and increasingly GSDF officers were those of diverse backgrounds and career pathways, with Major Tokunaga Katsuhiko J-CON commander from 2004 epitomizing the 'new UNDOF model' as an infantry Ranger officer, Command and General Staff Course graduate, who had completed the 'Humanitarian Challenge' and 'Human Rights' peacekeeping courses at the Pearson Peacekeeping Centre, Canada.[288] UNDOF epitomised the professionalization of JSDF ODO and for a minor expenditure provided a unique Force development opportunity.

Legacies of ODO

The first decade of JSDF overseas despatch operations provided the Forces with a real operational focus that they had previously lacked beyond domestic disaster rescue and relief duties. International operational experience raised challenges scarcely imagined and provided unrivalled opportunities for development and improvement, even in roles in which the Forces considered themselves highly competent, such as medical care, engineering, and transport. From the first minesweeping mission the MSDF were confident of their technical abilities, but rapidly appreciated that distant multi-national taskforce duty was rather more challenging than exercising with the USN in home waters. They were also exposed to new techniques, such as mine-hunting drones rather than manual diving, in the context of international 'best-practice;' as one UNTAC commander had noted, the JSDF had to learn what was normal practice for other nations.[289] UN-PKO 'best practice' allowed the Forces to contribute proficient water supply and civil-military relations methodologies as well as engineering and communications. This was also the case in cooperation between defence civilians, as seen in the UK-Japan efforts in Nairobi, and between NGO, officials, and the JSDF. The corpus of overseas operational experience made the JSDF more aware of its abilities and deficiencies and professionalised many areas of their work, reaching its apex in UNDOF, with concomitant benefits for later operations.

Despite this new operational stance there were problems accruing from perceived success. With no Force casualties or major failures, achieved through diligent middle-level military and civilian leadership that at times ignored legal limitations, there was little momentum to develop doctrine or operation-specific training until UNDOF. JSDF niche ODO could be a source of legitimate pride, but it scarcely developed beyond engineering and medical services. While the IPCL was passed, it hardly constituted a legislative panacea, and despite revisions it remained an awkward tool for troops and politicians, like the JSDF compromised at birth. Unlike the German government's 1994 Constitutional Court referral of overseas missions to clarify their legitimacy, Japanese governments consistently avoided any such clarification, partly fearing escalating controversy, and partly as addressing ODO constitutional legitimacy could proliferate to encompass the legitimacy of the JSDF and 'Yoshida doctrine' legalities.[290] Until 2015, little was done to address concerns of risk and use of force, the Forces expected to 'make do' with imperfect laws as they had with equipment, training, and experience deficiencies. Japan continued to be regarded as a 'risk averse' actor while extending ODO reach and range, a dilemma that would have implications for later operations and partnership building aspirations.

Only a minority of personnel experienced overseas missions, and among the GSDF 'majority,' armour, artillery, and aviation 'career elite' specialists were notably scarce. Established career pathways initially avoided distracting 'adventures' from career focus, and it would not be until 2005 before an ODO participant, Banshō Kōichirō, gained Major-General rank. The relevance of ODO for the ASDF and MSDF was generally less appreciated. Only logistical support elements were operationally engaged, hardly prime routes to senior command. The ASDF continued to struggle for ODO relevance, despite becoming the lead Force in Iraq/Kuwait following GSDF withdrawal in 2006. The vast majority of air personnel remained detached from the sterling work of 1st Tactical Airlift Group (1TAG) and its C-130H crews. The MSDF would realise niche ODO activities from basic 'delivery' roles (Turkey), to complex HA/DR projection (Aceh), and eventually engaged in anti-piracy and counter-terrorism support operations in addition to conventional assistance and relief roles. There was no joint ODO doctrine, repository of knowledge nor lessons-learned capacity (until 2007), Force investment in 'learning' having rarely been prioritised and doctrine development long neglected. Former Defense Vice-Minister Natsume Haruo even suggested in 2008 that a 'growing number of Japanese have started supporting the SDF after seeing their activities overseas' with some JSDF officers becoming 'excessively self-confident' and 'arrogant.'[291] There seemed little foundation for hubris given the limits of JSDF ODO.

Overseas operations had varied effects upon JSDF procurement. The 1989 MSDF Designs Office 5,500-tonne helicopter-capable LST was rejected (by JDA and MOF), but the first highly versatile *Ōsumi* LST orders were achieved in 1993 under the precept of ODO-support necessity, demonstrating cunning internal-external pressure management.[292] Three relatively inexpensive vessels enabled the MSDF to conduct a far greater range of missions, including helicopter-minesweeping, of relevance to both national defence and ODO, enabling naval leadership of the first JSDF joint operation. The ASDF, by contrast, didn't purchase a new type of large transport aircraft 1985–2005, and during 1991–6 relied upon ten-twelve C-130H aircraft, equivalent to Malaysia or Belgium, with payload-range limitations highlighted by Zaire and Honduras HA/DR deployments.[293] The ASDF record until 2005 was minimal airlift investment, adding several C-130H, and relying upon 1TAG professionalism to maintain operational support.[294] Eventually from 2006, four KC-767 strategic tanker-transporters were ordered, although primarily valued for re-fuelling fighter aircraft and lacking the ability to carry vehicles, bulk loads, or use less-prepared airstrips. The GSDF possessed significant domestic disaster relief niche capabilities, such as water purification equipment and 'one-piece' field kitchen and laundry trailers, Lt.-General Yamaguchi commenting on lessons learned from terrible wartime experiences.[295] The GSDF relied upon Type-82 six-wheeled armoured command-control vehicles in early operations, but based upon their excessive weight developed the effective Type-96 eight-wheel APC (*sōrinsōkōsha*), and the Light Armoured Vehicle

(LAV) (*keisōdōkidōsha*) from 2002.²⁹⁶ The ubiquitous, versatile LAV was highly evaluated by allied forces in Iraq, is readily air-mobile, costs one-third of the US M114 HUMVEE, and complements the soft-skinned High Mobility Vehicle (HMV *Kōkidōkuruma*).²⁹⁷ The JSDF, through harsh exposure to operational rather than purely budgetary or *kokusanka* priorities, was equipping for actual rather than potential operations.

Marginal changes in JSDF practice and culture derived from overseas operations and increased emphasis upon logistics and mobility would come to have unexpected consequences for national defence roles. Having extended operational reach to South-East Asia, Africa, and the Middle East, the JSDF would be required to address changing defence requirements in areas closer to home. These fundamental security challenges would call for far more radical defence reforms and eventually greater investments than the Forces required to conduct elective overseas operations, but the ODO cultivation of professional application and Force mobility would have unintentionally spin-off potential to address the emergent security challenges in East Asia.

3 Threats Close to Home: East Asia in the Corridor of Uncertainty

The third long-term factor for post-Cold War Japan would be the rise of regional security challenges in North-East Asia, not immediately apparent amid reduced tensions, warming Russia relations, and overwhelming US Cold War victory. Initial issues arose with the realisation that China was not converging and transforming into a liberal state, as predicted by Francis Fukuyama's 'end of history,' but as a rising power would assert its own agenda, with particular implications for the United States, Japan, Taiwan, and South China Sea littoral states, provoking 'clash of civilizations' concerns.²⁹⁸ As Japan-China relations had been warming from the early 1970s, Tokyo reluctantly imposed post-Tiananmen sanctions, and encouraged renewed trade.²⁹⁹ Few imagined that the PRC's 'dash for growth' would surpass Japan and feed the greatest modern expansion of Chinese military power and assertive foreign policy. The 'rising China' factor in Japanese security would be accompanied by an independently assertive North Korea, as rogue-state spoiler, extorting aid for a failing economic system deprived of Soviet sustenance. Pyongyang played to its strengths, twin threats of nuclear weapons and ballistic missiles, particularly sensitive for Japan to manage within its contradictory reliance upon non-nuclear principles and US nuclear umbrella.

The mid-1990s rise in East Asian tensions prompted the first significant revision of US-Japan Guidelines for two decades, enabling closer US military-JSDF working agreements. Parallels were evident with early 1970s détente succeeded by the 'second Cold War,' which was utilised to extract greater defence investment and enhanced US-Japan cooperation despite limited Japanese government enthusiasm. North Korea spurred Japan to its first major defence technology development project with the US (ballistic missile-defence: BMD). The rise of China, and its challenges to Japan, the US, and the extant norms of East Asia and international law would develop into one of the dominant issues of international affairs in the new century, which all countries struggled to manage. Japan laboured to adapt quickly or comfortably, attempting engagement, rebuke, re-engagement, and eventually the Koizumi chill. China utilised perceived historical-legacy insults for strategic ends, with the period characterised as Beijing bludgeoning Tokyo with unresolved historical legacy 'gifts' that Japan constantly presented to China. The first security challenge considered is Russia, the Cold War focus, and one-time best post-Cold War hope for Japan.

Regional Challenges: Russia

The end of the Cold War in Europe altered neither Japan's basic security stance nor JSDF planning. Large Soviet forces remained in close proximity, and concerns lingered that these forces were enhancing their capabilities.[300] Defence of the north continued to be the main focus of ground and air Forces, the GSDF investing in SSM batteries to dominate the contiguous Straits and deter invasion.[301] Russia was downgraded in JDA publications to a 'factor of instability' (1992), then 'a neighbour with an outstanding territorial dispute' (1996).[302] Progress led to Soviet President Mikhail Gorbachev visiting Japan in April 1991, and signing a joint statement with Prime Minister Kaifu Toshiki that four disputed Kuril Islands (the Northern Territories, *Hoppōryōdo*) be resolved by peace treaty.[303] The Agreement Concerning the Prevention of Incidents at Sea was signed with the Tokyo Declaration by Russian President Boris Yeltsin in 1993, encouraging the Peace Treaty Working Group, the Japan-Russia Joint Working Group, to reduce nuclear stockpiles and fissile material, and supporting a Japanese permanent UNSC seat.[304]

This was not a completely smooth transition. After the Tokyo Declaration there were fishing and earthquake aid disputes, but the trajectory was positive and by 1996–8 ASDF pilots were training on Russian fighter aircraft, the MSDF made the first Russian port call since 1925 with naval communications exercises, defence exchanges becoming normalised.[305] In April 1996, DG-JDA Usui Hideo signed a military cooperation protocol on military exercises, facilitating training and exchanging personnel and information, and Russia reduced its Pacific military personnel, particularly in the Northern Territories.[306] Prime Minister Hashimoto Ryūtarō had long advocated closer ties, and his first meeting with President Yeltsin in April 1996 developed into a warm relationship.[307] By 1997–8, they were holding 'no neckties' summits, the zenith of Russo-Japanese relations, Yeltsin surprising everyone with his resolution to conclude a peace treaty by 2000, creating a 'giddy mood of optimism' that could not be sustained.[308]

That treaty settlement and rapprochement stalled has been partly attributed to poor handling by Japanese politicians and diplomats.[309] Gilbert Rozman stated, 'the newly emerging 1990s atmosphere of somewhat muted Japanese arrogance toward Soviet weakness occurred with remarkable suddenness in the years 1988 to 1990.'[310] The Yeltsin years represented the peak of Russo-Japanese relations and the trough of Russian economic deterioration, with 'Japan offering the tantalizing possibility' of investment in Russia's Far East, but Yeltsin was opposed to selling its islands.[311] Some in Tokyo viewed such conditions as immutable, lending permanent advantage to Japan, as in the proverb that 'the misfortune of others tastes like honey,' but Russian revival under Putin and Japanese economic flat-lining illustrated that Japan, particularly MOFA, had 'missed the bus' on peace treaty and territorial issues.[312] The fading of fraternal relations and revival of Russian military investment resulted in rumblings of JSDF discontent, particularly naval, that the Russian threat had faded but would return.[313] Former diplomat Sono Akira spent a decade asserting that *perestroika* was a ruse to disarm and dominate Japan.[314] Negative Japanese reactions to Russian manoeuvres, political visits, and defence enhancements were notable for the scant regard they gave to how equivalent Japanese developments had been perceived in Moscow and Vladivostok.

Rising Forces, Declining Russia

Ironically, the 1990s saw the JSDF reach their 1976 NDPO goal of developing adequate Cold War defensive capabilities in land, sea, and air domains.[315] The Soviet Pacific Fleet had deployed the aircraft carrier *Minsk* and substantial amphibious capabilities to Vietnam, operated a huge submarine fleet, and a powerful air force. A decade later *Minsk* had been sold for scrap, eventually becoming a tourist attraction in China.[316] In 1994, four conscript sailors in the Pacific Fleet died of malnutrition, with over a thousand vessels discarded due to inadequate funds.[317] Three Pacific Fleet nuclear submarines were acting as electric-power generators for Kamchatka Peninsula towns while others were scrapped.[318] The Japanese government, alarmed by reports of Russian radioactive material dumped into the Sea of Japan, pledged aid for dismantling nuclear reactors and weapons.[319] From May 1999, the Japan-Russian Federation Joint Actions for Disarmament and Environmental Protection supported dismantling decommissioned nuclear submarines in the Russian Far East, with an initial pledge of $200 million, further extended from 2005.[320]

Yeltsin's embrace was economic while Japan's was political, with neither focusing upon security, defence cooperation therefore providing unexpected opportunities. In July 1997, MSDF destroyers *JS-Setogiri* and *JS-Sawayuki* sailed through the Sea of Okhotsk and the Urup Strait with Russian approval, once the Soviet Pacific Fleet's exclusive domain and closed to Japanese warships since 1945. Ferguson contends that this 'seemingly innocuous movement of two ships [...] was a dramatic symbol of the warming of relations between Tokyo and Russia.'[321] This blossoming relationship led to exchanges and port calls, a Russian warship entering the MSDF Yokosuka base, and Russian Border Guard vessels visiting the JCG Yokohama homeport and undertaking exercises for suitably neutral search and rescue (SAR) in 2000.[322] The ASDF Chief of Staff visited Moscow, and two veteran ASDF pilots trained on Su-27 jet fighters at Gromov AB near Moscow for forty-six days in 1998, investigating procuring aircraft for aggressor training.[323] The pilots and JDA were clearly impressed, which prompted media interest in Russian equipment, but the deal did not progress as the JDA wished to purchase only one or two fighters rather than Sukhoi's batch of six (denied by MOFA).[324] Russian amenability was illustrated by the test aircraft being part of a batch for China, the ASDF gaining data influencing development of the F-2 and F-15J upgrades.[325] With hindsight it appears a missed opportunity, one that the US grasped for its air-combat aggressor training units, a capability Japan lacked.

Russia-China

Russian defence technology exports to China and North Korea became a concern, including advanced missiles, warships and submarines, and the Su-27 fighter complicated by Chinese tendencies to 'improve' designs and self-produce. Worryingly for Japan the first Sino-Russian exercises for forty years, 'Peace Mission 2005,' involving 10,000 personnel, featured such technology as warships, fighters, and strategic-bombers, in air superiority, maritime blockade, and amphibious-airborne landings that 'caused some controversy, and was seen by some as preparation for a Chinese invasion of Taiwan.'[326] Despite being conducted under the Shanghai Cooperation Organisation (SCO) banner as anti-terrorism and peacekeeping, the exercises emphasised high-intensity assault, in contrast to 2002–03 SCO exercises, 'Peace Mission 2007' reducing China's contingent and including other SCO countries.[327] Russia also struggled to deal with the 'China Factor' as a potential economic, political, and military threat to its Asian territories and Central Asian 'area of influence,' adopting close engagement and strategic convergence, but also distancing itself from burgeoning Chinese disputes with the US and Japan, and embracing relations with Asian states similarly troubled by burgeoning Chinese power.[328] The Russian Foreign Affairs and Defense Policy Council had even proposed in 1997 that Russia should develop closer security ties with the US, ROK, and Japan, but James Brown clearly illustrates Putin's avoidance of Japanese attempts to pivot Russia.[329] Ferguson quotes Harry Gelman suggesting that China and Russia were 'in the process of trading traditional places' regarding the US-Japan security alliance, China locking itself into a 'Cold War' confrontation, while Russia attempted to benefit by balancing, hedging, and forming associations of advantage.[330]

Cooling

Disturbances to the defence relationships arose from Japanese interest in US BMD joint projects due to the 1998 North Korean missile launch.[331] Russia's response was initially muted, but disquiet increased, not least through consultation with China, an example of a purely defensive measure provoking fears of aggression among neighbouring states.[332] There was also a scandal in 2000 involving MSDF Lt-Commander Hagisaki Shigehiro, who passed secret intelligence material to the Russian naval attaché in Tokyo, which illustrated both lax JDA intelligence management procedures, and limited secrets legislation, all the more remarkable given the 1980 case of retired GSDF Major-General Miyanaga Yukihisa and two former-subordinates arrested for passing military secrets to the Soviet military attaché.[333] Miyanaga had been a leading GSDF Soviet-intelligence expert, and received the maximum SDF Law one-year imprisonment term.³³⁴ Twenty years later Hagisaki was sentenced to only ten months.³³⁵ Interestingly, both cases involved secret information concerning Chinese not Japanese military capabilities.³³⁶ In the Miyanaga case this apparently caused concern that 'could dampen enthusiasm for the exchanges of good-will delegations that Peking recently has been promoting with the Self-Defense Forces.'³³⁷ By 2015, another Russian defence attaché scandal concerned JSDF tactics and defensive capacity.³³⁸

Enthusiasm for closer ties with Moscow was significantly dampened by the outstanding scandal of amicable Russo-Japanese relations: Suzuki Muneo, former LDP Minister of State for Okinawa and Northern Territories Affairs and Deputy-Cabinet Secretary.³³⁹ His disgrace, resignation, and conviction for corruption and perjury impacted upon relations with Russia, Japan suddenly switching from 'two-plus-two,' accepting return of two Russian-held islands, while hoping for eventual return of the others, to 'all or nothing.'³⁴⁰ 'Muneo' casualties included Cabinet Secretary Nonaka Hiromu and Kuril Islanders living astride what Paul Richardson has termed the 'hyper-border.'³⁴¹ Most damaging, MOFA engagement specialists Togo Kuzuhiko and Nishimura Mutsuyoshi were discarded, attitudes hardened, and relations stalled.³⁴² President Putin and Prime Minister Koizumi agreed the 2003 Action Plan, including 'Action as Strategic Partners,' but this muted declaration lacked focus.³⁴³ Relations revived under Prime Minister Abe, but the defence relationship never returned to 1998 levels, Putin/Medvedev Far East investment plans dramatically changing Kuril Islanders' opinions regarding reversion to Japan, which was reinforced by President Dmitri Medvedev's 2010 visit.³⁴⁴ In February 2011, Medvedev announced upgraded military capabilities, 'in order to ensure the security of the islands as an integral part of Russia,' which was deemed 'incompatible with Japan's position and regrettable' by Abe.³⁴⁵ Russian defence budgets outstripped Japanese, two French *Mistral* amphibious warfare ships were ordered for the Far East, and Russia annexed Crimea from Ukraine (leading to *Mistral* cancellation) as Russian military mass exercises emphasised 'forcible entry' and 'encirclement forces.'³⁴⁶ These developments were not allowed to damage the warm Abe-Putin relationship, and surprisingly a Russia-Japan 'two-plus-two' summit of November 2013 brought together security issues for discussion, but 'Abe-optimism' appeared misplaced.³⁴⁷ In November 2017 Putin re-introduced the Soviet precept that the US-Japan alliance required 'modification' as a peace and territory agreement pre-condition, indicating the political and security costs expected for any territorial concessions.³⁴⁸

Conclusion

From the heights of burgeoning MSDF, ASDF, and coast guard interactions, Japanese perceptions of Russia became increasingly negative and interactions stalled, with opportunities lost due to Russia's Putin revival, and Japanese incompetence and arrogance. The relative lack of GSDF-Russian engagement was due to obviously limited opportunities, but in the post-Cold War period the Force would play a unique role in defence diplomacy and functional engagement with their Chinese counterparts. Predictably in Sino-Japanese relations the common concern was a legacy of war.

Regional Challenges: China

'Chinese conventional military power is declining [...] Beijing has experienced increasing fiscal deficits [...] the last five years there has been almost zero real term growth in [...] revenues. In this sense, China is not a modern nation even compared with India and Pakistan.'[349] Far from the conventional 'Rising China' narrative, contrary journalist Taoka Shunji's 1997 statement illustrates that Japanese perceptions of Chinese economic and military power were nuanced and conflicted during the post-Cold War period. Taoka commented at the tipping point when perceptions of a poor, developing China shifted to that of an emerging superpower, but when Sino-Japanese relations appeared positively disposed, many scholars anticipated future Sino-Japanese competition but also cooperation with minimal military challenges.[350] The range of Chinese challenges to Japan, many economic, some obviously military, require examination, including Chinese defence budget increases, maritime and airspace intrusions, and aggressive regional actions. This is the only challenge that appears to pose full-spectrum threats, and it is inextricably tied to Japan's past and its strategic present.

China is the challenge that Japan has failed to effectively meet through engagement or other means. Post-war governments attempted to rebuild economic ties to prevent Japan, isolated from Chinese markets, being doomed to depression, the allure that had led to imperial aggression. JCP-Chinese Communist Party (CCP) connections helped develop a Japan-China Fishery Council to manage fishing disputes, disrupted after a Korean-Chinese-Japanese spy ring in 1957 was discovered, Japanese fishing vessels subsequently attacked and seized by Chinese authorities, which illustrated Sino-Japanese relations' political sensitivity beyond security considerations.[351] The 1970s brought détente and burgeoning exchanges until Tiananmen Square events in 1989 impacted the 'China progress' thesis. The first 'Chinese Cold War' concluded between US recognition in 1971 and Japan's Treaty of Peace and Friendship, 1978 coinciding with China's 'opening' to the West.[352] Prime Minister Tanaka Kakuei visited China in September 1972, his joint communiqué with Zhou Enlai declaring that 'the abnormal state of affairs that has hitherto existed' was at an end. 'Neither of the two countries should seek hegemony in the Asia-Pacific region and each is opposed to efforts by any other country or group of countries to establish such hegemony.'[353] Despite this anti-hegemony, Zhou Enlai withdrew opposition to the US-Japan alliance, supporting Tokyo's Northern Territories claims, as Mao had done, and encouraging JSDF capabilities particularly for sea lane air defence, with Central Military Commission chairman Deng Xiaoping even suggesting that Japan double its defence budgets.[354]

Confrontational 'Rise of China' narratives have become so normalised that alternatives have been neglected. Even during the Korean War, Yoshida was eager to build relations and trade, Michael Green illustrating how fraternal mercantilism was an intrinsic 'Yoshida Doctrine' element.[355] If anything, limited exchanges cultivated nostalgia for old bonds, and for China's ancient culture, fanned by NHK's 'epic televisual poem' *Silk Road* documentary, 'the most fruitful Sino-Japanese cultural exchange in postwar history.'[356] The bloody Tiananmen Square 'incident' (*jiken*) made 1989 a turning point, attempts to draw China into Western spheres and institutions stalled, and defence cooperation halted. Japan regarded this more as pausing than halting.

Troubled Relations

At which point the Japan-China relationship became 'troubled' isn't clear, as Japan's Cold War policy remained consistent: trade and cultural engagement.[357] Reinhard Drifte describes how the '1983–4 period was therefore referred to as the best in the 2000-year history of Japanese-Chinese relations.'[358] By contrast, US policy sharply veered between strict containment and enthusiastic engagement, 'Washington's grand plans to refurbish the Chinese armed forces' including vital intelligence assistance by President Carter, and nuclear weapon technology by President Reagan.[359] Japan avoided defence cooperation, as some in Washington had ironically accused her of 'punching [...] holes in the umbrella we hold over them' by selling defence-sensitive technology to China, but Italian missiles, French helicopters, and

British Harrier jets competed for Chinese orders.[360] Prime Minister Ōhira's rejection of military aid to China and the lack of regular defence exchanges demonstrated limited trust.[361] Alarmed by Reagan rhetoric and escalating US and Japanese defence spending, the Chinese began to regard Japan as a threat, aggravated by Prime Minister Nakasone visiting Yasukuni Shrine in 1985, and Education Minister Fujio Masayuki's outrageous anti-Chinese comments compelling Nakasone to dismiss him.[362]

Aggressive depictions of Japan, regressing to historical martial identities, have been common in Chinese education and culture, used to emphasise CCP-PRC achievements and reinforce the 'China as Victor/Victim' narrative, so embedded that the Cannes Grand Prix winning war film *Devils on the Doorstep* (*Guizi laile*) was censored for depicting 'Chinese civilians [...] [who] don't hate the Japanese.'[363] Restrained Japanese responses to the Tiananmen Square killings produced unexpected results; General-Secretary Jiang Zemin clamped down on not only dissent but also anti-Japanese patriotic demonstrations, prompting international criticism of Japan for its 'vacillating and ambivalent policy predominantly governed by economic motives.'[364] In August 1991, Prime Minister Kaifu became the first G7 leader to visit after 1989, followed in October 1992 by the previously unthinkable first visit of a Japanese Emperor.[365] Kaifu's visit recalibrated Japan's significant ODA with four criteria: military spending, weapons of mass destruction (WMD), arms sales, and promoting democracy, human rights, and liberal economics, indicating that Chinese military power was a cause of concern.[366] Subsequently, non-LDP liberal-pacifist statements of Japanese war responsibility (Kōno et al) coincided with warming relations, but PRC defence spending concerns continued.[367] Japan could pay largely symbolic attention to domestic abuses of power, but would be fully attentive to aggressive expressions of regional military power.

Taiwan

In the summer of 1995, massive PLA military exercises were held near Taiwan, including amphibious landings. These were accorded significant Chinese media coverage, signalling Beijing's displeasure at Taiwanese President Lee Teng-hui's June US visit.[368] Lee consciously stoked controversy for election purposes, skilfully manipulating media coverage to promote a democratizing Taiwan contrasted with repressive China, enraging Beijing by arms deals and statements of pride in Taiwanese rather than Chinese identity. The PLA held further exercises around Taiwan immediately preceding the elections, including intensive firing missiles near Taiwanese ports.[369] President Clinton dispatched the *USS Nimitz* carrier group through the Taiwan Strait in December 1995, followed by two carrier-group exercises near Taiwan in 1996. Michael O'Hanlon considered that China (in 2000) lacked the military capabilities to conquer Taiwan, even without US intervention, based upon the lack of precision-guided munitions (PGM) and 'poor quality [...] PRC aircraft.'[370] In 2013, however, the Taiwan Ministry of National Defense predicted that Chinese military power would be capable of invasion by 2020, regardless of US responses, indicative of China's qualitative military expansion.[371] Beijing demonstrated its unification aims to any countries interfering in 'one-China' affairs.

Both dovish and hawkish China specialists agree that despite growing capabilities military domination is not PRC methodology, David Kang detailing how China has avoided military confrontations beyond minor conflicts, the Five Principles of Peaceful Coexistence significantly influencing security doctrine.[372] Even realist-pessimists, such as Lee Kuan Yew and Michael Pillsbury, identify the avoidance of conflict as vital to the economic-strategic core of a 'rising China.'[373] The Hashimoto administration carefully avoided involvement, ignoring local requests for protection when one PLA missile landed sixty km from Yonaguni-jima, receiving limited Washington and JDA communications, despite the ASDF and MSDF assisting US forces with reconnaissance and refuelling.[374] Tokyo avoided the opprobrium heaped upon Washington despite Beijing noticing that Japanese bases facilitated US military intervention in 'China matters.'[375] For Japan, regional crises brought familiar conflicted fears of US entrapment and abandonment, of being drawn into war by its alliance, or being left exposed if failing to demonstrate sufficient support to Washington. Alliance communications and coordination were inadequate for security contingencies short of conventional war, and in the event of war there were few measures nor exercises to ensure effective cooperation: the Japan-US Security Consultative Committee did not meet from November 1978 to January 1982, failing to operationalise the Guidelines.[376] A passive Tokyo and base facilities-focused Washington hardly formed an ideally balanced partnership.[377]

Changes in Japanese Defence

In IR studies, the search for the point of 'securitization of China by Japan,' the tipping point when Japan switched from engagement to containment including by military means, has become a sub-genre of its own.³⁷⁸ This is a valuable but too fastidiously narrow focus which risks missing the constant presence of both elements and how they interacted within Japanese foreign, defence, and alliance policies. Soeya Yoshihide illustrates how, following the 1994 Korean peninsula crisis, US-Japan Guideline reviews began in 1995, delayed by political issues until 1996, by which time the Taiwan crisis further demonstrated alliance coordination problems.³⁷⁹ The Japan-U.S. Joint Declaration on Security of 17 April 1996 revised the 1978 Japan-US Guidelines on Defense, consolidating the Reciprocal Provision of Logistic Support, Supplies and Services Agreement signed two days previously.³⁸⁰ This first USFJ-JSDF cross-servicing agreement indicated poor Cold War defence contingency planning and the changing post-Cold War necessity, portrayed in Chinese media as a 'dangerous signal [...] bound to evoke the vigilance [...] against Japan's advance toward becoming a military power.'³⁸¹ The Joint Declaration had been preceded by the 1995 National Defense Program Outline (NDPO), the first post-Cold War review of Japanese defence. Prime Ministers Miyazawa and Hosokawa both established security panels, and Miyazawa's 'Committee on Asia, the Pacific and Japan in the 21st Century' resulted in recommendations for cooperative Asian mechanisms to aid transparency and reduced military tensions. It was eventually encapsulated in the ASEAN Regional Forum (ARF), 'conceived as an inclusive group not directed against any country.'³⁸² Hosokawa's committee, however, had a direct influence upon Japanese post-Cold War defence planning and immediately shaped the 1995 NDPO.

The Higuchi Report (August 1994) of the 'Advisory Group on Defense Issues' (*Bōeimondaikondankai*) chaired by Higuchi Hirotaro, with Watanabe Akio as the key specialist, proposed development of regional and global security cooperation, bolstering alliance functionality, and developing JSDF capabilities within a comprehensive security framework. It suggested personnel reductions, building reserve forces, developing intelligence and BMD capabilities, and strategic transport and aerial refuelling. It referenced declining Soviet threats and potential military challenges from China, and recommended that JSDF overseas operations, particularly UN-PKO, be regarded equally alongside alliance and regional security considerations.³⁸³ Drifte, Hughes, and Green examined how China threat references were 'weeded out,' leaving the Korean peninsula as prime regional security concern, which resulted in the 1995 NDPO becoming a nuanced diplomatic document rather than a detailed defence statement.³⁸⁴ These efforts were apparently due to opposition pressure, avoidance of potential Senkaku Islands and WMD crises, and a desire to avoid controversy, relying upon DPRK issues to promote defence (and Guidelines) reform.[385] The NDPO was complemented by the Nye Report (*United States Security Strategy for the East Asia-Pacific Region*, February 1995), which reassured that 'Our security alliance with Japan is the linchpin of United States security policy in Asia.'[386] The Nye Report was also interpreted as indicating Japanese utility to Washington as an equalising regional balance against China, with dissonance between Departments of State and Defense. State emphasised China engagement while Defense saw 'Rising China' not as an opportunity but a challenge and threat. Controversy concerning Japan's potential new security identity occurred during this State-Defense tussle, according to Chalmers Johnson, when DOD 'young Turks' overreacted to the Higuchi Report 'that Japan was about to slip the leash [...] about to step forth on its own,' despite little evidence beyond UN-PKO participation and oil trading with Iran.[387]

It seems that a presumption of martial revisionism and a misreading of innocuous statements was not the preserve of Beijing, reviving the post-war 'cork in the bottle' thesis of 'independent' Japan automatically reverting to imperial-militarism. Despite such analytical baggage, Patrick Cronin and Michael Green cogently argued that (their perception of) Japan's new obsession with an international military role (UN-PKO) was a potentially damaging distraction from vital security concerns, ODO best undertaken in concert with Washington.[388] Sebata Takao suggests that the Cronin-Green paper 'influenced the formation of the New NDPO of 1995 and the New Guidelines,' regarding their concerns of a 'free-radical' Japan, but that Watanabe Akio had recognised this possibility yet insisted JSDF ODO complemented the US alliance, the Outline and Guidelines both products of sustained Japan-US mediation.[389] Civilian security architecture was also reformed: the National Security Policy Division was established within MOFA's Foreign Policy Bureau (1993) for ARF support, and the JDA International Policy Planning Division likewise established within the Defense Policy Bureau for multilateral security initiatives. Yuzawa Takeshi suggests that these constituted Asian confidence-building, China-management security measures complementing the US alliance.[390]

The 1995 NDPO provided quantitative JSDF reductions and qualitative improvements, cutting GSDF personnel from a notional 172,000 (actual 167,000) regular personnel to 147,000, plus 2,006 ready-reserves.[391] There were MSDF AEGIS destroyer capability enhancements with aviation cuts reflecting Russian decline, enhancements for ASDF F-15DJ fighters, and investment in surface-to-air missiles, transport helicopters and aircraft, with slight reductions in GSDF tank, APC, artillery, and aviation procurement.[392] Higuchi panel members and Hosokawa sought major GSDF cuts, even halving divisional numbers, but were deflected by stubborn JDA-JSDF resistance.[393] Even MSDF and ASDF senior officers hoping that GSDF reductions could free funds maintained gradual Force transitions and 'balancing' of resources, without interference from transient politicians: balance being 'an important value in itself.'[394] The NDPO asserted greater JSDF mobility, redefining secondary duties as 'response to large-scale disasters and various other situations,' third-line duties involving 'creation of a more stable security environment,' which was code for ODO.[395] Despite lighter vehicles and *Ōsumi*-class LST, there were few mobility enhancements or signs that Chinese military power was significantly influencing defence policy, and no preparation for Taiwan or Korean *shūhen* operations, despite obvious concerns of Chinese intent. One Higuchi panel member felt that the transition to the Murayama cabinet sapped the zest for radical reforms.[396]

In 1995, the ASDF first intercepted a People's Liberation Army Air Force (PLAAF) aircraft in Japanese controlled airspace, indicating future challenges.[397] The revised US-Japan Guidelines clause that the 'situations in areas surrounding Japan, is not geographic but situational,' amplified rather than clarified the ambiguity.[398] As Reinhard Drifte and Funabashi Yoichi relate, Japan utilised this operational-ambiguity to manage critical Chinese comments and domestic concerns of US entanglement/abandonment.[399] However, due to US-Japan dissonance, and Japanese politicians' gaffes, by 2000 it was 'not surprising that the Chinese don't seem to have any doubt about Taiwan's inclusion in the guidelines.'[400] China apparently understood that Japan's *shūhen* included Taiwan, in 'Beijing's opinion, the redefined U.S.-Japan alliance presages Washington-Tokyo domination of regional affairs and smacks of an ulterior intention to marginalize China.'[401] Both countries aspired to engage Chinese economic power while containing Chinese military power, the high-profile Armitage report (2000) urging encouragement for China 'to become a positive force in regional political and economic affairs.'[402]

Chinese concern over US-Japan BMD cooperation escalated with fears that AEGIS destroyers could defend Taiwan, nullifying PLA Second Artillery Force missiles, with President Bush denying Taiwan AEGIS technology in 2001.[403] The 1996 US-Japan agreement to study theatre missile defence (TMD) following DPRK developments provoked 'clearly aimed at China' responses from Beijing.[404] China conducted over forty nuclear warhead tests, but the ninth since 1990 in August 1995 prompted Japanese ODA sanctions, despite China having 'the most restrained pattern of deployment' with eighty warheads.[405] China's compliance with the Comprehensive Test-Ban Treaty (CTBT) from 1997 resulted in ODA revival, but ODA 'had long been considered reparations in disguise,' and required disentangling from historical legacies, being terminated in 2005 due to worsening relations and shifting economic realities of a modernising China.[406]

From the 1997–2000 interlude when premiers Hashimoto and Li Peng exchanged visits, President Jiang signing a 1998 cooperation agreement in Tokyo, relations rapidly became embittered under Koizumi.[407] China's unprecedented economic growth and military spending made lingering Japanese ODA appear anachronistic within the 'new high ground' of Chinese diplomacy.[408] Such concerns were obvious in 1992 when a Japanese Vice-Foreign Minister criticised Chinese aircraft carrier purchase plans, and in 1993 Prime Minister Miyazawa expressed concerns about China's military expansion.[409] In 1992, China's Law on Territorial Waters and Contiguous Areas claimed sovereignty over all islands in the South China Sea and the Senkaku Islands in the East China Sea, linking two disputes with deep implications.[410] The Senkaku issue had largely been in abeyance since returning from US administration in 1972, Tokyo denying either sovereignty dispute or 'shelving' complicity with Beijing.[411] The South China Sea also had obvious strategic concerns for Japanese energy imports, contested islands controlled by Vietnam and Taiwan providing obvious potential flashpoints, yet Japan attempted to engage China in defence diplomacy.

JSDF Engages China

Amid Sino-Japanese rancour, Japanese troops cooperated with PLA colleagues on Chinese soil following a 1990 request by the Chinese Government to dispose of war-legacy chemical weapons, denied until US archive documentation proved the Imperial Army had used and buried them in China.[412] Japan and China ratified the Chemical Weapons Convention (CWC) in 1995 and 1997 respectively, Japan assuming Abandoned Chemical Weapons (ACW) obligations, resulting in a 1999 Memorandum of Understanding, and excavations from September 2000, which recovered 50,000 ACW by December 2012 with 400,000–700,000 remaining.[413] The project, originally due for completion in 2007, was dogged by scandals involving private contractors, following which the GSDF assumed greater responsibilities.[414] It has been the longest Japanese-PLA functional engagement programme, and despite obvious tensions the 'mil-mil' cooperation proceeded smoothly, managing a literally toxic war-legacy issue.[415] From 1997, Japan and China agreed to exchange defence civilians, officer cadets, and academics. The GSDF Chief of Staff met his PLA counterpart, agreeing unit inspections and defence medicine exchanges, the first in January 1999, a functional, engaging, 'less military' defence interface.[416] China refrained from exchanges following the 2012 Senkaku nationalisation, but from spring 2018 these were revived, managed by the Sasakawa Peace Foundation as Track 1.5 engagement to avoid political complication.[417]

Several GSDF officers have spoken with regret at the failure to equally engage with Chinese colleagues through UN-PKO, despite JDA efforts.[418] Some note the qualitative improvement in PLA officers despatched to peacekeeping training and operations, with increasingly sophisticated international perspectives and English skills.[419] Limited engagement was influenced by the highly political-strategic nature of Chinese ODO, but it has been suggested that fundamental conflicts separate the PLA and CCP regarding UN-PKO.[420] Suzuki Shogo illustrates how these primarily relate to Chinese principles of non-interference in state internal affairs, and the prevalence in post-Cold War UN-PKO for free and fair election mission goals, with potential parallels for China, Taiwan, and Tibet.[421] Furthermore, throughout the 1990s, the PRC signalled its disquiet with UN Charter Chapter VII mandates sanctioning Peace-Enforcement Operations (PEO), even when endorsing them in the Security Council.[422] As Marc Lanteigne and Hirono Miwa assert, changing attitudes derived from China's self-perception transformation, from 'activist' Middle Power 'norm-taker' of (Western) models, to 'norm-maker' Great Power promoting alternative, non-Western models.[423] Japan also had Chapter VII concerns, but the JSDF had few problems cooperating with UN agencies, NGO, civilians, and media, unlike their Chinese counterparts. Unlike in Japan, Chinese HA/DR are established and managed through completely separate means to UN-PKO, which somewhat limits cross-domain consolidation for human security ends.[424] The PLA has tended to be media-shy in UN-PKO, and pressured to simultaneously present a friendly face and yet conform to CCP doctrine and policy.[425] Japan appeared content to be a semi-activist Middle Power, but Chinese Foreign Minister Qian Qichen considered that Japan was 'not reconciled to being only an economic power but hopes to play a major role as a big power in international affairs,' with UNTAC participation provided as 'evidence of its political ambitions.'[426] Japan has achieved cooperation with China in multilateral anti-piracy operations under EU leadership, PLAN-MSDF cooperation perhaps providing a key to future 'mil-mil' engagement.

Colder Relations

Despite defence diplomacy efforts and exchanges the China-Japan defence relationship failed to reach cordial Russia-like levels, Senkaku, Yasukuni, and legacy issues contributing to sub-crisis discontent, which contrasted with a brief warming in US-China relations that aggravated fear of US abandonment and 'Japan passing' anxieties amid economic atrophy.[427] War legacy issues do not cause but frequently irritate the troubled relationship. This is inextricably linked to representations of Japan as a military power, and its failing to repent its war crimes through textbook screening, flag recognition, and political statements, which has been extensively documented by Hatano Sumio as representing Japanese neglect and Chinese exploitation.[428] Even Tokyo Governor Ishihara Shintarō's ludicrous April 2000 *sangokujin* speech defaming ethnic-Korean/Chinese residents of Japan, unfortunately urging JSDF personnel to 'not only fight against disasters but also maintain public security' against foreigners in Japan, provided the means for extensive Chinese policy exploitation.[429]

Prime Minister Koizumi Junichirō kept his election pledge to the War Bereaved Families Association (*izokukai*) to annually visit Yasukuni Shrine. The condemnations from Seoul and Beijing were expected, but less so his relatively positive visit to Beijing in October 2001. Gavan McCormack characterised Koizumi's nationalism as 'more pose than substance. Faithful to Washington on almost all issues [...] he has to disguise himself with strong Japanese national accents and posture.'[430] Sheila Smith details how Koizumi attempted to retain his Yasukuni pledge and manoeuvre sufficiently to assuage Chinese criticism, but ultimately failed, and placed faith in his anointed successor, Abe Shinzo, to repair relations.[431] Most Japanese politicians have been bland, but Koizumi was an exceptional kabuki actor, mesmerizing audiences of limited patience.

Patience was limited in Beijing beyond Koizumi and Yasukuni. The CCP was disturbed by US-led 'regime change,' the apparently accidental 1999 bombing of the Chinese Embassy in Belgrade during the Kosovo campaign, which was considered deliberate in Beijing, provoking a strong Chinese rebuke at the UN.[432] 'China perceived itself to be facing a United States bent on global domination and the permanent separation of Taiwan from China', prompting closer Russian relations, and heightening suspicions of US allies.[433] As June Teufel Dreyer outlines, the PLA considered that Kosovo displayed '"hyperconventional" features suggesting that information warfare (*xinxi zhanzheng*) was a vital future operational realm.'[434] The Belgrade bombing was 'proving once again the continuing applicability of People's War, the lessons being "the greatest deterrent to any enemy involves paying close attention to and doing a good job of national defense education and patriotic education and fostering a sense of national pride and confidence."'[435] Japan adopted a low-key approach during the Kosovo crisis and the April 2001 Hainan Island incident, when a USN EP-3E signals-intelligence aircraft and PLAAF J-8 fighter collided, despite the EP-3E being based at Kadena AB, Okinawa.[436] Provocation for Japan came from Chinese maritime surveying and SIGINT monitoring, and particularly the rise of cyber intrusions and attacks after 1999 as China operationalised its asymmetric information warfare doctrines. Japanese ministries were attacked in 2000 and 2004, seemingly related to historical legacy issues, but in 2005 technology corporations were attacked in data theft attempts, repeated several times, most notably when Mitsubishi, Kawasaki, and other defence contractors were targeted in 2011.[437] Approximately 40 per cent of cyber attacks on Japan were being ascribed to Chinese origin in 2014, although some sources ascribed attacks to non-state citizen 'hactivists,' and by 2017 the MOD was openly according responsibility to Chinese official and criminal groups, including PLA units, as a distinctive Chinese 'hybrid warfare' approach emerged.[438]

Despite burgeoning hybrid conflict, Japan proved accommodating towards China's bid for World Trade Organisation (WTO) membership, and despite Koizumi's Yasukuni toxicity, 'a key problem—not a problem-solver in this worsening of Sino-Japanese relations,' he was invited to attend the Track II Boao Asia Forum in 2002.[439] However, anti-Japanese demonstrations 2003–5 also reflected an uneven political transition from Jiang Zemin to Hu Jintao, issues and leaders 'hijacked by nationalism in policymaking.'[440] Chinese nationalism grew from policies 'of national defense education and patriotic education [...] fostering a sense of national pride and confidence,' and as a permitted proxy protest issue. However, as Wang Zheng has identified, the CCP slogan 'wu wang guo chi'—'never forget national humiliation,' has been operationalised as a social control norm and as a diplomatic tool.[441] Moderate and nuanced views by Japan specialists were overwhelmed by those of general historians, who placed Japan within the context of Chinese politics and history, while activists utilised history as a political tool.⁴⁴² Chilled relations could not be completely separated from Japan-US alliance issues. President GW Bush's announcement of a 'Global War on Terrorism' in 2001 and Koizumi's JSDF ODO reinforced Chinese perceptions of hegemon and ally. For Japan, the dilemma appeared to be that benevolent hegemonic power was in danger of being displaced by a less benevolent challenger, and that the much cultivated and ODA-supported economic interdependence, in Sheila Smith's phrase, 'seen as the salve that would heal the wounds of Japan's wartime invasion and subsequent defeat,' was losing its healing properties.⁴⁴³ China had finely honed historical disputes as tools to attack Japan while laying claim to Japanese East China Sea territory, paralleling expansive South China Sea claims that also provoked fears for Japanese maritime trade. The outstanding feature of the Senkaku dispute is that the CCP chose to highlight the issue of an arrested trawler captain in 2010, applying 'rare earth' de facto economic sanctions to reinforce the diplomatic message, and felt unable to refrain from escalation when the Noda Yoshihiko cabinet purchased several islands from private ownership in September 2012 to prevent Ishihara Shintarō, or Chinese buyers, doing so for nationalist ends. Stuart Harris depicts Japanese escalation as a sovereignty issue, but it appears that the JCG regarded it as a maritime safety and therefore legal issue, which was the Kan cabinet position until Chinese pressure damaged Japanese interests.⁴⁴⁴ Chinese state-nationalist expressions shocked Japanese public opinion into drastic threat perceptions of China parallel to Taepodong-1 in 1998, with coastguard, naval, and air forces drawn into proximity and occasional confrontation from which it is difficult to envisage mutually satisfactory peaceful and constructive outcomes.

Beyond Post-Cold War China

China faces problems familiar to Japan, 'the Chinese themselves are very worried about their future […] the economic downturn […] social instability […] will the CCP be able to handle this situation?', not least facing huge and rapidly ageing population pressures.⁴⁴⁵ Many studies emphasise the 'middle kingdom' traditional world view, that 'rising China' issue is actually 'returning China,' with Yong Deng stating that 'Chinese officials and analysts alike have, since the mid-1990s, evoked "international status" (*Guoji diwei*) as if it were the most desirable value, the one that leads to power, security, and respect […] the PRC may very well be the most status-conscious country in the world.'⁴⁴⁶

Dittmer and Kim identified the importance of 'national identity' 'mythical' discourses to China's international relations, mirroring tensions between myths, realities, values, and status-desire in pre-war Japan.[447] IR theories proposes that the 'rise of China' is more significant than recognition hunger, neo-realism suggesting that status quo challengers provoke conflict, power competition being unrelenting—in John Mearsheimer's iconic statement, 'great powers are primed for offense.'[448] Barry Buzan utilises English School methodologies to assess how China is 'rising' as a challenger to global international society (GIS) or as an actor within the international system with 'the rise of the rest' representing a new 'deep pluralism.' He concludes that China cannot simply be regarded as a 'status quo revisionist' as it works within and defends elements of that order, such as at the UN, while largely rejecting broader GIS in East Asia as 'China champions the narrow view as part of its defence against democracy and human rights' and asserts its territorial 'historical rights,' with potentially worrying implications for Japan.[449] Graham Allison insists that China and America can 'escape Thucydides' trap,' while Steinberg and O'Hanlon acknowledge elite capacities to cooperate and avoid conflict.[450][451] Mearsheimer's thesis that 'China and the United States are destined to be adversaries as China's power grows,' with Japan caught between competing hegemonic powers, constitutes a bleak assessment.[452] It is therefore worth assessing what fuels China's military and broader strategic expansion.

Chinese growth 1978–2017 was estimated by the World Bank to have lifted over 800 million people out of poverty and averaged 9.7 per cent (1978–2005), compared to Japan's 1.2 per cent, surpassing Japan as the second largest economy in 2010.[453] China built upon this growth with strategic initiatives from 2013: the Asian Infrastructure Investment Bank (AIIB) and the 'Belt and Road Initiative' (BRI) projects, both perceived as challenges to US-led norms and institutions, although, as Jeffrey Wilson and Shaun Breslin note, China not only wished to be a challenger, but also to raise its status as a responsible great power.[454] With Britain, Australia, Korea, and Canada attracted into the AIIB-bloc, the US and Japan stood in isolated opposition.[455] President Xi Jinping's goals appear economically geostrategic, stoking fears of possible conflict with the US and regional powers, such as India.[456]

Prime Minister Abe's 2007 'arc of freedom and prosperity' was a scarcely concealed effort to counter Chinese geo-strategic economic initiatives, such as the 'string of pearls' Indian Ocean project.[457] He attempted to woo India as a trading and security 'hedge' against Chinese influence in 'an association in which we share fundamental values such as freedom, democracy and respect for basic human rights as well as strategic interests.'458 Abe's notion of a 'broader Asia' encompassed the Japan, India, Australia, and United States 'Quad' as an ideational norm-based constellation appealing to Asian partners, but the scale and ambition of AIIB-BRI appear overwhelming. As Cai, Pillsbury and others have identified, economic power is vital for Chinese and CCP status and survival, but defending that power remains a prime consideration.459

China's defence spending is less easily gauged than economic growth, but the Stockholm International Peace Research Institute (SIPRI) estimates approximately 2 per cent of GNP 1996–2016, decreasing from approximately 9.5 per cent to 5 per cent of government expenditure.460 Examining Japanese defence spending illustrates that Chinese opacity is not unique. SIPRI includes Japan's Special Action Committee on Okinawa (SACO) budget and excludes military pensions, most assessments varying between the official sub-1 per cent to approximately 1.3 per cent of GNP.461 China's 2004 defence white paper claimed the budget amounted to 3.11 per cent of GDP, the State Council Research Office director insisting that despite discrepancies there was 'nothing secret.'462 The official 2017 defence budget was 1.044 trillion yuan ($151.43 billion), an annual 7 per cent increase, after two decades of double-digit increases.463 SIPRI estimates Chinese expenditure in 1990 at less than 60 per cent that of Japan, reaching parity by 1999, double Japan's spending by 2006, triple by 2010, reaching $215.18 billion, almost five times the Japanese level by 2016, with The International Institute for Strategic Studies (IISS) producing even higher purchasing-power parity estimates.464 The US estimated that 'China's total military-related spending for 2015 exceeded $180 billion U.S. dollars,' with 'poor accounting transparency.'465 Liff and Erickson contend that obsession with budgets distracts from equitable consideration of China's security requirements, Aizawa Kōetsu even suggesting defence excesses would entail the 'death of the Chinese economy by military power.'466

'Rising China' appears more menacing than 'Rising Singapore' due to scale and 'offensive' doctrine despite nuclear 'no first-use' policy, as 'China upholds the path of peaceful development and pursues a defensive defense policy.'467 Cold War offensives were limited to Tibet, Korea, bombarding Taiwanese islands, and conflicts with India, the USSR, and Vietnam, securing, stabilising, and slightly expanding its borders. Deng states that the US and Japan 'used China's military threat to achieve their ulterior motives,' erroneously alleging Japanese UN-PKO legislation had been passed by invoking 'China Threats.'468 A 2006 Cabinet response to an 'inquiry about the Chinese threat,' was that 'only when "power" sufficient for invasion and "intention" that allows one to use such power can the term "threat" materialize.' The government under the 1978 treaty stated 'we do not hold the notion that China has an "intention" to invade Japan. Hence we [...] do not regard China as a threat.'[469] After 2006, that stated position had shifted. Chinese military technology dramatically improved, submarines entered Okinawan waters, and interceptions of Chinese aircraft rose, including of PLAAF Su-27, the 'only aircraft of concern to Japanese defence officials' up to 2010, yet with little open sense of military conflict.[470] JSDF officers commented upon the startling pace and quality of Chinese developments, a USAF officer observed that J-15/J-16 fighters would 'not be game changers' in East Asian security, but would require 'changes in operational sense [...] changed scenario planning,' attention on J-20/31 stealth aircraft distracting from conventional fighters of greater operational concern.[471] PLAAF introduced advanced support aircraft (EW, tanker, AEW), domestic production reflecting embargo fears, such as Israel-China *Lavi*-fighter and *Phalcon*-AEW projects blocked by US pressure.[472]

The ASDF scramble rate increased from 2004, reaching the Cold War peak (944 in 1984) by 2014, and 1,168 interceptions in 2016, with 851 of them of PRC aircraft.[473] The first confirmed Chinese incursion into Japanese territorial airspace in December 2012, near the Senkaku Islands, prompted a review of ASDF procedures (see Chapter Four).[474] These campaigns increased after the shock announcement of China's East China Sea Air Defense Identification Zone (ADIZ) in November 2013, with thirteen PLAAF aircraft transiting between Okinawan islands in one incident.[475] The ADIZ surprise was cautiously received by Japan, but robustly challenged by US and Korean military flights demonstrating disdain for the measure.[476] Somewhat surprisingly, MSDF perceptions of the first PLAN aircraft carrier *Liaoning* (001), a refitted Ukrainian vessel, have been generally less alarmist than media reporting.[477] The 'mature,' limited vessel is regarded as a training tool absorbing a great deal of time, money, and energy, but the next indigenous carrier (001A) is larger, approximately 50,000 tonnes, while the third and fourth carriers (002/055) will likely introduce advanced catapult technology, the MSDF anticipating a PLAN carrier force of at least four vessels.[478] Of more direct concern have been developments in Chinese amphibious warfare and anti-ship missiles, which could pose direct threats to Japanese islands and USN carrier groups. Since 2006, China has commissioned large Type-071 Landing Dock LPD ships, accompanied by major 'island-capturing' exercises in 2013–15,

Newsham and Collin suggesting that China may have been influenced by the US Marine Corps Marine Expeditionary Unit model, and recommending the GSDF follow likewise to meet the Chinese challenges.[479] China's great missile forces include hypersonic anti-ship 'carrier-killer' (DF-21D) and land-target 'Guam-killer' (DF-26) versions, estimated as more powerful and difficult to intercept than any comparable system.[480]

Yoshihara and Holmes' impressive study of Chinese naval doctrine contentiously suggests the PLAN blends Mahan and Mao within expansive Chinese naval strategy and tactics, whereas Michael Swaine emphasises CCP doctrinal supremacy, supported by Saunders and Scobell dismissing notions of military shaping of policy.[481] From 2004, the Central Military Commission (CMC) had no military uniformed representation, as the central policy and strategy body, with implicit civilian control, PLA ground forces' influence dissipated under strict CCP supervision.[482] The PLAN aims for greater reach and capabilities, with major exercises in the Western Pacific from 2008, including China's first RIMPC participation in 2014.[483] Chinese survey vessels have replicated Soviet patterns, gathering data on Japanese straits and possibly signals intelligence, with seventy Japan EEZ intrusions logged in 1998–2000, with Chinese intelligence vessel *Haibing-723* even having circumnavigated Japan, transiting the Tsugaru Strait three times.[484] When the *USNS Impeccable* attempted a similar oceanic survey 100km south of Hainan Island in 2009, Chinese vessels sabotaged its survey equipment by aggressive action.[485] PLAN exercises have been closely monitored transiting Japanese straits, matched by fleet manoeuvres in the Indian Ocean. Here, parallels between China and Japan include establishing their first overseas bases in Djibouti for anti-piracy duties but with (seemingly) broader security intentions.[486]

Unlike air incidents, there have been few PLAN-MSDF confrontations. A submerged PLAN nuclear submarine was detected by an MSDF P-3C aircraft on 10 November 2004, near Sakishima in the ECS, tracked until it departed the Japanese ADIZ on 12 November without surfacing despite requests. Following a MOFA protest, on 16 November Vice-Minister Wu Dawei stated 'we have confirmed that the submarine in question is a Chinese nuclear-powered submarine. It got into the Ishigaki Channel of Japan by mistake from a technical cause during [...] training [...] and we [...] regret that the incident happened,' one MSDF submariner apparently accepting that this could have been a simple error.[487] Far more serious was the confrontation of PLAN frigates and an MSDF destroyer more than 100km north of the Senkaku Islands in January 2013, the Chinese vessel locking its fire-control-system (FCS) radar onto the destroyer at approximately 3km, and then onto its helicopter.[488] Initially, China claimed Japanese 'fabrication,' which by March had become an admission of an 'emergency decision' by the commander, who claimed PLAN communications technology 'is not as advanced as those of Japan.'[489] Despite new maritime liaison mechanisms, PLAN civilian control and naval command concerns remain.[490]

The number of Chinese ships, coastguard and commercial, intruding into Japanese EEZ and territorial waters has been far greater than that of naval vessels, despite the Japan Coast Guard managing such encounters.[491] The JCG has borne the brunt of the Senkaku issue, its impressive resources becoming stretched, but, as Lindsay Black illustrates, neither new legal 'fighting' powers nor investments have 'navalised' the JCG, which remains distinct from the MSDF, and it has operated with deft subtlety as the primary legal and security buffer in the East China Sea.[492] Confrontations of naval and air forces are more serious, with greater potential for unintended conflict and therefore requiring cautious command and control;' as Reinhard Drifte details, East China Sea confrontations could potentially escalate to disputes in the South China Sea.[493]

Conclusion

The rise of China has become the primary security concern for Japan, overshadowing all other security challenges by proximity, scale, nature of economic dependence, and forms of unavoidable military and para-military challenges. Japan faces the dilemma of engagement or confrontation, of attempting to lessen disputes by developing closer relations, potentially even (unlikely) military relations, with consequences for its core US alliance, or depending upon that alliance and attempting to circumscribe and contain Chinese power expansion. Neither are appealing options and therefore Tokyo has combined both elements in policy. Suggestions, such as by Kai Schulze, that 'the Japanese government had started securitizing moves towards China as early as in 2007' are based upon MOD and MOFA papers rather than more detailed examination of policy shifts from 1995.[494] Schulze is correct on an explicit 'China threat' in policy, but this does not explain earlier developments, nor later cautious avoidance of China-related scenarios for the controversial 2015 security laws, demonstrating nuanced Japanese approaches (see Chapter Four).

China-Japan defence and security cooperation have been limited, in contrast with peak Russian defence engagement, despite seemingly unlikely functional cooperation in extra-regional UN-PKO, multilateral counter-piracy, and development cooperation within ASEAN. Whether expanded engagement would be able to overcome the intrinsic strategic challenges of China seems remote, particularly under the strident Xi, but such avenues of communication could help manage the nature of strategic frictions. The escalation of the 'Rising China' challenge under President Xi has been measured in scale of strategic application, and willingness to assert China's military identity even in the face of Japanese, US, Taiwanese, and South-East Asian protests. For the JSDF, the China issue has had a post-Cold War transformative effect, shifting emphasis from far north to south-west, with belated development of joint operations, air and amphibious mobility, and JCG coordination, examined in Chapter Four. BMD capabilities, despite Beijing's suspicions, were not motivated by Chinese power, but by North Korean WMD and missile programmes.

Regional Challenges: The Democratic People's Republic of Korea (DPRK)

The DPRK security challenge is of a failing, isolated state seeking to survive by deft manipulation of limited options, extracting concessions and surviving two generational leadership transformations since 1990. The China challenge prompted JSDF reforms, but the DPRK challenge has involved Japan in armed combat and brought consideration of offensive capabilities. Japanese-DPRK Cold War security concerns primarily related to North Korean citizens in Japan, abductees, and insurgents, but Christopher W. Hughes illustrates Japanese consternation in the early 1990s concerning DPRK efforts to exploit US-ROK divisions, uncertainties regarding President Bill Clinton's alliance commitments, and confused responses to DPRK nuclear gamesmanship.[495] The oddity was that this followed a 1990 rapprochement with Premier Kim Il Sung and subsequent negotiations, which Iokibe Makoto considers failed due to LDP grandee Kanemaru Shin, arrested for outrageous tax evasion, symbolising the slow collapse of LDP governance.[496] Compared to deftness in Seoul, 'which showed the desire and ability to link its national interests with the dramatic international changes then taking place, the Japanese government lacked an international sense of direction and found itself adrift.'[497] Failure was attributed to Kanemaru's naivety, Kim's charms, or, as a Japanese ruse, Washington urging reassertion of 'official-civilian control' over Japan-DPRK relations.[498] Seoul's defence minister in April 1991 conjectured an 'Osirak solution,' referencing Israel's 1981 Iraq nuclear-facility air strike, but there was no consensus for a high-risk military operation, and the DPRK withdrew from the Non-Proliferation Treaty (NPT).[499]

The Korean crisis unravelled, whereby conflict was narrowly averted in June to October 1994, prompting former President Jimmy Carter's shuttle diplomacy, and special envoy William Perry's later admission that the US was planning for war.[500] The crisis, amid Japan's diverse Hosokawa-Hata-Murayama coalition governments, complicated responses, compounding decades of contingency planning neglect, and prompting Prime Minister Hata to establish the 'Korean emergency study group' to investigate sanctions and the anticipated backlash. Despite Guidelines, US-Japan contingency planning was inadequate, leaked study group reports revealing that authorities considered deploying JSDF units for internal security, as police and coastguard plans were considered inadequate to counter DPRK infiltrators or Korean refugees.[501] While the 1960 Security Treaty provided for Japanese support to US forces, Tokyo was clearly perturbed by potential US requests for JSDF facilities, ports, intelligence, and possibly MSDF contributions given Cold War divisions of responsibilities, but a 1994 Korean minesweeping encore was unthinkable.[502]

North Korea extracted enough fuel-rod plutonium in 1989 for 'a "starter kit" toward a nuclear arsenal.' International Atomic Energy Agency (IAEA) inspection demands were rebuffed with a 'state of readiness for war' declaration and NPT withdrawal in March 1993.[503] The Pentagon developed Yongbyon reactor 'Osirak strike solutions,' which 'would hardly be surgical in its overall effect' with a million war fatalities predicted.[504] Defense Secretary Perry recalled the US was 'within a day of making major additions to our troop deployments to Korea, and [...] an evacuation of American civilians' which the DPRK would have considered a preliminary to conflict.[505] Luckily, Jimmy Carter's efforts enabled negotiations, Michishita Narushige illustrating that the DPRK 'military-diplomatic campaign' delivered significant economic gains amid domestic crisis, to be repeated.[506] The Korean Peninsula Energy Development Organization (KEDO) implemented the 1994 Agreed Framework, supplying a light-water reactor and oil, freezing plutonium extraction for eight years, with inspections, but without eliminating threats or modifying DPRK behaviour.[507]

The 1998 Taepodong-1 ballistic missile launch immediately followed President Kim Dae-jung's 'Sunshine Policy' announcement of DPRK engagement, and transformed the security challenges and Japan's responses.[508] Taepodong-1 produced an unprecedented social and political shock as it flew across Honshu, the second-stage landing only 60km from Japan's Pacific shore.[509] This exceeded the 1976 shock, with Pyongyang's satellite launch claims dismissed, the Japanese government and media considering the flight as demonstrating nascent inter-continental ballistic missile (ICBM) capability, although Taoka Shunji naturally disagreed.[510] As John Swenson-Wright states, the launch, 'by highlighting Japan's strategic vulnerability, had a catalyzing effect on Japanese public opinion, abruptly shaking it out of the postwar psychological cocoon,' followed by seven smaller missile tests.[511] Japanese officials, politicians, and Forces appeared rattled, unsure how to react, but Japan declared its intention to join the US Navy Theater-Wide Defense (NTWD) system, and by 2007 the ASDF had introduced the PAC-3 ground-based point-defence system, with four MSDF BMD-capable AEGIS warships in service by 2012.[512] Nuclear warhead tests in 2006–17 were equally worrying, Pyongyang attempting to keep states off balance and extract concessions, but DPRK honesty would prove equally alarming to Japan.[513]

Prime Minister Koizumi's visit to Pyongyang in September 2002 led to Kim Jong-Il stunning his guest by admitting that eight Japanese had been abducted between 1977 and 1983 by DPRK agents. Few who witnessed the television images of smiling Kim shaking hands with an ashen, shaken Koizumi could forget the impact. Pyongyang's disclosure buried its ICBM-WMD 'freeze' pledges under abduction debris.[514] Many on the left felt betrayed. Many on the right felt vindicated.[515] Politicians wondered how to resolve the abduction issue (*rachimondai*). Five of the abductees were allowed to visit Japan, all remaining, waiting several years for family members to join them.[516] Abduction issues created alliance tensions as Washington's primary concerns were ICBM-WMD, while DPRK spying and smuggling of drugs and counterfeit currency with *yakuza* crime gangs had long concerned the NPA and MSA (from 2000 JCG), becoming broader border security issues.[517]

A suspected infiltration boat had been discovered at Mihama, Fukui, in 1990, but two suspected DPRK spy ships off the Noto Peninsula, Ishikawa Prefecture, in March 1999 led to a joint MSA-MSDF operation, and the first operational application of Japanese combat power. MSDF destroyers *JS-Haruna* and *JS-Myōkō* fired thirty-five five-inch shells, MSA vessels fired warning shots, and MSDF P-3C aircraft dropped depth-charges and nets before the fast vessels escaped.[518] The MSDF and MSA were unable to fire directly at the ships under their ROE: the SDF Law allowed force to prevent invasion not incursion, the Police Duties Execution Act (1948) allowed use of force for 'prevention of a criminal's escape' but 'shall not inflict injury upon any person' unless unavoidable.[519] MSA-MSDF ROE grey zones, and dissonance between legal, security, and diplomatic priorities, contributed to operational confusion, compounded by Obuchi Keizō PMO micro-management to depict Japan as non-aggressive rather than to secure borders.[520] One positive consequence was a joint JDA-MSA Manual on Joint Strategies Concerning Unidentified Vessels.[521] *Yomiuri Shimbun* polls found 36 per cent of respondents opposed to firing live rounds, with 32 per cent supportive.[522] After two years, responses would demonstrate significant shifts in opinions.

The ultimate engagement occurred in December 2001, with a running battle off Kyushu, both sides sustaining damage and casualties, before the DPRK ship sank with fifteen fatalities.[523] The converted fishing vessel, weapons, personal effects, and two bodies were expensively recovered from China's EEZ and, following extensive negotiation and compensation, the craft and equipment were put on public display in Yokohama.[524] The MSDF provided surveillance data to the JCG, including US satellite intelligence, naval P-3C being shot at but not returning fire based upon lessons from 1999.[525] This JCG-MSDF joint operation had been enabled by legal revisions, faster vessels, and improved coordination. The first state use of lethal combat power was by the JCG rather than the MSDF, Koizumi confidently devolving tactical responsibility despite combat in China's EEZ with obvious diplomatic ramifications. Dramatic fire-fight videos rather overwhelmed legal points, JCG 'near warning-shots,' 'hit warning-shots,' and 'defence shots' potentially justifying the intense DPRK fire, which left three JCG wounded. JCG claims that the ship 'exploded and sank by unknown causes' rather than by cannon-fire, which somewhat supports 'minimal force' assertions.[526] Despite this epochal moment, when 'pacifist' Japan inflicted fatalities, there was surprisingly little public concern. DPRK threats and violence seemingly counteracted expressions of guilt or doubt, and did not hinder Koizumi's Pyongyang visit the next year.

DPRK: Next Generation

Under the succeeding Kim Jong-un regime, the DPRK appeared to refine its asymmetric security challenges, with an increased emphasis upon integrated cyberconflict for gathering intelligence, illegal funds, and disabling overseas targets, and the development of a viable nuclear deterrent in a renewed *juche* 'self-reliance' effort for great power status.[527] This had been enhanced by the 2015 testing of submarine-launched ballistic missiles (SLBM), warhead and mobile-launcher developments, an improved SLBM launched in October 2019 that landed in Japan's EEZ, and short-range missiles tested in March

2020.[528] As Michishita Narushige outlines, the desire for proven warhead and missile systems essentially repeated 1994 negotiation-by-threat approaches.[529] The risk level elevated with missiles capable of reaching Guam and Hawaii by 2015, and by 2017 the continental US.[530] Japanese BMD capabilities escalated expectations for missile defence not only of itself but also for the United States. Rapidly reacting to threats provides immense technical, legal, and political challenges, with potentially vast consequences of either successful or failed interceptions, possibly provoking a DPRK 'second strike,' while Washington's reaction to Tokyo not attempting interception would not be easily assessed.

The J-Alert warning-system was activated during 2017 by DPRK missiles (July, Hwasong-14; August, Hwasong-12) at extraordinary altitudes over Hokkaido beyond JSDF BMD capabilities.[531] This engendered public confusion and government concern, regarding North Korean actions but also potential Trump Administration 'fire and fury' responses. The alerts provided further impetus for the Japanese government to raise defence expenditure and investigate procurement of the AEGIS-Ashore BMD system.[532] Public perception was generally supportive, hastened by J-Alert drills, but essentially 'cocooned' with little public discourse concerning BMD consequences.[533] As with the 2001 maritime incident, there was much discussion of defence and little consideration of the consequences of combat. The missile-defence issue, while regarded as 'purely defensive,' held potential for progression to belligerency.

Conclusion

Korean peninsula crises encouraged Japanese governments to reconsider defence and contingency planning, contributing to the 1995 NDPO and Revised Guidelines, and forced reconsideration of national security presumptions within peaceful Japan, mirroring Korean War developments. The JCG were reconfirmed as first-line defenders against low-intensity threats to sovereignty and citizens, the JSDF as high-intensity defenders, of both Japan and the US against WMD and missile threats, also influenced by the strategic challenge of increasing Chinese power. As Reinhard Drifte has related, 'the North Korean threat became a diplomatic code word in Japan for anxieties about China's growing military potential and future intentions, and the need to enhance the deterrence element.'[534] When mention of Chinese power was deemed too sensitive, North Korea became the substitute threat, as it had clearly demonstrated such threatening capability, and with near-zero trade value was more easily 'vilifiable.' The DPRK, from minor irritant and diplomatic blank sheet, developed into a potentially existential threat for which JSDF missile defence was greatly expanded, but constituted a significantly less comprehensive strategic challenge than China.

Chapter Conclusion

The transformation of Russia in North-East Asia and brief post-Cold War détente with Japan was a sign of possible defence diplomacy engagement that was wastefully dissipated and could not readily be rekindled, of opportunities lost due to Japanese arrogance and lack of urgency, and of obsession with a territorial dispute it was within signing distance of resolving. The JSDF were not involved in the dispute, but defence engagement could have provided an interface to aid resolution, even though, given lost opportunities and the lack of product from Abe-Putin diplomacy, this seems a vain hope. This unfortunate narrative did not distract from the eventual displacement of perceived Cold War Soviet threat by that of post-Cold War China, but Japan and China had assiduously courted each other over two decades. There was no sudden, comprehensive militarisation of Sino-Japanese disputes or abrupt dive into mutual securitisation, but rather a gradual loss of trust, partly due to Chinese assertiveness towards the East China Sea and extant historical disputes, but largely due to the overall strategic assertiveness of the PRC, its burgeoning military power and willingness to risk civil disputes and military conflict with other states, and the ambient diminishing of hopes that China could converge with liberal-internationalist values as it transformed into a developed state. China's blanket rejection of the 2016 Permanent Court of Arbitration tribunal ruling on UNCLOS, which found in favour of the Philippines, and Beijing's continuation of SCS maritime and resource claims, with military-base construction, pose a major challenge for international norms, law, UNCLOS, and the UN.[535] China was not securitised in Japanese policy at a fixed point, nor was 2016 the moment China rejected world order norms, but it was a hinge moment when the limits of normative constraints were exposed. Japan is not the only country to claim to defend the international legal order, nor the only one reticent to defend it with military force.

Cold War concepts of solely national defence security had been displaced by international engagement through JSDF ODO to meet complex post-Cold War security challenges. This placed new, previously unacceptable demands upon Japan, with the Forces and Japanese policy adopting innovatively nuanced responses signalled in the Higuchi Report. The MSDF pioneered engagement through training cruises and minesweeping, but the GSDF was presented with the primary role and sustained its pioneering ODO innovations, adapting niche domestic disaster relief and civil support roles to Peace Support duties. With large and small footprint mission models, Japanese ODO became emblematic not only of the Forces but of the nation, providing valuable international contributions of distinctive character although limited range, while China also focused upon developing its broader contributions to UN missions. Japan's armed forces did become the legitimate, designated national representatives in liberal-international operations to a degree that could have been scarcely imagined a decade earlier, raising their profile and prestige, but the effort appeared to stall in the late 1990s with limited deployments and innovations. The question lingers as to whether JSDF ODO achieved their intended results. They deflected US and other criticism of 'cheap-riding' Japan, raised the possibility of a permanent UNSC seat, allowed for broader and more diverse engagement with security partners, and normalised a policy option long considered taboo to national leaders. Unintentionally, they contributed to legitimising the Forces within society, helped sustained their generous budgets, and provided precedents for the diverse operations to follow in the next century, but they did not deliver Japan from US pressure for greater contributions. The pattern was set for each Japanese expansion to be countered by inflated US expectations, and subsequent disappointment, thereby adding little to alliance amity. The UNSC 'holy grail' became a mythical quest divorced from actual policy or strategy goals, and faded with fraternal feelings towards China and Russia, Japan 'missing the bus' as it had for the Northern Territories. Ironically, liberal-international engagement was realised and normalised through JSDF ODO in parallel with Cold War-legacy defensive capabilities being reassessed and recalibrated to meet regional security challenges, ODO therefore becoming increasingly viewed within the rubric of an overly 'militarised' Japanese strategic response.

Strategic deterrence began to look more and more beyond conventional JSDF national defence, addressing DPRK 'missile rattling,' but mainly China's regional power projection, re-imagining Japanese deterrence as potentially embracing economic strategies and non-alliance partnerships, Forces developing potential kinetic and cyber offensive capabilities beyond the imaginings of 'defensive defence.' The defenders of Japan could be seen to be facing the three dilemmas of how to *shape* the security environment to manage escalating and diversifying risks and threat assessments, how to *deter* threats from becoming actual attacks, and how to develop the capacity to *counter* any such offensive actions during the second decade of the twenty-first century. These developments and the Self-Defense Forces' ability to sustain reforms, secure financial and human resources, and adapt their cultures and doctrines to future defence challenges will be investigated in Chapter Four.

4

DEFENDERS OF JAPAN PRESENT AND FUTURE

Beyond the post-Cold War era, how did Japan adapt to the emerging security challenges of the twenty-first century, up to the security legislation reforms of 2015–16, coinciding with Donald Trump's election aiming to 'make Japan pay' for its defence, and beyond? This century saw the Forces face their greatest ever operational challenge as defenders of civil society against natural disaster in 2011, and also encountered close proximity to combat in the Middle East and Africa. The defenders of Japan were therefore facing more intense versions of previous post-Cold War challenges, but close to home the security challenges appeared to have drastically changed. North Korean missiles proliferated in type and capability with seemingly credible nuclear warheads, raising implications for missile defence, the challenges of terrorism loomed large in the aftermath of the 9/11 tragedies, and cyber security shifted from purely criminal to increasingly strategic security concerns. However, beyond these peaks of alarm, the long-term strategic shift provided the greatest challenge. China's rise and increasingly assertive approach to maritime, territorial, and diplomatic issues, with burgeoning economic and military power, provides a global challenge for the western-liberal order with distinct implications for Japan and the JSDF. Tokyo has three territorial disputes with neighbouring states, but only in the Senkaku Islands 'non-dispute' with China is there credible risk of conflict.

In 2013, Prime Minister Abe announced 'Japan is back!' with keystone statements on 'proactive contributions to peace' and partnerships with other western-liberal states, but it wasn't clear from where or how Japan had returned, nor for what purpose.[1] Nor was it altogether clear what 'proactive pacifism' would entail for the JSDF or whether policy would move beyond 'Yoshida Doctrine' norms, requiring reforms of Force configuration, practice, doctrine, and culture. Chapter Four examines the Self-Defense Forces as Japan's primary defenders, and their ability to adapt to extant and emerging twenty-first century security challenges, and how their country regards, resources, and intends to utilise them.

Terrorism posed Japan's first major twenty-first century security crisis, resulting in the JSDF refuelling foreign warships and operating in southern Iraq. Neither was seemingly relevant to the 9/11 2001 terrorist attacks upon the US, but both were inextricably linked with alliance demands and responsibilities beyond the security treaty, repeating the pattern of Kuwait and Cambodia. JSDF ODO had become normalised, expanded into anti-piracy, sanctions patrols, and 'partnership-building,' integrating more with foreign militaries and becoming more obviously strategic. Japanese forces shifted 'south-west,' into the East China Sea, South China Sea, Indian Ocean, and beyond for ODO and national defence. How would the Forces defend Japan in an age of such transformational security challenges? How did the JSDF reform and adapt, and how well coordinated have they been with each other and national strategy, compared to 'stovepiped' Cold War approaches when each Force planned separate national defences? Indeed, how well-prepared are the Forces to sustain themselves amid economic atrophy, declining and ageing population, and rising and diversifying security challenges? Also, what do the changes in Japanese defence and security in this century indicate about future developments of the Forces? This chapter addresses these questions, initially by examining post-Cold War defence reforms.

Changing Defence

Japanese defence reform became more frequent during the post-Cold War period, quality driven, without the vast budgetary expansions of previous decades. JSDF qualitative reforms beyond Cold War 'build-up' were signposted by the National Defense Program Outline/Guidelines (NDPO/NDPG), from 1976: the first post-Cold War guidelines (1995); the post-9/11 guidelines (2004); the Democratic Party of Japan (*Minshutō* DPJ) guidelines (2010); and the second Abe administration plans (2013/2018). The obvious features were increased reform frequency and general continuity despite tremendous changes to the security environment. The 1995 NDPG was significant but not comparable to NATO nations' contemporary reforms, with modest personnel reductions compared with Higuchi Report recommendations mentioned in Chapter Three, the GSDF reorganised from twelve-divisions/two-brigades to eight-divisions/six-brigades (ten divisions remained in 2004), with a quarter of tanks cut and 10 per cent of artillery. The MSDF lost half of its minesweeping flotillas, maritime patrol aircraft were cut by 17.5 per cent, but retained escort-fleet and submarine capabilities. The ASDF reorganised early-warning systems and reduced combat aircraft (by one squadron).[2]

The 2004 NDPG continued the trends, with further tank and artillery reductions (from 900 to 600 each), GSDF regular personnel increased to 148,000, with 8,000 fewer ready-reserves. There were slight reductions in MSDF warship and aircraft but quality improvements, and conclusion of close air-support (CAS) 'fiction' as new 'support fighters' (F-2 replacing F-1) were transferred to air-defence roles with subsidiary strike-swing roles.[3] The most significant changes were a GSDF Central Readiness Force (CRF) from 2007, directly under the Ground Staff Office (GSO), later the Joint Staff, as the JDA was elevated to Ministry of Defense status gaining enhanced domestic and alliance standing. The CRF combined 1st Airborne Brigade's central role with the small Special Operations Group of approximately 300 troops established in 2004 from 1st Airborne with US training (from 2008 Special Forces Group *Tokushusakusengun*), the CRF becoming (with the Ground Research Command and PKO Training Center) the ODO experience repository, and primary conduit for domestic disaster relief despatch.[4] Regional Army (RA) 'rotational' duty providing units/individuals for overseas duties was replaced by CRF requests to RA, encouraging niche capability development, with Joint Staff liaison providing air and sealift. Command by a three-star general, for a brigade-sized force (GSDF two-star, NATO/Commonwealth one-star), indicated CRF importance, a 2006 Joint Staff reform also creating a joint operational planning cell.[5] Experience with Aceh and Iraq deployments seemingly drove reforms, regarding operational planning as 'imminent' rather than for distant 'times of contingency,' and constituting a more significant reform than hardware procurement.[6]

The 1995 and 2004 NDPG retained the Basic Defense Force Concept which 'rather than preparing to directly counter a military threat, Japan, as an independent state, should maintain the minimum necessary basic defense forces lest it becomes a destabilizing factor in the region by creating a power vacuum [...] combined with the Japan-U.S. Security Arrangements.'[7] However, from 2004 this was modified to demonstrate both increased independence of action from and improved coordination with US forces, amid JSDF Iraq and Indian Ocean missions, balancing independence and alliance, emphasising both anti-terrorism efforts and countering DPRK 'Intrusion of Armed Special-Purpose Ships.'[8] There was also the first designation of ASDF-MSDF 'Assets for Ballistic Missile Defense' in the wake of the 1998 shock. The retention of *senshūbōei* 'exclusively defensive-defence' orientation to reassure against 'militarising' policy particularly irritated Watanabe Akio in the context of missile or terrorist attacks.[9] The 2004 Guideline was a mediation between LDP and Komeito coalition partners: GSDF counter-invasion capabilities were retained despite threats evaporating, comprehensive role-conversion proving too expensive.[10] Measures countering 'Invasion of Japan's Offshore Islands' were introduced, MSDF supporting the GSDF Western Army Infantry Regiment (WAIR), the primary air-mobile and increasingly amphibious rapid-response unit for island defence. This light unit of 600 Ranger-course graduates established in 2002 provided the first tangible manifestation of 'moving south-west' to deter/counter threats to Japan's 5,000–6,800 barely populated islands, 90 per cent within Western Army area.[11] WAIR pioneered combined amphibious exercises (Iron Fist 2006), introducing new approaches and expectations by exposure to US methods.[12]

The aim was a 'Multi-Functional Flexible Defense Force,' able to span operations from national defence, including missile defence, through anti-terrorism, to international engagement.[13] The problem, as Tatsumi Yuki illustrated, was that JDA aims clashed with Ministry of Finance means—that there was a hope to improve capabilities without increasing budgets: 'the Japanese government has set an impossible goal for itself—doing more with fewer resources. How is this possible?'[14] The UK cut defence budgets by one-third 1990–2001, yet greatly increased the number, tempo, diversity, and distance of operations, and the JDA showed interest in the UK Strategic Defence Review (SDR, 1997–8) without any sense of being able or willing to implement an equivalent for Japan.[15] One neglected SDR aspect was open, public consultation that could have greatly aided defence reforms, but which apparently struck fear among Japanese politicians decrying public ignorance of security issues but avoiding engaging in security discussions with civil society.

The 2004 NDPG indicated defence concerns regarding North Korea and China, thereby creating controversy despite having been included in defence white papers for several years. 'North Korea is engaged in the development, deployment and proliferation of weapons of mass destruction and ballistic missiles [...] a major destabilizing factor to regional and international security, and [...] a serious challenge to international non-proliferation efforts.' China 'has a major impact on regional security, continues to modernize its nuclear forces and missile capabilities as well as its naval and air forces [...] is also expanding its area of operation at sea. We will have to remain attentive to its future actions.' Hardly jingoistic language. The NDPG continued the procurement of four KC-767 air-refuelling tanker-strategic transport 'swing-role' aircraft, and armour-modified CH-47 helicopters, Christopher Hughes and others presuming armour indicated deployments to Iraq and/or Afghanistan, and the KC-767/F-2 combination strengthening power-projection capabilities.[16] The CH-47 were not despatched to Iraq/Afghanistan but to Western Japan, despite sources relating that the UK in particular hoped for such a deployment, the tankers providing power-projection potential but primarily sustaining ASDF air-interception scrambles, mainly in the south-west.[17] The F-2 is capable of strike roles, but these were neglected in training and doctrine, modified F-15J would be better suited, and acquisition of air-launched cruise missiles would reduce strike tanker-dependence.[18] Hughes identified the ASDF's first ground-attack PGM, Joint Direct-Attack Munitions (JDAM) procurement as important for a strike role, several decades after USAF introduction, with modifications to E-767 AWACS aircraft complementing BMD efforts.[19] He also stressed F-35A stealth capabilities, 'and its greater associated strengths as an air defence penetration fighter, rather than air superiority fighter, suggests a future interest in developing an offensive counter-air (OCA) doctrine for the ASDF' (examined below).[20]

The 2010 NDPG was the major defence reform during three years of DPJ administrations under Prime Ministers Hatoyama, Kan, and Noda, but is most notable for continuity with preceding and succeeding LDP-dominated plans. The review was launched amid Hatoyama Yukio's emulation of his grandfather, Ichirō's less alliance-focused foreign policy that embraced Asian partnerships within *yūaigaikō*, 'fraternal diplomacy.' This caused consternation in Washington, not least through campaign promises to remove the MCAS Futenma base from Okinawa contrary to bilateral agreements.[21] With Kan Naoto succeeding as prime minister, the August 2010 report of The Council on Security and Defense Capabilities in the New Era created defence review foundations.[22] Most of its recommendations were included in the NDPG, but without permitting weapon exports, despite Keidanren lobbying.[23] Improved JSDF joint-working, mobility, south-west movement, and attention to missile and WMD threats continued from 2004, as did US nuclear deterrent dependence. It also stated that 'China is strengthening its capability for extended-range power projection [...] expanding and intensifying its maritime activities in the surrounding waters [...] with insufficient transparency over China's military forces and its security policy.'[24] GSDF armour and artillery were further reduced (to 400 each), while MSDF AEGIS destroyers were increased from four to six, primarily for BMD, and the submarine force from sixteen to twenty-two boats, for intelligence gathering and as an East China Sea and key-straits deterrent, disrupting the established construction schedule.[25] This could be construed as Japan's Anti-Access Area Denial (A2/AD) capability effort, China's espoused counter to USN 'Air-Sea Battle Plan' dominance.[26] China greatly augmented its ocean-floor monitoring equipment to prevent MSDF submarines accessing SCS 'near seas,' which they may extend into the ECS, but the stealthy Japanese diesel-electric craft are able to operate with considerably more freedom than large USN nuclear boats.[27]

The 'Rising China' issue also involved the trivial matter of a Chinese fishing boat skipper refusing Japan Coast Guard orders to stop and be searched for illegal fishing around the Senkaku Islands in September 2010. Several incursions had previously occurred, including Taiwanese protestors colliding with JCG vessels, but Taipei and Tokyo calmed the situation.[28] The 2010 incident was remarkable for its rapid escalation by Beijing, including de facto 'rare earth' sanctions against Japan, with large scale anti-Japanese demonstrations, and four Fujita Corporation employees arrested, ironically while planning chemical weapons disposal.[29] Tokyo was left flat-footed as it considered the case a legal rather than political issue.[30] The politically managed fishing crew release eased tensions, but widespread perception of 'China's growing assertiveness' and 'Japan's weak diplomacy' shocked society and made Kan appear weak rather than wise.[31] However, DPJ policy specialists, such as Maehara Seiji, focusing on security issues almost in lock-step with LDP counterparts, such as Ishiba Shigeru, signalled expiration of Cold War binary norms and development of emergent consensus on defence, security, and perceptions of regional threats.

The 2013 NDPG was introduced by the second Abe administration following the fall of the Noda DPJ cabinet, and increased GSDF personnel (4,000 regular, 1,000 reserve) for rapid-deployment forces, including an amphibious brigade in the most obvious 'movement south-west' with operationally integrated joint-working aspirations.[32] Although tanks and artillery were further reduced (300 each, by 2020), naval forces were increased, from forty-seven to fifty-four destroyers (eight AEGIS), and confirmation of twenty-two submarines, but without detailing how they would be effectively crewed amid challenging demographics. F-35A fighters were included, although AWACS and tanker aircraft would have greater impact upon capabilities.[33] The GSDF Basic Force Concept, eight/six divisions/brigades, was to be replaced by 7th Armoured Division, plus the new amphibious and four other rapid deployment brigades, and three rapid deployment divisions.[34] No detail was provided on such 'rapid deployment' formations, other than that new AFV and helicopters, AH-64D Apache gunship procurement, suspended from 2008 was cancelled after only thirteen purchased of sixty planned, with no planned replacement for ageing AH-1 Cobras.[35] For armoured units the Type-10 main battle tank provided Type-90-level firepower and protection with 'C4I' network-capability for enhanced situational awareness and mobility, complemented by light, fast eight-wheeled Type-16 Manoeuvre Combat Vehicles (MCV-*kidōsentōsha*) with Type-74 tank level firepower, complementing wheeled APC. Forty-one (refurbished) AAV-7 amphibious carriers were ordered for the amphibious brigade, the only APC purchased, in a continuation of firepower priorities with more mobile systems.[36]

The AAV-7 procurement was linked with that of (initially) twelve MV-22 Osprey tilt-rotorcraft, so controversial that the 2016 defence white paper listed all US accidents, each one newsworthy, which contributed to delaying JSDF Osprey transfer from Chiba to Saga.[37] Osprey came to symbolise the troubled nature of US-Japan defence relations, admired by the JSDF, considered dangerous by many citizens, and galling for US personnel when the response to an Okinawa-based Osprey crashing off the Australian coast during exercises consisted of Okinawan political leaders venting anger, surprisingly echoed by Defense Minister Onodera, and which contrasted with sympathy in Australia.[38] Public concern was understandable, given twenty aviation incidents in Okinawa involving US forces in 2016, and eroding Operation Tomodachi goodwill and shaking confidence.[39]

The 2013 Guidelines constituted continuation and evolution in defence, with gradually increasing defence budgets, and considered within Abe cabinet strategic reviews there emerged the sense of burgeoning reform. Critical China references were longer, specifying A2/AD, maritime incursions and ADIZ, Chinese warships and aircraft 'expanding their operational areas which include areas north of Japan.'[40] It also mentioned 'North Korea's nuclear and missile development, coupled with its provocative rhetoric and behavior, such as suggesting a missile attack on Japan, pose a serious and imminent threat to Japan's security.'⁴¹ Use of 'serious and imminent threat' was provocative, describing the basis upon which Japan has asserted its right of pre-emptive strike.

Revision of the US-Japan Guidelines and the raft of Abe cabinet security measures entailed a 2018 NDPG influenced by the Advisory Panel on Security and Defense Capabilities, established mainly with academics who considered papers prepared by MOFA, MOD, and NSS officials.⁴² This continued much from the previous NDPG, but concentrated less on traditional defence and more on cyber, space, and emerging domains with a 'Multi-domain Defense Force,' an Abe-LDP agenda.⁴³ The tangible consequences of the NDPG and Medium Term Defense Program (MTDP) in December 2018, however, were announcements of orders for traditional 'industrial military' jet fighters and studies of strike missiles, observers noting limited joint innovations, particularly the failure to establish a Permanent Joint Headquarters (PJHQ), demonstrably required to coordinate HA/DR activities and south-west defences.⁴⁴ Despite innovative references to Whole of Government 'strategic communications,' there was relatively little on basic joint approaches, and the term 'strategic communications' appeared slightly skewed in the Japanese version.⁴⁵ The government seemingly attempted to communicate greater strategic focus without having first achieved elementary JSDF joint focus, but the NDPG did achieve a cogent simplification of defence aims over the confusion of previous reforms, to create a desirable security environment, deter aggression, and counter threats.⁴⁶ The MTDP contained plans to establish small ASDF space and joint cyber security units, and mysteriously two Aegis Ashore BMD systems under GSDF rather than MSDF or ASDF units, but the clear desire to develop aircraft carriers and build a new stand-off strike missile capability overshadowed many of the programme's innovations.⁴⁷

Striking Power

Beyond the NDPG, 2017 DPRK missile tests near and over Japan prompted planned enhancement of JSDF capabilities. Abe's August 2017 denial of planning strikes against DPRK sites was followed by OCA strike capabilities confirmed as under consideration and constitutional as 'pre-emption' in July 2020.⁴⁸ In December 2017, a cruise missile study to counter North Korean threats was announced as Japan's first 'strategic deterrent,' '"stand-off" missiles that can be fired beyond the range of enemy threats.'⁴⁹ The MOD listed

Norwegian JSM (500km range), US LRASM (Long Range Anti-Ship Missile), and JASSM (Joint Air-to-Surface Stand-off Missile) (both 900km) as being considered for integration on F-35A and F-15J fighters, rather than F-2 (without explanation), or rather than developing the Type-12 SSM.[50] DG-JDA Ishiba Shigeru had considered cruise missiles in 2005, but this proved too controversial despite some opposition support.[51]

A significant problem for Japan's 'deterrent' is an understanding of what it is aiming to deter, particularly concerning conventional defence against a nuclear-armed state. An official was quoted as stating MOD 'thinking about introducing missiles nowadays is that the longer the range the better. Our main target will be ships at sea,' displacing DPRK missile threat scenarios with East China Sea PLAN A2/AD.[52] Defense Minister Onodera Itsunori stated that missiles could be used 'to protect Aegis-equipped destroyers responsible for missile defense and [...] to defend Japan as a whole. The defense of remote islands is included in the defense of Japan.'[53] The *Mainichi Shimbun* quoted 'a senior Defense Ministry official' that 'obtaining public understanding would be easier' if strike-missile purchases were connected to North Korean missile and WMD programmes, placating the LDP's cautious Komeito coalition partner, reinforcing Reinhard Drifte's observations regarding earlier 'North Korean ciphers' for China-threat messaging.[54]

Despite being controversial, responses were muted, partly as pre-emptive strike concepts dated to Prime Minister Hatoyama Ichirō's 1956 Diet statement: 'In the event that an imminent illegal invasion is carried out against our country [...] through guided missiles, I cannot believe that it is the constitution's intention for us to sit and wait for our own destruction [...] Taking the minimum measures [...] to protect against such attacks—such as attacking missile bases in order to defend against missile attacks, only if no other measures are available, is legally within the scope of self-defence.'[55] This interpretation was rephrased by DG-JDA Ishiba Shigeru in 2003: 'imagine if every possible diplomatic effort has been used to avoid such a situation, but unfortunately such a situation becomes reality. If North Korea both declares that it will turn Tokyo into ashes and raises a missile, I believe that counts as starting to launch.'[56] The extent to which the bipolar world of Japanese security politics had been usurped is evident in the Ishiba-Maehara exchanges detailed by Takahashi Sugio. Both were outliers in their respective parties as realist, policy experts who agreed that possessing the right without the means to strike was an aberration masked by reliance upon US 'spear' and 'umbrella' capabilities.[57] A MOFA official insisted that three conditions were required for legitimate

JSDF strikes: 'an imminent and unlawful attack against Japan [...] no other appropriate measures to eliminate or deter this attack [...] use of force shall be the minimum possible.' When asked what would constitute 'an imminent and unlawful attack,' it was helpfully suggested: 'Maybe we have to wait and see when that kind of situation really happens.'[58]

The 2013 NDPG reiterated the Japan-US alliance 'shield and spear' for 'appropriate role and mission sharing between Japan and the U.S. [...] Japan will study a potential form of response capability to address the means of ballistic missile launches.'[59] In 1999, senior JDA official Moriya Takemasa stated: 'According to our nation's interpretation [...] the constitution does not allow our nation to possess weapons that are devoted to causing catastrophic damage to another country,' referencing nuclear weapons, which were roundly rejected by Japanese society and most politicians.[60] Strike-missile deterrence by contrast could be regarded as the logical extension of 'minimum defence' if Japan faced an existential missile threat, but usage would be deeply uncomfortable for a society that largely rejects belligerency. As opposition leader Edano Yukio stated, 'Are they going to introduce (cruise missiles) only so that Japan has the ability to strike enemy bases? If that's not strictly the case, then what checks are there on the missiles' use?'[61] Utilisation of 'strategic deterrents' could be hazardous if the targeted country considered it an existential threat, thereby creating escalatory pathways envisaged in NATO's 'flexible response' Cold War nuclear planning. Japan from 2017 was seemingly developing a strategic deterrent and accompanying strategy, but in September 2020 Ishiba admitted that advances in ballistic missile technology from 2003 had almost closed the window of legitimate Japanese OCA utilisation as a 'defensive-offensive' measure, casting doubt upon OCA utility within strategy.[62]

Strategic Approaches

The second Abe Shinzo administration from December 2012 attempted to reform the Japanese security landscape and thereby posed challenges to postwar socio-political norms. The cabinet published a National Security Strategy (NSS), established a new National Security Council (NSC) and Secretariat, reinterpreted the constitution to allow collective self-defence (CSD), and passed laws that operationalized the reinterpretation allied to newly strengthened Japan-US Security Guidelines. This was achieved despite significant public disquiet, with the perceived forced passage of 2015 new security laws (NSL) provoking nationwide anti-militarist demonstrations not seen since the

Vietnam War. As one commentator suggested, thanks to these laws, 'utopian pacifism is back again at the center of Japanese politics.'[63] Abe repeatedly stated that the reforms reinforced Japan's security and defended international law, highlighting UN-PKO and maritime safety as distinct Japanese contributions. Since the NSL generated such critical reactions, had Abe crafted a paradox of greater legal despatch capability yet reduced legitimacy for JSDF operations?

In countering peace education and pacifism in Japanese society, the government attempted multiple, innocuous measures 'salami slicing' extant norms for accumulative effect yet avoiding monolithic confrontations. This could be seen as far back as Yoshida, whose Doctrine could be considered one such slice, as well as later developments such as the 1992 IPCL, JSDF ODO, and the 2003 Contingency Law (*yūjihōsei*), Japan's first law formalising countermeasures in case of armed attack, passed due to terrorist rather than invasion threats.[64] Abe's slicing included educational restrictions, and appointment of key allies to the NSC, and Komatsu Ichiro as Cabinet Legislative Bureau (CLB) Director-General, which 'changed the nature of the Legislation bureau that had maintained a certain degree of independence as a group of legal experts.'[65] The disclosure under DG-CLB, Yokobatake Yūsuke, that there had been no dissenting CLB voices during reinterpretation of collective self-defence and 2015 NSL issues provoked incredulity.

Abe continued many DPJ Kan and Noda administration reform measures and reconstituted the 2007 Advisory Panel on Reconstruction of the Legal Basis for Security, which recommended many of the legislative and policy changes introduced, including revising the self-declared CSD prohibition.[66] The report considered complex 'grey zone' operations, such as territorial intrusion by non-military/para-military personnel, to be paramount concerns, exposing gaps between legislation and security capabilities.[67] However, the eventual 2015 bills and cabinet justifications drove some panel members to surprisingly scathing critiques regarding 'grey zones,' contingency scenarios, and prioritisation of controversy avoidance over policy effect.[68] The first realisation steps came with the National Security Strategy and 2013 NDPG, and the 2014 Protection of Specially Designated Secrets Act.[69] Post-war Japan's first and controversial secrecy bill designated state secrets as including 'operation of the Self-Defense Forces or assessments, plans or studies relevant thereto,' possibly including this book. Passage was considered vital to protect against leaks detailed in Chapter Three, and to promote revised Japan-US Guidelines coordination, but was compromised by failure to provide evidence to the Board of Audit, and by former-GSDF Lt.-Gen. Izumi Kazushige passing data to a Russian diplomat while cognisant of its illegality.[70]

The NSS motto was 'pro-active contribution to peace,' rhetoric commonly associated with UN-centricity, but clearly focused upon demonstrating regional security.[71] JSDF NSS roles were noted as disaster relief and international peace support, US security cooperation without *shūhen* or doctrinal references, intelligence gathering, and missile defence. The National Security Council (NSC) was established with a supporting Secretariat conducting continuous reviews of strategy and approaches not always possible within ministries, as well as providing a forum to address policy issues. The Secretariat is divided into administration and strategy sections, with an intelligence section, and subsidiary project groups handling standing or ad hoc issues, separating long-term issues and immediate contingencies.[72] While the previous Security Council met a maximum of seventeen times (in 2010), the new NSC met forty-eight times in 2016.[73]

The Medium-Term Defense Program (FY2014–18) accompanying the NDPG accelerated movement south-west, including an AEW group to Okinawa and a coastal observation force to Yonaguni-jima, integrated with Japan-US Guidelines revision. The US Security Treaty 'has probably been the single most discussed issue of postwar Japanese foreign policy,' and Japan has 'always regarded its relations with the U.S. as the kingpin of its foreign policy, even while trying to make the relationship less irksome.'[74] It remains the kingpin, but 1978 and 1997 US-Japan Guidelines revisions improved cooperative perceptions rather than more meaningful Japanese contributions with familiar, recurring problems: revision rhetoric, raised expectations, deflated hope, cooling, stasis, renewed 'meaningful' revision. Guidelines revision began with a U.S.-Japan Security Consultative Committee (SCC) statement in October 2013, emphasising conventional joint/combined working, contingency planning, and missile-defence, and also areas of stated cooperation rarely undertaken.[75] The new Guidelines established a 'whole-of-government mechanism for Alliance coordination, enabling a seamless response in all phases, from peacetime to contingencies,' forming an 'Alliance Coordination Mechanism.'[76] The Subcommittee for Defense Cooperation (SDC) drafted recommended revisions, with particular attention to space and cyber security issues, BMD, and HA/DR as a 2011 legacy.[77] More than six months prior to Guidelines publication Prime Minister Abe pledged to pass new security laws addressing 'grey zone' issues, 'operationalization' beginning in July 2014 with a revised interpretation of Japan's right of collective self-defence (*shūdantekijieiken*).[78] Despite the rational reasons for revision the pace was startling, as was re-interpretation and Guidelines revision preceding legislation.

The long and bitter campaign to pass the NSL in 2015 was characterised by the administration attempting to demonstrate necessity through two major security crisis scenarios involving the JSDF: rescuing Japanese nationals from conflict, and minesweeping in the Straits of Hormuz during conflict.[79] The major problem for NSC/NSS officials was that justifying the legal revisions required more pertinent scenarios, but for obscure reasons Chinese threats, Korean contingencies, DPRK missile attacks, and scenarios risking JSDF combat were prohibited from official discourse, presumably so as not to raise East Asian tensions nor disquiet a public worried by opposition portrayal of 'war laws.' Few ministers grasped that rescue and Hormuz scenarios had been conducted under existing legislation: Thailand (1997, prompting SDF Law reform in 1999) and Iraq (ten civilians evacuated, 2004), and the 1991 post-conflict minesweeping mission, in addition to MSA Korean War minesweeping.[80] Vitally, neither scenario appeared to pose obvious existential threats to Japan, supposedly the legal rationale, cabinet insistence that mined Straits would result in economic collapse convincing few.

The prime minister even became a reform obstacle, depicted as an extreme nationalist, a revisionist longing for empire, despite Abe's character being considerably more complex.[81] Soeya Yoshihide depicts Abe as suffering from a 'sense of trauma regarding defeat' in 1945—Abe 'has not hidden his basic approach [...] to defy defeat and reform the occupation regime'—thereby challenging the post-war international status quo, the very issue which he utilised to berate China.[82] The close Abe-Putin relationship, despite territorial dispute, was possibly eased by mutual grievances with the international order.[83] Many suspect that Abe was driven to emulate his grandfather, Prime Minister Kishi Nobusuke, unkind wags commenting that they generated similar protests.[84] Advisors close to Abe relate how he diligently attended to work, spending 'after hours' with his friends talking in expansive terms of recasting society and instilling patriotism, only the next morning to dutifully return to work, and ultimately damage his health.[85] Constitutional revision was his ultimate legacy goal, but 2007 failure prompted indirect efforts, hence gradual constitutional erosion, with JSDF operations providing an example of liberal-establishment norms being 'salami-sliced' by the NSL.

The NSL were revisions except for the new International Peace Support Law (IPSL: *Kokusaiheiwashienhō*) replacing the IPCL. The IPSL umbrella enabled despatch legislation to be passed within seven days through each Diet chamber, and renewal within two years, which was slightly more restrictive than preceding legislation.[86] The 'three new conditions' were:

(1) When an armed attack against Japan occurs or when an armed attack against a foreign country that is in a close relationship with Japan occurs and as a result threatens Japan's survival and poses a clear danger to fundamentally overturn people's right to life, liberty and pursuit of happiness,
(2) When there is no other appropriate means available to repel the attack and ensure Japan's survival and protect its people,
(3) Use of force limited to the minimum extent necessary. As a matter of course, use of force must be carried out while observing international law. In certain situations this is based on the right of collective self-defense under international law.[87]

The NSL seemed far less ambitious than 'war laws' and 'Hitler Abe' denouncers assumed.[88] JSDF NSL operations included logistical support for US operations or assisting states in crisis, but enabling legislation had provided for these since 2001. Other operations envisaged included supporting US forces defending Korea, a scenario the JSDF explored in the 1960s but found unacceptable in either Japan or Korea with little sense that this had changed by 2015. UN-PKO partners would be reassured by the changed interpretation of collective self-defence, given previous JSDF refusals to cooperate while practicing de facto collective self-defence, until the JSDF faced a real defence situation in South Sudan.

Abe security reforms produced curious reactions. Conservative-realists found themselves somewhat satisfied with cogent, whole-of-government strategy.[89] Liberal-pacifists were generally appalled, but reassured by the reforms empowering and uniting generations of dissenters, such as 'SEALDs' (Students Emergency Action for Liberal Democracy), OLDs (retirees), MIDDLEs ('40s and 50s'), and Mothers Against WAR.[90] Given Japanese demographics, and the greater voter turnout among retirees, Japanese politicians were attentively concerned by such groups in the 2016 elections.[91] Passage of the Laws resulted in the abeyance of demonstrations, but few would have imagined that such controversial reforms would rapidly pass against determined opposition in the land of glacial reform and conflict avoidance.

The parallel pursuit of constitutional revision almost derailed the Laws, for at a hearing of the Diet Commission on the Constitution, three noted constitutional scholars, including one selected by the LDP, criticised constitutional reinterpretation. The 'government scholar' Hasebe Yasuo opined that 'allowing the use of the right of collective self-defense cannot be explained within the framework of the basic logic of the past government views,' and that the 'silent majority of Japanese might think that Abe's reinterpreted collective self-defense is unconstitutional.'[92] Revision remains an LDP goal, and both support and resistance have hardened positions, much to the frustration to those who seek practical mediation, or those such as Inoue Tatsuo who decry both sides' illiberal and unprincipled positions and would prefer to see Article 9 abolished.[93]

Consequences of revised Guidelines and NSL were limited. In November 2016, the first 'new regime' exercise despite major media attention demonstrated few innovations, other than reports of JSDF members concerned about increased risks.[94] A poignant 'drama without drama' involved the symbolic and unnecessary escorting of a USN tanker through Japanese waters by MSDF flagship *JS-Izumo*.[95] Unfortunately for JSDF personnel in South Sudan during July 2016, despite UN collective self-defence rhetoric the government lacked the will to undertake tasks for which the hard legal and sociopolitical battles had apparently been fought, as examined below. Defence budget increases were extremely limited, not greatly contributing to strategic 'rebalancing' or 'resetting' defence. The low-point was ¥4.65 trillion in 2012, while annual increases from 2013 to 2017 equated to 1.08 per cent, the highest being 2.2 per cent in 2014, reaching ¥4.9 trillion in 2017, and ¥5.07 trillion in 2020, mostly consumed by fuel and equipment costs.[96] These are substantial sums, but given massive increases in Chinese spending, NATO's nominal 2 per cent of GNP 'minimum standard,' and the stated aims to recast the JSDF, resources in ratio to stated territorial and economic threats make such reticence difficult to understand from Realist-theory perspectives. DPJ reticence would be understandable, but Kan-Noda cabinets sanctioned similar increases. Abe cabinets from 2012, often depicted as Realist-revisionists 'remilitarising' Japan, largely followed DPJ patterns of incremental increases. It might almost be imagined that Abe was thinking like a Realist and acting like a Liberal, and he certainly sought liberal partners.

Partnerships

An international-liberalist aspect of NSS-based policy has attempted to build non-alliance 'partnerships,' a strategic effort to coordinate foreign and defence, aid and economic-industrial policies, matching those efforts to deepen, strengthen, and operationalise the US-Japan alliance, with a proliferation of military-military exchanges, training exercises, capacity building initiatives, and formal agreements on cross-servicing, status of forces, and even contingency measures.[97] The most significant have been with Australia, with whom Japan shares many security interests as well as difficulties as middle-power allies of an increasingly demanding US. Both countries developed a 'special strategic partnership' with their Joint Declaration on Security Cooperation in March 2007.[98] The fourth 'two-plus-two' Foreign and Defence Ministerial Consultation in 2012 resulted in the 'Common Vision and Objectives' as partnership development continued seamlessly under DPJ and LDP cabinets, Abe's warm relationship with Prime Minister Tony Abbot obvious in his parliamentary speech.[99] A perceived 'China Gap' between the partners was evident as Australia engaged with China, with a 2015 Free-Trade Agreement and in defence diplomacy far more than Japan had attempted, with a finely US-China-balanced 2016 Defence White Paper. This altered from 2016–17, with South China Sea issues, concerns over Chinese investments, and disclosure of Chinese interference in Australian politics.[100] The trade, media, and diplomatic spats between Beijing and Canberra in 2020 refocused attention upon Japan as a partner and the possibilities for security cooperation in Asia.

There was enhanced JSDF bilateral activity with Australian Defence Forces (ADF) in the South China Sea and ASEAN area, consolidating ODO cooperation in Cambodia, Iraq, and Operation Tomodachi, two ADF staff embedding with the JSDF contingent in South Sudan, until the unfortunate Japanese withdrawal.[101] The 2013 Australian National Security Strategy stated an intention to 'build a comprehensive and proactive strategic agenda with Japan,' reinforced by the 2014 Agreement Concerning the Transfer of Defence Equipment and Technology, and three Cross-Servicing Agreements.[102] A bilateral Reciprocal Access Agreement (RAA) drafted from 2018 with only 'agreement in principle' (in November 2020), partly due to Japanese caution about a unique 'standing-SOFA' step with a (non-alliance) partner, serving as a template for other partnership RAA, with Canberra concerns of Japan's death penalty potentially applying to ADF members.[103] For the MSDF, Japan-US-Australia comprehensive annual trilateral joint naval exercises began from 2007, while the ASDF benefitted from Red Flag, Alaska and Cope North Guam exercises leading to inaugural bilateral Japan-Australia and trilateral exercises with the US in 2011, with a Japan-Australia Information Security Agreement (ISA) in 2013 potentially aiding all Forces.[104]

After Australia, the relationship with India has perhaps shown the greatest transformation, for until 1998 MOFA scarcely acknowledged India beyond ODA and nuclear proliferation. The shift was particularly rapid in maritime relationships, with coast guards leading the way, and Malabar multinational naval exercises often including Japan, as in 2007, MSDF absence until 2015 attributed to unconfirmed Chinese pressure on India, which, if true, was disregarded thereafter, such as the 2016 exercises near Okinawa, which attracted Chinese naval surveillance vessels.[105] 'Developing the trilaterals' has been extended to ASEAN nations, with JSDF defence diplomacy efforts, training exercises, and donations of military equipment, the JSDF engaging through the ADMM Plus Experts Working Groups which Japan co-chaired on HA/DR (2010–13) and military medicine (2014–15), and the 2016 'Vientiane Vision: Japan's Defense Cooperation Initiative with ASEAN' providing a nexus of UN-PKO-HA/DR training.[106] The MSDF made significant visits to Vietnam and the Philippines in 2016, SAR exercises providing non-combat functional engagement points, and Japan donating retired naval vessels and aircraft in coordination with the US and Australia.[107] MSDF and JCG diplomatic efforts have often been closely coordinated, and yet quite distinct, such as 17 JCG exercises with Indian counterparts 2000–2017.[108] The ODO relationship with the Philippines intensified due to UNDOF cooperation and HA/DR despatch, and with Indonesia by HA/DR operations in 2005. The development of Asian strategic partnerships is aimed to provide sub-alliance security mechanisms, 'international order' and 'status quo' rhetoric differentiating Chinese and Japanese approaches. In Japanese diplomacy 'respect for international law' has been mobilised in the battle for legitimacy in Asia, JSDF defence diplomacy and 'softer power' efforts integrated within that campaign. Security partnerships in Asia are also predicated upon increased Forces mobility.

Mobility

Since the 2004 NDPG, each defence review has stressed force mobility and transferred units to south-western Japan. During the Cold War, northwards reinforcement exercises were infrequent, the first held in 1977, and the first GSDF-US exercises in 1981.[109] Middle Army's Northern Manoeuvre Special Exercises (*Hokuhōkidō tokubetsuenshū*) were held eight times (1987–2017), in summer, with light units of approximately 2,000 troops.[110] The three 2013–17 exercises included amphibious embarkation-disembarkation training with MSDF landing vessels and Landing Craft Air-Cushion (LCAC), but only for one day, main transport being commercial ferries, the same pattern as in other RA, with implications for contingency planning.[111] Combined training with US forces was more frequent, under the *Yamasakura* (YS) banner, emphasizing command coordination, but critics relate coordinated but separate small units of different doctrines, minimally interacting.[112] The fast catamaran ferry *Nanchan-World* shipped GSDF forces to Kyushu for exercises from October 2011, prompting speculation that the MSDF would invest in these vessels for mobile force posture.[113] The rail network was utilised for movements (with weight and width limitations, as Type-90 tanks could not be moved by rail), and in Hokkaido GSDF tanks drove to Tomakomai West Port on four occasions in 2011–2017, taking more than eight hours to complete 30km, with whole neighbourhoods woken as witnesses to the nocturnal, rumbling snail-like 'rapid reaction reinforcement' demonstration.[114]

Given that GSDF brigade-level amphibious operations were established by 2020 (see below), the relative lack of MSDF amphibious and logistical capacity is remarkable. The UK developed extensive sealift capacity after the Falklands Conflict revealed alarming weaknesses, peaking between the 1998 Strategic Defence Review (SDR) and 2010 Strategic Defence and Security Review (SDSR). A Japanese-built sealift 'ro-ro' (roll-on/roll-off ferry) was commissioned into the Royal Fleet Auxiliary (*RFA Sea Crusader*), succeeded by six purpose-built *Point*-class RFA-Private Finance Initiative (PFI) vessels.[115] This relatively cheap sealift capacity was complemented by four large Spanish-Dutch-designed RFA amphibious landing-dock auxiliaries and RN amphibious-warfare vessels.[116] RFA crews varied from seventeen to sixty, so that a typical destroyer complement (200) could theoretically provide at least three transport vessel crews, two *Point*-class accommodating approximately an armoured brigade's vehicles, more than the three MSDF *Ōsumi*-class combined. *Ōsumi* are more flexible ships, more survivable, performing multiple naval roles, but the MSDF has generally avoided large, cheap transporters that Japanese shipbuilders export.

Similarly, the MSDF has only five AOE to replenish warships, amphibious forces' considerable consumption of supplies rendering them operationally limited without logistic reinforcement.[117] In 1981, the logistics officer of Britain's 3 Marine Brigade displayed three days' training exercise supplies, shocking troops who later realised they required 9,000 tonnes of supplies, not including vehicles, in the Falklands Conflict.[118] Such conspicuous operational consumption would be a major concern for the Forces as the ammunition budget declined more than 20 per cent 1990–2011, despite being a constant US focus for improvement.[119] Sealift was partly addressed by the radical step of establishing a 'special shipping company,' Kosoku Marine Transport, with two ferries, the fast *Nacchan World* (Hokkaido), and slow *Hakuo* (Osaka), used commercially and for JSDF exercises and contingencies, crewed ultimately by twenty-one MSDF reservists, the first post-war civilian naval 'operational reserves.'[120]

DEFENDERS OF JAPAN PRESENT AND FUTURE

Civilians Serving

Civilians have always actively engaged in Japan's defence, and, as Chapter One demonstrated, Japanese defenders were all civilian until JSDF 'special civil servants' assumed responsibilities. This book cannot provide extensive detail for all non-JSDF personnel, particularly the broad work of police and coast guards. The JCG in particular being a national, armed security force of over 14,000 personnel, with sixty-six large patrol vessels and eighty-five aircraft, has played a frontline role in Japanese maritime security and counter-terrorism, and is the only service to have engaged in combat. JCG assertion of its 'new fighting power' (*aratana senryoku*), to deal with DPRK vessels, prompted Richard Samuels to refer to it as a 'fourth branch of the Japanese military', but this represents neither its role nor capabilities.[121] The JCG has supported the JSDF, but the Forces primarily support the Coast Guard in their legal enforcement and safety roles. Other than the JCG, JSDF reservists, MOD officials, and intelligence personnel deserve particular attention.

Reserves

Within the JSDF, only the GSDF initially organised reserves, and with former regular personnel as casualty replacements, many apparently wondered why the reserves existed, and the Forces devoted little attention and resources to them during the Cold War.[122] GSDF reserves were formed into Regular Reserves (*yobijieikan*), Ready Reserves (*sokuōyobijiekan*) from 1998, and Candidate Reserves (*yobijiekanhō*) from 2002, Ready and Regular being retired JSDF personnel with reserve liabilities. Ready Reserves volunteer for enhanced training and service liabilities, thereby providing a rapid-deployment capability, but despite an establishment of over 8,000, the actual serving total declined from 6,201 in 2005 to 4,330 in 2018. Similarly, Candidates are volunteer-reservists, many with prized civilian skills (foreign languages, medical, technical) without call-up liability but able to volunteer for service, but despite an establishment of 4,600, less than half the positions are usually filled.[123] 160 Ready and Candidate Reservists served in the response to the 2016 Kumamoto earthquake, their second such mobilisation, but in contrast to 2011 mobilisation was limited to local personnel, ensuring a high response rate and useful local knowledge within regular GSDF units.[124] Twenty-one equivalent MSDF transport reservists, recruited from 2017, faced seamen's union opposition.[125]

During 'Three Arrows' contingency planning in 1963, proposals were aired for forming Local Defense Corps (*Kyōdobōeitai*), air-raid precaution and firefighting units attached to JSDF and civil authorities, but once exposed they rapidly evaporated.[126] Veteran LDP politicians' suggestions for expending Cold War reserves were dismissed as delusions, the GSDF in 1980 resorting only to providing reservists with badges, symbolising completing qualification training, and consistently provided obsolete training equipment.[127] The GSDF developed reserves due to personnel cuts while facing potentially increased contingency duties, and reserves are prohibited from overseas despatch or compulsory mobilisation, limiting their utility.[128] Ishiba Shigeru regretted that in 2006 there were only two retired JSDF Diet members, Nakatani Gen (GSDF, Lieutenant) and Tamura Hideaki (ASDF, Lieutenant-General), compounding politicians' limited grasp of defence issues and highlighting the civilian-military gap.[129]

Officials

JSDF performance has been influenced by limited civilian-staff support. JDA personnel declined to 1994 (18,043), rising thereafter (23,262 in 2007), with the JDA/MOD having a uniformed-civilian personnel ratio of 11.7 to one in 2006–07 compared to 3.4 to one for Australia, reflecting long-term civilian investment deficiencies.[130] Japan's regular Forces in 1990 had just under 250,000 personnel, and those of Britain 306,000, admittedly with much larger reserve forces, and yet UK MOD civilian personnel outnumbered the JDA more than four to one. By 2010, JSDF/MOD numbers had scarcely altered, while UK forces were below 180,000, supported by 73,000 MOD personnel, an approximate 2.5 to one ratio.[131] This civilian-military imbalance is accentuated by the small MOFA establishment, despite diplomats having played key roles in JSDF-US military relations and ODO. MOD/MOFA personnel became overloaded during major events, issues, or scandals, such as the 2015 NSL process when staff were evidently suffering from stress and fatigue, demonstrating insufficient spare capacity for contingencies. In ODO, MOD and MOFA staff significantly boosted Force capability, preparing facilities, liaising, and bridging communication divides. There are also significant questions of physical and mental health issues, and legal requirement to prevent 'death from overwork,' *karoshi*, a significant problem in Japanese employment. The NSC Secretariat established issue groups divided from daily duties, and it appears that the MOD requires an equivalent institutional innovation, particularly when dealing with intelligence matters requiring high-volume, deep-analysis work detached from daily process.

Intelligence

Intelligence gathering has been a longstanding JSDF weakness despite each Force having extensive signals intelligence (SIGINT) experience and specialist units serving respective staff G2 offices, but with limited intelligence gathering capability, access to US intelligence, and independent analysis capacity. Ebata Kensuke conjectured in 2004 that Japan's intelligence-dependency placed it on the level of Denmark, an eager consumer of 'ready packaged' US analyses.[132] There have been significant efforts to remedy such faults, such as the GSDF-established Military Intelligence Command (MIC *Chuōjōhōtai*) from 2007, with its first official human intelligence (HUMINT) unit, the Local Intelligence Unit (*Genchijōhōtai*), and Intelligence School (*Jōhōkyōikubu*), and from 2010 intelligence officer specialists.[133] Retired USN Pacific Fleet director of intelligence Captain James Fanell praised JSDF SIGINT and maritime 'fine-grain intelligence that our forces might otherwise not collect.'[134] Richard Samuels details how the JSDF Intelligence Security Command (*Jieitaijōhō hozentai*) formed in 2009 as a joint counter-intelligence force, with 1,000 personnel directly under the Defense Minister, joint cells within each GSDF regional army, to prevent data leaks and espionage, and to bar the Forces spying upon citizens as had occurred in 2003, civilian control being integral to intelligence in Japan.[135]

The largest intelligence division with 2400 personnel reporting to the JSO is the Defense Intelligence Headquarters (DIH *Jōhōhonbu*), established in 1997, with particular SIGINT responsibilities.[136] JSDF 'military information gathering' duties 'gather, sort, and analyze military radio waves [...] reaching Japan from abroad.'[137] The Force Staff Offices also have direct pipelines from partner US forces, particularly MSDF-USN providing early warning of the 1998 Taepodong launch and 2001 DPRK spy ship incidents. The ASDF improved its ISR capabilities by acquiring Global Hawk UAV 'drone' capability (from 2020), their great range significantly augmenting intelligence-gathering, particularly as satellites are civilian controlled, and derived intelligence thereby filtered.[138] Increased costs and inability to provide 'real-time' moving-target tracking, such as shipping in the East China Sea, prompted Diet criticism that Japan invested in prestigious rather than efficacious systems.[139] The ASDF plans to improve F-15J and F-2 ISR capabilities, ensuring the Force is 'networked' with the F-35 and most MSDF operational units.

The main intelligence institutions are civilian (NPA, MSA/JCG, MOFA, Ministry of Justice), under nominal Cabinet Secretariat management, without equivalents of overseas Intelligence/Security/Secret Services. Japan particularly lacks African and Middle Eastern capabilities, civilian universities and research institutes notably reluctant to contribute to military intelligence, unlike in the UK, Australia, and France.[140] Japan's intelligence capabilities have been affected by what Kotani Ken has described as 'rampant sectionalism' within ministries/agencies, with 'stovepipe-silo' approaches precluding sharing, compounded by poor information security.[141] Fukuyama Takashi details JDA/MOD-MOFA sectional battles over intelligence sources, content, and analysis, and the confusion and conflicted loyalties for JSDF defence attachés within embassies, echoed by Tsukamoto Katsuichi who primarily identified the MOD Internal Bureau's 'capability ceiling' and insufficient funds and personnel for intelligence analysis inside the MOD and within civilian agencies as debilitating issues.[142]

Many civilian-managed intelligence functions counter North Korean, Russian and Chinese cyber threats, but the MOD also established the Defense Information Infrastructure (DII) and Command, Control, Communications and Computers (C4) System Command in 2008.[143] The civilian response was led by the NPA and Cabinet Office, with the 2005 establishment of the Information Security Policy Council (ISPC) and National Information Security Center (NISC) producing the First National Strategy on Information Security in 2006.[144] The JDA recruited civilian specialists for cyber-security, which was made more urgent by multiple cyber attacks upon MOD, NPA, and defence-contractor systems, but the first recognition of operational imperative came with the 'Six Pillars of Comprehensive Defense Against Cyber Attacks' (*Saibākōgekitaisho 6honchū*) placement of JSDF efforts within government systems.[145] The 2013 ISPC Strategy recognised cyberspace as 'a new "domain" [...] in which a variety of activities, such as intelligence, offence and defense, are carried out' by the JSDF, consolidated within the 2018 NDPG.[146] The Cyber Defense Unit (CDU) was established within a comprehensive whole-of-government Basic Act on Cybersecurity 2014 and 2015 Cybersecurity Strategy.[147] As Kallendar and Hughes state, this represented a centralisation and securitization of cyber security, JSDF development of doctrines and units 'indicating the broader militarization of cyberdefense and its potential stretching into formerly exclusive civilian domains across Japanese

DEFENDERS OF JAPAN PRESENT AND FUTURE

society.'[148] This has become embedded within international security relations, through JSDF-USFJ and broader bilateral strategic cooperation, and with institutional partners, such as the EU and NATO, and member states.[149] It could be said that Japan has better cyber-security partnerships than any other security domain, but sources suggest that fragmented institutional cyber-security approaches have complicated cooperation. It is unclear what degree the JSDF will undertake offensive cyber-retaliation but this would be the logical extension of strategy and defence policies into the cyber domain.

Space was also once solely a civilian, technical responsibility, which gradually developed a significant defence-intelligence-security role. The core Cabinet Intelligence Research Office (CIRO) (*Naikakujōhō chōsashitsu*) was established in 1986, with a Director of Cabinet Intelligence (DCI) from 1997, while the Cabinet Information Center (1996) and Cabinet Satellite Intelligence Center (CSIC *Naikakueiseijōhō sentaa*; 2001) consolidated the Cabinet Office coordination role, with NPA officials in leading roles.[150] CIRO and CSIC are particularly important given traditional dependence upon US intelligence, but Richard Samuels relates how 'silo' limitations even extended to the highest levels, with CIRO Director intelligence briefings extending no further than the prime minister and chief cabinet secretary.[151] Space utilisation for intelligence was complicated by the 1969 Diet resolution promoting 'non-military usage of space,' so that in 1991, Japan had no intelligence satellites and only ad hoc US data access, Suzuki Kazuto stating the JSDF became starkly aware of their limitations when monitoring DPRK shipping and missile sites.[152] Richard Samuels details how the Taepodong launch prompted a rush to acquire satellite capabilities, provided by a Mitsubishi Electric in-house design, launching four intelligence satellites (2003–07) and partially abandoning 'non-military space principles' in 2008.[153]

The military element became tangible with the May 2020 establishment of the ASDF Space Operations Squadron (*uchūsakusentai*). Initially only 20 personnel were tasked with ensuring Japanese satellite security, particularly with Chinese anti-satellite (ASAT) capabilities from 2007, complementing the Joint Staff's C4 Systems Department 'Space Domain Planning Section' and MOD space situational awareness (SSA) system.[154] Despite *kantei* coordination there was 'no system to integrate intelligence collected by each agency/ministry at the PM's Official Residence,' the Cabinet Secretariat having limited access until the NSC Secretariat somewhat centralised intelligence collection in 2014.[155] The operational satellite 'fleet' is eight (2020), five synthetic-aperture radar (SAR) and three optical, with an approximate five-year lifespan, costs reduced by series production and H-2A rocket reliability.[156] Civilian technological effects upon capabilities are evident, yet low-cost, and long-term investment in analysis and management systems is vital for augmenting JSDF capabilities and national security, a point often lost in procurement issues.

Technology Procurement

Defence Procurement

Japan has a chequered defence procurement history, with limited scope for competitive tendering, and subcontracting by large corporations (*Ōtekigyō*) to small-medium-sized (*Chūshōkigyō*) partners resulting in extensive contract dependency, such as 1,136 subcontractors for the F-15J.[157] *Kokusanka* domestic production prioritisation entailed drip-fed incremental orders prioritising corporate sustenance, but these were matched by substantial direct-imports and licensed-production agreements. Controversies and alliance contentions have mainly surrounded jet-fighter procurement, while missile and artillery technologies have been amicably imported or licensed. Domestic technology development has produced innovative and effective systems for the JSDF, but for an electronics superpower the lack of application to providing compatible communications systems between the Forces throughout their history is an outstanding anomaly that indicates an abdication of responsibility by politicians, officials, and the Forces. The constant focus of technology procurement has been high-profile combat systems. The MOF-MITI supported FSX/F-2 project suffered from political machinations and nationalism overriding security, with Michael Chinworth describing only the US contractor Lockheed-Martin as content.[158] After the F-1 debacle the ASDF demanded twin-engine safety, domestic or US design with 'open black-box' development rights.[159] The single-engine F-2 was late, over-budget, and neither original nor American. Cost-related limited procurement had been exacerbated by twelve F-2s written-off in the 2011 tsunami, and six more rebuilt at greater-than-original cost.[160] The F-2 has advanced Actively-Electronically Scanned Radar (AESA) and is highly capable, but it wasn't what the ASDF requested.[161]

In November 2011, the MOD chose the F-35A as the next-generation interim fighter. With increasing scramble rates, and fatigue-limited F-4EJ, the ASDF wanted the unavailable and painfully expensive F-22 Raptor.[162] The post-*Tomodachi* decision rendered non-US options untenable for the DPJ

Noda government, the MOD uniquely justifying the procurement process in seven pages of the defence white paper.[163] The F-35A was highly evaluated against US F/A-18E/F and F-15FX, and European Rafale and Typhoon for stealth and 'network centric capabilities,' although the ASDF only belatedly upgraded to Link-16, suggesting low priority status. The F-35A was the only aircraft not assessed for flight characteristics, and was praised for utilising the USAF boom in-flight refuelling system despite the RAF/USN drogue-probe system being optimal for fighters.[164] The F-35A, in spite of being marketed as possessing near-F-22 air-combat capabilities, Gen. Michael Hostage, USAF Air Combat Command, stated 'F-35 is not built as an air superiority platform. It needs the F-22,' with diplomats regretting that the F-35A was 'oversold.'[165] The F-35A was the only single-engine aircraft evaluated, a leaked test pilot report describing its inability to engage, escape from, or defend against a veteran F-16 in exercises.[166]

The replacement of 100 older F-15J was controversially decided in 2018 to be 63 F-35A conventional and 42 F-35B short-take-off-vertical-landing (STOVL) fighters, the latter operating from modified MSDF *Izumi*-class destroyer-helicopter-carriers. The 'Japanese carrier' issue distracted attention from whether this F-15J replacement plan would augment or degrade ASDF air-defence capabilities.[167] Mitsubishi HI closely cooperated with the MOD Technical Research and Development Institute (TRDI) and successor Acquisition, Technology and Logistics Agency (ATLA), producing ATD-X-2 'next generation aircraft' that flew in April 2016.[168] The Advanced Technology Demonstrator, Experimental-2 *Shin-shin* was a technology-demonstrator, but the 'Future Fighter-F-X,' from December 2019, was larger and more obviously F-22-influenced.[169] The Medium Term Defense Program (FY2014-FY2018) raised 'the possibility of international joint development of an aircraft to replace the F-2,' with Lockheed-Martin selected as main partner in December 2020.[170] Project feasibility depends upon whether Japan requires 'high-end' or 'lower-end' fighters or a mix, and the research and development (R&D) investment it is willing to make.[171]

Japan's defence-related R&D constituted just 4.5 per cent of the research budget in 1989, compared to 68.6 per cent in the US and 50.3 per cent in the UK.[172] The General Guidelines for Science and Technology Policy of 1986 (revised 1992) avoided defence-related research, yet the 1995 Science and Technology Basic Law (*Kagakugijutsukihon-hō*) raised 'a suspicion of future Japanese military adventures,' unrealised within the 2013 Science, Technology, and Information (STI) Strategy.[173] Limited R&D defence-focus stemmed from broader anti-war sentiments within the Science Council of Japan (SCJ) opposing government suggestions of defence-related research in universities and research institutes beyond JSDF-MOD personnel in graduate programmes.[174]

Defence Exports

On 1 April 2014, the government replaced the 'Three Principles of Arms Exports' (1967/1976), with the 'Three Principles of Defense Equipment Transfer,' twenty-one amendments and exceptions having eroded limitations 'while convincing domestic opposition factions and regional countries that policy amendment was necessary and non-threatening.' With the last 2011 Noda revision 'the arms transfer ban lost its force and was waiting for the last push,' permitting exports 'contributing to peace and promoting cooperation [...] to improve the performance of defense equipment and to deal with rising costs of equipment by participating in international joint development and production projects,' mediating between pacifist norms, liberal-international strategy, and cost reduction aims.[175] Bans were retained for states breaching or in conflict with UNSC resolutions and remained very restrictive, but prioritised Japanese security over prevention of harm.[176] TRDI/ATLA and MSDF cooperated with Augusta-Westland (later Leonardo) on MCH-101 minesweeping-helicopter technology, the company discovering that utilising innovations on other projects was prohibited, 'an invisible legal wall' obstructing 'export' of intangible defence technology, including mailing data within Japan to non-Japanese.[177] This highlighted complications for engaging with Japan's partners in technology programmes.

Post-2014 expectations that Japan would suddenly become a major defence technology exporter, mirroring car exports, did not eventuate, despite sustained efforts to sell submarines to Australia and maritime patrol aircraft to Britain, seemingly through lacking the project-export skills of competitors.[178] Japan did develop into a major 'security exporter,' embracing cyber, fire, maritime, and aviation safety and security services, becoming global 'number four' in 2017.[179] The first post-revision defence exports were missile components for Qatar, and ex-JSDF unarmed aircraft and ships for New Zealand, Philippines, and Indonesia.[180] In 2014, the MOD also first participated in the EUROSATORY, the defence trade fair in Paris, an NHK documentary showing staff eager to study Israeli drone technologies.[181] Export challenges became apparent with the submarine effort and tortuous attempts to sell unarmed

US-2 flying-boats to India.[182] Opportunities for synergies arose by marrying Japan's AAM-4 radar and European Meteor body-propulsion, potentially enhancing performance and (unlike AAM-4) fitting inside the F-35A weapons-bay.[183] Defence exports for strategic engagement buttressed diplomatic and military efforts in partnership building.

Overseas and Back

The Koizumi administration responded rapidly in support of Washington after the terror attacks of 9/11, initially with rhetorical flourishes, within the context of East Asian security and planned Pentagon cuts, but consolidated by JSDF deployments. Shinoda Tomohito illustrated how Koizumi acted with startling alacrity 'inspired largely by lessons Japan had learned during the 1990s.'[184] JSDF despatches to the Middle East and Indian Ocean seemingly became 'normal,' even while publicly recognised as abnormal. Nabers, Shinoda, and Hughes illustrate how Koizumi did not so much mediate between domestic and foreign pressures as navigate a new, direct course with little reference to public opinion, utilising the reformed, centralised powers of the PMO *kantei*, and Cabinet Secretariat (*Naikakukanbō*, CAS).[185] JSDF Indian Ocean, East Timor, and Iraq ODO rushed through cabinet and Diet despite public opposition, enabled by Koizumi's popularity and proven JSDF capability, Hughes asserting that extending JSDF 'operational reach' in the 1990s contributed to Japanese 'remilitarisation.'[186] This 'remilitarisation' thesis may seem easily refutable, but as with Tony Blair's UK foreign policy 'militarisation,' Japan's policy responses seemingly made JSDF utilisation the default measure, escalating commitments, expectations, and risks. Shinoda Tomohito has demonstrated the legal and policy progression from the 1992 IPCL to Iraq.[187] Takao Yasuo infers that post-1992 ODO were socio-politically distinct from post-9/11 despatches, but considering initial IPCL-UNTAC opposition and subsequent ODO 'normalisation,' the 'successor' thesis appears valid.[188]

Threats of terrorism and Koizumi's popularity allowed the government to rapidly formulate and pass previously controversial contingency legislation, terrorism 'thus achieved what the communist threat never could.'[189] The 2001 Anti-Terrorism Special Measures Law was passed within three days, and MSDF units were deployed rapidly as tangible demonstration of alliance solidarity. However, the Indian Ocean refuelling mission, an extension of the alliance naval relationship, was justified by Tokyo as a measure 'to ensure the peace and security of the international community,' whereas Washington placed it within US defence and the War on Terrorism, illustrating lingering legal, constitutional, and normative constraints.[190] JSDF Afghan operations were raised, and several 'insiders' relate intense discussions often favouring despatch, but the balance of risks and benefits precluded deployment until Iraq assumed hazardously combative characteristics, recreated in Afghanistan, thereby concluding discussions.

Indian Ocean

The Indian Ocean mission involved MSDF vessels refuelling warships of eleven navies in addition to transporting humanitarian relief equipment for Afghanistan.[191] Up to October 2007, approximately 480,000 kl of oil, as well as aviation fuel, water, and stores were provided, proving naturally popular with recipient navies.[192] The operation was discontinued, then resumed with restrictions from January 2008 due to opposition criticism of supporting US offensive actions.[193] Despite MSDF portrayals within the context of Proliferation Security Initiative (PSI) and counter-terrorism, there were no Japanese interdiction-boarding missions, PSI being primarily a JCG responsibility. 'Lead' vessels were logistical AOE/AOR, destroyers merely escorts for an obtuse mission.[194] MOFA indicated that terrorist arms and drug money passed through Karachi port, implying that funding would have been better spent on Pakistani law enforcement.[195] The mission concluded in 2010 under the DPJ (Ozawa Ichirō being a particular critic) without operational evaluation, having been launched and terminated due to political posturing rather than security efficacy.

Iraq

JSDF operations in Iraq 2003–09 were naturally controversial, with a widespread view that Prime Minister Koizumi forced the deployment despite major opposition, but, as Vosse and Midford demonstrate, polling data illustrates the difficulty of divining fluctuating public opinions.[196] Daniel Kliman suggests that JDA-DG Ishiba Shigeru envisaged significant JSDF Iraq War minesweeping and medical support roles, discounted due to risk, with choreographed *kantei* and White House preparations resulting in Iraq despatch that would ensure concomitant US commitment to Japanese and Korean security amid growing DPRK threats.[197] Koizumi referenced the constitution preface to emphasise the legitimacy of the Iraq despatch law, emphasising that 'all peoples of the world have the right to live in peace, free from fear and want [...] We, the Japanese people, pledge our national honor to accomplish these high ideals and purposes with all our resources,' using an appeal to high ideals to overcome principled objections based upon Article 9, high ideals being thereby harnessed to realist regional balance of power considerations to negate pacifist sentiment.[198] Such enraged sentiment enabled unique operational insight, as a journalist and an opposition politician subsequently leaked the normally barely revealed despatch histories of the mission.[199]

The July 2003 Iraq Special Measures Law enabled headquarter personnel to be deployed on 19 December, followed by thirty advance party troops on 9 January 2004.[200] The Japanese Iraq Reconstruction and Support Group (IRSG) of just under 600 GSDF troops operated in the Samawah area from February 2004 to July 2006, with MSDF logistics and transport forces, and an ASDF C-130H detachment running Kuwait-Baghdad and northern shuttle-flights until 2009 (when it was declared unconstitutional by the Nagoya High Court).[201] The IRSG arrival in Kuwait was rather confusing for USAF officers expecting an ASDF or JAL aircraft, as was seeing the GSDF emerge from a Phuket Air 747 due to risks for Japanese aircraft and the prohibitive costs quoted.[202] The contrast between the overlapping East Timor and Iraq missions was apparent, for although the Timor mission had the largest JSDF UN-PKO security profile it was dwarfed by IRSG force protection, despite operational roles resembling UN-PSO. In Iraq, the additional security provided by Dutch, Australian, and British forces was generally interpreted as mollycoddling by partners, rather than ODO-defence diplomacy and partnership cooperation, despite GSDF assertions of 'self-defence.' The initial JSDF coalition peace support operation raised issues of procedure, legality, and both civil-military and military-military cooperation. Aoi Chiyuki details how Dutch-Japanese cooperation was compromised by limited GSDF autonomy and 'situational awareness' due to poor intelligence, resulting in dependence on the Dutch, such 'lopsidedness was foreseeable, particularly given Japan's lack of experience in expeditionary missions.'[203] The Dutch, and Australians, were more capable of 'plugging-in' to US-UK plans than Japan, due to extensive coalition operational experience through NATO and ANZUS institutional frameworks.

A RAND study for the UK indicated that qualitative effects of information sharing in military operations varied due to top-down access-integration and bottom-up local network exploitation and collaboration. IRSG received intelligence seemingly below partners' levels, and commanders had less flexibility to modify operations and develop local intelligence sources.[204] Contingents gained experience and developed competence, but basic limitations upon intelligence, command and control, and collaboration remained, not helped by three-month troop rotations (six months for headquarter and support personnel) hindering lessons-learned.[205] IRSG did not fully integrate with the Multinational Force (MNF) command in Iraq, including in provincial CIMIC meetings, so despite command coordination this entailed ad hoc reliance upon partners.[206]

Dutch-Japanese cooperation has been described as 'accidental neighbours,' but van der Meulen and Kawano illustrate differences of motivations and operational modes, while Aoi describes Dutch pursuit of Japan for CIMIC-related funding as the Dutch self-envisaged robust security primacy while recovering from the 1995 Srebrenica shock.[207] The Japanese naturally focused upon humanitarian and human security-related duties, based upon PKO and HA/DR legacies, and also rejected security enforcement roles while embracing strong and stable 'allies,' both nations shying away from local 'authority' over Samawah's civil communities. Dutch commanders had the ability and confidence to interpret national orders, thereby gradually conducting reconstruction work beyond their mandate, contrasting with inflexible Japanese command and control structures, partly driven by 'civilian control' norms, and partly by the 'constitutional CSD curse,' despite collective defence being the JSDF ODO functional norm.[208]

The JSDF eventual coordinated defence information, sharing their local CIMIC community network and Dutch mortar-locating radar, while mainly focusing upon IRSG self-defence.[209] Aoi suggests the JSDF learned from Dutch-practice based CIMIC models, despite enduring problems with inflexible command and control, restrictive ROE, and the CSD issue, but also language limitations, even in English.[210] For the first time JSDF units were directly responsible for ODA projects, which received consistent public support, even when attacks upon the IRSG reduced positive mission sentiment.[211] The almost $5 billion ODA investment indicates the importance attached, and Yamaguchi Noboru details the intricate planning dedicated to integrating civilians into GSDF-led ODA projects.[212] The tangible effects were medical services that reduced neo-natal fatalities to one-third of the previous levels, and thirty-six schools repaired or constructed by the 5,600 Japanese troops that rotated through Iraq.[213] Surprisingly, CIMIC-project Japanese-Dutch competition emerged, whereby each attempted local 'hearts and minds' projects, with competition degrading cooperation and souring relations until

2005, when British and Australian troops replaced the Dutch.[214] There were thirteen attacks on the IRSG base causing slight damage but no casualties, all non-medical personnel being armed and trained on short ranges replicating close-quarters combat.[215] The GSDF created an IRSG pre-despatch operational handbook and constructed a replica 'mini-Samawah' training area in Japan, with riots, IEDs, and armed attacks, a significant innovation but standard procedure for many militaries.[216]

The leadership of Colonels Banshō and Satō were sources of GSDF pride, both having been 'recycled' through UN-PKO, demonstrating ODO professional career development. At the same time, zero JSDF fatalities was vital for the cabinet, despite four Japanese civilians being murdered pre-mid-deployment (one a former GSDF Airborne member), and five held hostage until the JSDF withdrew, though they were soon released. Attacks upon the IRSG were reported at the time, analysed by NHK reporter Degawa Nobuhisa in 2008, and repeated during the 2015 NSL controversies, yet were treated as revelations during the 2017 South Sudan 'morning report' scandal.[217] Despite Vosse and Midford's research, Kuroki Masanori discovered that perceptions of the JSDF, rather than the mission, degraded slightly among liberals uncomfortable with US-led wars, but also among conservatives, possibly due to absence of 'heroic acts.'[218] The official portrayal was positive, with Colonel '*hige no Sato*' and 'Kijima-couple' GSDF 'despatchees' portrayed as ODO models.[219] The tales of twenty-nine post-mission suicides (2004–14) indicate ODO stresses and the scale of mental health care required of the MOD, but the official histories detail major efforts to relieve tension through 'Dubai breaks,' counselling, family support, and other measures.[220]

Anti-Piracy

The anti-piracy mission in the Gulf of Aden from 2009 has been the longest MSDF ODO and one of the most innovative, working jointly with the GSDF and JCG law-enforcement officers, and establishing Japan's first permanent overseas facility in Djibouti, with MSDF officers holding post-war Japan's first multinational operational combined task force (CTF) command. The deployment can be traced to an upsurge in piracy against Japanese vessels in Asia, *Tenyu* (1998) becoming notorious for the disappearance of her crew, and *Alondra Rainbow* (1999) for the crew being set adrift, in John Bradford's term 'humanizing and "Japanizing" the impact of piracy.'[221] This prompted Japan's emergence as a civil maritime security innovator, with the Ministry of Transport leading establishment of the Regional Cooperation Agreement on

Combating Piracy and Armed Robbery (ReCAAP) to channel anti-piracy ODA.[222] Gradually, piracy reduced in East Asia only to rise in the Gulf of Aden, resulting in the 2009 UN Contact Group on Piracy off the Coast of Somalia (CGPCS) for coordinating countermeasures.[223] Japan joined as an 'independent deployer,' rather than working from within the EU's Operation ATALANTA established in December 2008 to protect World Food Program (WFP) humanitarian assistance vessels, the African Union Mission in Somalia (AMISOM), or NATO's Operation OCEAN SHIELD to avoid legal complications.[224]

Concerning whether naval or coastguard units should deploy, JCG despatch was somewhat disingenuously considered difficult 'not only because of legal aspects, but also the distance to the area of activities and the weapons that pirates use.'[225] The legal aspects were equally cumbersome, and the JCG had escorted radioactive fuel-recycling vessels between Japan and Europe with large, robustly-armed ships. The 'international trend that EU, NATO and other countries have dispatched warships' was the clinching argument, despite Turkey contributing coastguard vessels, MSDF prime qualifications being more ships with extensive aviation and C3 facilities that could be spared from other duties.[226] From June 2009, two Deployment Air Force for Counter-Piracy Enforcement (DAPE) P-3C supported *JS-Sazanami* and *Samidare*, which had patrolled from March, initially operating from US Camp Lemonnier at Djibouti's airport, until from July 2011 the Japanese Facility for Counter-Piracy Mission was established adjacent to the US base.[227] The MSDF and GSDF CRF guards established Japan's first standing overseas facility and second joint-unit operation to protect Japanese interests and trade.[228]

John Bradford illustrates the vital nature of the Malacca Straits to Japan's economy for energy resources motivating the securitization of South-East Asia piracy, while the same could not be said of the Gulf of Aden.[229] Japan developed its mission as part of broader engagement, moving away from bilateral security to multilateral-multi-institutional engagement with national characteristics.[230] Wilhelm Vosse demonstrates that through a practical marine trade security measure, Japan has been able to train and operate with the EU, NATO, and others, providing unparalleled opportunities for functional engagement with China, Korea, and Russia despite troubled bilateral relations.[231] From 2013 Japan joined the Combined Maritime Forces (CMF) CTF-151, with the US, UK, Korea, and Singapore, deepening coordination and integration, including for the 2014 detention of a suspected pirate vessel.[232] MSDF ships provided 'direct escort' or 'zone defence' responding to threats, P-3Cs contributing communication links and broader coverage. Embarked helicopters expanded patrol range and intervention speed, either for the Special Boarding Unit (*tokubetsukeibitai*) formed after the 2001 spy ship incident, or for eight JCG personnel who possess sole powers of arrest and detention, similar to US and Dutch naval-coastguard integration. The Forces were initially deployed under Article 82, SDF Law, thus separating JSDF and JCG despatches, protecting only Japanese ships and nationals, thereby limiting coalition cooperation, a 2009 Anti-Piracy Measures Law enabling unified and simplified cooperation.[233]

The total personnel comprised approximately 400 ships' crews, 170 DAPE crew and other base personnel, a CTF-151 headquarters cell (ten-twenty), and eight JCG officers, supported by visiting ASDF C-130H. The deployment was reduced to one destroyer from December 2016, justified by reduced threat perception, but also resource limitations.[234] The 'escort pool' required two deployed escorts, two working-up and transiting, another pair undergoing post-mission refit, and a further pair on stand-by, therefore, following 2008 reforms, two four-ship flotillas could be unavailable for other duties. With four-eight AEGIS destroyers on similar BMD-pool rotations, and DDH too expensive for anti-piracy operations, this left even the MSDF with a resource dilemma. Rear-Admiral Itō Hiroshi assumed command of CTF-151 for two months from May 2015, repeated in 2017 with Rear-Admiral Fukuda Tatsuya, based with the USN in Bahrain, thereby combining multilateral and MSDF-USN bilateral relations.[235] True to cautious form, the MOD stressed that the commander coordinated rather than commanded foreign naval vessels, calming fears of Japan engaging in collective security.[236] Cooperation between Japan, NATO, and the EU greatly expanded from 2014, as the 'declining number of maritime piracy incidences opened opportunities to conduct more joint military exercises and navigation maneuvers at sea.'[237] With zero Gulf of Aden piracy incidents in 2015, but those in South-East Asia rising to 147, the mission transitioned to a low-intensity reassurance operation providing training and cooperation opportunities, but with no 'shift eastwards' to South-East Asia indicating the specific nature of the Japanese deployment.[238] Based on a May 2014 Japan-NATO agreement, an MSDF destroyer, P-3C aircraft, and Danish naval 'suspect' vessel conducted boarding inspection exercises that illustrated the mission's value for functional engagement with partners.[239] The MOD despatched Lt-Colonel Kurita as an adviser to NATO Special Representative for Women, Peace and Security from December 2014 to deepen ties.[240] In 2015, Japan, together with other non-NATO states, joined NATO's CMX-15 crisis management exercise, and from

May 2018 had its Brussels Embassy upgraded to act also as the Japan Mission to NATO, for extended partnership building.²⁴¹

The Djibouti facility supported the UNMISS UN-PKO in South Sudan with extensive independent human security initiatives, becoming the hub for JSDF South Sudan rescue efforts.²⁴² There was speculation of another 'scramble for Africa,' pitting Japanese and Chinese public-private geo-political-commercial competing interests through the proxy of UN-PKO, but with 2017 UNMISS withdrawal, JSDF African grand strategy evaporated, limited to Djibouti and UN-PKO training courses.²⁴³ The anti-piracy mission could be referred to as Japan's first Ocean Peacekeeping Operation (OPKO), combining national strategy with 'Common Heritage of Mankind' concepts within international legal respect for maritime commons.²⁴⁴ Based upon the scale of piracy from 2016, and reduction in UN-PKO activity, it appears the Djibouti mission is an expensive defence engagement exercise, with the navy as JSDF ODO leaders.

Banda-Aceh

The despatch to Banda-Aceh in response to the 26 December 2004 tsunami was the much publicised first joint JSDF ODO, but the three Forces operated largely independently.²⁴⁵ Less recognised were three MSDF warships providing disaster relief in Phuket, Thailand, within days of the tsunami.²⁴⁶ The Aceh effort was considerable, Ōsumi-class *JS-Kunisaki* transporting vehicles and helicopters and providing a 'sea-base,' MSDF LCAC aiding coastal communities, with GSDF and ASDF providing medical and relief services.²⁴⁷ The response was not rapid, survey teams leaving Japan on 4 January 2005, with the first GSDF medical teams arriving on 16 January by ASDF C-130H, and *Kunisaki* and AOE *Tokiwa* arriving four weeks after the tsunami.²⁴⁸ Transport, emergency medical, and vaccination activities constituted the core mission, which concluded in March with a fine reputation, but Lam Peng Er criticised longer-term peace, recovery, and stabilisation missions indicating Japan's 'short attention span.'²⁴⁹ As in previous missions, there was little evidence of Japanese stabilisation doctrine or strategic approach, but within five years it would appear that the JSDF and the 'whole of government' had learned relevant lessons.

Haiti

The Force response to the devastating earthquake that struck Haiti on 13 January 2010, killing over 170,000 people, was based upon previous HA/

DR and yet proved highly innovative. A survey team was despatched within twenty-four hours, and an ASDF C-130H on exercise in the US was diverted, arriving in Haiti on 20 January with the GSDF medical assistance advance party, which commenced medical duties 21 January. A headquarters and coordination office was formed (civ-mil, Japanese-Haitian) for 104 medical personnel supported by sixty-two mainly ASDF logisticians.[250] Despatch speed compared favourably to Honduras and Banda-Aceh, as did the smooth combined-multi-agency working, the first JSDF operation within an existing UN-PKO (MINUSTAH) area, and uniquely the emergency response rather than withdrawing transformed into a sustained UN contribution.[251] This was not 'Honduras-model' light, but 'UNTAC-model' heavy-engineering plus large medical effort, with 150 vehicles, and 350 personnel with arms, for survey team members grasped the fragile security situation.[252] The ability to rapidly despatch troops for MINUSTAH was based, as Aoi Chiyuki details, upon the CRF centralising preparations and coordination, relieving the burden from Regional Army and Ground Staff Office (GSO) personnel.[253] Heavy lift was provided by two MSDF vessels, ASDF C-130H, B-747, and the initial KC-767 ODO airlift, as well as commercial Antonov lease.

This mission saw GSDF rebuilding and repair efforts in constant demand.[254] This comfortably fitted Japan's liberal-internationalist human security approaches, JSDF HA/DR-Peace Support profiles, and JSDF self-portrayal as noble, fraternal, near-heroic 'three-K' practitioners (*kiken, kitanai, kitsui*: dangerous, dirty, demanding). Even JSDF opponents could support the Haiti mission, with Prime Minister Hatoyama visiting personnel and families prior to departure, and Sado Akihiro demonstrating that public opinion was extremely supportive, with less than 2 per cent opposing participation.[255] This was the first operation launched after the 2007 establishment of the GSDF Japan Peacekeeping Training and Research Center as part of the measures to professionalise JSDF ODO 'core' rather than 'miscellaneous' duties, accompanying establishment of the MOD. The mission was withdrawn by February 2013, a joint JSDF-JICA civilian engineering education 'Kizuna Project' donating equipment.[256] Haiti, far from core Japanese security concerns, solely among JSDF ODO achieved a 'whole of government' strategic and tactical approach with the Forces as exemplary liberal-international actors, who again demonstrated technical skills and Force culture much admired during domestic HA/DR. Much of this achievement would be squandered by politicians during the South Sudan mission.

South Sudan

One reason for the Haiti withdrawal was the burden of maintaining a distant and 'heavy' mission while GSDF engineering units were stretched due to the South Sudan mission, and domestic demands following the 2011 tsunami. The UN Mission in South Sudan (UNMISS) was another UNTAC-model, but with unique strategic interests given the scale of Chinese involvement in the region and unique connection to the counter-piracy mission in Djibouti.[257] Operations from Somalia to Sudan had been considered but consistently failed to meet short-safe-significant 'UNTAC expectations'. UN requests for JSDF Sudan-South Sudan contingents, particularly for helicopters, were blocked by the GSO, UNMISS deployment being UNTAC-model without aviation, with the MOD adopting an almost paranoid avoidance of helicopters in UN-PKO on cost grounds.[258] Prime Minister Noda expended considerable energy overcoming GSDF resistance, partly due to engineering resources but mainly regarding unresolved ROE-legal issues and risks, prescient concerns given subsequent events.

Deployment was similar to Haiti: Initially, from November 2011, 210 GSDF engineering personnel were deployed (later 400), with personal weapons (one machine gun), for JICA-coordinated infrastructure projects, serving under the civilian SRSG rather than force commander.[259] UNMISS is depicted in the 2017 defence white paper as a highly professional mission, concluded due to changed circumstances.[260] This is not inaccurate but fails to reference the most outstanding elements: JSDF personnel uncertain amid conflict, a government which had struggled to enable robust contingency responses by passing the NSL, and petty scandals regarding documentation, cover-ups, and competence limitations. The government stated that withdrawal was not security-based, but 'morning report' (*nippō*) revelations that troops witnessed close-proximity combat (*sentō*) in July 2016, potentially triggering withdrawal under IPSL conditions, belied the claim.[261] Defense Minister Inada Tomomi claimed that 'combat' had not been stated in a legal sense, and her inability to explain 'lost morning reports' (later found), and MOD shortcomings, entailed a daily news cycle of farcical incompetence.[262] The scandals transformed UNMISS from a 'past-military' to 'prescient-political' problem, an existential threat to government credibility. The achievements of four years were assessed and the government decided that the mission's liabilities outweighed its assets and announced its conclusion.

Three UN-PKO withdrawals 2012–17 were remarkable. Unlike Haiti and Golan, the UNMISS retreat was a political farce, risks to the GSDF were marginalised, and rather than rationally assess operational reports, officials required troops compiling them to modify embarrassing vocabulary.²⁶³ Prime Minister Abe's 'pro-active' rhetoric, strategic shift, and 'Japan is Back!' re-affirmation did not suggest such timidity, nor did the 2014 CSD constitutional reinterpretation, 2015 NSL, and much vaunted *Kaketsukekeigo* ('rush and rescue') measures to rescue Japanese overseas amid conflict. Chief Cabinet-Secretary Suga Yoshihide stated in November 2016, 'Now the SDF can rescue people [...] when they call for help,' but when combat erupted in July, Japanese civilians in Juba often waited in vain for rescue.²⁶⁴ JICA-related staff were extracted, but CRF extraction troops did not know who or where other Japanese were, indicating dire situational awareness limitations, civilians depending upon their hotel staff and companies for safe transit.²⁶⁵

The highly capable UNMISS operation was compromised by poor political management, poor risk assessment, and poor coordination of legal, operational, and strategic aspects. The GSDF contingent appeared to have coped in July 2016, Col. Churiki Osamu detailing adequate contingency measures, although with obvious stress and PTSD issues to address.²⁶⁶ Media reports subsequently detailed over twenty cases of GSDF post-UNMISS PTSD cases and one suicide, indicating the potential for operational stress exacerbated by vague legal and limited social understanding.²⁶⁷ The JSDF performed well, but such was the political damage that as of 2020 no Japanese units serve in UN-PKO, and there appears to be little appetite for Japan to re-assert its peacekeeping credentials. With such limited leadership and strategic resolution it is difficult to understand why the Abe administration was so determined to pass the NSL. International credibility was damaged, and potential security partners warned of the wavering commitment of Japan to assume risk on behalf not only of others but even its own citizens.

Exercises

Japan has sought to establish international partnerships and engage in military training that complement ODO and US alliance exercises. Paul Midford suggests that 'Japan's decentring from the US after the Cold War' was designed to strengthen the US strategic relationship by complementary partner relationships cultivating economic development cooperation, but increasingly with security from 'softer' civilian maritime and cyber security, through to harder-power defence technology cooperation and exercises.²⁶⁸ Such partnerships may be intended as both alliance buttressing and hedging against US undependability, but administrations since 2016 have framed them within the unifying Free and Open Indo-Pacific (FOIP) Strategy, which by 2019 had become a 'Vision.'[269] Partnership exercises included the first by the GSDF with Australian and New Zealand forces (*Talisman Sabre*, 2015), which with US forces examined island defence and amphibious assault techniques of obvious relevance to the East China Sea.[270] This built upon Australia's first exercise in Japan for HA/DR in November 2014, complemented by US and New Zealand participation, consolidating 3.11 cooperation and the overlapping 'alliance-quad.'[271] Concerted efforts to 'develop the tri/quad-laterals' among US allies flourished, such as 2017 air force exercises, but potentially Japan's most strategically important tri-lateral could be with South Korea, a relationship constantly snagging on historical legacies.[272]

The inability of governments to bridge historical divides for mutual security benefit is evident with the GSOMIA imbroglio. Japan-Korea discussions of information sharing in 2011 eventually led (after one Korean cancellation) to the (in Seoul) controversial 2016 signing of the General Security of Military Information Agreement (GSOMIA). This followed the drawn-out US GSOMIA resolution in 2007 that smoothed the way for other agreements, the Korean GSOMIA providing direct mutual benefit for BMD and US alliance cooperation.[273] Korean court rulings on war-legacy slave-labour corporate liability issues in 2018 resulted in political friction and Japan's decision to suspend Korea's preferential trading status, with significant economic consequences. President Moon Jae-in's Democratic Party was far less amenable to cooperation with Japan than the preceding Park administration, particularly Park's 2015 Japan-Korea 'comfort women' issue (*ianfumondai*) agreement, indicating the challenges facing any Korean government aiming to cooperate with Japan. This broader friction provoked the August 2019 GSOMIA non-renewal announcement, a decision reversed in November under intense US pressure, but subsequently revived to threaten Japan for trade and war-legacy intransigence.[274] The importance for defence was emphasised by former Defense Minister Gen Nakatani who stated that Japanese BMD 'can't function' without GSOMIA, information having been provided twenty-nine times 2016–19.[275] Washington's frustration at the failure to secure the US alliance trilateral, with Seoul and Tokyo's barely bifurcated cooperation, is palpable, but despite Japanese 'US special relationship' assumptions the largest US Asian base is in Korea, and the ROK and US militaries operated a combined command system, unlike Japan.[276] The JSDF have become involved in this Japan-Korea dispute not only through GSOMIA and petty arguments regarding Japan's naval ensigns, but also when an MSDF P-1 aircraft was 'illuminated' by a Korean destroyer's fire-control radar in December 2018, resulting in highly public MOD claims and Korean counters that soured relations and stifled progress towards defence cooperation.[277]

Australia is one of few countries training Japanese intelligence personnel, with the Australian Secret Intelligence Service (ASIS) contracted since 2008, although not in espionage.[278] GSDF troops also participated in Vambrace Warrior (October 2016) in Wales, exercising with and being trained by British partners in Static Covert Surveillance (SCS) and Surveillance and Target Acquisition (STA), both for field intelligence gathering and forward air control CAS operations. Such realistic training as preparing to attack a nuclear power station in a multilateral context is commonplace in NATO, providing models for the Forces to use partnerships to 'plug-into' multi-lateral exercises, long neglected due to normative sensitivities and pre-occupation with US alliance development.[279] NATO and ANZUS partners allow for better training and US integration, re-assuring Washington that Japan is deepening alliance capability rather than seeking alternatives.

Combined multilateral approaches were also adopted during amphibious training exercises off Japan, Guam, and Tinian in 2017, with the French amphibious vessel *Jeanne d'Arc* hosting British and American forces, including RN helicopters embarked for six months.[280] Japanese Forces can scarcely imagine such embedded exchanges, for operational, personal, and legal reasons, but the limitations of short exercises and value of long-term engagements are evident, with British and Australian officers embedded with the US Seventh Fleet, Yokosuka, from 2015 to develop particular naval-tri/quad-laterals.[281] Japanese and British air forces had their first bilateral unit training exchanges in 2016, RAF Typhoon fighters and Voyager tanker-transporters in Japan October–November 2016 conducting the first non-US air-combat exercises in Japan with the ASDF.[282] Both sides were deeply impressed, the cooperation prompting a January 2017 Anglo-Japanese Acquisition and Cross-Servicing Agreement similar to the Australian ACSA, to facilitate future cooperative training.[283] The RAF 'first' was followed by the British Army consolidating upon Vambrace Warrior by despatching the Honourable Artillery Company (HAC) to Japan for GSDF exercises in late 2018, the first such non-US ground force training in Japan.[284] The HAC as an elite, reservist ISR force provided an interesting interface opportunity for GSDF units, with ISR and counter-terrorism, particularly with special-forces being British and Australian strengths, demonstrating elite reserve forces to reserve-negligent Japan.[285] Such international cooperation will likely increase as Japan buttresses the US alliance with defence and security partnerships, although the UK defence relationship appeared to 'plateau' after the Brexit referendum. Comments by Lt. Gen. Patrick Sanders, UK Commander Field Army, may have also caused some consternation: 'Japan remains one of our most important strategic partners in the Asia-Pacific region and we welcome the opportunity to develop strong bi-lateral ties [...] and we want to assure Japan that they will not have to fight alone either [...] This exercise is designed to promote peace and stability in the region with our natural partners whose values of respect and democracy we share.'[286] While reassuring, how deeply Japan will wish to embed within such activities, and with what limitations is not clear, as it appears deeply unwilling to assume risk for its partners. Japan remains a risk averse country even while its Forces take ever greater risks to protect its citizens, both at home and overseas. These risks became evident in March 2011.

JSDF and the 'Triple Crises'

The 11 March 2011 Great East Japan Earthquake (*Higashinihon daishinsai*), tsunami, and nuclear accident, the 'triple crisis' of 3/11, constituted the greatest domestic challenge since 1945 and the greatest operational challenge the Self-Defense Forces had confronted. Through the rescue, relief, and recovery phases the JSDF were major actors, closely cooperating with domestic and overseas civil and military organisations.[287] Disaster-response management had starkly improved since the 1995 Hanshin-Awaji earthquake, as had multifaceted Japan-US working relationships amid a controversy regarding Okinawa bases, but this and long-term JSDF constitutional and civilian-control issues were largely subsumed by the scale and nature of the crises.

JSDF Disaster Response Experience

Consideration of JSDF performance following 3/11 entails examining the 17 January 1995 Hanshin-Awaji earthquake, the largest Japanese quake since 1923. The response of the Murayama Tomiichi administration was slow and indecisive, compounding some local governments' disdain for the JSDF. The GSDF refrained from providing relief without JDA orders, rooted in 1951 NPR experience, Murayama not issuing orders for fear of being regarded as imposing 'military' solutions.[288] This public farce of ideological manners amid suffering effectively rendered ideological rhetoric obsolete.[289] The GSDF 3rd

Division (Itami) began rescue and relief work four hours after the quake upon Hyogo Prefectural Government request. Middle Army's full response was delayed for two days, which may have contributed 500 preventable fatalities, while companies, communities, and even *yakuza* criminal gangs mobilised in that critical period.[290] The Forces provided tremendous assistance for 100 days, even helping lost foreign volunteers, dealing with a disaster that claimed 6,434 lives.[291] This work, with UN-PKO, improved the Forces' public image, poor cabinet coordination for JSDF-USFJ cooperation being the only regrettable regression.[292] After the Hanshin-Awaji quake, the JSDF assisted with the sarin gas attack by the Aum Shinrikyo death-cult on the Tokyo Subway, with nuclear accident decontamination, earthquake rescue/relief, and volcanic evacuation roles, further developing proficiency and public support for these operations, as well as those overseas.[293] Civilian-control preoccupations were displaced by human security utility.

March 2011 Response

The contrast of the 3/11 JSDF response with Hanshin-Awaji was stark. Not only was the earthquake far stronger, and the effects of the tsunami unimagined, but the emerging Fukushima Dai-ichi plant meltdowns made JSDF duties far more complex than anything envisaged. GSDF Chief of Staff, Gen. Hibako Yoshifumi, unilaterally issued national response orders, confirmed by Defense Minister Kitazawa Toshimi's mobilisation orders.[294] Kitazawa, with Prime Minister Kan Naoto and Chief Cabinet-Secretary Edano Yukio, constituted the main leaders of JSDF response efforts, despite all being left-wing veterans.[295] From approximately 240,000 JSDF personnel, 100,000 were mobilised by 13 March, including the first reservist call-up.[296] 506 GSDF Reservists were initially mobilised, 2,210 operational in June, 496 with valued foreign language and technical skills, illustrating that reservists could sustain operations during major contingencies.[297] The initial JSDF rescue phase extracted 19,247 people, including a man rescued by the MSDF 14km offshore after two days on a roof, and a dog rescued by the JCG 1.8km offshore.[298] By 31 March, 70,000 GSDF, 15,100 MSDF, and 21,300 ASDF personnel were active within the relief area, and a further 500 attached to the Dai-ichi nuclear crisis management group.[299] Despite weaknesses in heavy airlift and amphibious capabilities, the Forces' extensive water-purification, bathing, cooking, and logistical equipment proved ideal for such contingencies. Only at the end of April did Kitazawa announce that half of ASDF/

MSDF and 30 per cent of GSDF units would stand down as intense operations had taken their physical and mental toll, with 67,200 GSDF, 10,600 MSDF, and 18,500 ASDF personnel remaining on 31 May.[300] Most evacuation shelters had a JSDF contingent, and the Forces effectively became transport suppliers, operating 'service stations' for civilians unable to buy fuel, and cheering up evacuees by band concerts and sports activities, collaborating with school, volunteer, and other groups.[301] More than at any time since 1945, the armed forces became integrated into and accepted by local civil society.

The challenges facing the JSDF first responders were daunting. Colonel Sasaki Toshio detailed how in Ofunato City, Iwate, he had difficulty with local civilian management rather than military command, but personnel recently returned from Haiti helped establish relief and CIMIC essentials.[302] The GSDF in particular received extensive coverage of their duties, but there was little coverage of how disparate units were despatched and immediately pressed into service. Saigō Kinya, an infantry company commander despatched from Yamaguchi Prefecture towards Kesennuma City, Miyagi, took fifteen hours to cover 170km through ruptured roads and debris.[303] Within three days his unit moved to liaise with 4th Division, recently arrived from Kyushu, met an old NDA classmate, thus ameliorating confusion caused by orders to contact an officer who did not exist, which was typical of the dislocation and poor initial communications.[304] JSDF cooperation with US forces provided transformative capability enhancement that in many ways transformed the perception of the US-Japan alliance.

JSDF-USFJ *Tomodachi*

On the evening of 11 March, Prime Minister Kan requested US Forces Japan assistance through Ambassador Roos, leading to USAF aircraft, 31st USMC Expeditionary Unit, and US Navy despatch.[305] The JSDF and USFJ formed Joint Task Force-Tohoku (JFT-TH) around the North-East Regional Army HQ, under Lt.-General Kimizuka Eiji, the first operational combined-command arrangement, USFJ efforts designated within *Operation Tomodachi* (friend). This was the culmination of decades of improving Japan-US security cooperation, from the Guidelines through RIMPAC and combined exercises, to Iraq despatch efforts, and, as Robert Eldridge states, this was vital to the success of US-Japan integration.[306] *JS-Hyūga* and *USS Ronald Reagan* providing respective flagships, exchanging flag personnel, and providing Tohoku-area airlift and ATC. Close US-Japan naval cooperation continued with *USS*

Tortuga transporting GSDF units from Hokkaido to Mutsu, Aomori, the first 'southward' brigade deployment.[307] The MSDF appeared initially overwhelmed by the scale of needs, with three *Ōsumi*-class amphibious vessels, four 500-tonne landing vessels, and only four AOE/AOR Combat Support Ships able to deliver fuel, stores, and provide local power and water to coastal communities, but in distant locations and facing difficulty operating inshore due to tsunami debris.[308] The MSDF was 'front-heavy tail-light,' with far less emphasis upon capability-multiplying support vessels than combat hulls, although DDH *Hyūga* and other aviation-capable warships helped rescue and comfort survivors.[309] Five MSDF LCAC hovercraft carried by the *Osumi*-class traversed debris-clogged waterways and slipways to access affected communities but there was a critical early-stage delay.[310] The inability to operate effectively inshore left communities with little fuel, power, or fresh water that ships could have abundantly provided, the first oil being delivered by the MSDF on 19 March, but naval vessels utilised helicopters to overcome obstacles.[311] The USN appeared to have learned lessons from Hurricane Katrina in 2005, lifting over 3,000 Marines from Okinawa, as well as GSDF units as the MSDF had few available resources.[312] However, expectations of two carriers operating as mobile helicopter-hospital bases were dashed by *USS George Washington* retreating to Sasebo, and the *USS Ronald Reagan* not treating evacuating Japanese, despite otherwise excellent assistance.

USFJ and civilian teams managed to clear enough Sendai Airport runway to allow helicopter landings, and C-130H from 16 March, the ASDF having previously 'written this airport off.'[313] Military flights increased until ATC passed to the JSDF on 1 April 2011, and to Sendai Airport Authority on 6 April, with civilian flights commencing less than one month after the tsunami.[314] The Sendai Airport mission was an extreme example of dynamic and imaginative US-support under a Japanese commander, Col. Kasamatsu Makoto, who admitted to embarrassment at having limited, constantly rotating JSDF support staff.[315] He acknowledged the dedication of civil airport workers, as well as the extraordinary energy and capabilities of USFJ personnel, rather understating his own contribution.[316] ASDF personnel concentrated upon reopening Matsushima base on 16 March, with dozens of aircraft written-off.[317] US Global Hawk unmanned aerial vehicles (UAV) flights mapped the devastation and monitored radiation for the cabinet.[318]

Such efforts contrasted with the often negative perceptions of USFJ, mainly due to Okinawa base issues. Despite comprising less than 1 per cent of Japanese territory, Okinawa hosts approximately 75 per cent of USFJ personnel, and safety, environmental, and crime concerns have fuelled protests and soured alliance relations for decades.[319] The 1995 rape of a twelve-year old girl enraged public opinion, and resulted in The Special Action Committee on Okinawa (SACO), the 1996 report of which provided for return of 20 per cent of land and a new Status of Forces Agreement (SOFA) governing treatment of US personnel under Japanese law.[320] The new SOFA did not materialise, but the redeployment of one-third of USMC units to Guam at Japanese expense was agreed in 2006, and a Futenma-Nago relocation plan, rejected by many locals, prompting Hatoyama Yukio to attempt re-location beyond Okinawa and Japan, his failure and downfall mirroring Tokyo's flawed policies.[321] *Operation Tomodachi* was not only a demonstration of capability but also of fraternity, a positive affirmation of loyalty contrasting with negative perception of burdens in Okinawa.[322] The abiding impression was of genuine friendship, represented by proliferation of a Japanese expression during the crises, *kizuna*, kinship although positive social *kizuna* impressions were matched by *kizuna* fatigue particularly in western Japan.[323] *Tomodachi kizuna* was organic and sustained, enabled by extensive civil-military cooperation and decades of USFJ-JSDF staff work. More than 18,000 US personnel participated before *Operation Tomodachi* wound down from 2 May.

Non-US Cooperation

International civilian and military support was coordinated by MOFA Korean and Australian air forces among the first responders, all three RAAF C-17 aircraft transporting GSDF units from Okinawa to Tohoku. One of the more unusual deployments was the Israeli Defense Force (IDF) Medical Aid Delegation in Minami-Sanriku, Miyagi, enabled by personal contact with the mayor, the IDF being the only such foreign medical team in Japan (three others had four members or fewer, and arrived at least a month after the IDF).[324] A MOFA official explained that communities would 'be very surprised if a foreign medical team arrived out of the blue,' as though surprise were fatal, a Health Ministry official insisting that the IDF only provided 'minimum necessary' care.[325] Thankfully, locals largely ignored the Ministries, and the IDF exception proved highly popular, the IDF donating their equipment, which illustrated the role of disaster relief work as valuable defence-diplomacy.[326] Eighteen countries provided 890 civilian Search and Rescue personnel with thirty-seven dogs, even though they could not be fully used due to lack of collapsed buildings. They were matched by international NGO, such as Peace Winds, with which the JSDF were able to cooperate effectively due to ODO experience, and the 2000 Japan Platform, a civil-military framework for public-private-voluntary sector cooperation, another Force niche CIMIC capability.[327] Oscar Gómez highlights the value of WFP contributions, such as prefabricated buildings, and those of other civilian groups being overshadowed by military efforts, a significant risk when focusing upon JSDF-USFJ work.[328]

Retired JSDF personnel serving with local governments provided effective conduits for communication and 'civil-interpretation,' 368 serving in 246 municipalities, forty-six prefectures by December 2015.[329] North-East Army despatched Liaison Officers to reinforce local coordination, consolidating Iwate-Miyagi-JSDF Disaster Response Exercises from 2008.[330] Miyagi Prefecture Governor Murai Yoshihiro being a former-GSDF Captain facilitated cooperation with JSDF rescue and relief efforts, reinforcing rather than undermining civilian control, although Richard Samuels supports Gómez' warnings of the potential for JSDF 'military takeover' in relief work amid weakened local civil authorities.[331] JCG coordinated with civil and military authorities, rescuing ships' crews, searching drifting ships, contributing fifty-four vessels and 2,492 personnel, rescuing 360 people, and recovering 391 bodies, as well as providing health, fire-fighting, and supply services.[332] In a legacy of 1995, over 130,000 volunteers joined in the recovery efforts, combining with international civilian, military, and JSDF personnel to make the Tohoku effort truly cosmopolitan. Even groups considered averse to the Forces, such as Peace Boat, recruited and managed volunteers in close coordination and cooperation with civil and military authorities.[333] This represented the transformative civil-military embodiment of *kizuna*.

Nuclear Operations

The JSDF provided support at the Dai-ichi reactors, building on GSDF responses to the 1999 Tokaimura Nuclear Incident explosion, and nuclear accident exercises in November 2003.[334] The CRF Central Nuclear Biological Chemical Weapon Defense Unit led the joint nuclear disaster relief mission.[335] Ground-spraying and hazardous GSDF helicopter 'water-bombing,' a move seemingly instigated by US pressure but which Isobe Kōichi details emerged from Cabinet-MOD deliberations, helped contain radioactive material.[336] Authorities were underwhelmed by Tokyo Electric

Power Company (TEPCO) leadership, which on 14 March asked Prime Minister Kan to make the JSDF responsible, which he forcefully rejected.³³⁷ The overall public-private effort was blighted by 'vertical sectionalism,' as 'nuclear village' experts closed ranks, and agencies argued over responsibilities, delaying US technical assistance and JSDF airborne-radiation monitoring, but not Force logistical support or debris removal with Type-74 tanks.³³⁸ US civil and military teams were deployed, initially hampered by US 80km exclusion rules, later relaxed, with support from reactor designers General Electric, as well as Russian, French and other atomic industries as a primarily civilian operation.³³⁹

Aftermath

Gradually, JSDF efforts reduced, after 19,286 rescued (70 per cent of total), 9,505 bodies recovered of 15,899 killed with 2,843 missing.³⁴⁰ However, the impact of JSDF efforts on Japanese society, politics, and geo-politics is less easily quantified. Tohoku, in contrast with Hanshin-Awaji, was relatively positively disposed towards the Forces, providing many recruits. Among affected citizens the general feeling was that the Japanese government had largely overlooked them, but this antipathy did not apply to the JSDF, nor to the JCG, with USFJ, volunteers, and particularly local authorities recognised as having conducted heroic duties in impossible situations. *Operation Tomodachi* was a success, both for its relief impact and the image of USFJ, previously often seen but rarely tangibly valued. While many countries aided Japan, they were overshadowed by US military aid, and it was notable that JSDF-USFJ cooperation was generally smooth and amicable, under Japanese control. Other countries stood out, such as Australia, demonstrating the value of active partnership with Canberra, and Korea, although relatively neglected.

For the Japan-US alliance, however, while its value was clearly demonstrated to the Japanese, as Richard Samuels states the 'only proof of concept [...] reaffirmed Japan's long-standing commitment to a cheap ride' at US expense, which apparently was 'acceptable in Washington,' so low were American alliance expectations.³⁴¹ Samuels bemoans initial Japanese conceptual responses and limited 'fungibility' to develop or extrapolate equivalent security cooperation from HA/DR cooperation, so that for the alliance 'there was no major Tohoku dividend'.³⁴² Japan viewed US-Japan 2013 HA/DR cooperation in the Philippines as 'Tomodachi Part-2,' but without equivalent sentiment in Washington.³⁴³ However, Samuels perhaps under-estimates the lingering positive impact upon Japanese society of USFJ *kizuna*, proof of concept that the alliance provided immense reassurance amid increasing recognition of climate change impact upon Japan's environment, and in an environment of increasing East Asian security threats.

Within Japan, those expressing interest in the JSDF hit a record high (69.8 per cent, January 2012), exceeding previous Gulf War (February 1991) and Iraq Despatch (February 2006) peaks, net positive responses recorded from December 1981, reaching 71.5 per cent in March 2015, with operations during the Tohoku crises producing a 97.7 per cent appreciative response, which actually increased by 2015.[344] Perception of USFJ-Operation Tomodachi was 79.2 per cent positive.[345] Appreciation of JSDF disaster-relief efforts became clear in polls from the 1960s, with over 70 per cent responding positively, even exceeding 90 per cent in 1995 for Hanshin-Awaji rescue and relief despite criticisms of delay.[346]

For JSDF personnel, the Triple Crisis brought mixed results. The words of Prime Minister Yoshida addressing the National Defense Academy appeared prescient: 'Many of you might finish your careers in the SDF without ever having been thanked or welcomed by the people [...] it is only when our nation is facing crisis and confusion [...] that the people will appreciate and praise the SDF.'[347] Never were the Forces more appreciated nor more thanked. This universally positive depiction was not always easily embraced. Many JSDF personnel attested to profound guilt, and commanders reported illness and fatigue when troops refused to rest, corpse removal especially traumatic for troops trying to 'handle the bodies carefully,' MSDF divers becoming particularly overworked, with significant PTSD risks.[348] Since 3/11, the systemised process for dealing with mental health issues in the JSDF recognised the burdens of disaster relief duties.[349] One GSDF Reserve medical officer was despatched with an infantry battalion from Koichi Prefecture on 23 March as a specialist in post-operational mental health.[350] Worryingly, although surveys in 2013 suggested that approximately 10 per cent of JSDF personnel could be suffering from depression or PTSD, it was left to individuals to seek assistance, much mental trauma attention being devoted to ODO veterans rather than accumulated 3/11 service.[351]

There were also operational issues to address. The Joint Task Force Headquarters in Sendai worked well with USFJ, but the commander was hampered by the GSDF Regional Army command structure and lacked any real control over ASDF and MSDF resources, some local communities being rendered negligible medical or logistical assistance.[352] Compared to the Hanshin-Awaji Earthquake, with almost 6,500 fatalities and 45,000 injuries, in Tohoku there were likely 18,000 fatalities and only 6,000 injuries but extensive hypothermia, as the tsunami killed but didn't injure. JSDF advanced medical resources were despatched while survivors really needed food, warmth, and shelter, indicating poor local situational awareness[353] A Finance Ministry study also showed that only 17.1 per cent of JSDF reservists deployed when requested, challenging the ¥8 billion reserve system's efficacy, the MOD having failed to track reservist employment and qualification data. While those who responded worked well, the rate of response was disappointingly low for the nation's greatest peacetime disaster.[354]

The MOD appeared to be attempting to learn lessons, but planned to utilise relief and recovery funds for procuring hardware of slight relevance to the crises.[355] The fundamental lessons of 3/11 were that the JSDF had proved their capabilities and necessity to the Japanese people as vital national defenders, with policies and politicians held up to fierce criticism, but rarely the Forces. Capability gaps outlined by Tatsumi Yuki included C4-ISR, joint-operation procedures, limited GSDF central-command, transport-logistics, and a civilian nuclear programme that depended upon military support were obvious matters of concern.[356] Reconfirmation of US dependability reaffirmed alliance centrality and clearly signalled relevance for security issues beyond Tohoku, thereby providing strategic 'fungibility'. The international engagement through rescue and relief work also brought home the connectivity of domestic and overseas policies, Japan's partners buttressing its core alliance, and demonstrating the utility of international engagement efforts. More crucially, the Forces proved their utility and legitimacy to the Japanese people and that not only their training but also fundamental institutional culture were in harmony with civil society.

Force Culture

Training and Education

JSDF training has attempted to meet the challenges of new security threats and accompanying technology amid efforts to maintain personnel amid the depopulating and ageing of society. Continuity is provided by the 1961 five principles of 'Self-Defense Force Member Mindset' (*jieikan no kokorogamae*), stressing public service, civilian control, and balancing individual rights and respect with group work and leadership that could be easily taken for post-war education policy rather than warrior ethos doctrine.[357] The Mindset stresses public service during peace and emergencies, and understanding *tadashiimin-*

zokuai, 'appropriate love of one's ethnicity,' which appears disconcerting but is contextualised in love and respect, contrasted with irresponsibility and political activity taboos.[358]

One of the obvious challenges facing the JSDF is securing enough young people to serve. The key target demographic of eighteen- to twenty-two-year-olds hit a peak in 1994 of seventeen million, but by 2015 had declined below eleven million (when over-eighties exceeded ten million), seeing the Forces engaged in a competitive market for recruits.[359] Studies also illustrate the self-isolating 'hermit-like' *hikikomori* problem, most prevalent among young men, with possibly over one million affected.[360] The JSDF spends increasing amounts for recruitment adding to personnel expenses, by 2016 consuming 44.2 per cent of the defence budget, and yet, as Robert Eldridge states, many of the alternatives, such as cuts or conscription, seem acceptable only to fringe activists.[361] Despite public opinion polls indicating respect for the Forces, and elevated threats to Japanese sovereignty, there has been little increase in JSDF career interest, and even when asked whether they would join the Forces if Japan were invaded, positive responses have barely changed over decades at approximately 6 per cent.[362] Acceptance has not equated to participation.

Whereas in some armed forces the initial period of basic training may be as short as six weeks, in the JSDF the shortest intake training is three months, and many recruits will complete five months before specialist programmes. Most of these training programmes have become coeducational, and from 2017 front-line combat training opened to female candidates. Veterans insist that twenty-first-century training has become more operational-scenario focused, balanced with complaints that modern recruits are treated as valuable commodities, due to bullying scandals and concerns for recruitment, retention, and mental health. A prominent case in 2004 involved the suicide of a young sailor due to bullying which resulted in the deceased's family winning damages.[363] This was not a unique MSDF or JSDF problem, bullying being a well-identified social concern, but scandals involving bullying in the ranks, and suicides, generate downward PR spirals.[364]

Apart from regular routes for joining the Forces through local recruitment centres, the GSDF has operated a Technical High School (*Kōteikōkagakkō*) since 1963, in many ways similar to a regular Japanese high school, the present GSDF High Technical School (*Shōnenkōkagakkō*) administered by the Eastern Army in Yokosuka. The school provides general, technical, and military education and accepts 320 male Junior High School graduates for three years, followed by required JSDF service (or NDA entry). The obvious benefit is free education, monthly stipend (¥96,000 in 2018) plus bonuses, uniforms, board and lodging, and a boost to JSDF careers, despite the calmly harsh discipline.[365] For less wealthy families this offers a tremendous opportunity in a society where the lack of a high school diploma generally equates to embarrassment and a life of menial work.[366]

Officer Training

The unique aspects of JSDF officer training are its length and that the National Defense Academy (*Bōeidaigakkō*) and National Defense Medical College (NDMC) (*Bōeiikadaigakkō*) are joint, coeducational, and that 'students' are paid. Both are as competitive as leading civil universities, the NDA consistently above 12:1 applicant/entrant ratios during the Cold War, exceeding 30:1 ratios 2011–15 while the NDMC averaged 87.6:1.[367] Education mirrors civilian universities, despite rising to bugle calls 'on-campus' and wearing uniforms, incoming NDA students (450–570) choose science or humanities courses for four years, as well as their prospective service. Common elements include ethics and social studies, mathematics, English and another language (from German, French, Russian, Chinese), and physical education.[368] There are foreign exchanges with sister academies, in western countries (US, UK, France, Germany, Australia), and also Qatar, Mongolia, Thailand, and despite diplomatic issues (sometimes) Korea and China, with 100 overseas cadets enrolled in 2018 from nine Asian countries.[369]

The oddity is that although approximately 10 per cent of cadets drop out over four years, none were required to serve in the Forces until 2014, those consequently leaving JSDF service within six years of graduation being liable for part of the estimated ¥2.5 million Academy costs, the full amount if declining to serve.[370] NDA graduates notably declined to serve in 1991 (19 per cent) and 2016 (11 per cent), both years of security legislation controversies, with prospects for high-risk overseas missions, only four having declined in 2012.[371] Those declining service have been prohibited from attending graduation ceremonies since 2014, rather than being lured into alternative JSDF reserve service as potential alternative-service assets.[372]

Unsurprisingly, NDMC entry is extremely competitive, civil medical schools being difficult to enter and expensive to graduate from, so the high quality, free College education is extremely appealing, students receiving a monthly allowance (¥113,300 in 2017) and bonuses. The post-graduation service obligation is for nine years, the penalty for early termination being repayment of up to ¥50 million. In 2013, 8,012 applicants competed for seventy-six places.[373] The issue of JSDF doctors retiring before completing nine years of service was identified in the 2005 white paper, thirty-two having not completed their terms, and in Japan it is notoriously difficult to impose punishments upon those who choose to leave the Forces, regardless of limiting rules.[374]

The JSDF reflects broader social norms in imposing restrictive age limits upon officer candidates. NDA entry is usually at eighteen, with some flexibility, whereas civilian officer-candidate entry is for twenty-two- to twenty-six-year-olds with only post-graduate study exceptions, while other-rank entry age limits are eighteen to twenty-seven. Age limits are relaxed for problematic retention specialisations, such as nurses (under thirty-six), doctors and dentists (no limit), and MSDF and ASDF technical officers (thirty-eight and forty-five respectively). For reservists, the normal age restrictions are eighteen to thirty-four, but again, for technically qualified candidates, those up to fifty-five are considered.[375] With high average ages, and recruitment largely restricted to the narrowest, youngest groups, the Forces are highly vulnerable to retention and demographic risks.

Of 42,024 JSDF officers serving in October 2016, 9,788 were NDA graduates, and 895 from NDMC, 9,830 with civilian degrees, while almost half were high school graduates (20,846), and 665 had only a junior-high school education, indicating that NDA education is a minority qualification.[376] The high number of officers without university degrees reflects a relatively egalitarian image where other-ranks can gain commissions, even though reaching senior command would be unlikely without NDA credentials, and in 2016 over 15 per cent of other-ranks (OR) or non-commissioned officers (NCO) were higher-education graduates, compared with 3 per cent in 1980.[377] There were even 356 OR/NCO who had attended the NDA.[378] The Joint Staff College (JSC *Tōgōbakuryōgakkō*) was established in 1961 to provide post-NDA education and professional training directly related to assuming staff positions, the NDA itself beginning MSc Science and Engineering courses in 1962, followed by the Graduate School of Security Studies in 1997.[379] The National Safety College, founded in 1952, became the National Defense College in 1954, and the National Institute for Defense Studies (NIDS) in 1985, indicating the shift from staff instruction and military history to policy studies research. This process accelerated with the move from its palatial Ebisu 'campus' to MOD headquarters, Ichigaya, in 2016, continuing higher research functions, its primary purpose having become MOD in-house think-tank.[380]

GSDF Training

For most of the Cold War, entry to the Ground officer candidate school was via the NDA or by competitive examination for university graduates, followed by seventeen to nineteen weeks of the officer candidate training programme, then commissioning as Second Lieutenants (*santōrikui*), with specialist training (sixteen to thirty-five weeks) followed by advanced training (four to fifty-two weeks).[381] Medical and nursing officer candidates' six-week training courses, without arms training, preceded commissioning with first postings equivalent to house officer/residency for two years, often in rural communities facing de-population and shortages of medical practitioners. Nurses proceed direct from commissioning to specialist training for sixteen to thity-six weeks, candidate pilots undertaking a fifty-five week course, with equivalent courses also open to Senior NCOs (eighty weeks), and Warrant Officers (WO) commissioned after a competitive examination and eight-twelve weeks' preparation courses.[382] GSDF officer training is long and expensive, but less so than the MSDF which invests more time and money in its officers than any other Force.

MSDF Training

Post-NDA naval officer training consists of one year at the Naval Academy, Etajima, Hiroshima, followed by commissioning as Ensigns (*santōkaii*), who embark upon a training cruise, their induction into sea service. Specialist training during the Cold War was five to seven weeks for the standard officer course (*ninmukatei*), ten to thirty-seven weeks for new officers' specialist courses, and ninety-two weeks for aircrew, but this has become more specialised, longer, and supposedly tougher in recent years, for example for aviation officers.[383] Only submarine service remains closed to women, and more than the other Forces the MSDF provides female recruits with progressive role models, including a Rear-Admiral, Kondo Natsue.[384] NCO and WO commissioning processes are similar to the GSDF, and those that attend the naval academy for six months participate in the prestigious ensign cruises, indicated by investment in technical and ensign training vessels, the purpose-built *Kashima*'s plush interiors symbolising the bubble-economy years, with classrooms and combat-system simulation rooms.[385] During such cruises for every ensign there are approximately three serving MSDF personnel, covering up to 33,000 nautical miles for five months during the vital formative experience of each naval officer, in which the MSDF invests so much.

ASDF Training

Post-graduation Air officer training originally lasted for thirty weeks for NDA graduates, and forty-three weeks for university graduates and non-commissioned ASDF personnel, while women from 1981 were given merely fifteen weeks, indicating their limited duties. Post-commissioning training required from thirty-one months to six weeks, illustrating speciality disparities.[386] By 2016, NDA graduates undertook twenty-three to forty-week courses before commissioning for specialist training, aircrew requiring a minimum of thirty-one months.[387] In an odd disparity of costs, an F-4EJ pilot (basic training to type-qualification) required 58.75 months, costing ¥521.3 million, while an F-15J pilot required fifty-five months and ¥548.4 million in 1999, but by 2016, the F-15J cost was ¥468 million.[388] More significant is that entry to all branches of the ASDF became more flexible and meritocratic rather than predestined by initial entry point, officers keenly stressing that their service remains free of the inflexibilities facing Ground and Maritime officers.[389]

Training Air Space

There are fifteen JSDF Training Air Spaces (TAS *kunrenkūiku*, A~U), plus nine under US management. The largest, G-TAS and C-TAS, are over the Sea of Japan, while A-TAS has the largest overland area (Hokkaido), with an additional twenty-six extraordinary zones (TAS X1–26 *rinjikunrenkūiku*).[390] The ASDF and MSDF have access to firing ranges, such as R-131 and R-129 inside B-TAS near ASDF Misawa AB and MSDF Hachinohe AS for cannon and air-surface ordnance.[391] US management has reduced, such as around USAF Yokota AB, Tokyo allowing expanded Haneda Airport movements from 2008, but remains strategically significant for Kuba and Taisho Islands, of the Senkaku group, US-managed since the 1972 Okinawa Reversion Agreement.[392] Katō Akira identifies Kuba as the only remaining privately-owned Senkaku Island, leased to the Japanese government, under USN air-bombing training control, although not used since 1978. Such facilities and areas 'shall be returned to Japan whenever they are no longer needed,' yet, despite the 2012 government Senkaku purchase, continued US management of 'the two islands implies that the United States itself is another actor in the Senkaku dispute.'[393] By implication, 'internationalizing' the Senkaku issue reinforces US defence responsibilities, discounted by US sources, who repeat the official US position that the islands as Japanese controlled territory shall be defended as per Japanese domains under the security treaty, without the US government committing to final sovereignty as yet to be determined. ASDF aircrew have trained in US airspace, on exercises and exchanges, but only joining the Red Flag multinational combat training exercises from 1996 (UK from 1977), bilaterally with the US rather than as a full participant due to CSD concerns. Red Flag participation has provided more experience for support crews than fighter pilots, in 2016 involving six F-15J (of almost 200), one E-767 AWACS (of four), and two KC-767 tanker-transporters (of four), indicating the relative importance of support aircraft, and the strain on limited resources of such deployments.[394]

Women

As detailed in Chapter Two, women were first admitted to the NSF in 1952 as nursing staff, allowed into GSDF support roles from 1968 and MSDF and ASDF from 1974, most non-combat roles from 1986 (GSDF) and 1993 (MSDF/ASDF), and into the NDA in 1992, but despite assertions that 'all restrictions for women had been lifted,' by 2000, several remain.[395] The JDA published its Basic Plan for Gender Equality in 2006, introducing broader career opportunities, mentoring and counselling systems, and a notional one-third quota for executive committees.[396] The ASDF removed restrictions upon fighter pilot training in 2015, the first woman fighter pilot qualifying in August 2018. The MSDF removed barriers in 2016, while GSDF limitations on front-line combat arms were abolished in 2017.[397] The remaining exclusions were mining (due to health effects), nuclear-biological-chemical duties (hazard), and submarines (proximity).[398] Frühstück rightly contends that 'the integration of women into the SDF has been a strictly regulated process, unilaterally driven by the needs of the military rather than by attempts to create equal career opportunities for women,' unlike in Europe, where EU equality legislation propelled reform.[399]

By the end of 2016, there were 13,989 female JSDF members, just over 6 per cent of the total, an increase from 10,439 in 2001. Despite the Abe government's 'society in which women shine' project, and MOD targets for doubling the number of female Force members by 2030 through the 2017 JSDF Female Personnel Empowerment Initiative, such recruitment efforts encounter the same obstacles as in civil society.[400] Frühstück details how many young women choose JSDF careers based upon economic factors, education expenses, or the allure of public service and job security. One member joined to become 'a kind of diplomat,' which she considered impossible through elite university-MOFA routes, while others considered public service as both fulfilling and less prone to discrimination and abuse than careers in companies.[401]

The JSDF expanded its recruitment budget from 2013, and used examples such as an MSDF rescue unit member as an appealing role model, demonstrating professional public service in a less combat-oriented role.[402] The MSDF provided high-profile female career progressions, the previously mentioned Rear-Admiral Kondo, and Commanders Otani Miho and Azuma Ryoko appointed to command *JS-Shimayuki* and *JS-Setoyuki* respectively in 2013. Otani assumed command of *JS-Yamagiri* in 2016, the first female combat command, followed in March 2018 by appointment of Captain Azuma as Commander Escort Division One, Yokosuka, with Japan's largest helicopter-carrier *JS-Izumo* as her flagship.[403] While MSDF progress may be considered slower than in the US (first female warship commander 1998), UK (2012) or France (2016), it has been a Forces pioneer.[404] Earlier but with less media fanfare, GSDF Lt.-Col. Nakagawa Misa was the first JSDF staff liaison officer to serve in a UN-PKO (UNDOF), other GSDF officers serving in similar roles and in NATO, illustrating the importance of international engagement roles.[405]

The role of 'operational women' gained particular prominence from 2002 in the East Timor UN-PKO, and in Iraq from 2004, where Sato Fumika details how images of women were utilised to project peaceful images at odds with operational realities.[406] Most images of women in operations have focused upon less-martial roles, particularly medical, the most comprehensive coverage naturally provided during the 2011 Triple Crises, where JSDF women were portrayed closely integrated with male colleagues, US troops, and civilians. The less-martial aspect was revived in media reports of women assisting local communities in the aftermath of the 2016 Kumamoto earthquake, which were dominated by images of bathing attendants posing with girls, which may seem both engaging and affectionate yet trivialised career professionals.[407] The official MOD magazine *Mamor* (*Mamoru* 'protect') featured female JSDF members or uniformed models as 'Monthly Venus,' or '*Sakimori-tachi no megami*,' 'Defence Godesses.'[408] While seemingly well-intentioned (by men), this scarcely constituted Force equality and professional ethos, appearing anachronistic in the context of the government's aim to promote women to 30 per cent of leadership roles by December 2020, a Koizumi-era policy dropped in July 2020, with women occupying less than 15 per cent of management positions.[409]

There have been two female defence ministers (2020). Koike Yuriko (later Tokyo Governor) served for less than sixty days in 2007, having become embroiled in a turf war with Administrative Vice-Minister of Defense Moriya Takemasa, who was imprisoned for corruption the following year. Koike resigned when she failed to receive sufficient cabinet support and due to an unrelated data-leak scandal.[410] Inada Tomomi became defence minister in August 2016, served for approximately one year, was a protégé of Prime Minister Abe, a loyal security reform proponent and mentioned as a possible Abe successor.[411] Unfortunately during Diet deliberations on security legislation she was unable to answer questions until repeatedly prompted by Foreign Minister Kishida Fumio, then managed to disclose classified documents to television cameras.[412] She also conveyed the impression that she expected all JSDF/JDA personnel to vote for the government in elections, prompting 'a source close to the prime minister' to comment 'I have no idea why she says the things she says,' and resigning amid escalating South Sudan 'morning reports' scandals.[413]

Luckily, JSDF women have displayed due diligence in their duties. Following the Triple Crisis, extensive references were made in defence white papers to the roles of female GSDF reservists, one retired GSDF Lt.-General praising their vital translation and communications work with US forces.[414] Successful career women have also, somewhat puzzlingly, had their status as wives and mothers held up for admiration, illustrating that the 'new Self-Defense Forces' allow for such a work-life balance for recruitment appeal. Personnel agree that more attention has been devoted to welfare issues, although many complain of sub-standard housing and poor facilities for families in Forces service, with frequently-voiced opinions that the move is motivated more by the wish to address retention and mental health issues than simply proving equality credentials.

Mental Health

The mental health of JSDF personnel has become a major concern, particularly since the strains of 3.11 operations, expressed by suicide and random acts that drew public attention to welfare issues. Far from being a recent phenomenon, the issue came to public notice when a 1964 Tokyo Olympics bronze medal-winning athlete, GSDF Lieutenant Tsuburaya Kōkichi, killed himself before the Mexico Olympics in 1968.[415] Suicide was the leading cause of death in Japan for those aged fifteen to thirty-nine in 2015, while for men it was the leading cause among 10 to forty-four-year olds, more than twice as prevalent as among women.[416] An MOD study discovered fifty-six suicides among JSDF personnel who had served overseas, with evidence of mental illness in fourteen cases, twenty-seven having served in MSDF Indian Ocean refuelling missions, and twenty-nine in Iraq, indicating that risk factors may be less important than separation from families.[417] While no direct causes can be traced, 2004–2015 Force suicide rates significantly exceeded those of civilians, while JSDF operations increased in distance, diversity, and intensity.[418]

Mental health care within the Forces has received greater attention in the twenty-first century. In 2003, the Defense Agency Headquarters for the Prevention of Suicide was established, and the 2005 white paper announced a mental health study group.[419] By 2012, the MOD had adopted Measures Aimed at Enhancing the Human Foundation, embracing mental health, gender equality, counselling, recruitment, and education aspects of service life, with psychiatrists visiting troops in South Sudan.[420] Kawano's study identified the stresses of ODO related to communication and inter-personal issues rather than danger or professional challenges as worrying most JSDF personnel, and it is likely that naval service could prove particularly challenging in those respects, with few 'releases' ashore or at sea.[421] Shimozono Sōta has demonstrated that JSDF personnel identifying aspects of life and work that cause stress and anxiety can thereby control the impact they have on their mental health, but that in intensive HA/DR operations this became almost impossible.[422] The nature of JSDF duties reduces self-control many aspects of life and work, thereby reducing individual determination of mental health. Progress made in two decades has been significant, but one suspects there is a great deal more to be accomplished, not least with MOD support often limited to awaiting personnel volunteering their mental health concerns.

Japan is Back!

In Washington DC in 2013, Prime Minister Abe announced 'Japan is back!,' rebooted and revived.[423] A prominent element of this revival was enhanced prioritisation of defence spending and partnership building. While Abe defence reforms built upon existing plans, the combination with new security strategy and Abe's active diplomacy and forging 'partnerships,' often with civilian/military security elements, created the impression of a new Japanese security approach. JSDF movement south-west for national security also had implications towards partner states, plans for enhanced mobility, adaptability, and engagement with Indo-Pacific and out-of-area partners raising the question of whether the Forces were being moulded into expeditionary actors. This suggests the possibilities of following a model, such as the USMC, British or Australian armed forces, and also broaches the issue of areas in which the Forces may be required to operate, operational roles, and the legality of such roles, not least in assuming risk for national or collective defence.

From 1991, there were expectations for extensions of Japan's reach and expeditionary capabilities. UN-PKO in Golan and Haiti, HA/DR in Zaire and Honduras, and counter-piracy were forwarded as examples of extended reach representing inflated ambition.[424] With less than ten JSDF personnel on UN-PKO duty after 2017, and deployments primarily for training and defence diplomacy, conjecturing on expeditionary capacities may seem fanciful. However, prominent among policy innovations have been the development of an amphibious brigade, study of strategic strike capabilities, fixed-wing ship-borne naval aviation, augmentation of ISR capabilities, and reinforcement of the south-west. Missile-defence and island defence are both dominated by air-sea space security, as 'the physical defense of Japan requires credible nautical power projection.'[425] Such power projection could adopt Royal Navy doctrine, with 'military,' 'constabulary,' and 'benign' naval roles, defining naval roles as 'war fighting, maritime security and Defence Engagement.'[426] Traditional views of power projection focused upon 'gunboat diplomacy,' 'a threat, however delicate and discreet, that naval force might actually be applied in support of specific diplomatic representations.'[427] Alternative power projection concepts have included security partnerships, even without military deployment, attempting to 'shape' the security environment whereby transition from power projection to deterrence becomes seamless.[428]

Patrick Morgan has detailed the elements of deterrence that include implicit and explicit threats, but unlike gunboat diplomacy, deterrence is distinct from 'compellance' threats to manipulate behaviour, which Morgan refers to as 'coercive deterrence' as opposed to ambient threats provoking (unilateral/multilateral) 'general deterrence.'[429] Japanese 'expeditionary capabilities' for national defence constitute 'general deterrence' towards North Korea and China, but only China deterrence requires capabilities to sustain operations over significant sea-air distance within the parameters of national defence, although the 'expeditionary' label is disputed.[430] The arena for such operations would be the East China Sea and near Western Pacific, the obvious scenarios beyond JCG managed 'harassment' would be interdiction of shipping, and seizure of Nanseishotō south-western islands between Taiwan, Okinawa, and Kyushu. The former scenario is closely aligned with MSDF Cold War defence planning schemes, while island seizure is not, despite denying communist control of the 'First Island Chain' being a core US Cold War aim, hence post-2010 refocusing upon amphibious capabilities.[431] Retired GSDF Lt-Gen. Banshō Kōichirō has highlighted the 'Southwestern Wall Strategy' reinforcing Japanese and US defence interests, but this hardly constitutes an island 'Maginot Line,' but rather a rectifying of decades of defence neglect.[432]

South-west island defence measures have involved moderate Nanseishotō militarisation, with ISR capabilities extended by a GSDF surveillance company (160) on Yonagunijima from 2016, the closest Japanese island to Taiwan, following a local referendum.[433] This was followed by larger units deploying to Miyakojima and Ishigakijima, with anti-shipping and surface-air missiles, 550 personnel on Amami-Ōshima, also with two missile units, a total increase of approximately 2,000 personnel.[434] The population of many islands is so low that the Diet passed a 2015 act effectively subsidising island communities to prevent undue foreign influence. Force personnel are generally welcomed, despite widespread distrust of USFJ and Japanese governments' motives among local conservatives and liberals.[435] The bases remain modest and the JSDF footprint small, but the trend is clear, enabled through consultation and referenda, such as authorities on Eniyabanarejima apparently welcoming MOD overtures regarding amphibious exercises.[436] Okinawa Prefectural politics facilitated this move, with significant support for JSDF investments on 'distant' islands opposing the anti-base activism of Naha, barely reflected in media beyond Ishigakijima's *Yaeyama Nippō* newspaper.[437] Yet trepidation throughout the islands appeared to increase following revelations of MOD Mobile Deployment Working Group (*KidōtenkaiWG*) scenario planning 2010–13 for re-taking islands from 'external' (Chinese) invasion with obvious parallels to the 1945 Battle of Okinawa.[438] Ishigakijima was highlighted as a prime invasion target, and scenarios prepared for 2,000 GSDF infantry dislodging 4,500 'enemy' troops in a reversal of conventional three to one offensive ratio plans.[439] A former GSDF major-general asserted that the JSDF 'also feels strongly that there must never be a repetition of the Battle of Okinawa, yet the discussion of resident protection is not moving forward' with civil-military, local-national disputation of responsibilities.[440] There were no solid proposals for moving ASDF fighters to Miyakojima, the largest airport in the area, but this may well prove the logical development, given the distance from Naha and increased scramble rates after 2010.

Many states have reduced Cold War legacy forces while developing air/sealift, amphibious capabilities, and brigade-level sustainable light forces operations. Japan slowly followed, but has been reluctant to eschew heavy, high-intensity defence capabilities.[441] MOD, JSDF and Diet measures 'started to enhance Japan's expeditionary capabilities since the latter half of the 2000s,' but it remains clear to the JSDF and their allies and partners that Japan was still 'punching below its weight.'[442] The formation of the Ground Component Command (*rikujōsōtai* GCC) in March 2018, sixty years after naval and air centralised commands, was one measure to increase operational tempo directly related to 3/11 despatch orders.[443] CRF units and roles were divided between the GCC and the new amphibious brigade, under the GCC with airborne/helicopter 'Adaptive Agile Ground Defense Force' brigades, but it is unclear why the four Northern Army formations will become 'mobile' (*kidōbutai*), in contrast to only one of three Western Army formations.[444] The movement of the GCC to Camp Zama, beside US Army headquarters in Japan, was designed to improve USFJ cooperation, following the transfer of the ASDF ADC and 800 personnel to USAF Yokota AB by December 2011.[445] While the latter has been regarded as successful and capability enhancing, particularly for BMD and intelligence, there have been grumblings of discontent regarding the relative lack of synergy between GSDF and US Army staff at Zama.

Development of JSDF expeditionary capabilities has been enhanced with ASDF C-2 transporters and ISR, while MSDF sealift has been slightly augmented by two civilian ferries and DDH airlift. GSDF developments from the WAIR have been greatly enhanced by the Amphibious Rapid Deployment Brigade (ARDB *Suirikukidōdan*) established in Sasebo, Nagasaki on 27 March 2018, with 2,100 troops (eventually expanding to three ARD Regiments and 3,000 troops), AAV-7A1 amphibious APC and MV-22 Osprey aircraft.[446] The ARDB is part of the 2013 Dynamic Joint Defense Force, but its development and supporting joint approaches require examination as it encapsulates the future joint-mobile configuration of the JSDF, relies upon extensive US support, and forms the core of Japan's south-western defence, deterrence, and counter-force.

Amphibious Jointness

GSDF amphibious training initiatives began from 2006 platoon-company WAIR-USMC 'Iron Fist' island-defence, high-intensity expeditionary exercise to also confer capacity for low-intensity HA/DR missions, driven by a GSDF-USMC agenda with support of the newly formed Joint Staff.[447] The first developments can be traced to Prime Minister Hashimoto's 1996 question regarding JSDF-USMC equivalence, and to a USMC initiative drawing together US Marine and Army officers, with GSDF Major-Generals Oriki Ryoichi (later Joint Chief of Staff) and Kimizuka Eiji (later *Tomodachi* JTF commander) in December 2001. This was innovative in that previous GSDF-USMC communications had been conducted via the MSDF.[448] The structured development of the ARDB began with a key decision to place USMC Col. Grant Newsham within the Ground Research Development Center. Newsham as liaison officer became the prime USMC-GSDF mentor-advisor, and considered the JSDF 'already had 90% of the hardware, but none of the know-how,' and that the great imperative was to get people committed to the amphibious force concept and joint architecture mindsets to realise the concept.[449] The GSDF initially devoted only ¥110 million ($1 million), Isobe suggests that resistance to developing expeditionary amphibious capacity beyond narrow 'defensive defence' was overcome by the example of the USMC in *Operation Tomodachi*, HA/DR effectively legitimising combat capacity.[450]

Newsham describes the navigation process as dependent upon key individuals committing to the concept. GSDF Chief of Staff Kimizuka, and his deputy Lt-Gen. Banshō Kōichirō (Iraq commander), Vice-Joint Chief of Staff Lt.-Gen. Isobe Kōichi, a USMC Command and Staff College graduate, MSDF Self-Defense Fleet Commander Kawano Katsutoshi (later longest-serving Chief of Staff, Joint Staff), and retired Vice-Admiral Kaneda Hideaki, as well as Japan-based USMC officers who fended off hostile US enquiries.[451] The first major exercise, 'Dawn Blitz,' California, 2013, involved GSDF units operating from three MSDF ships with USMC-USN cooperation, 'learning and growing' despite ambitious MOD Working Group plans for retaking occupied islands.[452] After the exercise Newsham handed over to Col. Jonathan Goff, USMC, who identified that beyond 'large ticket' AAV-7A and MV-22 items, multiple smaller investments were required, such as folding helicopter rotors, distilled water flushing to prevent corrosion, and new communications equipment, not attention grabbing but without which operations would be compromised.[453] Japanese command and control was 'a significant area of weakness,' as was joint working, with limited protocols, practice, and planning, and poor joint communications and data sharing.[454] The positive side of amphibious 'jointness' is that the Brigade is based near (but not with) the MSDF transport base, although there are no plans for a South-West Regional Joint Command, despite the obvious operational benefits, nor that the Forces would flexibly transfer command of units under 'other-Force' commanders.

The issue of joint Force capabilities reaches its nexus in the ARDB, for all amphibious expeditionary operations are joint. Defence white papers from the 1990s emphasised joint working, but with limited results, illustrated by General Isobe referring to an 'epoch-making event in the history of the JSDF [...] the first time that the three services had ever acted together to plan an amphibious operation' in Dawn Blitz 2013, non-epochal, routine training events in NATO during the 1980s.[455] Vice-Admiral Ota Fumio stated that 'joint doctrine has existed since 1968 and is continuously under review and revision,' but this appeared more faith based than operationally tangible, and Ota acknowledged greater Force keenness for US-combined training than joint JSDF exercises—though joint-combined approaches provided a virtuous coincidence.[456] Jointness should be integral rather than ad hoc sharing-joining, and central to joint integration are command, control, and communications, which, when applied to Nanseishotō defence, would integrate air-sea-land ISR and firepower. While the Forces have conducted joint shipping strike exercises, these are tame, planned events with no truly joint command and no contingency element (introducing uncertainties, friction, risk), characteristic of most JSDF training. Joint coordination of JSDF anti-ship systems is extremely difficult to achieve, more so with JCG participation to avoid friendly and/or civilian vessel targeting. Yet only after 2010 did the MSDF and ASDF share Link-16 data-systems (not universal in 2020), the previous ASDF Link-11 having been uniquely encrypted to prevent MSDF/USAF direct access, while GSDF and JCG lack either system.[457]

Poor joint approaches were obvious in ODO, HA/DR, and procurement, and yet seemingly contradicted by NDA joint education and the 2006 Joint Staff Office replacing the Joint Staff Council, which had hobbled jointness by separate reporting to the civilian head. Even where joint operational approaches are lauded, as in Aceh, they are often a veneer lacking joint command and control, let alone doctrine and institutional buttressing. *Operation Tomodachi* and the Joint Task Force was an ad hoc exception driven by extenuating circumstances, but provided a prescient demonstration of potential and limitation. The development of JSDF amphibious capabilities is driving joint progress 'but it remains a slow process fraught with many challenges.'[458] One of them is Force willingness to adopt a JTF commander from beyond their own Force. Would an MSDF admiral be willing to have the naval force placed under a GSDF or ASDF JTF commander? With the ARDB, the GSDF had found its mentor-mentee position with the USMC, mirroring naval and air special relationships, and therefore all three Forces may feel more comfortable under Combined (US-Japan) rather than Joint (JSDF) command. US largesse has allowed the JSDF to 'cheap-ride' in large-scale exercises, as Col. Goff stated that the MOD has been reluctant to invest in vital training 'where failure is allowed and units pushed to their failure point. The GSDF is an army of companies with almost no training at the regiment or above' with 'a budgeting process deficiency coupled with a planning process deficiency.'[459] Long-standing joint communications issues abound, such as GSDF ARDB units unable to communicate with MSDF landing ships, which hold such potential for compromising operational integrity while being astonishingly simple for electronics leviathan Japan to remedy that the lack of urgency is difficult to comprehend.[460] The GSDF without Link-16 platform cannot readily share data, such communication issues compounding the CAS legacy issue of how ARDB air support may be delivered without killing Japanese troops and civilians. Such capability gaps are often ascribed to ARDB novelty, but they are based upon decades of deficient joint consciousness and prioritisation of resources towards dazzling large-ticket combat systems.

The resource-jointness problem is potentially even greater when applied to logistics. Limitations of Japanese air and sealift have been noted, but ARDB operational issues suggest logistical bottlenecks, with requirements far exceeding the simple 'loading' data for force size.[461] It appears that JSDF amphibious missions would be conducted on a 'tight' basis by a JTF of one MSDF DDH (*Izumo*), and two LST/LSD (*Ōsumi*) with an embarked ARG (Amphibious Ready Group) of one Amphibious Rapid Deployment Regiment (ABDR *suirikukidōrentai*), and Brigade elements of combat landing (AAV-7A), reconnaissance, artillery, signals, engineer, and logistic support, plus headquarters, comprising over 1,000 personnel.[462] Therefore, one ARG could possibly fit within JTF vessels, but without all their equipment, and with little spare capacity to transport and support reserve ARG, drip-feed deploying in small 'waves.' GSDF helicopters providing CAS would entail additional DDH or reduced air-transport capacity, unless troops and equipment could be deployed direct by MV-22, but even their range could be inadequate in the vast Nanseishotō region, with limited refuelling potential.

Once ashore, further logistical problems arise as to how to support the ARG. As previously demonstrated, modern operations are major resource consumers, and with such limited MSDF transport, and the five AOE vessels presumably busy servicing warships, ARG replenishment would become a concern. Standard USN-MSDF procedure is to replenish at sea (RAS, or underwater replenishment, UNREP) every two to three days, an AEGIS destroyer's daily fuel consumption of approximately 155-tonnes increasing during operations.⁴⁶³ Supplying JTF vessels, with escorting flotilla (four destroyers), would exhaust the largest MSDF AOE within one week without refuelling LCAC, helicopters, vehicles, or supplying troops ashore. One JTF would therefore appear to require at least two AOE, with time for relay transit from the operational area to replenish and return. Japanese AOE are also not equipped to replenish major ordnance, placing escorts in a difficult position if in high-intensity operations. Short of combat stores ships (AFS), the US bought three veteran Tyne-built *Lyness/Sirius*-class from the British RFA in the early 1980s to support their '600-ship' navy expansion plan, and some equivalent innovation appears necessary to sustain JSDF amphibious capabilities.⁴⁶⁴ Once ashore, the ground logistics of moving ordnance, fuel, water, and other supplies consumes manpower and vehicles, including helicopters, and this element would struggle for sealift within the stated JTF.

This critique of JSDF amphibious capabilities is not intended to diminish the value of the ARDB, nor of efforts to produce a truly joint capability, but highlights efforts to undertake innovative, challenging, and complex operations with limited resources when attention is drawn towards combat system and BMD procurement rather than mundane, logistical capability enhancements. The present situation may be imperfect, but the JTF and ARDB provide the JSDF with greatly enhanced capabilities over what they possessed only a few years before, and would make valuable contributions to HA/DR or defence operations, including as a deterrent.⁴⁶⁵ The inherent hazard is that political leaders could assume a comprehensive amphibious capability without appreciating the operational limitations. The same is also true for associated air-support issues.

Amphibious Air-Support

ASDF ability to support Nanseishotō amphibious operations in air defence and CAS roles would be limited, given the great distances, even though aerial refuelling capabilities have improved. Reports in December 2017 indicated that the MOD was evaluating equipping DDH *JS-Izumo* with STOVL F-35B fighters, creating small aircraft carriers.⁴⁶⁶ This was easily dismissed as repeating prior fantasies that the flush-decked *Ōsumi*-class was designed for Harrier jets, MSDF-USN studies concluding that this would be possible, limited as it was by minimal operable aircraft per-ship and insufficient distilled water for flushing out seawater.⁴⁶⁷ Despite MOD denials the reports were confirmed in December 2018 by aircraft orders.[468] Fixed-wing carrier aviation remains controversial, but would appear logical, equivalent to Italian and Spanish capabilities, however in the context of East Asian relations such a development would more likely be ascribed motivations influenced by historical militarism than contemporary security concerns.[469]

Izumo-class STOVL carriers would have major limiting factors. The small flight deck would prevent operating the more effective F-35C or E-2C/D AEW catapult-launched aircraft. Eight AEW/ASW helicopters would permit only eight F-35Bs, marginal for combat operations, the similar purpose-built Italian *Cavour* STOVL carrier operating eight-ten F-35Bs.[470] For comparison, the huge *HMS Queen Elizabeth* will operate twelve F-35B and twelve helicopters, in emergencies increasing to thirty-six fighters plus helicopters.[471] Eight F-35B would provide combat air patrols (CAP) of two fighters, unless helicopters were reduced with significant operational consequences, or if both *Izumo*-class vessels operated together. A two-ship MSDF capability would provide fewer than twenty F-35B, which, while significant, would not be considered able to ensure air-defence integrity within range of Chinese land-based aircraft. It has been suggested that if undertaking both ASW and air-defence duties, then the maximum sustained capability would be six F-35B, meaning that it lacked comprehensive capability.[472] An *Izumo* carrier would become the flagship of an amphibious task force, but one vessel could not combine CAP-CAS roles, which would be further limited if the large MV-22 were also carried. Progression from *Hyūga* to *Izumo*-class is significant despite their 'flat-top' similarities, as *Hyūga* has destroyer systems and weapons with extensive aviation capabilities, while *Izumo* is not only larger, but also is internally configured like a carrier, with only point-defence weaponry but extensive command and control (C2) capabilities. *Izumo* would only seem tenable as a training carrier, possibly refitted with a ski-jump for enhanced F-35B performance, like the Chinese *Liaoning*, or for amphibious operations.

The risks of developing carrier capabilities could mislead politicians that Japan possessed aircraft carriers equivalent to other 'major middle-powers' (UK/France), plus the financial ability to shoulder the potentially huge costs involved in developing a carrier fighter force and cultivating joint ASDF-MSDF F-35B management.[473] Australia considered developing F-35B capability for its *Canberra*-class amphibious vessels but judged that the costs did not warrant the investment, which could 'raise unrealistic expectations' for a 'much more muscular strategic posture' and heighten tension without providing requisite capabilities.[474] If Japan wished to cheaply develop naval aviation capacity, an example could be *RFA Argus*, a container ship converted to aircraft transporter during the Falklands conflict, so useful it was purchased, updated, and used in operations in Sierra Leone and Bosnia as well as for RN aviation training. *Argus* also acts as Primary Casualty Receiving Ship (PCRS), deploying to the Caribbean in April 2020 to support British Overseas Territories' corona virus care measures, the MSDF having avoided PCRS or 'hospital ship' development despite prescient defence and HA/DR operational requirements.[475] Such aviation vessels and PCRS would provide cheap, flexible 'platforms' for operations, with secondary transport capabilities, and of hull types commonly produced by Japanese shipbuilders.

Expeditionary Challenges: East China Sea

Attempting to manage Chinese East China Sea (ECS) challenges is not only a JSDF joint amphibious concern, as it has also greatly stretched JCG resources. During 2014–16, Chinese Coast Guard (CCG) and other agency vessels intruded into Japanese territorial waters around the Senkaku Islands on ten to fifteen occasions per quarter, and in 2019, 1,097 Chinese vessels (including trawlers) intruded during 282 days.[476] While such incidents became commonplace, movements of PLAN warships through the Japanese 'first island chain' attracted great attention, such as a PLAN frigate and (presumed PLAN) submerged submarine that sailed through Japanese contiguous waters (within 24 nautical miles) in January 2018. However, the decision of Defence Minister Kōno Tarō to publicise a submarine's passage through Japanese south-western contiguous waters on 18–20 June 2020, and identify it as 'probably Chinese,' constituted signalling to Beijing of continuing Japanese attention and MSDF ASW capabilities.[477] The MSDF commissioned a new submarine surveillance vessel, *JS-Aki*, in January 2020, to complement two elder sisters (commissioned 1991–2), focused upon the south-western seas. As an MOD-insider commented upon existing ASW capacity, 'clearly the government does not think that is sufficient to adequately monitor the movements of Chinese submarines.'[478]

Scrambles caused by Chinese aircraft also increased, from thirty-one in 2008, to 306 in 2012, reaching 851 by 2016, with the ASDF as stretched as the JCG, particularly as several incidents in 2016–17 involved groups of aircraft making 'innocent passage' through Japanese airspace.[479] The great numbers of incidents and distances involved, especially with the ASDF Naha base over 400km from the Senkaku Islands, stretched resources and raised questions as to the ability of the Force to react, with cheap and plentiful

Chinese UAV 'drones' adding 'swarming' potential for unsustainable Japanese reactions.[480] An inauspicious equivalent to the '1976 shock' occurred when an unarmed, slow Chinese State Oceanic Agency Y-12 aircraft flew over the Senkaku Islands on 13 December 2012, the ASDF Miyakojima radar facility 200km away unaware until informed by a JCG vessel indicating limitations of the JADGE air defence system that replaced BADGE in 2009.[481] Eight fighters scrambled but could not intercept, prompting public concern and greater ASDF attention, which on 10 January 2013 resulted in a PLAAF Y-8 transport aircraft being intercepted over Chinese oil platforms. This provoked a PLAAF fighter counter-interception, and numerous 'close-flying' ECS confrontations.[482] Managing the scale and significance of such air defence duties has proved vexing. Retired USN Admiral Dennis Blair suggested adopting 'strategic silence,' only scrambling for the most pertinent intrusions, thereby conserving resources, while others have suggested forward deployment to Miyakojima.[483] In early 2019, the ASDF adopted multiple new approaches, scrambling when PLAAF aircraft were detected taking off eastwards from Fujian bases, scrambling four rather than two intercepting aircraft, and maintaining standing ECS patrols.[484] This appears unsustainable given equipment and personnel limitations, illustrates vital ASDF peacetime airspace policing duties similar to JCG-MSDF maritime management, and raises questions regarding concentrating scarce budget resources on high-end F-35s rather than a high-low aircraft mix, exacerbated by increasing scrambles for Russian aircraft.[485]

Gaps between high and low end capabilities, and between institutions and laws, could be exploited with 'grey zone' incidents, civilian incursions or potential military exploitation of civilian resources, which could lead to the JSDF becoming embroiled in proxy civilian disputes. The MSDF and JCG have narrowed their 'gaps' but problems remain. Despite Advisory Panel recommendations the government did not directly address grey zone 'salami slicing' depletion of Japanese control and sovereignty, such as by Russia's 'little green men' proxies in the 2014 Crimea hybrid warfare crisis, or by the 'little blue men' of China's Maritime Militia in the ECS.[486] Such swarming, accompanied by the CCG, embodies China's campaign of '"three warfares" (*san zhan*): public opinion warfare, psychological warfare, and legal warfare,' by which opponents' energy and resistance are sapped, media agenda seized, and doubts instilled in legal claims, avoiding application of traditional military power.[487] If the JCG were overwhelmed, calling upon the MSDF for assistance, the navy would be able to deal with conventional opponents, but it has little experience nor discernible doctrine for dealing with non-state actors, militia-proxies, or joint naval-coast guard roles in such hybrid operations. Despite having negotiated a Japan-China Maritime Liaison Mechanism from 2008 to prevent incidents escalating, it only became operational in 2018.[488] One incident in August 2016 involved more than ten CCG vessels 'accompanying' over 200 Chinese fishing vessels around the Senkaku, repeating 'swarm and swamp' tactics in countering Philippine maritime control efforts around Scarborough Shoals in 2012.[489] Conventional threats in the ECS are not easily deterred, but JSDF and USFJ capabilities are considerable. The outstanding problems are of fine gradations between incident and crisis, civilian and military, state and non-state, and the degrees of tactical or strategic advantage that may be gained. For the JSDF, such challenges are possibly even more challenging in the South China Sea.

South China Sea

Japan has no alliance commitments in the South China Sea (SCS) nor does it have territorial claims.[490] Its primary goal is an absence of security concerns, allowing Japan-related shipping to move freely, and for Japanese companies and partners to exploit maritime resources. This approach has been consistent, and considerable efforts have been made to build liberal-pacific-mercantile relations with ASEAN states with minimal military profile, more complicated as the SCS 'has become the showcase for how China is translating its considerable economic power into political and military power,' becoming a barometer of 'progress' or liberal-international 'regression.'[491] The most obvious exhibits are the reclaimed and vastly engineered 'enhanced-island' reef/atoll SCS bases, complete with weapon and shelter installations, without basis in international law and yet tangible demonstrations of China's ability to project power and assert its expansive SCS claims.[492] Despite insistence upon their civilian nature, Beijing proudly publicised them as bases for H-6K bombers and J-11B fighters, Fiery Cross alone possessing longer runways than most Japanese airports and bases.[493] Japan's previous absence of strategic profile entails that any initiatives or involvement in security-related matters are viewed antagonistically, while Chinese military expansion in the maritime commons raises Japanese suspicions. As Reinhard Drifte states, 'China's SCS policies therefore fit into Japan's narrative of the "China Threat," whereas Japan's SCS policies fit into China's narrative of Japan as a troublemaker at the side of the US.'[494]

The USN has frequently conducted freedom of navigation exercises (FONOPS) to assert unimpeded rights to SCS maritime commons, 'something akin to a "core interest"' of the US and its dependence upon naval power projection.⁴⁹⁵ As Denny Roy states, USN FONOPS claims of 'innocent passage' have been directly challenged by Chinese forces, but Beijing's position is not supported by UNCLOS, they have rejected international adjudication, and the Chinese themselves assert such rights, including naval surveillance, within Japan's EEZ.⁴⁹⁶ Australia has conducted air and naval FONOPS, challenged by Chinese authorities, and US European and Japanese allies are perceived to be under pressure to do likewise, with the RN expected to sail their new carrier through the SCS to Japan in 2021 as a right-of-passage 'demonstration.'⁴⁹⁷ JSDF Chief of Joint Staff Kawano commented in 2015 that Japan did not 'have any plans to conduct surveillance in the South China Sea currently but depending on the situation, I think there is a chance we would consider doing so;' for Tokyo, however, there are multiple problems relating to risk, law, and norms, with perception and reaction in Beijing and Washington as vital determining elements.⁴⁹⁸

Japanese naval vessels have transited the SCS for decades, particularly for cooperative exercises with ASEAN states and India, but they have not attempted FONOPS, nor established a standing presence in the region, despite some such interpretations of MSDF multilateral HA/DR and SAR exercises, and the more obviously naval ASW exercises in late 2018 with DDH *JS-Kaga*, two destroyers and submarine *JS-Kuroshio*.⁴⁹⁹ Rebuffing Chinese complaints, Defense Minister Onodera revealed that while this was the first public SCS ASW exercise, the MSDF had conducted such missions since 2003.⁵⁰⁰ The 2013 National Security Strategy explicitly stated the nature of Chinese SCS security challenges for Japan, and the relationship between SCS and ECS issues, criticality for Japan's economy, as well as the desire to see disputes settled 'not by force, but in accordance with the law and rules.'⁵⁰¹ Chinese maritime assertions based upon 'historical' claims and notional lines produced equivalent prosecution by civil and naval maritime incidents, and diplomatic and media campaigns. The MOD has also clearly appreciated the dangers of Chinese oil-gas platforms in the ECS being transformed into 'island bases,' more A2/AD than power-projection assets, with infra-red radar reportedly fitted in 2016.⁵⁰² Despite the obvious concerns expressed, Bill Hayton asserts that the much vaunted A2/AD capabilities have not unduly concerned US forces, so confident are they in their abilities to counter many of its key elements, while Chinese military sources express concern at continuing defensive weaknesses.⁵⁰³

The core of China's A2/AD issue is Beijing's 'option' of re-unification (with Taiwan) by force, and excluding US and Japanese counter-unification efforts.

This issue helped realise US-Japan Guidelines reforms, but little attention is devoted to possible JSDF cooperation in defence of Taiwan. Tokyo's position since 1972 has been recognising the PRC, while maintaining cordial, blurred relations with Taiwan, but following increasing Chinese provocations, with Taiwan the ECS-SCS gateway, potential Japan-Taiwan defence cooperation has been mooted, particularly since the 2016 election of Beijing-opposing President Tsai Ing-wen. Cooperation proposals predominantly originated with Taipei, and retired JSDF senior officers more concerned with US alliance implications, but even the suggestion of a Force simulation of Taiwan conflict with Japan 'observing' was sufficient to enrage Beijing.[504] There is no suggestion that the JSDF is engaging with Taiwan's military, although Singapore has uniquely combined sole recognition of Beijing with basing military training forces in Taiwan. Japan has managed to negotiate fishing and other agreements with Taiwan that avoid the disputed Senkaku and Okinotorishima issues, and have engaged through coastguard, police, and HA/DR operations indicating close, positive engagement, but this appears 'one partnership too far' for risk averse Tokyo.

Western Pacific

For Japan, legal and territorial issues define the SCS-ECS dilemma. China has undertaken surveillance within Japan's EEZ, asserting innocent passage to Japanese objections. This is particularly problematic in the Western Pacific around Okinotorishima, which Japan has concreted, establishing scientific posts, and asserting that these rocks and reefs constitute an island despite not meeting UNCLOS definitions, thereby greatly extending Japan's claimed/disputed EEZ while weakening its international law defence claims. The MOD has stressed the island's strategic position for Guam-Taiwan shipping, and that the area has been the subject of intensive Chinese surveys, including for ten days in July 2020, researching submarine routes, fisheries, and energy resources.[505] This illustrates the intricate connections between territorial, maritime, economic, political, and naval aspects, with the MSDF applying its extensive maritime surveillance capabilities to the ECS, West Pacific, and from 2017 the Yellow Sea.

Yellow Sea

JCG-MSDF joint efforts monitoring sanction breaches by DPRK vessels in the Yellow Sea represent a new and effective mission variant, with sixteen suspected breaches of UNSCR 2375 September from 2017 to February 2020 published by MOFA, based upon images provided by MSDF reconnaissance aircraft, demonstrating their reach and technical capabilities.[506] Despite little publicity, Yellow Sea monitoring has become a multilateral sanctions operation, Japan hosting the Enforcement Coordination Cell at Yokosuka for US, British, Australian, Canadian, New Zealand, Korean, and French naval forces.[507] This functional engagement is highly valued by the Forces and the government, for despite being low profile it confirms the centrality of Japan in international security efforts, strengthens the alliance and partnerships, and is regarded as reinforcing international laws, norms, and the United Nations system, as well as contributing to Japanese national security, perfectly encapsulating the JSDF mission statement.

Arctic

Japan has a long history of Antarctic exploration, the MSDF plum-red *Shirase* research vessel the ultimate expression of Japanese liberal-pacific navalism, but Arctic affairs received scant security attention. Global warming resulted in economic, geo-political, and security concerns, multiple agency responsibilities overlapping with scant coordination indicating limited Japanese engagement.[508] From 2013, Japan appointed an Ambassador for Arctic Affairs, gained observer status at the Arctic Council, the NSS stating 'the Arctic Sea is deemed to have enormous potential for developing new shipping routes and exploration of natural resources [...] such potential could provide new causes of friction.'[509] For Japan, the primary issues are (as in the SCS) freedom of navigation and adherence to international law, but Ishihara Takahiro has illustrated that Chinese ambitions and investments have raised security concerns with NATO that could have implications for Japan.[510] The MSDF and JCG would be obliged to conduct Arctic protection duties if requested by shipping companies.[511] Potentially huge numbers of Chinese vessels transiting Japan's EEZ and the Bering Strait would require JCG attention, and in the past Chinese shipping often disregarded Russian coast guard jurisdiction despite warnings, causing concern in Russia by references to Arctic 'public commons.'[512] As yet there is little sign that the Arctic is being militarised, but it represents diversifying defence and security demands made of the JSDF and JCG to which they and their masters must flexibly adapt, plan, and invest.

Conclusion

This chapter has illustrated defence reforms undertaken in the twenty-first century in order to meet the range of security challenges that Japan is likely to encounter. The movement of defence 'centre' south-west enhanced Force mobility, and the increased frequency, variety, and distances of training and exercises, including with international partners, indicates a sustainable trend, but JSDF education and training will have to adapt with these developments, as will resource provision. The lack of investment in such 'software' has degraded capability development. It appears that technology cooperation will also lead to greater international defence engagement, alongside cyber security and intelligence enhancements. The extent of international engagement through operations expanded after the ODO late 1990s hiatus, when new and challenging forms of operations were established, some of them highly controversial. However, despite apparent capability gaps, such as in joint operations, the JSDF proved adept at adapting, with field commanders proving particularly capable in managing resources and ensuring that personnel could provide significant mission contributions without incurring undue risks to life, or to legal, constitutional, or socio-political norms. Even in familiar UN-PKO or HA/DR Japanese contributions demonstrated innovation, particularly in Haiti, a decade of experience slowly resulting in professionalization of Japan's overseas contributions. The negative aspects were the continuing limited range of ODO, which demonstrated lack of ambition, imagination, and risk assumption, as well as withdrawals due to non-mission, non-operational issues, which damaged Japan's image as a dependable security partner in Golan and South Sudan. MSDF Indian Ocean and ASDF Iraq-Kuwait terminations provided poor examples of policy-strategy management, but South Sudan appeared to make a mockery of the NSL, strategy, and 'Japan is Back!' rhetoric. It could be said that JSDF ODO had run their course, but it seemed that just as Japan discovered cogent, stated strategy it lost sight of why it was engaging in overseas missions at all. Lessons were learned by the Forces but few by policy leaders.

The most significant, lauded, and traumatic JSDF operations were for the 2011 Triple Crises. Never had the JSDF been so comprehensively mobilised and engaged in such intense operations for so long, nor had they previously merged so completely into Japanese society. The culture of 'otherness', of serving civil society while being isolated from it, seemed distant, even if kinship was place and time specific. The Forces serving their people gained a level of trust rarely imagined by most personnel. Their trauma was also evident. The *kizuna* of *Operation Tomodachi* surprised many, given USFJ Okinawa issues, but the bonds that irritated also strengthened, and in Tohoku those bonds tied USFJ, JSDF, and local communities, and connected with Australia, Korea, Israel and elsewhere. Divisions between civilian and military blurred amid close cooperation between local authorities, NGO, volunteers, and the Forces. The problem remains that so few civilians wish to don JSDF uniforms, many doubting Japan's political leadership during challenging times.

The development of military capabilities to meet emerging security threats, and attendant strategy, policy, and legal reforms, particularly under the Abe administrations, threatened to fracture the *kizuna* spirit. The CSD reinterpretation, 2015–16 NSL process, and 'morning report' scandals reintroduced an air of cynical mistrust regarding defence matters, compounded by USFJ accidents and planning for dramatically enhanced military power beyond 'defensive defence'. Amphibious forces have not raised great public alarm, but the OCA cruise-missile announcement and F-35B carrier study caused shock and concern, even among those positively disposed towards the Forces. These three military capabilities could potentially provide the illusion of great power that statesmen find alluring, and tempt the less well defence-educated into pursuing adventurous policies of dubious provenance. Each of the capabilities has a sound strategic foundation, yet there is an implicit hazard. If national leaders can wisely coordinate partly-expeditionary Forces, in close coordination with civilian institutions, the effort will have been worthwhile. Questions remain as to Japanese capacities not only to operate jointly, between the Forces, but also with other agencies, and the difficulties of managing 'grey zone' hybrid contingencies appear not to have been given the attention they deserve. As in the Cold War, a conventional invasion assault, or maritime blockade of Japan are possible, but it appears far more likely that an 'attack' would arrive by terrorist, stealth, or 'hybrid' means, such as semi-state actors undermining Japanese control authority by operating in the gaps between military and civilian institutions. In this scenario as in many others, civilian control is less vital than civilian coordination.

Defence reforms have incrementally facilitated a changed balance of the Forces. The long-isolated GSDF has built an alliance-mentor relationship and multiple partnerships, and from the late Cold War gradually and significantly expanded its responsibilities from territorial defence to maritime security, seemingly leading the MSDF and ASDF in expeditionary amphibious operations. It was even granted, without apparent qualification, responsibility for the AEGIS Ashore system (since suspended). This demonstrates the prestige accumulated through HA/DR and ODO, but also the skill of the Ground Staff in shaping political perceptions of future defence and security imperatives. From a foundation of legitimacy deficit, the GSDF has risen rapidly and attained more prestigious high ground than appeared possible. The MSDF and ASDF retain exceptional capabilities and alliance relations, but their prestige and policy influence have been relatively reduced even as their national and regional security centrality have become yet more enhanced by the threats posed by China and North Korea. Of all the armed forces, the civilian JCG has perhaps grown most significantly in role, status, scale, and central crisis management. Whether the Forces are capable of dealing with the multi-domain security challenges they will face isn't clear. China has attempted to usurp Japanese authority in the ECS and assert its control over the Senkaku Islands through coastguard fisheries, and such finely calibrated proxy-offensive require equally subtle civil-military coordinated management, between the JSDF, JCG, and *kantei*.

The Yoshida Doctrine can be regarded as alive and well, for Japanese defence spending has barely altered in real terms over thirty years. US alliance dependency remains the strategic core, and despite 'salami slicing' norms, Japanese self-perception of a peaceful, pacific, non-belligerent state remains strong. This continuity is comforting for some, but alarming when considering the pressures of national debt, poor economic growth, and demographic challenges that will squeeze Force provision in the future, even if there is less pressure from post-Trump US administrations to contribute more to regional defences. Despite the vagueness of an 'Abe Doctrine' notion, the parameters of Japanese norms and restrictions have expanded, and recourse to military options has become normalised. There is greater sense of Japan potentially engaging in war beyond 2020 than there was during the Cold War, not due to Japanese belligerency, but rather as a result of the enhanced threats posed to Japanese territorial integrity and existential security by China and North Korea. The distinctive Abe contribution to Japanese security would be the sustained effort over both periods in office to build complimentary partnerships with liberal-democrat states in Asia and beyond, so as to buttress Japan and its US alliance. More than defensive reforms to deter or counter armed threats, this diplomatic effort to shape the security environment to more readily suit Japan's needs is an innovation that Yoshida may well have favoured.

CONCLUSION

'Everyone has roots. But they may extend from places scattered in space and time, and they may be roots from which one has become separated, or which have been designated in some way unsound.'[1]

The purpose of this book was to provide an insight into the nature of various incarnations of 'the defenders of Japan' after the Second World War and to attempt to solve the puzzle regarding their origins, development, status, nature, and capabilities. It is hoped that the puzzle has been largely if not completely solved and that connections between origins and capabilities, cultures and norms have been not only described but analytically examined and critically evaluated. Their roots were varied and of disparate degrees of acceptability to contemporary society. The salience of imperial legacy is the most difficult to analyse and understand, for it can be lauded and held up for institutional and international admiration, or damned into such submission that it becomes scarcely recognised. The Maritime Self-Defense Force is proud of its imperial heritage, it will take foreign visitors to the *Mikasa* museum, happily stand by the statue of Admiral Tōgō, and its officers recount tales of naval academy exercises where students re-fight, and win, the Battle of Midway. This is an institution comfortable with a lovingly crafted version of its past. The Air Self-Defense Force has likewise cherry-picked its heritage, from the dawn of powered flight, through the technical achievements and skill of the wartime air forces, and by association it taps the rich vein of American aviation history. The Ground Self-Defense Force are 'the other,' those with a legacy so tainted it is rarely acknowledged, the narrative of the Imperial Army so unremittingly negative that to claim ancestry of any constituent part could contaminate the modern whole. It took sixty-five years for the Force to openly associate itself with the legacy of the National Police Reserve, the most innocuous of bodies, and from which it unconsciously retains many less-martial traits evidently valued by the Japanese people.

The turmoil of imperialism was evident during the 1946–54 continuation of wars beyond Japanese state control, but with state knowledge and a degree of management. Startling inconsistencies between the reception of former Siberian POWs, and ex-imperial veterans caught up in conflicts beyond the surrender and treated with official disdain, illustrate the double standards applied to 'holdouts' emerging from jungles in the 1970s. Japanese Korean War casualties were barely recognised, the government avoiding acknowledgement or responsibility, as with those lost in Vietnam War service, Japan generally preferring to ignore the uncomfortable truth that its 'long peace' was blighted by war during its formative years. Yet, the MSA and NPR were formed during this post-war decade of conflict as distinctly civilian, performing vital para-military and 'para-naval' duties, and only transitioning to assume other roles and identities in the rapidly evolving Cold War and end of occupation period. The NSF was a pre-military, enabling the eventual development of clearly non-police armed forces that emerged as the JSDF, yet another 'non-military' which grew to closely resemble a conventional military, Korean War experience having particularly indicated the naval value of Japan to Washington. Each incarnation represented an evolving expression of what became known as the Yoshida Doctrine, the 'minimal possible demonstration' to retain US support and economic recovery—however, the more obviously military the Forces became, the more relevant was Ashida's critique and the more strain was placed upon the integrity of Article 9. The avoidance of such contradictions resulted in Force legitimacy deficit and efforts to redress this through promotion activities. The unintended consequences of disaster relief activities, however, would have a far greater positive impact upon Japanese social perceptions of the JSDF. The Forces thereby became the primary domestic defenders of Japan decades before they could make that claim for external security.

Such has been the profound change in Japanese society since 1945, and a remarkable transformation in military technology, that it is difficult to imply a great remaining imperial effect upon the modern armed forces. The MSDF display the greatest sense of continuity, with the institutions of Yokosuka and Etajima at its heart, and enjoying the perpetuation of great naval relationships, with the Royal Navy, US Navy and others. The MSA provided the MSDF with an unsullied platform upon which to build, and one tested in conflict, having sustained casualties in the cause of national and allied security, while

CONCLUSION

the GSDF struggled most with its sense of legitimacy, and its place within society and even in the defence of Japan. During the Cold War, the three Forces essentially planned separate and distinct defence campaigns, and while the GSDF depended upon the other Forces to aid their defence doctrines, it formed an almost insignificant part in their planning. GSDF non-military roles, the rescue, relief, and recovery aspects of its duties which became essential parts of its institutional culture and character, guaranteed it continuing local, national, political and financial support, and unexpectedly transformed into representing Japanese national character overseas. Endearment was slow to emerge, and subject to civilian control rebukes, the warmth from communities highly localised and perhaps short-lived, but as in a counter-insurgency campaign, Force influence slowly spread out from loyal bastions. The events of the 3/11 triple crises reconfirmed the dedication and value of the GSDF, not always apparent from its conventional defensive duties. The sense of searching for legitimacy within Japanese defence conflicts with the GSDF's general acceptance by civil society as 'less martial,' a para-military HA/DR emergency force.

The identity of the new Forces was humane, less martial, more humble, and dominated by public duty ethos, in stark contrast to imperial military traits. However, the GSDF also embraced the identity of a modern army, a technically advanced, heavy-hard armoured force escaping from one more IJA legacy. The purely domestic defence role also aided Force culture development by sanitary containment, preventing accusations of threatening 'power projection' from Hokkaido or Fuji. MSDF development was more easily accommodating of IJN legacies, and the navy felt able to refer to itself as such and engage with other navies upon a platform of shared cultural traits. The approach was far more expansive, little concerned with critiques of power projection, for the new navy, like the GSDF, had discovered roles that were sanitary, and un-besmirched by aggressive imperial strategies. Unlike the GSDF, these were direct legacies of imperial experience. Mine and antisubmarine warfare provided (initially) purely defensive roles to concentrate upon for professional fulfilment, with the added benefit of tutelage from the world's greatest navy. The role of the USN, from tutor to partner, was vital for the re-founding of the Japanese navy, not only as a capable force, but also as a respectable institution within Japan and overseas. Japanese naval capabilities had grown so greatly by the end of the Cold War that close mentoring was far less necessary, not least as the MSDF had conformed to USN strategic imperatives and effectively become semi-detached from Japanese policy and strategy by the 1970s. Adapting Paul Midford's concept, Japan's navy had 'de-centred' from Japanese defence. This appears in hindsight extremely worrying not only in terms of defence planning, but obviously also for civilian control issues, the dominating architecture of post-war Japanese defence, and yet one which the MSDF felt confident enough to effectively abdicate from as it felt appropriate. Both navies had become institutionally and culturally intimate and comfortable, the embrace of the democratic world's leading armed force being sufficiently re-assuring to allow flouting of a key aspect of democratic control, so that even without threats or operational focus the relationship would have likely continued. The demands of missile-defence and managing the rise of China, however, provided renewed focus for their intimacy. The ASDF struggled little with the legacy issue, but as with the other Forces it developed within an environment of stunted legitimacy, whereby defence expenditure and personnel were frequently derided, and where professional capacities were rarely tested or valued beyond the Force. When professional capacity was significantly tested in 1976, it was found to be wanting, and the air force was perhaps unlucky to be the only Force so operationally evaluated during the Cold War. Even between the Forces, such professional military-naval capacities were not assessed to any great extend, such was the sense of separation of operational doctrine. The stovepipe, silo culture of detachment, from society and from other Forces, became entrenched, and only began to erode after the Cold War, in overseas and disaster relief operations.

Civilian control could be blamed for such incidents or the prevailing environment, as it was viewed as avoidance of military infiltration of policy making and involvement in politics, effectively detaching policy from operational efficacy. This decapitation was accompanied by a neglect of that professional defence domain, by default such needs being met by uniformed officers, resulting in the disparate development of three national defence plans. Civilian control only embodied and institutionalised the prevailing social norms of anti-militarism, particularly anti-imperial militarism. That such pacifist norms remained so important in society, and, despite erosion, remain powerful symbols to the present day, is a matter this book cannot answer, but the contrast with West Germany is prescient. The rearmament of both countries occurred at approximately the same time, with foreign forces providing national defence, and yet the country with conscription, far larger foreign military presence, and far larger proportion of GNP expended upon defence was by far the less conflicted. Japan's rearmament took place without inclusive, multilateral institutions for defence or trade, largely without public conscious-

CONCLUSION

ness of imminent security threats, and despite the constitution seeming to bar such policies. Ashida was effectively justified in his denunciation of Yoshida, from the conservative perspective that they shared, that Japan required revival including a re-founded military acceptable to the people. Politicians from Hatoyama in the 1950s, through Koizumi and Abe, sought to utilise the preamble of the constitution to somehow override the uncomfortably restrictive technical aspect of Article 9, that military power and belligerency were forbidden. Constitutional reform is beyond the scope of this work, but the basic law cannot be avoided, nor the astonishing degree of dexterity displayed by Japan's leaders in avoiding its more obvious implications.

In terms of providing effective defence, without having been tested it is difficult to assess JSDF capabilities from 1954. The notion that Japan was capable of self-defence by the 1960s was and is largely derided, with near-independent capability only reached between the Nakasone cabinets and collapse of the Soviet Union, as the growth-trajectory of Japanese defence surpassed the decline of Russian Pacific power. Within this overall pattern, however, areas of particular strength and weakness are evident. The naval forces appeared to be the most effective and the most closely integrated with US forces, not unrelated aspects, and gradually built capabilities from minesweeping and coastal patrol foundations through ASW expertise. The development of ASW skills was far from a simple 'buy and build' process, but involved developing operational doctrine, which could not simply be used 'off the shelf' from USN models, given the disparities of resources, roles, and cultures. This was a long process, through which MSDF culture and command demonstrated deft suppleness, smoothly integrating land and sea-based air assets, and pushing ahead of JDA and PMO approaches in integrating with USN operational patterns and procedures to maximise operational effectiveness. The MSDF, like Genda Minoru, was haunted by the IJN ghosts of blockade by aircraft and submarine, and largely considered socio-political limitations upon its ability to 'secure Japan' as irrelevant, de jure restrictions eventuating into de facto 'civilian catch-up' as the JDA and PMO struggled to keep pace with duties the MSDF were planning or performing.

This naval approach clearly had implications for the other Forces, as it did for government. The ASDF was evidently unable to provide air-defence or maritime-strike for the beyond-coastal operations that the MSDF was planning, certainly until the 1980s, by which time the scope of naval operations had moved ever further off-shore with sea-lane defence policies. This fragmented scenario planning was far from ideal for overall defence and investment planning, but the demonstrable inability of the ASDF to secure its northern airspace was as alarming as Michael Hughes had related in 1972. The contemporary ASDF response had been to ridicule such poor assessments of Japanese air power, but it was clearly incapable of a core task, despite the peculiarities of the Belenko case, and ASDF establishment having been clinched by references to the RAF in the Battle of Britain. Despite the massive investments in training, procurement, and broader defence-industrial *kokusanka*, many wondered what had been the point. This was a view surely shared by many naval officers, but the great expansion of naval duties with little reference to the ASDF compounded the problem. The inability of the MSDF to realise the potential AEW capability it possessed in the 1950s demonstrates general culpability in failing to effectively prepare to defend Japan even by standards the Forces created for themselves.

Both air and naval Forces also had significant capability gaps for territorial defence. Ironically, the ASDF developed anti-shipping missiles and delivery aircraft before the MSDF acquired such ship-launched or air-borne capabilities, despite obvious improvements in Soviet surface warships and amphibious capabilities from the 1960s. Neither greatly invested in securing Hokkaido from such threats, echoing widespread scepticism of the Soviet invasion threat, and lending scant credence to the core GSDF defence role of deterring and countering amphibious and airborne invasion with coastal forces or CAS/interdiction-strike capabilities. ASDF inability to secure air-defence suggests that it was possibly incapable of expanding its capacities. The MSDF appeared uninterested in distractions from its core pursuit of ASW capacity within its own, and USN, operational scenarios, and perhaps rightly relied upon its nascent submarine deterrent force. The failure of the MSDF to adequately develop its own AAW capacities until the 1980s was more closely related to resource and technical difficulties that plagued other 'middle power' navies, although Australia managed despite facing lesser air threats. The poverty of efforts made to support GSDF movements through air and sealift were equally notable, and followed the established pattern of 'frontline-first' investment and attention. Most ASDF and MSDF shortcomings were addressed and by the 1990s they appeared to be far more capable and balanced, but logistical support to the GSDF remained low priority, as demonstrated in the efforts to transport troops and equipment overseas.

Such limitations remain in the twenty-first century, and provide a significant bottleneck in the development of mobile units for defending Japan's south-western islands. There appeared little point in developing such a capability and scale of mobile units if they were incapable of being deployed and sustained, but the investments required, such as in MSDF AOE and large transport vessels, based upon extensive civil marine engineering experience, would be relatively small. When faced with such logistical bottlenecks, other navies leased ro-ro or container ships, adapted overseas designs, or purchased used vessels from allies. The MSDF fleet of forty-six surface warships and three amphibious vessels in 2016 was supported by five AOE.[2] The equivalent Royal Navy force was nineteen surface warships, three amphibious warfare vessels, three auxiliary dock, four fast-transport vessels, and seven AOE/AO, the British amphibious and support vessels also being far larger than their Japanese equivalents and therefore able to sustain larger operations for longer periods.[3] This comparison reflects different notions of naval and amphibious operations and is not made to hold up British procurement as an unlikely model of efficiency, but to illustrate that even a shrunken and depleted RN recognised the value of its support 'tail.' The poverty of investment in support elements is matched by the relatively small establishments provided for civilian officials within the MOD and MOFA, and the range of civilian agencies that support intelligence and cyber aspects of security. Only the JCG appears to have received resources in accordance with its roles, and even this large force has become highly stressed by the burdens of ECS security management in confrontation with China.

Coordination limitations between the Forces have been associated with their lack of 'jointness,' but involve fundamental objections compounded by a lack of sense of urgency in developing common doctrines, procedures, institutions, and ethos. Other armed forces have developed joint capabilities under intense operational, financial, or political pressure. During the first seventy years of Japanese post-war defence there appeared to be few equivalent pressures in Japan. They had the advantages of the resources and relative freedom afforded by civilian control that largely disregarded operational issues, and the basis of the NDA, one of the world's few truly joint military academies that did provide 'cross-silo' relationships to aid those joint ventures that the Forces conducted. Despite references to joint operations and practices in 1985, little had been achieved until 2001, and the efforts beyond then were fractional.[4] Some joint approach innovations were attempted, most notably under DG-JDA Ishiba Shigeru, conscious of developments in the US, UK, and Australia, not least in Iraq and Afghanistan operations.[5] The much heralded new joint approach was launched in 2004, but lines of control remained direct from the DG-JDA to each Force Chief of Staff.[6] Military journalist Fukuyoshi

Shōji insists that initial joint efforts were driven by the JDA Internal Bureau, based on a March 2006 review which revealed that almost nothing had been achieved.[7] The Operations Planning Bureau was regarded as particularly important for joint planning and operations agenda setting and processing, but in the 2013 MOD restructuring the Bureau was abolished, its sections subsumed within the Defense Policy Bureau.[8] The Ministry of Finance as a restraining factor on expenditure also helped propel the joint-progress process by clearly indicating that reductions in budgets were not transitory but the new normal.[9] This tight financial control appeared to focus minds on the long-term efficiencies of joint efforts, but the development of amphibious forces and the extant and scarcely believable deficiencies of inter-Force communications entails fresh investment is required.

Politicians with defence interests and/or expertise were few, Nakasone unique in rising to the summit. The widely derided dearth of strategy was representative of a poverty of deep thought regarding national security, expressed in the concept of 'balancing' between the Forces, accepted with little question or deeper consideration. Given the great costs associated with maintaining GSDF manpower, cuts, as suggested by the Higuchi Report, would appear appealing. They would however be offset by the fear that such a decision would have distinctly uncomfortable consequences related to base closures in rural areas, loss of jobs, concerns regarding disaster relief capacities, and even of (unlikely) support to police. National leaders over the period consistently appeared to have little concern in the intricate details of Force configuration, nor in how they were to operate, or cooperate. Interest was rarely spiked, but usually occurred in reference to public failures (Belenko Incident), limitations of actions (Hanshin Earthquake), perceived infringements into civilian policy realms (Kurisu, Tamogami), or tragedies (ODO civilian deaths, suicide-bullying incidents). If the immediate post-war period is often regarded as a defence and security 'blank period' in Japan, much of the Self-Defense Forces' history could be regarded for most civilian leaders as a ledger with little detail, where funding was provided and Forces emerged but with little notion of how they were formed or why they emerged as they did. The obvious exceptions were MITI and *kokusanka* controls, the *bōeizoku* defence tribe members, and those few with exceptional knowledge and insight.

Despite the lack of expertise among politicians, the cogent critiques of Diet members during and after the Cold War were limited but significant, and despite the established binary left-right positions on JSDF constitutionality, such well-informed oversight was not confined to any single party or sympathy. The post-Cold War period saw the emergence of new generations of politicians, many with more pronounced security interests, less bound by previous prejudices, but also more willing to question both the extant norms of liberal-pacifism and assumptions of 'appropriate' defence expenditure and Force levels. In this the Diet was poorly served by standing committees until the twenty-first century, and there was no equivalently robust institution as the US Government Accountability Office or the UK National Audit Office, both of which serve the respective legislatures independent of executive control, and which provide effective sources of data and critical reports of defence expenditure. As in other countries experiencing such generational shifts, there has been concern that the cautions of the generation that experienced the Second World War and the harshness of the post-war period have been replaced by generations who were raised amid entitled privilege and displayed impatience and intolerance with security challenges and resistance to reform. Peter Katzenstein and others have described Japanese defence as a 'penetrated system,' where 'self-defense' was effectively harnessed by and for US interests, at the political level, and through military-military relationships.[10] This critique has an obvious basis in Cold War defence planning, and the ever more detailed Guidelines reforms would appear to support the 'penetrated' thesis. Abe Shinzo perhaps provides one of the most obvious counterpoints, for despite his obvious respect for the United States and the alliance, he appeared to be one of the strongest advocates for replacing 'penetrated' elements with 'Made in Japan' units, not least the constitution, for prestige and for the supposed limitations imposed upon policy and operations, particularly JSDF ODO.

JSDF overseas operations, launched as an extemporised form of alliance tension amelioration, proved of such great utility that momentum developed to continue and expand them. Notions of success built upon absence of fatalities as much as tangible achievements in a diplomacy driven process with scant regard for military evaluation. What became an identified Japanese 'PKO' model was actually several models firmly tied to a core of non-combative HA/DR and human security-based peace support functions that proved adaptable for UN and other missions, even in post-war Iraq. This brought advantages, such as avoiding having to address the constitutional issue of belligerency, but also constraints, as JSDF ODO failed to innovate and evolve to meet changing demands. The exceptions of Haiti and anti-piracy operations cast a shadow of stunted development on other missions, while withdrawal from South

Sudan proved a dismal nadir for Japan's international-liberal ventures. The Ground Staff had resisted the South Sudan mission due to risk-management concerns, but these had been overridden by a DPJ government, and further denigrated by LDP irresponsibility. Indian Ocean and Iraq-Kuwait terminations provided poor examples of policy-strategy management, but South Sudan appeared to make a mockery of the hard-fought NSL, National Security Strategy, and 'Japan is Back!' rhetoric. JSDF ODO had perhaps run their course, but as Japan discovered effective operational modes integrated with cogent strategy, it lost sight of why it was engaging in overseas missions. Important lessons were learned by the Forces but also by Japan's security partners. Japan did not burnish its reputation for dependability and resilience in a security-risk environment.

Despite depictions of success and achievement, it is unclear whether the operations achieved what the Japanese governments that launched them had expected. The first generation demonstrated burden-sharing and deflected international criticism of Japan as a free-rider, but it was unlikely to win a permanent UN Security Council seat. That failure was scarcely caused by JSDF ODO, and new operations were launched, some, like Iraq, with alliance-management intentions, others seemingly more equivalent to ODA projects, demonstrating Japanese international presence and international-liberal credentials. By doing so, they conversely also normalised the utilisation of armed forces in foreign contexts, an incremental 'militarisation' of policy, albeit within non-belligerent terms and legal restrictions, and opened up possibilities for defence engagement and strategic partnership, actively pursued in the twenty-first century. This partnership proliferation predated the Abe strategic reforms and only in hindsight assumed strategic purpose, but has developed significant momentum, not least with the burgeoning relationship with Australia, and potential for partnership with the EU under the 2018 Strategic Partnership Agreement (SPA).[11] Through such SPA the role of the Forces in foreign and broader security policies has become normalised for bilateral and multilateral engagement.

The periods of amicable détente Japan experienced with Russia and China illustrated the possibilities for regional engagement, including defence diplomacy and functional engagement, but the inherent difficulties of sustaining engagement with parties to territorial disputes became obvious, particularly those not adhering to liberal-democratic values. There was no sudden, comprehensive militarisation of Sino-Japanese disputes or precipitous dive into mutual securitisation, rather a gradual loss of trust, and increasing concern

CONCLUSION

with China's economic, military, and diplomatic developments, but the hinge period 2010–12 prompted the inescapable conclusion that China would not allow Japan to continue to ignore security disputes. Yet the Chinese challenge is not purely or primarily military, unlike that of North Korea, and can be neither disregarded nor readily managed, and developments of Japanese strategic and defensive elements to deter and counter Chinese and DPRK security challenges have been mildly transformative and consistent across both LDP and DPJ administrations. Yet there appears to be no formula or mechanism by which to solve the myriad Sino-Japanese problems, nor any framework to ameliorate their consequences. With such astonishing growth and power, China is attempting to dominate its surroundings, with an Asian Monroe Doctrine, but unlike the US in the nineteenth century, it is attempting to assume ownership or guardianship of major maritime commons and territorial features on the basis of spurious historical and *terra nullius* grounds. The ultimate prognosis for Japanese territorial integrity would be less than healthy, given Chinese insistence upon Senkaku sovereignty, increasing suggestions regarding all Nanseishotō, and the escalation of Chinese assertions under President Xi, 2016–20, hence the renewed efforts to ameliorate the US and solidify partnerships. Lingering use of North Korea as a cypher by which to build defence capacity to counter Chinese power, seemingly to avoid the excessive wrath of CCP denunciations and to calm ASEAN states more than any notion of deception, appeared hollow, reintroducing an 'Alice in Wonderland' element to Japanese defence planning.

Despite this minor oddity, the trend from 2004 involved movement of Japan's defence 'centre' south-west, with enhanced Force mobility, and the increased frequency, variety, and distances of training and exercises, including with international partners, previously avoided for both political and cost reasons. Defence reforms have allowed the GSDF to develop a US alliance-mentor relationship and multiple partnerships, significantly expanding responsibilities from territorial defence to maritime security, leading expeditionary amphibious capability development, and even carving out missile defence roles. The Ground Staff effectively influenced political perceptions of future defence and security imperatives, gaining prestige from decades of ODO and disaster relief duties, the first significant change in balance between the Forces, despite core MSDF and ASDF exceptional capabilities. Chinese attempts to bluntly swamp and subtly usurp Japanese authority in the ECS requires a symmetrically subtle civil-military coordinated management of armed forces, primarily the JCG, under close political direction, but doubts remain, not regarding the kinetic combat abilities of Japan's defenders, but related to 'whole of government' capability in strategic communication and hybrid security challenge management. There is a risk that three emergent military capabilities, amphibious forces (the ARDB), offensive counter-air (OCA) missile forces, and fixed-wing naval aviation (F-35B) could delude statesmen into risking adventurous policies of dubious provenance, with JSDF joint capabilities and civilian control less important in this context than civilian coordination and capacity limitation and situational awareness. In this as in many other elements of Japanese defence and security considerations the hardware and its operators are dependable, but their capabilities are diminished by relative lack of investment in and attention to the supporting 'software' of policy, education, and training, paralleling unbalanced investment in high-profile combat systems over capability enhancing supporting, linking, and enabling systems. More than hardware, the most innovative aspect of the 2018 defence review and Guidelines was the adoption of a cogent sense of mission for the Forces and for the 'whole of government': to *shape* Japan's security environment including by partnerships, ODO, and defence engagement, to *deter* potential foes from challenging sovereignty by the cost of engaging the JSDF and USFJ, and to *counter* any such challenges from proxy-hybrid efforts through to high-intensity kinetic combat. From 2018, Japanese defence at least appeared to have acquired strategic salience.

The various laws, reforms, re-interpretations, and re-structuring that were undertaken during the second Abe administration could be regarded as constituting such an investment in security 'software,' and the process up to 2016 was impressive, if failing to generate broad public support for many measures. They formed the most comprehensive revision of security mechanisms since 1954, complemented by unprecedented double revision of US-Japan Guidelines, and can be interpreted as both a more assertive and independent Japan, or as a reaffirmation of Japanese alliance loyalty. This potential ambiguity provides flexibility for Japanese policy in an increasingly uncertain security environment. The unease Japan has felt at US policy at various times since the Nixon shock, fearing both entanglement in foreign wars and abandonment by Washington, was compounded by the Trump administrations demands from 2016 for massively increased host nation support, possibly quadrupling with troop withdrawals as a potential coercive measure, and comments upon the unfair nature of the security treaty.[12] While the logic of the demand and the comment could be supported, the manner of delivery was alarming in Tokyo, not least due the huge efforts Prime Minister Abe had invested in currying presidential favour. As with previous defence procurement projects, large-item purchases of US systems were announced as major mitigation efforts that appeared only partially successful: F-35B, offensive strike missiles, and Aegis-Ashore.

The most significant JSDF operations were for 2011 Triple Crises rescue and relief, being mobilised, engaged, and integrated within Japanese society to the greatest extent in their history, enjoying public trust and experiencing personal trauma. The *kizuna* of *Operation Tomodachi* surprised many, but civilian-military distinctions blurred as did those of nationality amid close cooperation in an affirmation of alliance legacy and partnership promise. The domestic and overseas niche roles of the Forces were as evident as their ability to work so intimately with US forces, their legitimacy and popularity never greater. Yet despite this few civilians wished to serve, and the ability to sustain the Forces serving a diffident nation undergoing a dramatic demographic transformation to an ageing society, saddled with colossal public debt, does not bode well in a country with politicians and voters reluctant to embrace radical solutions and seemingly at ease with continuity into relative decline.

The Yoshida Doctrine could be regarded as alive and well, for Japanese defence spending has barely altered in real terms over thirty years, US alliance dependency remains the strategic core, and despite 'salami slicing' norms, Japanese self-perception of a peaceful, pacific, non-belligerent state remain strong. This continuity is comforting for some, but alarming when considering Japan's relative decline. Despite the vagueness of an 'Abe Doctrine' notion, the parameters of Japanese norms and restrictions have expanded, and recourse to military options has become normalised. The potentially radical aspect of an 'Abe doctrine' could be, as Christopher Hughes states, the aim to displace the 'Yoshida doctrine' and 'escape from the domestic and international constraints of the post-war regime', but whether such a doctrine would survive post-Abe is unclear, yet seems unlikely to endure like Yoshida's incarnation.[13] The distinctive Abe contribution to Japanese security would be the sustained effort over both periods in office to build complimentary partnerships with liberal-democrat states in Asia and beyond to buttress Japan and its US alliance. The constitutional revision process could have become a self-defeating process in this effort, but Abe's September 2020 resignation may have stilled the revision campaign. More than defensive reforms to deter or counter armed threats, sustained diplomatic efforts to shape the security environment to more readily suit Japan's needs constitutes a Yoshida-compliant approach.

Through assertions of 'pro-active contributions to peace' Japan has been attempting to demonstrate it is a newly assertive security actor to its ally and partners, while attempting to also demonstrate that it is a peaceful country to its own people and international society. It also attempts to assert its liberal-internationalist credentials through adherence to international law, and attempts to use this as a weapon against China, but compromises this by an 'UNCLOS-avoiding' approach to Okinotorishima, and insistence on prolonging a futile dispute with Korea over Takeshima (Dokdo). Abe attempted to draw as close to Putin and Russia as US alliance and UN sanctions permitted, wisely given the desire to conclude a peace treaty but less so when asserting international law and the sanctity of national territory. The government also appeared to have limited appreciation of how difficult it was for security partners to have faith in Japanese resolve and fidelity given the risk averse nature of policy and social opinion, compounded by the South Sudan imbroglio. In Cambodia and Iraq, attacks and civilian deaths shocked society but government determination and Force professionalism sustained the missions through difficult periods, illustrating what was possible, but each example of weakness, irresolution, or escape from crisis reduced the credibility and attractiveness of Japan as a security ally or partner.

Issues facing the defenders of Japan from the third decade of the century range from grand strategic issues of relative decline amid rising and assertive China in an 'unfriendly neighbourhood' through to becoming one of the major public actors in combating the corona virus pandemic. In the post-Abe world of Japanese politics and policy there is uncertainty that there are sufficient leaders with foreign and defence policy competence to match the somewhat lofty aims of strategic intent. The result of the US presidential election as ever will be a major factor, not least as Japan appears to extract itself from an embarrassingly clumsy process of preparing and purchasing extremely expensive and high-profile Aegis Ashore systems only to suspend plans in 2020 and examine a range of alternative options including installation on oil rigs, merchant vessels, and destroyers.[14] BMD remains a key but expensive area of defence investment, but public concern appears oddly fickle give the unpredictable nature of the Pyongyang regime, and given diverse defence budget pressures it remains to be seen whether the effort is sustained. There appears little impetus for Japan to return to comprehensive overseas operations, let alone embark upon expeditionary military operations, but the reform of the JSDF to become more mobile, agile, and adaptable seems likely to continue. There also appears to be as little appetite for significant increases in defence funding beyond the incremental rises from 2012 as there is for addressing the fundamental demographic trough facing all three Forces, with the GSDF most exposed. A record budget request for 2021 signifying up to a 3.3 per cent annual increase includes establishment for space and cyber units, as well as other capabilities noted.[15] What is clear is that the Self-Defense Forces will continue to be the primary defenders of Japan against external and natural security threats and given their deployment during the corona virus crisis they will be required to adapt to new contingencies in ways barely comprehensible from current perspectives.

This book attempted to solve a puzzle including whether the JSDF have proven themselves capable defenders who will be able to perform their duties in an age of increasingly diverse challenges and developing Japanese strategy? For most elements of the question the answers would be positive, that the Forces have developed and proven themselves capable, with evident caveats of 'software,' logistical support, and primarily civilian intelligence and cyber security aspects. The obvious unknowable factors relate to China, North Korea, and other state and non-state actors that could pose challenges in the future. The scale of China's challenges appear so comprehensive as to be beyond the capabilities of any one state to address them, and the Japanese shape, deter, counter approach would seem to be appropriate to national needs and capabilities. The North Korean threat is less dynamic and more narrowly military, but could pose unconventional threats to Japan not only with ballistic missiles and WMD but by straining the US alliance if Japan's leaders' reactions to time-constrained BMD decisions, or JSDF interception efforts failed to meet Washington's expectations. The difficulty of adapting to such unconventional threat dynamics is also symbolic of underlying defensive weaknesses.

What has become clear from this volume is that the Self-Defense Forces have been largely unconsciously transformed from often uncomfortable anomalies in post-war post-imperial Japan to representative of modern liberal-internationalist Japan. The breadth and depth of involvement in the rescue and recovery in Tohoku was astonishing, and many Japanese, even those positively disposed towards the JSDF were genuinely surprised that they had such good Forces. The JSDF, civilian volunteers, and local communities represented the hopeful aspects of Japan in crisis, facing appalling challenges, coping, helping, and emerging stronger for the effort. In some ways they resembled the veterans of war, carrying baggage of trauma and tragedy, but bearing it lightly and forging new futures. It is unlikely any of those veterans who returned to Japan after 1946 would have imagined that Japan would be such a peaceful and prosperous country in 2016. Nor that Japanese armed forces would be so respected in a society that does not want a large military or to participate in military service, but the story of the defenders of Japan has been a long and complex one where the ending was never clear, and nor shall it be. The police heritage of the GSDF was only belatedly recognised in 2015, but a sign of how the past returns was seen in April 2020, when a specialist Border Islands Security Force was established to defend the Senkaku and other south-western islands against illegal intruders. While seemingly in accordance with the 'south-western move' of defence, this Force is of police, led by an NPA assistant commissioner, its members armed with automatic weapons and helicopters, providing a capability that more closely resembles the NPR than any other.[16] In the past as in the present, legacies matter.

NOTES

PREFACE

1. Hosoya, Yuichi, Cannon, Tara (trans.), *Security Politics in Japan: Legislation for a New Security Environment* (Tokyo: Japan Library, 2019).

INTRODUCTION

1. Notable exceptions being Katzenstein, Peter J., *Cultural Norms and National Security: Police and military in post-war Japan* (New York: Cornell University Press, 1996); Samuels, Richard J., '"New Fighting Power!" Japan's Growing Maritime Capabilities and East Asian Security', *International Security*, 32–3 (Winter, 2007/2008), pp. 84–112.
2. Katzenstein, Peter J. and Okawara, Nobuo, 'Japan, Asian-Pacific Security, and the Case for Analytical Eclecticism', in Katzenstein, Peter J. (ed.), *Rethinking Japanese Security: Internal and External Dimensions* (Abingdon: Routledge, 2008), pp. 32–55; Hook, Glenn D., Gilson, Julie, Hughes, Christopher W., Dobson, Hugo, *Japan's International Relations: Politics, Economics, and Security*, second edition (Oxford: Routledge, 2005): 41–43.
3. Evans, David C., and Peattie, Mark R., *Kaigun: Strategy, Tactics, and Technology in the Imperial Japanese Navy 1887–1941* (Annapolis, MD.: Naval Institute Press, 1997): xxi.
4. Igawa, Kazuhisa, *Japanese Participants in the Vietnam War of Independence: Research based upon the evidence of the development of Japan-Vietnam relations (Betonamu dokuritsusensōsanka nihonjin no jiseki nimotozuku higoshino arikata ni kansurukenkyū)*, Research Report 2005–14 (Tokyo: Tokyo Foundation, October 2005); Fukatani, Toshi, *The Last Japanese Soldier to Return Home: Fukatani Yoshiharu and his Family (Nihonkoku saigono kikanhei-fukutaniyoshiharu to sonokazoku)*, (Tokyo: Shoeisha, 2014); Toi, Jugatsu, *Onoda Hiroo's Endless Battle (Onoda Hiroo no owaranaitatakai)* (Tokyo: Shinchosha, 2005); Okumura, Kazuichi and Sakai, Makoto, *I was an 'Ant Soldier': Japanese soldiers left behind in China (Watashi wa 'ari no heitai' datta-chūgokuni nokosareta nihonhei)* (Tokyo: Iwanamishoten, 2006); Smith, T.O., *Britain and the Origins of the Vietnam War: UK Policy in Indo-China, 1943–50* (Basingstoke: Palgrave MacMillan, 2007); Anderson, Benedict, *Java in a Time of Revolution: Occupation and Resistance, 1944–1946* (London: Cornell University Press, 1972).

5. Kurihara, Toshio, *Siberian POW—Incomplete Tragedy* (*Shiberia yokuryū-mikan no higeki*) (Tokyo: Iwanamishinsho, 2009); Dähler, Richard, 'The Japanese Prisoners of War in Siberia 1945–1956', *Internationales Asienforum*, Vol. 34 (2003) 3–4: 285–302; Maizuru City Archive Collection, *General Archive Materials Description* (*Omona shiryōno gayō*) (https://www.city.maizuru.kyoto.jp/kankou/cmsfiles/contents/0000 001/1474/siryougaiyou.pdf 1 Sept. 2016).
6. Kowalski, Frank (Katsuyama, Kinjirou translation) *The Rearmament of Japan: The Record of an American Army Civil Affairs Staff Officer* (*Nihonsaigunbi: beigun jiko mondan bakuryōchō nokiroku*) (Tokyo: Chuokoronshinsha, 1969/1999); Kowalski, Frank, (Eldridge, Robert D., ed./trans.), *An Inoffensive Rearmament: The making of the postwar Japanese Army* (Annapolis, MD.: Naval Institute Press, 2013).
7. French, Thomas W., *National Police Reserve: The Origin of Japan's Self Defense Forces* (Leiden: Brill / Global Oriental, 2014).
8. Hoshino, Yasusaburo and Hayashi, Shigeo, *JSDF: Their Two Faces* (*Jieitai: sono futatsunokao*) (Tokyo: Sanichishinsho, 1963/1970); Hook, Glenn D., *Militarization and Demilitarization in Contemporary Japan* (London: Routledge, 1996); Maeda, Tetsuo, *The Hidden Army: The Untold Story of Japan's Military Forces* (Carol Stream, IL.: edition q, 1995); Miyazaki, Kōki, Japan's Defence Organisation (*Nihonno bōeikikou*) (Tokyo: Kyoikusha, 1979); Yomiurishimbunsha (ed.), *Japan's Defence Combat Power 1—Ground Self-Defense Force: The Full Story of Ground Combat Power* (*Nihonno bōeisenryoku 1-rikujōjieitai: chijōsenryoku no zenyō*) (Tokyo: Yomiurishimbunsha, 1987).
9. Fukagawa, Takayuki, *Understand the JSDF in Three Hours by Manga* (*Jieitaino koto ga mangade 3jikantewakaruhon*) (Tokyo: Asakashuppansha, 2004).
10. Auer, James, E., *The Post-War Rearmament of Japanese Maritime Forces, 1945–1971* (New York: Praeger, 1973); Agawa, Naoyuki, *Friendship at Sea* (*Umi noyujo*) (Tokyo: Chuokoronsha, 2001); Graham, Euan, *Japan's Sea lane Security: A matter of life and death?* (Abingdon: Routledge, 2006); Patalano, Alessio, *Post-war Japan as a Sea Power: Imperial Legacy, Wartime Experience, and the Making of a Navy* (London: Bloomsbury, 2015).
11. Eldridge, Robert D., and Midford, Paul (eds.), *The Japanese Ground Self-Defense Force: Search for Legitimacy* (New York: Palgrave Macmillan, 2017); Morinogunjikenkyūsho (ed.), *Next Generation GSDF: This is the Way to Fight Future Wars* (*Jisedai no rikujōjieitaishoraisen wo kakutatakau*) (Tokyo: Kayashobou, 1996); Hunter-Chester, David, *Creating Japan's Ground Self-Defense Force, 1945–2015: A Sword Well Made* (Lanham, MD.: Lexington, 2016).
12. Yomiuri Shimbunsha (ed.), *Japan's Defence Combat Power 3—Air Self-Defense Force:* (*Nihon no bōeisenryoku3-kōkūjieitai*) (Tokyo: Yomiurishimbunsha, 1987); Tanaka Iwaki, *Scramble: Carrying out warning shots* (*Sukuranburu: keikoshageki wo jisshiseyo*) (Tokyo: Kojinsha, 2014).
13. Hughes, Michael Bryant, *Japan's Air Power Options: The Employment of Military Aviation in the Post-War Era*, Doctoral Thesis, Faculty of the Fletcher School of Law and Diplomacy, Tufts University (16 Aug. 1972).
14. Sado, Akihiro, *Post-war Politics and the JSDF* (*Sengoseiji to jieitai*) (Tokyo: Yoshikawahirobunkan, 2006); Sado, Akihiro, *JSDF Historical Treatise: 60 Years of*

Politicians, Bureaucrats, Military, Public (*Jieitaishiron: sei, kan, gun, min no60nen*) (Tokyo: Yoshikawahirobunkan, 2015).
15. Weinstein, Martin E., *Japan's Postwar Defence Policy 1947–1968* (New York: Columbia University Press, 1971); Katahara, Eiichi, 'Japan from Containment to Normalization', in Alagappa, Muthiah (ed.), *Coercion and governance: the declining political role of the military in Asia* (Palo Alto, CA.: Stanford University Press, 2001): 69–91; Soeya, Yoshihide, Tadokoro, Masayuki, Welch, David A., *Japan As A 'Normal Country'?: A Nation in Search of Its Place in the World* (Toronto: University of Toronto Press, 2011); Hughes, Christopher W., *Japan's Re-emergence as a 'Normal' Military Power* (Abingdon: OUP/IISS/Routledge, 2004/2005).
16. Hughes, Christopher W., *Japan's Remilitarisation* (Abingdon: IISS/Routledge, 2009); Samuels, Richard J., *Securing Japan: Tokyo's Grand Strategy and the Future of East Asia* (Ithaca, NY.: Cornell University Press, 2007); Pyle, Kenneth B., *Japan Rising: The Resurgence of Japanese Power and Purpose* (New York: Public Affairs, 2007); Smith, Sheila A., *Japan Rearmed: The Politics of Military Power* (Cambridge, MA.: Harvard University Press, 2019); Drifte, Reinhard, *Japan's Security Relations with China since 1989: From balancing to bandwagoning?* (Abingdon: RoutledgeCurzon, 2003); Green, Michael J., *Japan's Reluctant Realism: Foreign Policy Challenges in an Era of Uncertain Power* (Basingstoke: Palgrave Macmillan, 2003); Oros, Andrew L., *Japan's Security Renaissance: New Policies and Politics for the Twenty-first Century* (New York: Columbia University Press, 2017).
17. Smith's work was published while this volume was under review, therefore there is limited citation.

1. POST-WAR MILITARY ROOTS: JAPAN'S CONFLICTED MILITARY LEGACY

1. Kushner, Barak, "Imperial Loss and Japan's Search for Postwar Legitimacy," in Kushner, Barak and Muminov, Sherzod (eds.), *The Dismantling of Japan's Empire in East Asia: Deimperialization, postwar legitimation and imperial afterlife*, (Abingdon: Routledge, 2017), pp. 48–65.
2. Sado, Akihiro, *Post-war Politics and the JSDF* (*Sengoseiji tojieitai*), (Tokyo: Yoshikawahirobunkan, 2006): 44–60; Masuda, Hiroshi, *Birth of the JSDF: Japan's Rearmament and America* (*Jieitainotanjō: nihonnosaigunbi toamerika*), (Tokyo: Chuōkoronshinsha, 2004): 235–47.
3. Inoue, Kyoko, *MacArthur's Japanese Constitution: A Linguistic and Cultural Study of its Making* (Chicago: University of Chicago, 1991); Katahara, Eiichi, 'Japan from Containment to Normalization', in Alagappa, Muthiah (ed.), *Coercion and governance: the declining political role of the military in Asia* (Palo Alto, CA.: Stanford University Press, 2001), pp. 69–91.
4. Fukunaga, Akihiko, *A History of Post-war Military Equipment Manufacturing* (*Gunyōkiseizō no sengoshi*), (Tokyo: Fuyōshobō, 2016); Sado, Akihiro, *Post-war Politics and the JSDF*: 1–4.
5. Deutsch, Karl W. et al., *Political Community and the North Atlantic Area; International Organization in the Light of Historical Experience* (Princeton, NJ.:, Princeton University

Press, 1957); Schaller, Michael, *The American Occupation of Japan: The Origins of the Cold War in Asia* (New York: Oxford University Press: 1987).
6. Kowner, Rotem, 'The Repatriation of Surrendered Japanese Troops, 1945–1947', in Kushner, Barak and Levidis, Andrew (eds.), *In the Ruins of the Japanese Empire: Imperial Violence, State Destruction, and the Reordering of Modern East Asia* (Hong Kong: HKU Press, 2020), pp. 121–138.
7. Hasegawa, Tsuyoshi, *Racing the Enemy: Stalin, Truman, and the Surrender of Japan* (Cambridge, MA.: Belknap/Harvard, 2005): 255–85.
8. National Association of Forced Detainees Foundation, (*Zaidanhōjin zenkokukyōsei yokuryūshakyōkai*) (https://zaidan-zenyokukyo-com.ssl-xserver.jp/ 11 Feb. 2018); Takasugi, Ichirō *In a Harsh Light: Siberian POW Camp Record* (*Kyokkō no kage ni-Shiberiafuryoki*) (Tokyo: Iwanamibunko,1950/1991).
9. Toi, Jugatsu, *Onoda Hiroo's Endless Battle* (*Onodahiroo no owaranaitatakai*) (Tokyo: Shinchosha, 2005): 127.
10. Onoda, Hiroo, Terry, Charles Sanford (trans.), *No Surrender: My Thirty-Year War* (Tokyo: Kodansha, 1974/Annapolis, MD: Naval Institute Press, 1999): 7–10; Willacy, Mark, 'Japanese holdouts fought for decades after WWII' (Canberra: ABC, Aug. 12, 2010) (http://www.abc.net.au/lateline/content/2010/s3065416.htm 22 May 2017).
11. Kawasaki, Masumi, *The Taiwan-Japan Soldier Who Returned Home* (*Kaettekita taiwannihonhei*) (Tokyo: Bunshushinsho, 2003): 68–76.
12. Igawa, Kazuhisa, *Japanese Participants in the Vietnam War of Independence: research based upon the evidence of the development of Japan-Vietnam relations* (*Betonamudoku ritsusensōsankanihonjin no jiseki ni motozukuhigoshi no arikata nikansurukenkyū*), Research Report 2005-14 (Tokyo: Tokyo Foundation, Oct. 2005).
13. Lebra, Joyce C., *Japanese Trained Armies in Southeast Asia* (Hong Kong: Heinemann, 1977): 167–184; Fujiwara, Iwaichi, *F-Agency* (*F-Kikai*) (Tokyo: Bajiriko, 2012).
14. Igawa, Kazuhisa, *Japanese Participants in the Vietnam War of Independence*: 30–2.
15. Joint Chiefs of Staff, *General Order No. 1: Instruments for the Surrender of Japan*, J.C.S. 1467/2 (17 Aug. 1945) (http://csis.org/files/media/csis/programs/taiwan/timeline/sums/timeline_docs/CSI_19450902b.htm 7 Oct. 2016); Smith, T.O., *Britain and the Origins of the Vietnam War: UK Policy in Indo-China, 1943–50* (Basingstoke: Palgrave MacMillan 2007): 41.
16. Ibid: 45, 48–9.
17. McKay, Euan, 'Souvenirs of Internment: Camp Newspapers as a Tangible Record of a Forgotten Experience', in Carr, Gilly, and Mytum, Harold (eds.), *Cultural Heritage and Prisoners of War: Creativity Behind Barbed Wire* (Abingdon: Routledge, 2012): 121; Kowner, Rotem, 'The Repatriation of Surrendered Japanese Troops, 1945–1947': 126.
18. McKay, Euan, 'Waiting for their ship to come: Changing perceptions of the Japanese in postwar South-East Asia', in Jackson, Ashley; Khan, Yasmin; Singh; Gajendra (eds.), *An Imperial World at War: Aspects of the British Empire's war experience, 1939–1945* (Abingdon: Routledge, 2017), pp. 193–210: 194–6.
19. Aida, Yūji, *Rationalism* (*Gorishugi*) (Tokyo: Kodansha, 1966); Oba, Sadao, 'Recollections of Indonesia: 1944–1947', in Nish, Ian (ed.), *Indonesian Experience: The Role of Japan and Britain, 1943–1948*, (London: London School of Economics, 1979), pp. 1–34: 28–9.

20. 'The Parachute Battalion Mutiny', *The Spectator*, (11 Oct. 1946): 2, (http://archive.spectator.co.uk/article/11th-october-1946/2/the-parachute-battalion-mutiny 15 June 2015); McKay, Euan, 'Souvenirs of Internment': 121.
21. Ibid: 123.
22. Anderson, Benedict, *Java in a Time of Revolution: Occupation and Resistance, 1944–1946* (London: Cornell University Press, 1972): 78–83.
23. Ibid: 121–2; Sato, Mamoru, *Great East Asian War Ended on 30 April 1975* (*Daitōasensō wa shōwa50nen4gatsu30nichi ni shūketsushita*) (Tokyo: Seirindo, 2012): 87–8; Anderson, Benedict, *Java in a Time of Revolution*: 129.
24. Ibid: 142; Oba, Sadao, 'Recollections of Indonesia': 26.
25. Anderson, Benedict, *Java in a Time of Revolution*: 145–149.
26. Ibid: 147–9; McMillan, Richard, *The British Occupation of Indonesia 1945–1946: Britain, the Netherlands and the Indonesian revolution* (Abingdon: Routledge, 2005): 27.
27. Ibid: 26.
28. Ibid: 28–30, 65–75; Oba Sadao, 'Recollections of Indonesia': 26–7.
29. Anderson, Benedict, *Java in a Time of Revolution*: 150–5; McMillan, Richard, *The British Occupation of Indonesia*: 47.
30. Ibid: 76–8; Conversations with RMA faculty members, Sandhurst (Oct. 2013).
31. Oba, Sadao, 'Recollections of Indonesia': 33; SCAP, *Final Progress of Demobilization of the Japanese Armed Forces*, (Dec. 1946) (https://archive.org/stream/Japan-Occupation/Final%20Progress%20of%20Demobilization%20of%20the%20Japanese%20Armed%20Forces#page/n25/mode/2up 12 Feb 2018): 61.
32. McKay, Euan 'Waiting for their ship to come': 7–8.
33. McMillan, Richard, *The British Occupation of Indonesia*: 131; Oba, Sadao, 'Recollections of Indonesia': 24; Fraternal Welfare Association (*Fukushitomo nokai*) website (http://www3.nsknet.or.jp/~yoji-yoko/blog/hukusitomonokai/shuuhou.htm 16 Dec 2016).
34. Chō, Yōhiro, *Paying a Visit on Former Japanese Troops Remaining in Indonesia* (*Indoneshiazanryū motonihonhei wotazanete*), (Tokyo: Shakaihyōronsha, 2007): 104–5.
35. 'Marking the 69th Anniversary of Independence Government Officials, Ambassador Watch Over the Last Anniversary Under the Yudhoyono Administration' (*Dokuritsu69shunen iwao seifukankeisha, taishi mimamor yudoyon seikensaigo*)', *Jakarta Shimbun* (18 Aug. 2014) (http://www.jakartashimbun.com/free/detail/19758.html 12 Oct. 2015); 'Last former Japanese remaining soldier passes away, Ono Sakari, 94 years of age, interred in the cemetery of national heroes' (*Saigono motosanryunihonhei shibo onosakarisan, kyōnen94sai eiyūbochi nimaisou*), *Jakarta Shimbun* (26 Aug. 2014) (http://www.jakartashimbun.com/free/detail/19919.html 12 Oct. 2015).
36. Kurasawa, Aiko, Kitano, Sei (trans.) *Indonesian National Archives Compilation 'Two Red and White Flags-Indonesians' Comments on the Japanese Occupation Period'*" (*Indoneshia kokuritsubunshokan hencho [futatsuno kohakuhata-indoneshiajin gakataru nihonsenryōjidai]*) (Tokyo: Mokuseisha, 1996): 162–7; Atsushi, Ota, 'Indonesia in Memory: The Wartime Occupation in Japanese Novels, 1945–1970' (*Kiokusareruindoneshia—1945–70nenno nihonshosetsu nikakareru senjisenryō*) *Ajia taiheiyōtokyū*, No. 20 (Feb. 2013).
37. Seaton, Philip A. (ed.), *Local History and War Memories in Hokkaido* (Abingdon:

Routledge, 2016): 1–25, 48–51; Horton, William Bradley, 'Pramoedya and the Comfort Women of Buru: A Textual Analysis of *Perawan Remaja dalam Cengkeraman Militer (Teenage Virgins in the Grasp of the Military)*,' *Journal of Asia-Pacific Studies*, No. 14 (Waseda University, Mar. 2010).

38. Kowner, Rotem, 'The Repatriation of Surrendered Japanese Troops, 1945–1947': 130–2.
39. Gillin, Donald G., and Etter, Charles, 'Staying On: Japanese Soldiers and Civilians in China, 1945–1949', *The Journal of Asian Studies*, Vol. 42–3 (1983): 504–506, 511; Morris-Suzuki, Tessa, 'Post-War Warriors: Japanese Combatants in the Korean War', *The Asia-Pacific Journal*, 10–31–1 (July 2012) (http://japanfocus.org/-Tessa-Morris_ Suzuki/3803/article.pdf 22 Oct. 2016).
40. Okumura, Kazuichi and Sakai, Makoto, *I was an 'Ant Soldier': Japanese soldiers left behind in China (Watashiwa 'arinoheitai' datta-chugoku ni nokosaretanihonhei)* (Tokyo: Iwanamishoten, 2006).
41. Yeeshan, Chan, *Abandoned Japanese in Postwar Manchuria: The Lives of War Orphans and Wives in Two Countries* (Abingdon: Routledge, 2010): 56–7.
42. Fukatani, Toshi, *The Last Japanese Soldier to Return Home: Fukatani Yoshiharu and his Family (Nihonkoku saigono kikanhei-fukutaniyoshiharu to sonokazoku)*, (Tokyo: Shoeisha, 2014).
43. French, Thomas W., *A History of Japan's National Police Reserve 1950–1952: Army or Constabulary?*, PhD Thesis, (University of Southampton, 2010); French, Thomas W., *National Police Reserve: The Origin of Japan's Self Defense Forces* (Leiden: Brill / Global Oriental, 2014).
44. Weste, John, 'Great Britain and Japanese rearmament 1945–60,' in Iokibe, Makoto; Rose, Caroline; Tomaru, Junko; Weste, John, *Japanese Diplomacy in the 1950s: From Isolation to Integration* (Abingdon, Oxon: Routledge 2011), pp. 34–50.
45. Ibid: 44–5, 49.
46. Halliday, Jon, and Cumings, Bruce, *Korea The Unknown War: An Illustrated History* (London: Penguin, 1990): 32–54.
47. French, Thomas W., *A History Of Japan's National Police Reserve 1950–1952*: 128–46.
48. Auer, James, E., *The Post-War Rearmament of Japanese Maritime Forces, 1945–1971* (New York: Praeger, 1973); Patalano, Alessio, *Post-war Japan as a Sea Power*.
49. ASDF Exhibition Hall, Hamamatsu AB, Shizuoka; Ness, Leland S., *Rikugun: Guide to Japanese Ground Forces 1937–1945* (Solihull: Helion, 2014):14–5.
50. *United States Initial Post-Surrender Policy for Japan* (SWNCC150/4), The State-War-Navy Coordinating Committee (September 6, 1945), (http://www.ndl.go.jp/constitution/shiryo/01/022/022tx.html. 12 May 2018)
51. Ōnishi, Hiroshi, Kurida, Hisaya, Kokaze, Hidemasa, *The Sagami Bay Invasion Plan: The road to ending the second world war (Sagamiwanjōrikusakusen: dainijitaisenshūketsu eno michi)* (Yokohama: Yūrinshinsho, 1995); Harding, Stephen, 'The Last to Die,' *Air & Space Magazine* (Nov. 2008), (http://www.airspacemag.com/military-aviation/the-last-to-die-10099776/#4MZpZWwVp2XyLt0i.99 15 Oct. 2016).
52. SCAP, *Final Progress of Demobilization of the Japanese Armed Forces*, (Dec. 1946) (https://ia801308.us.archive.org/4/items/Japan-Occupation/Final%20Progress%20

of%20Demobilization%20of%20the%20Japanese%20Armed%20Forces.pdf 12 Feb 2018): 64.
53. Ibid: 80–8; SCAP Directive No. 2 (3 Sept. 1945): Auer, James, E., *The Post-War Rearmament of Japanese Maritime Forces, 1945–1971*: 42; MacArthur, Douglas, (General) and staff, *Reports of General MacArthur, MacArthur in Japan: The Occupation Phase, Volume I Supplement*, (http://www.history.army.mil/books/wwii/macarthur%20reports/macarthur%20v1%20sup/ch9.htm, 2 January 2010): 185, 284.
54. Appleman, Roy E., *United States Army in the Korean War: South to the Naktong—North to the Yalu (June–November 1950)*, CMH Pub 20-2-1 (Washington, DC.: Center of Military History, US Army, 1961): 525.
55. Pauley, Edwin Wendell, *Report on Japanese reparations to the President of the United States, November 1945 to April 1946*, Department of State (Far East Series 25/3174); Miwa, Ryōichi, 'Postwar Democratization and Economic Reconstruction', in Nakamura, Takafusa and Odaka, Konosuke (eds.), Brannen, Noah S. (trans.), *The Economic History of Japan, 1600–1990*, vol. 3: *Economic History of Japan 1914–1955: A Dual Structure* (Oxford: Oxford University Press, 2003): 336.
56. Finn, Richard B., *Winners in Peace: MacArthur, Yoshida and Postwar Japan* (Berkeley: University of California Press, 1992): 104; 'Reform of the Japanese Governmental System, Report by the State–War–Navy Coordinating Subcommittee for the Far East', (SWNCC 228, January 7, 1946), *Foreign Relations of the United States (FRUS)*, Vol. 8, (https://history.state.gov/historicaldocuments/frus1946v08/d116 7 January 2010).
57. Stevenson, William R. III, 'Japanese Soldier Writers and the American Postwar Purge of Militarists and Ultranationalists', *Journal of International and Advanced Japanese Studies*, University of Tsukuba, Volume 5 (Mar. 2013): 6 (http://japan.tsukuba.ac.jp/journal/pdf/05/5.1_Stevenson.pdf 17 Oct. 2016).
58. Dower, John, *Embracing Defeat: Japan in the Wake of World War II* (New York: Norton/New Press, 1999).
59. House of Representatives, 28 June 1946, in Nishi, Osamu, *The Constitution and the National Defense Law System in Japan* (Tokyo: Seibundo, 1987): 5.
60. Weinstein, Martin E., *Japan's Postwar Defence Policy*: 17–20; Shimazu, Naoko, *Japanese Society at War: Death, Memory, and the Russo-Japanese War* (Cambridge: Cambridge University Press, 2009): 37–8; *Shūgiingijisokkiroku* (26 June 1946), 90th Session, No. 6, Imperial House of Representatives, 4, (http://teikokugikai-i.ndl.go.jp/cgi-bin/TEIKOKU/swt_dispdoc.cgi?SESSION=6748&SAVED_RID=1&PAGE=0&POS=0&TOTAL=0&SRV_ID=5&DOC_ID=1935&DPAGE=1&DTOTAL=9&DPOS=5&SORT_DIR=1&SORT_TYPE=1&MODE=1&DMY=6772 12 Sept. 2016).
61. Weinstein, Martin E., *Japan's Postwar Defence Policy 1947–1968* (New York: Columbia University Press, 1971), 17–20; Ueda, Makiko (Rikki, Kersten, trans.), 'An Idea of Postwar Japan: Hitoshi Ashida and Japanese Liberalism', *Japanese Studies* (2011: 2), pp. 31–48, (http://japaninstitute.anu.edu.au/sites/default/files/u5/Ashida_Makiko_Ueda.pdf 22 June 2016).
62. Morris-Suzuki, Tessa, 'Democracy's Porous Borders: Espionage, Smuggling and the Making of Japan's Transwar Regime (Part I),' *The Asia-Pacific Journal: Japan Focus*, 12-40-4 (Oct 2014): 4.
63. Auer, James E., *The Post-war Rearmament of Japanese Maritime Forces*: 38–41.

64. Miwa, Yoshikazu, *Japanese Marine Transportation During the Occupation Period (Senryōki no nihonkaiun)* (Tokyo: Nihonkeizaihyoronsha, 1992): 88; Ishimaru, Yasuzo, 'Involvement of Japan in the Korean War: The Completely Forgotten Marine Transportation' (*Chōsensensoto nihon nokakawari: wasuresarareta kaijōyuso*),' *Senshikenkyūnenpo*, No. 11 (Mar. 2008), pp. 33–52: 37; Mooney, James L. (ed.), *Dictionary of American Naval Fighting Ships, Volume 4*, (Washington, DC.: Navy Department, Naval History Division, 1969): 597, 603; Takemae, Eiji, *The Allied Occupation of Japan* (New York: Continuum, 2002): 110–2.
65. NHK, 'Combined Fleet Youth: "Lucky Ship" *Yukikaze*'s War' (*Shōnentachi no rengōkantai—"kōunkan" yukikaze nosensō*), *NHK-BS1* (23 Aug. 2020) (https://www2.nhk.or.jp/hensei/program/p.cgi?area=001&date=2020–08–23&ch=11&eid=14868&f=2443 24 Aug. 2020).
66. *Reports of General MacArthur—MacArthur in Japan: The Occupation: Military Phase, Volume I Supplement* (Washington DC.: US Army, Reprint, 1994), (http://www.history.army.mil/books/wwii/macarthur%20reports/macarthur%20v1%20sup/ch5.htm 22 Oct. 2016): 145, 284.
67. Auer, James E., *The Post-war Rearmament of Japanese Maritime Forces*: 49–52; Agawa, Naoyuki, Yabuki, Hiraku (trans.), *Friendship Across the Seas: The US Navy and the Japan Maritime Self-Defense Force* (Tokyo: Japan Library, 2001/2019): 90.
68. *Reports of General MacArthur—MacArthur in Japan: Volume I Supplement*: 284; Operations and Plans Department of Maritime Staff Office (Ed.), *History of Sweeping Sea Lanes* (*Korokeikaishi*) (Tokyo: Maritime Staff Office, JMSDF, 1961): 4–5.
69. Patalano, Alessio '"Reclaiming the Trident": Japanese Minesweeping Operations in the Korean War and the Post-war Rearmament Process, 1950–1952', in *Quaderno SISM 2014 Naval History*, Italian Society for Military History: SISM Yearbook 2014, pp. 695–710: 697.
70. Dower, John W., *Empire and Aftermath: Yoshida Shigeru and the Japanese Experience, 1878–1954* (Cambridge, MA.: Council on East Asian Studies-Harvard University): 316; Murphy, Robert D., *Diplomat among Warriors* (Garden City, NY.: Doubleday, 1964): 347.
71. Mauch, Peter Cameron, *Sailor Diplomat: Nomura Kichisaburō and the Japanese-American War* (Cambridge, MA.: Harvard University Press, 2011): 240.
72. Drifte, Reinhard, 'Japan's Involvement in the Korean War,' Cotton, James and Neary, Ian (eds.), *The Korean War in History* (Manchester: Manchester University Press, 1989), pp. 121–34: 123.
73. Green, Michael J., *Arming Japan:* 31–33.
74. Appleman, Roy E., *United States Army in the Korean War*: 91.
75. Samuels, Richard J., *Rich Nation, Strong Army: National Security and the Technological Transformation of Japan* (Ithaca, NY.: Cornell, 1994): 138–9.
76. Hasegawa, Kenji, 'Anti-Americanism in the early *Zengakuren* and Japanese Communist Party', *Yokohamakokuritsudaigaku Ryūgakuseisentākiyō*, 12 (2005), pp. 111–31: 111–4.
77. Matray, James I., and Boose, Donald W. Jr., *The Ashgate Research Companion to the Korean War* (Abingdon: Ashton/Routledge, 2014/2016).
78. Field, James A. Jr., *History of United States Naval Operations—Korea: Chapter 11.*

Problems of a Policeman—3. Logistic Support (Washington DC.: Department of the Navy, 1962) (http://www.history.navy.mil/books/field/ch7a.htm, 28 April 2010): 3.
79. Boose, Donald W. Jr., *Over the Beach: US Army Amphibious Operations in the Korean War* (Fort Leavenworth, KS.: Combat Studies Institute Press, 2008): 65–6, 80.
80. Field, James A. Jr., *History of United States Naval Operations—Korea: Chapter 4. Help on the Way-2. Troops and Supplies*: 1; and *Chapter 5. Into the Perimeter-3. 3–30 July: The Pohang Landing*: 3.
81. Appleman, Roy E., *United States Army in the Korean War: South to the Naktong—North to the Yalu (June–November 1950)*, CMH Pub 20–2–1 (Washington, DC.: Center of Military History, US Army, 1961):394; Boose, Donald W. Jr., *Over the Beach*: 162.
82. Field, James A. Jr., *History of United States Naval Operations—Korea: Chapter 5. Into the Perimeter 3. 3–30 July: The Pohang Landing*: 3.
83. Boose, Donald W. Jr., *Over the Beach*: 317.
84. Ibid: 189, 242; *Evacuation Of Hungnam*, British Pathe News (1951) (https://www.youtube.com/watch?v=83YVbvd0lV8 12 Oct. 2016).
85. Drifte, Reinhard, 'Japan's Involvement in the Korean War': 129.
86. Field, James A. Jr., *History of United States Naval Operations—Korea: Chapter 11. Problems of a Policeman—3. Logistic Support*: 3.
87. Drifte, Reinhard, 'Japan's Involvement in the Korean War': 122–4.
88. Green, Michael J, *Arming Japan:* 31.
89. Field, James A. Jr., *History of United States Naval Operations—Korea: Chapter 2. Policy and Its Instruments-3. The Estimate of the Situation:* 2; Appleman, Roy E., *United States Army in the Korean War*: 486.
90. CNFE/S81 5451 (4 Oct. 1950), in Japan Maritime Self-Defense Force Staff Office (MSO), Defense Division (*Kaijōbakuryokanbubōeibu*) (ed.), *History of Japan's Turbulent Special Minesweeping Operations during the Korean War* (*Chōsendoran tokubetsusōkaishi*) (1 Feb. 1961), Additional Appendices (2010–13): 17.
91. The despatch received only fleeting media coverage: MSDF Staff Office, *History of Japan's Turbulent Special Minesweeping Operations during the Korean War*: 14; Hirama, Yoichi, *Japan's Value in the Korean War: Issues Surrounding the Dispatch of Minesweepers*, The Third Korean-Japan Security Shuttle Paper, (Seoul/Tokyo: The New Asia Research Institute/The Okazaki Institute, 1997); Tajiri, Seitsukasa, *1950 Wonsan Special Maritime Safety Memoire* (*1950nenwonsantokubetsusōkai no kaiko*) (Tokyo: MSDF/JDA, 1980/2002), (http://www.mod.go.jp/msdf/mf/touksyu/tokubetusoukai.pdf, 28 April 2010).
92. Agawa, Naoyuki, Yabuki, Hiraku (trans.), *Friendship Across the Seas*: 95.
93. Nakatani Sakataro, a 20-year old steward, was below deck, aft when the mine exploded: MSO, *History of Japan's Turbulent Special Minesweeping Operations during the Korean War*: 15–7, 53–4.
94. Appleman, Roy E., *United States Army in the Korean War*: 486.
95. MSO, *History of Japan's Turbulent Special Minesweeping Operations during the Korean War*: 44–5, 69–70, 75–80.
96. Hirama, Yoichi, *Japan's Value in the Korean War*; Cagle, Malcolm W., and Manson, Frank A., *History of United States Naval Operations—Korea: The Sea War in Korea-Chapter 5. The Battle of the Mines (Part II-Chinnampo)*, (Washington DC.: Department

97. MSO, *History of Japan's Turbulent Special Minesweeping Operations during the Korean War*: 105–8.
98. Ibid: 102–4,124; Agawa, Naoyuki, Yabuki, Hiraku (trans.), *Friendship Across the Seas*: 99.
99. MSO, *History of Japan's Turbulent Special Minesweeping Operations during the Korean War*: 115–23.
100. Ishimaru, Yasuzo, *The Impact on Japan from Mine Warfare during the Korean War*, Briefing Memo, NIDS Center for Military History (Feb. 2018) (http://www.nids.mod.go.jp/english/publication/briefing/pdf/2018/briefing_e201802.pdf 7 Oct. 2018); Agawa, Naoyuki, Yabuki, Hiraku (trans.), *Friendship Across the Seas*: 103–4.
101. Kimura, Yasuyuki, *The Defense Facilities Administration Agency: A Unique Support Organization for U.S. Forces in Japan*, Asia-Pacific Policy Papers Series (Edwin O. Reischauer Center for East Asian Studies, 2013): 18.
102. NHK, *Hidden "War Cooperation": Korean War and Japanese* (*Kakusareta "sensōkyōryoku" chōsensensōtonihonjin*), (18 Aug. 2019/ 15 Aug. 2020).
103. Morris-Suzuki, Tessa, 'Post-War Warriors: Japanese Combatants in the Korean War': 3–6
104. Ibid: 7.
105. Ishimaru, Yasuzo, 'Japanese Involvement in the Korean War: the forgotten story of maritime transport' (*Chōsensensoto nihonnokakawari: wasuresarareta kaijōyusō*), *Senshi kenkyūnenpo*, No. 11 (Mar. 2008), pp. 33–52: 35.
106. Patalano, Alessio '"Reclaiming the Trident"': 695–6.
107. E-mail with the author (2018).
108. Boose, Donald W. Jr., *Over the Beach*: 254.
109. Ibid: 255, 285.
110. CIA, *Probability of a Communist Assault on Japan in 1951: Indications of Soviet Intentions with Respect to Japan, Annex B to SE-11* (CIA-RDP79S01011A000 400050017–3).
111. 'For Japanese deserter from U.S. military in Vietnam, Constitution was a savior,' *Mainichi Shimbun*, (1 Jan. 2016) (http://mainichi.jp/english/articles/20160101/ p2a/00m/0na/025000c 4 Jan. 2016).
112. Hamasaki, Hashiharu and Higashino, Makoto, 'Ushiyama Junichi (*Nihonterebi*),' *Broadcast Research and Survey* (*Hōsōkenkyūto chōsa*), NHK, (May 2012).
113. Havens, Thomas RH., 'The Silent Partner,' in Large, Stephen S. (ed.), *Shōwa Japan— Political, economic and social history 1926–1989: Volume III 1952–1973* (London: Routledge, 1998): 159; Havens, Thomas RH., *Fire Across the Sea: The Vietnam War and Japan 1965–1975* (Princeton, NJ.: Princeton University Press, 1987): 5.
114. Ikeda, Tatsuo, '"Chartered Japanese, sacrifice for Vietnam War" astonishing report' (*[Yatowarenihonjin, betonamusensō degiseini] nohodoni kyōgaku*), *NPJ Tsushin*, (13 Aug. 2014) (http://www.news-pj.net/news/5781 12 Oct. 2016).
115. Fifth Session of Accounts Committee, 55th Diet Session, House of Representatives,

(21 Apr. 1967), (http://kokkai.ndl.go.jp/SENTAKU/syugiin/055/0106/0550421 0106005a.html 21 Oct. 2016); Havens, Thomas RH., *Fire Across the Sea*: 5.
116. Takarajimasha (ed.), *JSDF 60 Year History (Jieitai60nenshi)*, (Tokyo: Takarajimasha, 2015): 56; Turner, Matthew, 'The Vietnam War Deserters Who Sought Asylum in Sweden', *Lit Hub* (3 Aug. 2018), (https://lithub.com/the-vietnam-war-deserters-who-sought-asylum-in-sweden/ 12 Mar. 2020).
117. French, Thomas W., *A History Of Japan's National Police Reserve 1950*; French, Thomas W., *National Police Reserve*.
118. Kowalski, Frank, Eldridge, Robert D. (ed.), *An Inoffensive Rearmament:* 58–60; Ness, Leland S., *Rikugun*: 373–374; Kushner, Barak, *The Thought War: Japanese Imperial Propaganda* (Honolulu, HI.: University of Hawai'i Press, 2006): 180.
119. Memorandum by the Officer in Charge of Japanese Affairs (Green) to the Director of the Office of Northeast Asian Affairs (Allison), 'Limitations Imposed by FEC Decisions on Japanese Rearmament and Remilitarization', (19 July 1950) (694.001/7–1950), pp. 1244–46, in *FRUS*, 1950, Vol.VI: 1245.
120. Calder, Kent E., *Crisis and Compensation: Public Policy and Political Stability in Japan, 1949–1986* (Princeton, NJ.: Princeton University, 1988): 414–7.
121. Maeda, Tetsuo, *The Hidden Army: The Untold Story of Japan's Military Forces* (Carol Stream, IL.: edition q, 1995): 2, 6.
122. Ibid.
123. Ness, Leland S., *Rikugun:* 373–4.
124. Takemae, Eiji, *The Allied Occupation of Japan*, 458–62.
125. Shibayama, Futoshi, 'U.S. Strategic Debates over the Defense of Japan: Lessons for the Twenty-First Century,' *The Journal of American-East Asian Relations* 9–1/2 (Spring-Summer 2000), pp. 29–54.
126. Shibayama, Futoshi, *The Road to Japan's Rearmament (Nihonsaigunbi enomichi), 1945–1954* (Kyoto: Minervashobō, 2010): 26–29; 'Report by the National Security Council on Recommendations with Respect to United States Policy toward Japan,' NSC 13/2 (October 7, 1948), *FRUS*, 1948, vol. 6, (https://history.state.gov/historicaldocuments/frus1948v06/d588 18 Oct. 2018).
127. Kuzuhara, Kazumi, 'The Korean War and The National Police Reserve of Japan: Impact of the US Army's For East Command on Japan's Defence Capability,' *NIDS Security Reports*, No. 7 (Dec. 2006), pp. 95–116: 96–7.
128. 'Correspondence between General MACARTHUR and Prime Minister—General WHITNEY and Prime Minister,' (8 July 1950), *GHQ/SCAP Records*, Government Section, Box No. 2194, Sheet No.GS(B) 01751, National Diet Library; Kowalski, Frank, (Katsuyama, Kinjirō translation) *The Rearmament of Japan: The Record of an American Army Civil Affairs Staff Officer (Nihonsaigunbi: beigunjikomondan bakuryōchō no kiroku)* (Tokyo: Chuōkoronshinsha, 1969, reprinted 1999); Kowalski, Frank, (Eldridge, Robert D., ed.), *An Inoffensive Rearmament*. It is worth noting the criticisms of the Kowalski book (in Japanese) by French, who points out the time between its writing and the events, the career path of Kowalski, and how the Japanese version was the sole text for many scholars of the period. French, Thomas W., *National Police Reserve*.

129. Office of the Military History Officer, *History of the National Police Reserve of Japan* (HQ AFFE/US Eight Army, 1955): 1.
130. Kowalski, Frank, Eldridge, Robert D., (ed.), *An Inoffensive Rearmament*: 23.
131. Yamasaki, Takaharu, *Nine Years of the NPR, NSF, JSDF* (*Keisatsuyobitai, hoantai, jieitai no kyunenkan*) (Tokyo: Nihonbungakukan, 2010).
132. French, Thomas W., *A History Of Japan's National Police Reserve 1950–1952*: 72–3.
133. Takemae, Eiji, *The Allied Occupation of Japan*: 299.
134. Quoted in Pyle, Kenneth B., *Japan Rising: The resurgence of Japanese Power and Purpose* (New York: Public Affairs, 2007): 222.
135. Stevenson, William R. III, 'Japanese Soldier Writers and the American Postwar Purge of Militarists and Ultranationalists', *Journal of International and Advanced Japanese Studies*, Vol. 5, (Mar. 2013), pp. 1–15 (http://www.japan.tsukuba.ac.jp/journal/pdf/05/5.1_Stevenson.pdf 12 Oct. 2016): 2–3.
136. Masuda, Hiroshi, *Birth of the JSDF*: 11; Montgomery, John D., 'The Purge in Occupied Japan: A Study in the Use of Civilian Agencies under Military Government,' Technical Memorandum ORO-T-48 (FEC) (Chevy Chase, MD.: John Hopkins University, 1953).
137. Dower, John, and Hirata, Tetsuo (Middleton, Ben, trans.), 'Japan's Red Purge: Lessons from a Saga of Suppression of Free Speech and Thought,' *The Asia-Pacific Journal: Japan Focus*, (7 July 2007) (http://www.japanfocus.org/site/make_pdf/2462 17 Oct. 2016).
138. Samuels, Richard J., *Kishi and Corruption: An Anatomy of the 1955 System*, Japan Policy Research Institute Working Paper No. 83, (Dec. 2001).
139. 'Miners Seek Hearing,' and 'Red Purge Pledged', *The Examiner*, (Launceston, Tasmania) (26 Aug. 1949): 1.
140. Samuels, Richard J., *Machiavelli's Children: Leaders and Their Legacies in Italy and Japan* (Ithaca, NY.: Cornell University Press, 2003): 207.
141. Emmerson, John K., 'The Japanese Communist Party after Fifty Years,' *Asian Survey*, Vol. 12, No. 7 (July 1972), pp. 564–79: 569–70.
142. Weinstein, Martin E., *Japan's Postwar Defence Policy*: 17–20, 106.
143. Ueda, Makiko (Rikki, Kersten, trans.), 'An Idea of Postwar Japan'.
144. Masuda, Hiroshi, 'Ashida Hitoshi: The Intellectual and Cultured man as Politician,' in Watanabe, Akio (Ed.), Eldridge, Robert D. (Trans.), *The Prime Ministers of Postwar Japan, 1945–1995: Their Lives and Times* (Lanham, MD.: Lexington, 2016), pp. 55–70: 66–7.
145. Ueda, Makiko (Rikki, Kersten, trans.), 'An Idea of Postwar Japan': 41.
146. Ibid: 39.
147. Masuda Hiroshi, 'Ashida Hitoshi': 67–8.
148. Iokibe, Makoto (ed.), *The History of Post-war Japan's Diplomacy* (*Sengonihongaikōshi*), (Tokyo: Yūhikaku, 1999): 15.
149. Pyle, Kenneth B., *Japan Rising*: 230.
150. JDA (*Bōeichō-jieitai junenshihenshuiinkai*), *JSDF Ten Year History* (*Jieitaijunenshi*) (Tokyo: JDA, 1961): 28–30.
151. Takemae, Eiji, *The Allied Occupation of Japan*: 299.

152. JDA, *JSDF Ten Year History*: 285.
153. Maeda, Tetsuo, *The Hidden Army*: 15–8.
154. Kowalski, Frank, (Eldridge, Robert D., ed.), *An Inoffensive Rearmament*: 61–6.
155. Guillain, Robert, 'The Resurgence of Military Elements in Japan', *Pacific Affairs*, 25–3, (Sept. 1952), pp. 211–225: 213–4.
156. 'CIA files reveal militarist plot to kill Yoshida in '52', *The Japan Times*, (28 Feb. 2007): 1, 3.
157. Shibayama, Futoshi, *The Road to Japan's Rearmament*: 398–417.
158. 'Hattori Takushiro', *CIA Archives*, Vol. 1–7 (18 Dec. 1951), (https://ia601305.us.archive.org/29/items/HattoriTakushiro/HATTORI,%20TAKUSHIRO%20%20%20VOL.%201_0007.pdf 22 Oct. 2016); Vol. 2–45 (30 Jan. 1957), (https://ia601305.us.archive.org/29/items/HattoriTakushiro/HATTORI,%20TAKUSHIRO%20%20%20VOL.%202_0045.pdf 22 Oct. 2016).
159. Guillain, Robert, 'The Resurgence of Military Elements in Japan': 219.
160. Ibid: 220.
161. Kowalski, Frank, (Eldridge, Robert D., ed.), *An Inoffensive Rearmament*: 66, 84.
162. French, Thomas W., *A History Of Japan's National Police Reserve 1950–1952*: 156–7.
163. Ibid: 160–1.
164. Kuzuhara, Kazumi, 'The Korean War and The National Police Reserve of Japan': 101.
165. Kowalski, Frank, (Eldridge, Robert D., ed.), *An Inoffensive Rearmament*: 101.
166. French, Thomas W., *A History Of Japan's National Police Reserve 1950–1952*: 174–81.
167. French, Thomas, 'National Police Reserve': 141.
168. Ibid: 140.
169. Ibid: 142.
170. Ibid: 142–3.
171. Thompson, Leroy, *The M1 Carbine* (Botley, Oxon.: Osprey, 2011): 6–7; French, Thomas W., *A History Of Japan's National Police Reserve 1950–1952*: 137.
172. Yomiurishinbunshasengoshihan, *Showa post-war history*: 8–34.
173. French, Thomas W., *A History Of Japan's National Police Reserve 1950–1952*: 183–7; Hasegawa, Kenji, 'Anti-Americanism in the early Zengakuren and Japanese Communist Party'; Hayashi, Iwao, *The History of Post-war Japanese Tank Development (Sengonihonno senshakaihatsushi)* (Tokyo: Kojinsha NFBunko, 2005): 27–8, 35–47.
174. JDA, *JSDF Ten Year History*: 33–5.
175. CIA, *Strategic Importance of Japan* (CIA-RDP78-01617A003-200190001-5) (24 May 1948): 3.
176. Chandler, Michael J., *Gen Otto P. Weyland, USAF: Close Air Support in the Korean War*, School of Advanced Air and Space Studies, (Maxwell AF Base, AL.: Air University Press, Mar. 2007): 33–4.
177. Maeda, Tetsuo, *The Hidden Army*: 35.
178. Blackman, Raymond, VB., *Jane's Fighting Ships, 1969–70* (London: Jane's Yearbooks, 1969): 26–7, 53.
179. Auer, James, E., *The Post-War Rearmament of Japanese Maritime Forces*: 118.
180. Sebata, Takao, *Japan's Defense Policy and Bureaucratic Politics, 1976–2007*, (Lanham, MD.: University Press of America, 2010): xiv.

181. Uyehara, Cecil H., *The Subversive Activities Prevention Law of Japan: It's Creation, 1951–52* (Leiden: Brill, 2010).
182. JDA, *JSDF Ten Year History*: 60–1, 169–89.
183. Ibid: 34–5.
184. Ibid: 56–62, 172–182, 200.
185. Kusunoki, Ayako, 'The Early Years of the Ground Self-Defense Forces, 1945–1960,' in Robert D. Eldridge and Paul Midford (eds.), *The Japanese Ground Self-Defense Force*, pp. 55–132: 89.
186. Security Treaty Between the United States and Japan; September 8, 1951, The Avalon Project, Yale Law School, (http://avalon.law.yale.edu/20th_century/japan001.asp#1 12 Oct. 2018).
187. *Administrative Agreement under Article III of the Security Treaty between the United States of America and Japan* (28 Feb. 1952); The World and Japan Database, GRIPS-University of Tokyo, (http://worldjpn.grips.ac.jp/documents/texts/docs/19520228.T1E.html1 12 Oct. 2018).
188. Kusunoki, Ayako, 'The Early Years of the Ground Self-Defense Forces': 84.
189. Auer, James E., *The Post-War Rearmament of Japanese Maritime Forces*, 86.
190. Patalano, Alessio, *Post-war Japan as a Sea Power: Imperial Legacy, Wartime Experience, and the Making of a Navy* (London: Bloomsbury, 2015), 99.
191. Patalano, Alessio, '"A Symbol of Tradition and Modernity": Itō Masanori and the Legacy of the Imperial Navy in the Early Postwar Rearmament Process,' *Japanese Studies*, 34:1 (2014): pp. 61–82: 76.
192. JDA, *Ten Year history of the JSDF*: 57–60, 144–5, 226–8.
193. '60th Anniversary of the Establishment of the Maritime Self-Defense Force,' *Japan Defense Focus*, 29 (June 2012) (http://www.mod.go.jp/e/jdf/no29/topics.html 12 Sept. 2014).

2. COLD WAR DEFENDERS OF JAPAN

1. *Police of Japan, 2010* (Tokyo: NPA, 2010): 1–2.
2. Gow, Ian, 'Civilian Control of the Military in Postwar Japan', in Matsuyama, Keisuke, Matthews, Ron (eds.), *Japan's Military Renaissance?* (Basingstoke: Macmillan, 1993), pp. 50–68: 58; Graham, Euan, *Japan's Sea Lane Security: A Matter of Life and Death?*, (Abingdon: Routledge, 2006): 110.
3. Smith, Sheila A., *Japan Rearmed: The Politics of Military Power* (Cambridge, MA.: Harvard University Press, 2019): 249, note 10.
4. Hughes, Christopher W., *Japan's Remilitarisation* (Abingdon: IISS/Routledge, 2009).
5. Sugawa, Kiyoshi, *Time to Pop the Cork: Three Scenarios to Refine Japanese Use of Force*, Center for Northeast Asian Policy Studies, Working Paper, Brookings Institute (2000) (http://www.brook.edu/fp/cnaps/papers/2000_sugawa.htm 12 Nov. 2008).
6. *Handbook for Defense 1981* (*Bōeihandobukku showa56nenban*), (Tokyo: Asagumo-shinbunsha, 1981): 335–43; *Handbook for Defense 1985* (*Bōeihandobukku showa60nenban*), (Tokyo: Asagumoshinbunsha, 1985): 408–15; *Hand Book for Defense 1999* (*Bōeihandobukku heisei11nenban*) (Tokyo: Asagumoshinbunsha, 1999): 694–99.

7. *Charter of the United Nations* (http://www.un.org/en/sections/un-charter/chapter-vii/ 16 Feb. 2015).
8. Samuels, Richard J., *Politics, Security Policy, and Japan's Cabinet Legislation Bureau: Who Elected these Guys, Anyway?*, JPRI Working Paper 99 (2004).
9. *Defense of Japan 1998*: 150.
10. *Basic Policy for National Defense, 1957* (Tokyo: JDA, 1957).
11. Weinstein, Martin E., *Japan's Postwar Defense Policy*: 57; Drifte, Reinhard, *Japan's Quest for a Permanent Security Council Seat: A Matter of Pride or Justice* (London: St. Antony's Series-Macmillan, 2000): 13–6.
12. Sherif, Ann, *Japan's Cold War: Media, Literature, and the Law* (New York: Columbia University Press, 2009): 26.
13. *Hand Book for Defense 2002* (*Bōeihandobukku heisei14nenban*), (Tokyo: Asagumoshinbunsha, 2002): 613–19.
14. Auer, James E., *The Post-War Rearmament of Japanese Maritime Forces, 1945–1971* (New York: Preager, 1973): 145.
15. Calder, Kent E., *Crisis and Compensation: Public Policy and Political Stability in Japan, 1949–1986* (Princeton, NJ.: Princeton University, 1988): 423.
16. Sebata, Takao, 'Is Japan Becoming a "Normal State" in Civil-Military Relations?', *East-West Research* (*Tōyōkenkyū*) 20–1 (2008).
17. Hikotani, Takako, 'Civil-Military Relations in Japan: Past, Present, and Future' (*Shibiriankontrōru noshōrai*), *The Journal of International Affairs* (Kokusaianzenhoshō), 32–1 (2004): 27–29.
18. Yamaguchi, Noboru, 'Study of the military in politics' (*Seijiniokeru gunjinokenkyū*), *Chūōkōron* (Aug. 1991), pp. 158–70; Maeda, Tetsuo, *The Hidden Army: The Untold Story of Japan's Military Forces* (Carol Stream, IL.: edition q, 1995): 216–19; Olsen, Edward A., *U.S.-Japan Strategic Reciprocity: A Neo-Internationalist View* (Palo Alto, CA.: Hoover Institute, 1985): 86.
19. Johnson, Chalmers, *MITI and the Japanese Miracle: The Growth of Industrial Policy, 1925–1975* (Stanford, CA.: Stanford University Press, 1982); National Security Archive, *Takashi Maruyama Oral History Interview*, U.S.-Japan Project, (12 Apr. 1996), (https://nsarchive2.gwu.edu//japan/maruyamaohinterview.htm 25 July 2018); National Security Archive, *Seiki Nishihiro Oral History Interview*, U.S.-Japan Project, (16 Nov.1995), (https://nsarchive2.gwu.edu/japan/nishihiroohinterview.htm 22 Feb. 2018).
20. Gow, Ian, 'Civilian Control of the Military in Postwar Japan': 59–61.
21. Fujii, Haruo, *JSDF Coup d'Etat Strategy* (*jieitaikūdetasenryaku*) (Tokyo: Sanichishobō, 1974); Kotani, Hidejiro, *The Actual Condition of Defence: Dialogue with the JDA Big 4* (*bōeino jittai-bōeichōbiggu4 to notaidan*) (Tokyo: Nihonkyobunsha, 1972): 24–7; Maeda, Tetsuo, *Hidden Army*: 126–7, 150–5.
22. Taoka, Junji, '"Coup d'état Doctrine" Yelled Serving Major (Report JSDF)' ('*kūdetaaron' tonaetageneki 3sa no kyaria (ripōtojieitai)*), *Aera* (27 Oct. 1992): 20.
23. Andrews, William, *Dissenting Japan: A History of Japanese Radicalism and Counterculture from 1945 to Fukushima* (London: Hurst&Co., 2016): 61–3; Samuels, Richard J., *Special Duty: A History of the Japanese Intelligence Community* (Ithaca, NY.: Cornell University Press, 2019): 114–6.

24. Katzenstein, Peter J., *Cultural Norms and National Security: Police and Military in Postwar Japan* (Ithaca: Cornell University Press, 1996): 73; Eldridge, Robert D., 'The GSDF During the Cold War Years, 1960–1989', in Eldridge, Robert D., and Midford, Paul (eds.), *The Japanese Ground Self-Defense Force: Search for Legitimacy* (New York: Palgrave Macmillan, 2017), pp. 133–81: 141–5; National Security Archive, *Noboru Hoshuyama Oral History Interview*, U.S.-Japan Project, (19 April 1996), (https://nsarchive2.gwu.edu//japan/hoshuyamaohinterview.htm 22 July 2018).
25. Sado, Akihiro, *Post-war Politics and the JSDF*: 55–57.
26. Kirk, Donald, 'Sour Japan Greeting for U.S.S. Midway,' *Chicago Tribune* (6 October 1973): 2; 'USS Midway (CVB-41)', *Dictionary of American Fighting Ships and United States Naval Aviation, 1910–1995, Naval Historical Center* (http://www.navy.mil/navydata/ships/carriers/histories/cv41-midway/cv41-midway.html 12 Mar. 2017).
27. Hopkins, Robert S. III, *Spyflights and Overflights: US Strategic Aerial Reconnaissance, Vol. 1 1945–1960* (Manchester: Hikoki, 2016).
28. National Security Archive, *James Auer Oral History Interview*, U.S.-Japan Project, (Mar. 1996), (https://nsarchive2.gwu.edu//japan/auerohinterview.htm 22 Jan. 2018).
29. *Treaty of Mutual Cooperation and Security between the United States and Japan* (19 Jan. 1960), Columbia University (http://afe.easia.columbia.edu/ps/japan/mutual_cooperation_treaty.pdf 2 Oct. 2018).
30. JDA, *JSDF Ten Year History* (*Jieitaijunenshi*), (Tokyo: JDA, 1961): 284.
31. Ibid: 285.
32. JDA, *Defense of Japan 1970* (*Bōeihakushoshowa45nen*), (http://www.clearing.mod.go.jp/hakusho_data/1970/w1970_03.html 12 Aug. 2017).
33. JDA, *JSDF Ten Year History:* 287–8.
34. Interview, UK Armed Forces Recruitment Office, Middlesbrough (Sept. 2001).
35. Statistics Bureau, *Table 5 Population, percent of Population and Index of Population for Prefectures: 1920 to 1980*, e-Stat Official Statistics of Japan, Ministry of Internal Affairs and Communications, (file:///C:/Documents%20and%20Settings/Garren%20Mulloy/My%20Documents/Downloads/80a00500.pdf 12 Jan 2016).
36. *Handbook for Defense 1981*: 115–6.
37. Ibid: 104.
38. Eldridge, Robert D., and Midford, Paul (eds.), *The Japanese Ground Self-Defense Force*.
39. *Hand Book for Defense 1999*: 145.
40. Conversation, GSDF Colonel, Tokyo (June 2015).
41. Kotani, Hidejiro, *The Actual Condition of Defence*: 98–102.
42. Statistics Bureau, *31–5 Ships and Aircrafts etc. Held by the Defense Agency (1952–2004)*, (Tokyo: Statistics Bureau, Ministry of Internal Affairs and Communications, 2005), (http://www.stat.go.jp/english/data/chouki/31.htm 27 Oct. 2015).
43. 11th Budget Committee, House of Councillors, (11 Mar. 1963), (http://kokkai.ndl.go.jp/SENTAKU/sangiin/043/0514/04303110514011a.html 12 Mar. 2017).
44. Ibid.
45. *Hand Book for Defense 1999*: 72–3, 145–7.
46. National Security Archive, *Naotoshi Sakonjo Oral History Interview*, U.S.-Japan Project, (Apr. 1996), (https://nsarchive2.gwu.edu//japan/sakonjoohinterview.htm 2 Sept. 2018).

47. Doc.58, 'Memorandum From the Assistant Secretary of State for Far Eastern Affairs (Bundy) to the Deputy Under Secretary for Political Affairs (Thompson): Subject Japanese Defense Policy,' (20 Aug.1964), *FRUS, 1964–1968, Volume XXIX*, pp. 113–21: 119.
48. Fitzsimons, Bernard (ed.), *The Illustrated Encyclopedia of 20th Century Weapons and Warfare* (New York: Columbia House/Phoebus, 1978): 2184; *JSDF Equipment Yearbook 2016–2017*, (Tokyo: Asagumoshinbunsha, 2016): 30.
49. Kopp, Carlo, 'Soviet/Russian Cruise Missiles,' Technical Report APA-TR-2009–0805, *Air Power Australia* (Aug. 2009, updated 27 Jan. 2014) (http://www.ausairpower.net/APA-Rus-Cruise-Missiles.html#mozTocId937963 23 Feb. 2018); Hiranandani, GM, '1971 War: The First Missile Attack on Karachi', *Indian Defence Review* (1 Nov. 2017) (http://www.indiandefencereview.com/interviews/1971-war-the-first-missile-attack-on-karachi/0/ 23 Feb. 2018)
50. Yoshitomi, Nozomu, 'The Role of the Ground Self-Defense Force in Maintaining Maritime Traffic Security: For Japan's National Interests as a Global Maritime Nation' (*Kaijōkōtsū no anzenkakho ni okerurikujōjieitai noyakuwari*), *The Journal of International Security* (*Kokusaianzenhoshō*) 43–1 (June 2015): 106–122; Matsukane, Hisamoto, 'Japan and Security of the Sea Lanes', *Global Affairs*, Vol. 4 (Spring 1989), pp. 49–64.
51. JDA, *JSDF Ten Year History*: 88–90.
52. Ibid: 85–8.
53. *Hand Book for Defense 1999*: 145.
54. Ledwidge, Frank, *Investment in Blood: The Real Cost of Britain's Afghan War* (London: Yale University Press, 2014); Ferguson, James, *A Million Bullets: The real story of the British Army in Afghanistan* (London: Bantam, 2008); MOD, 'Reconstruction the key to progress in Helmand', *Military Operations* (MOD, 12 June 2007) (http://webarchive.nationalarchives.gov.uk/+/http://www.mod.uk/DefenceInternet/DefenceNews/MilitaryOperations/ReconstructionTheKeyToProgressInHelmandvideo.htm 27 July 2017).
55. Hunter-Chester, David, *Creating Japan's Ground Self-Defense Force, 1945–2015: A Sword Well Made* (Lanham, MD.: Lexington, 2016): 174–5.
56. Hayashi, Iwao, *The History of Post-war Japanese Tank Development* (*Sengonihon no senshakaihatsushi*) (Tokyo: Kojinsha, 2005): 27–30.
57. Eldridge, Robert D., 'The GSDF During the Cold War Years, 1960–1989': 139.
58. Sado, Akihiro, *The Self-Defense Forces and Postwar Politics in Japan*: 62–4.
59. Kotani, Hidejiro, *The Actual Condition of Defence*: 101–2.
60. Ibid: 100–1; *Hand Book for Defense 1999*: 145.
61. GSDF, *7th Armored Division History* (*Dai7shidan no enkaku*), (http://www.mod.go.jp/gsdf/nae/7d/enkaku.html 7 Mar. 2017).
62. Seaton, Philip A., 'Commemorating the War Dead at Hokkaido Gokoku Shrine', in Seaton, Philip A., (ed.), *Local History and War Memories in Hokkaido* (Abingdon: Routledge, 2016), pp. 161–78: 163–9.
63. GSDF, *7th Armoured Division, 73rd Tank Regiment History* (*Dai7kikoshidan dai73s-ensharentai enkaku*) (http://www.mod.go.jp/gsdf/nae/7d/hensei/team/73/enkaku/enkaku.html 7 Mar. 2017).

64. The British *Challenger 2* was in universal service within four years. Dunstan, Simon, *Challenger Main Battle Tank 1982–97* (Oxford: Osprey Publishing, 1998).
65. JDA, *Defense of Japan 1979* (http://www.clearing.mod.go.jp/hakusho_data/1979/w1979_02.html 23 Oct. 2017).
66. Kotani, Hidejiro, *The Actual Condition of Defence*: 120–1.
67. Otake, Hideo, *Japanese Defence and Domestic Politics: from détente to military* expansion (*Nihonno bōeito kokunaiseiji detantokara gunkakue*) (Tokyo: Sannichishoten, 1983): 31–2; Auer, James E., *The Post-war Rearmament of Japanese Maritime Forces*: 113–15.
68. Yomiurishimbunsha, *Japan's Defence Combat Power 1-GSDF* (*Nihonno bōeisenryoku1-rikujōkieitai*) (Tokyo: Yomiurishimbunsha, 1987): 14–6, 155–63; *Japan Self-Defense Forces Equipment Yearbook, 1987*: 48–77.
69. Sasaki, Tomoyuki, *Japan's Postwar Military and Civil Society: Contesting a Better Life* (London: Bloosmbury, 2015): 67.
70. Yamaguchi, Noboru, 'Evidence: 900 days of GSDF Iraq Dispatch' (*Kenshō, rikujōjieitaiirakuhaken no 900nichi*), *Close-up Gendai*, 2273, *NHK* (24 July 2006).
71. Yomiurishimbunsha, *Japan's Defence Combat Power 1*: 190–1.
72. Ibid: 191–2.
73. *Flight International* (1 Aug. 1981): 352; Yomiurishimbunsha, *Japan's Defence Combat Power 1*: 198.
74. Ibid, 112–8, 198–9; *Japan Self-Defense Forces Equipment Yearbook, 2016–2017*: 86, 92.
75. *Japan Self-Defense Forces Equipment Yearbook, 2016–2017*: 87.
76. Headquarters, US Joint Staff, *Joint Publication 1-02, Department of Defense Dictionary of Military and Associated Terms* (Washington, DC: Government Printing Office, 2010): 54.
77. Headquarters, Department of the Army, *Field Manual 3-04.126, Attack Reconnaissance Helicopter Operations* (Washington, DC: Government Printing Office, 2007): 1–4.
78. Yomiurishimbunsha, *Japan's Defence Combat Power 1*: 31–3.
79. *The Soviet Army: Troops, Organization, and Equipment*, Field Manual No. 100-2-3 Department of the Army (Washington, DC.: Department of the Army, June 1991): 4–26~ 4–116; Office of Soviet Analysis, *Reorganization of Soviet Ground Forces in East Germany (U): An Intelligence Assessment*, Directorate of Intelligence, HR70–14 (Aug. 1983): 5–17.
80. *The Soviet Army*: 4–149.
81. *Japan Self-Defense Forces Equipment Yearbook, 2016–2017*: 38, 51.
82. Yomiurishimbunsha, *Japan's Defence Combat Power 1*: 74–8; *'74 JSDF Equipment Yearbook* (*'74jieitai seibinenkan*) (Tokyo: Asagumoshimbunsha, 1974): 26.
83. *Japan Self-Defense Forces Equipment Yearbook, 2016–2017*: 18; National Archives, *Naval Leaders: Admiral of the Fleet Sir John Fisher, 1st Baron Fisher of Kilverstone 1841–1920*, (http://webarchive.nationalarchives.gov.uk/20090417210628/http://www.royalnavy.mod.uk/history/naval-leaders/john-fisher/ 22 Aug. 2017).
84. Sase, Masamori (Trans./Ed. Eldridge, Robert D; Leonard, Graham B), *Changing Security Politics in Postwar Japan: The Political Biography of Japanese Defense Minister Sakata Michita* (Lanham, MD.: Lexington, 2018): 58.

85. '74 JSDF Equipment Yearbook: 38–70; Takarajimasha (ed.), *JSDF 60 Year History* (*Jieitai60nenshi*), (Tokyo: Takarajimasha, 2015): 51.
86. '74 JSDF Equipment Yearbook: 59.
87. No. 58, Memorandum from the Assistant Secretary of State for Far Eastern Affairs (Bundy) to the Deputy Under Secretary for Political Affairs (Thompson), (20 Aug. 1965), Foreign relations of the United States, 1964–1968, Volume XXIX Pt. 2: Japan.
88. JDA, *Defense of Japan 1979* (http://www.clearing.mod.go.jp/hakusho_data/1979/w1979_9110.html 12 Jan 2018); (http://www.clearing.mod.go.jp/hakusho_data/1979/w1979_9140.html 12 Jan 2018).
89. SDF Law (*Jieitaihō*), Law No. 165 (9 June 1954) (http://law.e-gov.go.jp/htmldata/S29/S29HO165.html 26 July 2015).
90. Samuels, Richard J., *Special* Duty: 100–2.
91. Kusunoki, Ayako, 'The Early Years of the Ground Self-Defense Forces, 1945–1960,' in Eldridge, Robert D., and Midford, Paul (eds.), *The Japanese Ground Self-Defense Force*, pp. 55–132: 109.
92. Takarajimasha (ed.), *JSDF 60 Year History*: 46–7; Ota, Masakatsu, 'U.S. weighed giving Japan nuclear weapons in 1950s', *Kyodo/Japan Times* (23 Jan. 2015) (https://www.japantimes.co.jp/news/2015/01/23/national/history/u-s-weighed-giving-japan-nuclear-weapons-in-1950s/#.WaR5u9QS_Dc 24 Jan. 2015).
93. Ibid; Abiru, Rui, 'Japan's Self-Defense Forces Could Have Played a Larger Role in Fighting COVID-19, But...', *Japan Forward*, (3 June 2020) (https://japan-forward.com/japans-self-defense-forces-could-have-played-a-larger-role-in-fighting-covid-19-but/ 22 August 2020).
94. Shibayama, Futoshi, 'U.S. Strategic Debates over the Defense of Japan: Lessons for the Twenty-First Century,' *The Journal of American-East Asian Relations* 9–1/2 (Spring-Summer 2000), pp. 29–54.
95. Conversations, USMC Colonel, Tokyo and Fujisawa (2002).
96. National Security Archive, *Takashi Maruyama Oral History Interview*.
97. MOD, 'Kushiro garrison 63rd establishment anniversary, 27th Infantry Regiment 54th establishment anniversary parade' (*Kushirochūtonchi sōritsu63shunennarabi nidai27futsukarentai 54shunenkinengyoji*), *Higashi Hokkaido Dayori* (Aug. 2016): 2; *27th Infantry Regiment* (*Dai27futsukarentai*) (http://www.mod.go.jp/gsdf/nae/5d/01_unit/27i/00_27i.html 12 Aug. 2017).
98. Kurisu, Hiroomi, 'Soviet Military Land Here, Our Ways to Counterattack' (*Sorengunkokoejōriku, warerawo mukaeutsu*), *Gendai*, (Jan. 1980), pp. 54–86.
99. National Security Archive, *James Auer Oral History Interview*.
100. Ibid.
101. *Naotoshi Sakonjo Oral History Interview*.
102. Ibid; Morimoto, Satoshi, *The future of US–Japanese defence cooperation and its implications for regional security*, Proceedings of the Conference on Russia and Asia–Pacific Security, SIPRI (Tokyo, 19–21 Feb. 1999) (https://www.sipri.org/sites/default/files/files/misc/SIPRI99Chufrin.pdf 5 Sept. 2018) pp. 76–82: 77; US Forces Japan, *Command History, 1982* (https://nautilus.org/wp-content/uploads/2012/01/USFJ1982.pdf 22 May 2020): 60–4.

103. National Security Archive, *Seiki Nishihiro Oral History Interview*.
104. Smith, Sheila A., *Japan Rearmed*: 33–5.
105. 'Realisation of JSDF invitation strengthening: Prefecture and Gojo City' (*Jieitaiyūchijitsugen wokyōka-ken togojoshi*), *Nara Shimbun* (9 Apr. 2013) (http://www.nara-np.co.jp/20130409091645.html 27 Sept. 2016).
106. Murakami, Tomoaki, 'The GSDF and Disaster Relief Dispatches', in Eldridge, Robert D., and Midford, Paul (eds.), *The Japanese Ground Self-Defense Force*: 268–9.
107. Donovan, Matthew, and Grossi, Patricia, *1959 Super Typhoon Vera: 50-Year Retrospective* (Newark, CA.; Risk Management Solutions, 2009): 8–9.
108. Hoffman, Robert M., *1959 Annual Typhoon Report* (Guam: U.S. Fleet Weather Central/Joint Typhoon Warning Center, 1959): 189; Kurashina, Yuko, *Peacekeeping Participation and Identity Changes in the Japan Self Defense Forces: Military Service as 'Dirty Work'*, PhD Thesis (College Park, MD.: University of Maryland, 2005): 207–8.
109. Gifu Prefecture, *Hidagawa Bus Plunge Accident* (*Hidagawabasu tenrakujiko*), (http://www.pref.gifu.lg.jp/kurashi/bosai/shizen-saigai/11115/siryou/hidagawabasu.html 27 July 2017); MOD, *GSDF 10th Division Divisional History and Activities* (*Shidanno enkaku, katsudō*) (http://www.mod.go.jp/gsdf/mae/10d/10d/enkaku.htm 27 July 2017).
110. *Large-Scale Earthquake Countermeasures Law* (*Daikibojishintaisaku tokubetsusochihō*), Law 73 (15 June 1978) (http://law.e-gov.go.jp/htmldata/S53/S53HO073.html 27 July 2017).
111. Asahishimbunshakaibu (ed.), *JAL Jumbo Jet Crash: 24 Hours of the Asahi Shimbun* (*Nikkojyanbokitsuiryaku-asahishinbunno 24jikan*) (Tokyo: Asahibunko, 1990).
112. MOD, *North-Kanto Defense Bureau Paper* (*Kitakantō bōeikyokukōhō*), No. 77, (Apr.-May, 2014) (https://www.mod.go.jp/rdb/n-kanto/kouhou/pdf/77kouhou-140530.pdf 19 Sept. 2018): 2–3.
113. GSDF, *Engaru Garrison History* (*Engaruchūtonchino enkaku*), (http://www.mod.go.jp/gsdf/nae/2d/unit/butai/engaru/index.htm 27 July 2017).
114. Kamei, Kotaro, *Working in a GSDF Infantry Regiment* (*Rikjōjieitaifutsukarentai noshigoto*) (Tokyo: Kojinsha, 2013): 221–4.
115. Seaton, Philip A., (ed.), *Local History and War Memories in Hokkaido*.
116. Mason, Michele M., *Dominant Narratives of Colonial Hokkaido and Imperial Japan: Envisioning the Periphery and the Modern Nation-State* (New York: Palgrave MacMillan, 2012): 4.
117. Irish, Ann B., *Hokkaido: A History of Ethnic Transition and Development on Japan's Northern Island* (Jefferson, NC.: McFarland, 2009): 270.
118. Sasaki, Tomoyuki, *Japan's Postwar Military and Civil Society*: 67–8.
119. Ibid: 68–70.
120. Interview with former Ogose Junior High School student (Tokyo: Feb. 2018); Historical Outline (*Enkakugaiyō*), Ogose Junior High School (http://ogose-jh.com/history1.html 12 Feb. 2018).
121. Aspinall, Robert W., *Teachers' Unions and the Politics of Education in Japan*, (New York: SUNY Press, 2001).
122. Ogose Town, *Tomb for the Unknown Soldiers of the World* (*Sekaimumeisenshi no haka*),

(http://www.town.ogose.saitama.jp/kankonavi/meguri/1455863576470.html 12 Feb. 2018).
123. MOD, *History of Outside Construction* (*Bugaikōji norekishi*), (http://www.mod.go.jp/gsdf/neae/9d/9e/rekishi.pdf 14 Mar. 2017).
124. Sasaki, Tomoyuki, *Japan's Postwar Military and Civil Society*: 86–96.
125. Author's experience in Hokkaido and Utsunomiya.
126. Murakami, Tomoaki, 'The GSDF and Disaster Relief Dispatches': 284–5.
127. House of Councillors, 13th Diet Session, 40th Cabinet Committee (11 June 1952): 11 (http://kokkai.ndl.go.jp/SENTAKU/sangiin/013/0388/01306110388040.pdf 27 Nov. 2017).
128. Sato, Fumika, 'A Camouflaged Military: Japan's Self-Defense Forces and Globalized Gender Mainstreaming', *The Asia-Pacific Journal*, 10–36–3, (3 Sept. 2012).
129. Ibid; *Defense Handbook 1981* (*Bōeihandobukku56nenban*) (Tokyo: Asagumo, 1981): 107–8; *Defense Hand Book 1999*: 192–9.
130. *Defense Hand Book 1999*: 192; Fruhstuck, Sabine, *Uneasy Warriors: Gender, Memory, and Popular Culture in the Japanese Army* (Berkley, CA.: University of California, 2007); Sato, Fumika, *Military Institutions and Gender: The JSDF's Women*, (*Gunjisoshiki tojendaa–jieitaino joseitachi*) (Tokyo: Keio University, 2004): 188.
131. 'SDF sex harassment affects 18% of its women', *The Japan Times* (14 Jan. 1999), (http://search.japantimes.co.jp/cgi-bin/nn19990114b1.html, 12 March 2010).
132. Sato, Fumika, 'A Camouflaged Military.'
133. 'Emperor Showa's feelings should be respected,' *Nikkei Shimbun* (21 July 2006): 2, *US embassy cable—06TOKYO4084* (http://cables.mrkva.eu/cable.php?id=72098 12 Mar. 2017).
134. The author's late neighbour.
135. '2008 Hokkaido Gokoku Shrine Great Memorial Ceremony' (*2008nen Hokkaido gokokujinjaireitaisai*), *Asahikawa Peace Committee* (6 June 2008) (http://peace-asahikawa.cocolog-nifty.com/blog/2008/06/2008_f56c.html 22 Oct. 2016); Seaton, Philip A., 'Commemorating the War Dead at Hokkaido Gokoku Shrine', in Seaton, Philip A. (ed.), *Local History and War Memories in Hokkaido*, pp. 161–78.
136. Weeks, Eric N., 'A Widow's Might: Nakaya v. Japan and Japan's Current State of Religious Freedom,' *Brigham Young Law Review*, (1995) 2–11, pp. 691–730: 699.
137. Ibid: 702–3.
138. Ibid: 716.
139. 'FY2017 Memorial Service for Members of the JSDF Who Lost Their Lives on Duty,' *Japan Defense Focus*, No. 95 (Dec. 2017) (http://www.mod.go.jp/e/jdf/no95/activities.html#article02 7 Jan. 2018); JDA, *Defense of Japan 2004: 50th Anniversary* (*Bōeihakushoheisei16nen*) (Tokyo: JDA, 2004): 268.
140. Skabelund, Aaron, and Ishikawa, Akito, 'Japan', in Hassner, Ron. E., *Religion in the Military Worldwide* (Cambridge: Cambridge University Press, 2014), pp. 23–44: 33–9.
141. Ibid: 40.
142. Tahara, Soichiro, 'The Tamogami Essay: The Danger of Indignation is the Heart of the Problem,' *The Asia-Pacific Journal*, 47–8–08, (21 Nov. 2008), (https://apjjf.org/-Herbert-P.-Bix/2958/article.html 12 Nov. 2017).

143. Green, Michael J., 'Reviving Japan's Military,' *The Wall Street Journal* (15 Jan. 2007), (http://online.wsj.com/public/article/SB116881980420076629.html, 17 Jan. 2007).
144. GSDF, *Kasumigaura* Base Public Relations Center (*Kasumigaura chūtonchikōhōsentaa*) (http://www.mod.go.jp/gsdf/eae/eadep/sabu05.html 12 Feb. 2018); 'Casting wishes for fighter accident eradication 'Sky-goddess'' ('*Sentōkijikokonzetsuonegaiminage 'ōzorano megami'*'), *Sankei Shimbun* (7 Sept. 2017) (http://www.sankei.com/life/news/170907/lif1709070022-n1.html 12 Feb. 2018); Hertrich, André, 'War memory, local history, gender: Self-representation in exhibitions of the Ground Self-Defense Force,' in Seaton, Philip A., (ed.), *Local History and War Memories in Hokkaido*, pp. 179–98.
145. Kirishima, Shun, 'Administration in Disguise "Imperial Ideology"' (*Seiken wo ōu "kokokushisō"*), *AERA* (31 Aug. 2015): 63.
146. Smith, Rupert, *The Utility of Force: The Art of War in the Modern World*, (London: Penguin, 2006): 267–8.
147. Military Assistance and Advisory Group Japan (MAAG-J), 'Requirements for the Naval Defence of Japan,' in Ishii, Osamu, and Ono, Naoki (eds.), *Documents on the United States Policy towards Japan: Documents related to Diplomatic and Military Matters*, Volume 4 (Tokyo: Kashiwashobo, 1999): 398–405.
148. Nakayama, Takashi, *Sea of Japan-Military Tension* (*Nihonkai, gunjikinchō*) (Tokyo: Chuōkoronshinsha, 2002): 4.
149. SDF Law, Article 3.
150. Auer, James E., *The Post-war Rearmament of Japanese Maritime Forces*: 128.
151. All MSDF major combat ships are referred to as *Goeikan*, escort ships, but the Force assigns numbers and describes them as destroyers DD, or destroyer-escorts.
152. MSDF/MOD, 'Inaugural Reception of MSDF Hachinohe, 1957,' (http://www.mod.go.jp/msdf/hatinohe/images/about/history/history-1957.jpg 17 Mar. 2017).
153. Kevork, Chris, 'The Revitalisation of Japan's Submarine Industry: From Defeat to *Oyashio*,' *NIDS Journal of Defense and Security*, 14, (Dec. 2013), pp. 71–92: 76–77.
154. Ibid: 77–8.
155. Auer, James E., *The Post-war Rearmament of Japanese Maritime Forces*: 93–5, 153–5.
156. *JSDF Equipment Yearbook 2016–2017*: 175.
157. MAAG-J, 'Requirements for the Naval Defence of Japan,' in Ishii, Osamu, and Ono, Naoki (eds.), *Documents on the United States Policy towards Japan*: 398–405.
158. *Hand Book for Defense 1999*: 68, 145.
159. Ibid.
160. 11th Budget Committee, House of Councillors, (11 Mar. 1963) (http://kokkai.ndl.go.jp/SENTAKU/sangiin/043/0514/04303110514011a.html 24 June 2015).
161. Ibid.
162. Green, Michael J., *Bōeizoku: Defense Policy Formation in Japan's Liberal Democratic Party* (Cambridge, MA.: Massachusetts Institute of Technology, 1992).
163. Patalano, Alessio, Yabuki, Kei (trans.) 'From Navy to MSDF (1955–1976)' (*Kaigunkara kaiji*) *Gunjishigaku*, 44–4 (Mar. 2009).
164. Kevork, Chris, 'The Revitalisation of Japan's Submarine Industry': 79.
165. Boyd, Carl, and Yoshida, Akihiko, *The Japanese Submarine Force and World War II*, (Annapolis: Naval Institute Press, 1995/2002): 224.

166. Ibid: 4, 191–5.
167. Woodward, John Sandy, and Robinson, Patrick, *One Hundred Days: The Memoirs of the Falklands Battle Group Commander*, (London: Harper, 2012): 19–24.
168. Kevork, Chris, 'The Revitalisation of Japan's Submarine Industry': 84–87.
169. *All Ships of JMSDF 1952–2004, Ships of the World (Sekainokansen)*, No. 630 (Aug. 2004): 138; 'Development of JMSDF Submarines-Advent of Tear Drop Type Submarines,' *Ships of the World (Sekainokansen)* No. 821 (Sept. 2015), pp. 86–9.
170. Ibid: 'Development of JMSDF Submarines', pp. 90–3.
171. Patalano, Alessio, *Post-war Japan as a Sea Power: Imperial Legacy, Wartime Experience and the Making of a Navy* (London: Bloomsbury, 2015): 139.
172. Fairchild, Byron R., and Poole, Walter S. (eds.) *History of the Joint Chiefs of Staff: The Joint Chiefs of Staff and National Policy Vol. VII 1957–1960*: 77–82.
173. Kōda, Yōji, 'A New Carrier Race? Strategy, Force Planning, and JS Hyuga,' *Naval War College Review*, 64–3, (Summer 2011), pp. 31–60: 40.
174. Patalano, Alessio, *Post-war Japan as a Sea Power*: 139; *JSDF Equipment Yearbook 1997 (Jieitaisōbinenkan1997)* (Tokyo: Asagumoshinbunsha, 1997): 192, 242; *JSDF Equipment Yearbook 1993 (Jieitaisōbinenkan1993)* (Tokyo: Asagumoshinbunsha, 1993): 170–3.
175. Kōda, Yōji, 'A New Carrier Race?': 40.
176. Kōda, Yōji, 'Farewell to *Shirane* Class DDH,' *Ships of the World (Sekainokansen)* No. 858 (May 2017), pp. 141–7.
177. Yomiurishimbunsha (ed.), *Japan's Defence Combat Power 2—Maritime Self-Defense Force (Nihon no bōeisenryoku2-kaijōkieitai)* (Tokyo: Yomiurishimbunsha, 1987): 82–94.
178. Kōda, Yōji 'A New Carrier Race?': 43–4.
179. Congressional Budget Office, *The U.S. Sea Control Mission: Forces, Capabilities, and Requirements*, US Congress (June 1977): 7–9; Walsh, David M, *The Military Balance in the Cold War: US perceptions and policy, 1976–85* (Abingdon: Routledge, 2008): 131–2.
180. *All Ships of JMSDF 1952–2004*: 122, 154; Moore, John (ed.) *Jane's Fighting Ships 1974–75* (London: Jane's Yearbooks, 1974): 208.
181. Ishimaru, Yasuzo, *The Impact on Japan from Mine Warfare during the Korean War*, Briefing Memo, NIDS Center for Military History (Feb. 2018): 4–6.
182. Patalano, Alessio, *Post-war Japan as a Sea Power*: 138; Clarke, Barry, *et al*, *Coastal Forces*: 51–6.
183. *All Ships of JMSDF 1952–2004*: 146; Moore, John (ed.) *Jane's Fighting Ships 1974–75*: 93–4, 206; Ishimaru, Yasuzo, *The Impact on Japan from Mine Warfare during the Korean War*: 2.
184. *All Ships of JMSDF 1952–2004*: 72, 114.
185. Woolley, Peter J., *Japan's Navy: Politics and Paradox, 1971–2000* (Boulder, CO.: Lynne Rienner, 2000) 31–2; Kawabata, Osamu (ed.), *Operation Gulf Dawn: The 188 Day Minesweeper Force Deployment* ('*Wangan noyoake': sakusenzenkiroku–kaijōjieitai perushawan sōkaihaken taino188nichi*) (Tokyo: Asagumoshimbunsha, 1991): 202.
186. *All Ships of JMSDF 1952–2004*: 90, 149–50; Moore, John (ed.) *Jane's Fighting Ships 1974–75*: 205–6.

187. Clarke, Barry, *et al* (eds.), *Coastal Forces* (London: Brassey's, 1994): 118–27.
188. *All Ships of JMSDF 1952–2004*: 84–8, 116.
189. Ibid: 147; *1998 JSDF Equipment Yearbook* (*1998jieitai seibinenkan*) (Tokyo: Asagumoshimbunsha, 1998): 243.
190. Zumwalt, Elmo R. Jr., *On Watch: A Memoir* (New York: The New York Times, 1976): 57–83.
191. Moore, John (ed.) *Jane's Fighting Ships 1974–75*: 204.
192. MccGwire, Michael, *Military Objectives in Soviet Foreign Policy* (Washington, DC.: The Brookings Institution, 1987): 457–71.
193. Polmar, Norman, 'Norman's Corner: Analyzing Exercise Okean,' *Naval Historical Foundation*, (20 Feb. 2013), (http://www.navyhistory.org/2013/02/normans-corner-analyzing-exercise-okean/ 12 Oct. 2017).
194. Auer, James E., *The Post-war Rearmament of Japanese Maritime Forces*: 151.
195. National Security Archive, *James Auer Oral History Interview*.
196. Auer, James E., *The Post-war Rearmament of Japanese Maritime Forces*: 161.
197. Nishihara, Masashi, 'Expanding Japan's Credible Defense Role,' *International Security*, 8–3 (Winter 1983–84), pp. 180–205: 186; MSDF officer, in Samuels, Richard J., *Special Duty*: 110–111.
198. National Security Archive, *Seiki Nishihiro Oral History Interview*.
199. Aichi, Kiichi, 'Japan's Legacy and Destiny of Change,' *Foreign Affairs*, Vol. XLVIII, No. 1 (Oct. 1969) (https://www.foreignaffairs.com/articles/asia/1969-10-01/japans-legacy-and-destiny-change 8 Aug. 2017).
200. Auer, James E., *The Post-war Rearmament of Japanese Maritime Forces*: 163.
201. Walsh, David M., *The Military Balance in the Cold War:* 207.
202. Ibid: 199.
203. *All Ships of JMSDF 1952–2004*: 34, 64–5, 90–1; Moore, John (ed.) *Jane's Fighting Ships 1974–75*: 205–6.
204. Sase, Masamori (Trans./Ed. Eldridge, Robert D.; Leonard, Graham B.), *Changing Security Politics in Postwar Japan*; Chijiwa, Yasuaki, 'Unfinished "Beyond-the-Threat Theory": Japan's "Basic Defense Force Concept" Revisited', *NIDS Journal of Defense and Security*, (17, Dec. 2016) (http://www.nids.mod.go.jp/english/publication/kiyo/pdf/2016/bulletin_e2016_6.pdf 12 Feb. 2018), pp. 83–101; National Security Archive, *Takashi Maruyama Oral History Interview*.
205. Sebata, Takao, *Japan's Defense Policy and Bureaucratic Politics, 1976–2007*, (Lanham, MD.: University Press of America, 2010): 111–24.
206. Aizawa, Teruaki, 'The Defence Build-up Concept of the MSDF in the Post-Fourth Defense Build-up Program: The Modernisation of Maritime Forces and the "8 Destroyers-8 Helicopters Concept"' (*Posutoyojibō niokeru kaijōjieitaino bōeiryokuseibi kōsō nikansurukenkyū: kaijōbōeiryokukindaika to hachikanhachikitaisei*), *NIDS Military History Studies Annual Report*, No. 18 (Mar. 2015), pp. 27–55: 32.
207. National Security Archive, *James Auer Oral History Interview*.
208. Kotani, Hidejiro, *The Actual Condition of Defence*: 186.
209. 68th Diet Session, Cabinet Committee, No. 28, House of Representatives (*Shugiin*), (31 May 1972) (http://kokkai.ndl.go.jp/SENTAKU/syugiin/068/0020/06805310020028a.html 12 Mar. 2018).

210. Kotani, Hidejiro, *The Actual Condition of Defence*: 186–193.
211. Ibid: 198.
212. *Kaijōjieitai50nenshihensaniinkai*, 50-Year History of the MSDF (*Kaijōjieitai50nenshi*), (Tokyo: Bōeichō-kaijōjieitaibakuryōkanbu, 2003): 6–7.
213. Koyama, Takashi, 'Homeporting Issues for a US Navy Aircraft Carrier in the Yokosuka Base' (*Beikaigunyokosukakichi no beikūbo 'kūboka' nitsuite*), *Senshi*, NIDS (Mar. 2017), 1–43: 6 (http://www.nids.mod.go.jp/publication/senshi/pdf/201703/03.pdf 21 Mar. 2018).
214. Koyama, Takashi, 'Homeporting Issues for a US Navy Aircraft Carrier in the Yokosuka Base': 8–13; National Security Archive, *James Auer Oral History Interview*; Richard Nixon, 'Special Message to the Congress Proposing Reform of the Foreign Assistance Program', (15 Sept. 1970), Peters, Gerhard, and Woolley, John T., *The American Presidency Project*, UCSB (http://www.presidency.ucsb.edu/ws/?pid=2661 12 Aug. 2017).
215. National Security Archive, *James Auer Oral History Interview*.
216. Graham, Euan, *Japan's Sea Lane Security:* 108–9.
217. Kōda, Yōji 'A New Carrier Race?': 34–5.
218. Ibid.
219. Yoshitomi, Nozomu, 'The Role of the Ground Self-Defense Force in Maintaining Maritime Traffic Security: For Japan's National Interests as a Global Maritime Nation' (*Kaijōkōtsū noanzenkakho niokeru rikujōjieitai noyakuwari*), *The Journal of International Security* (*Kokusaianzenhoshō*) 43–1 (June 2015), pp. 106–122; Matsukane, Hisamoto, 'Japan and Security of the Sea Lanes,' *Global Affairs*, Vol. 4 (Spring 1989), pp. 49–64.
220. Sado, Akihiro, *Post-war Politics and the JSDF*: 145–7.
221. Sado, Akihiro, *History of the JSDF: 70 Years of Defence Policy* (*Jieitaishi: bōeiseisaku no70nen*) (Tokyo: Chikumashinsho, 2015): 155–62, 165–9; Agawa, Naoyuki, Yabuki, Hiraku (trans.), *Friendship Across the Seas: The US Navy and the Japan Maritime Self-Defense Force* (Tokyo: Japan Library, 2019): 192.
222. *Defense of Japan 1983* (Tokyo: JDA/Japan Times, 1983): 74–7.
223. National Security Archive, *James Auer Oral History Interview*.
224. Graham, Euan, *Japan's Sea lane Security*: 135–8; US Forces Japan, *Command History, 1982*: 72.
225. Green, Michael J., *By More Than Providence: Grand Strategy and American Power in the Asia Pacific Since 1783*, (New York: Columbia University Press, 2017): 405–6.
226. *Joint Communiqué of Japanese Prime Minister Zenko Suzuki and U.S. President Reagan*, Washington, DC.: 8 May 1981), 'The World and Japan' Database of Japanese Politics and International Relations, National Graduate Institute for Policy Studies (GRIPS), (http://worldjpn.grips.ac.jp/documents/texts/JPUS/19810508.D1E.html 12 Oct. 2017).
227. Green, Michael J., *By More Than Providence*: 405–6; National Security Archive, *Ohmori Keiji Oral History Interview*, U.S.-Japan Project, National Security Archive, (20 Dec. 1996), (https://nsarchive2.gwu.edu//japan/ohmoriohinterview.htm 12 Feb. 2018).
228. Woolley, Peter J., *Japan's Navy:* 70.

229. *Remarks of the President and Prime Minister Yasuhiro Nakasone of Japan Following Their Meetings in Tokyo* (Tokyo: 10 Nov. 1983), 'The World and Japan' Database, GRIPS, (http://worldjpn.grips.ac.jp/documents/texts/JPUS/19831110.O1E.html 12 Oct. 2017).
230. Main Question Submission No. 13, 98th Regular Diet Session, House of Councillors, (28 Apr. 1983), (http://www.sangiin.go.jp/japanese/joho1/kousei/syuisyo/098/syup/s098013.pdf 14 Oct. 2017).
231. Written Response No. 13, 98th Regular Diet Session, House of Councillors, Cabinet Opinion 98–13 (17 May 1983) (http://www.sangiin.go.jp/japanese/joho1/kousei/syuisyo/098/toup/t098013.pdf 14 Oct. 2017).
232. Chida, Tomohei, and Davies, Peter N., *The Japanese Shipping and Shipbuilding Industries: A History of Their Modern Growth* (London: Athlone, 1990): 189–90; Uttmark, Geoff, 'Japan-Finding the Dawn', *Marine Money Offshore* (https://www.marinemoneyoffshore.com/node/5754 12 Mar. 2017).
233. Ministry of Land, Infrastructure, Transport and Tourism, *The Current Situation of Japanese Shipping* (Tokyo: 2006): 4.
234. Graham, Euan, *Japan's Sea Lane Security*: 135–7.
235. Ibid: 144–7; *Hand Book for Defense, 1999*: 130–35.
236. JDA, *Defense of Japan 1986 (Bōeihakusho1986)*, (http://www.clearing.mod.go.jp/hakusho_data/1986/w1986_02.html 2 Oct. 2017).
237. Moore, John (ed.) *Jane's Fighting Ships 1974–75*: 205–6; 'All Ships of JMSDF 1952–2004': 100, 250; Yomiurishimbunsha (ed.), *Japan's Defence Combat Power 2*: 98–102; 'Memorandum of a Conversation, (26 June 1957),' *FRUS, 1955–1957, Japan*, Volume XXIII, Part 1, Document 196; Auer, James E., *The Post-war Rearmament of Japanese Maritime Forces*: 249.
238. Kōda, Yōji 'A New Carrier Race?': 40.
239. 'All Ships of JMSDF 1952–2004': 102–3.
240. Ibid: 66–7.
241. Ibid: 157.
242. Kaijōjieitai50nenshihensaniinkai, *50-Year History of the MSDF*: 277–9.
243. Moore, John (ed.) *Jane's Fighting Ships 1974–75*: 182–196.
244. 'All Ships of JMSDF 1952–2004': 132; Saunders, Stephen (ed.), *Jane's Fighting Ships 2001–2002* (Coulsdon, Surrey: Jane's Information Group, 2001): 380.
245. 'All Ships of JMSDF 1952–2004': 104, 128; Saunders, Stephen (ed.), *Jane's Fighting Ships 2001–2002*: 379–81.
246. Yomiurishimbunsha (ed.), *Japan's Defence Combat Power 2*: 32–64; Kodansha (ed.), *Japan's Defensive Power-JSDF present condition in illustrations and photographs (Nihonno bōeiryoku-jieitai no genkyō wotsukaito shashinde)* (Tokyo: Kodansha, 1983): 64–7. MSDF researcher on the Falklands War: "suddenly we could see how vulnerable we were, and how expensive operations could become."
247. Cabinet Office, 'Maritime Surveillance and Intelligence Collection (1) JGSDF and JMSDF' (*Keikaikanshijōhō noshūshūtaisei (1): rikujōoyobikaijōjieitai*), Materials, Fifth Security and Defence Power Colloquium, (29 June 2004) (http://www.kantei.go.jp/jp/singi/ampobouei/dai5/5siryou.pdf 12 Aug. 2017).

248. Sekino, Hideo, 'Japan and Her Maritime Defense,' *Proceedings*, USNI (May 1971), (https://www.usni.org/document/sekino-hideo-1971-97-5-819pdf 23 Aug. 2017).
249. Ball, Desmond, and Tanter, Richard, *The Tools of Owatatsumi: Japan's Ocean Surveillance and Coastal Defence Capabilities* (Canberra: NU Press, 2015): 55–78.
250. Conversations with the author.
251. 'All Ships of JMSDF 1952–2004': 170, 199–200, 205; Saunders, Stephen (ed.), *Jane's Fighting Ships 2001–2002*: 388–91.
252. JDA, *JSDF Ten Year History*: 53–7.
253. Masuda, Hiroshi, *Birth of the JSDF*: 168–79; Yomiurishinbunsha Sengoshihan, *Showa post-war history: the pathway to 'rearmament'*: 477–82.
254. Auer, James E., *The Post-war Rearmament of Japanese Maritime Forces*: 94–6.
255. 'Memorandum of a Conversation, 26 June 1957,' FRUS, 1955–1957, Volume XXIII, Part 1, Japan, Document 196.
256. JDA, *JSDF Ten Year History*: 227, 234–7.
257. *Kaijōjieitai50nenshihensaniinkai*, *50-Year History of the MSDF*: 40–42.
258. Auer, James E., *The Post-war Rearmament of Japanese Maritime Forces*: 96–7.
259. '40 Years After the Incident "The Lockheed Scandal" New Facts Imminent! Pending Scandal' (*Jikenkara40nen rokkiidojiken no shinmajitsu ni semaru! Mikaiketsujiken*), File.5 Lockheed Scandal, NHK (http://www6.nhk.or.jp/nhkpr/post/original.html?i=06801 25 Mar. 2017).
260. Aizawa, Teruaki, 'The Defense Build-up Concept of JMSDF in the Post-Fourth Defense Build-up Plan: Modernization of the JMSDF's Aviation Component and "100 P-3C Patrol Aircrafts-Based Structure,"' *NIDS Journal of Defense and Security*, (Dec. 2016), pp. 103–25: 108–16.
261. Ibid: 116–120.
262. Aizawa, Teruaki, 'The Defence Build-up Concept of the MSDF in the Post-Fourth Defense Build-up Program: The Modernisation of Maritime Forces and the "8 Destroyers-8 Helicopters Concept"' (*Posutoyojibō ni okeru kaijōjieitai no bōeiryokuseibi kōsō ni kansurukenkyū: kaijōbōeiryokukindaika to hachikanhachikitaisei*), NIDS Military History Studies Annual Report, No. 18 (March 2015), pp. 27–55: 40–42.
263. Aoki, Yoshitomo, 'From HSS-1 to SH-60K, the Development of ASW Helicopters,' *Ships of the World* (*Sekai no kaizen*), No. 696 (Oct. 2008), pp. 88–91.
264. Ishikawa, Junichi, 'MSDF Shipborne Aviation Force Development History' (*Kaijōjieitaikansaikōkūbutaihattatsushi*), *Ships of the World* (*Sekai no kaizen*), No. 584 (July 2001), pp. 96–9.
265. Patalano, Alessio, *Post-war Japan as a Sea Power*; Agawa, Naoyuki, *Friendship at Sea (Umi noyujo)* (Tokyo: Chuokoronsha, 2001); Koizumi, Masayoshi, *The Making of the MSDF: The JSDF for Recruits* (*Kaijōjieitainotsukurikata: rikurūtu no jieitai*) (Tokyo: Kojinsha, 2008).
266. Hillenbrand, Laura, *Unbroken: A world war II story of survival, resilience, and redemption* (New York: Random House, 2010).
267. Skabelund, Aaron and Ishikawa, Akito, 'Japan,' pp. 23–44 in Hassner, Ron. E., *Religion in the Military Worldwide* (Cambridge: Cambridge University Press, 2014): 33–5.
268. Conversations during MSDF Fleet Review, (14 Oct. 2012).
269. Blackman, Raymond, VB., *Jane's Fighting Ships, 1969–70* (London: Jane's Yearbooks,

1969): 26–7, 53; Auer, James E., *The Post-War Rearmament of Japanese Maritime Forces*: 118.
270. Auer, James E., *The Postwar Rearmament of Japanese Maritime Forces*: 107; Graham, Euan, *Japan's Sea lane Security*: 97.
271. MOD, *Defense of Japan 2014*: 359.
272. *Kaijōjieitai50nenshihensaniinkai*, 50-Year History of the MSDF: 252; and author's experience of 2012.
273. *Hidagawa Bus Plunge Accident*.
274. Interview, Hirano, Ryuichi, Director, Secretariat, International Peace Cooperation Headquarters, Cabinet Office, Tokyo (11 June 2009); Auer, James E., *The Postwar Rearmament of Japanese Maritime Forces*: 121.
275. Woolley, Peter J., *Japan's Navy*: 49.
276. *Defence Handbook 1989*: 443; *Defence Handbook 1999*: 229.
277. Woolley, Peter J., *Geography and Japan's Strategic Choices: From Seclusion to Internationalization*, (Dulles, VA.: Potomac, 2005): 119–21, 155.
278. Conversation with Ebata Kensuke, and MSDF Captain, Tokyo, (Oct. 2004).
279. Hood, Christopher P., *Dealing with Disaster in Japan: Responses to the Flight JL123 Crash* (Abingdon: Routledge, 2012): 83.
280. MLIT, 'Submarine *Nadashio* Pleasure Fishing Vessel *Dai-ichi Fujimaru* Collision Incident' (*Suisenkannadashio yūgyosenDaiichifujimaru shōtotsujiken*), Japan Marine Accident Tribunal (10 Aug. 1990) (http://www.mlit.go.jp/jmat/monoshiri/judai/judai.htm 12 June 2017).
281. Hood, Christopher P., *Dealing with Disaster in Japan*: 176–8. Conversations with the author, Sheffield (Sept. 2018).
282. SCAP, *Final Progress of Demobilization of the Japanese Armed Forces*, (Dec. 1946) (https://ia801308.us.archive.org/4/items/Japan-Occupation/Final%20Progress%20of%20Demobilization%20of%20the%20Japanese%20Armed%20Forces.pdf 12 Feb 2018): 64.
283. *Seijikeizaikenkyukai*, *History of the JSDF: To Defend the Motherland* (*Jieitaishi: mamorutowa*) (Tokyo: Seijikeizaikenkyukai, 1997): 219.
284. Masuda, Hiroshi, *Birth of the JSDF: Japan's Rearmament and America* (*Jieitai notanjō: nihonno saigunbi toamerika*) (Tokyo: Chuōkoronshinsha, 2004): 172–3; Okumiya, Masatake, and Horikoshi, Jirō, Caidi, Martin (trans.), *Zero: the story of Japan's air war in the Pacific, as seen by the enemy* (New York: ibooks, 2004); Yates, Ronald E., 'Japan's Last War Leader Tells Of Lifelong Regret,' *Chicago Tribune* (21 Sept. 1989), (http://articles.chicagotribune.com/1989-09-21/news/8901140836_1_japan-didn-t-late-emperor-foreign-ministry 14 Mar. 2015).
285. Masuda, Hiroshi, *Birth of the JSDF*: 172–3; Shibayama, Futoshi, *The Road to Japan's Rearmament* (*nihonsaigunbi enomichi*), *1945–1954* (Kyoto: Minerva Shobō, 2010): 405–20, 528–66.
286. Masuda, Hiroshi, *Birth of the JSDF*: 174–6.
287. Yomiurishinbunsha Sengoshihan, *Showa post-war history: the pathway to 'rearmament'* (*Showasengoshi saigunbi nokiseki*) (Tokyo: Chukobunko, 2015): 479–84.
288. Ibid: 483.
289. Hughes, Michael Bryant, *Japan's Air Power Options: The Employment of Military*

Aviation in the Post-War Era, Doctoral Thesis, Faculty of the Fletcher School of Law and Diplomacy, Tufts University (16 Aug. 1972): 138–40; Shibayama, Futoshi, *The Road to Japan's Rearmament*: 552–5.

290. The Acting Secretary of State to the Embassy in Japan (794.5/10–2052: Telegram No. 608) (28 Oct. 1952), *FRUS, 1952–1954*, Volume XIV, Part 2, China and Japan, Document 608.
291. Hughes, Michael Bryant, *Japan's Air Power Options*: 141.
292. JDA, *JSDF Ten Year History*: 71–3.
293. The Acting Secretary of State to the Embassy in Japan (794.5/10–2052: Telegram No. 608) (28 Oct. 1952).
294. Asagumoshinbunsha henshūkyoku (ed.), *For the Blue Sky: 50 years of the ASDF* (*For the Blue Sky-ASDFno 50nenōgatahon*) (Tokyo: Asagumoshimbunsha, 2005): 18–20; JDA, *JSDF Ten Year History*: 71–3.
295. 'Japan Armed Forces Reactivated; Leaders Appeal for United Defense', *Pacific Stars and Stripes* (Tokyo-Yokohama) (2 July 1954): 6, (https://newspaperarchive.com/pacific-stars-and-stripes-jul-02-1954-p-6/ 12 Apr. 2016).
296. Maeda mistakes Uemura as Murakami: Maeda, Tetsuo, *The Hidden Army*: 76.
297. *Seijikeizaikenkyūkai, History of the JSDF*: 219–21.
298. Acting Secretary of State to the Embassy in Japan (Telegram No. 608), *FRUS*.
299. JDA, *JSDF Ten Year History*: 57, 236; '60th Anniversary of the Air Self-Defense Force', *Japan Defense Focus*, 53 (June 2014) (http://www.mod.go.jp/e/jdf/no53/topics.html 2 July 2014).
300. JDA, *JSDF Ten Year History*: 251–2; Asagumoshinbunsha henshūkyoku (ed.), *For the Blue Sky*: 20.
301. 'Memorandum of a Conversation, Department of State,' (Washington DC.: 31 Aug. 1956), *FRUS, 1955–1957, Japan*, Vol. XXIII, Part 1, Document 96: 215 (https://history.state.gov/historicaldocuments/frus1955–57v23p1/pg_214 22 June 2016).
302. Weintraub, Sidney, *Japanese Military Situation*, Background Paper, Office of Northeast Asian Affairs, KIV8/3a, (17 June 1957), *Foreign Relations of the United States, 1955–1957, Japan*, Volume XXIII, Part 1, Document 175: 352.
303. 'Memorandum of a Conversation, Pentagon,' (Washington DC.: 26 June 1957), *FRUS, 1955–1957, Japan*, Volume XXIII, Part 1, Document 196, (https://history.state.gov/historicaldocuments/frus1955–57v23p1/d196 12 Mar. 2017).
304. Weintraub, Sidney, *Japanese Military Situation*: 353.
305. JDA, *JSDF Ten Year History*: 116–20.
306. Ibid: 116–23; Otake, Hideo, *Japanese Defence and Domestic Politics*: 92–9.
307. Seiki Nishihiro Oral History Interview.
308. Memorandum of a Conversation, *FRUS*, Document 196; Samuels, Richard J., *Rich Nation, Strong Army: National Security and the Technological Transformation of Japan* (Ithaca, NY.: Cornell, 1994): 148–9.
309. JDA, *JSDF Ten Year History*: 137.
310. *Defense of Japan 2002*: 439, 442.
311. Hughes, Michael Bryant, *Japan's Air Power Options*: 17.
312. JDA, *Defense of Japan 1976* (*Bōeihakusho1976*), (http://www.clearing.mod.go.jp/hakusho_data/1976/w1976_04009.html 12 Nov. 2017).

313. Takarajimasha (ed.), *All About the ASDF* (*Kōkūjieitai nosubete*) (Tokyo: Takarajimasha, 2015): 98–9; Asagumoshinbunsha henshūkyoku (ed.), *For the Blue Sky*: 114–24.
314. *SDF Law*, articles 28–30.
315. JDA, *Defense of Japan 1970* (*Bōeihakusho1970*), (http://www.clearing.mod.go.jp/hakusho_data/1970/w1970_03.html 27 Mar. 2017).
316. Takarajimasha (ed.), *All About the ASDF*: 64.
317. Lorell, Mark A., *Troubled Partnership: A History of U.S.-Japan Collaboration on the FS-X Fighter* (Santa Monica, CA.: RAND, 1995): 58.
318. Johnson, Chalmers, *MITI and the Japanese Miracle: The Growth of Industrial Policy, 1925–75* (Stanford, CA.: Stanford University Press, 1982).
319. Samuels, Richard J., *Rich Nation, Strong Army*: 210–14; Maema, Takanori, *The Men Who Built Japan's Own Passenger Plane: YS-11* (*YS-11: Kokusanryokakūki wo tsukuttaotokotachi*) (Tokyo: Kodansha, 1994).
320. Yamamura, Takashi, *The Tragedy of the YS-11: The Collapse of a Special Corporation* (*YS-11 no higeki: arutokushuhojin nohokai*) (Tokyo: Nihonhyoronsha, 1995).
321. *Flight International* (1 Aug. 1981): 352; *JSDF Equipment Yearbook 1990* (*Jieitaisōbinenkan1990*) (Tokyo: Asagumoshimbunsha, 1990): 339; *The Military Balance 1990–1991* (London: IISS/Brassey's, 1990): 59.
322. *JSDF Equipment Yearbook 1990*: 336; *JSDF Equipment Yearbook 2016–2017*: 354.
323. Green, Michael, J., *Bōeizoku*.
324. *JSDF Equipment Yearbook 2016–2017*: 331, 346.
325. Samuels, Richard J., *Rich Nation, Strong Army*: 208–10; Fitzsimons, David (ed.), *The Illustrated Encyclopedia of 20th Century Weapons and Warfare* (London: Latimer House/Phoebus, 1977): 2498.
326. Samuels, Richard J., *Rich Nation, Strong Army*: 208–10; *Defense of Japan* 2008 (Tokyo: MOD, 2008): 543.
327. Samuels, Richard J., *Rich Nation, Strong Army*: 223–4; MIAC, *18–8 Foreign Exchange Rates (1950–2005)* (Tokyo: Statistics Bureau, Ministry of Internal Affairs and Communications, 2005) (http://www.stat.go.jp/english/data/chouki/18.htm, 10 May 2010).
328. Lambert, Mark, 'Japan's Aerospace Industry,' *Flight International* (9 Oct. 1976): 1146; JDA, *Defense of Japan 1980* (*Bōeihakushoshowa55nen*) (http://www.clearing.mod.go.jp/hakusho_data/1980/w1980_02001.html; http://www.clearing.mod.go.jp/hakusho_data/1980/w1980_02002.html 15 July 2017).
329. 'Telegram From the Embassy in Japan to the Department of State', (20 Dec. 1957), *FRUS, 1955–1957, Japan*, Volume XXIII, Pt.1-Doc.252, (https://history.state.gov/historicaldocuments/frus1955–57v23p1/d252 12 Mar. 2017).
330. Yomiurishimbunsha, *Japan's Defence Power 3: Air Self-Defense Force* (*Nihonno bōeisenryoku3 kōkūjieitai*) (Tokyo: Yomiurishimbunsha, 1987): 80–4; *'74 JSDF Equipment Yearbook*: 314.
331. 'Memorandum of a Conversation', (26 June 1957), Doc.196, *FRUS*.
332. 'Telegram From the Embassy in Japan to the Department of State', (29 Nov. 1957), *FRUS, 1955–1957, Japan*, Volume XXIII, Part 1, Document 246: 539–40.
333. 'Memorandum of a Conversation', (26 June 1957), Doc. 196, *FRUS*.

334. Ibid.
335. Ball, Desmond, and Tanter, Richard, 'The Transformation of the JASDF's Intelligence and Surveillance Capabilities for Air and Missile Defence', *Security Challenges*, 8–3 (Spring 2012), pp. 19–56: 34–5.
336. 'Ministry of Defense extends the air defence identification zone, 26km west above Yonaguni Island' (*Bōeishō, bōkūshikibetsuken wo kakudaiyonagunijōkūnominishikata 26kiro*), *Ryūkyūshimpo*, (25 June 2010) (http://ryukyushimpo.jp/news/prentry-164039.html 21 Feb. 2017).
337. JDA, *Defense of Japan 1976/2017* (http://www.clearing.mod.go.jp/hakusho_data/1976/w1976_04.html; http://www.clearing.mod.go.jp/hakusho_data/2017/html/n3121000.html#zuhyo03010205 21 Nov. 2017).
338. Abeyratne, Ruwantissa, 'In search of theoretical justification for air defence identification zones', *International Foundation For Aviation And Development* (http://aviationdevelopment.org/eng/sites/default/files/2011111501_Publication.pdf 21 Feb. 2017).
339. Civil Aviation Bureau, *Flight Information Region (FIR) and Control Area*, Ministry of Land, Infrastructure and Transport (https://www.mlit.go.jp/koku/15_hf_000050.html 12 Mar. 2017); MOFA, *ADIZ Air Defense Identification Zone in East Asia*, Embassy of Japan in Guatemala, (http://www.gt.emb-japan.go.jp/Politica/Mapa_del_Mar_de_China_Oriental_24.11.2013.pdf 12 Mar. 2017).
340. 'Background paper by Sidney Weintraub, Office of Northeast Asian Affairs, KIV8/3a, (Washington DC., 17 June 1957), "Japanese Military Situation,"' *FRUS*, 1955–1957, Japan, Volume XXIII, Part 1, Document 175: 354 (https://history.state.gov/historicaldocuments/frus1955–57v23p1/pg_354 7 Mar. 2017).
341. Memorandum of a Conversation, Pentagon, Washington, (26 June 1957), *FRUS*.
342. 'Telegram From the Embassy in Japan to the Department of State,' (19 Aug. 1957) *Foreign Relations of the United States, 1955–1957*, Volume XXIII, Part 1, Japan, Document 210: 452–3.
343. Samuels, Richard J., *Special Duty*: 113.
344. Hughes, Michael Bryant, *Japan's Air Power Options*: 330.
345. Yomiurishimbunsha (ed.), *Japan's Defence Power 3*: 50–1; MOD, *Statistics on scrambles through fiscal year 2016*, Joint Staff Press Release, (13 Apr. 2017).
346. Takarajimasha (ed.), *All About the ASDF*: 98–9.
347. Hughes, Michael Bryant, *Japan's Air Power Options*: 344.
348. JDA, *Defense of Japan 1977* (http://www.clearing.mod.go.jp/hakusho_data/1977/w1977_04.html 25 Aug. 2017); Samuels, Richard J., *Special Duty*: 112.
349. Sase, Masamori, *Changing Security Politics in Postwar Japan*: 115.
350. Ibid: 106–9.
351. Mladenov, Alexander, *Soviet Cold War Fighters* (Stroud: Fonthill, 2016): 233–6.
352. 78th Diet Session, Cabinet Committee, No. 1, House of Representatives (*Shūgiin*), (7 Oct. 1976): 8–21 (http://kokkai.ndl.go.jp/SENTAKU/syugiin/078/0020/07810070020001.pdf 7 Aug. 2017); Hughes, Michael Bryant, *Japan's Air Power Options*: 333–6.
353. Sase, Masamori, *Changing Security Politics in Postwar Japan*: 73–4; Kōsaka, Masataka;

Sako, Susumu; Abe, Bunji, *Chronology of Postwar Japan-US Relations* (*Sengo nichibeikankei nenpyō*) (Tokyo: *PHPkenkyūshō*, 1995): 137.
354. Takarajimasha (ed.), *All About the ASDF*: 17; *Japan Self-Defense Forces Equipment Yearbook 2016–2017*: 331, 348–9.
355. JDA, *10 Year History of the JSDF*: 205.
356. 'Naval Early Warners: No. 849: A Unique Fleet Air Arm Squadron', *Flight*, (22 Oct. 1954): 604–5, (https://www.flightglobal.com/pdfarchive/view/1954/1954%20-%202897.html 12 Aug. 2017); 'Radar-plus for AEW Nimrod', *Flight International*, (12 Mar. 1977): 636, (https://www.flightglobal.com/pdfarchive/view/1977/1977%20-%200676.html?search=shackleton%20AEW 12 Aug. 2017); Boyne, Walter J., 'That First Look,' *Air Force Magazine*, (1 Jan. 2007), (https://www.airforcemag.com/article/0107firstlook/ 12 May 2020); A British AN/APS-20 and its aircraft are on display at the Science and Industry Museum, Manchester (https://collection.sciencemuseumgroup.org.uk/objects/co8418680/an-aps-20-radar-scanner-aeroplane-component 12 May 2020).
357. Asagumoshinbunsha henshūkyoku (ed.), *For the Blue Sky*: 133, 139–40; MOD, *2012 Policy Evaluation Report (Post-action Evaluation)* (*Heisei24nendo seisakuhyōkasho (jigono jigyōhyōka)*), MOD (2013), (http://www.mod.go.jp/j/approach/hyouka/seisaku/results/24/jigo/honbun/05.pdf 12 Aug. 2017).
358. Otake, Hideo, *Japanese Defence and Domestic Politics*: 31–2.
359. Yomiurishimbunsha (ed.), *Japan's Defence Power 2*: 111–19.
360. JDA, *Defense of Japan 1977* (http://www.clearing.mod.go.jp/hakusho_data/1977/w1977_03.html 12 Sept. 2017).
361. 'Japan', *Flight International*, (9 Oct. 1976): 1145–6.
362. Lorell, Mark A., *Troubled Partnership*: 64–5.
363. 'Senior Defense Official Tells Diet-U.S. Planes May Refuel SDF Fighters', *The Japan Times* (25 Feb. 1984), DOD, Reading Room: International Security Affairs, (http://www.dod.gov/pubs/foi/Reading_Room/International_Security_Affairs/93-F-2563_DOCUMENTS_ABOUT_US_JAPAN_RELATIONS_FINAL_RESPONSE_GRANTS.pdf 5 Aug. 2017).
364. Yomiurishimbunsha (ed.), *Japan's Defence Power 3*: 58–9.
365. Ibid.
366. Drifte, Reinhard, 'High Technology in the Japanese-American Defense Relationship and Northeast Asia', *Korean Journal of Defense Analysis*, 1–2 (1989): 77–103.
367. Sase, Masamori, *Changing Security Politics in Postwar Japan*: 111–4.
368. *Defence Handbook 1981*: 94–5; *Defense of Japan 2000* (*Bōeihakushoheisei12nen*): 327.
369. *Hand Book for Defense 1999*: 158–9.
370. JDA, *Defense of Japan 1977* (*Bōeihakushoshowa52nen*) (Tokyo: JDA, 1977): 72–3; *Hand Book for Defense 1999*: 148–9.
371. Hughes, Michael Bryant, *Japan's Air Power Options*: 59 (quoting *Koku Shimbun*, (21 July 1971): 9).
372. Ibid: 48–9.
373. Hughes, Michael Bryant, *Japan's Air Power Options*: 328–9.
374. Lorell, Mark A., *Troubled Partnership*: 62; Reed, Arthur, *SEPECAT Jaguar* (Shepperton: Ian Allan, 1982): 46–8.

375. Ebata, Kensuke, *Insufficient Military Power for Japan* (*Nihonni tarinaigunjiryoku*) (Tokyo: Seishunshuppansha, 2008): 12.
376. Hughes, Michael Bryant, *Japan's Air Power Options*: 48–9; JDA, *Defense of Japan 1980* (http://www.clearing.mod.go.jp/hakusho_data/1980/w1980_03.html 12 Oct. 2017); Yomiurishimbunsha (ed.), *Japan's Defence Power 3*: 87–9; JDA, *Defense of Japan 2004* (http://www.clearing.mod.go.jp/hakusho_data/2004/2004/pdf/1623 0000.pdf 12 Oct. 2017): 96.
377. Ebata, Kensuke, *Insufficient Military Power for Japan*: 142–3; *Hand Book for Defense 2016* (*Bōeihandobukku heisei28nenban*) (Tokyo: Asagumoshinbunsha, 2016): 134–5.
378. Butler, Amy, 'USAF To 'Re-Energize' Debate On Future Of CAS,' *Aviation Week & Space Technology*, (25 Feb. 2015) (http://aviationweek.com/defense/usaf-re-energize-debate-future-cas 21 Feb. 2017).
379. Reed, Arthur, *SEPECAT Jaguar*: 15.
380. Hughes, Michael Bryant, *Japan's Air Power Options*: 324–9.
381. Conversations, USAF Lt.-Colonel, Tokyo (Oct. 2015, Feb. 2016).
382. Vick, Alan J., *Air Base Attacks and Defensive Counters Historical Lessons and Future Challenges*, RAND Corporation (2015): 50–4.
383. Sidoti, S. J., *Airbase Operability: A Study in Airbase Survivability and Post-Attack Recovery*, (Canberra: Aerospace Centre, 2001).
384. Hughes, Michael Bryant, *Japan's Air Power Options*: 60–1.
385. Yomiurishimbunsha (ed.), *Japan's Defence Combat Power 3—Air Self-Defense Force*: (*Nihonno bōeisenryoku3-kōkūjieitai*) (Tokyo: Yomiurishimbunsha, 1987): 10–13.
386. Newsham, Grant, presentation, *Japanese defense after the security legislation*, Institute of Contemporary Asian Studies, Temple University, Tokyo (26 Oct. 2015).
387. Kaihara, Osamu, *My Own National Defence White Paper* (*Watakushino kokubōhakusho*), (Tokyo: Jijitsūshinsha, 1975): 140–2.
388. Yomiurishimbunsha (ed.), *Japan's Defence Power 3*: 58–9.
389. Grube, Michael, *Autobahn-Flugplätze (Notlandeplätze NLP-Str)* (*Autobahn Airstrips-Emergency Landing Strip*) (http://www.geschichtsspuren.de/artikel/luftfahrt-luftwaffe/113-autobahn-notlandeplaetze-nlp.html 17 Mar. 2017); *C-160 & C-130 Landing On Autobahn*, (https://www.youtube.com/watch?v=bLEbV_CehWs 17 Mar. 2017).
390. Reed, Arthur, *SEPECAT Jaguar*: 27, 30, 107; 'Talk about a blast from the past! A Jag in the fast lane...', *The Blackpool Gazette*, (25 Apr. 2015) (http://www.blackpoolgazette.co.uk/news/community/memory-lane/talk-about-a-blast-from-the-past-a-jag-in-the-fast-lane-1-7228373#ixzz3zOYFj6ZR 12 Mar. 2017).
391. *Handbook for Defense 1981*: 183–5; *Hand Book for Defense 1999*: 303–4.
392. *Hand Book for Defense 2016*: 334.
393. ASDF, *Hofu Kita Air Base Introduction* (http://www.mod.go.jp/asdf/hofukita/about/introduction.html 17 Mar. 2017).
394. Secretary of the Air Force, *Air Force Instruction 11–2F-16, Volume 3: Flying Operations-F-16 Operations Procedure* (1 July 1999); Hange, Craig, *Short Field Take-Off and Landing Performance as an Enabling Technology for a Greener, More Efficient Airspace System*, NASA, (https://ntrs.nasa.gov/archive/nasa/casi.ntrs.nasa.gov/20090036801.pdf 15 Apr. 2017).

395. Honda Airways (http://www.honda-air.com/index.html 12 Apr. 2017); Aviation Law (*Kōkūhō*) (15 July 1952), Law 231 (http://law.e-gov.go.jp/htmldata/S27/S27HO231.html 17 Mar. 2017).
396. ASDF, *Yakumo Sub-Base* (*Yakumo buntonkichi*) (https://www.mod.go.jp/asdf/yakumo/index.html 29 Oct. 2018).
397. ASDF, *Special Feature 012: Civil Engineer at Base*, ASDF Iruma Air Base (http://www.mod.go.jp/asdf/iruma/special/012/p1.html 17 Mar. 2017); *Unit Introduction: Mobile Construction Group Commander* (*Butai Shokai: Kido Shisetsutai Shirei*), MSDF, *Hachinohe Naval Air Station* (http://www.mod.go.jp/msdf/hatinohe/about/squadron/mcg.html 17 Mar. 2017).
398. *Hand Book for Defense 2016*: 334.
399. USAF, *51ˢᵗ Security Forces Squadron: Osan Air Base*, (22 Apr. 2016), (http://www.osan.af.mil/About-Us/Fact-Sheets/Display/Article/740339/51st-security-forces-squadron/ 12 Mar. 2017).
400. Hughes, Michael Bryant, *Japan's Air Power Options*: 344.
401. Asagumoshinbunsha henshūkyoku (ed.), *For the Blue Sky*: 115.
402. JDA, *JSDF Ten Year History*: 190–1, 330.
403. *Japan Self-Defense Forces Equipment Yearbook 2016–2017*: 28, 376–80; JDA, *Defense of Japan 1989* (http://www.clearing.mod.go.jp/hakusho_data/1989/w1989_03.html 12 Apr. 2017).
404. *Flight International* (1 August 1981): 351.
405. ASDF, 'Base History,' *Iruma Air Base*, (http://www.mod.go.jp/asdf/iruma/about/history/index.html 19 Mar. 2017); Air Force Historical Research Agency, *U.S. Air Force Fact Sheet: 35 Operations Group* (PACAF) (http://www.afhra.af.mil/factsheets/factsheet_print.asp?fsID=9683 19 Mar. 2017); *U.S. Air Force Fact Sheet: 336 Fighter Squadron* (ACC), (http://www.afhra.af.mil/factsheets/factsheet_print.asp?fsID=10671 19 Mar. 2017); *U.S. Air Force Fact Sheet: 3 Wing* (PACAF) (http://www.afhra.af.mil/factsheets/factsheet_print.asp?fsID=9596&page=1 19 Mar. 2017).
406. Ball, Desmond and Tanter, Richard, 'US signals intelligence (SIGINT) activities in Japan 1945–2015: A Visual Guide,' *Nautilus Institute*, Special Report (Dec. 2015): 223.
407. Ibid: 225–8; conversations, Mergel, Edward J. Jr., ex-USAF, Daito Bunka University, Saitama (2003–19); Asagumoshinbunsha henshūkyoku (ed.), *For the Blue Sky*: 31, 124; Reed, Robert F. *The US-Japan Alliance: Sharing the Burden of Defense*, National Security Affairs Monograph Series 83–7 (Washington, DC.: National Defense University Press, 1983): 52–3.
408. Asagumoshinbunsha henshūkyoku (ed.), *For the Blue Sky*: 31; Memorandum of a Conversation, (26 June 1957), Document 196, *FRUS*.
409. Asagumoshinbunsha henshūkyoku (ed.), *For the Blue Sky*: 56.
410. Ibid: 104; USAF, *432 Wing (ACC)*, Air Force Historical Research Agency, (http://www.afhra.af.mil/About-Us/Fact-Sheets/Display/Article/433132/432-wing-acc/ 19 June 2017).
411. 'North Koreans Down Navy Recon Plane', *Pacific Stars and Stripes* (17 Apr. 1969); Homan, Richard, 'Lost Plane a Pueblo-Type Spy,' *The Washington Post* (16 Apr. 1969),

(http://www.willyvictor.com/History/Korean_Shootdown/Korea.html 12 Aug. 2017).
412. Takarajimasha (ed.), *All About the ASDF*: 30.
413. Midford, Paul, 'The GSDF's Quest for Public Acceptance and the "Allergy" Myth', in Eldridge, Robert D., and Midford, Paul (eds.), *The Japanese Ground Self-Defense Force*, pp. 297–345, 305.
414. Asagumoshinbunsha henshūkyoku (ed.), *For the Blue Sky*: 55.
415. Hirano, Keiji, 'Group saves records of fatal U.S. fighter jet crash', *Kyodo/Japan Times* (28 Sep. 2012) (http://www.japantimes.co.jp/text/nn20120928f2.html, 30 Sept. 2012).
416. Ishiba, Shigeru, *Official Blog* (8 Apr. 2016) (http://ishiba-shigeru.cocolog-nifty.com/blog/2016/04/post-a738.html 27 Mar. 2017); Sakaida, Henry, *Japanese Army Air Force Aces, 1937–1945*, (Oxford: Osprey, 1997): 75.
417. MOD, *Press Conference by the Defense Minister*, (4 Nov. 2011) (http://www.mod.go.jp/e/press/conference/2011/11/04.html 12 Jan. 2012); 'F15 Crash: Pilot Error, System Failure Cause, ASDF Evaluation Results' (*F15tsuiraku: sojyuushishikisoushitsu ga genin koukuujietai ga chousakekka*), *Mainichi Shimbun* (9 Nov. 2011) (http://mainichi.jp/select/jiken/news/20111110k0000m040093000c.html, 27 Feb. 2012).
418. ASDF, *50 Years Since No. 110 Accident* (*110gokijikokara50nen*), ASDF Miho, (http://www.mod.go.jp/asdf/miho/topics_c-46_sinobutudoi.html 12 Feb. 2017).
419. Vasconcelos, Miguel, *Civil Airworthiness Certification: Former Military High-Performance Aircraft* (Washington, DC.: US Department of Transportation/FAA, 2013): 2–14–5.
420. 'ASDF Crash, High-Tension Power Lines Severed: Tokyo, Saitama 800,000 Homes Power-Cut' (*Kūjitsuiraku de kōatsusensetsudan*), *Asahi Shimbun* (23 Nov. 1999): 1.
421. Third Security Committee Meeting, 147th Diet Session, House of Representatives (13 Apr. 2000) (*Dai147kaikokkai anzenhoshōiinkaidai3gō*), (http://kokkai.ndl.go.jp/SENTAKU/syugiin/147/0015/14704130015003a.html 23 Apr. 2017).
422. 27th Cabinet Response to Tabled Questions, 147th Diet Session, House of Representatives (30 May 2000) (*Dai147kaikokkai naikakushūshitsu27gō*), (http://www.shugiin.go.jp/internet/itdb_shitsumona.nsf/html/shitsumon/b147027.htm 23 Apr. 2017).
423. Ministry of Transport, *White Paper 1973: III Aviation, Chapter 2 Air Accidents* (*Showa47nendo unyūhakushoIIIkoukuu dai2shokoukūjiko*), (http://www.mlit.go.jp/hakusyo/transport/shouwa47/ind100206/frame.html 17 Mar. 2017).
424. Asagumoshinbunsha henshūkyoku (ed.), *For the Blue Sky*: 42–3.
425. Ibid: 61.
426. Hood, Christopher P., *Dealing with Disaster in Japan*: 62.
427. Ibid: 61; Asahishimbunshakaibu, *JAL Jumbo Jet Crash*: 14–22.
428. Hood, Christopher P., *Dealing with Disaster in Japan*: 64–5; Asahishimbunshakaibu, *JAL Jumbo Jet Crash*: 15–32.
429. Asagumoshinbunsha henshūkyoku (ed.), *For the Blue Sky*: 32.
430. Hughes, Michael Bryant, *Japan's Air Power Options*: 102.
431. JAXA, *JAXA's Astronauts: Yui Kimiya*, Japan Aerospace Exploration Agency (JAXA) (http://iss.jaxa.jp/astro/yui/ 21 Oct. 2017).

432. Mizokami, Kyle, 'Nukes, Carriers and Boomers: The Dream of General Tamogami', *Japan Security Watch* (16 May 2011) (http://jsw.newpacificinstitute.org/?p=6071 21 May 2011); 'Ex-ASDF chief found guilty of bribing campaign staff', *Mainichi Japan*, (22 May 2017) (http://mainichi.jp/english/articles/20170522/p2g/00m/0dm/062000c 23 May 2017).
433. Takarajimasha (ed.), *JSDF 60 Year History*: 16–21; Hongo, Jun, and Nagata, Kazuaki, 'Tamogami ups nationalist rhetoric: War justified, Constitution needs change, axed general tells Diet', *The Japan Times* (12 Nov. 2008) (http://search.japantimes.co.jp/cgi-bin/nn20081112a1.html, 12 Nov. 2008).
434. *Hyakuri Base Protest Action Page* (*Hyakurikichihantaiundo nopeeji*) (http://www.cam.hi-ho.ne.jp/kuri777/ 12 Mar. 2017); *Hyakuri Peace Park in the Middle of the Base: The Hill of Peace that the Base Despises* (*Kichino mannakaniaruhyakuriheiwakoenkichi wo miorosukyūjō nooka*) (http://www.cam.hi-ho.ne.jp/kuri777/ 12 Mar. 2017).
435. *Emergency Measures Act Relating to the Preservation of Security at Narita International Airport* (*Naritakokusaikūkō noanzenkakuho nikansuru kinkyūsochihō*), 27 November 2013, Law No. 86.
436. 'ASDF displays cluster bomb before banned; ASDF hates to give up 'satanic weapons'', *Tokyo Shimbun*, (19 Nov. 2008), in *Wikileaks, Cablegate: Daily Summary of Japanese Press*, US Embassy, Tokyo, (20 Nov. 2008):22, (http://www.scoop.co.nz/stories/WL0811/S01534/cablegate-daily-summary-of-japanese-press-112008.htm 12 Mar. 2017); Glionna, John M., 'Farmers wage turf battle with Japan air force', *Los Angeles Times*, (10 Sept. 2009) (http://articles.latimes.com/2009/sep/10/world/fg-japan-peacepark10/2 12 Mar. 2017).
437. Asagumoshinbunsha henshūkyoku (ed.), *For the Blue Sky*: 31–2, 44–5, 85.
438. Ibid: 32.
439. 'Bid-rigging at the ASDF', *Asahi Shimbun*, (26 Mar. 2010), (http://www.asahi.com/english/TKY201003260324.html 31 Mar. 2010).
440. Sasaki, Tomoyuki, *Japan's Postwar Military and Civil Society*: 96–106.
441. Hoshino, Yasusaburo and Hayashi, Shigeo, *JSDF: Their Two Faces* (*Jieitai: sonofutatsu nokao*) (Tokyo: Sanichishinsho, 1963/1970) ninth edition: 13–5.
442. Ibid: 16–7.
443. ASDF, *Air Rescue Wing: Cooperation Activities-cinema, drama, animation* (http://www.mod.go.jp/asdf/arw/satueikyouryoku/eiga-dorama.html 17 Feb. 2018); JDA, *Defense of Japan 1999* (http://www.clearing.mod.go.jp/hakusho_data/1999/honmon/frame/at1105010200.htm 18 Feb. 2018).
444. Asagumoshinbunsha henshūkyoku (ed.), *For the Blue Sky*: 51.
445. Frühstück, Sabine, *Uneasy Warriors*.
446. *Hand Book for Defense 1999*: 192.
447. *Hand Book for Defense 2016*: 194.
448. Tōba, Hajime, *Japan's Military Power: The Inside Story of the JSDF* (*Nihonno gunjiryoku-jieitai no uchimaki*) (Tokyo: Yomiurishimbunsha, 1963): 138.
449. *Dream News* (*doriimunyūzu*), 'Yokohama Dreamland Defence Expo' (*yokohamadoriimurando daibōeihaku*), (10 Mar. 1966) (eighth edition):1–4.
450. Aoi, Chiyuki, 'Japan's Civil Military Relations: Separation, Control and Effectiveness from an Operational Perspective', in Bruneau, Thomas C. and Croissant, Aurel (eds.),

Civil-Military Relations: Control and Effectiveness Across Regimes (Boulder, CO.: Lynne Rienner, 2019), pp. 69–84.
451. Smith, Sheila A., *Japan Rearmed*: 250, note 13; Sebata, Takao, *Japan's Defense Policy and Bureaucratic Politics*: 151.

3. TRANSITION TO POST-COLD WAR CHALLENGES

1. MOFA, *Diplomatic Bluebook 1991* (http://www.mofa.go.jp/policy/other/bluebook/1991/1991-4-1.htm#Section 1. Asia-Pacific 10 Dec. 2017).
2. Pyle, Kenneth B., *Japan Rising: The resurgence of Japanese Power and Purpose* (New York: Public Affairs, 2007): 3.
3. Glosserman, Brad, *Peak Japan: The End of Great Ambitions*, (Washington, DC.: Georgetown University Press, 2019): 26–30.
4. MIAC, '31–1 National Defense Expenditure (F.Y.1950—2006)', *Historical Statistics of Japan* (Tokyo: Statistics Bureau, Ministry of Internal Affairs and Communications, 2017) (http://www.stat.go.jp/english/data/chouki/31.htm 12 Mar. 2018).
5. JDA, *Defense of Japan 2002* (Tokyo: Urban Connections/JDA, 2002): 384–5.
6. *Hand Book for Defense 2017* (*Bōeihandobukku heisei29nenban*), (Tokyo: Asagumoshinbunsha, 2017): 284.
7. OECD, *Gross domestic product (GDP)Total, US dollars/capita, 2016*, (https://data.oecd.org/gdp/gross-domestic-product-gdp.htm 23 Oct. 2017).
8. Shirakawa, Masaaki, *Demographic Changes and Macroeconomic Performance: Japanese Experiences*, Opening Remark at 2012 BOJ-IMES Conference, (30 May 2012), Bank of Japan/Institute for Monetary and Economic Studies: 5–9; Imam, Patrick, *Shock from Graying: Is the Demographic Shift Weakening Monetary Policy Effectiveness*, IMF WP/13/191 (Washington, D.C.: International Monetary Fund, 2013): 5; *Monthly Report of Prospects for Japan's Economy*, Macro Economic Research Center Economics Department, The Japan Research Institute, Limited (Tokyo: September 2016).
9. Statistics Bureau, *Japan Statistical Yearbook 2020* (Tokyo: Statistics Bureau, Ministry of Internal Affairs and Communications, 2020), (https://www.stat.go.jp/english/data/nenkan/69nenkan/index.html 27 Feb 2020).
10. e-Stat, *Table 10. Population by Age (3 Groups) for Prefectures (as of October 1 of Each Year)—Total population (from 1970 to 2000): Population Estimates—Time Series Population Estimates of Japan 1920–2000*, (https://www.e-stat.go.jp/en/stat-search/files?page=1&layout=datalist&toukei=00200524&tstat=000000090001&cycle=0&tclass1=000000090004&tclass2=000000090005&stat_infid=000000090270 12 Jan 2018).
11. *Hand Book for Defense 1999* (*Bōeihandobukku heisei11nenban*) (Tokyo: Asagumoshinbunsha, 1999): 188–90.
12. *Hand Book for Defense 2019* (*Bōeihandobukku2019*) (Tokyo: Asagumoshinbunsha, 2019): 208–9.
13. 'JSDF, Money and Organisation' (*Jieitaino kaneto soshiki), Weekly Tōyō Keizai* (13 May 2017), pp. 26–67.
14. MOD, *MOD, JSDF Personnel Configuration* (*Bōeishō, jieitaino jininkōsei*) (31 Mar. 2017) (http://www.mod.go.jp/j/profile/mod_sdf/kousei/ 19 Mar. 2018); 'SDF des-

perately trying to recruit high school students', *Japan Press* (JCP) (23 December 2014) (http://www.japan-press.co.jp/modules/news/index.php?id=7828 10 Jan. 2015).

15. '71% of Japanese firms short of workers: survey', *Mainichi News* (1 Feb. 2018), (https://mainichi.jp/english/articles/20180201/p2a/00m/0na/005000c 2 Feb. 2018).
16. Calder, Kent E., *Crisis and Compensation: Public Policy and Political Stability in Japan, 1949–1986* (Princeton, NJ.: Princeton University Press, 1988): 420.
17. Sugawa, Kiyoshi, *Time to Pop the Cork: Three Scenarios to Refine Japanese Use of Force*, Working Paper, Center for Northeast Asian Policy Studies, Brookings Institute (2000) (http://www.brook.edu/fp/cnaps/papers/2000_sugawa.htm 12 Nov. 2008).
18. Hook, Glenn D., and McCormack, Gavan, *Japan's Contested Constitution: documents and analysis* (London: Routledge, 2001): 8.
19. Midford, Paul, *Rethinking Japanese Public Opinion and Security: From Pacifism to Realism?* (Stanford, CA.: Stanford University Press, 2011): 82–109.
20. Katahara, Eiichi, 'Japan from Containment to Normalization', in Alagappa, Muthiah (ed.), *Coercion and governance: the declining political role of the military in Asia* (Palo Alto, CA.: Stanford University Press, 2001): pp. 69–91, 70.
21. Pitman, Joanna, 'Fighting talk sinks Japan's embattled defence minister', *The Times* (3 December 1993): 17; Sanger, David, E., 'Japan Aide Ousted; He'd Criticized Arms Role', *The New York Times* (3 December 1993) (http://www.nytimes.com/1993/12/03/world/japan-aide-ousted-he-d-criticized-arms-role.html?scp=35&sq=Japan%20peacekeeping&st=cse, 8 June 2010).
22. The *Yomiuri Shimbun* published constitutional revision proposals (1994, 2000, 2004): '2004 Yomiuri Shimbun Proposal for Constitutional Revision', *The Daily Yomiuri* (3 May 2004): 14–6.
23. Aoi, Chiyuki, *Peace Support Operations: Contemporary Challenges and the Role of Japan*, RIPS' Policy Perspectives 3 (Tokyo: Research Institute for Peace and Security, 2007).
24. *The Council on Security and Defense Capabilities Report–Japan's Visions for Future Security and Defense Capabilities (The Araki Report)* (2004): 52–3.
25. Shimura, Hisako, 'Should Japan participate in UN peacekeeping operations?', *Asia-Pacific Review*, 3–1 (1996): 137–44.
26. Armacost, Michael H., *Friends or Rivals: The Insider's Account of US-Japan Relations*, (New York: Columbia, 1996): 107; 'The Scrooge of Asia', *The Economist* (1 September 1990).
27. Togo, Kazuhiko, *Japan's Foreign Policy 1945–2003: The Quest for a Proactive Policy* (Leiden: Brill, 2005): 77.
28. Weisman, Steven R., 'Confrontation in the Gulf; Japan Defends Aid in Mideast Effort', *The New York Times*, (14 September 1990) (http://www.nytimes.com/1990/09/14/world/confrontation-in-the-gulf-japan-defends-aid-in-mideast-effort.html?scp=53&sq=Japan%20peacekeeping&st=cse, 10 Dec. 2009); Friedman, Thomas L., 'Baker Asks Japan to Broaden Role', *The New York Times* (12 Nov. 1991), (http://www.nytimes.com/1991/11/12/world/baker-asks-japan-to-broaden-role.html?scp=61&sq=Japan%20peacekeeping&st=cse&pagewanted=2, 19 July 2010).
29. Funabashi, Yoichi, 'Japan and the New World Order', *Foreign Affairs* (Winter 1991): pp. 58–74: 58; Bridges, Brian, 'South Korea and the Gulf crisis', *The Pacific Review*, 5–2 (2007), pp. 141–48.

30. Shinoda, Tomohito, *Koizumi Diplomacy: Japan's Kantei Approach to Foreign and Defense Affairs* (Seattle, WA., University of Washington, 2007).
31. Okamoto, Yukio, 'Toward Reconstruction Aid for Iraq: A Path via the Indian Ocean and the Nile', *Gaiko Forum* (Summer 2003): 7.
32. Henrich, L. William Jr. *et al*, *United Nations Peace-keeping Operations*: 9; Pan, Liang, *The United Nations in Japan's Foreign and Security Policymaking, 1945–1992* (Cambridge, MA.: Harvard University, 2005): 186.
33. Kozai, Shigeru, *UN Peacekeeping Operations* (*Kokurenno heiwaijikatsudō*) (Tokyo: Yuhikaku, 1991): 485.
34. MOFA, *The Present Condition of Japan's Foreign Policy* (*Wagagaikō no kinkyō*) (1958): 8.
35. Murakami, Tomoaki, 'The UN Foreign Policy of the Kishi Administration: the Lebanon crisis as Japan's first PKO opportunity' (*Kishinaikakuto kokurengaikō-PKO gentaikentoshite norebanonkiki*), *Journal of International Cooperation Studies* (*Kokusaikyōryokuronshu*), 11–1 (Sept. 2003), pp. 141–63: 155.
36. Tanaka, Akihiko, 'The Domestic Context: Japanese Politics and UN Peacekeeping', in Harrison, S. Selig, and Nishihara, Masashi, (eds.) *UN Peacekeeping: Japanese and American Context* (Washington DC.: Carnegie Endowment for International Peace, 1995), pp. 89–108: 90–1.
37. Bōeikenkyūkai, *Japan Defense Agency, Japan Defense Force* (*Bōeichōjieitai*) (Tokyo: Kayashōbō, New Edition, 1996): 90–2.
38. MOFA, *Issues Related to UN Peace Cooperation* (*Kokurenkyōryokuhoan nitsuite*), (27 Jan. 1966).
39. MOFA, 'Speech of Prime Minister Satō Eisaku at the National Press Club' (*Nashonaru puresukurabu niokeru satōeisaku sōri-daijinenzetsu*) (11 Nov. 1969), *Blue Book* (*Gaikōseisho*) (Tokyo: MOFA, 1970): 369–76; MOFA, 'Speech of Foreign Minister Aichi to the 25th Session of the UN General Assembly, 18 September 1970', *Blue Book* (*Gaikōseisho*) (Tokyo: MOFA, 1971): 396–402.
40. Interview, Policy Advisor, Legislation Office, Cabinet Secretariat, Tokyo (May 2009).
41. Drifte, Reinhard, *Japan's Quest for a Permanent Security Council Seat*: 16–18.
42. UN, *Prevention and removal of threats to peace and of situations which may lead to international friction or give rise to a dispute*, Working Paper, A/AC.182.L.38, GA (39) Suppl., 33–34, (Repertory Supplement 6), III (1979–1984) (http://untreaty.un.org/cod/repertory/art34/english/rep_supp6_vol3_art34_e.pdf, 28 Dec. 2009): 146.
43. Dore, Ronald, *Japan, Internationalism, and the UN* (London: Routledge, 1997): 112; Watanabe, Hirotaka, 'Japan's UN Diplomacy: History and Current Issues', *Japan Echo* 32, (2005) (http://www.japanecho.co.jp/sum/2005/32sp07.html, 23 Dec. 2009).
44. Drifte, Reinhard, *Japan's Quest for a Permanent Security Council Seat*: 41.
45. Interview, Murakami Tomoaki, Tokyo (June 2009); Murakami, Tomoaki, 'The Yoshida Way and PKO Participation Problem' (*Yoshidarosen toPKO sankamondai*), *International Politics* (*Kokusaiseiji*), 151 (2008), pp. 121–39: 121–2.
46. 'Gov't to review UN peacekeeping law', *Nikkei Shimbun* (5 Jan. 1993), (http://telecom21.nikkei.co.jp/nt21/service/ENGD021/ENGD241?cid=NDJEDB1993010500101029&madr=TOP&kdt=19930105&dk=8ab2414c&reservedtp=ENGD021g6ir2iik&ftrmode=ENGD031&hltid=206chh4opa2e0, 7 Mar. 2010); 'Weekly Announce-

ment (December 19~25)' (Shūkanhōkoku (12gatsu 19nichi~12gatsu 25nichi)), Asahi Shimbun (27 December 1993): 5.
47. 'UN Accept Macedonia', *The Guardian* (8 April 1993): 5.
48. Samuels, Richard J, *Politics, Security Policy, and Japan's Cabinet Legislation Bureau.*
49. *Defence Handbook 1989*: 201, 219, 443; *Defence Handbook 1999*: 229; MOFA, *UN Peacekeeping Operations* (2000), (http://www.mofa.go.jp/policy/un/pamph2000_archive/pko.html, 23 Aug. 2007).
50. Yamamoto, Ryo, 'Legal Issues Concerning Japanese Participation in United Nations Peace-Keeping Operations (1991–2003),' *The Japanese Annual of International Law* 47 (2004): pp. 136–67: 139.
51. *Minutes of the Plenary Session, House of Councillors, 19th Session, 57*, (2 June 1954): 34–35; *Minutes of the Plenary Session, House of Councillors, 122nd Session, 5*, (4 Dec. 1991): 8; Yamamoto, Ryo, 'Legal Issues Concerning Japanese Participation in United Nations Peace-Keeping Operations': 140–4.
52. 'SDF officers on leave should work in PKO, Ouchi says', *Nikkei Shimbun* (13 May 1991) (http://telecom21.nikkei.co.jp/nt21/service/ENGD021/ ENGD241?cid=NDJEDB19910513000101448&madr=TOP&kdt=19910513&dk=e57f3c9&reservedtp=ENGD021g6iskv47&ftrmode=ENGD031&hltid=206chh4opa2e0, 10 Mar. 2010).
53. Iokibe, Makoto, Itō, Motoshige, and Yukushiji, Katsuyuki, *Witness of the 90s: Drastic Change in Foreign Policy, Former MOFA Administrative Vice-minister Yanai Shunji (90nendai no shōgen, gaikōgekihen, motogaimushōjimujikan yanaishunji)* (Tokyo: Asahishimbunsha, 2007): 52–3.
54. Yamaguchi, Jirō, 'The Gulf War and the Transformation of Japanese Constitutional Politics', *Journal of Japanese Studies*, 18–1 (1992), pp. 155–72: 166.
55. *Act on Cooperation for United Nations Peacekeeping Operations and Other Operations, Act No. 79* (19 June 1992) (Tokyo: IPCH, 2009) (http://www.pko.go.jp/PKO_J/data/law/pdf/law_e.pdf 10 April 2010); 'Japan's U.N. peacekeeping law has name changed', *Nikkei Shimbun* (3 July 1992), (http://telecom21.nikkei.co.jp/nt21/service/ENGD241?cid=NDJEDB1992070300101577&madr=TOP&kdt=19920703&dk=7ac6a127&reservedtp=ENGD021g6irgpax&ftrmode=ENGD031&hltid=206chh4opa2e0, 7 Mar. 2010).
56. MOFA, *Bluebook 1992* (http://www.mofa.go.jp/policy/other/bluebook/1992/1992-2-1.htm#4. 12 Dec. 2017).
57. Ru, Pechun (ed.), *PKO: What are Asians and Japanese Thinking About? (PKO: ajiajintonihonjin nokōkōseiwa dōkangaeteiruka)* (Tokyo: Nashinokisha, 2003): 208; Quoted in Pyle, Kenneth B., *Japan Rising*: 266.
58. Bessho, Koro, *Identities and Security in East Asia*, Adelphi Paper 325 (Oxford: OUP, 1999).
59. Iokibe, Makoto, *et al, Witness of the 90s:* 57–8.
60. Samuels, Richard J., *Securing Japan*: 74; *International Peace Cooperation Corps* (http://www.pko.go.jp/PKO_E/organization/organization02.html, 6 Jan. 2010).
61. JDA, *Defense of Japan 1998*: 150; JDA, *Defense of Japan 2005* (Tokyo: JDA/Urban Connections, 2005): 65.
62. *The Council on Security and Defense Capabilities Report*: 20.

63. MOD, *Defense of Japan 2008*: 114–16.
64. MOFA, *Japan's Efforts on Peacebuilding: Towards Consolidation of Peace and Nation Building* (2007): 15 (http://www.mofa.go.jp/policy/un/pko/effort0704.pdf, 12 Jan. 2010).
65. MOD, *Defense of Japan 2008*: 115.
66. Exceptions are for non-JSDF duties, or when the Diet is not in session, approval being provided/withheld for Cabinet Orders (*Seirei*) during subsequent sessions: IPCL, Articles 6, 7.
67. MOFA, *Current Issues Surrounding UN Peace-keeping Operations and Japanese Perspective* (1997).
68. JDA, *Defense of Japan 2002*: 224–6, 255.
69. Ibid.
70. Mulloy, Garren, *Adapting Militaries to Peacekeeping and Policing Roles: The Effects of Peacekeeping on Militaries and the Stresses and Strains of Operations*, HUMSEC Working Paper Series (Graz: HUMSEC, 2007): 9; Forster, Anthony, *Armed Forces and Society in Europe* (Basingstoke: Palgrave Macmillan, 2006): 202–6.
71. Hirano, Ryuichi, 'Our Country's IPCA and its Issues' (*Wagakuni no kokusaikyōryo-kukatsudō to sonokadai*), *Overseas Affairs* (*Kaigaikōtojō*) (May 2009): pp. 18–36: 28.
72. *Act on Cooperation for United Nations Peacekeeping Operations and Other Operations*: 3.
73. Ibid: 11–13.
74. Ibid: 12.
75. JDA, *Defense of Japan 1998*: 150.
76. 'Japan's Diet To Approve Revisions To PKO Law,' *Nikkei Shimbun* (4 June 1998), (http://telecom21.nikkei.co.jp/nt21/service/ENGD021/ENGD241?cid=NDJED B1998060400101471&madr=TOP&kdt=19980604&dk=7ad121aa&nhpjnl= &reservedtp=ENGD025g6istatw&ftrmode=ENGD031&hltid=206chh68apmvc, 10 Mar. 2010).
77. 'The Issue of PKF Main Force Frozen Duties: the statement of position and opinions of various parties' (*Iwayuru PKF hontaigyōmu no tōketsu kaijō nomondai nitsukimashite wa...samazamana tachibakara no goiken ga shimesareteoruko to moshōchi woitashiteor-imasu*); *Minutes of the 144th Meeting of the Special Committee on Fiscal Structural Reform of the House of Representatives*, 5 (*Dai 144kai Shuugiinzaiseikvōzōkaikaku ni kansurutokubetsuiinkaikaigiroku dai5gō*) (8 Dec. 1998): 7; 'PKF Frozen Activities, Hatoyama looking positive' (*PKF tōketsukaijō,Yushi ga maemuki*), *Nikkei Shimbun* (9 Jan. 1999): 2.
78. 'DPJ to back expansion of PKO law: Limits on SDF Arms Use to Ease,' *The Japan Times* (29 October 2001) (http://search.japantimes.co.jp/cgi-bin/nn20011029a1.html,10 March 2010).
79. MOD, *Defense of Japan 2008*: 288–9.
80. Shinoda, Tomohito, *Koizumi Diplomacy*: 146.
81. Singh, Bhubhindar, 'Japan's Security Policy: From a Peace State to an International State,' *The Pacific Review* 21–3 (2008): pp. 303–25, 311.
82. *Cabinet Office Survey 2004* (http://www8.cao.go.jp/survey/h16/h16-gaikou/2-7.html, 1 Mar. 2010); *Cabinet Office Survey, 1991* (http://www8.cao.go.jp/survey/h02/H02-10-02-14.html, 10 Mar. 2010).

83. Conversations, Katakura Kunio, Daito Bunka University (2003–04).
84. Hook, Glenn D., *Militarization and Demilitarization in Contemporary Japan*: 89.
85. 'ASDF conducts first overseas transport aircraft exercise: For possible international assistance' (*Kōkūjietaino yusōkiga shonokaigaikunren: kokusaienjowo nentōni*), *Asahi Shimbun* (3 March 1995): 33.
86. 'Analysis: Hashimoto's SDF evacuation attempt backfires', *Nikkei Shimbun* (15 July 1997), (http://telecom21.nikkei.co.jp/nt21/service/ENGD021/ENGD241?cid= NDJEDB19970715001013888&madr=TOP&kdt=19970715&dk=106aeb3d&nhp jnl=&reservedtp=ENGD021g6iswkzl&ftrmode=ENGD031 &hltid=206chh6ax4 ekw, 8 March 2010).
87. 'Persian Gulf Peace Proposal, Personnel Despatch, Legal Revision the Focal Point also "Assistance Force" Enabling Laws' (*Perushawangan waheikōkensaku, yōinhaken, hōkaiseiga shōten "enjotai" shinrippōmo*), *Yomiuri Shimbun* (18 Aug. 1990, Tokyo, morning): 2.
88. Hook, Glenn D., *et al, Japan's International Relations*: 384.
89. Woolley, Peter J., *Japan's Navy*: 31–2; 108th Diet Session, Second Meeting, Special Security Council (26 Dec. 1987), House of Representatives, (http://kokkai.ndl.go.jp/ SENTAKU/syugiin/108/0770/10805260770002c.html 9 Jan. 2018).
90. Kawabata, Osamu (ed.), *Operation Gulf Dawn: The 188 Day Minesweeper Force Deployment* ('*Wangannoyoake': sakusenzenkiroku–kaijōjieitai perushawan sōkaihaken taino188nichi*) (Tokyo: Asagumoshimbunsha, 1991): 202; *Hand Book for Defense 1999*: 597–8.
91. Ochiai, Jun, *Operation Gulf Dawn* (*Wanganno yoakesakusen*), JDA, (Oct. 2001), (http://www.mod.go.jp/msdf/mf/other/history/img/001.pdf 12 May 2015).
92. Woolley, Peter J., *Japan's Navy*: 31; Kawabata, Osamu (ed.), *Operation Gulf Dawn*: 202.
93. Hook, Glenn D., *Militarization and Demilitarization in Contemporary Japan*: 90; Kawabata, Osamu (ed.), *Operation Gulf Dawn*: 190–1.
94. Kawabata, Osamu (ed.), *Operation Gulf Dawn*: 165, 191.
95. Takeda, Yasuhiro, 'Japan's Role in the Cambodian Peace Process: Diplomacy, Manpower, and Finance,' *Asian Survey* 38–6 (1998): MOFA, 553–68; Press Statement, 'Joint statement of Foreign Minister Aichi and Secretary of State Rodgers' (*Aichigaimudaiji– Rojaazukokumuchōkankyōdōseimei*) (24 June 1970), *The Diplomatic Bluebook*, (1971), (http://www.mofa.go.jp/Mofaj/gaiko/bluebook/1971/s46-shiryou-3-3.htm 9 December 2009).
96. Tomoda, Seki, 'The Novelty of the Cambodia Assistance Policy' (*Kanbojiaenjoseisaku no atarashisa*), *Gaiko Forum*, 54, (March 1993), pp. 28–34.
97. Ikeda, Tadashi, *The Road to Peace in Cambodia* (*Kanbojiaheiwa eno michi*) (Tokyo: Toshishunpan, 1996): 179–81; Berger, Thomas U., *Cultures of Antimilitarism*: 191.
98. UNDPKO, *UNTAC Mandate*, (http://www.un.org/Depts/dpko/dpko/co_mission/ untacmandate.html, 19 Aug. 2009).
99. Sanderson, John M., 'Dabbling in War: The Dilemma in the Use of Force in United Nations Intervention', in Otunnu, Olara A., and Doyle, Michael W., (eds.), *Peacemaking and peacekeeping for the new century* (Lanham, MD.: Rowman & Littlefield, 1998), pp. 145–168: 154.

100. Berdal, Mats, and Leifer, Michael, 'Cambodia', in Berdal, Mats, and Economides, Spyros, (eds.) *United Nations Interventionism 1991–2004* (Cambridge: Cambridge University Press, 2007), pp. 32–64: 32.
101. Sanderson, John, Book Review, *International Affairs* 71–4 (1995), pp. 914–6.
102. UNDPKO, *Background to UNTAC Mission* (http://www.un.org/Depts/dpko/dpko/co_mission/untacbackgr2.html#two, 8 Aug. 2009).
103. Ibid.
104. Cain, K., Postlewait H., Thomson, A., *Emergency Sex (and Other Desperate Measures)* (London: Ebury Press, 2005).
105. Ghosh, Amitav, 'The Global Reservation: Notes toward an Ethnography of International Peacekeeping,' *Cultural Anthropology* 9–3 (1994), pp. 412–22: 418–420.
106. Conversation with Sanderson, John, UNU, Tokyo (22 Oct. 1999).
107. Fujiwara, Kiichi, 'Cambodian settlement points way to peace,' *Asahi Shimbun: Asia Network* (2000), (http://www.asahi.com/english/asianet/report/eng_2000_02.html 16 May 2004).
108. Findlay, Trevor, *Cambodia*: 130.
109. Akashi, Yasushi, 'In a Hurry to Live' (*Ikirukoto nimo kokoroseki*) (Tokyo: Chuokoronshinsha, 2001), in Watanabe, Takashi, *The PKO in Cambodia-Lessons Learned*: 92.
110. *Kanbojia kokusaiheiwakyōryoku chōsadan*; Interview, Liefland, Karl, Minister, Embassy of Sweden, Tokyo (Apr. 2001).
111. 'Gov't to send PKO survey mission to Cambodia,' *Nikkei Shimbun* (5 Aug. 1992), (http://telecom21.nikkei.co.jp/nt21/service/ENGD021/ENGD241?cid=NDJEDB 1992080500101562&madr=TOP&kdt=19920805&dk=e28b08b6&reservedtp= ENGD021g6irgpax&ftrmode=ENGD031&hltid=206chh4opa2e0, 10 Mar. 2010); Interview, Yamazaki, Hiroto, Tokyo (2009).
112. *Hand Book for Defense 1999*: 615–7.
113. Ibid: 617.
114. Ibid: 618.
115. Kitajima, Takao, *Cambodia Dispatch Outline* (*Kanbojiahaken nogaiyō*), MOD, Tokyo (http://www.mod.go.jp/gsdf/crf/pa/closeuphaken/3gou/hotta.html, 17 Dec. 2009); Interviews, GSDF Lt-Colonel (Aug. 2007), and GSDF Lt-Colonel (July 2009), Tokyo.
116. Conversation GSDF Major, Tokyo (Oct. 2007).
117. *JSDF Equipment Yearbook 1997*: 91, 396; Miyajima, Shigeki, *Ah, Magnificent JSDF*: 63–74.
118. 'JMSDF's PKO Sealift Force Leaves Japan for Cambodia,' *Ships of the World* (*Sekainokansen*) 458 (1992): 21–5; 'Kyamputakeo', *Japan Military Review* (Jan. 1993): 19–34.
119. Ledgerwood, Judy, L., quoting *Japan Review*, Summer 1993, in *UN Peacekeeping Missions: The Lessons from Cambodia*, Asia Pacific Issues, East-West Center 11 (Mar. 1994): 8; Correspondent Asami, 'PKO Main Unit enters Phnom Penn: 600 man engineering battalion ready for real operations' (*PKOhontai, punonpen iri-shisetsu daitai600nin, honkakukatsudōhe*), *Nikkei Shimbun* (14 Oct. 1992): 1.

120. NHK, 'Negotiator Akashi' (*Kōshōjin akashi*), *Bakumon, Gakumon*, File 105, NHK-General (6 Apr. 2010) (http://www.nhk.or.jp/bakumon/previous/20100406.html, 12 May 2010).
121. Conversation with Akashi Yasushi, UNU, Tokyo (22 Oct. 1999).
122. 'Defense Agency chief ready for PKO in Cambodia', *Nikkei Shimbun* (31 July 1992), (http://telecom21.nikkei.co.jp/nt21/service/ENGD021/ ENGD241?cid=NDJE DB1992073100101572&madr=TOP&kdt=19920731&dk=fb26f01&reservedtp= ENGD021g6irgpax&ftrmode=ENGD031&hltid=206chh4opa2e0, 10 Mar. 2010).
123. Shenon, Philip, 'Actions of Japan Peacekeepers in Cambodia Raise Questions and Criticism', *The New York Times* (24 Oct. 1993), (http://www.nytimes.com/1993/10/24/world/actions-of-japan-peacekeepers-in-cambodia-raise-questions-and-criticism.html?scp=1&sq=Japan%20peacekeeping&st=cse&pagewanted=2, 10 May 2010).
124. Ledgerwood, Judy, L., *UN Peacekeeping Missions*: 6; Shenon, Philip, 'Actions of Japan Peacekeepers in Cambodia Raise Questions and Criticism'.
125. Correspondent Asami, 'Unable to operate due to landmines, heatstroke, the main unit also appears to be 'homeless': PKO Cambodia Report' (*Katsudō habamu jirai, mōshō, hontaimotōmen wa 'yadonashi' (PKOkanbojiahōkoku)*, *Nikkei Shimbun* (14 Oct. 1992): 17.
126. IPCH, *International Peace Cooperation Assignment in Cambodia*, (http://www.pko.go.jp/PKO_E/result/cambo/cambo02.html, 12 May 2007);[126] Yanai, Shunji, 'UN Peace Operations and the Role of Japan: A Japanese Perspective', in Morrison, Alex, and Kiras, James, (eds.) *UN Peace Operations and the Role of Japan* (Clemensport, Nova Scotia: Canadian Peacekeeping Press, 1996), 75–81: 79.
127. Suzuki, Katsunari, 'Japan Gets Unfair Blame on Peacekeepers', *The New York Times* (11/20 Nov. 1993), (http://www.nytimes.com/1993/11/20/opinion/l-japan-gets-unfair-blame-on-peacekeepers-172493.html?scp=8&sq=Japan%20 peacekeeping&st=cse, 10 May 2010).
128. Imagawa, Yukio, *Cambodia and Japan* (*Kanbojiato nihon*) (Tokyo: Rengo, 2000): 187–188.
129. Heinrich, L. William Jr., Shibata, Akiho, Soeya, Yoshihide, *United Nations peace-keeping operations: a guide to Japanese policies*, (Tokyo: UNU Press, 1999): 90; IPCH, *International Peace Cooperation Assignment in Cambodia*.
130. Azimi, Nassrine (ed.), *The United Nations Transitional Authority in Cambodia (UNTAC): Debriefing and Lessons, Report and Recommendations of the International Conference, Singapore, August 1994* (London: Kluwer Law International/UNITAR, 1995): 13.
131. Even Watanabe Akio, commented that JSDF personnel were dispatched to Cambodia, "practically without any arms": Watanabe, Akio, 'Is Now a Good Opportunity for Japan to Show the Flag,' *Asia Perspectives* (Spring 2002), pp. 6–9: 7; *Hand Book for Defense 1999*: 618.
132. Watanabe, Takashi, 'In the Field of Cambodia-A Recollection of the Japanese Commander in UNTAC' (*Genbano hokori-UNTAC hakenjieitaishikikan nokaisō*), in Military History Society of Japan (ed.), *Peacekeeping Operations in Historical Perspective*, pp. 152–166: 161–2.

133. Interview, GSDF Lt. Col., Tokyo (June 2009).
134. JDA, *PKO, JSDF, and International Emergency Relief Operations* (*PKO oyobi kokusai kinkyuenjo katsudō tojieitai*) (Tokyo: JDA, 1992), in Chuma, Kiyofuku, 'The Debate over Japan's Participation in Peace-keeping Operations', *Japan Review of International Affairs* 6–3 (1992), pp. 239–54: 243.
135. Conversation with Sanderson, John, UNU, Tokyo (1999); Sanderson, John, book review, *International Affairs*.
136. 'SDF officers' duties in Cambodia questioned', *Nikkei Shimbun* (4 Feb. 1993), (http://telecom21.nikkei.co.jp/nt21/service/ENGD021/ENGD241?cid=NDJEDB19930 20400101504&madr=TOP&kdt=19930204&dk=2c9072a&reservedtp= ENGD 021g6ir2iik&ftrmode=ENGD031&hltid=206chh4opa2e0, 10 July 2010).
137. Buckingham, Antony, *RACMP in Cambodia-The UNTAC Military Police Company*, (http://home.iprimus.com.au/buckomp/MPCambodiaUNTAC.htm, 12 June 2010).
138. Takeda, Yasuhiro, 'Japan's Role in the Cambodian Peace Process, pp. 553–68: 561; Watanabe, Takashi, 'In the Field of Cambodia': 163.
139. Hook, Glenn D., *Militarization and Demilitarization in Contemporary Japan*: 97; 'JSDF in Cambodia: commencement of port improvement construction' (*Kanbojia no jieitai, kōwankairyōkōjichakushu he*), *Kyodo/Nikkei Shimbun* (27 May 1993): 3.
140. Dore, Ronald, *Japan, Internationalism, and the UN*: xv.
141. Shirohama, Tatsuoki, *Knowledge I wish to put in place: 'Disaster' seen from a medic's eyes-preparation, limitation, and then cooperation* (*shitteokitaiishi no mekaramita 'saigai'—sonoe, saizensen, soshiterenkei*) (Tokyo: Naigai, 2005): 76, 84; Fujii, Tatsuya, 'The facts of PKO medical duties' (*PKO iryō gyomu no jissai*), pp. 14–20, Nakayama, Taro (ed.), *International Medical Cooperation: medicine without borders* (*Kokusai iryō kyoryoku: iryō ni kokkyōnashi*) (Tokyo: Simul Press, 1993): 15–7.
142. Fujii, Tatsuya, 'The facts of PKO medical duties': 20.
143. Nakayama, Taro, 'International Medical Cooperation' (*Kokusai iryō kyoryoku*), in Nakayama, Taro (ed.), *International Medical Cooperation*: 23.
144. Shirohama, Tatsuoki, *Knowledge I wish to put in place:* 76; Fujimoto Atsuhito, 'The utility of medical origins' (*Iryō no genten nitatsu*), in Nakayama, Taro (ed.), *International Medical Cooperation*, pp. 20–22: 21.
145. Heininger, Janet E., *Peacekeeping in Transition: The United Nations in Cambodia* (New York: Twentieth Century Fund, 1994): 75.
146. *Fourth Progress Report of the Secretary-General on the United Nations Transitional Authority in Cambodia*, UN Document S/25719 (3 May 1993): 3; Findlay, Trevor, *Cambodia*: 75–7.
147. Ōishi, Akatsuki, "JSDF Trial by PKO' The World and Japan, Part 6' (*JieitaiPKO heiwaeno shiren' sekaito nihondairokubu*), *Yomiuri Shimbun* (7 Apr. 1993) (http://nippon.zaidan.info/seikabutsu/2002/01257/contents/337.htm, 12 Aug. 2004).
148. Mickolus, Edward F., and Simmons, Susan L., *Terrorism, 1992–1995: a Chronology of Events and a Selectively Annotated Bibliography* (Westport, CT.: Greenwood, 1997): 365; *Fourth progress report of the Secretary-General on the United Nations Transitional Authority in Cambodia*: 26; 'Second PKO Contingent: first part of the main unit,

300troops, leaves the Chitose Base', (*Kanbojia 2ji PKO, hontaidaiichijinga shuppatsu-300nin, chitosekichikara*), *Nikkei Shimbun* (7 Apr. 1993): 17.

149. "Five conditions' unconnected with JSDF dispatch, announces Commissioner Ogata ('*Gogensoku' kankeinakujieitaino hakenwo, PKOde Ogatabenmukan*), *Nikkei Shimbun* (13 April 1993): 9.
150. Findlay, Trevor, *Cambodia*: 78; Ratner, Steven R., *The New UN Peacekeeping*: 161–2.
151. Kurokawa, Uchitaka, "JSDF Trial by PKO' The World and Japan, Part 5 of 6 Parts', *Yomiuri Shimbun* (10 Apr. 1993) (http://nippon.zaidan.info/seikabutsu/2002/01257/contents/341.htm, 12 Aug. 2004).
152. Ibid.
153. Imagawa, Yukio, *Cambodia and Japan*: 203–6; 'Negotiator Akashi' *Bakumon, Gakumon*, NHK.
154. Iokibe, Makoto, *et al*, *Witness of the 90s:* 104–5; Kurokawa, Uchitaka, "JSDF Trial by PKO' The World and Japan, Part 5 of 6 Parts'; Hook, Glenn D., *Militarization and Demilitarization in Contemporary Japan*: 97.
155. *JSDF Equipment Yearbook 1997*: 74–5.
156. Izumi, Nobumichi, 'Japanese troops should play full role in U.N. missions', (4 Sept.1995), *The Nikkei Weekly*: 7.
157. Maeda, Tetsuo, *The Hidden Army:* 297.
158. Maeda, Tetsuo, *JSDF and PKO Verification*: 53.
159. Ibid: 63–4.
160. Interview, GSDF Captain (1993), Tokyo (June 2009).
161. Izumi, Nobumichi, 'Japanese troops should play full role in U.N. missions'.
162. Ōishi, Akatsuki, "JSDF Trial by PKO' The World and Japan, Part 2 of 6 Parts', *Yomiuri Shimbun* (7 Apr. 1993) (http://nippon.zaidan.info/seikabutsu/2002/01257/contents/337.htm, 12 Aug. 2004).
163. Watanabe, Takashi, *The PKO in Cambodia-Lessons Learned*: 101.
164. Ōishi, Akatsuki, "JSDF Trial by PKO' The World and Japan, Part 6'.
165. Sanderson, John M., 'Dabbling in War': 155.
166. 'JSDF Cambodia Dispatch Objection Recited' (*Jieitaikanbojiahaken niigiwo tonaeta*), *Asahi Shimbun* (7 May 1993): 7.
167. Mikuriya, Takashi, and Nakamura, Takafusa; George, Timothy S. (trans.), *Politics and Power in 20th-Century Japan: The Reminiscences of Miyazawa Kiichi*, (London: Bloomsbury Academic, 2015): 205–6.
168. Takeda, Yasuhiro, 'Japan's Role in the Cambodian Peace Process': 561.
169. Seki, Hajime *et al*, *The Truth About PKO*: 73–4.
170. Iokibe, Makoto, *et al*, *Witness of the 90s*: 95.
171. Heinrich, L. William, Jr., *et al*, *United Nations Peace-keeping Operations*: 90; Interviews: GSDF Major, Tokyo (June 2009); GSDF Captain, Tokyo (Nov. 2009).
172. Interview, Karl Liefland, Minister, Embassy of Sweden, Tokyo (Apr. 2001).
173. Dalairre, Romeo, *Shake Hands With the Devil: The Failure of Humanity in Rwanda* (London: Arrow, 2004): 245–6, 316–7, 400, 423–6.
174. Sanderson, John, *A Review of Recent Peacekeeping Operations*, presentation, Dacca, (10 Jan. 1994), in Findlay, Trevor, *Cambodia*: 117, 142.

175. Findlay, Trevor, *Cambodia*: 142.
176. Pyle, Kenneth B., *The Japanese Question: Power and Purpose in a New Era*, second edition (Washington, DC.: AEI Press, 1996): 155.
177. Goulding, Marrack, *Peacemonger*, (Baltimore, MD.: Johns Hopkins University Press, 2003): 263.
178. Watanabe, Takashi, *The PKO in Cambodia-Lessons Learned*: 99.
179. McNamara, Robert S, *The Essence of Security: Reflections in Office*, in Clutterbuck, R.L., 'Fingers in the Mangle: British Military Commitments in the Third World', *Brassey's Annual* (London: Brassey's, 1972), pp. 10–22: 19.
180. Fick, Nathaniel, 'Fight Less, Win More', *The Washington Post* (9 Aug. 2007) (http://www.washingtonpost.com/wp-dyn/content/article/2007/08/09/AR2007080900667.html, 12 Aug. 2007).
181. *Nontraditional Roles of the Military and Security in East Asia* (Executive Summary) (Tokyo: NIDS, 2003): 16.
182. Findlay, Trevor, *Cambodia*: 80.
183. *The Military Balance 1990–1991*: 165.
184. Krishnasamy, Kabilan, 'Pakistan Peacekeeping Experiences': 110–111.
185. Interview, Kawano, Hitoshi, NDA, Yokosuka (June 2001).
186. Kurashina, Yuko, *Peacekeeping Participation and Identity Changes in the Japan Self Defense Forces: Military Service as 'Dirty Work,'* PhD Thesis (College Park, MD.: University of Maryland, 2005): 207–8.
187. Ledgerwood, Judy, L., quoting *Japan Review* (Summer 1993), *UN Peacekeeping Missions*: 8; Conahan, Frank C., *UN Peacekeeping*: 7; Findlay, Trevor, *Cambodia*: 141; Buckingham, Antony, *RACMP in Cambodia*.
188. Pringle, James, 'Sex and inflation end the UN honeymoon in Cambodia', *The Times* (26 Nov. 1992): 13.
189. Ledgerwood, Judy, L., *UN Peacekeeping Missions*: 7–8.
190. Findlay, Trevor, *Cambodia*: 141.
191. Ibid: 140.
192. Watanabe, Takashi, *The PKO in Cambodia-Lessons Learned*: 99.
193. Ohta, Kiyohiko, 'A Public Relations Officer's Experiences in UNTAC' (*KanbojiaPKO to kōhōkatsudō*), in Military History Society of Japan (ed.), *Peacekeeping Operations in Historical Perspective (PKO no shitekikenshō)* (Tokyo: Nishikitadashisha, 2007), pp. 167–183: 168, 171–2.
194. JDA, *Defense of Japan 1994 (Bōeihakusho heisei6nen)* (Tokyo: JDA, 1994): 162–3, 221–6.
195. JDA, *Defense of Japan 1996 (Bōeihakusho heisei8nen)*, (Tokyo: JDA, 1996):105; JDA, *Defense of Japan 1998 (Bōeihakusho heisei10nen)*, (Tokyo: JDA, 1998): 189, (http://www.clearing.mod.go.jp/cgi/hakusho_search.cgi?query=UNTAC&from=1995 &to=2000 12 Feb. 2018).
196. The author was denied access to UNTAC despatch history under freedom of information mechanisms.
197. Sanger, David, E., 'U.N. Chief Presses Japan for Peacekeeping Troops', *The New York Times* (19 Feb. 1993) (http://www.nytimes.com/1993/02/19/world/un-chief-

presses-japan-for-peacekeeping-troops.html?scp=3&sq=Japan%20 peacekeeping&st=cse, 18 July 2010).
198. Nakanishi, Harufumi, 'Troop dispatches the bailiwick of politicians', *The Nikkei Weekly* (8 Mar. 1993): 7.
199. *Hand Book for Defense 1999*: 640.
200. UN, *Report of the Secretary-General on the United Nations Operation in Mozambique*, Doc.S/1994/89 (28 Jan. 1994), (http://daccessdds.un.org/doc/UNDOC/GEN/N94/047/14/PDF/N9404714.pdf?OpenElement, 9 Aug. 2009); UN, *Report of the Security Council Mission Established Pursuant to the Statement Made by the President of the Security Council at the 3406th Meeting*, Doc.S/1994/1009 (29 Aug. 1994) (http://daccessdds.un.org/doc/UNDOC/GEN/N94/343/60/PDF/N9434360.pdf?OpenElement, 9 Aug. 2009).
201. UN, *UN Security Council Resolution 797 (1992)*, UN Document S/RES/797 (1992) (16 December 1992) (http://daccess-dds-ny.un.org/doc/UNDOC/GEN/N92/824/85/IMG/N9282485.pdf?OpenElement, 7 July 2004).
202. UNDPKO, *ONUMOZ Background* (http://www.un.org/Depts/dpko/dpko/co_mission/onumozFT.htm, 19 Aug. 2009).
203. Vines, Alex, 'Disarmament in Mozambique', *Journal of Southern African Studies* 24–1 (1998), pp. 191–205: 192; UNDPKO, *The United Nations and Mozambique, 1992–1995* (New York: UN Department of Public Information, 1995).
204. UN, *Final Report of the Secretary-General on the United Nations Operation in Mozambique*, Doc.S/1994/1449 (23 Dec. 1994): 7.
205. UNDPKO, *Mozambique ONUMOZ Background* (http://www.un.org/en/peacekeeping/missions/past/onumozFT.htm#ONUMO, 9 Aug. 2009).
206. Much of this section relies upon an interview: Colonel Nakano, Shegenori, Camp Asaka (20 July 2007).
207. Nakano, Shegenori, 'Mozambique Life Diary', *Securitarian*: 35.
208. *Hand Book for Defense 1999:* 640.
209. Ibid: 641.
210. 'Mozambique PKO unit members sent New Year goods by air from Komaki Base (Nagoya)', (*MozambiikuPKO notaiinni shōgatsuyōhinkūyukomakikichi (Nagoya)*), *Asahi Shimbun* (29 Dec. 1993): 2.
211. *Hand Book for Defense 1999*: 630–1.
212. Interview, Colonel Nakano Shigenori (2007).
213. Synge, Richard, *Mozambique*: 16.
214. UN, *Further Report of the Secretary-General on the United Nations Operation in Mozambique*, UN Document S/1994/1002 (26 Aug. 1994): 4.
215. Interviews: GSDF Colonel, and JDA officials supporting ONUMOZ.
216. UN, *Report of the Security Council Mission Established Pursuant to the Statement Made by the President of the Security Council at the 3406th Meeting (S/PRST/1994/35)*, UN Document S/1994/1009 (29 Aug. 1994), (http://daccessdds.un.org/doc/UNDOC/GEN/N94/343/60/PDF/N9434360.pdf?OpenElement, 1 Aug. 2009).
217. Maeda, Tetsuo, *JSDF and PKO Verification*: 136–7.
218. MOFA, *Japanese Participation in UN Peacekeeping: UN Peacekeeping Operations in*

Mozambique, (http://www.mofa.go.jp/policy/un/pko/pamph96/02_3.html, 2 Jan. 2010).
219. *Hand Book for Defense 1999*: 642; Sato, Chigumi, 'Transformation of UN PKO and Japanese Military Contribution from 1992 to 2009', *IPCH Journal Collection* (*Koku saiheiwakyōryokuronbunshū*), (2010).
220. Maeda, Tetsuo, *JSDF and PKO Verification*: 138–9.
221. JDA, *Defense of Japan 2003* (Tokyo: JDA/Urban Connections, 2003): 261; Synge, Richard, *Mozambique*: 92.
222. Maeda, Tetsuo, *JSDF and PKO Verification*: 140–141.
223. Nakano, Shiginori, 'Mozambique Duty Roster' (*Mozanbiiku doumuban*), *Securitarian* (October 1993), pp. 20–5: 21; UN, *Financing of the United Nations Operation in Mozambique: Report of the Secretary-General*, Doc.A/51/807 (25 Feb. 1997): 14–5; 'Mozambique Note' (*Mozanbiikutayori*), *Securitarian* (Sept. 1993): 34.
224. UN, *Further Report of the Secretary-General on the United Nations Operation in Mozambique*: 4–5.
225. MacQueen, Norrie, *United Nations Peacekeeping in Africa Since 1960* (Harlow: Longman, 2002): 64–80.
226. IPCH, *International Peace Cooperation Assignment for Rwandan Refugees: Outflows of Rwandan Refugees*, (http://www.pko.go.jp/PKO_E/result/rwanda/rwanda03.html, 17 July 2009).
227. Murayama had strongly protested against UNTAC despatch. See, Hook, Glenn D., et al, *Japan's International Relations*: 382–4.
228. 'Socialist party OKs sending SDF personnel to Rwanda', *Nikkei Shimbun* (17 Aug. 1994), (http://telecom21.nikkei.co.jp/nt21/service/ENGD021/ENGD241?cid=NDJEDB1994081700101372&madr=TOP&kdt=19940817&dk=5dfc7af4&reservedtp=ENGD025g6iqtoy6&ftrmode=ENGD031&hltid=206chh4opa2e0, 10 March 2010); *Hand Book for Defense 1999*: 644; Ishizuka, Katsumi, *Peacekeeping and National Interests: Positive Factors Influencing Potential Contributing States*, Kyōei University Research Report Collection (*Kyōeidaigakukenkyūronshū*) (2002): 11.
229. *Defense Yearbook 1995* (*Bōeinenkan1995*) (Tokyo: Bōeinenkankankōkai, 1995): 108–9; MOFA, *Map Around Billeting Area*, (http://www.mofa.go.jp/policy/un/pko/pamph96/3_1.html, 17 July 2009).
230. Interviews: JDA officials, GSDF Lt-General, ASDF Lt.-Colonel; Kamimoto, Mitsunobu, *Rwanda Refugee Relief Unit: 80 Days in Goma, Zaire* (*Ruwandananminkyūentaizaiiru, goma no 80nichi*) (Tokyo: Uchisotoshuppan, 2007): 6.
231. 'Gov't mulls beefing up PKO mission to Rwanda', *Nikkei Shimbun* (1 Sept. 1994) (http://telecom21.nikkei.co.jp/nt21/service/ENGD021/NGD241?cid=NDJEDB1994090100101045&madr=TOP&kdt=19940901&dk=d444e582&reservedtp=ENGD025g6iqtoy6&ftrmode=ENGD031&hltid=206chh4opa2e0, 10 Mar. 2010).
232. *Hand Book for Defense 1999*: 648; Yanai, Shunji, 'UN Peace Operations and the Role of Japan': 79.
233. Interviews with two JDA officials who served in Nairobi, 1994 (Tokyo, 2008).
234. Kamimoto, Mitsunobu, *Rwanda Refugee Relief Unit*: 20; *Hand Book for Defense 1999*: 654–5.
235. *Hand Book for Defense 1999*: 656; *Japanese Contributions to International*

Humanitarian Relief Operations, Rwanda: International Relief Cooperation Assignments for Rwandan refugees, MOFA (http://www.mofa.go.jp/policy/un/pko/pamph96/03.html, 17 July 2009); Interview, Karl Liefland (Apr. 2001); Kamimoto, Mitsunobu, *Rwanda Refugee Relief Unit*: 84–8.
236. Ibid: 16.
237. Ibid: 144–58; IPCH, *International Peace Cooperation Assignment for Rwandan Refugees: Refugees Relief Units*, (http://www.pko.go.jp/PKO_E/result/rwanda/rwanda03.html, 17 July 2009)
238. *Hand Book for Defense 1999*: 656.
239. Interview, JDA official, Tokyo (May 2007).
240. 'First of 120 GSDF Rwanda Refugee Relief Unit members strike camp' (*Dai1jin 120ninga gomawo tesshū, rikujiruwandananminkyūentai*), *Asahi Shimbun* (16 Dec. 1994): 1.
241. Takahara, Takao, 'Japan', in Findlay, Trevor, (ed.), *Challenges for the New Peacekeepers*, SIPRI Research Report No. 12 (Oxford: OUP, 1996): 52–67, 62.
242. 'Cambodia was 'Protect', Goma was 'Get stuck in': five people who experienced two PKO' (*Kanbojiawa 'mamori', gomawa 'seme': futatsuno PKOtaikenshita5nin*), *Asahi Shimbun* (30 Dec. 1994): 26.
243. Interview, Morioka, Takashi, Head of General Affairs, NDA (June 2001).
244. 'JSDF shall not search for missing Briton: JDA insists it is the principle of service in Zaire' (*Eikokujin no fumeishasōsaku ni jieitaihakensezu: bōeichou ga hōshinzaiiru*), *Asahi Shimbun* (1 Dec. 1994): 34; Kamimoto, Mitsunobu, *Rwanda Refugee Relief Unit*: 209–11.
245. Ibid: 90–105, 278–9; Slim, Hugo, 'The Stretcher and the Drum: Civil-Military Relations in Peace Support Operations', *International Peacekeeping* 3-2 (1996), pp.123–140: 127.
246. Kamimoto, Mitsunobu, *Rwanda Refugee Relief Unit*: 212–5; '5 dead in plane crash chartered from Nairobi, journalists from Kyodo and Fuji TV covering Goma among the dead' (*Gomashuzai 5nintsuirakushi kyodo, fujitv kisharanairobidechaataaki*), *Asahi Shimbun* (7 Dec. 1994): 1.
247. 'British aid for hurricane victims', *BBC News* (4 Nov. 1998) (http://news.bbc.co.uk/2/hi/uk_news/207924.stm, 12 Nov. 2008); UNDP, *Mitch+5 Regional Forum Report*, UN Development Program/Coordination Center for the Prevention of Natural Disasters in Central America (2004): 46 (http://www.preventionweb.net/files/2960_mitch5forumreporteng.pdf, 2 Aug.2010).
248. *Hand Book for Defense 1999*: 678.
249. JDA, *Defense of Japan 2002*: 234–5; Watanabe, Makiko, 'Japan's humanitarian assistance,' *Human Practice Network* 26 (2004) (http://www.odihpn.org/report.asp?id=2617, 12 Mar. 2008); Interview, Hirano, Ryuichi, Cabinet Office, Tokyo (2009).
250. *Hand Book for Defense 1999*: 678; MOFA, *Dispatch of Japan Disaster Relief Team (SDF Units) to Honduras*, (13 Nov. 1998) (http://www.mofa.go.jp/announce/announce/1998/11/1113.html, 2 May 2008).
251. Satō, Yūji, 'Strong Expression of International Aid by the JSDF, First Honduras Dispatch is completed' (*Kokusaienjo ni tsuyomihakkijieitai, honjurasue shinha-*

kenshuryō), *Asahi Shimbun* (4 Dec. 1998: Nagoya): 30; JICA, *Japan Disaster Relief Team (Kokusaikinkyūenjotai JDR)*, (http://www.jica.go.jp/jdr/about.html, 11 July 2010).

252. ASC, *International Emergency Assistance Implementation Plan for the Republic of Honduras (Hondyurasukyowakoku ni taisuru kokusaikinkyūenjojisshikeikaku)*, ASC Report 108 (13 Nov. 1998): 5, 19.
253. ASC, *International Emergency Assistance Implementation Plan for the Republic of Honduras*: 4; MOFA, *Dispatch of Japan Disaster Relief Team (SDF Units) to Honduras*.
254. ASC, *International Emergency Assistance Implementation Plan for the Republic of Honduras*: 12; Sato, Yūji, 'Strong Expression of International Aid by the JSDF, First Honduras Dispatch is completed'; GSDF, *Dispatch of Japan Disaster Relief Team (SDF Units) to Honduras*; *Honduras International Disaster Relief Medical Unit (Honjurasukokusai kinkyūiryōenjotai)*, Middle Army (http://www.mod.go.jp/gsdf/mae/MAkatudou/kokusai/honjyurasu/index.html, 12 Aug. 2010).
255. GSDF, *Dispatch of Japan Disaster Relief Team (SDF Units) to Honduras: The 1990s*, Middle Army (http://www.mod.go.jp/gsdf/mae/50univ/MA/50th_90yphoto.html, 12 Aug. 2010).
256. *Hand Book for Defense 1999*: 679.
257. Satō, Yūji, 'Strong Expression of International Aid by the JSDF, First Honduras Dispatch is completed'.
258. Shirohama, Tatsuoki, *Knowledge I wish to put in place*: 75–77; 'JSDF Despatched to Honduras Disaster, Groping for the Path to Disaster Relief' (*Saigai honjurasu hakennorikuji, kinkyūenjoni aratanamichi mosaku*), *Asahi Shimbun* (24 Nov. 1998): 3.
259. Shirohama, Tatsuoki, *Knowledge I wish to put in place*: 77.
260. 'Record of Experience in the International Disaster Relief Team, Honduras' (*Hondurasu kokusaikinkyūenjotaitaikenki*), *Securitarian* (May 1999): 46–8.
261. *Hand Book for Defense 1999*: 679.
262. Interview, Mendez, Ruben, Tsukuba University (12 Mar. 2001).
263. 'Record of Experience in the International Disaster Relief Team, Honduras', *Securitarian*; 'JSDF Dispatched to Honduras Disaster', *Asahi Shimbun*.
264. Satō, Yūji, 'Strong Expression of International Aid by the JSDF, First Honduras Dispatch is completed'; 'JSDF Dispatched to Honduras Disaster', *Asahi Shimbun*.
265. Interview, Lt.-General Yamaguchi, Noboru, Camp Asaka (Aug. 2007).
266. Hong, Kyudok, 'South Korean Experiences in Peacekeeping and Plan for the Future,' in Caforio, Giuseppe (ed.), *Advances in Military Sociology: Essays in Honor of Charles C. Moskos, Part A* (Bingley: Emerald Group, 2009), pp. 173–87: 177.
267. JDA *Defense of Japan 2004*: 288–9.
268. Koyama, Shukuko, and Myrttinen, Henri, 'Unintended consequences of peace operations on Timor Leste from a gender perspective,' in Aoi, Chiyuki, de Coning, Cedric, Thakur, Ramesh (eds.), *Unintended Consequences of Peacekeeping Operations*, pp. 23–43: 37.
269. Japan Platform, *East Timor Humanitarian Assistance* (*Higashitimorujindōshien*), (http://www.japanplatform.org/programs/east-timor/ 1 Feb. 2018); JICA, *Understanding Japanese NGOs from Facts and Practices* (http://open_jicareport.jica.go.jp/pdf/11881265.pdf 12 Jan. 2018).

270. Marza, Vasile I., *On the Death Toll of the 1999 Izmit (Turkey) Major Earthquake*, European Seismological Commission (2004) (http://www.esc-web.org/papers/potsdam_2004/ss_1_marza.pdf, 17 Aug. 2010).
271. *Hand Book for Defense 2002* (*Bōeihandobukku heisei14nenban*), (Tokyo: Asagumoshinbunsha, 2002): 706.
272. JDA, *Defense of Japan 2000* (Tokyo: JDA/Urban Connections, 2000): 171.
273. Ibid.
274. *Hand Book for Defense 2002*: 690.
275. Ibid: 682; 'Saving East Timor: Nations in the region must take the lead,' *The Guardian* (3 Sept.1999): 19.
276. JDA, *Defense of Japan 2002*: 231.
277. Satō, Masahisa, 'From the Golan Heights to Iraq: a JGSDF Commander's Experience in the Middle East' (*Gorankōgenkara irakue shikikanno chūtōkeiken*), in Military History Society of Japan (ed.), *Peacekeeping Operations in Historical Perspective*, pp. 308–25: 320; Goulding, Marrack, *Peacemonger*: 41.
278. 'SDF may go to Golan: Mission', *Nikkei Shimbun* (20 Apr. 1995) (http://telecom21.nikkei.co.jp/nt21/service/ENGD021/ ENGD241?cid=NDJEDB1995042000101 036&madr=TOP&kdt=19950420&dk=eee016b6&reservedtp=ENGD025g6iqto y6&ftrmode=ENGD031&hltid=206chh4opa2e0, 10 Mar. 2010); Izumi, Nobumichi, 'Japanese troops should play full role in U.N. missions'; 'The practical terms of forceful cooperation' (*PKO sekkyokukyōryoku no yūgenjikkō wo*), *Yomiuri Shimbun* (1 Aug. 1994), (http://nippon.zaidan.info/seikabutsu/2002/01257/contents/346.htm, 1 May 2008).
279. *Hand Book for Defense 1999*: 659–660.
280. Heinrich, L. William, Jr. *et al*, *United Nations Peace-keeping Operations*: 82.
281. Satō, Masahisa, *Iraq JSDF 'Action Report'* (*Irakujieitai 'sentōki'*) (Tokyo: Kodansha, 2007).
282. Interview, Kawano, Hitoshi, NDA (June 2001).
283. *Golan: The UNDOF Journal*, 106: 14; *Moderne Alpinausrüstung für die höchste UN-Position der Welt*, Austrian Army, 2007 (http://www.bmlv.gv.at/ausle/undof/artikel.php?id=1815, 12 Aug. 2007); 'Listening to the Eastern Army GOC' (*Tōbuhōmensōkan ni kiku*), *Securitarian* (Apr. 1997): 6–10; *MOD UNDOF Data Index August 2009* (http://www.mod.go.jp/gsdf/crf/pa/overseas/undof/undofindex.html, 30 Aug. 2010).
284. Seki, Hajime, *et al*, *The Truth About PKO*: 108.
285. Kojima, Nobuyoshi, 'Self-Defense Force in the Middle East: An Observation by a Defense Attaché': 199–200; Rafferty, Kevin, 'Japan sharpens military role,' *The Guardian* (22 Dec. 1995): 11.
286. 'Austrian Golan PKO members shot dead on patrol' (*GoranPKO no ousutoriajintaiin, patorōruchū ni shasatsu*), *Asahi Shimbun* (31 May 1995): 3; Tortolani, Benjamin C. (ed.), *Annual Review of Global Peace Operations 2010*: 272.
287. MOFA, *UNDOF and Japan's Contribution*; Karube, Masakazu, 'UNDOF Round Table Discussion': 26.
288. *Golan: The UNDOF Journal* 100 (2004): 3.
289. Aizawa, Teruaki, 'Briefing Memo: Significance and Lessons of the Persian Gulf

Minesweeping Despatch' (*Buriifingumemo, perushawansōkaiteihaken noigito kyūkun*), *NIDS News* (Dec. 2014), (http://www.nids.mod.go.jp/publication/briefing/pdf/2014/briefing_193.pdf 12 Dec. 2016): 3

290. Philippi, Nina, 'Civilian Power and war: the German debate about out-of-area operations 1990–1999', in Harnisch, Sebastian, and Maull, Hanns W., (eds.), *Germany as a Civilian Power: The Foreign Policy of the Berlin Republic* (Manchester: Manchester University Press, 2001), pp. 49–67: 61.

291. 'SDF's rise in '90s behind Tamogami's challenge,' *Kyodo/The Japan Times* (28 Nov. 2008) (http://search.japantimes.co.jp/cgi-bin/nn20081128f1.html, 29 November 2008).

292. *JSDF Equipment Yearbook 1975 (Jieitaisōbinenkan1975)* (Tokyo: Asagumoshinbunsha, 1975): 203–5; *JSDF Equipment Yearbook 1997 (Jieitaisōbinenkan1997)* (Tokyo: Asagumoshinbunsha, 1997): 192, 242, *JSDF Equipment Yearbook 1993*: 170–3, 220–1.

293. IISS, *The Military Balance 1990–1991*: 59, 166, 170; *The Military Balance 1996–1997* (London: IISS/OUP, 1996): 191.

294. MOD, *ASDF Base Local Information (Kōkūjieitaikichishōzaichi)* (http://www.mod.go.jp/asdf/about/organization/shozaichi/, 10 May 2010).

295. *JSDF Equipment Yearbook 2004–2005*: 165–72; *Defense of Japan 2002*: 236–7; Interview, Yamaguchi, Noboru (Tokyo, Aug. 2007); Yamaguchi, Noboru, 'Evidence: 900 days of GSDF Iraq Dispatch' (*Kenshō, rikujōjieitai irakuhaken no900nichi*), *Close-up Gendai*, 2273, NHK (24 July 2006); *JSDF Equipment Yearbook 2004–2005 (Jieitaisōbinenkan2004–2005)* (Tokyo: Asagumoshinbunsha, 2004): 160.

296. *JSDF Equipment Yearbook 1998*: 556–68.

297. *JSDF Equipment Yearbook 2001*: 575; 'Up-Armored HUMVEE', *Defense Update*, 3, (2004) (http://www.defense-update.com/features/du-3-04/up-armored-humvee.htm, 8 Apr. 2008).

298. Fukuyama, Francis, 'The End of History?', *The National Interest*, No. 16 (Summer 1989), pp. 3–18; Huntington, Samuel P., *The Clash of Civilizations and the Remaking of World Order* (NY: Simon & Schuster, 1996).

299. Drifte, Reinhard, *Japan's Security Relations with China since 1989: From balancing to bandwagoning?* (Abingdon: RoutledgeCurzon, 2003): 29–30, 123.

300. JDA, Security Council Resolution, (19 Dec. 1990), *Defense of Japan 1992 (Bōeihakushoheisei4nen)* (http://www.clearing.mod.go.jp/hakusho_data/1992/w1992_9126.html 7 Jan. 2018).

301. CIA, *Soviet Amphibious Forces: Tasks and Capabilities in General War and Peacetime*, National Foreign Assessment Center, (Mar. 1979): 7–11.

302. JDA, *Defense of Japan 1992* (http://www.clearing.mod.go.jp/hakusho_data/1992/w1992_01.html 15 Mar. 2018); *Defense of Japan 1996* (http://www.clearing.mod.go.jp/hakusho_data/1996/102.htm 15 Mar. 2018).

303. MOFA, *Diplomatic Bluebook 1991* (http://www.mofa.go.jp/policy/other/bluebook/1991/1991–4–4.htm 19 Nov. 2017)

304. MOFA, 'Agreement Between the Government of Japan and the Government of the Russian Federation Concerning the Prevention of Incidents at Sea beyond the

Territorial Waters and Air Space Above Them', *Japan's Policy on the Russian Federation* (http://www.mofa.go.jp/region/europe/russia/russia_policy.html 24 Sept. 2017); *Tokyo Declaration on Japan-Russia Relations*, (13 Oct. 1993), (http://www.mofa.go.jp/region/n-america/us/q&a/declaration.html 24 Sept. 2017).

305. 'Japan warship sails to Russian parade', *UPI* (22 July 1996), (http://www.upi.com/Archives/1996/07/22/Japan-warship-sails-to-Russian-parade/4770838008000/?spt=su 24 Sept. 2017); '2 ASDF Pilots "Training" on Russian Jet Fighter'(*Roshiasentōki "kenshū" ni kūji2hikōshi*), *Asahi Shimbun* (24 Jan. 1998) morning edition: 3.

306. Ferguson, Joseph, *Japanese-Russian Relations, 1907–2007* (Abingdon: Routledge, 2008): 84.

307. *Press Conference by the Press Secretary 30 April 1996*, MOFA, (http://www.mofa.go.jp/announce/press/1996/4/430.html#3 22 Sept. 2017).

308. Ferguson, Joseph, *Japanese-Russian Relations*: 84–5; MOFA, *Press Conference by the Press Secretary April 17, 1998*, MOFA, http://www.mofa.go.jp/announce/press/1998/4/417.html#10

309. Togo, Kazuhiko, *The Inside Story of the Northern Territories Negotiations: Five Lost Opportunities for a Settlement* (*Hoppōryōdokōshōhiroku: ushinawaretagodo no kikai*) (Tokyo: Shinchōsha, 2007); Hasegawa, Tsuyoshi, 'Gorbachev's Visit to Japan and Soviet-Japanese Relations', *Acta Slavica Iaponica*, 10, (1992), pp. 65–91.

310. Rozman, Gilbert, *Japan's Response to the Gorbachev Era, 1985–1991: A Rising Superpower Views a Declining One* (Princeton, NJ.: Princeton University Press, 1992): 7.

311. Richardson, Paul B., *At the Edge of the Nation: The Southern Kurils and the Search for Russia's National Identity* (Honolulu, HA.: University of Hawai'I Press, 2020): 31, 37.

312. Ibid: 42–3; Togo, Kazuhiko, *The Inside Story of the Northern Territories Negotiations*; Sugiura, Masaaki, *A "Hell" for Putin is the Real Chance for the Russo-Japanese Territorial Talks*, CEAC Commentary, No. 98 (28 Apr. 2016), (http://www.ceac.jp/e/commentary/160428.pdf, 11 May 2016).

313. Conversations with three MSDF Officers (Tokyo, July 2008).

314. Sono, Akira and Yoshinari, Taishi, *Sono Akira's "World Situation Peepshow": Read the Reverse Side of 21-Gorbachev "Pliable Diplomacy"* (*Sonoakira no 'sekaijōseinozokimegane' 21gorubachofu 'jūnangaikō' no ura wo yome* (Tokyo: Bungeijunjū, 1985).

315. JDA, *Defense of Japan 1977* (*Nihon no bōei*): 144–7.

316. 'Soviet-era ship leaves Shenzhen', *Shenzhen Daily* (4 Apr. 2016), (http://www1.szdaily.com/content/2016-04/04/content_12991857.htm 22 Sept. 2017)

317. Mulvey, Stephen, 'Russia's rusting navy', *BBC News Online*, (23 Mar. 2004), (http://news.bbc.co.uk/2/hi/europe/880220.stm 12 July 2015).

318. Krupnick, Charles, *Decommissioned Russian Nuclear Submarines and International Cooperation*, (Jefferson, NC.: McFarland & Co., 2001): 20, 84–9.

319. Usui, Naoaki, 'Russian Radwaste Dumping in Sea of Japan Mars Bilateral Entente', *Nucleonics Week* (21 Oct. 1993): 4–5; Swinbanks, David, 'Japan To Study Damage From Russian Dumping', *Nature*, 365–28 (Oct. 1993): 777.

320. MOFA, *Japan's Assistance Programs for Russia* (Mar. 2001), (http://www.mofa.go.jp/region/europe/russia/assistance/index.html 4 Mar. 2016); Ilyukhov, Anatoly, 'Japan set to continue atomic submarine scrapping program', *RIA Novosti*, (11 July 2005) (http://sputniknews.com/world/20050711/40882906.html#ixzz3QOFyBfav 31 Jan. 2015)
321. Ferguson, Joseph, *Japanese-Russian Relations*: 87.
322. Ibid: 107, 229; MOFA, *Press Conference by the Press Secretary April 24, 1998*, (http://www.mofa.go.jp/announce/press/1998/4/424.html#6 12 Mar. 2017).
323. Jackson, Paul (ed.), *Jane's All the World's Aircraft 2000–2001* (Coulsdon, Surrey: Jane's Information Group, 2000): 446.
324. Michael Green asserts that several aircraft were purchased, but without evidence: Green, Michael J., *Japan's Reluctant Realism*: 315, note-41; 'Russia Test Flight, Confidential' (*Roshiakishijō, hikōkai*), *Asahi Shimbun* (30 Mar. 1998) morning edition: 1; '2 ASDF Pilots "Training" on Russian Jet Fighter,' *Asahi Shimbun* (24 Jan. 1998): 3; MOFA, *Press Conference by the Press Secretary 7 May 1996*, MOFA (http://www.mofa.go.jp/announce/press/1996/5/507.html 17 Oct. 2017).
325. Ferguson, Joseph, *Japanese-Russian Relations*: 86–7; MOFA, *Press Conference by the Press Secretary 14 May 1996*, (http://www.mofa.go.jp/announce/press/1996/5/514.html#1-b 17 Oct. 2017).
326. de Haas, Marcel, *The 'Peace Mission 2007' Exercises: The Shanghai Cooperation Organisation Advances*, Defence Academy of the United Kingdom (Sept. 2007), (https://www.files.ethz.ch/isn/92599/07_Sept_Peace.pdf 17 Oct. 2017): 6.
327. Ibid.
328. Hyōdō, Shinji, 'National Security Policy of the Russian Federation' (*Roshiano kokkaanzenhoshō seisaku*), *The Journal of International Security* (*Kokusaianzenhoshō*) (June 2011) 39–1, pp. 1–11: 6–7; Brown, James D. J., *Japan, Russia and their Territorial Dispute: The Northern Delusion*, (Abingdon: Routledge, 2017): 58.
329. Ibid; Azizian, Rouben, 'Japan's Relations with Russia: The Painful Search for a New Paradigm', in Sato, Yoichiro, and Limaye, Satu P., *Japan in a Dynamic Asia: Coping with the New Security Challenges* (Oxford: Lexington Books, 2006), pp. 157–78: 170.
330. Ferguson, Joseph, *Japanese-Russian Relations*: 141.
331. *Hand Book for Defense 1999*: 142–4; JDA, *Defense of Japan 1999* (http://www.clearing.mod.go.jp/hakusho_data/1999/honmon/frame/at1103010402.htm 13 Dec. 2017).
332. 'China, Russia Consult for Response to TMD' (*ChūroTMDtaiōkyōgi*), *Tokyo Shimbun* (12 Mar. 1999): 3.
333. Maeda, Tetsuo, *The Hidden Army*: 239–40.
334. Jameson, Sam, 'Japanese officials fear increase in drug use', *The Los Angeles Times*, in *The Stanford Daily*, 177–1, (4 Feb. 1980): 2 (http://stanforddailyarchive.com/cgi-bin/stanford?a=d&d=stanford19800204-01.2.12&e=———en-20—1—txt-txIN———18 May 2015).
335. 'MSDF lieutenant sentenced to 10-month term for spying', *The Japan Times* (8 Mar. 2001): 1–2.
336. 'Secret data on Chinese navy found at Hagisaki's home; Japan's intelligence-gather-

ing capability might have been exposed,' *Mainichi Shimbun* (30 Sept. 2000), Daily Summary of Japanese Press, American Embassy, Tokyo (3 Oct. 2000): 4.
337. Oka, Takashi, 'Spy scandal shakes Japan; US secrets lost?', *The Christian Science Monitor*, (21 Jan.1980) (http://www.csmonitor.com/1980/0121/012155.html 18 May 2015).
338. 'Ex-Russian Diplomat, at Center of SDF Info Leak, Releases Book on SDF', *Jiji Press*, (11 Dec. 2015) (http://jen.jiji.com/jc/eng?g=eco&k=2015121000941, 14 Dec. 2015).
339. Katō, Akio, *The Anatomy of Muneo Suzuki (Suzukimuneokenkyū)*) (Tokyo: Shinchōsha, 2002). Seemingly, most of the books written about Suzuki are self-authored.
340. Mulgan, Aurelia George, *Power and Pork: A Japanese Political Life* (Canberra: ANU E Press and Asia Pacific Press, 2006): 150–203.
341. Richardson, Paul Benjamin, 'Beyond the nation and into the state: identity, belonging, and the 'hyper-border,'' *Transactions of the Institute of British Geographers*, 41 (2016), pp. 201–15.
342. Ferguson, Joseph, *Japanese-Russian Relations*: 108–10, 161–3; Conversations with Togo Kuzuhiko.
343. MOFA, *Japan-Russia Action Plan* (http://www.mofa.go.jp/region/europe/russia/pmv0301/plan.html 12 Nov. 2017).
344. Richardson, Paul Benjamin, 'Beyond the nation and into the state': 210–1.
345. Ibid: 211; *Japan Military Review (Gujikenkyū)*, 46–5 (May 2011): 126–8; Putz, Catherine, 'Full speed ahead: Russia to accelerate construction in the Kurils', *The Diplomat* (9 June 2015) (http://thediplomat.com/2015/06/full-speed-ahead-russia-to-accelerate-construction-in-the-kurils/ 25 July 2015); Ryall, Julian *et al*, 'Russia deploys Bal and Bastion-P missile systems to disputed Kuril Islands, says report', *IHS Jane's Defence Weekly*, (23 Nov. 2016) (http://www.janes.com/article/65714/russia-deploys-bal-and-bastion-p-missile-systems-to-disputed-kuril-islands-says-report 26 Nov. 2016); 'Abe Says Russia's Missile Deployment Regrettable', *Jiji Press*, (25 Nov. 2016) (http://jen.jiji.com/jc/eng?g=eco&k=2016112500420 26 Nov. 2016).
346. Bodner, Matthew, 'Russia's Military Will Get Bigger and Better in 2015', *The Moscow Times*, (8 Dec. 2014), (http://www.themoscowtimes.com/business/article/russia-s-military-will-get-bigger-and-better-in-2015/512753.html, 27 Feb. 2015); Palmer, Diego A. Ruiz, *Theatre operations, high commands and large-scale exercises in Soviet and Russian military practice: insights and implications*, NATO Defense College Monograph Series-12 (Rome, 2018): 36; Richardson, Paul B., *At the Edge of the Nation*: 154–8.
347. 'Abe Stresses "Win-Win" Development of Isles Disputed with Russia', *Jiji Press* (22 Nov. 2016) (http://jen.jiji.com/jc/eng?g=eco&k=2016112200422, 22 Nov. 2016); Brown, James D. J., *Japan, Russia and their Territorial Dispute*: 60–1.
348. Eyal, Jonathan, 'Russian President Vladimir Putin imposes new conditions to normalise Moscow's relations with Tokyo', *RUSI Commentary*, (14 Nov. 2017) (https://rusi.org/commentary/japan%E2%80%93russia-another-fine-mess 19 Nov. 2017); Pinchuk, Denis, 'Putin links Japan peace treaty to Tokyo's alliances', *Reuters* (11 Nov. 2017) (https://www.reuters.com/article/us-apec-summit-russia-japan/putin-links-japan-peace-treaty-to-tokyos-alliances-idUSKBN1DB0BZ?il=0 19 Nov. 2017).

349. Taoka, Shunji, *The Japanese-American Security Treaty Without a U.S. Military Presence*, Japan Policy Research Institute, Working Paper No. 31 (Mar. 1997) (http://www.jpri.org/publications/workingpapers/wp31.html 12 Mar. 2017)
350. Taylor, Robert, *Greater China and Japan: Prospects for an Economic Partnership in East Asia* (Abingdon: Routledge, 1996): 178–88.
351. Dreyer, June Teuful, *Middle Kingdom & Empire of the Rising Sun* (New York: Oxford University Press, 2016): 95, 103–4.
352. MOFA, *Treaty of Peace and Friendship between Japan and the People's Republic of China* (12 Aug. 1978) (http://www.mofa.go.jp/region/asia-paci/china/treaty78.html, Article II 13 Dec.2017).
353. MOFA, 'Joint Communiqué of the Government of Japan and the Government of the People's Republic of China' (29 Sept. 1972), (http://www.mofa.go.jp/region/asia-paci/china/joint72.html 13 Dec.2017).
354. Dreyer, June Teuful, *Middle Kingdom & Empire of the Rising Sun*: 109; Drifte, Reinhard, *Japan's Security Relations with China since 1989: From balancing to bandwaggoning?* (Abingdon: RoutledgeCurzon, 2003): 24–5.
355. Buckley, Roger, 'Hong Kong and San Francisco: Anglo-American debate on East Asia and the Japanese peace settlements', *Japan Forum*, Vol. 15, No. 3 (2003), pp. 435–50; Ferretti, Valdo, 'In the shadow of the San Francisco peace settlement: Yoshida Shigeru's perception of Communist China and Anglo-American relations', *Japan Forum*, Vol. 15, No. 3 (2003): pp. 425–34; Green, Michael J., 'Japan, India, and the Strategic Triangle with China', in Tellis, Ashley J.; Tanner, Travis; Keough, Jessica (eds.), *Strategic Asia 2011–12: Asia responds to its Rising Powers China and India* (Seattle, WA: The National Bureau of Asian Research, 2011), pp. 131–60: 133.
356. NHK, 'Silk Road', *50 Years of NHK Television* (http://www.nhk.or.jp/digitalmuseum/nhk50years_en/history/p20/index.html 21 Feb. 2007).
357. Hosoya, Chihiro, 'From the Yoshida Letter to the Nixon Shock', in Iriye, Akira, and Cohen, Warren I. (eds.), *The United States and Japan in the Cold War World* (Lexington, KY.: The University Press of Kentucky, 1989), pp. 21–35.
358. Drifte, Reinhard, *Japan's Security Relations with China since 1989*: 25.
359. Pillsbury, Michael, *The Hundred Year Marathon: China's Secret Strategy to Replace America as the Global Superpower* (New York: St. Martin's Griffin, 2016): 72–3; Tyler, Patrick, *A Great Wall: Six Presidents and China: An Investigative History*, (New York: Public Affairs, 1999): 338.
360. '126. Memorandum From Alfred Jenkins of the National Security Council Staff to the President's Special Assistant (Rostow),' (18 June 1968), *FRUS 1964–1968, Vol. XXIX, Pt. 2, Japan* (https://history.state.gov/historicaldocuments/frus1964-68v29p2/d126 13 Mar. 2017); 'Chinese pilot has flown Harrier', *Flight International* (18 Nov. 1978), (https://www.flightglobal.com/pdfarchive/view/1978/1978%20-%202913.html?search=Harrier%20China 16 Mar. 2017); Albers, Martin, *Britain, France, West Germany and the People's Republic of China, 1969–1982: European Dimension of China's Great Transition* (London: Palgrave Macmillan, 2016): 161–2.
361. Drifte, Reinhard, *Japan's Security Relations with China since 1989*: 26.
362. Dreyer, June Teuful, *Middle Kingdom & Empire of the Rising Sun*: 179–80; Hattori,

Ryūji, *Diplomatic Document: History Recognition* (*Gaikōdokyumento rekishininshiki*) (Tokyo: Iwanamishinsho, 2015): 57–67.
363. Gries, P.H. *China's New Nationalism: Pride, Politics and Diplomacy*, (Berkeley, CA.: University of California Press, 2004): 79.
364. Kesavan, K. V., 'Japan and the Tiananmen Square Incident: Aspects of the Bilateral Relationship', *Asian Survey*, 30–7 (July 1990), pp. 669–81: 669.
365. Shambaugh, David, 'China and Japan towards the Twenty-First Century: Rivals for Pre-eminence or Complex Interdependence?', in Howe, Christopher (ed.), *China and Japan: History, Trends, and Prospects*, (Oxford: Oxford University Press, 1996), pp. 83–97: 86–7.
366. Ibid.
367. Cabinet Office, *Policy Speech by Prime Minister Hosokawa Morihiro to the 127th Session of the National Diet*, 23 August 1993, (http://japan.kantei.go.jp/127.html 22 June 2017); MOFA, *Statement by the Chief Cabinet Secretary Yohei Kono on the result of the study on the issue of "comfort women,"* MOFA, (4 Aug. 1993), (http://www.mofa.go.jp/policy/women/fund/state9308.html 22 June 2017); MOFA, *Statement by Prime Minister Tomiichi Murayama, On the occasion of the 50th anniversary of the war's end* (15 Aug. 1995) (http://www.mofa.go.jp/announce/press/pm/murayama/9508.html 22 June 2017).
368. Scobell, Andrew, *Show of Force: The PLA and the 1995–1996 Taiwan Strait Crisis*, (http://aparc.fsi.stanford.edu/sites/default/files/Scobell.pdf 27 Dec. 2017): 5.
369. Tyler, Patrick, *A Great Wall: Six Presidents and China: An Investigative History*, (New York: Public Affairs, 1999): 21–4.
370. O'Hanlon, Michael, 'Why China Cannot Conquer Taiwan', *International Security*, 25–2 (Fall, 2000), pp. 51–86: 53, 66.
371. Gold, Michael, 'Taiwan says China could launch successful invasion by 2020', *Reuters*, (9 Oct. 2013) (http://www.reuters.com/article/2013/10/09/us-taiwan-china-idUSBRE99809020131009 30 Dec. 2014).
372. Kang, David C., *China Rising: Peace, Power, and Order in East Asia* (New York: Columbia University Press, 2007): 83–90.
373. Pillsbury, Michael, *The Hundred Year Marathon*: 140, 229–33
374. Funabashi, Yoichi, *Alliance Adrift* (New York: Council on Foreign Relations Press, 1999): 394.
375. Ibid: 394–400; Drifte, Reinhard, *Japan's Security Relations with China since 1989*: 65–70.
376. 'Security Consultations and the Way of Studying Emergencies in the Far East', *Nikkei Shimbun* (10 Jan. 1982): 2, JPRS ID: 10293 Japan Report, FBIS, (https://www.cia.gov/library/readingroom/docs/CIA-RDP82-00850R000500030001-2.pdf 15 Apr. 2017).
377. Ibid; Drifte, Reinhard, 'Japan's Involvement in the Korean War': 120.
378. Schulze, Kai, 'Japan's new assertiveness: institutional change and Japan's securitization of China', *International Relations of the Asia-Pacific*, 18–2, (May 2018), pp. 221–247.
379. Soeya, Yoshihide, 'A 'Normal' Middle Power: Interpreting Changes in Japanese Security Policy in the 1990s and After', in Soeya, Yoshihide, Tadokoro, Masayuki,

Welch, David A., *Japan as a Normal Country?: A Nation in Search of Its Place in the World*, (Toronto: University of Toronto Press, 2011), pp. 72–97: 84–5.

380. MOFA, *Japan-U.S. Joint Declaration on Security-Alliance for the 21st Century* (17 Apr. 1996) (http://www.mofa.go.jp/region/n-america/us/security/security.html 17 May 2017).
381. Ross, Robert S., *Managing a Changing Relationship: China's Japan Policy in the 1990s*, Strategic Studies Institute, US Army War College (30 Sept. 1996):9.
382. *United States Security Strategy for the East Asia-Pacific Region*, (27 Feb. 1995), 'The World and Japan' Database (Tanaka, Akihiko) GRIPS, (http://worldjpn.grips.ac.jp/documents/texts/JPUS/19950227.O1E.html 19 Nov. 2017).
383. Advisory Group on Defense Issues, *The Modality of the Security and Defense Capability of Japan* (Higuchi Report) (12 Aug. 1994): 5–6, 11–8.
384. JDA/MOFA, *National Defense Program Outline in and after FY 1996* (Dec. 1995), (http://www.mofa.go.jp/policy/security/defense96/ 19 Dec 2017); *Hand Book for Defense 1999*: 118–27.
385. Drifte, Reinhard, *Japan's Security Relations with China since 1989*: 88–90; Hughes, Christopher W., *Japan's Economic Power and Security: Japan and North Korea*, (Abingdon: Routledge, 1999): 190–3.
386. *United States Security Strategy for the East Asia-Pacific Region*.
387. Johnson, Chalmers, *The Okinawan Rape Incident and the End of the Cold War in East Asia*, JPRI Working Paper No. 16 (Feb. 1996), (http://www.jpri.org/publications/workingpapers/wp16.html 27 June 2014).
388. Cronin, Patrick M., and Green, Michael J., *Redefining the U.S.-Japan Alliance: Tokyo's National Defense Program*, National Defense University, McNair Paper 31 (1994).
389. Sebata, Takao, *Japan's Defense Policy and Bureaucratic Politics, 1976–2007* (Lanham, MD.: University Press of America, 2010): 263, 270–1; Conversations with Watanabe Akio (2002–2005).
390. Yuzawa, Takeshi, *Japan's Security Policy and the ASEAN Regional Forum: The Search for Multilateral Security in The Asia-Pacific* (Abingdon: Routledge, 2007): 44–52.
391. *Hand Book for Defense 1999*: 138.
392. Ibid: 118–31.
393. Sebata, Takao, *Japan's Defense Policy and Bureaucratic Politics*: 266–9.
394. Campbell, John Creighton, 'Japanese Budget *Baransu*', in Vogel, Ezra, F. (ed.), *Modern Japanese Organization and Decision Making* (Berkley/Los Angeles: University of California, 1975), pp. 71–100: 81.
395. JDA, *Defense of Japan 2002* (Tokyo: Urban Connections/JDA, 2002): 101–3.
396. Conversation with author, Tokyo (Nov.-Dec. 2002).
397. Drifte, Reinhard, *Japan's Foreign Policy for the 21st Century: From Economic Superpower to What Power?* (New York: St. Martin's Press, 1998): 59.
398. MOD, *The Guidelines for Japan-U.S. Defense Cooperation*, (23 Sept. 1997), (http://www.mod.go.jp/e/d_act/anpo/pdf/19970923.pdf 12 May 2017): 6.
399. Drifte, Reinhard, *Japan's Security Relations with China since 1989*: 95–9; Funabashi, Yoichi, *Alliance Adrift*: 398–429.
400. Drifte, Reinhard, *Japan's Security Relations with China since 1989*: 99
401. Wu, Xinbo, *U.S. Security Policy in Asia: Implications for China-U.S. Relations*, CNAPS

working paper, Brookings Institution (Sept. 2000), (http://www.brook.edu/fp/cnaps/papers/2000_wu.htm#FN4_BACK 22 Feb. 2007).

402. *The United States and Japan: Advancing Toward a Mature Partnership*, INSS Special Report (11 Oct. 2000): 7.
403. Boese, Wade, 'Bush Approves Major Arms Deal To Taiwan, Defers Aegis Sale,' *Arms Control Today*, (1 May 2001) (https://www.armscontrol.org/act/2001_05/taiwan 27 Nov. 2017).
404. Ross, Robert S., *Managing a Changing Relationship: China's Japan Policy in the 1990s*, Strategic Studies Institute, US Army War College (30 Sept. 1996): 9.
405. Lewis, Jeffrey G., *The Minimum Means of Reprisal: China's Search for Security in the Nuclear Age*, (Cambridge, MA.: MIT Press, 2007): 1; Hiramatsu, Shigeo, China's Military Power (*Chūgoku no gunjiryoku*): 35–8.
406. Dreyer, June Teufl, *Middle Kingdom & Empire of the Rising Sun*: 192; MOFA, *Diplomatic Bluebook 1999* (http://www.mofa.go.jp/policy/other/bluebook/1999/I-b.html#1 16 Feb. 2018); 'Nuclear Weapons, Continuing Increase Decrease Trends, China Increases' (*Kakuheiki, sakugenkeikōsuzukuchūgoku wazōka*), *Nikkei Shimbun* (3 June 2013) (http://www.nikkei.com/article/DGXNASGM0300S_T00C13A6EB2000/ 30 Aug. 2015).
407. MOFA, *Recent Developments in China and Japan-China Relations* (Dec.1999) (http://www.mofa.go.jp/region/asia-paci/china/relations.html 12 Feb. 2018).
408. Drifte, Reinhard, 'The ending of Japan's ODA loan programme to China—All's well that ends well?', *Asia-Pacific Review*, (2006) 13:1, pp. 94–117; JICA, *Activities in China: List of On-going Technical Cooperation Projects*(https://www.jica.go.jp/china/english/activities/ongoing.html 10 Mar. 2018); Wang, Yizhou, *Creative Involvement: A New Direction in China's Diplomacy* (Abingdon: Routledge, 2017): vii.
409. Yuzawa, Takeshi, *Japan's Security Policy and the ASEAN Regional Forum*: 46.
410. Drifte, Reinhard, *Japan's Foreign Policy for the 21st Century*: 59; Lam, Peng Er, 'Japan and the Spratlys Dispute: Aspirations and Limitations', *Asian Survey*, 36–10, (Oct. 1996), pp. 995–1010.
411. Takahara, Akio, with Smith, Sheila A., Podcast-Episode 2: *The Competing Nationalisms of Japan and China*, Council on Foreign Relations, (4 Nov. 2017), (https://www.cfr.org/podcasts/episode-2-competing-nationalisms-japan-and-china 27 Feb. 2017).
412. Gao, Wanglai, 'China's Battle with Abandoned Chemical Weapons', *The RUSI Journal*, 162:4 (2017), 8–16.
413. ACWO, *Excavation and recovery operation in Beian City, Heilongjiang Province (Sep. 2000)*, Cabinet Office, (http://wwwa.cao.go.jp/acw/en/jigyobetsu/jigyobetsu_kaisyu1.html 12 Jan. 2018); ACWO, *Development of the ACW projects*, Cabinet Office, (http://wwwa.cao.go.jp/acw/en/keii/keii.html#sec1 12 Jan. 2018).
414. 'Another PCI scandal', *The Asahi Shimbun*, (19 Oct. 2007), (http://www.asahi.com/english/Herald-asahi/TKY200710190055.html 16 April 2008);
415. MOD, *Defense of Japan 2016* (http://www.mod.go.jp/e/publ/w_paper/pdf/2016/DOJ2016_3-2-4_web.pdf 17 Feb. 2018): 354.
416. JDA, *Defense of Japan 1999* (http://www.clearing.mod.go.jp/hakusho_data/1999/honmon/frame/at1103040302.htm 17 Feb. 2018).
417. 'Japan-China defense exchange program to resume,' *NHK* (6 Feb. 2018) (https://

www3.nhk.or.jp/nhkworld/en/news/20180206_01/ 10 Feb. 2018); *2019 Japan–China Field Officer Exchange Program organized by the Sasakawa Peace Foundation*, Sasakawa Peace Foundation (23 Apr. 2019) (https://www.spf.org/en/spfnews/press-release/20190423.html 29 Oct. 2019).
418. Kato, Hisanori, *China's Military Modernization and Japan-China Relations*, Institute for International Policy Studies, (June 1999).
419. 'Accidental Explosion or Maturity? The Future of China's Expanding Military Power: Capability and Intentions Analyzed by Former Senior Leaders of the Japan Self-Defense Forces' (*Bohatsuka seijukuka, gunkakuchūgoku no yukusue jieitaimotokanbu ga bunsekisuru 'noryoku' toito'*), *Chūokoron*, (Sept. 2013): 2837. (Translation, Japan Foreign Policy Forum, Sept. 2013); *NIDS China Security Report 2012* (Tokyo: NIDS, 2012): 13.
420. Murai, Tomohide, 'JSDF Overseas Despatch and Japan-China Relations' (*Jieitaino kaigaihaken to nicchūkankei*), *RIPS' Eye* (RIPS, Tokyo), 83 (4 Jan. 2008).
421. Suzuki, Shogo, 'Why Does China Participate in Intrusive Peacekeeping? Understanding Paternalistic Discourses on Development and Intervention', in Lanteigne, Marc, and Hirono, Miwa, China's Evolving Approach to Peacekeeping (Abingdon: Routledge, 2011), 29–44.
422. Lanteigne, Marc, and Hirono, Miwa, 'Introduction: China and UN Peacekeeping,' in Lanteigne, Marc, and Hirono, Miwa, *China's Evolving Approach to Peacekeeping*, 1–15: 8.
423. Ibid: 4–9.
424. de Haas, Marcel, *The 'Peace Mission 2007' Exercises*: 6; Hirono, Miwa, 'Impact of China's decision-making process on international cooperation: cases of peacekeeping and humanitarian assistance/disaster relief', *Australian Journal of International Affairs*, 74–1, (Feb. 2020), pp. 54–71.
425. Conversations with Hirono Miwa, Brisbane (July 2016), Singapore (July 2019).
426. Ross, Robert S., *Managing a Changing Relationship: China's Japan Policy in the 1990s*, Strategic Studies Institute, US Army War College (30 Sept. 1996): 3.
427. Kamachi, Noriko, 'Japanese writings on post-1945 Japan-China relations', in Lam, Peng Er, *Japan's Relations With China: Facing a Rising Power* (Abingdon: Routledge, 2006), 50–68: 61.
428. Hatano, Sumio, *State and History: Post-war Japan's History Issues* (*Kokka to rekishi: sengonihon no rekishimondai*), (Tokyo: Chūokōronshinsha, 2011).
429. Larimer, Tim, 'Rabble Rouser,' *Time Asia*, (24 Apr. 2000), 155–16 (http://cgi.cnn.com/ASIANOW/time/magazine/2000/0424/cover1.html 18 June2008).
430. McCormack, Gavan, 'Koizumi's Japan in Bush's World: After 9/11', PFO 04–46A (8 Nov. 2004), (http://www.nautilus.org/fora/security/0446A_McCormack.pdf 25 May 2008): 16.
431. Smith, Sheila A., *Intimate Rivals: Japanese Domestic Politics and a Rising China* (New York: Columbia University Press, 2015): 83–6.
432. UN, *China, at Security Council Meeting, Registers Strongest Possible Protest over Attacks Against its Embassy in Belgrade*, UNSC Press Release SC/6674/Rev.1* (8 May 1999) (http://www.un.org/press/en/1999/19990508.SC6674.R1.html 28 Nov. 2017); Sweeney, John; Holsoe, Jens; Vulliamy, Ed, 'Nato bombed Chinese deliberately: Nato

hit embassy on purpose', *The Guardian* (17 Oct. 1999) (https://www.theguardian.com/world/1999/oct/17/balkans 28 Nov. 2017).

433. Shambaugh, David, *Modernizing China's Military: Progress, Problems, and Prospects* (Berkeley, CA.: University of California Press, 2002): 4–6, 302.
434. Dreyer, June Teufel, 'The PLA and Kosovo: A Strategy Debate', in Marble, Andrew D. (ed.), *Special Issue: The China Threat Debate, Issues and Studies*, 36–1, (Jan./Feb. 2000): 4–5.
435. Ibid: 9.
436. Kan, Shirley A. (ed.), *China-U.S. Aircraft Collision Incident of April 2001: Assessments and Policy Implications*, CRS Report for Congress,(10 Oct. 2001), (https://fas.org/sgp/crs/row/RL30946.pdf 28 Nov. 2017): 34–6.
437. Faligot, Roger, Lehrer, Natasha (trans.), *Chinese Spies: From Chairman Mao to Xi Jinping* (London: Hurst & Co., 2019): 323, 334–5; 'No defense info leaked in Internet attack: MHI', *Kyodo/The Japan Times* (21 Sept. 2011) (http://search.japantimes.co.jp/cgi-bin/nn20110921a4.html 22 Sept. 2011).
438. Vosse, Wilhelm, 'Japan's Cyber Diplomacy', *EU Cyber Direct* (https://eucyberdirect.eu/wp-content/uploads/2019/10/vosse_rif_topublish.pdf 22 June 2020); MOD, *Defense of Japan 2017* (https://www.mod.go.jp/e/publ/w_paper/pdf/2017/DOJ2017_1-3-5_web.pdf 2 Feb. 2020); Patalano, Alessio, 'When strategy is 'hybrid' and not 'grey': reviewing Chinese military and constabulary coercion at sea', *The Pacific Review*, 31:6 (2019), pp. 811–39, Harris, Stuart, *China's Foreign Policy* (Cambridge, Polity, 2014): 109.
439. Drifte, Reinhard, *Japan's Security Relations with China since 1989*: 129; Lam, Peng Er, 'Japan's Deteriorating ties with China: The Koizumi Factor', *China: An International Journal* 3–2, (Sept. 2005), pp. 275–91.
440. Fukuda, Madoka, 'Japan's Koizumi years, a time of lost opportunities', *East Asia Forum*, (14 Oct. 2015) (http://www.eastasiaforum.org/2015/10/14/japans-koizumi-years-a-time-of-lost-opportunities/ 29 Nov. 2017); Kitazume, Takashi, 'Sino-Japan Policy Dialogue Held Hostage by Nationalistic Fervor', *The Japan Times*, (24 Dec. 2005), (http://www.brook.edu/views/interviews/fellows/huang20051224.htm 22nd February 2007).
441. Dreyer, June Teufel, 'The PLA and Kosovo': 9; Wang, Zheng, *Never Forget National Humiliation: Historical Memory in Chinese Politics and Foreign Relations* (New York: Columbia University Press, 2012).
442. Reilly, James, 'China's History Activists and the War of Resistance against Japan: History in the Making', *Asian Survey*, 44–2, pp. 276–94.
443. Smith, Sheila A., *Intimate Rivals*: 33.
444. Harris, Stuart, *China's Foreign Policy*: 84.
445. Takahara, Akio, *The Competing Nationalisms of Japan and China*.
446. Roy, Denny, *Return of the Dragon: Rising China and Regional Security*, (New York: Columbia University Press, 2013); Deng, Yong, *China's Struggle for Status: The Realignment of International Relations* (Cambridge: Cambridge University Press, 2008): 9.
447. Dittmer, Lowell and Kim, Samuel S., 'In Search of a Theory of National Identity', pp. 1–31; 'Wither China's Quest for National Identity?', pp. 237–90, in Dittmer,

Lowell and Kim, Samuel S. (eds.), *China's Quest for National Identity* (Ithaca: Cornell University Press, 1993); Pyle, Kenneth B., *Japan Rising*: 133–6.

448. Mearsheimer, John J., *The Tragedy of Great Power Politics* (New York: W. W. Norton, 2003): 3.

449. Buzan, Barry, 'China's rise in English school perspective', *International Relations of the Asia-Pacific*, Vol. 18, (2018), pp. 449–476: 462.

450. Allison, Graham, *Destined for War: Can America and China escape Thucydides' Trap?*, (London: Scribe, 2017); Steinberg, James and O'Hanlon, Michael E., *Strategic Reassurance and Resolve: U.S.-China Relations in the Twenty-First Century* (Princeton, NJ.: Princeton University Press, 2014).

451. Steinberg, James and O'Hanlon, Michael E., *Strategic Reassurance and Resolve: U.S.-China Relations in the Twenty-First Century* (Princeton, NJ.: Princeton University Press, 2014).

452. Mearsheimer, John J., *The Tragedy of Great Power Politics*: 83.

453. World Bank, *World Development Indicators* (http://databank.worldbank.org/data/reports.aspx?source=world-development-indicators 27 Feb. 2018); 'World Bank chief says China's poverty reduction effort is historic', *Xinhua* (13 Oct. 2017) (http://www.xinhuanet.com/english/2017–10/13/c_136675677.htm 27 Feb. 2018).

454. Wilson, Jeffrey D., 'The evolution of China's Asian Infrastructure Investment Bank: from a revisionist to status-seeking agenda', *International Relations of the Asia-Pacific*, Vol. 19, (2019), pp. 147–176; Breslin, Shaun, 'China and the global order: signalling threat or friendship?', *International Affairs*, 89–3, (2013), pp. 615–34.

455. '(Update) Japan's Aso Seeks "Bold" Reforms of ADB', *Jiji News*, (4 May 2015), (http://jen.jiji.com/jc/eng?g=eco&k=2015050400310 6 May 2015); Branigan, Tania, 'Support for China-led development bank grows despite US opposition', *The Guardian* (14 Mar. 2015), (http://www.theguardian.com/world/2015/mar/13/support-china-led-development-bank-grows-despite-us-opposition-australia-uk-new-zealand-asia 14 Mar. 2015).

456. Cai, Peter, *Understanding China's Belt and Road Initiative*, Lowy Institute (Mar. 2017) (https://www.lowyinstitute.org/sites/default/files/documents/Understanding%20China%E2%80%99s%20Belt%20and%20Road%20Initiative_WEB_1.pdf 12 Feb. 2018); Taneja, Kabir, 'A Game Changer for China and India in Sri Lanka?', *The Diplomat*, (25 Jan. 2015) (http://thediplomat.com/2015/01/a-game-changer-for-china-and-india-in-sri-lanka/ 6 Feb. 2015).

457. Khurana, Gurpreet S., 'China's 'String of Pearls' in the Indian Ocean and Its Security Implications', *Strategic Analysis*, 32:1(2008), pp. 1–39.

458. 'Japanese PM calls for 'arc of freedom' democratic alliance,' *Taipei Times* (23 Aug. 2007), (http://www.taipeitimes.com/News/front/archives/2007/08/23/2003375416 8 Nov. 2014).

459. Cai, Peter, *Understanding China's Belt and Road Initiative*.

460. *Military expenditure by country as percentage of gross domestic product, 1988–2016* SIPRI (2017), (https://www.sipri.org/sites/default/files/Milex-share-of-GDP.pdf 21 Feb. 2018); Gady, Franz-Stefan, 'China's Defense Budget to Increase 10 Percent in 2015', *The Diplomat*, (4 Mar 2015), (http://thediplomat.com/2015/03/chinas-defense-budget-to-increase-10-percent-in-2015/ 21 Feb. 2018).

461. See Mulloy, Garren, *Japan Self-Defense Forces' Overseas Dispatch Operations in the 1990s: Effective International Actors?*, Doctoral Thesis, University of Newcastle upon Tyne (2011): 55–6.
462. *China's National Defense in 2004* (27 Dec. 2004) (http://www.china.org.cn/e-white/20041227/ 23 Nov. 2017); Cordesman, Anthony H., *Estimates of Chinese Military Spending*, CSIS (21 Sept. 2016), (https://csis-prod.s3.amazonaws.com/s3fs-public/publication/160928_AHC_Estimates_Chinese_Military_Spending.pdf 17 Feb. 2018); Martina, Michael, and Blanchard, Ben, 'China confirms 7 percent increase in 2017 defense budget', *Reuters* (6 Mar. 2017), (https://www.reuters.com/article/us-china-parliament-defence/china-confirms-7-percent-increase-in-2017-defense-budget-idUSKBN16D0FF 6 Mar. 2017).
463. Cordesman, Anthony H., *Estimates of Chinese Military Spending*.
464. SIPRI, *Military expenditure by country, in constant (2015) US$ m., 1988–2016*, SIPRI (2017), (https://www.sipri.org/sites/default/files/Milex-constant-2015-USD.pdf 21 Feb. 2018); IISS, *The Military Balance, 2006–2015*.
465. DOD, *Annual Report to Congress: Military and Security Developments Involving the People's Republic of China 2016*, Office of the Secretary of Defense (RefID: 117FA69) (26 Apr. 2016): 77
466. Liff, Adam P. and Erickson, Andrew S., 'Demystifying China's Defence Spending: Less Mysterious in the Aggregate', *China Quarterly* (Mar. 2013), pp. 805–30: 806–7; Aizawa, Kōetsu, *Death of Chinese Economy by Military Power* (*Gunkjiryoku ga chūgokukeizaiwo kurosu*), (Tokyo: Kōdansha, 2014).
467. Kulacki, Gregory, *The Chinese Military Updates China's Nuclear Strategy* (Mar. 2015), Union of Concerned Scientists (Cambridge, MA.); Martina, Michael, and Blanchard, Ben, 'China confirms 7 percent increase in 2017 defense budget'.
468. Deng, Yong, *China's Struggle for Status*: 105, 109.
469. Matsuda, Yasuhiro, 'Japanese Assessments of China's Military Development,' *Asian Perspective*, 31–3 (2007), pp. 183–93: 187.
470. 'Chinese Military Aircraft Increase' (*Chūgokugunki gakyūzo*), *Asagumo News* (28 Apr. 2005), (http://www.asagumo-news.com/news.html 12 July 2007); Drifte, Reinhard, *Japan's Security Relations with China since 1989*: 53; Conversations with ASDF officers (Oct. 2016), MSDF officers (Feb. 2017), Tokyo; Roblin, Sebastien, 'China's New J-16D Aircraft Might Have a Terrifying New Military Capability', *The National Interest* (30 Nov. 2017) (http://nationalinterest.org/blog/the-buzz/chinas-new-j-16d-aircraft-might-have-terrifying-new-military-23427 12 Dec. 2017).
471. Conversation with USAF Major (Tokyo: Oct. 2017); 'J-20 stealth fighter's capabilities to be enhanced', *China Daily*, (13 Mar. 2018) (http://en.people.cn/n3/2018/0313/c90000–9436307.html 19 Mar. 2018).
472. *NIDS China Security Report 2016* (Tokyo: National Institute for Defense Studies, 2016): 26–35.
473. MOD, 'Statistics on scrambles through fiscal year 2016,' *Joint Staff Press Release* (13 Apr. 2017); 'Japan scrambled jets a record 1,168 times in FY 2016', *Mainichi Japan/Kyodo* (14 Apr. 2017) (https://mainichi.jp/english/articles/20170414/p2g/00m/0dm/027000c 14 Apr. 2017).
474. Reynolds, Isabel, 'Chasing Chinese Planes 400 Times a Year Is Wearing Out Japan's

Top Guns', *Bloomberg* (6 Mar. 2015) (http://www.bloomberg.com/news/articles/2015-03-05/chasing-chinese-planes-400-times-a-year-stretches-japan-top-guns 8 Mar. 2015).
475. 'Japan scrambled jets a record 1,168 times in FY 2016', *Mainichi Japan/Kyodo*.
476. Nagaiwa, Toshimichi, *A Technical Aspect of ADIZ*, AJISS-Commentary No. 190 (17 Jan. 2014); Huang, Zijuan 'Japan's provocative 'reconnaissance' in the East China Sea Air Defense Identification Zone,' *People's Daily Online*, (12 Aug. 2014), (http://en.people.cn/n/2014/0813/c98649–8768976.html
477. 'J-15 Aboard Carrier: Chinese news report, close to completion?', (*Kūbokansai-ki 'zen15' wo chūgokushihōdōkanseimajika*), *Sankei Shimbun/Kyodo* (27 Apr. 2011), (http://sankei.jp.msn.com/world/news/110210/chn11021023330005-n1.htm, 5 Apr. 2012).
478. Ohara, Bonji, 'Threat Assessment of China's Four Aircraft Carriers' (*Chūgokunokūbo 4sekitaisei wakyōika*), *Ships of the World* (*Sekainokansen*), 907 (Sept. 2019), pp. 110–3.
479. Tate, Andrew, 'PLAN commissions three more LSTs', *IHS Jane's Navy International* (13 Mar. 2016) (http://www.janes.com/article/58743/plan-commissions-three-more-lsts?utm_campaign=PC6110_E16%20DF%20NL%20Naval%2003_15_16&utm_medium=email&utm_source=Eloqua 16 Mar. 2016); Tate, Andrew, 'China launches fifth LPD for PLAN', *IHS Jane's Navy International* (16 June 2017), (http://www.janes.com/article/71491/china-launches-fifth-lpd-for-plan 30 June 2017); *NIDS China Security Report 2016*: 10; Newsham, Grant, and Collin, Koh Swee Lean, 'Can China Copy the U.S. Marine Corps?', *The National Interest* (29 Jan. 2016) (http://nationalinterest.org/feature/can-china-copy-the-us-marine-corps-1505 19 Feb. 2016).
480. McCabe, Thomas, R., 'Air and Space Power with Chinese Characteristics: China's Military Revolution', *Air and Space Power Journal*, 34–1 (Spring 2020), pp. 19–42:
481. Yoshihara, Toshi and Holmes, James R., *Red Star over the Pacific: China's Rise and the Challenge to U.S. Maritime Strategy* (Annapolis: Naval Institute Press, 2012): 30; Swaine, Michael D. *The Role of the Chinese Military in National Security Policymaking* (Santa Monica, CA.: RAND, 1998); Saunders, Phillip C., and Scobell, Andrew (eds.), *PLA Influence on China's National Security Policy* (Palo Alto, CA.: Stanford University Press, 2015).
482. Central Military Commission (CMC) (http://eng.mod.gov.cn/cmc/index.htm 12 Jan. 2018); Cliff, Roger, *China's Military Power: Assessing Current and Future Capabilities* (New York: Cambridge University Press, 2015): 12–4, 29–36.
483. *NIDS China Security Report 2016*: 11–3.
484. NIDS, *East Asian Strategic Review 2001* (Tokyo: NIDS, 2002): 199–203.
485. NIDS, *East Asian Strategic Review 2011* (Tokyo: The Japan Times, 2011): 122–4.
486. Clover, Charles, and Fei Ju, Sherry, 'Chinese military base takes shape in Djibouti', *The Financial Times* (12 July 2017) (https://www.ft.com/content/bcba2820–66e1–11e7–8526–7b38dcaef614 12 July 2017).
487. Miyoshi, Masahiro, 'The Submerged Passage of a Submarine Through the Territorial Sea: The incident of a Chinese atomic-powered submarine,' *Singapore Year Book of International Law* (2006), pp. 243–50: 244; Smith, Sheila A., *Japan Rearmed: The Politics of Military Power* (Cambridge, MA.: Harvard University Press, 2019): 113.

488. MOD, *Defense of Japan 2014* (http://www.clearing.mod.go.jp/hakusho_data/2014/html/n1132000.html 12 Jan. 2018); *NIDS China Security Report 2013* (Tokyo: National Institute for Defense Studies, 2014): 38–9.
489. 'China accuses Japan of falsifying information', *NHK News* (8 Feb. 2013) (http://www3.nhk.or.jp/daily/english/20130208_36.html, 8 Feb. 2013); 'Chinese officials admit to MSDF radar lock allegations', *Kyodo/Japan Times* (18 Mar. 2013) (http://www.japantimes.co.jp/news/2013/03/18/national/chinese-officials-admit-to-msdf-radar-lock-allegations/#.UUaDfTdlASk 18 Mar. 2013).
490. 'Japan, China Agree to Work for Early Start of Maritime Liaison Mechanism', *Jiji* (18 May 2015) (http://jen.jiji.com/jc/eng?g=eco&k=2015051800845, 24 May 2015).
491. MOFA, *Status of activities by Chinese government vessels and Chinese fishing vessels in waters surrounding the Senkaku Islands* (18 Aug. 2016).
492. Black, Lindsay, *Japan's Maritime Security Strategy: The Japan Coast Guard and Maritime Outlaws* (New York: Palgrave Macmillan, 2014).
493. Drifte, Reinhard, *Japan's Policy towards the South China Sea—Applying "Proactive Peace Diplomacy"?*, PRIF Report No. 140, Peace Research Institute Frankfurt (PRIF) (2016).
494. Schulze, Kai, 'Japan's new assertiveness': 224.
495. Hughes, Christopher W., *Japan's Economic Power and Security: Japan and North Korea* (Abbingdon: Routledge, 1999): 93.
496. Curtis, Gerald L., *The Logic of Japanese Politics: Leaders, Institutions, and the Limits of Change* (New York: Columbia University Press, 1999): 92–7.
497. Iokibe, Makoto, 'Japanese diplomacy after the Cold War', in Iokibe Makoto (ed.), *The Diplomatic History of Postwar Japan*, pp. 173–209: 177.
498. Martin, Bradley K., *Under the Loving Care of the Fatherly Leader: North Korea and the Kim Dynasty* (New York: St. Martin's Press, 2004): 439–42.
499. Ibid: 439–46.
500. *Engaging North Korea II: Evidence from the Clinton Administration*, National Security Archive, (https://nsarchive.gwu.edu/briefing-book/korea/2017-12-08/engaging-north-korea-ii-evidence-clinton-administration 22 Jan. 2018).
501. Hughes, Christopher W., *Japan's Economic Power and Security*: 93–5.
502. Ibid.
503. Carter, Ashton B., 'The Korean Nuclear Crisis: Preventing the truly dangerous spread of weapons of mass destruction', *The Harvard Magazine*, (Sept.-Oct. 2003), (http://harvardmagazine.com/2003/09/the-korean-nuclear-crisi.html 25 Sept. 2016); Michishita, Narushige, *North Korea's Military-Diplomatic Campaigns, 1966–2008* (Abingdon: Routledge, 2010): 93–5.
504. Ibid; Carter, Ashton B., 'The Korean Nuclear Crisis'.
505. McIntyre, Jamie, 'Washington was on brink of war with North Korea 5 years ago: Pentagon had predicted up to 1 million deaths', *CNN*, (4 Oct. 1999), (http://edition.cnn.com/US/9910/04/korea.brink/ 11 June 2014).
506. Michishita, Narushige, *North Korea's Military-Diplomatic Campaigns*: 93.
507. *Korean Peninsula Energy Development Organization (KEDO)*, Nuclear Threat

Initiative (http://www.nti.org/learn/treaties-and-regimes/korean-peninsula-energy-development-organization-kedo/ 27 Jan. 2018).
508. Michishita, Narushige, "Playing the Same Game: North Korea's Coercive Attempt at U.S. Reconciliation," *The Washington Quarterly*, 32:4 (Oct. 2009), pp. 139–152: 140.
509. JDA *Defense of Japan 1999* (http://www.clearing.mod.go.jp/hakusho_data/1999/honmon/frame/at1106020102.htm 12 Jan. 2018).
510. Taoka, Shunji, (Hasegawa, Kenji, trans.) 'Japanese Government Misinformation On North Korea's Rocket Launch', *The Asia-Pacific Journal: Japan Focus*, 14–8–1, (Apr. 2016).
511. Swenson-Wright, John, 'The Limits to 'Normalcy': Japanese-Korean Post-Cold War Ineractions', in Soeya, Yoshihide, Tadokoro, Masayuki, Welch, David A., *Japan as a Normal Country?*, pp. 146–92: 157.
512. Takahashi, Sugio, 'Emerging Missile Defence Issues', *NIDS News* (Aug.-Sept. 2007) 114, pp. 1–7: 1,4.
513. Michishita, Narushige, 'Playing the Same Game: North Korea's Coercive Attempt at U.S. Reconciliation', *The Washington Quarterly* (Oct. 2009), 32–4, pp. 139–52.
514. *Policies and Concrete Measures for Resolving the Abduction Issue*, Headquarters for the Abduction Issue (http://www.rachi.go.jp/en/shisei/taisaku/images/20130125honbukettei.en.pdf 22 Nov. 2017); MOFA, *Prime Minister Junichiro Koizumi's Visit to North Korea* (17 Sept. 2002) (http://www.mofa.go.jp/region/asia-paci/n_korea/pmv0209/index.html 29 Dec. 2017).
515. Nakata, Sachio, 'Japan's Shifting North Korean Policy under Koizumi Administration: Toward Responsive Engagement', *Ritsumeikan International Affairs* (2004) Vol. 2, pp. 141–57.
516. Cabinet Office, *Abductions of Japanese Citizens by North Korea*, Headquarters for the Abduction Issue (http://www.rachi.go.jp/en/ratimondai/jian.html 20 Dec. 2017).
517. Nakayama, Takashi, *Sea of Japan-Military Tension* (*Nihonkai, gunjikinchō*) (Tokyo: Chuōkoronshinsha, 2002): 5–8.
518. MLIT, *Japan Coast Guard Annual Report 2001* (*Kaijōhoanrepōto*), (http://www.kaiho.mlit.go.jp/info/books/report2001/chapter1/03.html 12 Nov. 2017); JDA, *Defence of Japan 1999* (http://www.clearing.mod.go.jp/hakusho_data/1999/honmon/frame/at110 6030000.htm 21 Dec. 2017); Nakayama, Takashi, *Sea of Japan-Military Tension*: 9–12.
519. Black, Lindsay, *Japan's Maritime Security Strategy*: 107–8; *The Police Duties Execution Act* (Act No. 136, 12 July 1948) (http://www.japaneselawtranslation.go.jp/law/detail/?id=2229&vm=04&re=02 12 Mar. 2018).
520. Black, Lindsay, *Japan's Maritime Security Strategy*: 104–9.
521. MOD, *Defense of Japan 2015*: 226.
522. Oros, Andrew L., *Normalizing Japan: Politics, Identity and the Evolution of Security Practice* (Palo Alto, CA.: Stanford University Press, 2008): 181.
523. NPA, North Korea's Espionage Operations in Japan, National Police Agency, February 2004 (http://www.npa.go.jp/keibi/kokutero1/english/0402.html 19 Oct. 2017).

524. Nakayama, Takashi, *Sea of Japan-Military Tension*: 12–7; Black, Lindsay, *Japan's Maritime Security Strategy*: 109–13.
525. JDA, *Defense of Japan 2002* (http://www.clearing.mod.go.jp/hakusho_data/2002/honmon/frame/at1403020104.htm 21 Dec. 2017).
526. MLIT, *Coast Guard Annual Report 2002* (http://www.kaiho.mlit.go.jp/info/books/report2002/special/01_01.html#4 17 Mar. 2017); Black, Lindsay, *Japan's Maritime Security Strategy*: 109–13.
527. Park, Seong-Yong, 'North Korea's military policy under the Kim Jong-un regime,' *Journal of Asian Public Policy*, 9:1 (2016), pp. 57–74; Raska, Michael, 'North Korea's evolving cyber warfare strategy', *East Asia Forum* (24 Sept. 2020) (https://www.eastasiaforum.org/2020/09/24/north-koreas-evolving-cyber-warfare-strategy/#more-301023 24 Sept. 2020).
528. 'N. Korea Apparently Fires Missile from Submarine', *Jiji Press* (23 Apr. 2016) (http://jen.jiji.com/jc/eng?g=eco&k=2016042300326, 24 Apr. 2016); McCurry, Justin, 'North Korea may have ability for miniaturised nuclear warhead, Japan says', *The Guardian*, (8 Aug. 2017) (https://www.theguardian.com/world/2017/aug/08/north-korea-nuclear-miniaturised-warhead-advanced-considerably-japan 8 Aug. 2017); 'North Korea likely fired submarine-launched ballistic missile: South Korea', *Kyodo News* (2 Oct. 2019), (https://english.kyodonews.net/news/2019/10/bbbc09310edc-breaking-news-n-korea-fires-unidentified-projectile-s-koreas-military.html 12 Feb. 2020); Masterson, Julia, 'North Korea Tests First Missiles of 2020', *Arms Control Association* (Apr. 2020) (https://www.armscontrol.org/act/2020-04/news/north-korea-tests-first-missiles-2020 11 May 2020).
529. Michishita, Narushige, "Playing the Same Game," *The Washington Quarterly*, October 2009.
530. Ryall, Julian, 'US & Japan vow action on 'growing direct' North Korea threat', *Deutsche Welle*, (9 Aug. 2017) (http://www.dw.com/en/north-koreas-nuclear-advances-raise-alarm-in-japan/a-40020768 10 Aug. 2017).
531. 'North Korea's Kim Jong Un says ICBM an Independence Day 'gift' to 'American b**tards': KCNA', *Straits Times/AFP*, (5 July 2017) (http://www.straitstimes.com/asia/east-asia/north-koreas-kim-jong-un-says-icbm-an-independence-day-gift-to-american-btards-kcna 8 July 2017); 'North Korean 'Hwasong-12' launch test confirmation announced' (*Kitachōsen 'kasei12gata' no hashakunren wo jisshishitahappyō*), *NHK*, (16 Sept. 2017) (http://www3.nhk.or.jp/news/html/20170916/k10011141791000.html?utm_int=all_side_ranking_social_003 16 Sept. 2017); 'N. Korea's missile could be advanced IRBM: defense minister', *Mainichi Japan*, (29 August 2017) (https://mainichi.jp/english/articles/20170829/p2a/00m/0na/018000c 29 August 2017).
532. 'Ministry seeks 730 mil. yen for land-based Aegis missile system', *Mainichi Japan/Kyodo*, (10 Dec. 2017) (https://mainichi.jp/english/articles/20171210/p2g/00m/0dm/039000c 10 Dec. 2017); MOD, *Defense of Japan 2018* (*Bōeihakusho heisei30nenban*) (2018) (http://www.clearing.mod.go.jp/hakusho_data/2018/html/nc020000.html 22 Jan. 2019).
533. 'Japan holds first civilian missile evacuation drill', *Mainichi Japan/AP*, (17 Mar. 2017) (http://mainichi.jp/english/articles/20170317/p2g/00m/0dm/072000c 17 Mar.

2017); Cabinet Secretariat, *Civil Protection Portal Site*, (http://www.kokuminhogo. go.jp/en/pc-index_e.html 12 Jan. 2018).

534. Drifte, Reinhard, *Japan's Security Relations with China since 1989*: 77.
535. Kotani, Tetsuo, 'The South China Sea Arbitration: No, It's Not a PCA Ruling,' *Maritime Issues* (17 Nov. 2016) (http://www.maritimeissues.com/south-china-sea-arbitration-ruling/the-south-china-sea-arbitration-no-its-not-a-pca-ruling.html 12 Sept. 2018).

4. DEFENDERS OF JAPAN PRESENT AND FUTURE

1. MOFA, *Japan is Back: Shinzo Abe, Prime Minister of Japan* (2013), (https://www.mofa.go.jp/announce/pm/abe/us_20130222en.html 22 Mar. 2017).
2. MOD, *Defense of Japan 2017* (Tokyo: MOD, 2017): 226, (http://www.mod.go.jp/e/publ/w_paper/pdf/2017/DOJ2017_2-2-1_web.pdf 7 Nov. 2017).
3. PMO, *National Defense Program Guidelines, FY 2005* (10 Dec. 2004), (http://japan.kantei.go.jp/policy/2004/1210taikou_e.html 12 Feb. 2015).
4. Oriki, Ryoichi, *Responsibility to Defend the Country: former top JSDF officer tells all* (*Kuniwo mamorusekinin, jieitaimotosaikōkanbu wakataru*) (Tokyo: PHPShinsho, 2015): 136–7; MOD, *GSDF Order No. 22* (*rikujōjieitai kunreidai22go*) (29 Mar. 2004) (http://www.clearing.mod.go.jp/kunrei_data/a_fd/2003/ax20040329_00022_000.pdf 12 Sept. 2018).
5. Yamaguchi, Noboru, 'Thoughts about the Japan-US Alliance after the Transformation. With a Focus on International Peace Cooperation Activities'. *NIDS News*, No. 96 (Jan. 2006) (http://www.nids.mod.go.jp/english/publication/briefing/pdf/2006/096.pdf 12 Oct. 2017); MOD, *Joint Staff, Organization* (http://www.mod.go.jp/js/e_organization.htm 12 Oct. 2017).
6. Oriki, Ryoichi, *Responsibility to Defend the Country*: 135–8.
7. PMO, *National Defense Program Guidelines, FY 2005*.
8. Ibid.
9. Fouse, David, 'Japan's FY 2005 National Defense Program 2005 National Defense Program Outline: New Concept Outline: New Concepts, Old Compromises', *Asia-Pacific Center for Security Studies*, 4–3, (Mar. 2005): 4 (http://apcss.org/Publications/APSSS/JapansFY2005NationalDefenseProgramOutline.pdf 27 Nov. 2017).
10. Ibid: 3.
11. Islands (*tōsho*) increased 5,000 to 6,800 (*shimajima*) 2002–2016: JDA, *Defense of Japan 2002*, (http://www.clearing.mod.go.jp/hakusho_data/2002/column/frame/ak143005.htm 12 Feb. 2017); *Defense of Japan 2016* (http://www.mod.go.jp/j/publication/wp/wp2016/html/n3121000.html 22 Feb. 2018).
12. JDA, *Defense of Japan 2006*, (http://www.clearing.mod.go.jp/hakusho_data/2006/2006/html/i62c2000.html 12 Feb. 2017); Fuentes, Gidget, 'Iron Fist 2017: Japan Under Time Crunch to Establish New Amphibious Unit', *USNI News* (28 Feb. 2017) (https://news.usni.org/2017/02/28/iron-fist-2017-japanese-forces-time-crunch-establish-new-amphibious-unit-camp-pendleton-calif-rough-seas-queasy-stomachs-tested-350-japanese-soldiers-command 12 June 2017).
13. JDA, *Defense of Japan 2006*: 100.

14. Tatsumi, Yuki, 'National Defense Program Outline: A New Security Policy Guideline or a Mere Wish List?', *Japan Watch*, CSIS (20 Dec. 2004).
15. Mulloy, Garren, 'A British Way in War and Peace: UK Post-Cold War Defence Reform' (*Igirisuryū sensotoheiwa*), *The Journal of International Security (Kokusaianzenhoshō)*, 29–3 (Dec. 2001), pp. 43–65.
16. Hughes, Christopher W., *Japan's Remilitarisation*, (Abingdon: Routledge/IISS, 2014): 41–2.
17. Conversations with JDA/MOD officials and JSDF personnel (2006–2010).
18. Lind, Jennifer M., 'Pacifism or Passing the Buck?: Testing Theories of Japanese Security Policy,' *International Security*, 29–1 (2004), pp. 92–121: 98.
19. Hughes, Christopher W., *Japan's Remilitarisation*: 42.
20. Hughes, Christopher W., *Japan's Foreign and Security Policy under the 'Abe Doctrine': New Dynamism or New Dead End?* (Basingstoke: Palgrave Macmillan, 2015): 33–4.
21. McCormack, Gavan, 'The Battle of Okinawa 2010: Japan-US Relations at a Crossroad', *The Asia-Pacific Journal*, 45–4–10, (8 Nov. 2010).
22. Cabinet Office, *Japan's Visions for Future Security and Defense Capabilities in the New Era: Toward a Peace-Creating Nation*, The Council on Security and Defense Capabilities in the New Era (Aug. 2010); MOD, *National Defense Program Guidelines, for FY 2011 and beyond: Approved by the Security Council and the Cabinet on December 17, 2010* (http://www.mod.go.jp/e/d_act/d_policy/pdf/guidelinesFY2011.pdf 22 Feb 2014).
23. 'Kitazawa: Review of Arms Ban May be on the Cards', *Asahi Shimbun*, (12 Oct. 2010) (http://www.asahi.com/english/TKY201010120151.html 21 Oct. 2010); Nippon Keidanren, *Proposal for the new National Defense Program Guidelines*, (20 July 2010) (http://www.keidanren.or.jp/en/policy/2010/067proposal.pdf 22 Feb 2016).
24. MOD, *National Defense Program Guidelines, for FY 2011 and beyond*: 4.
25. Ibid: 20.
26. Nagaiwa, Toshimichi, 'U.S. Defense Strategy vis-à-vis China's A2/AD: A Japanese Perspective' (*Beikokuno taichūgunjisenryaku to nihonnotaiō*), *Kokusaianzenhoshō* (*The Journal of International Security*), 41–1 (June. 2013), pp. 60–72: 66–9; Yagi, Naoto, 'Background of Air/Sea-Battle' (*Eashiibatoru nohaikei*), *Japan Maritime Self-Defense Force Command and Staff College Review* (*Kaikankōsenryakukenkyū*), 1–1, (May 2011): 4–22; Takahashi, Sugio, 'Counter A2/AD in Japan-U.S. Defense Cooperation: Toward 'Allied Air-Sea Battle'', *Futuregram* 12–03 (https://pdfs.semanticscholar.org/59e9/2dc4a8c4dfc0ba3faaba31b8ecebaf6c94ab.pdf 22 Feb. 2018); Friedberg, Aaron L., *Beyond Air-Sea Battle: The Debate Over US Military Strategy in Asia* (Abingdon: IISS/Routledge, 2014): 116–21.
27. Kazianis, Harry, 'China's Underwater A2/AD Strategy', *The Diplomat* (6 May 2014), (https://thediplomat.com/2014/05/chinas-underwater-a2ad-strategy/ 22 July 2015); 'Exploring China's Unmanned Ocean Network', *Asia Maritime Transparency Initiative*, CSIS, (16 June 2020) (https://amti.csis.org/exploring-chinas-unmanned-ocean-network/ 12 Sept. 2020).
28. Yoshida, Reiji, 'Taiwanese patrol ships join intrusion: Protest boat, escorts make Senkaku foray,' *The Japan Times* (17 June 2008) (http://search.japantimes.co.jp/cgi-bin/nn20080617a1.html 18 June 2008).
29. Hagström, Linus, ''Power Shift' in East Asia? A Critical Reappraisal of Narratives on

the Diaoyu/Senkaku Islands Incident in 2010', *The Chinese Journal of International Politics*, Vol. 5, (2012), pp. 267–297: 274.
30. MOFA, *Major Exchanges between Japan and the People's Republic of China concerning the Collision Incident between Japan Coast Guard Patrol Vessels and a Chinese Fishing Trawler in Japanese Territorial Waters off the Senkaku Islands* (Oct. 2010), (http://www.mofa.go.jp/region/asia-paci/china/r-relations/major_e.html 12 Dec. 2017); Choong, William, *The Ties that Divide: History, Honour and Territory in Sino-Japanese Relations*, Adelphi Series, 54:445 (Abingdon: Routledge/IISS, 2014): 77–8.
31. Tanaka, Hitoshi, 'The Senkaku Islands and Mending Japan–China Relations', *East Asia Insights*, (Nov. 2010) (http://www.jcie.org/researchpdfs/EAI/5-5.pdf 29 Feb. 2014): 2.
32. MOD, *National Defense Program Guidelines, for FY 2014 and beyond* (17 Dec. 2013).
33. Ibid; Waldron, Greg, 'Japan KC-46 acquisition moves forward', *Flight International*, (26 Dec. 2017) (https://www.flightglobal.com/news/articles/japan-kc-46-acquisition-moves-forward-444457/ 24 Feb. 2018).
34. MOD, *National Defense Program Guidelines, for FY 2014 and beyond*: 31.
35. Hirokawa, Seiji, 'Japan to halt AH-64D Apache orders after 13th airframe', *Flight International* (10 Sept. 2007) (https://www.flightglobal.com/news/articles/japan-to-halt-ah-64d-apache-orders-after-13th-airframe-216559/ 12 Dec. 2017); Grevatt, Jon, 'Japan not currently considering more Apaches', *IHS Jane's Defence Weekly* (5 Feb. 2015) (http://www.janes.com/article/48735/japan-not-currently-considering-more-apaches, 9 Feb. 2015).
36. MOD, *Defense of Japan 2016* (http://www.clearing.mod.go.jp/hakusho_data/2016/pdf/28knmt04.pdf 22 Dec. 2017); *JSDF Equipment Yearbook, 2016–2017*, (Tokyo: Asagumoshinbunsha, 2016): 38–44, 505.
37. MOD, *Defense Programs and Budget of Japan: Overview of FY2016 Budget Request* (Tokyo: MOD, 2015): 8; MOD, *Defense of Japan 2016* (http://www.clearing.mod.go.jp/hakusho_data/2016/html/ns042000.html 12 Dec. 2017) and (http://www.clearing.mod.go.jp/hakusho_data/2016/html/nc006000.html 22 Dec. 2017); 'Japan Defense Ministry to deploy Osprey aircraft to Chiba Pref. base', *Mainichi Japan* (27 Mar. 2018) (https://mainichi.jp/english/articles/20180327/p2a/00m/0na/015000c 27 Mar. 2018).
38. McCormack, Madura, and Viellaris, Renee, 'US Osprey may have smashed into ship during landing off central Queensland', *The Courier-Mail* (7 Aug. 2017) (http://www.news.com.au/national/queensland/us-osprey-may-have-smashed-into-ship-during-landing-off-central-queensland/news-story/c5dc96472d04fcee4763ed12f5bbd3fc 26 Feb. 2018); 'US military head in Okinawa sees no need to refrain from Osprey flights', *Mainichi Japan* (8 Aug. 2017) (https://mainichi.jp/english/articles/20170808/p2g/00m/0dm/065000c 26 Feb. 2018).
39. 'No end to US military aircraft accidents', *NHK News* (6 Jan. 2018) (https://www3.nhk.or.jp/nhkworld/en/news/20180106_23/ 8 Jan. 2018).
40. MOD, *National Defense Program Guidelines, for FY 2014 and beyond*: 3–4.
41. Ibid: 3.
42. Schoff, James L., Romei, Sayuri (eds.), *The New National Defense Program Guidelines:*

Aligning U.S. and Japanese Defense Strategies for the Third Post-Cold War Era, Sasakawa Peace Foundation (2019), (https://spfusa.org/programs/japans-new-ndpg/ 17 Jan. 2020); Conversation with member (Aug. 2020).
43. MOD, *National Defense Program Guidelines for FY 2019 and beyond* (18 Dec. 2018): 10, (https://www.mod.go.jp/j/approach/agenda/guideline/2019/pdf/20181218_e.pdf 22 Feb. 2019); Conversation with member (Aug. 2020).
44. MOD, *Medium Term Defense Program (FY 2019-FY 2023)* (18 Dec. 2018), (https://www.mod.go.jp/j/approach/agenda/guideline/2019/pdf/chuki_seibi31-35_e.pdf 22 Feb. 2019).
45. Ibid: Aoi, Chiyuki, 'Japanese Strategic Communication: Its Significance as a Political Tool', *Defence Strategic Communications*, NATO Strategic Communications Centre of Excellence, Vol. 3 (Autumn 2017), pp. 69–98.
46. MOD, *National Defense Program Guidelines for FY 2019 and beyond* (18 Dec. 2018): 8.
47. MOD, *Medium Term Defense Program (FY 2019-FY 2023)*: 36.
48. 'Abe Hints at Possible Study on Enemy Base Attack Capability', *Jiji Press* (22 Nov. 2017) (https://jen.jiji.com/jc/eng?g=eco&k=2017112201197 28 Nov. 2017); 'Pre-emptive first strike on enemy missile base constitutional: Japan defense minister,' *Mainichi Japan* (9 July 2020) (https://mainichi.jp/english/articles/20200709/p2a/00m/0na/001000c 10 July 2020).
49. Sieg, Linda, 'Japan to acquire air-launched missiles able to strike North Korea', *Reuters* (8 Dec. 2017) (https://www.reuters.com/article/us-northkorea-missiles-japan/japan-to-acquire-air-launched-missiles-able-to-strike-north-korea-idUSKBN1E20YR 10 Dec. 2017).
50. Ibid; 'SDF to equip fighter jets with standoff missiles', *NHK News* (8 Dec. 2017) (https://www3.nhk.or.jp/nhkworld/en/news/20171208_22/ 10 Dec. 2017).
51. Shimoyachi, Nao, 'Japan Mulled Buying Cruise Missiles for Pre-emptive Self-Defense: Ishiba,' *The Japan Times*, (25 Jan. 2005), (http://www.japantimes.co.jp/news/2005/01/25/national/japan-mulled-buying-cruise-missiles-for-pre-emptive-self-defense-ishiba/#.WYjiE02Wzct 22 Feb. 2012).
52. 'Japan eyes budget for long-range cruise missiles amid N. Korea threat', *Kyodo/Mainichi Japan* (6 Dec. 2017) (https://mainichi.jp/english/articles/20171206/p2g/00m/0dm/024000c 7 Dec. 2017).
53. MOD, *Press Conference by Defense Minister Onodera* (8 Dec. 2017), (http://www.mod.go.jp/e/press/conference/2017/12/08.html 12 Feb. 2018).
54. 'Justification shaky for Japanese government's cruise missile plans', *Mainichi Japan*, (22 Dec. 2017) (https://mainichi.jp/english/articles/20171222/p2a/00m/0na/021000c#cxrecs_s 24 Dec. 2017).
55. Cabinet Committee, House of Representatives, 24th Diet session, (Statement of Hatoyama Ichirō by Foreign Minister Funada, Naka) (29 Feb.1956) (http://kokkai.ndl.go.jp/SENTAKU/syugiin/024/0388/02402290388015a.html 24 Sept. 2017).
56. Budget Committee, House of Representatives, 156th Diet (Minister of Defense Ishiba Shigeru) (24 Jan. 2003), (http://kokkai.ndl.go.jp/SENTAKU/syugiin/156/0018/15601240018004a.html 24 Sept. 2017).
57. Takahashi, Sugio, 'Dealing with the Ballistic Missile Threat: Whether Japan Should Have a Strike Capability under its Exclusively Defense-Oriented Policy,' *NIDS Security*

Studies, 8–1 (Apr. 2006) (http://www.nids.mod.go.jp/english/publication/kiyo/pdf/bulletin_e2006_4_takahashi.pdf 23 July 2017).
58. MOFA, *Press Conference by the Press Secretary: Deputy Press Secretary Masaki Okada* (5 Mar. 1999) (http://www.mofa.go.jp/announce/press/1999/3/305.html#5 28 Sept. 2017).
59. MOD, *National Defense Program Guidelines, for FY 2014 and beyond*: 20.
60. Security Committee, House of Representatives, 145th Diet (1999) (Moriya Takemasa, 9 Feb. 1999), (http://kokkai.ndl.go.jp/SENTAKU/syugiin/145/0015/14502090015002a.html 24 Sept. 2017).
61. 'Justification shaky for Japanese government's cruise missile plans', *Mainichi Japan*.
62. Ishiba, Shigeru, *LDP Presidential Candidate*, The Foreign Correspondents' Club of Japan, (11 Sept. 2020) (http://www.fccj.or.jp/news-and-views/club-news-multi-media/2257-shigeru-ishiba-member-of-house-of-representatives-ldp-ldp-presidential-candidate-september-11-2020.html 11 Sept. 2020).
63. Miyake, Kunihiko, *Another Debate on Constitutionality*, Canon Institute for Global Studies, (10 July 2015), (http://www.canon-igs.org/en/column/security/20150710_3195.html 23 July 2016).
64. E-Gov., *Armed attack contingency law* (*Buryokukōgekijitai taishokanrenhō*) (6 June 2003), (https://elaws.e-gov.go.jp/search/elawsSearch/elaws_search/lsg0500/detail?lawId=415AC0000000079 17 Apr. 2017).
65. 'Cabinet Legislation Bureau chief defends self over process of reinterpreting Article 9', *Mainichi Shimbun*, (17 Mar. 2016) (http://mainichi.jp/english/articles/20160317/p2a/00m/0na/014000c 18 Mar. 2016).
66. 'Abe's security panel moves toward weakening Constitution', *Akahata* editorial, (10 Feb. 2013), (http://www.japan-press.co.jp/modules/news/index.php?id=5086 10 Feb. 2013).
67. The Advisory Panel on Reconstruction of the Legal Basis for Security, *Report of the Advisory Panel on Reconstruction of the Legal Basis for Security*, (15 May 2014).
68. 'Discussion of Issues Concerning the Right of Collective Self-Defence', Panel, *JAIS 2014 Conference*, (7 Dec. 2014), Kokushikan University, Tokyo.
69. The Act on the Protection of Specially Designated Secrets (SDS Act) (Act No. 108 of 2013); Cabinet Office, *Overview of the Act on the Protection of Specially Designated Secrets (SDS)*, Cabinet Secretariat, Cabinet Intelligence and Research Office (http://www.cas.go.jp/jp/tokuteihimitsu/gaiyou_en.pdf 12 Nov. 2017).
70. 'Cabinet Secretariat kept Board of Audit out of the loop on special state secrets', *Mainichi Japan*, (3 May 2016) (http://mainichi.jp/english/articles/20160503/p2a/00m/0na/007000c 4 May 2016); 'Former-GSDF Officer Information Leak' (*Rikujimotokanbu jōhōrōei*), *Sankei Shimbun*, (4 Dec. 2015) (https://www.sankei.com/affairs/news/151204/afr1512040047-n1.html 21 July 2016).
71. Cabinet Office, *National Security Strategy* (17 Dec. 2013), (https://www.cas.go.jp/jp/siryou/131217anzenhoshou/nss-e.pdf 12 Feb. 2014).
72. Sunohara, Tsuyoshi, *What is Japan's Version of the NSC?* (*NihonbanNSC towananika*), (Tokyo: Shinchōsha, 2014): 155–66.
73. *Hand Book for Defense 2017* (*Bōeihandobukku heisei29nenban*) (Tokyo: Asagumo-shinbunsha, 2017): 26.

74. Stockwin, JAA., "Continuity and Change in Japanese Foreign Policy," pp. 123–138, in Large, Stephen S. (ed.) *Shōwa Japan—Political, economic and social history 1926–1989: Volume III 1952–1973* (London: Routledge, 1998): 132.
75. MOD, *Joint Statement of the Security Consultative Committee: Toward a More Robust Alliance and Greater Shared Responsibilities* (3 Oct. 2013) (http://www.mod.go.jp/j/approach/anpo/pdf/js20131003_e.pdf 25 June 2016).
76. MOD, *The Guidelines for Japan-U.S. Defense Cooperation*, (27 Apr. 2015), (http://www.mod.go.jp/e/d_act/anpo/pdf/shishin_20150427e.pdf 25 June 2016).
77. Ibid.
78. 'Abe pledges to prepare security legislation', *NHK News*, (26 Oct. 2014), (http://www3.nhk.or.jp/nhkworld/english/news/20141026_15.html, 26 Oct. 2014).
79. 'Abe: Japan should join mine-sweeping', *NHK News*, (3 Mar. 2015), (http://www3.nhk.or.jp/nhkworld/english/news/20150303_22.html, 3 Mar. 2015); Lies, Elaine, 'Japan should consider military undertaking overseas rescues: PM', *Reuters*, (1 Feb. 2015) (http://www.reuters.com/article/2015/02/02/us-mideast-crisis-japan-military-idUSKBN0L602C20150202 12 Feb. 2015).
80. JDA, *Defense of Japan 2004: 50ᵗʰ Anniversary* (*Bōeihakushoheisei16nen*) (Tokyo: JDA, 2004): 148–9; *Act on Measures to Secure Peace and Security in Japan in Periphery Situations*, (*Shūhenjitai nisaishite wagakuni noheiwa oyobianzen wo kakuhosurutame nosochi ni kansuruhōritsu*), House of Representatives, (26 May 1999) (http://www.shugiin.go.jp/internet/itdb_housei.nsf/html/housei/h145060.htm 12 June 2015).
81. Harris, Tobias S., *The Iconoclast: Shinzo Abe and the New Japan* (London: Hurst & Co., 2020); Smith, Sheila A., and Takahara, Akio, 'Episode 2: The Competing Nationalisms of Japan and China', Podcast: *Northeast Asian Nationalisms and the U.S.-Japan Alliance*, Council on Foreign Relations (4 Nov. 2017), (https://www.cfr.org/podcasts/episode-2-competing-nationalisms-japan-and-china 6 Mar. 2018).
82. Smith, Sheila A., and Soeya, Yoshihide, 'Episode 3: The Divide Between Japan and South Korea', Podcast: *Northeast Asian Nationalisms and the U.S.-Japan Alliance*, Council on Foreign Relations (https://www.cfr.org/podcasts/episode-3-divide-between-japan-and-south-korea 6 Mar. 2018).
83. Rozman, Gilbert, 'Unanswered Questions about Japan-Russia Relations in 2017', *Asia-Pacific Review*, 24:1 (2017), pp. 74–94; Walker, Joshua W., and Azuma, Hidetoshi, 'Abe and Putin Make Peace: Why Japan and Russia Are Working Together', *Foreign Affairs*, (15 Sept. 2016) (https://www.foreignaffairs.com/articles/japan/2016-09-15/abe-and-putin-make-peace, 12 Nov. 2017).
84. 'Abe's desire to inherit grandfather's legacy lies behind railroading of security bills', *Mainichi Japan*, (19 Sept. 2015) (http://mainichi.jp/english/english/perspectives/news/20150919p2a00m0na012000c.html 22 Sept. 2015).
85. Conversation, Tokyo (June 2016).
86. Cabinet Office, *Outline of Peace Security Legislation* (*Heiwaanzenhōsei no gaiyo*), Cabinet Secretariat/Cabinet Office/Ministry of Foreign Affairs/Ministry of Defence (2015): 13.
87. Cabinet Office, *'Japan's Legislation for Peace and Security', and Outline: Seamless Responses for Peace and Security of Japan and the International Community* ('*Heiwaanzenhoshōhōsei' nogaiyō: wagakuni oyobikokusaishakai noheiwa oyobianzen*

notame nokireme nonaitaisei noseibi) (May 2015). The Japanese version has eighteen pages, the English version eight.
88. Author's experience, Sapporo (10 Oct. 2015).
89. Nishihara, Masashi, 'Debates on National Security Should Rule Out One-nation Pacifism', *Discuss Japan-Japan Foreign Policy Forum*, No. 27 (2015).
90. 'Young protesters against security laws, support SDF deployment to save Japanese: survey', *Mainichi Japan*, (3 Apr. 2016) (http://mainichi.jp/english/articles/20160403/p2a/00m/0na/013000c 4 Apr. 2016); SEALDs (http://www.sealds.com/ 24 Nov. 2015); OLDs (*Otoshiyori* for Liberal Democracy) (https://www.facebook.com/groups/1473622819616176/permalink/1474289316216193/?__mref=message_bubble 24 Nov. 2015); Mothers Against WAR (*Anpokanrenho taiosuru mamanokai*) (http://mothers-no-war.colorballoons.net/mothers-no-war/ 24 Nov. 2015).
91. 'Mothers Against War circulation of Senior Network poster campaign' (https://www.facebook.com/mothersagainstwareng/photos/a.810418715737983.1073741828.809986525781202/837003723079482/?type=1&theater 15 Apr. 2016).
92. 'All three experts decry security bills as unconstitutional at Diet panel', *Mainichi Japan*, (5 June 2015) (http://mainichi.jp/english/english/newsselect/news/20150605p2a00m0na005000c.html 5 June 2015); Miyake, Kunihiko, 'Another Debate on Constitutionality', *JBpress/Canon Institute for Global Studies* (29 June 2015) (http://www.canon-igs.org/en/column/security/20150710_3195.html 12 July 2015).
93. Inoue, Tatsuo, *What's Liberalism? What's the Philosophy of Law?* (2016) (https://www.u-tokyo.ac.jp/en/whyutokyo/science_17_2.html 11 July 2020).
94. '1st joint Japan-US drill based on security laws', *NHK News* (7 Nov. 2016) (http://www3.nhk.or.jp/nhkworld/en/news/20161107_35/ 7 Nov. 2016); 'Japan SDF Personnel Nervous about Arms Use under New Laws', *Jiji Press*, (4 Apr. 2016) (http://jen.jiji.com/jc/eng?g=eco&k=2016040101025 Apr. 2016).
95. Author interviewed, *BBC World* (1 May 2017); 'Izumo helicopter carrier's escort mission more symbolic than practical', *Mainichi Japan*, (2 May 2017), (http://mainichi.jp/english/articles/20170502/p2a/00m/0na/018000c 2 May 2017).
96. MOD, *Defense of Japan 2020* (*Bōeihakusho reiwa2nensaku*) (Tokyo: MOD, 2020): 26.
97. MOD, *Japan's Defense Capacity Building Assistance* (2016) (https://www.mofa.go.jp/files/000146830.pdf 21 May 2018).
98. Wilkins, Thomas S., 'From Strategic Partnership to Strategic Alliance? Australia-Japan Security Ties and the Asia-Pacific', *Asia Policy*, No. 20 (July 2015), pp. 81–111: 82.
99. MOFA, *Australia and Japan-Cooperating for peace and stability Common Vision and Objectives*, (https://www.mofa.go.jp/files/000034392.pdf 22 July 2018); *Remarks By Prime Minister Abe to the Australian Parliament* (8 July 2014) (https://japan.kantei.go.jp/96_abe/statement/201407/0708article1.html 25 June 2015).
100. Greene, Andrew, 'Australian warships challenged by Chinese military in South China Sea', *ABC* (20 Apr. 2018) (http://www.abc.net.au/news/2018-04-20/south-china-sea-australian-warships-challenged-by-chinese/9677908 21 Apr. 2018); Kassam, Natasha, 'Great expectations: The unraveling of the Australia-China relationship',

Brookings (20 July 2020) (https://www.brookings.edu/articles/great-expectations-the-unraveling-of-the-australia-china-relationship/ 12 Sept. 2020).

101. MOD, 'Japan-Australia Cooperation in South Sudan-Interview with Australian Liaison Officers', *Japan Defense Focus*, No. 63 (Apr. 2015) (https://www.mod.go.jp/e/jdf/sp/no63/sp_specialfeature.html 5 Aug. 2015).

102. Department of the Prime Minister and Cabinet, *Strong and Secure: A Strategy for Australia's National Security* (Jan. 2013) (https://www.files.ethz.ch/isn/167267/Australia%20A%20Strategy%20for%20National%20Securit.pdf 22 June 2015); MOFA, *Signing of the Agreement between the Government of Japan and the Government of Australia concerning the Transfer of Defence Equipment and Technology* (8 July 2014) (http://www.mofa.go.jp/press/release/press4e_000349.html 25 June 2015); *Agreement between the Government of Australia and the Government of Japan concerning Reciprocal Provision of Supplies and Services between the Australian Defence Force and the Self-Defense Forces of Japan* (14 Jan. 2017), (https://www.aph.gov.au/Parliamentary_Business/Committees/Joint/Treaties/SingaporeFTA-Amendment/Report_172/section?id=committees%2Freportjnt%2F024074%2F24690 9 Oct. 2018).

103. Bosack, Michael MacArthur, 'Slowly Blazing the Trail with the Australia-Japan Reciprocal Access Agreement', *The Diplomat*, (10 Apr. 2019) (https://thediplomat.com/2019/04/slowly-blazing-the-trail-with-the-australia-japan-reciprocal-access-agreement/ 23 Sept. 2020); The Prime Minister of Australia, *Media Statement* (17 Nov. 2020)(https://www.pm.gov.au/media/reciprocal-access-agreement 19 Nov. 2020).

104. Ishihara, Yusuke, 'Japan-Australia Defence Cooperation in the Asia-Pacific Region', *NIDS* (2014), (http://www.nids.mod.go.jp/english/publication/joint_research/series10/pdf/06.pdf 7 Aug. 2017): 98–100; MOFA, *Entry into Force of the Japan-Australia Information Security Agreement (ISA)* (22 Mar. 2013) (https://www.mofa.go.jp/press/release/press6e_000011.html 5 Aug. 2017).

105. Pant, Harsh V., 'India, Japan, Australia, and the US: The Return of Asia's 'Quad,'' *The Diplomat*, (28 Apr. 2017) (https://thediplomat.com/2017/04/india-japan-australia-and-the-us-the-return-of-asias-quad/ 12 July 2017); 'Chinese spy ship shadows US, Japanese, Indian naval drill in the Western Pacific', *Reuters*, (15 Jun 2016) (http://hawaiipublicradio.org/post/pacific-news-minute-chinese-vessels-shadow-us-japan-and-india-naval-exercise-okinawa, 16 Jun 2016).

106. Mulloy, Garren, 'Japan, Asian, and Global broader peace operations: functional engagement amid regional estrangement', *Australian Journal of International Affairs*, 74–1 (Feb. 2020), pp. 14–34; 'Japan, Vietnam to step up defense cooperation', *NHK News*, (28 May 2016) (http://www3.nhk.or.jp/nhkworld/en/news/20160528_26/, 28 May 2016).

107. 'Japan eyes lease deal for MSDF aircraft to Philippines in May', *Mainichi Shimbun*, (30 Apr.2016), (http://mainichi.jp/english/articles/20160430/p2g/00m/0dm/004000c, 30 Apr. 2016).

108. JCG, *We will send a patrol ship to prevent piracy!* (*Kaizokutaisaku notameni junshisentsugaru wo hakenshimasu!*) (20 Dec. 2017) (http://www.kaiho.mlit.go.jp/01kanku/kouhou/anken/01_1kanku/171220_tsugaruhaken.pdf 23 Feb. 2018);

Bhatt, Arunkumar, 'India, Japan conduct anti-piracy exercise', *The Hindu* (5 Nov. 2004) (http://www.thehindu.com/2004/11/05/stories/2004110502251300.htm 26 Mar. 2016).

109. MOD, *Shinkashitsukeru JGSDF-Nihon tosekai noheiwa toantei notameni*, JSDF-Joint Staff Office (24 Dec. 2015) (https://www.youtube.com/watch?v=sn3EXXigT7I 12 Feb. 2016).

110. MOD, *Regional Army History*, GSDF Middle Army (2013) (http://www.mod.go.jp/gsdf/mae/syoukai/index.01.html 12 Feb. 2018); GSDF, *GSDF News Release*, Ground Staff Public Information Office (26 May 2017) (http://www.mod.go.jp/gsdf/news/press/2017/pdf/20170526_10d.pdf 12 Feb. 2018).

111. GSDF, *Army*, No. 78 (Autumn 2017): 13 (http://www.mod.go.jp/gsdf/about/pamphlet/pdf/army78.pdf 12 Feb. 2018); *GSDF Press Release*, Ground Staff Public Information Office (20 June 2013) (http://www.mod.go.jp/gsdf/news/press/2013/20130620.html 12 Feb. 2018); (24 Sept. 2013) (http://www.mod.go.jp/gsdf/news/press/2013/20130924_1.html 12 Feb. 2018).

112. GSDF, *Army*, No. 78: 14; Conversations with former-USMC officer, GSDF officer (Tokyo, 2016).

113. Togo, Yukinori, 'Japan's Defence Capability Structural Reform and Highspeed Ferry Natchan' (*Bōei ryokukōjōrōdomappu tokōsokuferii [nacchan]*), *Ships of the World* (*Sekainokansen*), No. 750 (Nov. 2011): 154–7; Takarajimasha, *JSDF, New Generation Weaponry: Perfect Book 2035 Weaponry Catalogue* (*Jieitaishinsetaiheiki Perfect Book2035nenheikikatarogu*), (Tokyo: Takarajimasha, 2011): 52–5.

114. *Japan Military Review* (*Gunjikenkyū*), (Jan. 2012): 17–9; Noguchi, Takuya, Ibid, pp. 20–1; Simpson, James, 'T-90s to Leave Higashi-Chitose for Oita Tomorrow Morning', *Japan Security Watch* (5. Nov. 2011) (http://jsw.newpacificinstitute.org/?p=8753#comment-2939 16 Nov. 2016); 'GSDF 2Div Takes Ferry to Kyushu, First Participation of New Type-10 Tanks' (*Rikuji2shidan gaferiide kyushue saishinei 10shikisensha gahatsusanka*) *Tomakomaiminpo* (1 Nov. 2014) (https://www.tomamin.co.jp/news/area1/3983/ 16 Nov. 2016).

115. Critchley, Mike, *British Warships and Auxiliaries 2003/2004* (Liskeard: Maritime Books, 2002): 45–8; House of Commons, *Strategic Lift: Eleventh Report of Session 2006–07*, House of Commons Defence Committee HC 462 (London: The Stationery Office, 5 July 2007).

116. Ibid; Saunders, Stephen (ed.), *Jane's Fighting Ships, 2001–2002*, (Coulsdon, Surrey: Jane's Information Group, 2001): 780.

117. Johnson, Michael, and Coryell, Brent, 'November–December 2016 Army Sustainment Logistics Forecasting and Estimates in the Brigade Combat Team', (http://www.alu.army.mil/alog/2016/NOVDEC16/PDF/176881.pdf 12 June 2017).

118. Privratsky, Kenneth L., *Logistics in the Falklands War: A Case Study in Expeditionary Warfare* (Barnsley: Pen&Sword, 2014/2016): 33.

119. MOD-Accounting and Procurement Bureau, *Armoured Vehicles, Artillery, and Ammunition Development and Procurement*, (Feb. 2011): 3.

120. 'Ferry company launched under Defense Ministry plan to use private ships in emergencies', *Mainichi Japan* (17 Mar. 2016) (http://mainichi.jp/english/articles/

20160317/p2a/00m/0na/007000c#csidx501fd20284239f6927cc1deda8c196a 23 Mar. 2016).

121. Samuels, Richard J., '"New Fighting Power!" Japan's Growing Maritime Capabilities and East Asian Security', *International Security*, 32–3 (2007), pp. 84–112: 84; JCG, *Annual Report 2006* (https://www.kaiho.mlit.go.jp/info/books/report2006/topics/p009.html 22 Feb. 2018).

122. Ishiba, Shigeru, and Kiyotani, Shinichi, *Talking About Peace in Ignorance of Military Affairs: Issues of Japanese Defense* (*Gunjiwo shirazushiteheiwa wokotaru*), (Tokyo: KKbesutoserāzu, 2006): 91–2.

123. *Hand Book for Defense 2002*, (*Bōeihandobukku heisei14nenban*) (Tokyo: Asagumoshinbunsha, 2002): 212; *Hand Book for Defense 2016*, (*Bōeihandobukku heisei28nenban*) (Tokyo: Asagumoshinbunsha, 2016): 194; *Hand Book for Defense 2019* (*Bōeihandobukku2019*) (Tokyo: Asagumshimbunsha, 2019): 210; 'SDF Reserve Law Change', *The Daily Yomiuri* (6 Feb. 2001): 2; MOD, *SDF Reservist Topics* (*Yobijieikantopikusu*), (http://www.mod.go.jp/gsdf/reserve/topics/katagata/index.html, 12 Mar. 2009).

124. GSDF, *2016 Kumamoto Earthquake Disaster Role Assembly* (*Hesei28nen kumamotojishin niokeru saigaitō shōshū*), GSDF Video Channel (https://www.youtube.com/watch?v=hhzt-XAkdr8 12 Apr. 2016).

125. 'Seamen's union protests plan to make civilian ship workers SDF reservists', *Mainichi Japan*, (30 Jan. 2016) (http://mainichi.jp/english/articles/20160130/p2a/00m/0na/011000c 31 Jan. 2016).

126. Higuchi, Tsuneharu, 'Local Defense Corps: Fallen Vision', (*Kyōdobōeitai kōsōno shōchō*), *Bulletin of the Japanese Institute of Political Studies*, No. 22, (Jan. 1998) Kokushikan University, p. 113–33: 126.

127. Ibid: 127; JDA, *Awarding Preliminary JSDF Reservist Official Badges* (*Yobijieikanshirushibata no oriatsukai nitsuite*) (1 July 1980) (http://www.clearing.mod.go.jp/kunrei_data/f_fd/1980/fz19800701_00266_000.pdf 21 Apr. 2018).

128. Ishiba, Shigeru, and Kiyotani, Shinichi, *Talking About Peace in Ignorance of Military Affairs*: 93–4.

129. Ibid: 96–7.

130. *JSDF Equipment Yearbook 1994* (*Jieitaisōbinenkan1994*) (Tokyo: Asagumoshinbunsha, 1994): 551; DOD, *Defence Annual Report, 2006–2007* (Canberra: Department of Defence, 2007): 128; JDA, *2006 Defense Budget Provision Request* (*Heisei18 nendōbōeiyosan nogaiyō (an)*) (Tokyo: JDA, 2006): 38–9.

131. *The Military Balance 1990–1991*; *The Military Balance 2011*; Morgan, Bryn, *Defence Statistics 1997*, Research Paper 97/135, House of Commons Library (8 Dec. 1997); National Statistics, *Civilian Workforce by Grade Equivalence and Budgetary Area*, CPS01, (1 Oct. 2010), (https://assets.publishing.service.gov.uk/government/uploads/system/uploads/attachment_data/file/280104/1-october-2010.pdf 21 May 2015).

132. Ebata, Kensuke, *Information and the State* (*Jōhōtokokka*) (Tokyo: Kōdanshagendaishinsho, 2004): 168–78.

133. Samuels, Richard J., *Special Duty: A history of the Japanese intelligence community* (Ithaca, NY.: Cornell University Press, 2019): 187–8.

134. Newsham, Grant, 'The case for bringing Japan into the Five Eyes', *Asia Times*, (24 Aug.2020), (https://asiatimes.com/2020/08/the-case-for-bringing-japan-into-the-five-eyes/ 25 Aug. 2020).
135. Samuels, Richard J., *Special Duty*: 188–9.
136. DIH, *Defense Intelligence Headquarters Outline* (*Jōhōhonbu nogaiyō*), (http://www.mod.go.jp/dih/gaiyou.html, 12 Aug. 2010); *Defense Intelligence Headquarters* (http://www.mod.go.jp/dih/bosyu.pdf, 12 Aug. 2010).
137. JDA, *Defense of Japan 2002*: 139–40.
138. MOD, *Defense of Japan 2017* (http://www.clearing.mod.go.jp/hakusho_data/2017/html/n2423000.html 22 May 2018).
139. Shirai, Ryoji, *Incorporating Unmanned Aerial Systems Into The Japan Air Self-Defense Force*, Brookings, Policy Paper (Sept. 2014) (https://www.brookings.edu/wp-content/uploads/2016/06/Incorporating-UAS-Into-JASDF-Formatted-91914.pdf 19 Oct. 2017); 'Price spike sparked defense ministry struggle over Global Hawk drone: internal docs', *Mainichi Japan*, (22 Aug. 2017) (https://mainichi.jp/english/articles/20170822/p2a/00m/0na/018000c 23 Aug. 2017); Fifth Meeting, Security Committee, 201st Session, House of Representatives (16 June 2020) (http://www.shugiin.go.jp/Internet/itdb_kaigiroku.nsf/html/kaigiroku/001520120200616005.htm 10 June 2020).
140. Dorril, Stephen, *MI6: fifty years of special operations* (London: Fourth Estate, 2000): 761.
141. Kotani, Ken, 'Current State of Intelligence and Intelligence Issues in Japan', *National Institute of Defense Studies News* 100, (2006), (http://www.nids.go.jp/english/publication/briefing/pdf/2006/100.pdf, 15 Aug. 2010): 2.
142. Fukuyama, Takashi, *MOD and MOFA: Two Distorted Intelligence Organizations*, (*Yugandafutatsu no interijensusoshiki*) (Tokyo: Gentosha, 2013): 77–84; Tsukamoto, Katsuichi, *JSDF Intelligence War* (*Jieitaino jōhōsen*), (Tokyo: Soshisha, 2008): 201–12.
143. MOD, *Defense of Japan 2017*: 201–3.
144. ISPC/NISC, *The First National Strategy on Information Security* (2 Feb. 2006) (https://www.nisc.go.jp/eng/pdf/national_strategy_001_eng.pdf 22 Mar. 2016).
145. 'Government websites hit by cyberattacks traced to China', *Kyodo/ The Japan Times*, (20 Sep. 2011), (http://search.japantimes.co.jp/cgi-bin/nn20110920a3.html 22 Sept. 2011); MOD, *Defense of Japan 2017*: 358–60.
146. ISPC/NISC, *Cybersecurity Strategy: Towards a world-leading, resilient, and vigorous cyberspace* (10 June 2013): 41–2 (http://www.nisc.go.jp/eng/pdf/cybersecuritystrategy-en.pdf 24 mar. 2016).
147. NICS, *Cybersecurity Strategy*, Cabinet Decision: The Government of Japan (4 Sept. 2015) (https://www.nisc.go.jp/eng/pdf/cs-strategy-en.pdf 12 Apr. 2016).
148. Kallendar, Paul, Hughes, Christopher W., 'Japan's Emerging Trajectory as a 'Cyber Power': From Securitization to Militarization of Cyberspace', *Journal of Strategic Studies*, 40:1–2 (2017), pp. 118–45: 129.
149. MOD, *Defense of Japan 2017*: 201–3; Vosse, Wilhelm M., 'Japan's Cyber Diplomacy', *EU Cyber Direct* (https://eucyberdirect.eu/wp-content/uploads/2019/10/vosse_rif_topublish.pdf 22 June 2020).
150. Samuels, Richard J., *Special Duty*: 96.

151. Ibid: 178.
152. Aoki, Setsuko, *Significance of 1969 Diet Resolution on Peaceful Uses of Outer Space in the Era of Weaponisation* (*Tekihonauchū no gunjiriyōketteikijun toshiteno kokkaiketsu ginoyūyōsei*), Keio University, Working Paper 68: 16 (http://spacelaw.sfc.keio.ac.jp/archive/WP68.pdf 18 Mar. 2008); Suzuki, Kazuto, *Space: Japan's New Security Agenda: The Diet's 1969 Resolution on "Exclusively Peaceful Purposes"*, RIPS' Policy Perspectives 5, (2007) (http://www.rips.or.jp/english/publications/policy_perspectives/pp005.html#point04, 10 Mar. 2008); JAXA Document Library (13 July 1969), (http://www.jaxa.jp/library/space_law/chapter_1/1-1-1-5_j.html, 14 May 2010).
153. Samuels, Richard J., *Securing Japan*: 104; Yoshimura, Keisuke, 'Not registered with the UN: Japan's spy satellites are an open secret', *Kyodo News/Japan Times* (15 June 2007), (http://search.japantimes.co.jp/cgi-bin/nn20070615f1.html 17 June 2007); 'Diet OK's military use of space', *Yomiuri Shimbun* (22 May 2008) (http://www.yomiuri.co.jp/dy/national/20080522TDY01305.htm 26 May 2008).
154. MOD/ASDF, *About the New Edition Space Operations Squadron* (*Uchūsakusentai noshinpennitsuite*) (18 May 2020) (https://www.mod.go.jp/asdf/news/release/2020/0518/ 12 July 2020); 'Japan sets up its first 'Space Operations Squadron,'' *Janes Defence News* (18 May 2020) (https://www.janes.com/defence-news/news-detail/2020/05/18/242b253c-349b-4ace-96fb-52c08c033596 12 July 2020).
155. PMO, *Protocol of the 7th administrative reform conference*, (1997) (http://www.kantei.go.jp/jp/gyokaku/0312dai7.html 23 June 2008); Sunohara, Tsuyoshi, *What is the Japanese Version of NSC?* (*NihonbanNSC towananika*) (Tokyo: Shinchōsha, 2014): 155–71.
156. 'Japan successfully launches intelligence-gathering satellite', *Mainichi Japan*, (17 March 2017) (http://mainichi.jp/english/articles/20170317/p2g/00m/0dm/069000c 18 March 2017); Hughes, Christopher W., *Japan's Re-emergence as a 'Normal' Military Power* (Abingdon: Routledge, 2005): 87; 'Japan launches, puts in orbit new intelligence-gathering satellite', *Kyodo News* (9 Feb. 2020), (https://english.kyodonews.net/news/2020/02/95de6d601433-japan-launches-intelligence-gathering-satellite-after-delay.html 9 July 2020).
157. Ikegami-Andersson, Masako, 'Japan', in Singh, Ravinder Pal (ed.), *Arms Procurement Decision Making Volume I*, pp. 131–76: Note 82, 159–60.
158. Lorell, Mark A., *Troubled Partnership: A History of U.S.-Japan Collaboration on the FS-X Fighter* (Santa Monica, CA.: RAND, 1995): 66–71; Chinworth, Michael W., Presentation, *Security Trade Management in the United States, Science*, Technology and Global Governance Seminar, Kiroro, Hokkaido (5 Aug. 2004); Conversations, Michael Chinworth, Tokyo, Hokkaido (2003–04).
159. Chinworth, Michael W., and Matthews, Ron, 'Defense Industrialisation Through Offsets: The Case of Japan', in Martin, Stephen (ed.), *The Economics of Offsets: Defence Procurement and Countertrade* (Amsterdam: Harwood Academic/OPA, 1996), pp. 177–218: 183–4; Aoki, Yoshitomo, *How Strong are JSDF Fighters?* (*Jieitaisentōki wa doredaketsuyoinoka*) (Tokyo: SoftBank Creative, 2010): 154–5.
160. Watanabe, Takashi, 'Air SDF to scrap 12 fighters, citing tsunami damage', *Asahi Shimbun* (16 Sept. 2011) (http://www.asahi.com/english/TKY201109150442.html,

9 Oct. 2011); Komine, Takao, *Revived Wings F-2B (YomigaerutsubasaF-2B)* (Tokyo: Namikishobō, 2017).
161. Conversations with ASDF officers, Tokyo (2004–12).
162. GAO, *Defense Acquisitions: Assessments of Selected Weapon Programs*, United States Government Accountability Office, Report to Congressional Committees, GAO-11-233SP, (March 2011) (http://www.gao.gov/assets/320/317081.pdf 11 July 2016).
163. MOD, *Defense of Japan 2012*: 151–7.
164. MOD, *Defense of Japan 2012*: 156.
165. Mehta, Aaron, 'Air Combat Command's challenge: Buy new or modernize older aircraft', *Air Force Times*, (2 Feb. 2014) (http://www.airforcetimes.com/article/20140202/NEWS04/302020005/Air-Combat-Command-s-challenge-Buy-new-modernize-older-aircraft 22 June 2015); Comments by US Embassy and US defence company staff, Tokyo (2015).
166. Axe, David, 'Read for Yourself—The F-35's Damning Dogfighting Report: Test pilot reveals stealth fighter's vulnerability', *War is Boring*, (1 July 2015) (https://medium.com/war-is-boring/read-for-yourself-the-f-35-s-damning-dogfighting-report-719a4e66f3eb 18 July 2015); Jennings, Gareth, 'JPO counters media report that F-35 cannot dogfight', *IHS Jane's Defence Weekly*, (1 July 2015) (http://www.janes.com/article/52715/jpo-counters-media-report-that-f-35-cannot-dogfight?utm_campaign=[PMP]_PC5308_J360%2003.07.2015%20_KV_Deployment&utm_medium=email&utm_source=Eloqua 12 July 2015).
167. Gady, Franz-Stefan, 'Japan to Continue Assembling F-35A Fighter Jets at Home', *The Diplomat*, (8 Jan. 2020) (https://thediplomat.com/2020/01/japan-to-continue-assembling-f-35a-fighter-jets-at-home/ 7 Mar. 2020); Kinoshita, Noriaki, 'Japan to introduce 'aircraft carriers' to counter China; defense role to be emphasized', *Mainichi Japan* (28 Nov. 2018) (https://mainichi.jp/english/articles/20181128/p2a/00m/0na/008000c 30 Nov. 2018).
168. 'National Stealth Fighter, First Test Flight Expected in August, Half a Year Later Than Initial Plans' (*Kokkusansuterusu sentōki, hatsushikenhiko 8gatsu nitosho keikakuyori hantoshiokure*), *Nikkei Shimbun*, (15 Feb. 2015) (http://www.nikkei.com/article/DGXLASFS14H0L_U5A210C1PE8000/ 17 Feb. 2015); Miyakawa, Junichi *et al*, 'Research of Flight Control System for High Maneuver Aircraft' (*Kōndohikōseigōshisutemu nokenkyū*), Special Report (*Tokushūronbun*) Mitsubishi Heavy Industries Technology Review (*Mitsubishijūkogiho*) 45–4 (2008), pp. 58–61 (http://www.mhi.co.jp/technology/review/pdf/454/454058.pdf#page=2 17 Feb. 2015).
169. MOD, *Defense of Japan 2016* (http://www.clearing.mod.go.jp/hakusho_data/2016/html/nc044000.html 24 June 2017).
170. MOD, *Medium Term Defense Program (FY2014-FY2018)*: 27.
171. Bitzinger, Richard A., *The X-2 ADT-X: Japan's Last Chance Fighter Jet?*, RSIS Commentary (6 April 2016) (https://www.rsis.edu.sg/rsis-publication/rsis/co16075-the-x-2-adt-x-japans-last-chance-fighter-jet/#.WwU6kNQS_Dd 26 Feb. 2018); Host, Pat, 'Replacing the F-2: Japan's complex effort to procure a new fighter jet', *Jane's Defence Weekly* (5 Jan. 2020) (https://www.janes.com/images/assets/498/92498/

Replacing_the_F-2_Japans_complex_effort_to_procure_a_new_fighter_jet.pdf 6 Jan. 2020).
172. Ota, Hiroshi, 'New Technology: The Japanese Perspective', in Ball, Desmond, and Wilson, Helen (eds.), *New technologies: Implications for Regional and Australian Security*, Canberra Papers on Strategy and Defence No. 76 (Canberra: ANU, 1991), pp. 20–42: 25.
173. Hemmert, Martin, and Oberländer, Christian, 'The Japanese System of Technology and Innovation: preparing for the twenty-first century', in Hemmert, Martin, Oberländer, Christian (eds), *Technology and Innovation in Japan: Policy and management for the twenty-first century* (London: Routledge, 1998), pp. 3–20: 9; MEXT, 'Development of Science and Technology Policy,' in *"White Paper on Science and Technology 2014—Building a Human Resources System That Maximizes Potential,"* Ministry of Education, Culture, Sports, Science and Technology-Japan (Tokyo: January 2015) (http://www.mext.go.jp/english/whitepaper/1354396.htm 12 Jan 2016), pp. 197–213: 206–7.
174. 'Gov't council looking to promote joint military-civilian research', *Mainichi Japan*, (3 Feb. 2017) (http://mainichi.jp/english/articles/20170203/p2a/00m/0na/009000c 5 Feb. 2017); 'Military and Security Related Research' (*Gunjitekianzenhoshōkenkyū nitsuite*) *Science Council of Japan* (13 Apr. 2017) (http://www.scj.go.jp/ja/member/iinkai/anzenhosyo/pdf23/170413-houkokukakutei.pdf#page=12 12 June 2017).
175. Sato, Heigo, 'From the "Three Principles of Arms Exports" to the "Three Principles of Defense Equipment Transfer,"' *AJISS Commentary*, No. 197 (14 May 2014); Cabinet Office, *Statement by the Chief Cabinet Secretary, On Guidelines for Overseas Transfer of Defense Equipment*, (27 Dec. 2011).
176. Cabinet Office, *Three Principles of Arms Exports*, (1 Apr. 2018) (http://www.mofa.go.jp/files/000034953.pdf 12 Jan. 2018).
177. Conversations with UK embassy staff, Tokyo (2011–12), and Center for Information on Security Trade Controls staff (Tokyo, 2012–14); CISTEC Brochure (http://www.cistec.or.jp/about/cistec/ebook/001/_SWF_Window.html 12 June 2016).
178. Kitagawa, Keizo, 'Maritime Patrol Aircraft: A Japanese Perspective', *RUSI Defence Systems*, (8 Dec. 2014) (https://www.rusi.org/publications/defencesystems/ref:A54859791DBFF7/#.VK-laMm3uH8, 10 Jan 2015); Nicholson, Brendan, 'Japan's subs bid is seen as the weakest', *The Australian* (21 April 2016), (http://www.theaustralian.com.au/national-affairs/defence/japans-subs-bid-is-seen-as-the-weakest/news-story/45dae566e2c5f2f5c4ba3f603178ed29 3 May 2016).
179. DIT/DSO, *UK defence and security export statistics for 2017*, Department for International Trade/Defence and Security Organisation (14 Mar. 2019) (https://www.gov.uk/government/publications/defence-and-security-exports-for-2017/uk-defence-and-security-export-statistics-for-2017 12 Aug. 2020).
180. 'Japan to allow first arms export under new guidelines', *Nikkei Asian Review*, (6 July 2014), (http://asia.nikkei.com/Politics-Economy/Policy-Politics/Japan-to-allow-first-arms-export-under-new-guidelines 9 July 2014); 'Japan, Philippines to sign defense equipment deal', *NHK News* (26 Feb. 2016), (http://www3.nhk.or.jp/nhkworld/en/news/20160226_19/, 26 Feb. 2016); 'Air Force to Upgrade Ten Aircraft for Training', *New Zealand Defence Force*, (29 July 2009) (http://www.defense-aero-

space.com/cgi-bin/client/modele.pl?shop=dae&modele=release&prod=107102&cat=3 2 May 2015).
181. NHK, 'Weapons Exports' ('*Bukiyushutsu*'), (21:00–21:50, 5 Oct. 2014), *NHK-General*; 'Missions of ATLA', *ATLA*, (http://www.mod.go.jp/atla/en/soubichou_gaiyou.html 27 Nov. 2017); Kelly, Tim, and Kubo, Nobuhiro, 'Exclusive: Japan civilian R&D agency to get military role to spur arms innovation-sources', *Reuters*, (20 Mar. 2015) (https://www.reuters.com/article/us-japan-r-d-military/exclusive-japan-civilian-rd-agency-to-get-military-role-to-spur-arms-innovation-sources-idUSKBN0MF2K520150320 22 Feb. 2018).
182. Kando, Yoshihiro, Konno, Shinobu, 'India Considering Introducing US-2 from Japan as used by JSDF' (*Indo, nihonkara hikōteidōnyūkentōkaiji moshiyō noUS2*), *Asahi Shimbun*, (2 Mar. 2015): 7.
183. Perrett, Bradley, 'Japan, Britain To Collaborate On Meteor Guidance', *Aviation Week* (17 July 2014), (http://aviationweek.com/awin-only/japan-britain-collaborate-meteor-guidance 7 Jan. 2017); Grevatt, Jon, 'Japan points to potential to expand missile technology ties with UK', *IHS Jane's Defence Industry* (14 Mar. 2017) (http://www.janes.com/article/68690/japan-points-to-potential-to-expand-missile-technology-ties-with-uk 14 Mar. 2017).
184. Shinoda, Tomohito, *Koizumi Diplomacy: Japan's Kantei Approach to Foreign and Defense Affairs* (Seattle: University of Washington Press, 2007): 91.
185. Nabers, Dirk, 'Culture and Collective Action: Japan, Germany, and the United States After September 11, 2001'; Shinoda, Tomohito, *Koizumi Diplomacy*; Hughes, Christopher W., *Japan's Re-emergence as a 'Normal' Military Power*.
186. Hughes, Christopher W., *Japan's Remilitarisation*.
187. Shinoda, Tomohito, *Koizumi Diplomacy*: 146.
188. Takao, Yasuo, *Is Japan remilitarising? The politics of norm formation* (Melbourne: Monash University Press, 2008).
189. Delamotte, Guibourg, 'Globalization's impact on threat perception and defence postures in Northeast Asia', in Till, Geoffrey, Chew, Emrys, Ho, Joshua (eds.), *Globalization and Defence in the Asia-Pacific: Arms Across Asia* (Abingdon: Routledge, 2009), pp. 73–89: 75.
190. Aoi, Chiyuki, and Yokota, Yozo, 'Avoiding a Strategic Failure in the Aftermath of the Iraq War: Partnership in Peacebuilding', in Samii, Cyrus, and Thakur, Ramesh (eds.), *The Iraq War and the World Order* (Tokyo: International Peace Academy/UN University Press, 2006), pp. 282–97: 292.
191. Antiterrorism Law extended, *Kyodo/The Daily Yomiuri*, (12 Oct. 2003): 1.
192. MOD, *Japan is playing an important role in the International Community's fight against Terrorism*, (http://www.mod.go.jp/e/publ/pamphlets/pdf/trr_0710/p2–3.pdf 19 Oct. 2010).
193. 'Refueling Cover-up', editorial, *The Asahi Shimbun* (23 Oct. 2007): 23.
194. MOFA, *The Proliferation Security Initiative (PSI) Maritime Interdiction Exercise "Team Samurai 04"(Overview and Evaluation)*, (28 Oct. 2004) (https://www.mofa.go.jp/policy/un/disarmament/arms/psi/overview0410.html 27 Mar. 2017).
195. MOD, *Japan is playing an important role in the International Community's fight against Terrorism*.

196. Vosse, Wilhelm M., 'Japan', in Sobel, Richard, Furia, Peter, Barratt, Bethany (eds.), *Public Opinion and International Intervention*, (Dulles, VA.: Potomac, 2012), pp. 109–36; Midford, Paul, *Rethinking Japanese Public Opinion and Security: From Pacifism to Realism?* (Stanford, CA.: Stanford University Press, 2011).
197. Kliman, Daniel M., *Japan's Security Strategy in the Post-9/11 World: Embracing a New Realpolitik*, (Westport, CT.: CSIS/Praeger, 2006): 121–8.
198. MOFA, *Press Conference by Prime Minister Junichiro Koizumi*, (9 Dec. 2003), (https://www.mofa.go.jp/region/middle_e/iraq/issue2003/pmpress0312.html 7 Aug. 2018); *The Constitution of Japan*, (https://japan.kantei.go.jp/constitution_and_government_of_japan/constitution_e.html 7 Aug. 2018).
199. GSDF-Ground Staff Office (GSO), *Iraq Reconstruction Activities History* (*Iraku fukkōshienkatsudō kōdōshi*), Tsujimoto Kiyomi blog, (1 July 2015) (https://www.kiyomi.gr.jp/blog/5969/ 21 Aug. 2018).
200. 'Act on Special Measures concerning Humanitarian Relief and Reconstruction Work and Security Assistance in Iraq'; *Hand Book for Defense 2017*: 849–51.
201. Katsumata, Hidemichi, 'Court leaves ASDF Iraq mission up in air', *The Daily Yomiuri*, (23 Apr. 2008), (http://www.yomiuri.co.jp/dy/national/20080423TDY04303.htm 24 Apr. 2008), GSDF-GSO, *Iraq Reconstruction Activities Official History*: 29–34.
202. Conversations with GSDF staff officer, Tokyo (2004–09), according to whom, Phuket Air tender price was $2-million, JAL $4-million, and USAF $8-million, the USAF figure for US-Japan-Kuwait round-trip.
203. Aoi, Chiyuki, 'Conditions for Effective Intelligence and Information-Sharing: Insights from Dutch–Japanese Cooperation in Iraq, 2003–2005', in Goldenberg, Irina, Soeters, Joseph, Dean, Weylon H. (eds.), *Information Sharing in Military Operations* (New York: Springer, 2016), pp. 147–63: 148.
204. Perry, Walter L., and Moffat, James, *Information Sharing Among Military Headquarters: The Effects on Decisionmaking* (Santa Monica, CA.: RAND/UK MOD, 2004).
205. *Hand Book for Defense 2017*: 849–51.
206. van der Meulen, Jan, and Kawano, Hitoshi, 'Accidental Neighbours: Japanese and Dutch troops in Iraq', in Soeters, Joseph, and Manigart, Philippe (eds.), *Military Cooperation in Multinational Peace Operations: Managing Cultural Diversity and Crisis Response* (Abingdon: Routledge, 2008), pp. 166–179.
207. Ibid; Aoi, Chiyuki, 'Conditions for Effective Intelligence and Information-Sharing': 149–50.
208. Aoi, Chiyuki, 'Conditions for Effective Intelligence and Information-Sharing': 153–5.
209. Ibid: 156–7.
210. Ibid: 157–160.
211. Sakaemura, Yoshiyuki, 'Practical Activities and Lessons-Learned of the JGSDF's Civil-Military Cooperation on Humanitarian and Reconstruction Assistance in Iraq' (*Irakufukkōshien niokeruminsei kyōryokukatsudōno jissento kyōkun*), *The Journal of International Security* (*Kokusaianzenhoshō*) 38–4 (Mar. 2011), pp. 38–56: 39–40; Vosse, Wilhelm M., 'Japan'; Aoi, Chiyuki, and Yokota, Yozo, 'Avoiding a Strategic Failure in the Aftermath of the Iraq War': 294.
212. Sakaemura, Yoshiyuki, 'Practical Activities and Lessons-Learned of the JGSDF's Civil-Military Cooperation on Humanitarian and Reconstruction Assistance in Iraq': 45–9;

Yamaguchi, Noboru, 'Self Defense Forces in Peace Building Missions: What Japan Learned from its Experiences in Iraq?' (*Heiwakōchikuto jieitai-irakujindōfukkōshien wochūshinni*), *The Journal of International Security* (*Kokusaianzenhoshō*) 34–1 (June 2006), pp. 17–34: 24–6; MOFA, *Japan's Assistance for the Reconstruction of Iraq* (Tokyo: July 2006).

213. Ibid; *Hand Book for Defense 2017*: 851–3.
214. Aoi, Chiyuki, 'Conditions for Effective Intelligence and Information-Sharing': 160–1.
215. 'Veterans of Japan's Iraq mission explain dangers of overseas operations', *Mainichi Japan*, (19 Sept. 2015) (http://mainichi.jp/english/english/newsselect/news/20150919p2a00m0na018000c.html 21 Sept. 2015).
216. Yamaguchi, Noboru, in 'Evidence: 900 days of GSDF Iraq Dispatch' (*Kenshō, rikujōjieitaiirakuhaken no900nichi*), *Close-up Gendai*, 2273, NHK (24 July 2006); GSDF-GSO, *Iraq Reconstruction Activities Official History, Part 1*: 84–6.
217. Degawa, Nobuhisa, 'Covering the Activities of Self-Defense Forces inside Iraq' (*Jieitaihaken wo irakudeshuzai*), *The Journal of International Security* (*Kokusaianzenhoshō*) 36–1 (June 2008), pp. 125–50: 138–9; Shiba, Rei, and MOD, *JSDF Iraq Morning Report: 295 Days in Baghdad, Basra* (*Jieitaiirakunippō-bagudaddo-bazura no295nichikan*), (Tokyo: Kashiwashobō, 2018); 'Veterans of Japan's Iraq mission explain dangers of overseas operations', *Mainichi Japan*; 'GSDF logs on Iraq mission lack info on period when security worsened', *Mainichi Japan*, (18 Apr. 2018) (https://mainichi.jp/english/articles/20180418/p2a/00m/0na/010000c 19 Apr. 2018).
218. Kuroki, Masanori, 'The Deployment of the Japan Self-Defense Forces in Iraq and Public Trust Among Different Ideological Groups', *Defence and Peace Economics*, 25:3 (2014), pp. 281–89: 288.
219. JDA, *Defense of Japan 2006*: 289–91.
220. Answers to written questions, 189th Diet Session, No. 288, House of Representatives (30 June 2015) (http://www.shugiin.go.jp/internet/itdb_shitsumon.nsf/html/shitsumon/b189288.htm 10 July 2020); GSDF-GSO, *Iraq Reconstruction Activities Official History, Part 1*: 43–51.
221. Bradford, John F., 'Japanese Anti-Piracy Initiatives in Southeast Asia: Policy Formulation and the Coastal State Responses', *Contemporary Southeast Asia*, 26–3, pp. 480–505: 486.
222. Black, Lindsay, *Japan's Maritime Security Strategy: The Japan Coast Guard and Maritime Outlaws* (Basingstoke: Palgrave Macmillan, 2014): 1, 119–22; 'ReCAAP Ensures the Safety of Asian Waters', *We are Tomodachi* (Winter 2017) (https://www.japan.go.jp/tomodachi/2017/autumn-winter2017/reaccp_ensures_the_safety.html 22 Mar. 2018)
223. Bradford, John F., 'Japanese Anti-Piracy Initiatives in Southeast Asia'.
224. EU, *European Union Naval Force (EU NAVFOR) Somalia Operation ATALANTA* (Sept. 2012) (http://eunavfor.eu/wp-content/uploads/2011/08/20120912_Informationbroschure_english.pdf 25 Oct. 2016); NATO, NATO Counter-piracy operations (http://www.nato.int/cps/en/natolive/topics_48815.htm 23 April 2016).
225. Sakurai, Tetsuhisa, Kawashima, Takashi (trans.), *The Fact sheet of Anti-piracy Activities off the Coast of Somalia and the Gulf of Aden*, Japan Peacekeeping Training and Research

Center, MOD, (31 Mar. 2013) (http://www.mod.go.jp/js/jsc/jpc/english/research/image/eng01.pdf 27 Sept. 2016): 22.
226. 171st Session, House of Representatives, Special Committee on Anti-Piracy Response, No. 4 (17 Apr. 2009): 27.
227. Sakurai, Tetsuhisa, Kawashima, Takashi (trans.), *The Fact sheet of Anti-piracy Activities off the Coast of Somalia and the Gulf of Aden*: 21–2.
228. MOD, *Japan Defense Focus* (Oct. 2011) (http://www.mod.go.jp/e/jdf/no23/topics01.html 24 Mar. 2015); CAS, *Annual Report 2014: 'Japan's Actions against Piracy off the Coast of Somalia and in the Gulf of Aden'*, (Mar. 2015) (https://www.cas.go.jp/jp/gaiyou/jimu/pdf/siryou2/counter-piracy2014.pdf 27 Sept. 2017).
229. Bradford, John F., 'Japanese Anti-Piracy Initiatives in Southeast Asia': 485.
230. Vosse, Wilhelm M., 'Learning multilateral military and political cooperation in the counter-piracy missions: a step towards de-centering of Japan's security policy?', *The Pacific Review*, 31:4, (2018), pp. 480–497.
231. Ibid: 486–7.
232. CAS, *Annual Report 2014*.
233. MOD-MOFA sources use both anti-/counter-piracy terms. Sakurai, Tetsuhisa, Kawashima, Takashi (trans.), *The Fact sheet of Anti-piracy Activities off the Coast of Somalia and the Gulf of Aden*: 21.
234. MOD, *Defense of Japan 2017* (http://www.mod.go.jp/e/publ/w_paper/pdf/2017/DOJ2017_3-2-2_web.pdf 28 Apr. 2018).
235. MOD, *Defense of Japan 2017*: 383.
236. 'SDF officer to head anti-piracy force off Somalia', *NHK News* (3 Feb. 2015) (http://www3.nhk.or.jp/nhkworld/english/news/20150203_15.html 3 Feb. 2015).
237. Vosse, Wilhelm M., 'Learning multilateral military and political cooperation in the counter-piracy missions': 489.
238. MOD, *Defense of Japan 2017*: 359.
239. 'Japans SDF holds joint drill with NATO forces', *NHK News* (27 Sept. 2014) (http://www3.nhk.or.jp/nhkworld/english/news/japan.html 27 Sept. 2014).
240. MOD, 'Dispatch of Female SDF Personnel to NATO Headquarters', *Japan Defense Focus*, No. 59 (Dec. 2014) (http://www.mod.go.jp/e/jdf/no59/activities.html 12 Mar. 2015).
241. NATO, *NATO conducts Annual Crisis Management Exercise (CMX)*, Press Release (3 Mar. 2015) (https://www.nato.int/cps/en/natohq/news_117862.htm 21 Sept. 2017); NATO, *Allies agree Japan's Mission to NATO* (24 May 2018) (https://www.nato.int/cps/ic/natohq/news_154886.htm?selectedLocale=en 28 May 2018).
242. MOD, *Defense of Japan 2012 (Bōeihakushoheisei24nen)*: 292–305; 'Japan to Beef Up SDF Unit in Djibouti', *Jiji News* (24 June 2015) (http://jen.jiji.com/jc/eng?g=eco&k=2015062400867 25 June 2015).
243. MOD, *Defense of Japan 2017*: 390–1; Handa, Shigeru, *Verification-JSDF-South Sudan PKO: melting civilian control (Kenshō jieitaiminamisūdan PKO: yūkaisuru shibiriankontorōru)*, (Tokyo: Iwanamishoten, 2018): 51–6.
244. Susumu, Takai, and Kazumine, Akimoto, 'Ocean-Peace Keeping and New Roles for Maritime Force', NIDS Security Reports, 3 (1999): 60 (http://www.nids.mod.go.jp/english/publication/kiyo/pdf/bulletin_e1999_3.pdf 7 May 2017).

245. Arcala Hall, Rosalie, 'Civil-military cooperation in international disaster response: the Japanese Self-Defense Forces' deployment in Aceh, Indonesia', *Korean Journal of Defense Analysis*, 20:4, (2008), pp. 383–400.
246. JDA, *Defense of Japan 2005* (http://www.clearing.mod.go.jp/hakusho_data/2005/2005/html/17415300.html 22 Feb. 2018).
247. Yamashita, Hiroji, 'Indonesia International Team Activities in Retrospect' (*Indoneshiakokusaikatsudō wo furikaette*), *Bouei News* (1 May 2005) (http://www.boueinews.com/news/2005/20050501_5.html 9 Oct. 2009).
248. JDA, *Defense of Japan 2005* (http://www.clearing.mod.go.jp/hakusho_data/2005/2005/html/17415300.html 22 Feb. 2018).
249. Peng Er, Lam, *Japan's Peace-Building Diplomacy in Asia: Seeking a More Active Political Role* (Abingdon: Routledge, 2009): 70.
250. *Hand Book for Defense 2017*: 811–3.
251. MOD, *Defense of Japan 2010* (http://www.clearing.mod.go.jp/hakusho_data/2010/2010/html/mc334000.html 25 Feb. 2018).
252. *Hand Book for Defense 2017*: 759–63; Conversation with survey team member (Cabinet Office, 2010).
253. Aoi, Chiyuki, 'Punching Below Its Weight: Japan's Post-Cold War Expeditionary Missions', in Patalano, Alessio (ed.), *Maritime Strategy and National Security in Japan and Britain* (Leiden/Boston: Global Oriental, 2012), pp. 132–156: 143.
254. Watanabe, Takahiro, *Working with the Engineering Troops of Different Countries*, IPCH, (Oct. 2012) (http://www.pko.go.jp/pko_e/liaison/liaison18.html 12 Jan. 2017).
255. Sado, Akihiro, *The End of the Cold War and Japan's Participation in Peacekeeping Operations: Overseas Deployment of the Self-Defense Forces*, Japan Digital Library, JIIA: 7 (http://www2.jiia.or.jp/en/digital_library/japan_s_diplomacy.php 29 Dec. 2016); MOD, *Defense of Japan 2010* (http://www.clearing.mod.go.jp/hakusho_data/2010/2010/html/m3312200.html 21 Feb. 2018).
256. Okuma, Kiyoshi, 'Moving Toward Recovery in Haiti', IPCH, (Aug. 2012) (http://www.pko.go.jp/pko_e/liaison/liaison17.html 12 Jan. 2017).
257. Koma, Yuichiro, *One-Year-Old South Sudan and the Work of Logistics Officers*, IPCH, (Oct. 2012) (http://www.pko.go.jp/pko_e/liaison/liaison20.html 12 Feb. 2018).
258. Heinrich, L. William Jr., *et al*, *United Nations peace-keeping operations: a guide to Japanese policies*, (Tokyo: UNU Press, 1999): 26–7; 'SDF Dispatch to Darfur Considered', *The Japan Times/Kyodo*, (http://search.japantimes.co.jp/cgi-bin/nn20070708a9.html 8 July 2007).
259. *Hand Book for Defense 2017*: 782–99; Koma, Yuichiro, *One-Year-Old South Sudan and the Work of Logistics Officers*.
260. MOD, *Defense of Japan 2017*: 387–90.
261. CAS, *On the Termination of Activities of SDF Construction Units in UNMISS: basic considerations* (*UNMISS niokeru jieitai shisetsubutai nokatsudōshūryō nikansuru kihontekinakangaekata*), Cabinet Secretariat (10 Mar. 2017); Handa, Shigeru, *Verification-JSDF-South Sudan PKO*: 131–7.
262. 'Defense Minister Suggests Word 'Combat' in GSDF Report 'not used in legal sense'',

Mainichi Japan, (9 Feb. 2017) (http://mainichi.jp/english/articles/20170209/p2a/00m/0na/017000c, 11 Feb. 2017); Handa, Shigeru, *Verification-JSDF-South Sudan PKO*: 141–68; 'Defense Minister Inada denies daily reports hidden' (*Inadabōeishōnippōinpei wo ryōshōshita jijitsunai tohitei*), *NHK* (19 July 2017) (http://www3.nhk.or.jp/news/html/20170719/k10011064771000.html?utm_int=news_contents_news-main_003 19 July 2017).

263. 'SDF Leader Tells Officers What "Combat" Means Legally', *Jiji Press* (9 Feb. 2017) (http://jen.jiji.com/jc/eng?g=eco&k=2017020901224 12 Feb. 2017).
264. Kamata, Tomoko, 'New Duties for Japan's SDF', *NHK News* (15 Nov. 2016) (http://www3.nhk.or.jp/nhkworld/en/news/editors/5/newdutiesforjapanssdf/, 27 Nov. 2016).
265. Conversations with family of civilian worker in Juba, 2016 (Saitama, Oct.-Dec. 2016); 'Japanese aid workers extracted from S. Sudan amid violence', *Mainichi Japan/Kyodo* (14 July 2016) (http://mainichi.jp/english/articles/20160714/p2g/00m/0dm/010000c 16 July 2016).
266. 'GSDF colonel recalls bullets flying over camp during S. Sudan PKO', *Mainichi Japan*, (17 Nov. 2017) (https://mainichi.jp/english/articles/20171117/p2a/00m/0na/009000c 17 Nov. 2017).
267. Fukuura, Atsuko, *Ambiguous Positioning of Military Wives: Exclusion and Reliance Techniques in Japan*, Working paper No. 266 (Shiga University, 2017); Mulloy, Garren, *Adapting Militaries to Peacekeeping and Policing Roles: The Effects of Peacekeeping on Militaries and the Stresses and Strains of Operations*, HUMSEC Working Paper Series (Graz: HUMSEC, 2007).
268. Midford, Paul, 'Japan's Multilateral Security Cooperation with East Asia', in Vosse, Wilhelm and Midford, Paul (eds.) *Japan's New Security Partnerships: Beyond the Security Alliance* (Manchester University Press, 2018), pp. 89–111: 89.
269. MOFA, *Diplomatic Bluebook 2017*, (https://www.mofa.go.jp/policy/other/bluebook/2017/html/chapter1/c0102.html#sf03 12 Feb. 2020); MOFA, *Foreign Policy Speech by Foreign Minister MOTEGI Toshimitsu on the occasion of The 1st Tokyo Global Dialogue* (2 Dec. 2019) (https://www.mofa.go.jp/fp/pp/page3e_001133.html 12 Feb. 2020).
270. 'Japan GSDF Joins Australia-U.S. Military Exercise', *Jiji Press*, (5 July 2015) (http://jen.jiji.com/jc/eng?g=eco&k=2015070500105, 6 July 2015).
271. 'Japan's GSDF, Australian troops plan joint drills', *NHK News*, (31 July 2014) (http://www3.nhk.or.jp/nhkworld/english/news/20140731_35.html, 4 Aug. 2014); Robson, Seth, 'Royal New Zealand Air Force squadron visits Yokota', *Stars and Stripes* (19 May 2016), (https://www.stripes.com/news/royal-new-zealand-air-force-squadron-visits-yokota-1.410329#.WORRXLiguH9 5 Apr. 2017).
272. 'Cope North Guam: Japan-U.S. Australia Joint Exercise in Guam', *Japan Defense Focus*, No. 86 (Mar. 2017) (http://www.mod.go.jp/e/jdf/no86/activities.html 28 Oct. 2017); Sneider, Daniel C., Sohn, Yul, and Soeya, Yoshihide, *U.S.-ROK-Japan Trilateralism: Building Bridges and Strengthening Cooperation*, NBR, Special Report No. 59 (July 2016).
273. NATO (2010), France (2011), Australia (2012), the UK (2013), India (2015) and Italy (2016) GSOMIA; Samuels, Richard J., *Special Duty*: 194–200.

274. Kim, Seung-yeon, 'S. Korea warns Japan of rolling back decision to suspend GSOMIA's termination', *Yonhap* (9 Jan. 2020) (https://en.yna.co.kr/view/AEN20200109003200325 22 Mar. 2020).
275. Tanabe, Yusuke and Furukawa, Shu, 'Japan fears S. Korea's scrapping of military info pact could hinder response to N. Korea', *Mainichi Japan* (23 Aug. 2019) (https://mainichi.jp/english/articles/20190823/p2a/00m/0na/005000c 24 Aug. 2019).
276. Botto, Kathryn, *Overcoming Obstacles to Trilateral U.S.-ROK-Japan Interoperability*, Carnegie Endowment for International Peace (Mar. 2020) (https://carnegieendowment.org/2020/03/18/overcoming-obstacles-to-trilateral-u.s.-rok-japan-interoperability-pub-81236 27 June 2020).
277. MOD, *Regarding the incident of an ROK naval vessel directing its fire-control radar at an MSDF patrol aircraft* (https://www.mod.go.jp/e/d_act/radar/index.html 12 June 2019); Lee Sung-eun, and Seo Seung-wook, 'Japan demotes Korea on defense', *Korea JoongAng Daily* (30 Dec. 2018) (https://koreajoongangdaily.joins.com/2018/12/30/politics/Japan-demotes-Korea-on-defense/3057536.html 21 June 2019).
278. Maley, Paul, 'Spies like us: ASIS training Japanese', *The Australian*, (21 Mar. 2015), (http://www.theaustralian.com.au/national-affairs/foreign-affairs/spies-like-us-asis-training-japanese/story-fn59nm2j-1227272245838?sv=f409313688bf4a84a2c72d13b230ba2c 16 Nov. 2015).
279. FCO, 'Britain and Japan conduct joint training in discreet capabilities', British Embassy Tokyo, (2 Nov. 2016) (https://www.gov.uk/government/world-location-news/britain-and-japan-conduct-joint-training-in-discreet-capabilities 15 May 2017); Wyn-Williams, Gareth, 'Watch troops launch mock attack on Gwynedd airfield and nuclear power station', *Daily Post*, (11 Oct. 2016) (http://www.dailypost.co.uk/news/north-wales-news/watch-troops-launch-mock-attack-12011103 15 May 2017).
280. 'Joint Training Exercise involving Japan, France, the United Kingdom and the United States', *Japan Defense Focus*, No. 89 (June 2017) (http://www.mod.go.jp/e/jdf/pdf/jdf_no89.pdf 23 Sept. 2017); RN/MOD, *Royal Navy and Royal Marines train alongside partner naval forces* (17 July 2017), (https://www.royalnavy.mod.uk/news-and-latest-activity/news/2017/july/17/170717-royal-navy-and-royal-marines-train-alongside-partner-naval-forces 23 Sept. 2017).
281. Ryall, Julian, 'Why a Royal Navy officer is serving with the Japanese', *Daily Telegraph*, (24 Apr. 2015) (http://www.telegraph.co.uk/news/worldnews/asia/japan/11562537/Why-a-Royal-Navy-officer-is-serving-with-the-Japanese.html 29 Apr. 2015).
282. 'Japan and Britain hold joint aerial drills', *NHK News*, (23 Oct. 2016), (http://www3.nhk.or.jp/nhkworld/en/news/20161023_05/, 23 Oct. 2016).
283. 'Japan, Britain ink logistics sharing pact to beef up defense ties', *Kyodo/Mainichi Japan*, (27 Jan. 2017) (http://mainichi.jp/english/articles/20170127/p2g/00m/0dm/003000c 27 Jan. 2017).
284. 'HAC first British troops to deploy in Japan', *The Military Times* (12 Oct. 2018) (https://www.themilitarytimes.co.uk/news/hac-first-british-troops-to-deploy-in-japan/ 14 Oct. 2018).
285. Ishihara, Yusuke, 'Japan-Australia "New Special Relationship,"' *NIDS Commentary*,

No. 44 (4 Apr. 2015); Nilsson-Wright, John, *UK Election Notes: Foreign Policy Opportunities—Security Cooperation with Japan* (23 Apr. 2015) (https://www.chathamhouse.org/expert/comment/17500, 25 Oct. 2015).

286. 'HAC first British troops to deploy in Japan', *The Military Times*.
287. MOFA, *Current situation and the Government of Japan's response*, (http://www.mofa.go.jp/j_info/visit/incidents/index.html 5 May 2011).
288. "Thinking of the Constitution': incapable of function or authority, contingencies and risk management' (*'Kenpō wokangaeru' kikikanriyūjinisokuō dekinukinō, kengen*), *Sankei Shimbun* (4 May 1995) (http://nippon.zaidan.info/seikabutsu/2002/01257/contents/531.htm, 2 Jan. 2010).
289. 'Hanshin Disaster, Post-war Resolution Request Cabinet Vote of No-confidence, Governing-Opposition Members of the Current Diet Look Back' (*Hanshindaishinsai, sengoketsugi, naikakufushinninanyoyatōgiin, konkokkai wofurikaeru*), *Asahi Shimbun*, (14 June 1995): 7.
290. Iokibe, Makoto, 'Crisis management: Administrative Response' (*Kikikanrigyōsei notaiyō*), in Hanshin-Awajidaishinsaihenshūiinkai (ed.), *Great Hanshin-Awaji Earthquake* (*Hanshin-Awajidaishinsai*) (Tokyo: Asahishimbunsha, 1996): 360–2; Conversations with Eric Johnston, *The Japan Times*, Osaka (30 May 2015); Ono, Keishi, 'Cooperation between the Self-Defense Forces (SDF) and Civil-sector Medical Institutions-Lessons from the Great East Japan Earthquake', *The National Institute for Defense Studies News*, (10 July 2012), pp. 1–4: 1.
291. JDA, *Defense of Japan 1995* (http://www.clearing.mod.go.jp/hakusho_data/1995/ara26.htm 27 Nov. 2017); Author's experience, Kobe (Mar. 1995).
292. 'Lessons for Japan From Kobe Quake', *The Diplomat*, (23 Mar. 2011), (https://thediplomat.com/2011/03/lessons-for-japan-from-kobe-quake/ 24 Oct. 2017).
293. *East Asian Strategic Review*, NIDS (2006) (http://www.nids.go.jp/english/publication/east-asian/pdf/2006/east-asian_e2006_08.pdf 22 May 2010): 236–8.
294. 'Regional security worries paved way for unified HQ for Japan's land forces', *Mainichi Japan*, (23 Mar. 2018) (https://mainichi.jp/english/articles/20180323/p2a/00m/0na/015000c#cxrecs_s 24 Mar. 2018).
295. Kitazawa, Toshimi, *Reasons Japan Needs the JSDF* (*Nihonni jieitaiga hitsuyōriyū*) (Tokyo: KadokawaOneteema21, 2012).
296. MOD, *Outline of Defense Minister's Extraordinary Press Conference* (*Daijinrinjikaikengaiyō*) (19 Mar. 2011) (http://www.mod.go.jp/j/press/kisha/2011/03/19.pdf 17 Mar. 2017).
297. MOD, *Disaster Call-Up of Reserve/Ready Reserve Personnel*, Press Release (16 Mar. 2011), (http://www.mod.go.jp/e/pressrele/2011/110316.html 23 March 2011); 'Aid Japan With All Strength!' (*Chikara wo awasetenihon wo sukuō!*), *Mamor*, 52 (June 2011), 4–27: 17; MOD, *Defense of Japan 2011* (http://www.clearing.mod.go.jp/hakusho_data/2011/2011/html/nt400000.html 14 Mar. 2017).
298. 'Aid Japan With All Strength!', *Mamor*, (June 2011): 6–7; MLIT, *Japan Coast Guard Annual Report 2012* (http://www.kaiho.mlit.go.jp/info/books/report2012/html/tokushu/p022_02_01.html 12 Feb. 2018).
299. Ibid: 16–7.

300. Takarajimasha, *JSDF vs. East Japan Great Earthquake* (*Jieitai vs. higashinihondaishinsai*), (Tokyo: Takarajimasha, 2011): 16–7.
301. Kurashina, Yuko, *Peacekeeping Participation and Identity Changes in the Japan Self Defense Forces: Military Service as 'Dirty Work'*, PhD Thesis (College Park, MD.: University of Maryland, 2005): 2.
302. MOD, *Defense of Japan 2011*, (http://www.clearing.mod.go.jp/hakusho_data/2011/2011/html/nct30000.html 3 Nov. 2017).
303. Saigō, Kinya, *Great East Japan Earthquake Record of a GSDF Officer's 138 Days* (*Higashinihon daishinsai rikujōjieikan toshiteno 138nichikannokiroku*), (Tokyo: ImpressR&D, 2016): 19–27.
304. Ibid: 39–44.
305. *US Assistance-Operation Tomodachi*, Vanderbilt University, Center for US-Japan Studies and Cooperation (http://www.vanderbilt.edu/publicpolicystudies/usjc/Quake/US%20Assistance.pdf 5 May 2011)
306. Eldridge, Robert D., 'Information Sharing Between U.S. and Japanese Forces Before, During, and After Operation Tomodachi', in Goldenberg, Irina, Soeters, Joseph, Dean, Weylon H. (eds.), Information Sharing in Military Operations (New York: Springer, 2016), pp. 135–46.
307. *Japan Military Review* (*Gunjikenkyū*) (May 2011): 33–4; Kawakami, Hirotaka; Kanari, Ryuichi; Fujita, Naotaka, 'U.S. military providing huge disaster relief effort', *Asahi Shimbun*, (24 Mar. 2011) (http://www.asahi.com/english/TKY201103230212.html 26 Mar. 2011).
308. Imagawa, Yukio, *Cambodia and Japan* (*Kanbojia tonihon*) (Tokyo: Rengo, 2000): 187–8.
309. MOD, *Lessons Learned of Responses to the Great East Japan Earthquake: final report* (*Higashinihondaishinsai enotaiō nikansurukyōkunjikō (saigotorimatome)*) (Nov. 2012) (http://www.mod.go.jp/j/approach/defense/saigai/pdf/kyoukun.pdf 7 Oct. 2016).
310. Takarajimasha, *JSDF vs. East Japan Great Earthquake*: 36–43; Kajimoto, Tetsushi, 'MSDF Hovercraft debuts in Oshima disaster drills', *The Japan Times*, (16 June 1998) (http://search.japantimes.co.jp/cgi-bin/nn19980616a8.html 28 April 2011).
311. *Japan Military Review* (*Gunjikenkyū*) (May 2011): 28–31; MOD, *Lessons Learned of Responses to the Great East Japan Earthquake*.
312. Kawakami, Hirotaka *et al*, 'U.S. military providing huge disaster relief effort'; Jackson, Tim, 'Sea Power and Domestic Disaster Response: Exploring the Role of Naval Vessels during Hurricane Katrina', *Liaison*, 4:1, (2008) (http://www.coe-dmha.org/Publications/Liaison/Vol_4No_1/Dept07.htm 14 Mar. 2011).
313. Takarajimasha, *JSDF vs. East Japan Great Earthquake*: 70–3; Tritten, Travis J., 'Marines help clear out Sendai Airport after tsunami', *Stars and Stripes*, (24 Mar. 2011) (http://www.stripes.com/marines-help-clear-out-sendai-airport-after-tsunami-1.138774# 28 Mar. 2011); US State Department, *Reopening of the Sendai Airport*, Teleconference Briefing (15 Apr. 2011) (https://2009-2017-fpc.state.gov/161156.htm 14 Oct. 2017).
314. Ibid; Tokyo Aviation Bureau Sendai Airport Office (*Tōkyōkōkūkyoku sendaikūkōjimusho*), (http://www.mlit.go.jp/common/000231873.pdf 12 Oct. 2017).
315. Mori, Eisuke, 'Operation Tomodachi, US Soldiers didn't even take a shower: Part 3'

(*Tomodachisakusen, beiheiwa shawāsura abinakatta: dai 3-kai*), *Nikkei Business Online* (10 Mar. 2015) (http://business.nikkeibp.co.jp/article/interview/20150306/278346/ 12 Oct. 2017).
316. Conversation with Col. Kasamatsu Makoto, Tokyo (Oct. 2012).
317. Takarajimasha, *JSDF vs. East Japan Great Earthquake*: 44–51.
318. Kawakami, Hirotaka *et al* 'U.S. military providing huge disaster relief effort'.
319. Inoue, Masamichi S., *Okinawa and the U.S. Military: Identity Making in the Age of Globalization* (New York: Columbia, 2017).
320. MOFA, *The Japan-U.S. Special Action Committee (SACO) Interim Report* (15 April 1996) (http://www.mofa.go.jp/region/n-america/us/security/seco.html 22 Mar. 2017).
321. 'DPJ government never committed to Futenma alternatives', *Asahi Shimbun*, (4 May 2011) (http://www.asahi.com/english/TKY201105040063.html 8 May 2011).
322. Tritten, Travis J., 'Marines help clear out Sendai Airport after tsunami'.
323. Glosserman, Brad, *Peak Japan: The End of Great Ambitions*, (Washington, DC.: Georgetown University Press, 2019): 155–60.
324. Gómez, Oscar, A., 'Human Security After the Great East Japan Earthquake: Rethinking the Role of External Assistance', in Hernandez, Carolina G, *et al* (eds.), *Human Security and Cross-Border Cooperation in East Asia* (London: Palgrave Macmillan, 2019), pp. 65–86: 72.
325. Ito, Masami, 'First foreign doctors arrive to help victims', *The Japan Times*, 28 March 2011 (http://search.japantimes.co.jp/cgi-bin/nn20110328a4.html 28 Mar. 2011).
326. Ueda, Mayumi; Ito, Hiroki; Inoue, Michio, 'Israel medical team heads home after quake aid mission', *Asahi Shimbun*, (16 Apr. 2011) (http://www.asahi.com/english/TKY201104150133.html 19 Apr. 2011).
327. MOFA Schedule (http://www.mofa.go.jp/j_info/visit/incidents/pdfs/rescue.pdf 1 May 2011); *Japan Platform* (http://www.japanplatform.org/work/index.html, 17 July 2010); *Japan Earthquake and Tsunami Update*, Center for Excellence in Disaster Management and Humanitarian Assistance, (21 Mar. 2011) (http://www.coe-dmha.org/Research/ResearchInfoMgmt/Japan/Japan03212011.pdf 24 Mar. 2011).
328. Gómez, Oscar, A., 'Human Security After the Great East Japan Earthquake': 78.
329. MOD, *Ability to live with local governments* (*Chihōkōkyōdantai de ikirunōryoku*), (http://www.mod.go.jp/gsdf/retire/chihou/index.html 12 Mar. 2018); MOD, *Retired SDF Useful as Disaster Prevention/Crisis Management Officials!* (*Bōsaikikikanrishokuin toshite taishokujiei-kan ga oyakunitachimasu!*) (http://www.mod.go.jp/pco/kanagawa/engo/1bousai.pdf 15 Mar. 2018).
330. MOD-Tohoku Defense Bureau, *Great East Japan Earthquake Tohoku Defense Bureau Activity Record* (*Higashinihondaishinsai niokeru Tōhokubōeikyoku nokatsudōkiroku*) (29 Mar. 2013): 17–20, (http://www.mod.go.jp/rdb/tohoku/sinsaikiroku/para8.pdf 23 Mar. 2018).
331. Samuels, Richard J., *3.11*: 194–5.
332. Takarajimasha, *JSDF vs. East Japan Great Earthquake*: 99; MLIT, *Japan Coast Guard Annual Report 2012*; JCG, *Record Related to the East Japan Great Earthquake*

(*Higashinihondaishinsai enotaiō nokiroku*), (Jan. 2012) (http://www.kaiho.mlit.go.jp/info/kouhou/jisin/20110311miyagi/120123_taiou.pdf 7 Feb. 2018).

333. Peace Boat, *Peace Boat Great East Japan Earthquake and Tsunami Disaster Relief Operations* (http://peaceboat.jp/relief/wp-content/uploads/2011/04/Ishinomaki-midtermreport.pdf 12 Apr. 2018).
334. JDA, *Defense of Japan 2000*, (http://www.clearing.mod.go.jp/hakusho_data/2000/honmon/frame/at1204010402.htm 10 Feb. 2018); JDA, *Defense of Japan 2004*, (http://www.clearing.mod.go.jp/hakusho_data/2004/2004/html/163433.html 10 Feb. 2018).
335. Yoshizaki, Tomonori, 'The Military's Role in Disaster Relief Operations: A Japanese Perspective', *NIDS* (2011), pp. 71–89: 79 (http://www.nids.mod.go.jp/english/event/symposium/pdf/2011/e_06.pdf 22 Nov. 2017).
336. Isobe, Kōichi, *The Frontline of Operation Tomodachi: Lessons from US-Japan Alliance Cooperation Considering the Fukushima Nuclear Accident* (*Tomodachisakusen nosaizensen-fukushimagenpatsujiko nimiru nichibeidōmeirenkei nokyōkun*) (Tokyo: Sairyūsha, 2019): 47–54.
337. 'TEPCO wanted to withdraw all nuclear plant workers 3 days after quake', *Mainichi Shimbun*, (18 Mar. 2011) (http://mdn.mainichi.jp/mdnnews/news/20110318p2a00m0na009000c.html 22 Mar. 2011).
338. Hongo, Jun, 'Panel lays bare Fukushima recipe for disaster', *The Japan Times*, (29 Feb. 2012), (http://www.japantimes.co.jp/text/nn20120229a1.html 29 Feb. 2012); MOD, *Lessons Learned of Responses to the Great East Japan Earthquake*.
339. Akiyama, Nobumasa, 'Self-Defense Forces and the US-Japan Alliance in the Fukushima Nuclear Crisis' (*Genpatsukiki niokeru jieitainichibeidōmei*), *The Journal of International Security* (*Kokusaianzenhoshō*), 41–2 (Sept. 2013), pp. 45–63.
340. Yoshizaki, Tomonori, 'The Military's Role in Disaster Relief Operations': 79; NPA, *Police Countermeasures and Damage Situation associated with 2011 Tohoku district—off the Pacific Ocean Earthquake* (10 June 2020) (https://www.npa.go.jp/news/other/earthquake2011/pdf/higaijokyo_e.pdf 4 July 2020).
341. Samuels, Richard J., *3.11: Disaster and Change in Japan* (Ithaca, NY.: Cornell University Press, 2013): 108–9.
342. Samuels, Richard J., *3.11*: 108–9; Yeo, Yezi, 'De-militarizing Military: Confirming Japan's Self-defense Forces' Identity as a Disaster Relief Agency in the 2011 Tohoku Triple Crisis', *Asia Journal of Global Studies*, 5–2 (2012–13), pp. 71–80.
343. Mori, Eisuke, 'Operation Tomodachi, US Soldiers didn't even take a shower'.
344. *Hand Book for Defense 2017*: 863; MOD, *Outline of "Public Opinion Survey on the Self-Defense Forces (SDF) and Defense Issues"*, Cabinet Office (Mar. 2012): 2 (http://www.mod.go.jp/e/d_act/others/pdf/public_opinion.pdf 17 Nov. 2017).
345. Ibid: 9–10; *Hand Book for Defense 2017*: 870.
346. *Hand Book for Defense 1999* (Tokyo: Asagumoshimbunsha, 1999): 711.
347. Martin, Alex, 'Military Wins Hearts and Minds', in *3.11: The Japan Times Special Report* (Tokyo: The Japan Times, 2011), pp. 49–50.
348. Kimizuka, Eiji, 'The Great East Japan Earthquake and the Self-Defense Forces' (*Higashinihondaishinsai tojieitai*), *The Journal of Military History*, 48–1: 6, 9; Takarajimasha, *JSDF vs. East Japan Great Earthquake*: 64–9.

349. Harada, Nahoko *et al*, 'Mental health and psychological impacts from the 2011 Great East Japan Earthquake Disaster: a systematic literature review', *Disaster and Military Medicine*, 1–17 (2015).
350. 'Call for Immediate Reserve Response: Kochi Area—Great East Japan Earthquake Disaster—Lieutenant Kominami (doctor) Sets Off, Heading for the Affected Area' (*Sokuōyobiji wo shōshūkōchiiimoto higashinihondaishinsai ni wazawaiha kominami2jō (ishi)ga hisaichiemuke, shuppatsu*), *Bōeinyūzu* (1 Apr. 2011) (http://www.boueinews.com/news/2011/20110401_3.html 22 Oct. 2017).
351. '10% of SDF personnel showed signs of depression, PTSD in fiscal 2013: survey', *Mainichi Japan* (11 Mar. 2017) (http://mainichi.jp/english/articles/20170311/p2a/00m/0na/026000c 12 Mar. 2017).
352. Tatsumi, Yuki, *Great Eastern Japan Earthquake: "Lessons Learned" for Japanese Defense Policy*, (Washington, DC.: Stimson Center, Nov. 2012).
353. Ono, Keishi, 'Cooperation between the Self-Defense Forces (SDF) and Civil-sector Medical Institutions': 2.
354. '17% of SDF reserves ready on 3/11', *Kyodo/The Japan Times*, (4 July 2012), (http://www.japantimes.co.jp/text/nn20120704a5.html 4 July 2012).
355. MOD, *Lessons Learned of Responses to the Great East Japan Earthquake*; 'Used C130 Transport Aircraft for MSDF Enhanced Deployed Transport Capacity' (*Chūkono C130yusōki, kaijihaibie yusōryokuzōkyō*), *Yomiuri Shimbun* (6 Sept. 2011) (http://www.yomiuri.co.jp/politics/news/20110905-OYT1T01172.htm 2 Nov. 2011).
356. Tatsumi, Yuki, *Great Eastern Japan Earthquake*.
357. *Hand Book for Defense 2015* (*Bōeihandobukku2015*) (Tokyo: Asagumshimbunsha, 2015): 240–1.
358. Ibid.
359. MOD, *Defense of Japan 2012*: Table III-4-1-3 (http://www.clearing.mod.go.jp/hakusho_data/2013/2013/html/n3412000.html 19 Jan. 2018).
360. Kawakami, Norito, *Actual Condition and Related Factors of 'Hikikomori' in Japan: World Mental Health Japan Survey* (*Wagakuni niokeru 'hikikomori' nojittai tokanrenyōin: sekaiseishinhoken nihonchōsa kara*) (13 Feb. 2010) (http://www8.cao.go.jp/youth/suisin/pdf/hikikomori/s1-2.pdf 24 May 2015); Ministry of Health, Labour, and Welfare, *Withdrawal Policy Issues* (*Hikikomorishisaku ni tsuite*) (2 Feb. 2010) (http://www.mhlw.go.jp/seisaku/2010/02/02.html 12 Feb. 2016); Zielenziger, Michael, *Shutting Out the Sun: How Japan Created Its Own Lost Generation* (New York: Doubleday, 2006).
361. Eldridge, Robert D., 'Japan's Changing Demographics and the Impact on Its Military', *Education About ASIA*, 22–3 (Winter 2017), pp. 27–30; Miura, Ruri, *War and Peace in the 21st Century: Why Conscription System is Needed Again* (*21sekino sensōtoheiwa: chōheisei wanaze futatabihitsuyō tosareteirunoka*), (Tokyo: Shinchosha, 2019).
362. *Hand Book for Defense 2019*: 904.
363. 'MSDF Bullying Suicide Lawsuit Plaintiff Appeal, Unauthorised Death Compensation Objection' (*Kaijiijime jisatsusoshō de genkokukōso shibōbaishōfunintei nifufuku*), *Japan Press Network/Kyodo* (4 Feb. 2011) (http://www.47news.jp/CN/201102/CN2011020401000457.html 22 Feb. 2011).

364. 'Serving JSDF Member who Unveiled the Darkness of the JSDF (*Jieitaino yamifuseiwo abaitagenekijieikan*) *Nippon Terebi* (23 Feb. 2014), (http://www.ntv.co.jp/document/back/201402.html 27 Aug. 2016).
365. *GSDF High Technical School Student Recruitment Guide* (*Kōteikōkagakkō seitōboshuannai*), MOD/JSDF (2015): 4; 'Non-fiction: Irons in the Fire—15 Years Old, A Boy's JSDF Tale' (*Zanonfikushon tetsuwaatsuiuchi ni-15-saishōnenjieitaimonogatari*), *Fuji Television* (2012), (http://nviewer.mobi/player?video_id=sm188 33390 12 June 2016).
366. GSDF, *Outline of the High Technical School* (*Kōteikōkagakkō nogaiō*), (http://www.mod.go.jp/gsdf/yt_sch/setumei/index.html 12 June 2016); *GSDF High Technical School Student Recruitment Guide* (2015): 2–3.
367. *Hand Book for Defense 2017*: 198; Bōeikenkyūkai (ed.), *JDA-JSDF* (*Bōeichō-jieitai*) (Tokyo: Kayashobō, 1996)): 378–9.
368. Bōeikenkyūkai (ed.), *JDA-JSDF*: 380–2.
369. NDA, *International Exchange Program* (http://www.mod.go.jp/nda/english/exchange/exchange.html 12 May 2018).
370. 'Defense Academy graduates to reimburse tuition for refusing to be commissioned', *Mainichi Japan*, (10 Feb. 2012), (http://mdn.mainichi.jp/mdnnews/news/20120 210p2a00m0na008000c.html, 11 Feb. 2012).
371. 'More defense academy graduates refusing to become SDF officers', *Mainichi Japan*, (https://mainichi.jp/english/articles/20160322/p2a/00m/0na/012000c 24 Mar. 2016).
372. Ibid.
373. *Hand Book for Defense 2017*: 198; NDMC, *Student position, repayment* (*Gakuseino mibun, shōkankin*), (http://www.ndmc.ac.jp/about/identification/ 14 Jan. 2018).
374. JDA, *Defense of Japan 2005*: 75 (http://www.mod.go.jp/e/publ/w_paper/pdf/2005/5.pdf 12 Jan. 2018).
375. *Hand Book for Defense 2017*: 201–3.
376. Ibid: 206.
377. *Handbook for Defense 1981* (*Bōeihandobukku56nenban*) (Tokyo: Asagumoshimbunsha, 1981): 117.
378. *Hand Book for Defense 2017*: 206.
379. NDA, *Graduate School of Science and Engineering* (http://www.nda.ac.jp/cc/gsse/ 12 June 2016); *Graduate School of Security Studies* (http://www.nda.ac.jp/cc/gsss/eng_intro.html 12 June 2016).
380. NIDS, *The Role of the National Institute for Defense Studies (NIDS)*, (http://www.nids.mod.go.jp/english/about_us/index.html 16 Jan. 2018).
381. *Handbook for Defense 1981*: 142; *Establishment Purpose* (*Setsuritsumokuteki, enkaku*), NDMC (http://www.ndmc.ac.jp/about/university_summary/history/ 24 Oct. 2017).
382. *Hand Book for Defense 2017*: 248.
383. Ibid; *Handbook for Defense 1981*: 142–4.
384. MOD, *Defense of Japan 2017* (http://www.mod.go.jp/e/publ/w_paper/pdf/2017/DOJ2017_feature3_web.pdf 12 Apr. 2018)
385. *JSDF Equipment Yearbook 1994*: 255–6.

386. *Handbook for Defense 1981*: 142–4.
387. *Hand Book for Defense 2017*: 250.
388. *Hand Book for Defense 1999*: 281; *Hand Book for Defense 2017*: 286.
389. Ibid; Asagumoshinbunsha henshūkyoku (ed.), *For the Blue Sky: 50 years of the ASDF* (*For the Blue Sky-ASDF no 50nenōgatahon*) (Tokyo: Asagumoshimbunsha, 2005): 28–32; Takarajimasha (ed.), *Everything About the ASDF* (*Kōkūjieitai no subete*) (Tokyo: Takarajimasha, 2015): 22–8.
390. MLIT-Aviation Bureau, *Concerning Safe and Efficient Aircraft Operations* (*Kōkūki no anzen katsu kōritsu-tekina na unkō ni tsuite*) (25 Feb. 2004), (http://www.mlit.go.jp/kisha/kisha04/12/120226/04.pdf: 12; 12 Mar. 2017); *Self-Defense Force High Altitude Training Airspace and Temporary Training Airspace (X-1~26)*, (*Kōkōdokunrenshikenkūiki oyobi rinjikunrenkūiki (X-1~26)*) (http://www.shiokawa-tetsuya.jp/field/img/140606kunren-kuiki.pdf 12 Mar. 2017).
391. MOD, *Northern Section, Northern Air Defense Command Jurisdiction* (*Hokubukōkū-hōmentaikannai*), (http://www.mod.go.jp/j/approach/chouwa/firing/hokubu.html#misawaoki_rinzi 12 Mar. 2017); MOD, *Misawa Special Open Sea Zone (Misawa Okirinji)*, (http://www.mod.go.jp/j/approach/chouwa/firing/images/misawa_atoa.pdf 12 Mar. 2017).
392. MOFA, *Security Consultative Committee Document U.S.-Japan Alliance: Transformation and Realignment for the Future*, (29 Oct. 2005) (http://www.mofa.go.jp/region/n-america/us/security/scc/doc0510.html 13 Mar. 2017); USFJ, *U.S. military returns portion of Yokota air space to Japan*, (25 Sept. 2008) (http://www.usfj.mil/Media/Press-Releases/Article-View/Article/563064/us-military-returns-portion-of-yokota-air-space-to-japan/ 13 Mar. 2017); MOFA, *Senkaku Islands Q&A*, (http://www.mofa.go.jp/region/asia-paci/senkaku/qa_1010.html#q15 13 Mar. 2017).
393. MOFA, *Agreement under Article VI of the Cooperation and Security between the United States of America, Regarding Facilities and Areas and the Status of United States Armed Forces in Japan*, (1960): 2 (http://www.mofa.go.jp/mofaj/area/usa/sfa/pdfs/fulltext.pdf 11 Mar. 2017); Kato, Akira, "The United States: The Hidden Actor in the Senkaku Islands", *Asia Pacific Bulletin* (East-West Center), No. 205 (Apr. 2013) (https://www.eastwestcenter.org/sites/default/files/private/apb205.pdf 11 Mar. 2017).
394. MOD, *USAF Exercise Participation* (*Beikūgunenshū eno sankanitsuite*), Official News Release, ASDF (20 May 2016) (http://www.mod.go.jp/asdf/news/houdou/H28/0520.html 11 Mar. 2017).
395. Frühstück, Sabine, 'The Modern Girl as Militarist: Female Soldiers In and Beyond Japan' Self-Defense Forces', *The Asia-Pacific Journal*, 12–44–3, (10 Nov. 2014).
396. JDA, *JDA Basic Gender Equality Plan* (*Bōeichō niokeru danjokyōdōsankaku nikakawaru kihon keikaku nitsuite*), (12 July 2006) (http://www.mod.go.jp/j/press/news/2006/07/12.pdf 12 Feb. 2010).
397. Woman qualifies to become fighter jet pilot for 1st time in Japan, *Mainichi Japan/Kyodo* (24 Aug.2018) (https://mainichi.jp/english/articles/20180823/p2g/00m/0fp/088000c 24 Aug.2018).
398. 'Women to pilot Self-Defense Forces fighters', *NHK News* (11 Nov. 2015), (http://www3.nhk.or.jp/nhkworld/english/news/20151111_13.html 11 Nov. 2014); 'Defense Ministry to abolish gender restrictions in almost all SDF units', *Mainichi*

Japan, (18 Apr. 2017) (https://mainichi.jp/english/articles/20170418/p2a/00m/0na/018000c#cxrecs_s 19 Apr. 2017).

399. Frühstück, Sabine, 'The Modern Girl as Militarist'; Gee, David, *Informed choice? Armed forces recruitment practice in the United Kingdom* (2007) (https://www1.essex.ac.uk/armedcon/story_id/000733.pdf 22 Feb. 2018).

400. MOFA, *Address by Prime Minister Shinzo Abe, at The Sixty-Eighth Session of The General Assembly of The United Nations* (26 Sept. 2013) (http://japan.kantei.go.jp/96_abe/statement/201309/26generaldebate_e.html 25 June 2016); 'JSDF Female Personnel Empowerment Initiative', *Japan Defense Focus*, No. 88 (May 2017) (http://www.mod.go.jp/e/jdf/no88/specialfeature.html 27 July 2017).

401. Frühstück, Sabine, 'The Modern Girl as Militarist'.

402. 'SDF's New Recruitment Tactics', *NHK News*, (24 Mar. 2016), (http://www3.nhk.or.jp/nhkworld/en/news/editors/3/2016032402/, 4 June 2016).

403. MOD, *Defense of Japan 2013*, (http://www.mod.go.jp/e/publ/w_paper/pdf/2013/46_Part3_Chapter4_Sec1.pdf, 4 June 2016); 'First female commander of MSDF division inaugurated at Yokosuka naval base', *Mainichi Japan*, (7 Mar. 2018) (https://mainichi.jp/english/articles/20180307/p2a/00m/0na/002000c, 9 Mar. 2018).

404. 'JMSDF Appointed the First Female Officer to Command a Destroyer', *Navy Recognition* (2 Mar. 2016) (http://www.navyrecognition.com/index.php?option=com_content&task=view&id=3637, 4 June 2016).

405. MOD, *I'm Walking Through my own Dream* (*Jibunjishinde yumeno ichizuo aruiteiru*) (Mar. 2007) (http://www.mod.go.jp/gsdf/html/qu_rikujitaiin/nakagawa/index.html 5 March 2008); MOFA, *Dispatch of a female Self-Defense Force personnel to NATO headquarters* (4 Nov. 2014) (http://www.mofa.go.jp/press/release/press4e_000488.html 2 Oct. 2016).

406. Sato, Fumika, 'A Camouflaged Military: Japan's Self-Defense Forces and Globalized Gender Mainstreaming', *The Asia-Pacific Journal*, 10–36–3, (3 Sept. 2012).

407. 'Despatched from Tohoku, Female GSDF Members Receive Thanks for Constructing 'Ladies' Bath'', (*Kasetsu 'onayu' nikansha nokoe tohokukarahaken no rikujijoseitain ga katsuyaku*), Sankei Shimbun (21 Apr. 2016) (http://www.sankei.com/affairs/news/160421/afr
1604210049-n1.html 22 Oct. 2016).

408. MOD, *Mamor* (http://www.mod.go.jp/j/publication/book/mamor/ 21 Mar. 2018).

409. 'Japan to give up raising women's share of leadership to 30% by 2020', *Mainichi Japan/Kyodo* (16 July 2020) (https://mainichi.jp/english/articles/20200716/p2g/00m/0na/013000c 17 July 2020).

410. Aihara, Jun, 'JDA to MOD, 10 Years Elevation Increased Presence, Questionable Ministerial Quality' (*Bōeichō-shō, shōkaku10nen masuonzaikan, towaretadaijinshishitsu*) (12 Sept. 2017) (https://www.asahi.com/articles/ASK9C4F9PK9CUTFK00F.html 27 Sept. 2017); 'Ex-vice defense chief Moriya gets 2 1/2-year term for bribery', *Kyodo/The Japan Times*, (6 Nov. 2008), (https://www.japantimes.co.jp/news/2008/11/06/national/ex-vice-defense-chief-moriya-gets-2–12-year-term-for-bribery/#.WrpAjdQS_Dc 22 Oct. 2010).

411. Shimizu, Masatomo, 'Seeking Abe's successor: Will LDP's 'Joan of Arc' become Japan's

first female PM?', *Nikkei Shimbun* (29 June 2015) (http://asia.nikkei.com/Japan-Update/Will-LDP-s-Joan-of-Arc-become-Japan-s-first-female-PM?page=2, 8 July 2015).
412. Live coverage of Diet proceedings, *NHK-General*, (30 Sept.-4 Oct. 2016); 'Inada's inconsistent remarks raise questions over qualifications as defense minister', *Mainichi Japan*, (15 Oct. 2016), (https://mainichi.jp/english/articles/20161015/p2a/00m/0na/011000c 17 Oct. 2016).
413. 'Inada's call for votes as defense minister raises doubts about her qualifications', *Mainichi Japan*, (29 June 2017) (http://mainichi.jp/english/articles/20170629/p2a/00m/0na/018000c 29 June 2017); Mulloy, Garren, 'Japan is back! From South Sudan', *East Asia Forum*, (15 July 2017) (http://www.eastasiaforum.org/2017/07/15/japan-is-back-from-south-sudan/ 15 July 2017); 'Sudden Conflict and PKO Cessation: South Sudan Despatched Unit Morning Reports, Government Failure to Explain: MOD (*Toppatsutekisentō ya PKOteishi mo-minamisūdanhakenbutai no nippōkōkaiseifusetsumeitozure bōeishō*), *Jiji*, (7 Feb. 2017), (http://www.jiji.com/jc/article?k=2017020701049&g=soc, 9 Feb. 2017).
414. MOD, *Defense of Japan 2013*: 287; MOD, *Plus Value*, GSDF Reserve Candidate Publicity Pamphlet (2014); Conversations with author, Tokyo (Nov. 2014, Oct. 2015).
415. '"I Cannot Run Out Exhausted": The life of Yukichi Tsuburaya who committed suicide after the Tokyo Olympic Games' (*Tsukarekitte hashiremasen" tōkyōgoringo jisatsushita tsuburayakōkichi nojinsei*), (21 Sept. 2013), *Shūkan Asahi* (27 Sept. 2013), (https://dot.asahi.com/wa/2013091900031.html?page=2 17 Mar. 2017).
416. Ministry of Health Labour and Welfare, *An overview of population dynamics monthly report yearly total (approximate number): 2015* (*Heisei27-nen jinkōdōtaitōkei geppōnenkei (gaisū) nogaikyō*), (http://www.mhlw.go.jp/toukei/saikin/hw/jinkou/geppo/nengai15/dl/gaikyou27.pdf 17 Oct. 2017).
417. 'Japan in Depth', *NHK News*, (9 June 2015), (http://www3.nhk.or.jp/nhkworld/english/news/japanindepth/2015060901.html, 27 June 2015).
418. 'Mental diseases blamed for some SDF members' suicides after missions abroad', *Mainichi Japan*, (6 June 2015) (http://mainichi.jp/english/english/newsselect/news/20150606p2a00m0na007000c.html 7 June 2015)
419. JDA, *Defense of Japan 2005* (http://www.mod.go.jp/e/publ/w_paper/pdf/2005/5.pdf 12 Jan. 2018); MOD, *Defense of Japan 2012* (http://www.mod.go.jp/e/publ/w_paper/pdf/2012/40_Part3_Chapter4_Sec1.pdf 12 Jan. 2018).
420. Ibid: 346–7; IPCH, *FAQ on Japan's International Peace Cooperation Assignment in South Sudan* (Oct. 2012) (http://www.pko.go.jp/pko_e/faq/faq_s_sudan.html 22 Nov. 2017).
421. Kawano, Hitoshi, 'The Positive Impact of Peacekeeping on the Japan Self Defense Forces', in Parmar, Leena (ed.), *Armed Forces and the International Diversities*, (Jaipur: Pointer, 2002), pp. 254–83: 265–7.
422. Shimozono, Sōta, *JSDF Mental Health Education Officer Teaches: Techniques for Removing Fatigue of the Soul* (*Jieitaimentarukyōkan gaoshieru kokorono tsukarewo torugijutsu*) (Tokyo: Asahishinso, 2013): 189–230.
423. MOFA, *Japan is Back*.

424. Hughes, Christopher W., *Japan's Re-emergence as a 'Normal' Military Power*: 10–5, 76–88.
425. Yoshihara, Toshi and Holmes, James R. (2018) 'Japanese Maritime Thought: If Not Mahan, Who?', *Naval War College Review*, 59–3–4: 4.
426. UK MOD, *UK Maritime Power*, Joint Doctrine Publication 0–10 (5th Edition), (Oct. 2017): 7 (https://assets.publishing.service.gov.uk/government/uploads/system/uploads/attachment_data/file/662000/doctrine_uk_maritime_power_jdp_0_10.pdf 21 Dec. 2017).
427. Cable, James, *Gunboat Diplomacy: Political Applications of Limited Naval Force* (New York: Praeger, 1971): 21.
428. Lindsey, Scott, 'Deep Coalitions: Alternative Power Projection', *Proceedings*, 125/1/1–151 (Jan. 1999), (https://www.usni.org/magazines/proceedings/1999-01/deep-coalitions-alternative-power-projection 2 Mar. 2018).
429. Morgan, Patrick M., *Deterrence Now* (Cambridge: Cambridge University Press, 2003): 2–5, 81–7.
430. Bansho, Koichiro, 'Japan's New Defense Strategy in the Southwest Islands and Development of Amphibious Operations Capabilities', *US-Japan Alliance Conference*, RAND (2018), pp. 8–15, (https://www.rand.org/content/dam/rand/pubs/conf_proceedings/CF300/CF387/RAND_CF387.pdf 22 May 2019).
431. Kitamura, Jun, *JSDF That Cannot Protect Senkaku* (*Senkakuwo mamorenaijieitai*) (Tokyo: Takarajimasha shinsho, 2012); Umetsu, Hiroyuki, 'Communist China's entry into the Korean hostilities and a U.S. proposal for a collective security arrangement in the Pacific offshore island chain', *Journal of Northeast Asian Studies*, 15 (1996), pp. 98–118.
432. Bansho, Koichiro, 'Japan's New Defense Strategy in the Southwest Islands and Development of Amphibious Operations Capabilities': 10.
433. 'GSDF unit deployed to Japan's westernmost island', *NHK News* (28 Mar. 2015), (http://www3.nhk.or.jp/nhkworld/en/news/20160328_22/, 29 Mar. 2015).
434. MOD, *Defense of Japan 2016*: 288–90 (http://www.mod.go.jp/e/publ/w_paper/pdf/2016/DOJ2016_3-1-2_web.pdf 22 Oct. 2017); 'Japan to boost defense in remote islands', *NHK News* (28 Mar. 2015), (http://www3.nhk.or.jp/nhkworld/en/news/20160328_25/, 29 Mar. 2015); MOD/GSDF, *New Structure of the GSDF* (*Rikujōjieitai no shintaisei*) (27 Mar. 2018) (http://www.mod.go.jp/gsdf/about/structure/index.html 31 Mar. 2018).
435. 'Japan enacts law to protect remote islands near borders', *Kyodo/Mainichi Japan*, (20 Apr. 2016) (http://mainichi.jp/english/articles/20160420/p2g/00m/0dm/064000c 21 Apr. 2016); Taira, Yoshitoshi, 'The Rift Between Okinawa and the Japanese Mainland: Historical Memory and Political Space', in Iokibe, Kaoru *et al* (Uleman, Fred *et al*, trans.), *History, Memory & Politics in Postwar Japan* (Boulder, CO.: Lynne Rienner, 2020), pp. 79–94.
436. MOD, *Extra Press Conference by the Defense Minister Onodera* (7 June 2014) (http://www.mod.go.jp/e/press/conference/2014/06/07.html 12 Jan. 2018).
437. Nakashinjo, Makoto, "Yaeyama Nippo' Provides Counterpoint to Anti-military Newspapers in Okinawa', *Japan Forward/Sankei* (5 June2017), (https://japan-for-

ward.com/yaeyama-nippo-provides-counterpoint-to-anti-military-newspapers-in-okinawa/ 12 Mar. 2018).
438. 4th Security Committee Meeting, 197th Diet Session, House of Representatives (29 Nov. 2018) (http://www.shugiin.go.jp/internet/itdb_kaigiroku.nsf/html/kaigiroku/001519720181129004.htm 14 May 2020).
439. 'Ishigakijima Invasion Assumption, MOD Operational Analysis' (*Ishigakijimaeno shinkōsōtei, bōeishōga sakusenbunseki*), Okinawa Times, (30 Nov. 2018) (https://www.okinawatimes.co.jp/articles/-/352371 21 May 2020).
440. 'SDF strengthening in southwest Japan includes plan for military clash, not residents' evacuation', *Ryukyu Shimpo*, (23 June 2019) (http://english.ryukyushimpo.jp/2019/06/28/30673/ 18 May 2020).
441. Yamaguchi, Noboru, 'Balancing Threat Perceptions and Strategic Priorities: Japan's Post-war Defence Policy', in Patalano, Alessio (ed.), *Maritime Strategy and National Security in Japan and Britain* (Leiden/Boston: Global Oriental, 2012), pp. 81–103.
442. Aoi, Chiyuki, 'Punching Below Its Weight: Japan's Post-Cold War Expeditionary Missions', in Patalano, Alessio (ed.), *Maritime Strategy and National Security in Japan and Britain*, pp. 132–56: 132–3.
443. 'Regional security worries paved way for unified HQ for Japan's land forces', *Mainichi Japan*.
444. MOD/GSDF, *Roles* (http://www.mod.go.jp/gsdf/english/roles/ 12 May 2018); MOD/GSDF, *New Structure of the GSDF* (*Rikujōjieitai no shintaisei*) (27 Mar. 2018) (http://www.mod.go.jp/gsdf/about/structure/index.html 31 Mar. 2018).
445. MOD, *Defense of Japan 2012*: 259.
446. GSDF Osprey are due to be based in Oita Prefecture near Sasebo, but as of 2020 have been based in Kisarazu, near Tokyo due to opposition in Oita.
447. Isobe, Kōichi, 'An Insider's View of the History, Evolution, and Prospects of Japan's Amphibious Rapid Deployment Brigade', *US-Japan Alliance Conference*, RAND (2018), pp. 16–24: 19.
448. Ibid: 17–8.
449. Newsham, Grant, 'How Japan got an Amphibious Rapid Deployment Brigade', *Asia Times* (27 Mar. 2018) (http://www.atimes.com/article/japan-got-amphibious-rapid-deployment-brigade/ 12 Apr. 2018).
450. Isobe, Kōichi, 'An Insider's View of the History, Evolution, and Prospects of Japan's Amphibious Rapid Deployment Brigade': 19–20; MOD, *Defense of Japan 2013*: 117, (http://www.mod.go.jp/e/publ/w_paper/pdf/2013/27_Part2_Chapter2_Sec3.pdf 23 Feb. 2018).
451. Newsham, Grant, 'How Japan got an Amphibious Rapid Deployment Brigade'.
452. Newsham, Grant, 'Japanese Amphibious Development: The bulldog and the salamander', *Marine Corps Gazette* (Dec. 2014), pp. 72–5; Ryall, Julian, 'Japan and US have secret invasion plans for disputed Diaoyu/Senkaku islands', *South China Morning Post*, (26 Jan. 2016) (http://www.scmp.com/news/asia/east-asia/article/1905469/japan-and-us-have-secret-invasion-plans-disputed-diaoyusenkaku 31 Jan. 2016).
453. Kallender-Umezu, Paul, 'Japan's Amphib Capabilities Struggle With Rivalries, Budgets', *Defense News* (12 Oct. 2015), pp. 22, 28: 22.

454. Hicks, Kathleen H. *et al*, *Landing Together: Pacific Amphibious Development and Implications* (Washington DC.: CSIS, 2016): 62.
455. Isobe, Kōichi, 'An Insider's View of the History, Evolution, and Prospects of Japan's Amphibious Rapid Deployment Brigade': 20.
456. Ota, Fumio, 'Jointness in the Japanese Self-Defense Forces', *Joint Force Quarterly*, (Winter 2000–2001), pp. 57–60: 59.
457. Ball, Desmond and Tanter, Richard, 'The Transformation of the JASDF's Intelligence and Surveillance Capabilities for Air and Missile Defence', *Security Challenges*, 8–3, (2012), pp. 19–56: 47–8; JDA, *1998 Policy evaluation report* (*Heisei20nendo seisakuhyōkasho*), (https://www.mod.go.jp/j/approach/hyouka/seisaku/results/20/jizen/honbun/13.pdf 12 Feb. 2018).
458. Hornung, Jeffrey W. 'Japan's Amphibious Joint Pain', *US-Japan Alliance Conference*, RAND (2018), pp. 25–46: 26.
459. Kallender-Umezu, Paul, 'Japan's Amphib Capabilities Struggle With Rivalries, Budgets': 28.
460. Hornung, Jeffrey W. 'Japan's Amphibious Joint Pain': 35–6.
461. Hicks, Kathleen H *et al*, *Landing Together: Pacific Amphibious Development and Implications*: 1–2.
462. MOD/GSDF, *ARDB* (http://www.mod.go.jp/gsdf/gcc/ardb/hensei/link1.html 12 May 2018).
463. Brown, Gerald G., *et al*, 'Steaming on Convex Hulls', *Informs*, Naval Postgraduate School, 37–4, (July/August 2007), pp. 342–52: 343–8.
464. Sharpe, Richard (ed.), *Jane's Fighting Ships 1991–92* (Coulsdon: Jane's Information Group, 1991): 778. *RFA Stromness* (later *USNS Saturn*) won a Falklands Conflict battle honour, for RAS, support, and landing over 400 Royal Marines under air attack: 'RFA Stromness', *Historical RFA* (http://www.historicalrfa.org/rfa-stromness 16 May 2020).
465. Newsham, Grant, 'Japanese Amphibious Development'.
466. Kubo, Nobuhiro, and Kelly, Tim, '*Izumo*-class destroyers under carrier-ization scrutiny: F35B utilisation mooted by insiders' (*Izumogatagoeikan no kūboka wokentō, F35B wo unyōkankeisha*), *Reuters* (26 Dec. 2017) (https://jp.reuters.com/article/2018-views-japan-ian-bremmer-idJPKBN1EN0JS 27 Dec. 2017); 'Defense Ministry considers procuring dozens more F-35 fighters', *Mainichi Japan* (31 Dec. 2017) (https://mainichi.jp/english/articles/20171231/p2a/00m/0na/011000c 2 Jan. 2017).
467. Saunders, Stephen (ed.), *Jane's Fighting Ships 2001–2002* (Coulsden: Jane's Information Group, 2001): 384; Conversations with USN officers (Tokyo: 2004–06).
468. Aibara, Ryo, 'ANALYSIS: Japan's defense to mark historic change if Izumo becomes flattop', *Asahi Shimbun* (27 Dec. 2017) (http://www.asahi.com/ajw/articles/AJ201712270020.html 29 Dec. 2017); MOD, *Defense of Japan 2019* (http://www.clearing.mod.go.jp/hakusho_data/2019/html/nc013000.html 6 Jan. 2020).
469. Wang, Zhaokun, 'Tokyo unveils new carrier', *Global Times* (7 Aug. 2013), (http://www.globaltimes.cn/content/802056.shtml#.UgFl9ZI3tsk 28 Mar. 2018); 'China urges Japan to follow the road of peaceful development', *Xinhua* (26 Dec. 2017), (http://www.xinhuanet.com/english/2017–12/26/c_136853292.htm 2 Jan. 2018).

470. Marina Militare, *Cavour: Portaerei (CVH)—Classe Cavour*, (Italian), (http://www.marina.difesa.it/uominimezzi/navi/Pagine/Cavour.aspx 4 Jan. 2018).
471. House of Commons, 'Carrier Strike Capability', *Hansard*, (10 May 2012): Column 140–152 (https://publications.parliament.uk/pa/cm201213/cmhansrd/cm120510/debtext/120510-0001.htm#12051029000006 12 Jan. 2018).
472. Okabe, Isaku, 'If Our Flat-Top DDHs Get F-35B' (*KaijiDDH ga F-35B wo tōzaisuruhi*) *Sekkai no Kansen* (May 2017): 102–5.
473. Handa, Shigeru, *Proceed Under Security Legislation! JSDF able to pre-emptively attack* (*Anpohōseika desusumu! senseikōgekidekiru jieitai*), (Tokyo: Akebishobō, 2019): 73–80.
474. Kerin, John, 'PM's floating fighter jet plan quietly sunk by Defence', *The Australian Financial Review* (7 July 2015) (http://www.afr.com/news/politics/pms-floating-fighter-jet-plan-quietly-sunk-by-defence-20150707-gi6qxj?stb=twt 12 July 2015).
475. Bush, Steve, *British Warships and Auxiliaries 2010/2011* (Liskeard: Maritime Books, 2010): 47; Allison, George, 'RFA Argus sails for Caribbean to support British Overseas Territories', *UK Defence Journal* (3 Apr. 2020) (https://ukdefencejournal.org.uk/rfa-argus-sails-for-caribbean-to-support-the-british-overseas-territories/ 12 May 2020); Spurlock, Kenneth R., 'Hospital Ships: A Transformational Necessity for Japan', *NIDS Bulletin* (June 2008) (http://www.nids.mod.go.jp/english/publication/kiyo/pdf/2008/bulletin_e2008_6.pdf 12 Oct. 2019).
476. MOD, *Defense of Japan 2020*: 17.
477. MOD, Press Conference (23 June 2020) (https://www.mod.go.jp/j/press/kisha/2020/0623a.html 17 July 2020).
478. Ryall, Julian, 'Japan builds new surveillance warship targeting Chinese, North Korean submarines', *South China Morning Post* (11 Mar. 2020) (https://www.scmp.com/week-asia/politics/article/3074680/japan-builds-new-surveillance-warship-targeting-chinese-north 12 May 2020).
479. MOD, *Defense of Japan 2016*: 340–2; MOD/Joint Staff, *Statistics on scrambles through FY2019* (9 Apr. 2020) (https://www.mod.go.jp/js/Press/press2020/press_pdf/p20200409_02.pdf 2 July 2020); 'Chinese Bombers Fly between Southern Japan Islands', *Jiji Press* (21 May 2015), (http://jen.jiji.com/jc/eng?g=eco&k=2015052100958 21 May 2015).
480. Moss, Trefor, 'Here Come…China's Drones', *The Diplomat* (2 Mar. 2013) (https://thediplomat.com/2013/03/here-comes-chinas-drones/ 12 May 2015).
481. Japan Aerospace Defense Ground Environment (JADGE). MOD, *Defense of Japan 2009* (*Bōeihakusho2009*) (http://www.clearing.mod.go.jp/hakusho_data/2009/2009/html/l3131000.html 21 Jan. 2018).
482. Drifte, Reinhard, 'The Japan-China Confrontation Over the Senkaku/Diaoyu Islands: Between "shelving" and "dispute escalation,"' *Asia-Pacific Journal-Japan Focus* (27 July 2014), 12–30–3, (https://apjjf.org/2014/12/30/Reinhard-Drifte/4154/article.html 18 May 2015).
483. Oguro, Masataka, *Ensuring Japan's Future Air Security: Recommendations for Enhancing the JASDF's readiness to Confront Emerging Threats*, Brookings (Sept. 2018) (https://www.brookings.edu/wp-content/uploads/2018/09/FP_20180925_JASDF_readiness.pdf 7 Feb. 2020): 12.

484. 'Japan now instantly scrambles jets against China's from Fujian', *Kyodo* (19 July 2020) (https://english.kyodonews.net/news/2020/07/c0f33e803562-japan-now-instantly-scrambles-jets-against-chinas-from-fujian.html 19 July 2020).
485. MOD/Joint Staff, *Statistics on scrambles through FY2019*.
486. Erickson, Andrew S. and Kennedy, Conor, 'Directing China's 'Little Blue Men': Uncovering the Maritime Militia Command Structure', *Asia Maritime Transparency Initiative*, (11 Sept. 2015) (https://csis-website-prod.s3.amazonaws.com/s3fs-public/publication/170505_GreenM_CounteringCoercionAsia_Web.pdf?OnoJXfWb4A5gw_n6G.8azgEd8zRIM4wq 22 May 2019).
487. Cheng, Dean, 'Winning without Fighting: Chinese Legal Warfare', Heritage Foundation (21 May 2012) (https://www.heritage.org/asia/report/winning-without-fighting-chinese-legal-warfare 21 Feb. 2019); Green, Michael J, *et al*, *Countering Coercion in Maritime Asia: The Theory and Practice of Gray Zone Deterrence*, CSIS (May 2017) (https://csis-website-prod.s3.amazonaws.com/s3fs-public/publication/170505_GreenM_CounteringCoercionAsia_Web.pdf?OnoJXfWb4A5gw_n6G.8azgEd8zRIM4wq 12 May 2019).
488. McLellan Ross, Marta, *The Japan-China Maritime and Air Communication Mechanism: Operational and Strategic Considerations*, JIIA, (30 June 2015) (https://www2.jiia.or.jp/pdf/fellow_report/150630_Ms_Ross_ECS.pdf 21 Nov. 2017); 'Japan-China communication mechanism launched to avert clash at sea', *Kyodo* (8 June 2018), (https://english.kyodonews.net/news/2018/06/d690bde410a4-update1-japan-china-communication-mechanism-launched-to-avert-clash-at-sea.html 12 Jan. 2019).
489. MOFA, *Confirmation of Chinese government vessels in Japan's maritime areas surrounding the Senkaku Islands* (17 Aug. 2016) (https://www.mofa.go.jp/press/release/press4e_001245.html 22 Mar. 2017); Pajon, Céline, 'Japan's Coast Guard and Maritime Self-Defense Force in the East China Sea: Can a Black-and-White System Adapt to a Gray-Zone Reality?', *Asia Policy*, 23 (Jan. 2017), pp. 111–30: 118.
490. Sato, Yoichiro, 'Japan and the South China Sea Dispute: A Stakeholder's Perspective', in Storey, Ian, and Lin, Cheng-yi, *The South China Sea Dispute: Navigating Diplomatic and Strategic Tensions* (Singapore: ISEAS, 2016), pp. 272–90: 273.
491. Drifte, Reinhard, *Japan's Policy towards the South China Sea—Applying "Proactive Peace Diplomacy"?*, PRIF Report 140 (2016): 1.
492. Asia Maritime Transparency Initiative, *China Island Tracker* (https://amti.csis.org/island-tracker/china/ 12 Sept. 2020).
493. 'Air Force bombers land on island airport for first time', *China Daily* (19 May 2018), (http://en.people.cn/n3/2018/0519/c90000–9461810.html 21 May 2018); 'China showcases jet fighters at South China Sea island', *Global Times*, (1Dec. 2017) (http://en.people.cn/n3/2017/1201/c90000–9299186.html 21 May 2018).
494. Drifte, Reinhard, *Japan's Policy towards the South China Sea*: 1.
495. Roy, Denny, 'The United States and the South China Sea: Frontlin of Hegemonic Tension?', in Storey, Ian, and Lin, Cheng-yi, *The South China Sea Dispute*, pp. 228–46: 233.
496. Ibid: 236.
497. Wingfield Hayes, Rupert, 'Australia conducting 'freedom of navigation' flights in South China Sea', *BBC News*, (15 Dec. 2015) (http://www.bbc.com/news/maga-

zine-35031313 17 Dec. 2015); Werner, Ben, 'Future South China Sea FONOPS Will Include Allies, Partners', *USNI* (12 Feb. 2019), (https://news.usni.org/2019/02/12/41070 23 May 2019).

498. Drifte, Reinhard, *Japan's Policy towards the South China Sea*: 21.
499. *U.S., partner navies sail together in South China Sea*, Commander, US Pacific Fleet (8 May 2019) (https://www.cpf.navy.mil/news.aspx/110737 12 Mar. 2020); *Indo-Pacific Deployment 2019(IPD19)*, JMSDF (Aug. 2019) (https://www.mod.go.jp/msdf/en/operation/IPD19.html 12 Mar. 2020); DeAeth, Duncan, 'US, Japan, India, Philippines conduct joint naval patrol through South China Sea', *Taiwan News*, (9 May 2019) (https://www.taiwannews.com.tw/en/news/3698009 12 Mar. 2020).
500. 'Japan denies submarine drill in South China Sea is a warning to Beijing', *Kyodo/South China Morning Post*, (18 Sept. 2018) (https://www.scmp.com/news/asia/east-asia/article/2164664/japan-denies-submarine-drill-south-china-sea-warning-beijing 12 Oct. 2018).
501. CAS, *National Security Strategy* (17 Dec. 2013): 8–9, 12–3, 17, 24.
502. Drifte, Reinhard, *Japan's Policy towards the South China Sea*: 6–7.
503. Hayton, Bill, *The South China Sea: The Struggle for Power in Asia* (New Haven: Yale University Press, 2014): 221–2.
504. Teufel Dreyer, June, 'Security, Defense Cooperation Puts Japan-Taiwan Relations Back on Track', *Japan Forward* (13 July 2018) (https://japan-forward.com/security-defense-cooperation-puts-japan-taiwan-relations-back-on-track/ 11 Feb. 2020); Watanabe, Yoshikazu, *et al*, *Taiwan Contingency and Japan's Security* (*Taiwanyūjito nihonnoanzenhoshō*) (Tokyo: Wanipurasu, 2020).
505. MOD, *Defense of Japan 2017*: 311; Yoshikawa, Yukie, 'Okinotorishima: Just the Tip of the Iceberg', *Harvard Asia Quarterly*, 9–4 (Fall 2005), pp. 51–61; 'Japan protests Chinese maritime survey off southern islets', *The Asahi Shimbun/AP* (21 July 2020) (http://www.asahi.com/ajw/articles/13564077 22 July 2020).
506. MOFA, *Suspicion of illegal ship-to-ship transfers of goods by North Korea-related vessels*, (19 Feb. 2020) (https://www.mofa.go.jp/fp/nsp/page4e_000757.html 22 Mar. 2020); MOD, *Suspicion of illegal transshipment of goods offshore by North Korean vessels* (*Kitachōsenkanrensenpaku niyoru ihōnayōjō deno busshino tsumikaeno utagai*) (24 Jan. 2018) (http://www.mod.go.jp/j/press/news/2018/01/24a.html 27 Jan. 2018); 'Japan plane sees N. Korea, C'wealth of Dominica tankers' contact', *Mainichi Japan/Kyodo* (25 Jan. 2018) (https://mainichi.jp/english/articles/20180125/p2g/00m/0dm/070000c#cxrecs_s 26 Jan. 2018).
507. 'Royal Navy Deploys Third Ship for North Korea Patrols', *MAREX* (11 Apr. 2018) (https://www.maritime-executive.com/article/royal-navy-deploys-third-ship-for-north-korea-patrols#gs.Pg3iC8g 14 Apr. 2018); Government of Canada, *Operation Neon* (https://www.canada.ca/en/department-national-defence/services/operations/military-operations/current-operations/operation-neon.html 19 May 2020).
508. Tonami, Aki, and Watters, Stewart, 'Japan's Arctic Policy: The Sum of Many Parts', *Arctic Yearbook 2012*: 94–5 (https://arcticyearbook.com/images/Articles_2012/Tonami_and_Watters.pdf 12 Jan. 2016).
509. *Charting Japan's Arctic Strategy*, Brookings (19 Oct. 2015) (https://thearcticreport.

com/arctic-report-articles/charting-japans-arctic-strategy/ 12 Mar. 2018); CAS, *National Security Strategy* (17 Dec. 2013): 9.
510. Ishihara, Takahiro, 'China's Arctic Activities and the Impact of the Ice Silk Road Concept on the International Security Environment' (*Hyōjōshirukurōdokōsōga kokusaianzenhoshōkankyō niataerueikyō, nitsuite-chūgokuno hokkyokushinshutsu nikansuru anzenhoshōmenkara nokōsatsu*), *The Journal of International Security (Kokusaianzenhoshō)*, 47–1 (June 2019), pp. 52–71.
511. Tonami, Aki, and Watters, Stewart, 'Japan's Arctic Policy': 95, 99.
512. 'Maritime organization approves Bering Strait shipping routes', *Mainichi Japan*, (26 May 2018) (https://mainichi.jp/english/articles/20180526/p2g/00m/0in/ 032000c 26 May 2018); conversations with Tonami Aki (Hong Kong, June 2016; Tokyo, January 2017); Brown, James D. J., *Japan, Russia and their Territorial Dispute: The Northern Delusion*, (Abingdon: Routledge, 2017): 54–5; Loy, Jennifer, 'Russia in the Arctic: Friend or Foe?', *Geopolitical Monitor* (19 Apr. 2018), (https://www. geopoliticalmonitor.com/russia-in-the-arctic-friend-or-foe/ 5 June 2018).

5. CONCLUSION

1. Meek, James, 'The Leopard', *The London Review of Books*, 36–12 (19 June 2014), pp. 3–10: 3.
2. *JSDF Equipment Yearbook 2016–2017*: 173, 214–5, 221–2.
3. Bush, Steve, *British Warships and Auxiliaries 2016/2017* (Liskeard: Maritime Books, 2016); RN-MOD, *Ships* (https://www.royalnavy.mod.uk/the-equipment/ships 11 Dec. 2017).
4. MOD,'Document 30: Concerning the Mid-T erm Defence Capability Improvement Plan' (*Shiryō30 chūkibōeiryokuseibikeikaku nitsuite*), (9 Sept. 1985) Decision of the National Defense Council,*Defense White Paper 1985,* (http:// www.clearing.mod. go.jp/hakusho_data/1986/w1986_9130.html 7 Aug. 2018).
5. MOD, *Defense of Japan 2015*, (Tokyo: Ministry of Defense, 2015): 408.
6. JDA, 'Establishment of New Joint Operations Procedures' (*Aratanatōgōunyōtaisei no seibi*) *Defense White Paper 2005*(http://www.clearing.mod.go.jp/ hakusho_data/ 2005/2005/html/17242100.html 12 Mar. 2017).
7. Fukuyoshi,Shōji, *Japan Military Review* (*Gunji Kenkyū*), 53–1 (Jan. 2018): 86–7.
8. MOD, *Concerning Structural Re-organisation (MOD Reform)* (*Soshikikaihen (bōeishō kaikaku) nitsuite*) (1 Oct. 2015) (http://www.mod.go.jp/j/approach/others/ kaikaku/pdf/h27_kaihen.pdf 28 May 2017).
9. Hughes, Christopher W., *Japan's Remilitarisation* (Abingdon: IISS/Routledge, 2009): 35–40; Maruyama, Takashi, 'Oral History Interview', Tanaka, Akihiko, Murata, Koji (12 Apr. 1996), *National Security Archive: U.S.-Japan Project*, NSA (https:// nsar-chive2.gwu.edu//japan/maruyamaohinterview.htm 12 Mar. 2018).
10. Katzenstein, Peter J., *Cultural Norms and National Security: Police and Military in Postwar Japan* (Ithaca: Cornell University Press, 1996).
11. MOFA, *Japan-EU Strategic Partnership Agreement (SPA)*, (17 July 2018), (https://www.mofa.go.jp/files/000381942.pdf 25 Feb.2020).

12. 'Trump: Japan-US Security Treaty is unfair', *NHK*, (29 June 2019), (https://www3.nhk.or.jp/nhkworld/en/news/20190629_31/ 30 June 2019); 'US demanded Japan pay $8bn annually for troops: Bolton', *Nikkei-Asia/Kyodo*, (22 June 2019), (https://asia.nikkei.com/Politics/International-relations/US-demanded-Japan-pay-8bn-annually-for-troops-Bolton 30 June 2019).
13. Hughes, Christopher W., *Japan's Foreign and Security Policy under the 'Abe Doctrine': New Dynamism or New Dead End?* (Basingstoke: Palgrave Macmillan, 2015): 29.
14. Ishikawa, Junichi, 'Aegis Ashore 'Top Secret SPY-7 Radar" (*Iijisuashoa 'gokuhi SPY-7reedaa'*), *Japan Military Review* (*Gunjikenkyū*), (Mar. 2020), pp. 36–45; Fujita, Naotaka, 'Former SDF chief blasts scrapping of Aegis Ashore defense system', *The Asahi Shimbun*, (15 July 2020) (http://www.asahi.com/ajw/articles/13546952 16 July 2020).
15. 'Japan seeks record defense budget to boost capabilities in new areas', *Mainichi Japan*, (30 Sept. 2020), (https://mainichi.jp/english/articles/20200930/p2g/00m/0na/109000c 30 Sept. 2020).
16. 'Police force established to repel invaders of outlying islands', *The Asahi Shimbun*, (2 Apr. 2020) (http://www.asahi.com/ajw/articles/13266097 7 Apr. 2020).

INDEX

Note to Index: This index includes references to the main text, with incidents and places specific to one country being categorised together with that country. Non-state organisations, such as companies, international waters, technology and other items regarded as non-state or not limited within one country are listed independently. No titles are provided for individuals, other than for military personnel (last known rank), unless primarily known as a civilian (such as Prime Minister Nakasone, previously a naval officer).

AAM-1/Type-69 (missile), 97
AAM-4 (missile), 217
AAV-7 (APC), 197, 250–1, 253
Abandoned Chemical Weapons (ACW), 172
Abe, Shinzo, xvi, 65, 119, 122, 127, 164, 174, 177–8, 187, 191–2, 194, 196–206, 227, 244, 246–7, 263–4, 269, 273–4, 276, 278
'Abe-nomics', 119
'Abe doctrine', 264, 277
Abbot, Anthony 'Tony' John, 206
Actively-Electronically Scanned Radar (AESA), 214
Advanced Technology Demonstrator, Experimental-2 (ATD-X-2) Shin-shin, 215
AEGIS (naval system), 84–5, 90, 101, 170–1, 184, 196–7, 199, 223, 253–4
Aegis Ashore, 186, 198, 263, 277–8

AERA, 65
Afghanistan, 51, 76–7, 113, 153, 195, 218, 271
African Union (AU), 222
   Mission in Somalia (AMISOM), 222
Agawa, Naoyuki, 7, 19, 22, 87
AH-1/AH1S Huey Cobra, 54, 197
AH-64D Apache, 197
Aichi, Kiichi, 76
Aida, Yūji, 14
AIM-4 Falcon (AAM), 97
AIM-7 Sparrow (AAM), 97
AIM-9 Sidewinder (AAM), 97
Airborne Early Warning (AEW), 100–2, 107, 112–3, 179, 202, 255, 270
Airborne Warning and Control Systems (AWACS), 195, 197, 244
Air-launched cruise missiles, 195, 199–200

INDEX

Aizawa, Kōetsu, 178
Aizawa, Teruaki, 77, 86
Ajello, Aldo, 144
Akashi, Yasushi, xii, 132–4, 137, 140, 142
Alice in Wonderland, 275
Allison, Graham, 177
All Nippon Airways (ANA), 109
Alondra Rainbow (merchant vessel), 221
Amami-Ōshima, 249
Amphibious capabilities/operations, 21–2, 50, 56–9, 65–7, 74, 76, 83, 162–4, 167, 179, 182, 194, 196–7, 207–8, 228–9, 231, 233, 248–56, 263, 270–2, 275–6
AMX-10P (MICV), 55
AN/APS-20 (radar), 100–1
AN/APG-36 (radar), 101
Antarctic, 85, 261
Anti-Access Area Denial (A2/AD), 103, 196–7, 199, 259
Anti-satellite (ASAT) capabilities, 213
Antonov aircraft, 145, 149, 225
Anti-aircraft warfare (AAW), 49, 55, 72–3, 79, 83–4, 106–7, 110
ANZUS, 219, 229
AOE Fast combat support ship, 73, 85, 131, 134, 154, 208, 218, 224, 233, 253–4, 271
Aoi, Chiyuki, x, 114, 122, 219–20, 225
Araki Report, 122, 127
Arctic, 261
Arctic Council, 261
Armacost, Michael Hayden, 123
Armitage Report, 171
Armitage, Richard Lee, 171
Armoured fighting vehicles (AFV), 49, 53, 55, 65, 197
Armoured personnel carriers (APC), 49, 55, 65–6, 138, 158, 171, 197, 250

Armoured reconnaissance vehicles (ARV), 65
Artillery, 15–6, 22, 32–4, 36, 49–51, 53–6, 65–6, 97, 157, 171, 193, 196, 214, 253
Asahi Shimbun, 25
Ashida, Hitoshi, 19–20, 29, 35, 37, 113, 266, 269
Asian Infrastructure Investment Bank (AIIB), 177–8
ASM-1 Type-80 (missile), 83, 103
ASROC (ASW), 83
Association of Southeast Asian Nations (ASEAN), 169, 182, 206–7, 258–9, 275
 ASEAN Defence Ministers' Meeting (ADMM), 207; ASEAN Regional Forum (ARF), 169–70
Atomic/nuclear energy/power, 42, 75, 78, 90, 162, 180, 182, 196, 235–6, 229, 230, 231, 235–8
Atomic/nuclear weapons, 25, 27, 42, 57, 104, 107, 159–60, 166, 171, 178, 182–5, 191, 195–7, 199–200, 206, 244
Auer, James E., 7–8, 17, 22, 43, 58–9, 68, 75–6, 78, 80, 90
Augusta-Westland, 216
Australia, 17, 28, 53, 66, 83, 89, 133, 137, 142, 177–8, 197, 205–7, 210, 212, 216, 219, 221, 228–9, 236, 240, 248, 255, 259, 263, 270–1, 274
 Australian Defence Forces (ADF), 206, 219
 Australian Secret Intelligence Service (ASIS), 229;
 National Security Strategy, 206
 Royal Australian Air Force (RAAF), 234
 Royal Australian Navy (RAN), 67, 229, 261

INDEX

Canberra-class, 255
Austria, 156
Azuma, Ryoko, Captain, 245

BAe (British Aerospace), 96
Baker, James Addison, 123
Bahrain, 223
Ball, Desmond, 84
Ballistic missile submarines (SSBN), 75
Bangladesh, 142, 145
Banshō, Kōichirō, Lt.-General, 157, 221, 249, 251
Bashi Channel, 80
Battle of Britain, 92, 270
Battle of Midway, 265
Belenko, Victor, Lt., 98–101, 107, 270, 272
Belgium, 96, 158
Bering Strait, 261
Black, Lindsay, 181
Blair, Anthony 'Tony' Charles Lynton, 217
Blair, Dennis Cutler, Admiral, 257
BMD (mechanized infantry combat vehicle MICV), 55
BMP (MICV), 55
Boeing-727, 109
Boeing-747, 95, 105, 219, 225
Bosnia-Herzegovina, 144, 256
Boyd, Carl, 70
Bradford, John F., 221–2
Bradley (MICV), 55
Breslin, Shaun, 177
Brown, James D.J., 163
Buddhism, 64, 87, 123
Bulgaria, 142
Bundy, William P., 56
Bush, George Walker, 171, 176
Buzan, Barry, 177

C-1, 96

C-2, 250
C3 (Command, Control, Communications), 149, 222, 252
C4-ISR (Command, Control, Communications, Computers-Intelligence, Surveillance, Reconnaissance), 212–3, 238
C-17, 234
C-46, 96, 101, 108
C-130H, 96, 109, 130, 134, 145, 149, 151, 158, 219, 223–5, 233
Cai, Peter, 178
Calder, Kent, 43, 121
Cambodia, xv, 88, 120, 125, 129, 130–43, 144, 146, 147, 150, 192, 206, 278
  Khmer Rouge, 132, 140–2
  Paris Peace Accords, 132
  Sihanouk, Norodom, Prince, 132
  Supreme National Council of Cambodia (SNC), 132
  United National Front (FUNCINPEC), 132
Canada, 177
  Royal Canadian Navy (RCN), 89, 156, 177, 261
Caribbean, 256
Carter, James 'Jimmy' Earl Jr., 166, 183
CH-47, 195
Chemical weapons, 55, 172, 196, 235, 244
Chemical Weapons Convention (CWC), 172
China (People's Republic of China), xvi, 5, 7, 16, 24, 25, 30, 36, 45, 53, 84, 112, 117, 123, 125, 133, 159–60, 162–3, 165–82, 185, 186–8, 191–2, 194, 195–7, 199, 203, 205–6, 211, 212, 213, 214, 222, 226, 240, 248–9, 255, 256, 257–9, 260, 261, 264, 268, 271, 274–5, 278–9

INDEX

Belt and Road Initiative (BRI), 177–8
Central Military Commission, 166, 180
Chinese Coast Guard (CCG), 256
Chinese Communist Party (CCP), 166
Chinese State Oceanic Agency, 257
Defence budget, 178
East China Sea Air Defense Identification Zone (ADIZ), 98, 179
Fishing vessels, 176, 196, 256, 258
Five Principles of Peaceful Coexistence, 168
Hainan Island, 175, 180
Information warfare (*xinxi zhanzheng*), 175, 257
Law on Territorial Waters and Contiguous Areas, 172
Maritime Militia, 257
Oil-gas platforms, 257, 259
People's Liberation Army (PLA), 142, 167, 171, 172–3, 175, 180
People's Liberation Army Air Force (PLAAF), 98, 171, 178, 179, 256–7
People's Liberation Army Navy (PLAN), 174, 179–81, 199, 207, 256
  Aircraft carrier development, 172
  Haibing-723, 180
  Liaoning, 179, 255
  Type-071 (LPD), 179
Re-unification, 259–60
Shanghai Cooperation Organisation (SCO), 163
Sino-Russian Military exercises, 163
  Peace Mission 2005, 163
  Peace Mission 2007, 163
'Three warfares' (*sanzhan*): public opinion warfare, psychological warfare, legal warfare, 257; Tiananmen Square/Incident, 117, 159, 166–7; UAV, 257
Chinese Civil War, 16, 30
Chinworth, Michael W., 214
Christianity, 64–5
Churiki, Osamu, Colonel, 227
Civil-military cooperation (CIMIC), 3, 6, 9, 60–1, 63, 66, 154, 157, 219, 220, 232, 234–5, 264, 275
Clark, Mark W., General, 92
Climate change/Global warming, xii, 237, 261
Clinton, William 'Bill' Jefferson, 168, 182
Close Combat Attack (CCA), 54
CMX-15 exercise, 223
Collin, Koh Swee Lean, 180
Combat information centre (CIC), 84
Combat stores ship (AFS), 254
Combined Maritime Forces (CMF) CTF-151, 222–3
Combined task force (CTF), 221
The Commonwealth, 51, 54, 193
Comprehensive Test-Ban Treaty (CTBT), 172
Conscription, 13, 52, 58, 162, 239, 268
Constabulary Forces, 12, 17, 33
Container ship, 145, 154, 256, 271
Corona virus, new (Covid-19), ix, xii, 63, 256, 278–9
Coup d'état, 43–4
Crimea, 164, 257
Cronin, Patrick M., 170
Cruise missiles, *see also* air launched cruise missiles, 198, 200
Cuba, 50
Cyber attacks, 175, 212

Degawa, Nobuhisa, 221
Demobilization, disarming, and reintegration (DDR), 137, 144

INDEX

Democratic People's Republic of Korea (DPRK), 5, 23, 25, 32, 45, 73, 106, 112, 117, 123, 159, 162, 170, 182–8, 212, 248, 260, 264, 275, 279
   DPRK Spy Ships, 185, 194, 209, 211, 213
   Juche 'self-reliance', 185
   WMD/Missile Programmes, 91, 98, 160, 163, 171, 182–6, 191, 194–5, 197–9, 203, 211, 213, 218
Deng, Xiaoping, 166
Deng, Yong, 176, 178
Denmark, 58, 73, 83, 211, 223
Deterrence, 9, 31, 42, 50, 70, 75, 99, 110, 160, 175, 185, 186, 188–9, 194, 196, 198–200, 248, 250, 254, 258, 264, 270, 275–7, 279
Devils on the Doorstep (*Guizi laile*) (film), 167
DF-21D, 180
DF-26, 180
Dittmer, Lowell, 177
Djibouti, 180, 221–2, 224, 226
Dore, Ronald Philip, 123
Dower, John, 18, 28
Dreyer, June Teufel, 175
Drifte, Reinhard, x, 8, 21, 42, 124, 166, 169, 171, 181, 186, 199, 258
Dubai, 131, 221
Dulles, John Foster, 26–7, 30

E-2C/D, 100, 255
E-767 AWACS, 195, 244
East Timor, *see* Timor-Leste
Ebata, Kensuke, 103, 211
Ebola, 153
Edano, Yukio, 200, 231
Egypt, 104, 123
Eldridge, Robert D., 7, 26, 232, 239
Electronic Intelligence (ELINT), 84, 99

Emperor Heisei (Akihito), 167
Emperor Showa (Hirohito), 64
Endō, Ayako, 64
EP-3E, 175
Erickson, Andrew S., 178
European Union (EU), 174, 213, 222, 223, 244, 274
EUROSATORY, 216
Evans, David C., 6
Ezaki, Masumi, 78

F-1, 97, 103, 106–7, 193, 214
F-2, 162, 193, 195, 199, 211, 214–5
F-4/F-4EJ/ F-4EJ*kai*, 96–7, 99, 101, 103, 106–8, 109, 214, 243
F-14, 101
F-15/F-15DJ/ F-15J/F-15J*kai*, 82, 100, 101–2, 162, 170, 195, 199, 211, 214, 243–4
F-15FX, 215
F-16, 101, 215
F-22 Raptor, 214–5
F-35A/B/C, 195, 197, 199, 212, 214–5, 217, 254–5, 257, 263, 276–7
F-86D/F, 93–4, 96–7, 99, 101, 102–3, 106, 109
F-104/104J, 96, 99, 101, 106–7, 108–9
F/A-18E/F, 215
Falkland Islands (Conflict/War), 71, 84, 208, 256
Fanell, James E., Captain, 211
Fast combat support ship, *see* AOE
Federal Republic of Germany (FRG)/ West Germany, 12, 17, 26, 58, 83, 103, 105, 109, 268
Ferguson, Joseph, 162–3
Fick, Nathaniel, 141
Fiery Cross, 258
Findlay, Trevor, 133
First Island Chain, 249, 256
Fisher, Jackie, Lord, 56

391

INDEX

'Five Eyes' intelligence network, 84
Foreign Affairs, 76
Forward air control (FAC), 65, 102, 229
France, 14, 103, 133, 134–5, 138, 141–2, 148–9, 166, 212, 236, 240, 245, 255
   French National Gendarmerie, 32
   Marine Nationale, 90, 229, 261
      Jeanne d'Arc, 229
      Mistral-class, 164
Free and Open Indo-Pacific (FOIP), 228
Freedom of Information, 6
Freedom of navigation exercises (FONOPS), 258
French, Thomas W., 7, 28, 31–3
Frente de Libertação de Moçambique (Liberation Front of Mozambique, FRELIMO), 144
Frühstück, Sabine, 111, 244
Fuji Heavy Industries, 93, 110
Fujii, Tatsuya, 136
Fuji Maru No. 1, 89
Fujio, Masayuki, 167
Fujita Corporation, 196
Fujita, Nobuo, 65
Fujita, Tamiko, 65
Fujiwara, Kiichi, 133
Fujiyama, Aiichirō, 98, 124
Fukuda, Tatsuya, Rear-Admiral, 223
Fukui, Yusuke, Colonel/Maj.-General, 139
Fukuyama, Yoshihiro Francis, 159
Fukuyama, Takashi, 211–2
Fukuyoshi, Shōji, 271–2
Fulda Gap, 58
Funabashi, Yoichi, 171
Funada, Naka, 52, 71, 101
Future Fighter-F-X, 215

G-2 (staff intelligence), 26–7, 29, 31, 211
Gas-turbine propulsion, 83
Gelman, Harry, 163
Genda, Minoru, General, 93, 98–9, 102, 109–110, 269
Geneva Convention, 14
Germany, 12, 128, 136, 142, 144, 240
   Constitutional Court, 157
Ghana, 153
Global Hawk (UAV), 211, 233
Glosserman, Brad, 117
Godzilla, 12, 113
Goff, Jonathan, Colonel, 251, 253
Gokoku Shrines, 64
Golan Heights, 147, 154–6, 226, 248, 262
Gómez, Oscar A., 235
Gorbachev, Mikhail Sergeyevich, 160
Gorshkov, Sergey Georgyevich, Admiral, 75
Goulding, Marrack, 140
Gow, Ian, 43
Gracey, Sir Douglas David, Maj.-Gen., 14
Graham, Euan, 7, 79, 80
Great Lakes Refugee Crisis, 148–51, 153, 158, 248
Green, Michael J., 8, 26, 166, 169–70
Greenland-Iceland-UK Gap, 84
Guam, 80, 151, 180, 186, 206, 229, 234, 260
Guillain, Robert, 30
Gulf of Aden, 153, 221–3
Gulf War (1990–91), 5, 88, 123, 130, 133, 237
Gunboat diplomacy, 248

H-2A (rocket), 214
H-6K, 258
H-19/S-55 (helicopter), 54
Hagisaki, Shigehiro, Lt-Comm., 163
Hague Convention, 14

INDEX

Haig, Alexander Meigs Jr., 81
Haiti, 148, 151, 153, 224–6, 232, 248, 262, 273
Hardened Aircraft Shelters (HAS), 104
Harpoon (SSM), 83
Harrier (fighter), 103, 105, 167, 254
Harris, Stuart, 176
Hasebe, Yasuo, 204
Hashimoto, Ryūtarō, 130, 161, 168, 172, 251
Hata, Tsutomu, 148, 183
Hatakeyama, Shigeru, 138
Hatano, Sumio, 174
Hatoyama, Ichirō, 195, 199, 269
Hatoyama, Yukio, 195, 225, 234
Hattori, Takushiro, 27
Hayashi, Keizo, 27
Hayashi, Shūzomac;, 123
Hayton, Bill, 259
Hertrich, André, 65
Hibako, Yoshifumi, General, 231
High Mobility Vehicle (HMV), 159
Higuchi, Hirotaro, 169
Higuchi Report (*Advisory Group on Defense Issues (Bōeimondaikondankai)*), 169–71, 188, 193, 272
Hikotani, Takako, 43
Hino, Ashihei, 18
Hirano, Ryuichi, 128
Hirata, Tetsuo, 28
Hirono, Miwa, xi, 173
Ho, Chi Minh, 14
Holmes, James R., 180
Honduras, 147, 151–3, 158, 225, 248
Hood, Christopher, 89, 109
Hook, Glenn D., 6, 41, 131
Horsey, Outerbridge, 98
Hoshina, Zenshiro, Admiral, 94
Hoshuyama, Noboru, 77
Hosokawa, Morihiro, 148, 169

Hospital ship, 256
Hostage, Gilmary Michael III, General, 215
HSS-1 (S-58), 86
HSS-2 (S-62) Sea King, 86
Hughes, Christopher W., xi, 8, 103, 169, 182, 195, 212, 217, 277
Hughes, Michael, 8, 102, 270
Hu, Jintao, 175
Humanitarian assistance/disaster relief (HA/DR), 60, 65, 66, 88, 130, 148–153, 154, 158, 173, 198, 202, 207, 220, 225, 228, 230–8, 247, 248, 250, 251–2, 254, 256, 259–60, 262, 264, 267, 273
Human intelligence (HUMINT), 211
Hunter-Chester, David, 51
Hurd, Douglas, 125
Hurricane Mitch, 151
Hutu, 148
Hwasong-14, 186
Hwasong-12, 186
Hybrid operations/warfare, 175, 257–8, 263, 276

Ibuki, Shoichi, Vice-Admiral, 34
Ikeda/Robertson Talks, 43
Imam, Patrick, 119
Imagawa, Yukio, 137
Improvised Explosive Device (IED), 221
Inada, Tomomi, 226, 246
India, 136, 165, 177–8, 206, 217, 259
  Malabar naval exercises, 206
Indian Ocean, 131, 177, 180, 192, 194, 217, 218, 247, 262, 274
Indonesia, 13, 15–6, 30, 137, 153, 207, 216
  Banda-Aceh, 158, 224
  Bandung, 15
  Jakarta, 16

393

INDEX

PETA (*Pembela Tanah Air*—Defenders of the Homeland), 15
Surabaya, 15
Inoue, Tatsuo, 205
Integrated combat system (ICS), 83
Intelligence, Surveillance, Reconnaissance (ISR), 211, 229, 238, 248–50, 252
Inter-continental ballistic missile (ICBM), 184
International Atomic Energy Agency (IAEA), 183
International Force East Timor (INTERFET), 154
International Institute for Strategic Studies (IISS), 178
International Military Tribunal for the Far East, 19
International Monetary Fund (IMF), 119
International Relations (IR) theory, xv, 4, 6, 7, 205
Iokibe, Makoto, 182
Iraq, 51, 120, 123, 126, 129, 153, 155, 158–9, 182, 192–3, 194–5, 203, 206, 217, 218–21, 232, 237, 245, 247, 251, 262, 271, 273, 274, 278
Iran, 131, 153, 170
Ireland, 142
Ishiba, Shigeru, 196, 199–200, 210, 218, 271
Ishida, Suteo, Admiral, 78, 80
Ishigaki Channel, 180
Ishihara, Shintarō, 174, 176
Ishihara, Takahiro, 261
Ishikawa, Akito, 65, 87
Ishikawa, Junichi, 86
Ishimaru, Yasuzo, 23
Ishioroshi, Yoshio, Colonel, 138
Isobe, Kōichi, 235, 251–2
ISR: *see* Intelligence, Surveillance, Reconnaissance (ISR)

Israel, 50, 77, 155–6, 179, 182, 216
Israeli Defense Force (IDF), 148, 234, 263
Italy, 74, 103, 128, 145, 166
Italian Navy, 83, 255
Cavour, 255
Itaya, Takaichi, Admiral, 33
Itō, Hiroshi, Rear-Admiral, 223
Itō, Masanori, 35
Itō, Masayoshi, 81
Izumi, Kazushige, Lt.-General, 201

J-8, 175
J-11B, 258
J-15/J-16, 179
J-20/31, 179
Jaguar (fighter aircraft), 103, 105
Japan
  1955 System, 37, 69
  2–26 incident, 87
  Abduction issue (*rachimondai*), 184
  Advisory Panel on Reconstruction of the Legal Basis for Security, 201
  Advisory Panel on Security and Defense Capabilities, 198
  Air-Defense Identification Zone (ADIZ), 80
  Air traffic control (ATC), 94–5, 97–8
  Anti-piracy/ counter-piracy, 153, 221–4, 226, 248, 273
  Anti-Piracy Measures Law, 223
  Anti-terrorism legislation, 129, 217
  ASEAN-Japan Relations, 169, 182, 207, 258–9, 275
  ASEAN Defence Ministers' Meeting (ADMM) Plus Experts Working Groups, 207
    Vientiane Vision: Japan's Defense Cooperation Initiative with ASEAN, 207

INDEX

Astronauts, 110
Aum Shinrikyo, 231
Australia-Japan Relations, 17, 89, 178, 205–7, 228–9, 234, 236, 240, 261, 263, 274
   Agreement Concerning the Transfer of Defence Equipment and Technology, 206
   Common Vision and Objectives, 206
   Cross-Servicing Agreements, 206
   Free-Trade Agreement, 206
   Information Security Agreement (ISA), 206
   Joint Declaration on Security Cooperation March 2007, 206
   Reciprocal Access Agreement (RAA), 206
Autonomous defence (*jishubōei*), 100
Aviation ban, 93
Aviation Law (*Kōkūhō*), 105
Aviation Preparation Office (*Kōkūjunbishitsu*), 91
Ballistic missile defence (BMD), 98, 160, 163, 169, 171, 182, 184, 186–7, 191, 194–6, 198, 202, 223, 228, 248, 250, 254, 268, 275, 278–9
Basic Policy for National Defense (*Kokubōno kihonhōshin* BPND), 42
Blank period (*kūhakuki*), 11, 12, 17
Board of Audit, 201

Cabinet Legislation Bureau (*Naikakuhōseikyoku*, CLB), 41, 43, 88, 124, 125, 201
Cabinet Information Center, 213
Cabinet Intelligence Research Office (CIRO) (*Naikakujōhō chōsashitsu*), 213
Cabinet Office (*Naikakufu*), 127
Cabinet Satellite Intelligence Center (CSIC *Naikakueiseijōhō sentaa*), 213

Cabinet Secretariat (*Naikakukanbō*, CAS), 212–3, 217
Civilian Merchant Marine Committee, 19
Coastal Safety Force (CSF), 33–5, 36, 37, 93
Collective self-defence (CSD), 200–1, 220, 227, 244, 264
Combined Annual Plan (CAP), 58
Constitution, xvi, 1–4, 11–2, 18–9, 23, 27, 29, 35, 39–41, 43, 52, 64, 82, 112–3, 122–7, 129, 133, 146, 157, 198–200, 204, 218–220, 227, 230, 262, 269, 272–3
Constitutional Revision, 122, 203, 204, 269, 277
Contingency Law (*Yūjihōsei*), 201
Control Authority for the Japanese Merchant Marine (SCAJAP), 19, 21
Cooperation for United Nations Peacekeeping Operations and Other Operations Act (*Kokusairengō heiwaijikatsudōtō nitaisurukyoryoku ni kansuruhōritsu*), 126
Council on Security and Defense Capabilities, 195
Cyber Security, 175, 185, 188, 191, 198, 202, 212, 216, 227, 262, 271, 279
   Basic Act on Cybersecurity, 212
   Cyber Defense Unit (CDU), 212
   Cybersecurity Strategy, 212
   Information Security Policy Council (ISPC), 212
   ISPC Strategy, 211–2
   National Information Security Center (NISC), 211–2
   National Strategy on Information Security, 211–2
   Six Pillars of Comprehensive Defense Against Cyber Attacks (*Saibākōgekitaisho 6honchū*), 212

INDEX

Defense attaché staff (*bōeichūzaikan*), 88, 125, 212
Defence Budget, 40, 48, 52, 69, 79, 94, 96–8, 113–5, 117–8, 121, 166, 178, 197, 205, 208, 214, 239, 245, 257, 278–9
Defense Build-up Plan (DBP), 43, 49, 51, 53, 69, 71–2, 75–6, 77, 94, 103, 106
Defence Expo (*Daibōeihaku*), 113
Defence Exports, 195, 216–7
Defence Procurement, 40, 70, 84, 86, 94, 158, 171, 186, 193, 195, 197, 214–5, 252, 254, 270–1, 277; Defense Facilities Administration Agency (*Bōeishisetsuchō* DFAA), 40
Defence/Defense White Paper (1970), 45, 76, 95, 100
Defence/Defense White Papers, 6, 45, 52, 58, 76, 80, 82, 95, 99–100, 109, 115, 127, 143, 194, 197, 206, 215, 226, 241, 246–7, 252
Demilitarisation, 2–4, 11, 17–8, 20
Democratic Liberal Party, 28
Democratic Party of Japan (*Minshutō* DPJ), 192, 195–6, 201, 205–6, 214, 218, 274–5
Director of Cabinet Intelligence (DCI), 213
Disaster Relief Law, 126

Emergency services, 60–1
Equality legislation/measures, 244–7
Exclusive Economic Zone (EEZ), 67, 80, 98, 180–1, 185, 259–61

Five Conditions for PKO Participation (PKO *sankagogensoku*), 122, 127, 137, 146
First National Strategy on Information Security, 212

Flight Information Regions (FIRs), 98
Flag recognition/ controversies, 87, 174, 229

Gaiatsu, external pressure, 82, 94, 121
General Maritime Bureau (Transport Ministry), 19
Great East Japan Earthquake (*Higashinihon daishinsai*), 63, 230–8
Greater East Asia Co-prosperity Sphere (*Daitōa-kyoeiken*), 14
Grey zones, 184, 201–2, 257, 263

Hanshin-Awaji earthquake, 60, 63, 230–1, 236–7, 272
Hidagawa Bus Accident, 60, 88
Hikikomori: *see* Self-isolating *hikikomori*
Hiroshima Atomic Bombing, 2
Hokkaido, 24–5, 31–2, 46–7, 50, 52, 55, 57–9, 61–2, 66, 68, 71, 92, 98, 99, 102, 15–7, 110, 155, 186, 208, 233, 243, 267, 270

Imperial Household, 31, 64, 95, 167
Imperial Japanese Army (IJA *Teikokurikgun*), 12–6, 18–9, 27–32, 43, 46, 52–3, 62, 64, 87–8, 91–3, 105, 107–9, 267
Imperial Japanese Navy (IJN *Teikokukaigun*), 12, 15–20, 27–31, 33–5, 44, 46, 64–5, 69–70, 73, 77, 83–5, 87–8, 90–5, 105, 108–10, 267, 269
Yamato, 64, 87
Yukikaze, 19
India-Japan Relations, 177–8, 206–7, 217, 259
International Peace Cooperation Corps (IPCC), 126–8, 133–4, 151
International Peace Cooperation Headquarters (*Kokusaiheiwakyōryoku*

INDEX

honbujimukyoku IPCH), 127–8, 135, 138–9, 146, 151
International Peace Cooperation Law (*Kokusaiheiwakyōryokuhō* IPCL), 125–9, 133–5, 137–8, 144, 146, 148, 154, 157, 201, 203, 217
International Peace Support Law (*Kokusaiheiwashienhō* IPSL), 203–5, 226
Invasion of Japan, actual/planning for, 13, 18, 20, 24, 31–3, 50, 52, 56, 58–9, 66, 76–7, 79, 82, 106, 112, 160, 179, 184, 194, 199, 201, 249, 263, 270; Iraq Law, 129; Ise Bay Typhoon, 60

J-Alert warning-system, 186
Japan-China relations, *see also* China-Japan relations
    Chinese surveys of Japanese (claimed) waters, 260
    Japan-China Fishery Council, 166
    Japan-China Maritime Liaison Mechanism, 258
    PLAN passage through Japanese waters, 256
    Scrambles due to Chinese aircraft, 256–7
    Treaty of Peace and Friendship, 166
Japan Coast Guard (JCG *Kaijōhoanchō*), 87, 162, 176, 181–2, 184–6, 196, 207, 209, 212, 218, 221–3, 231, 235–6, 248, 252, 256–7, 260–1, 264, 271, 275
    Special Boarding Unit (*Tokubetsukeibitai*), 223
Japan Communist Party (JCP), 26, 28–9, 31–2, 37, 41, 120, 165
Japan Defense Agency (*Bōeichō* JDA), 40
    Basic Plan for Gender Equality, 244

JDA Defense Policy Bureau, 78, 170
    International Policy Planning Division, 170
JDA Establishment Law, 88, 125
JDA Headquarters for the Prevention of Suicide, 247
JDA Internal Bureau, 43, 70, 80, 101
JDA Operations Planning Bureau, 272
JDA personnel, 150, 210, 246
JDA Regional Liaison Office (RLO), 64
Japanese Islands
    Eniyabanarejima, 249
    Ishigakijima, 249
    Miyakojima, 249, 257
    Nanseishotō south-western islands, 248–9, 252–4, 275
    Okinotorishima, 260, 278
    Senkaku Islands, 169, 172–4, 176, 179–81, 191, 196, 243, 256–8, 260, 264, 275, 280; Yonagunijima, 168, 249
Japan International Cooperation Agency (JICA), xii, 149, 151–2, 154, 225–7
Japan-Korean Relations
    Comfort women issue (*ianfumondai*), 228
    General Security of Military Information Agreement (GSOMIA), 228
    Korean court rulings on slave-labour issues, 228
Japan Platform, 154, 235
Japan-Russia Relations
    Agreement Concerning the Prevention of Incidents at Sea, 160
    Japan-Russian Federation Joint Actions for Disarmament and Environmental Protection, 162;

INDEX

Japan-Russia Joint Working Group (nuclear issues), 160
Kuril Islands, 13, 160
Military cooperation protocol, 161
Peace Treaty issues, 160-2
Peace Treaty Working Group, 160
Tokyo Declaration (1993), 160
Japan Socialist Party (JSP), 29, 41, 43, 57, 148
Japanese Surrendered Personnel (JSP), 14-16
Japan Teachers' Union (*Nikkyōso*), 62
Japan Technical Committee for Assistance to US Anti-War Deserters (JATEC), 25
Japan-US relations
   Dawn Blitz exercise, 251
   Guidelines (US-Japan Security), 45, 59, 76, 78, 80, 115, 160, 168-71, 183, 186, 198, 200-2, 205, 232, 260, 273, 276
   Iron Fist exercise, 250
   Japanese-American Committee on Security, 98
   Japan-US Alliance, 12, xvi, 3, 8, 12, 14, 25, 42, 44-5, 56, 59, 78-82, 88, 90, 107, 117, 120-1, 123-4, 163-4, 166, 168-71, 176, 181-2, 184, 188, 192-5, 200, 202, 205, 214, 217, 227, 228-30, 232, 234, 236-8, 258, 26-1, 263-4, 273, 274-9
   Japan-US Security Consultative Committee, 168
   Japan-US Security Subcommittee, 82
   Reciprocal Provision of Logistic Support, Supplies and Services Agreement, 169
   Security Treaty (1951), *Treaty of Mutual Cooperation and Security Between the United States and Japan* (*Anpō*), 20, 34-5
   Status of Forces Agreement (SOFA), 81, 234
   JL123 crash, 60, 91

Kaketsukekeigo ('rush and rescue'), 227
Karoshi (death from overwork), 210
KB-thesis, 77; Keidanren, 195
Kokusanka (prioritisation of domestic development and production), 51, 51-2, 85-6, 95-6, 100-1, 106, 112, 114, 159, 214, 270, 272
Komeito, 194, 199
Kumamoto earthquake, 209

Large-Scale Earthquake Countermeasures Law, 60
Law Concerning Dispatch of International Disaster Relief Teams (IDR Law), 151
Liberal-Democratic Party (*Jimintō* LDP), 41, 43, 63, 94, 100, 114, 126, 143, 148, 155, 164, 167, 182, 194-6, 198-9, 204, 206, 210, 274-5
LDP Policy Affairs Research Council (*Seimuchōsakai* PARC), 70
PARC divisions (*bukai*), 70
Local Defense Corps (*Kyōdobōeitai*), 210
Lockheed scandal, 86, 99-100

M-Fund, 28
Manual on Joint Strategies Concerning Unidentified Vessels (JDA-MSA), 185
Maritime Safety Agency (MSA *Kaijōhoanchō*), 19-20, 22-4, 35-6, 184-5, 203, 212, 266
MS14, 22-3
MS30, 22

INDEX

Maritime Safety Board (MSB), 19
Maritime Safety Force (MSF), 17, 27
Merchant shipping, 19, 21, 67, 75, 79–82, 163, 221–4, 263, 269, 278
MIDDLEs, 204
Mid-Term/Medium-Term Defense Program (MTDP), 82, 198
Militarisation, 9, 17–8, 20, 26, 37, 40, 187, 212, 217, 249, 274
Militarism, 3–4, 12, 17, 18, 41, 65, 170, 255
Military Aviation Reconstruction Group (*Kōkūsenryoku saikengurūpu*), 91
Ministry of Defense (MOD *Bōeishō*), 3, 23, 127, 155, 175, 181, 198–9, 209–10, 212–6, 221, 223, 225–6, 229, 235, 238, 241, 244, 245–7, 249–51, 253–6, 259–60, 271–2
  Acquisition, Technology and Logistics Agency (ATLA), 215
  Command, Control, Communications and Computers (C4) System Command, 211–2
  Defense Information Infrastructure (DII), 211–2
  Defense Policy Bureau, 272
  Measures Aimed at Enhancing the Human Foundation, 247
  Mobile Deployment Working Group (*KidōtenkaiWG*), 249, 251
  'Southwestern Wall Strategy', 249
  Space situational awareness (SSA), 213
  South Sudan 'morning report' scandal, 221, 226, 246, 263
Ministry of Finance (MOF *Zaimushō*), 40, 43, 49, 69, 70–1, 82, 86, 100, 111, 115, 158, 214
Ministry of Foreign Affairs (MOFA *Gaimushō*), 3, 20, 23, 40, 80–1, 99, 124–6, 130, 132, 134, 143, 146–7, 149, 151–2, 155, 161–2, 164, 180–1, 198–9, 206, 210, 212, 218, 234, 245, 261, 271
  Foreign Policy Bureau, 170
  National Security Policy Division, 170
Ministry of Health and Welfare (*Kōseishō*), 19
Ministry of Internal Affairs and Communications (*Sōmushō*, formerly Home Ministry, *Naimushō*), 93;
Ministry of International Trade and Industry (MITI *Tsūshōsangyōshō*, now Ministry of Economy Trade and Industry, METI *Keizaisangyōshō*), 40, 82, 96, 100–1, 214, 272
Ministry of Justice (MOJ *Hōmushō*), 211–12
Ministry of Land, Infrastructure, Transport and Tourism (MLIT *Kokudokōtsūshō*), 105–6
Ministry of Transportation/Transport (*Unyushō*), 22, 82, 106, 111, 221
Mothers Against WAR, 204

Nagoya High Court, 219
'Nakamura Lines', 80
National Defense Council (*Kokubōkaigi* NDC), 40, 99
National Defense Program Outline (*Taikō* NDPO), 76–7, 97, 102, 114, 161, 169–71, 186, 192
National Diet (*Kokkai*), 6, 23, 27–8, 57, 59, 63, 64, 69–70, 78, 81, 88, 94, 100, 102, 109, 114, 124, 126, 127, 199, 203–4, 210–1, 213, 217, 246, 249, 250, 272–3
Bōeizoku 'defence tribe', 70, 96, 114, 272

399

INDEX

Diet Commission on the Constitution, 204
House of Councillors (*Sangiin*), 125
House of Councillors Budget Committee, 69
House of Representatives (*Shūgiin*), 100
National Headquarters for Earthquake Disaster Prevention, 60
National Information Security Center (NISC), 212
National Police Agency (NPA *Keisatsuchō*), 40, 133, 184, 212–3, 280
National Police Reserve (NPR *Keisatsuyobitai*), 12, 17, 26–36, 40, 47–8, 56, 59–60, 92, 230, 266, 280; National Rural Police (NRP *Kokkachihōkeisatsu*), 27–8, 30–1
National Safety Agency (*Hoanchō* NSA), 35
National Safety Forces (*Hoantai* NSF), 32–7, 40
National Safety College, 241
NSF Air Section, 93
NSF Aviation School, 36, 93
National Security Council (NSC *Kokkaanzenhoshōkaigi*), 200
National Security Secretariat, 200
National Security Strategy (NSS), 198, 200, 258
Neutrality, 18–9, 25, 29, 87, 124, 126–7
New Party Sakigake, 148
New security laws (NSL), xvi, 200–6, 210, 226–7, 262–3, 274
Nippon Hōsō Kyōkai (NHK), 23, 86, 166, 216, 221
Silk Road, 166
Nipponkaigi, 65
Northern Territories (*Hoppōryōdo*), 65, 160

Nuclear Accidents/Incidents, 230–1, 233–6, 238, 244

Official Development Assistance (ODA), 124–6, 167, 172, 176, 206, 220, 222, 274
ODA Charter, 126
Ōfuna Transitory Prison Camp, Kamakura, 87
Okinawa Prefecture, 44, 80, 88, 94–7, 105–6, 119, 134, 164, 175, 178–9, 195, 197, 202, 207, 230, 233–4, 243, 248–9, 263
  Battle of Okinawa, 249
  Border Islands Security Force, 280
  Crime, 234
  Okinawa Reversion Agreement, 243
  Special Action Committee on Okinawa (SACO *Okinawanikansuru tokubetsukōdōiinkai*), 178, 234
OLDs (retirees), 204
Opinion polls, 108, 126, 185, 237, 239
Organisational Investigation Committee (*Seidochōsaiinkai*), 69
Partnerships, 157, 192, 205–6, 217, 219, 224, 228, 236, 247, 260, 274, 277
Peacetime defence capability (*heiwajino bōeiryoku*), 100
'Pojiristo'-'Negaristo', 128
Police (Japanese), 3–4, 12, 17, 19–20, 25–34, 36–7, 40, 43–4, 48, 56, 59, 62, 93, 99, 109, 127–8, 132–4, 139, 183–4, 209, 260, 272, 280
  Border Islands Security Force, 280
  Nagano Prefectural Police, 109
  Okayama Prefectural Police, 139
  Police Duties Execution Act (1948), 184
Population, 4–5, 45–6, 61, 117–20,

INDEX

141, 192, 239, 241–2, 149, 264, 277–8
Prime Minister's Office (PMO), 19, 22, 30, 35, 40, 43, 60, 66, 69, 114–5, 146, 185, 217, 269
Prisoners of War (POW), 13–4, 87
Procurement Agency (*Chōtatsuchō*), 40
Protection of Specially Designated Secrets Act, 201
Protests, 17, 61–2, 110, 203, 234
Purges, 18, 20, 28–9, 44

Rearmament, 2, 11, 19, 24, 26–7, 29–30, 33–5, 37, 42, 268
Regional Armies (*hōmentai*), 18, 36, 51–2, 55, 58, 62, 134, 151, 193–4, 207, 211, 225, 231–7, 239, 250; Regional Crisis Law, 129
Research and development (R&D), 215–6
Rules of Engagement (ROE), 122, 129, 139, 156, 184, 220, 226

Safety Security Force (*Keibitai* SSF), 35
Science Council of Japan (SCJ), 216
Science and Technology Basic Law (*Kagakugijutsukihonhō*), 215
Science, Technology, and Information (STI) Strategy, 215
SEALDs (Students Emergency Action for Liberal Democracy), 204
Sea Lines Of Communications (SLOC), 79–82, 86
Self-Defense Forces Law (*Jieitaihō*), 42, 56, 60, 67, 95, 123, 125, 127, 129–31, 163, 184, 203, 223; Self-isolating *hikikomori*, 239
Shipbuilding, 69, 208, 271
Six Pillars of Comprehensive Defense Against Cyber Attacks (*Saibākōgekitaisho 6honchū*), 212

Standard defence posture (*kibanteki bōeiryoku*), 77
Status of Forces Agreement (SOFA), 81, 149, 206, 234
Strategic communication, 198, 276
Strategic deterrent, 198, 200, 263, 276
Strikes/industrial unrest, 22, 26, 28, 33
Submarine Study Group (informal-veterans), 70
Submarine Study Group (Kawasaki-Mitsubishi), 70
Suicide (in civil society), 246
Suita Incident, 32
Supreme Court, 16, 64

Technical Research and Development Institute (TRDI), 70, 215
  'Undersea Weapons Study Group', 70
Textbook screening, 174
'Three Arrows' controversy (1963), 43–4, 59
Toho Studio strike, 33

United States-Japan relations
  Alliance Coordination Mechanism, 202
  Security Consultative Committee (SCC), 202
  Subcommittee for Defense Cooperation (SDC), 202
  US 'shield and spear', 79, 81, 199–200
  US 'nuclear umbrella', 159, 166, 199
  Yamasakura exercises, 207

Veterans, 11, 12, 13
Volunteer Fighting Corps (*Kokumingiyōsentōtai*), 18
Volunteering, 231, 235–6, 263, 279

War Bereaved Families Association (*Izokukai*), 174

401

INDEX

Whole of Government approach, 9, 198, 202, 204, 212, 224–5, 276
Working Conditions of JDA Officials Despatched to International Organizations Act, 129
Y-committee, 35
Yakuza crime gangs, 184, 231
Yasukuni Shrine, 36, 64, 167, 174–5
Zaibatsu, 20

Japan Airlines, 60, 89
Japan Self-Defense Forces
    Airlift, 90, 135, 141, 149, 151–2, 158, 225, 231–2, 250
    Allied-Support Operations (ASO), 130
    Air-Self Defense Force (ASDF *Kōkūjieitai*)
        1st Tactical Airlift Group (1TAG), 158
        2 Wing, 106
        3 Wing, 106
        7 Wing, 107
        Air Civil-Engineering Groups (*Kōkūshisetsutai*), 106
        Air Command (*Kōkūshūdan*), 95
        Air Defense Command (ADC *Kōkūsōtai*), 95, 250
        Air Development and Test Command (ADTC), 95
        Air Materiel Command Headquarters (AMCH), 95
        Air Rescue Wing (*Kōkūkyūnandan*), 95, 111
        Air Staff Office, 95
        Air Support Command (ASC *Kōkūshienjūdan*), 95
        Air Training Command (ATgC *Kōkūkyōikushūdan*), 95
        Base Air Defense Ground Environment (BADGE) System, 98, 107, 109, 257

        Base Resilience, 103–7
        Blue Impulse, 108, 112
        Central Air Defense Force (CADF), 95
        Close Air Support (CAS), 50, 54–5, 65, 99, 102–4, 106, 112, 193, 229, 253–5, 270
        Crash Record, 98, 108–9, 112
        In-flight refuelling, 100–1, 134, 151, 168–9, 195, 215, 254
        JADGE (Japan Air Defense Ground Environment) system, 257
        Iraq-Kuwait operation, 261–2, 274
        Maritime strike, 102–3, 269–70
        Northern Air Defense Force (NADF), 95, 106
        Precision-guided munitions (PGM), 103, 195
        Scrambles, 99, 101, 106, 109, 112, 179, 195, 214, 224, 249, 256–7
        Southwestern Composite Air Division, 95
        Space Operations Squadron (*Uchūsakusentai*), 213
        Special Airlift Group (SAG *Tokubetsukōkūyusōtai*), 95
        Su-27 Flanker (ASDF pilot training), 162
        Training costs, 243
        Transport Command (*Yusōdan*), 95
        Western Air Defense Force (WADF), 95
    Ammunition reserves, 58, 83, 155, 208
    Branch Billeting Areas (*hakenchi*), 135
    Camp Takeo, 134–7, 141, 145
    Civilian control, 2, 4, 9, 39,

INDEX

42–3, 59, 60, 90, 95, 98, 114, 128, 180–2, 211, 220, 231, 235, 238, 263, 267–8, 271, 276
Counter-Terrorism Operations (CTO), 130
Cyber Defense Unit (CDU), 212
Defense Intelligence Headquarters (*Jōhōhonbu* DIH), 211
Despatch histories, 6, 143, 219
Disaster Relief, xii, 1, 9, 53, 60, 88, 111, 115, 125–6, 130, 136, 151–3, 158, 188, 193, 202, 224, 230–8, 266, 268, 272, 275
Dynamic Joint Defense Force, 250
Exercises, 44–5, 50, 57–9, 62, 75, 78, 80, 89, 154, 194, 197, 205–8, 223–4, 225, 227–30, 232, 235, 244, 249, 250–3, 258–9, 262, 265, 275
Expeditionary capabilities, 5, 219, 247–8, 249–56, 256–61, 263, 275, 278
Explosive Ordnance Disposal (*fuhatsudanshori* EOD), 60
Female Personnel Empowerment Initiative, 244
Firing ranges, 243
Force Culture, 62–5, 87–9, 111, 142, 225, 232–5, 238–40, 267
Ground Self-Defense Force (GSDF *Rikujōjieitai*)
  1st Helicopter Brigade, 53
  2nd Division, 58
  3rd Division, 230–1
  4th Division, 232
  5th Division, 58
  7th Division, 49, 52, 54
  10th Division, 60
  11th Division, 58
  Adaptive Agile Ground Defense Force, 250

Airborne forces, 53, 57, 65, 193, 221, 250
Amphibious Rapid Deployment Brigade (ARDB *Suirikukidōdan*), 254, 276
Amphibious Rapid Deployment Regiments (ARDR *Suirikukidōrentai*), 250
Aviation, 50, 53–4, 153, 195, 197, 235
Basic Force Concept, 197
Brigades (*ryōdan*), 34, 51–5, 60, 66, 193, 196–7, 208, 233, 248–51, 253
Central Readiness Force (CRF), 193, 222, 225, 227, 250
Central Nuclear Biological Chemical Weapon Defense Unit, 235
Combined brigades (*konseidan*), 51
Divisions (*shidan*), 49, 51–5, 58, 60–1, 197, 230–2
Eastern Army, 239
Engineer Units, 53–4, 62–3, 133–43, 154–7, 225–7, 253
Ground Component Command (*Rikujōsōtai* GCC), 250
Ground Research Command, 193
Ground Staff Office (GSO), 193, 225–6
Intelligence School (*Jōhōkyōikubu*), 211
Intelligence Training Academy (*Chōsagakkō*), 57
Japan Peacekeeping Training and Research Center, 193, 225
Joint Staff, 33, 58, 104, 193, 213, 250–2, 259
Local Intelligence Unit (*Genchijōhōtai*), 211

403

INDEX

Medical Units, 53, 55, 136–7, 140–1, 149–53, 156–7, 209, 218, 224–5, 237–8, 242, 245
Middle Army, 134, 151, 231
Military Intelligence Command (*Chuōjōhōtai* MIC), 211
'Mini-Samawah' training area, 221
North-East Army, 232, 238
Northern Army, 51–2, 55, 58, 62, 250
Northern Manoeuvre Special Exercises (*Hokuhōkido tokubetsuenshū*), 207
Rangers, 53, 156, 194
Regional forces (*kankutai*), 51
Research Division, 152
Reserves, 209:
  Candidate Reserves (*Yobijiekanhō*), 209
  Ready Reserves (*Sokuōyobijiekan*), 209
  Regular Reserves (*Yobijieikan*), 209
  Reservist call-up, 231
School of Field Medicine, 152
Snow capabilities, 53, 61, 155
Special Forces, 53, 65, 113, 229
Special Forces Group (*Tokushusakusengun*), 193
Special Operations Group, 193
Staff College, 57
Technical High School (*Kōteikōkagakkō*)/High Technical School (*Shōnenkōkagakkō*), 239
Western Army Infantry Regiment (WAIR), 194, 250
Humanitarian Assistance/Disaster Relief Operations (*Jindōshien/kinkyūenjo katsudō* HA/DR), 60,
65–6, 88, 130, 148–54, 158, 198, 202, 207, 220, 225, 228, 232–8, 247–8, 250–2, 254, 256, 259–60, 262, 264, 267, 273

Intelligence Security Command (*Jieitaijōhō hozentai*), 211
Interest in the JSDF, 237
Iraq Reconstruction and Support Group (IRSG), 219–21
Island defence, 194, 228, 248–54, 275

Japanese contingent (J-CON, UNDOF), 155–6
Joint Staff College (JSC *Tōgōbakuryōgakkō*), 241
Joint Staff Council, 252
Joint Staff Office, 252
Joint Operations/Institutions, 'Jointness', 3, 9, 48, 54, 57, 59, 60, 65, 90, 95–6, 101, 103–4, 113, 145, 153, 158, 182, 184–5, 193, 195–6, 198, 202, 206, 211, 222–5, 232, 235, 237, 240–1, 250–4, 256, 258, 260, 262, 271–2, 276
Joint Task Force-Tohoku (JFT-TH), 232–8
JSDF Central Hospital, 136
JSDF Cooperation Associations (*Jieitaikyōryokukai*), 62
JSDF Veterans Association (*Kaikōsha*), 64

Kodaira Foreign Language School, 144

Logistics, 73, 85, 90, 96, 112, 134, 140, 147–8, 151–2, 155, 157–8, 204, 208, 218, 231, 237, 253–4, 270–1, 279

Maritime Self-Defense Force (MSDF *Kaijōjieitai*)

INDEX

Antisubmarine warfare (ASW), 68–72, 75–6, 79, 82–3, 86, 112, 255–6, 259, 269–70
Coastal Defense Group (*Bōbitai*), 74
Command of CTF-151, 223
Deployment Air Force for Counter-Piracy Enforcement (DAPE), 222
Designs Office, 158
Escort Division One, 245
Fleet Air Force, 68
Fleet Escort Force, 68
Fleet Rehabilitation and Modernization (FRAM), 84
Fleet Review, 87
Fleet Submarine Force, 68, 70–1, 196, 270
Hakuo, 208
Helicopter carrier (CVH), 71–2
Indian Ocean refuelling, 217–8, 261
Japanese Facility for Counter-Piracy Mission (Djibouti), 222
Japanese Ship (JS) Aki, 256
JS Akitsugi, 87
JS Akuzuki-class (1960), 83
JS Amatsukaze, 83
JS Asuka, 85
JS Bungo, 154
JS Hamana, 73
JS Haruna-class, 72
JS Hatsushima-class, 131
JS Hatsuyuki-class, 83
JS Hayase, 131
JS Hyūga, 87, 232, 255
JS Ichigo-class, 74
JS Ise, 87
JS Ishikari (1981), 83
JS Izumo, 205, 245 253–5
JS Kasado-class, 74
JS Kashima, 85, 242
JS Kongō, 84
JS Kunisaki, 224
JS Kurobe, 85
JS Miura, 134
JS Nadashio, 89
JS Ojika, 134
JS Ōsumi-class (1961), 74
JS Ōsumi-class (1998), 72
JS Oyashio, 71
JS Sagami, 73
JS Samidare, 222
JS Sawayuki, 162
JS Sazanami, 222
JS Setogiri, 162
JS Setoyuki, 245
JS Shimayuki, 245
JS Shirane-class, 72
JS Shirase, 85, 261
JS Tachikaze-class, 84
JS Takami-class, 74
JS Takatsuki-class, 84
JS Tenryu, 85
JS Tokiwa, 131, 224
JS Towada-class, 85, 134
JS Uzushio-class, 71
JS Yamagiri, 245
JS Yamagumo-class, 83
Korean destroyer radar lock-on incident, 229
Kosoku Marine Transport special shipping company, 208
Maritime Staff Office (MSO), 68, 70–1, 131
Mine Warfare Force, 68, 71–4, 83, 86, 90, 112, 120, 123, 130–1, 143, 156–8, 183, 188, 193, 203, 216, 218, 269
Nanchan-World, 208
Naval Academy, 242
Naval divers, 60, 88, 157, 237
Navy curry, 87
Officer Candidate School (*Kanbukohoseigakkō*), 68

INDEX

Operation Tomodachi, 197, 206, 232–8, 251–2
Radar Lock-on Incidents, 180–1, 229
Regional District Forces (*Chihōtai*), 68
Reservists, 208
Sealift, 90, 193, 208, 249–50, 253–4, 270
Second Fleet Air Wing (*Dai2kōkūgun*), 68
Self-Defense Fleet (*Jieikantai*), 34, 68, 78, 85, 251
Training cruises, 88, 123, 188, 242

Memorials, 64
Mental health, 210, 221, 232, 237, 239, 246–7
Multi-Functional Flexible Defense Force, 194
National Defense Academy (NDA *Bōeidaigakkō*), 8, 46, 63, 232, 239–45, 252, 271
National Defense College, 241
National Defense Medical College (NDMC *Bōeiikadaigakkō*), 240–1
National Institute for Defense Studies (NIDS *Bōeikenkyūsho*), 8, 122, 241
Graduate School of Security Studies, 241
Overseas despatch operations (ODO), xv, 5, 9, 23, 42, 63 120–59, 170–1, 176, 187–8, 192–3, 201, 206–7, 210, 217, 219–21, 224, 225, 227, 235, 237, 247, 252, 262, 264, 272, 273–6
Peacekeeping Operations (UN-PKO *heiwaijikatsudō*), xv, 74, 120–48, 153–7, 169–70, 173, 178, 182, 193, 201, 203–4, 207, 219–221, 224–7, 231, 245, 248, 262, 273

Peace Support Operations (PSO *heiwashien katsudō*), 127, 130, 138, 219
Permanent Joint Headquarters (PJHQ), 198
Recruitment, 45–9, 52, 63, 92, 111, 114, 119–20, 239, 241, 244–7
Rules of Engagement (ROE), 122, 129, 139, 156, 184, 220, 226
Self-Defense Force Member Mindset (*Jieikan no kokorogamae*), 238
Signals Intelligence (SIGINT), 98, 175, 211
Space Domain Planning Section, 213
Suicide in the JSDF, 221, 227, 239, 246–7, 272
Tele-medicine, 152
Training, 43–6, 48, 53–4, 57, 59, 61–2, 65–6, 68, 71, 73, 83–6, 88–90, 92–7, 100, 103, 106–11, 123, 125, 133–4, 136, 140, 142, 144–5, 147, 154–7, 161–2, 188, 193, 195, 205–10, 221, 223–5, 227, 229, 238–44, 248, 50, 252–3, 255–6, 260, 262, 270, 272, 275–6
Training Air Spaces (TAS *kunren kūiku*), 243
Training Areas, 57, 62, 155, 221, 243
Women in the JSDF, 63, 111, 114, 152, 223, 242, 243, 244–6

Jiang, Zemin, 167, 172, 175
Johnson, Chalmers, 96, 170
Joint Air-to-Surface Stand-off Missile (JASSM), 199
Joint Direct-Attack Munitions (JDAM), 195
Joint Strike Missile (JSM), 199
Joy, Charles Turner, Vice-Admiral, 22

INDEX

Kaifu, Toshiki, 123, 126, 160, 167
Kaihara, Osamu, 27, 79, 94, 99, 105
Kallendar, Paul, 211
Kamimoto, Mitsunobu, Lt.-Colonel, 150
Kan, Naoto, 176, 195, 196, 201, 205, 231–2, 236
Kaneda, Hideaki, Vice-Admiral, 251
Kanemaru, Shin, 182
Kang, David, 168
Katahara, Eiichi, 121
Katayama, Tetsuo, 29
Katō, Akira, 243
Katzenstein, Peter J., 6
Kawano, Hitoshi, 220, 247
Kawano, Katsutoshi, Admiral, 251, 259
Kawasaki Heavy Industries (KHI), 70, 96, 175
KC-767, 158, 195, 225, 244
Kennan, George Frost, 27–8
Kevork, Chris, 69
Kim, Dae-jung, 183
Kim, Il Sung, 182
Kim Jong-Il, 184
Kim Jong-Un, 185
Kim, Samuel S., 177
Kimizuka, Eiji, Lt.-General, 232, 251
Kimura, Tokutarō, 44, 93
Kimura, Yasuyuki, 23
Kinugasa, Hayao, 53
Kiroku, Hanai, 138
Kishi, Nobusuke, 94, 98, 114, 124, 203
Kishida, Fumio, 246
Kitamura, Kenichi, Vice-Admiral, 78
Kitazawa, Toshimi, 231
Kliman, Daniel M., 218
Kobayashi, Teruhiko, Major, 108
Kodama, Yoshio, 30
Kōda, Yōji, 72, 79, 84
Koike, Yuriko, 245
Koizumi, Junichiro, 123, 139, 160, 164, 172, 174–6, 184, 185, 217, 218, 245, 269
Kōkū Shimbun, 99
Komatsu, Ichiro, 201
Komura, Jutarō, 20
Kondo, Natsue, Rear-Admiral, 242
Kōno, Yōhei, 137, 143
Korea (Republic of Korea, ROK)
  Incheon, 21–2
  Korean Airlines Flight 007, 98
  Korean Constabulary, 17
  Korean War (1950–53), 3, 11, 16, 20–25, 26, 27, 29, 36, 37, 45, 67, 92, 103, 120, 130, 166, 186, 203, 266
  Relations with Japan, 21, 25, 32, 59, 92, 97–8, 154, 174, 177, 179, 183–6, 203–4, 222, 228–9, 234, 236, 240, 261, 263, 278
  ROK Air Force, 234
  ROK Navy, 22, 229, 261
  Sunshine Policy, 183; Wonsan, 21
Korean Peninsula Energy Development Organization (KEDO), 183
Kosovo, 174
Kotani, Ken, 211–2
Kowalski, Frank, 7, 28, 31
Kowner, Rotem, 16
Kubo, Takuya, 77–8
Kuomintang (KMT), 16
Kurisu, Hiroomi, General, 33, 43, 58, 272
Kurita, Chizu, Lt.-Colonel, 223
Kuriyama, Shōichi, 126
Kuroki, Masanori, 221
Kusunoki, Ayako, 34, 57
Kuwait, 120, 125–6, 130, 158, 192, 219, 262, 274
Kuzuhara, Kazumi, 27, 31, 33

Lam, Peng Er, 224

INDEX

Landing Craft Air-Cushion (LCAC), 207, 224, 233, 254
Landing Ship, Tank (LST), 21, 25, 72, 74, 134, 154, 158, 171, 253
Landmines, 20, 134–5
Lanteigne, Marc, 173
Lavi (fighter), 179
Lebanon, 123–4
Ledgerwood, Judy, 142
Lee, Kuan Yew, 132, 168
Lee, Teng-hui, 167
Leonardo, 216
Light Armoured Vehicle (LAV), 158–9
Li, Peng, 172
Liff, Adam P., 178
Link-11, 252
Link-16, 215, 252–3
Lockheed-Martin, 214–5
Long Range Anti-Ship Missile (LRASM), 199
Lucky Dragon No. 5, 23

M1 (carbine), 32
M-20 (bazooka), 56
M-24 (tank), 32
M-41 (tank), 49
M114 HUMVEE, 159
MacArthur, Douglas II, 98
Maeda, Tetsuo, 27, 33, 138
Maehara, Seiji, 196, 199
Mahan, Alfred Thayer, 180
Mainichi Shimbun, 199
Malacca Straits, 222
Malaysia, 131, 158
Maldives, 149
Mamor, 245
Manga, 7
Mao, Zedong, 166, 180
Map Exercise Fuji, 57
Marder (MICV), 55
Marquat, William Frederic, Maj.-General, 28

Marshall Islands, 151
Maruyama, Takashi, 43
Masuda, Hiroshi, 28, 92
Masuhara, Keikichi, 31, 71, 93
Matsudaira, Kōtō, 123
MccGwire, Michael, 75
McCormack, Gavan, 41, 174
MCH-53 Sea Stallion, 86
MCH-101, 216
McKay, Euan, 14–5
McMillan, Richard, 15
McNamara, Robert Strange, 140
Mearsheimer, John Joseph, 177
Mechanized infantry combat vehicle (MICV), 55
Medvedev, Dmitry Anatolyevich, 164
Mergel, Edward J. Jr., x, 314
Meteor (missile), 217
van der Meulen, Jan, 220
Mexico City Olympic Games, 246
Michishita, Narushige, 183, 186
Midford, Paul, xi, 7, 26, 108, 218, 221, 227, 268
MiG-25, 76, 98–100, 102
Mihara, Asao, 81
Mikasa, 88, 265
Miki, Takeo, 25, 77, 100
Militia, 52
Mindan, 23
Minesweepers, 2, 17–8, 22, 24, 68, 74, 85, 131, 154
Mishima, Yukio, 43–4, 109
Mitsubishi Electric, 213
Mitsubishi Heavy Industry (MHI), 54, 70, 97, 175, 215
Miyanaga, Yukihisa, Maj.-General, 163
Miyashita, Sohei, 133–4
Miyazawa, Kiichi, 100, 125–6, 134, 169, 172
Miyazawa, Yasushi, 100
Mongolia, 240

INDEX

Montgomery, John, 28
Moon, Jae-in, 228
Morgan, Patrick, 248
Moriya, Takemasa, 200, 246
Morris-Suzuki, Tessa, 19, 23
Motor-torpedo boats (MTB)/coastal forces, 68, 74, 270
Mountbatten, Lord Louis Francis Albert Victor Nicholas, Admiral, 14
Mozambique, 143–7
Multinational Force (MNF) Iraq, 220
Monroe Doctrine, 275
Murai, Yoshihiro, 235
Murakami, Tomoaki, 125
Murakami, Yasusuke, 126
Murata, Keijiro, 139
Mutō, Kabun, 137
Murayama, Tomiichi, 60, 63, 148–9, 155, 171, 183, 230
Murphy, Robert Daniel, Ambassador, 20
MV-22 Osprey, 197, 250–1, 253, 255

Nabers, Dirk, 217
Nakagawa, Misa, Lt.-Colonel, 245
Nakamura, Ryuhei, General, 49
Nakamura, Teiji, Admiral, 77, 80
Nakamura, Teruo, Pvte., 13
Nakanishi, Keisuke, 121
Nakano, Shigenori, Colonel, 145
Nakasone, Yasuhiro, 23, 81, 83, 86, 100, 114, 118, 130, 167, 269, 272
Nakatani, Gen, 210, 228
Nakaya, Takafumi, 64
Nakaya, Yasuko, 64
Nairobi hub, 145
NATO North Atlantic Treaty Organisation, 51, 55, 58, 103–5, 130, 193, 200, 205, 213, 219, 222–4, 229, 245, 252, 261
Natsume, Haruo, 158

Netherlands, 14, 133, 148, 208, 219–21, 223
Netherlands East Indies (NEI), 15
Nepal, 148, 153
Newsham, Grant, Colonel, 180, 251
The New York Times, 135
New Zealand, 17, 17, 53, 89, 153, 216, 228, 261
NGOs, 141, 150, 154 157, 173, 235, 263
Nike-Hercules (surface-to-air missile SAM), 49, 106–7, 110
Nikkei Shimbun, 135
Nishihiro, Seiki, 40, 43, 59, 76–7, 94
Nishimura, Mutsuyoshi, 164
Nixon, Richard Milhous, Nixon doctrine, 78
Nixon shock, 77, 276
Noda, Yoshihiko, 176, 195–6, 201, 205, 215–6, 226
Nonaka, Hiromu, 164
Non-Proliferation Treaty (NPT), 182
North Korea, *see* Democratic People's Republic of Korea (DPRK)
Norway, 58
Nuclear, biological, chemical (NBC), 55, 244
Nukaga, Fukushiro, 151
Nye, Joseph Samuel Jr., 170
Nye Report (*United States Security Strategy for the East Asia-Pacific Region*), 170

Oba, Sadao, 15
Obuchi, Keizō, 129, 185
Offensive counter-air (OCA) doctrine/capability, 195, 200
Ogata, Kagetoshi, 110
Ogata, Sadako, xii, 133, 137, 148
Ogawa, Raita, 99
O'Hanlon, Michael E., 168

INDEX

Ōhira, Masayoshi, 77, 167
Ōide, Shun, 100
Oil shock, 77, 100
Ōka (rocket aircraft), 65, 110
Okawara, Nobuo, 6
Ōkubo, Takeo, 22
Okumura, Waichi, 16
Olympic Games, 108, 113, 246
Ono, Sakari, 16
Onoda, Hiroo, Lt. (IJA), 13
Onodera, Itsunori, 197, 199, 259
Operation ATALANTA, 222
Operation Enduring Freedom-Maritime Interdiction Operation, 153
Operation OCEAN SHIELD, 222
Operation Tomodachi, 197, 206, 214, 232–4, 236–7, 251–2, 263, 277
Organisation for Economic Cooperation and Development (OECD), 119
Oriki, Ryoichi, General, 251
Oros, Andrew L., 8
Osaka World Exposition (1970), 108
Osirak reactor air strike, 182–3
Ota, Atsushi, 16
Ota, Fumio, Vice-Admiral, 252
Otani, Miho, Commander, 245
Ozawa, Ichirō, 126, 218

P-1, 229
P2V-7/P2J Neptune, 85, 100
P-3C, 82, 86, 180, 184–5, 222–3
P-51, 108
PAC-3, 184
Pakistan, 50, 131, 142, 153, 165
Park, Geun-hye, 228
Patalano, Alessio, xi, 7, 17, 19, 22, 24, 35, 71–3, 87, 90
Pauley Report, 18
Peace Boat, 235
Pearson Peacekeeping Centre, Canada, 156

Peattie, Mark R., 6
Perestroika, 161
Permanent Court of Arbitration, 187
Perry, William, 59
Persian Gulf, 123
Phalcon (AEW), 179
Philippines, 13, 130, 187, 258
Phuket Air, 219
Pillsbury, Michael, 168, 178
Plutonium, 183
Police (non-Japanese), 17, 128, 132
Portugal, 145
Post-Traumatic Stress Disorder (PTSD), 136, 150, 227, 237
Potsdam Declaration, 21
Primary Casualty Receiving Ship (PCRS), 256
Prisoners of War (POW), 7, 13–4, 23, 87
Proliferation Security Initiative (PSI), 218
PS-1, 85
Putin, Vladimir Vladimirovich, 161, 163–5, 187, 203, 278
Pyle, Kenneth B., 8, 117, 140

Qatar, 216, 240
Qian, Qichen, 173
The Quad (Japan, India, Australia, US), 178, 228–9
Quill, Jeffrey, 103

Radiation, 23, 42, 162, 222, 233, 235–6
Rafale (fighter), 215
RAND Corporation, 219
Rare earth minerals, 196
Rb08A (SSM), 50
Reagan, Ronald Wilson, 80–1, 166–7
Red Cross, 136
Red Flag exercises, 206, 244

INDEX

Regional Cooperation Agreement on Combating Piracy and Armed Robbery (ReCAAP), 221–2
Religion, 64–5, 87, 110, 123
Remarque, Erich, 18
Replenish(ment) at sea (RAS, or underway replenishment, UNREP), 68, 73–4, 85, 131, 134, 208, 253–4
RF-4B, 108
Richardson, Paul B., 164
RIMPAC, Rim of the Pacific (naval exercises), 89, 232
Roos, John Victor, 232
Ro-ro (roll-on/roll-off ferry), 208, 271
Roy, Denny, 259
Royall, Kenneth, 27
Rozman, Gilbert, 161
Russia, 5, 117, 153, 159–65, 170, 174–5, 181, 187–8, 201, 212, 222, 236, 240, 257, 261, 269, 274, 278
    Foreign Affairs and Defense Policy Council, 163
    Russian Border Guard, 162
    Siberia, 7, 16, 266
Rwanda, 140, 145, 148, 153

S2F-1 Tracker, 85
S-3 Viking, 86
Sado, Akihiro, 8, 51, 80, 225
Saigō, Kinya, Major, 232
Sakata, Michita, 56, 77, 96, 99–100, 102
Sakishima, 180
Sakonjo, Naotoshi, Vice-Admiral, 59
Samuels, Richard J., 8, 20, 28–9, 57, 96, 125, 209, 211, 213, 235–6
Sanagi, Sadamu, General, 93
Sanders, Patrick, Lt.-General, 230
Sanderson, John, Lt.-General, xii, 132, 136, 139–40
San Francisco Peace Treaty, 34

Sankei Shimbun, 23, 35
Sarin gas, 231
Sasakawa Peace Foundation, 173
Sasaki, Tomoyuki, 61
Sasaki, Toshio, Colonel, 232
Satō Eisaku, 124
Sato, Fumika, 63, 245
Satō, Gisen, 123
Sato, Masahisa, 155, 221
Saudi Arabia, 104
Saunders, Phillip C., 180
Scarborough Shoals, 258
Schlesinger, James, 56
Schulze, Kai, 181
Scobell, Andrew, 180
Sea Control Ship, 72
Sea Mines, 19, 22, 43, 73–4, 131
Sea of Okhotsk, 162
Sea Sparrow (SAM), 84
Sebata, Takao, 34, 170
Sekino, Hideo, 73, 84
Sexually transmitted disease, 142
Sexual harassment, 63, 142
Seychelles, 149
Shepherd, Winfield, Maj.-General, 28
Sherif, Ann, 42
Shibayama, Futoshi, 30, 57, 92
Shiina, Etsusaburo, 25
Shinoda, Tomohito, 129, 217
Shinto, 64–5, 110
    Shinto Association of Spiritual Leadership (*Shintoseijirenmei*), 65
Short-take-off and landing (STOL), 96, 105, 215
Sidoti, S. J., 104
Sierra Leone, 256
Singapore, xi, 131–2, 178, 222, 260
Singh, Bhubhindar, 129
Skabelund, Aaron, 65, 87
SM-1MR (SAM), 84
Smith, Sheila A., 8, 174

INDEX

Soeya, Yoshihide, 169, 203
Somalia, 144, 222, 226
Sono, Akira, 161
Sound Surveillance System (SOSUS), 84
South China Sea, 75, 159, 172, 176, 181, 187, 192, 196, 206, 258–61
South-East Asia Command (SEAC), 14
South Sudan, 148, 204–6, 221, 224–6, 262, 274, 278
Soya Straits, 73, 76
Spain, 208, 255
Special Air Service (SAS), 53
Srebrenica massacre, 220
Sri Lanka, 130
SS-N-2 (SSM), 50
Static Covert Surveillance (SCS), 229
Steinberg, James, 177
Stockholm International Peace Research Institute (SIPRI), 178
Straits of Hormuz, 23, 203
Su-27 Flanker, 162, 179
Submarine-launched ballistic missiles (SLBM), 185
Suga, Yoshihide, 227
Sugawa, Kiyoshi, 121
Sugihara, Arata, 71
Surveillance and Target Acquisition (STA), 229
Suzuki, Katsunari, 135
Suzuki, Kazuto, 213
Suzuki, Muneo, 63, 164
Suzuki, Shogo, 173
Suzuki, Zenkō, 80–1, 83, 114
Swaine, Michael D., 180
Sweden, 50, 56, 58, 83, 104–5, 133, 140
Swenson-Wright/Nilsson-Wright, John, xi, 184
Switzerland, 18, 29, 52, 104–5, 136

Synthetic-aperture radar (SAR), 213
Syria, 155–6

T-1A, 93
T-33A, 93, 109
Taepodong-1 (ballistic missile), 98, 102, 176, 183, 211, 213
Taiwan (Republic of China), 13, 16, 19, 36, 80–1, 96–7, 104–5, 159, 163, 167–9, 171–3, 175, 178, 182, 196, 248–9, 259–60
  Ministry of National Defense, 168
  Republic of China Navy (ROCN), 19
Taiwan Strait, 168
Takada, Haruyuki, Inspector, 139
Takahara, Takao, 150
Takahashi, Hajime, 110
Takahashi, Sugio, 199
Takao, Yasuo, 217
Takeshima/Dokdo, 97, 278
Takeshita, Noboru, 124
Talisman Sabre (exercise), 228
Tamogami, Toshio, General, 110, 272
Tamura, Hideaki, 210
Tamura, Kyuzō, 19, 22
Tanaka, Jirō, 63
Tanaka, Kakuei, 99–100, 114, 166
Tanter, Richard, 84
Taoka, Shunji, 165, 184
Tartar (SAM), 83
Tatsumi, Yuki, 194, 238
TBM-Avenger, 100
Tenyu (merchant vessel), 221
Terauchi, Hisaichi, Field Marshal, 15
Thailand, 130, 133–6, 142, 149, 153, 203, 224, 240
Theatre missile defence (TMD), 171
Theater-Wide Defense (NTWD), 184
Tibet, 173, 178
Timor-Leste/East Timor, 148, 153–4, 217, 219, 245

INDEX

Tinian, 229
Tōgō, Heihachirō, Admiral, 88, 265
Togo, Kuzuhiko, 123, 164
Tōgō Shrine, 87
Tōjō, Hideki, 64
Tokunaga, Katsuhiko, Major, 156
Tokyo Electric Power Company (TEPCO), 235–6
Tokyo Foundation, 14
Tokyo Olympic Games (1964), 108, 246
Tokyo Shimbun, 138
Tomb for Unknown Soldiers of the World (*Sekaimumeisenshi no haka*), 62
Toncontin Airport, 151
Tōyō Keizai, 120
Toyota Motor Corporation, 16, 139
Truman, Harry S., 27
Truman Doctrine, 27
Trump, Donald J., 5, 186, 191, 264, 276
Tsai, Ing-wen, 260
Tsuburaya, Kōkichi, Lt., 246
Tsugaru Strait, 76, 180
Tsukamoto, Katsuichi, 212
Tsushima, Juichi, 98
Tsushima Straits, 76
Tu-16J Badger, 99
Tu-22 Backfire, 73
Tu-95B Bear, 107
Tunisia, 139
Turkey, 153–5, 158, 222
Tutsi, 148
Type-10 (main battle tank, MBT), 197
Type-12 (SSM), 199
Type-16 (Manoeuvre Combat Vehicle MCV *kidōsentōsha*), 197
Type-60 (AFV, self-propelled recoilless rifle), 49
Type-60 (armoured personnel carrier APC), 55
Type-61 (MBT), 49
Type-64 Medium Anti-Tank (MAT) (anti-tank guided weapon ATGW), 55
Type-73 (APC), 55
Type-74 (MBT), 52, 55, 197, 236
Type-82 (AFV), 138, 158
Type-88 (land-based surface-to-surface anti-ship missiles SSM), 50
Type-89 (MICV), 55
Type-90 (MBT), 52, 197, 208
Type-96 (APC), 158
Typhoon (fighter), 215, 229

U-125, 96
UH-1 Huey (helicopter), 54
Ueda, Kaneo, 16
Ueda, Katsurō, 69
Ueda, Makiko, 29
Uemura, Kentarō, 93
Ugaki, Kazushige, 30
Ukraine, 164, 179
Unexploded ordnance (UXO), 60, 136
Union of Soviet Socialist Republics (USSR), 12–3, 24, 31, 45, 50, 52, 55, 58–9, 66–7, 69–71, 73, 75–7, 79, 83–4, 92, 98–102, 105–7, 112, 117, 146, 149, 159–64, 169, 180, 187, 269–70
  Exercise Okean (Ocean), 75
  Siberia, 7, 13, 16, 266
  Soviet Navy, 55, 67, 71, 75–6, 83, 102, 161–2
    Minsk, 161
  Soviet Naval Infantry, 55
  Soviet naval vessel 'attacked' in ASDF exercise, 102
  Soviet Pacific Fleet, 55, 75, 83, 161–2
United Kingdom (UK), xiii, 14–8, 46, 53, 55, 58, 65–6, 71, 84, 88, 92, 101,

413

INDEX

105, 125, 128, 149–50, 157, 167, 177, 194–5, 208, 210, 212, 215–7, 219, 221–2, 229–30, 240, 244–5, 247, 254–6, 261, 270–1, 273
Anglo-Japanese Acquisition and Cross-Servicing Agreement (ACSA), 229
Brexit, 230
British Army, 14–5, 58, 65, 219, 229
  Honourable Artillery Company (HAC), 229
British Overseas Territories, 256
National Audit Office (NAO), 273
Private Finance Initiative (PFI), 208
Royal Air Force (RAF), 101, 215, 229, 270
Royal College of Defence Studies (RCDS), 150
Royal Marines, 208, 3
  Marine Brigade, 208
Royal Navy, xi, 22, 67, 71, 90, 101, 229, 248, 256, 259, 266, 271
  HMS *Queen Elizabeth*, 255
Royal Fleet Auxiliary (RFA), 208, 254
  Lyness/Sirius-class, 254
  RFA Argus, 256
  RFA Point-class, 208
  RFA Sea Crusader, 208
Strategic Defence Review (SDR, 1997–8), 194
Strategic Defence and Security Review (SDSR 2010), 208
United Nations (UN), xii, 1, 19, 23–4, 41–2, 88, 120–48, 153–7, 169–70, 173–4, 177–8, 182, 187–8, 201–2, 204–5, 207, 219, 221–2, 224–7, 231, 245, 248, 261–2, 273–4, 278
Civilian police (CIVPOL), 133
Enforcement Coordination Cell, 261

Special Representative of the Secretary-General (SRSG), 132, 134, 137, 142, 144, 226
UN Contact Group on Piracy off the Coast of Somalia (CGPCS), 222
UN Convention on the Law of the Sea (UNCLOS), 187, 259–60, 278
UN Department of Peacekeeping Operations (UNDPKO, from 2019
UN Department of Peace Operations, UNDPO), 129
UN Educational, Scientific and Cultural Organization (UNESCO), 7
UN High Commissioner for Refugees (UNHCR), 133, 137, 144, 148–50, 154
UN military observers (UNMOs), 133, 135, 13941, 144
UN peacekeeping operations (UNPKO), 120–5, 129–33, 139–48, 153–5, 157, 169–70, 173, 178, 182, 201, 204, 207, 219, 221, 224–7, 231, 245, 248, 262
UN Disengagement Force (UNDOF), 147, 155–7, 207, 245
UN Mission in South Sudan (UNMISS), 148, 224, 226–7
UN Mission of Support for East Timor (UNMISET), 148, 154
UN Observation Group in Lebanon (UNOGIL), 123
UN Operation in Mozambique (ONUMOZ), 143–8
UN Stabilization Mission in Haiti (MINUSTAH), 224–6, 232, 248, 262, 273
UN Transitional Authority for

INDEX

Cambodia (UNTAC), xii, 131–45, 147–51, 154–5, 157, 173, 217, 225–6
UN Security Council, 41, 123–5, 144, 160, 173, 188, 216, 261, 274
UN Volunteer (UNV), 132
World Food Program (WFP), 222, 235
US-2, 217
United States of America (USA)
    US Air Force (USAF), 71, 85, 91–8, 100–03, 106–10, 148–9, 151, 179, 195, 215, 219, 232, 243, 250, 252
    USAF 51st Fighter Wing, 106
    US Army, 21, 23–4, 26–7, 31, 33, 48, 57, 59, 250
    LT-636, 23
    Central Intelligence Agency (CIA), 24, 30, 32–3, 57
    Command and General Staff College, 57
    Department of Defense (DOD), 80, 92–3, 170
    Far East Command (FEC, FECOM), 24, 26–8, 92
    Foreign Military Sales (FMS), 101
    Government Accountability Office (GAO), 273
    US Forces Japan (USFJ), 35, 42, 44–5, 57, 59–60, 68, 78, 80, 94, 97, 105, 108, 110, 169, 213, 231–7, 249–50, 258, 263, 276
    Hawaii, 88, 151, 186
    Joint Chiefs of Staff (JCS), 57, 71, 92
    US Joint Strategic Plans Committee, 71
    US Marine Corps (USMC), 51, 54, 58, 71, 105, 108, 232–4, 247, 250–2
    Marine Expeditionary Unit (MEU), 51
    31st USMC Expeditionary Unit, 232
    USMC Command and Staff College, 251
    Military Assistance Program (MAP), 49, 71, 86, 94
    Military Assistance and Advisory Group Japan (MAAG-J), 72, 86
    Military Sea Transportation Service (MSTS), 21
    Mutual Defense Assistance Office (MDAO), 86
    Mutual Defense Assistance Plan (MDAP), 34
    US Navy (USN)
        Air-Sea Battle Plan, 196
        USNS Impeccable, 180
        USS Arleigh Burke, 84
        USS George Washington, 233
        USS Midway, 44
        USS Nimitz, 168
        USS Pueblo, 107
        USS Ronald Reagan, 232–3
        USS Tortuga, 232–3
    US Seventh Fleet, 71, 75, 78, 229
    USN Ship Repair Facility (SRF), 78
    Offshore procurement (OSP), 56; State Department, 26, 56, 92; Strategy, 4, 11, 26, 37, 75, 115; Supreme Commander of the Allied Powers (SCAP), 18, 20, 22, 26–30, 69, 92
University of Tokyo, x, 137
Uno, Shōji, Lt.-General, 134
Ura, Shigeru, General, 91
Uruguay, 137, 142
Urup Strait, 162
Usui, Hideo, 161

INDEX

V-107/CH-46 (helicopter), 53
Vambrace Warrior (exercise), 229
Voyager (aircraft), 229
Vietnam, 11, 14, 21, 23, 25, 36, 44, 75, 101–4, 107, 162, 172, 178, 201, 207, 266
Viet-min, 14
Vietnam War, 11, 25, 36, 44, 75, 101–4, 107, 201, 266

Walsh, David, 76
Wang, Zheng, 175
War criminals, 28, 64
Warrior (MICV), 55
Watanabe, Akio, x, 124, 169–70, 194
Watanabe, Michio, 121
Watanabe, Takashi, Colonel, 133, 140, 143
Weapons of Mass Destruction (WMD), 167, 169, 182, 184, 186, 196, 199, 279
Weinberger, Casper Willard, 81
Weinstein, Martin E., 8, 29, 32
Shimozono, Sōta, 247
Western Pacific, 180, 248, 260
West Timor, 153–4
Weyland, Otto P., General, 92–3
Willoughby, Charles Andrew, Maj.-General, 26–7, 30–1
Wilson, Jeffrey D., 177
Woolley, Peter J., 81
World Bank, 177
World Trade Organisation (WTO), 175
Wu, Dawei, 180

Xi, Jinping, 177, 182, 275

Y-8, 257
Y-12, 257
Yaeyama Nippō, 249
Yamada, Akira, 110
Yamada, Makoto, 92
Yamaguchi, Jirō, 126
Yamaguchi, Noboru, Lt.-General, xii, 152, 158, 220
Yamamoto, Kiyokatsu, Brig-General, 44
Yamamoto, Moichirō, Maj-General, 15
Yamamura, Takashi, 96
Yamazaki, Hiroto, Superintendent, 133
Yamazaki, Takeshi, 29
Yanai, Shunji, 126, 138
Yatabe, Minoru, Major, 65
Yellow Sea, 260
Yeltsin, Boris Nikolayevich, 160–2
Yokobatake, Yūsuke, 201
Yokohama Dreamworld, 113
Yomiuri Shimbun, 139, 185
Yonai, Mitsumasa, Admiral, 19
Yoshida, Akihiko, 70
Yoshida, Shigeru, 18–20, 26–7, 29–30, 32, 37, 42, 44, 92, 112–4, 166, 237, 269
Yoshida Doctrine, 4–5, 37, 126, 157, 166, 192, 201, 264, 266, 277
Yoshihara, Toshi, 180
Yoshimatsu, Tamori, Vice-Admiral, 70
YS-11, 85, 96
Yui, Kimiya, 110
Yuzawa, Takeshi, 170

Zaire, 145, 148–50, 153, 158, 248
Zamperini, Louis, 87
Zhou, Enlai, 166
Zumwalt, Elmo R. Jr., Admiral, 72